Object-Oriented Application Development
Using Java

Object-Oriented Application Development Using Java

E. Reed Doke and John W. Satzinger, Series Editors

E. Reed Doke
John W. Satzinger
Susan Rebstock Williams

COURSE
TECHNOLOGY
TM
THOMSON LEARNING

Australia • Canada • Mexico • Singapore • Spain • United Kingdom • United States

COURSE TECHNOLOGY
THOMSON LEARNING™

Object-Oriented Application Development Using Java

by E. Reed Doke, John W. Satzinger, and Susan Rebstock Williams

Senior Editor:
Jennifer Muroff

Associate Product Manager:
Janet Aras

Cover Designer:
Steve Deschene

Managing Editor:
Jennifer Locke

Editorial Assistant:
Christy Urban

Compositor:
GEX Publishing Services

Development Editor:
Lisa Ruffolo, The Software Resource

Production Editor:
Jennifer Goguen

Manufacturing Coordinator:
Alexander Schall

Disclaimer
Course Technology reserves the right to revise this publication and make changes from time to time in its content without notice.

ISBN 0-619-03565-X

Contents

BRIEF

TABLE OF
Contents

8. Additional Inheritance Concepts and Techniques   241

9. Implementing Association Relationships   279

Preface

This text covers object–oriented application development using Java, emphasizing business information systems for CIS and MIS students and practitioners. We assume readers have some introductory computer programming experience, but experience with object-oriented programming and the Java programming language in particular are not required. The text therefore takes readers who know a little about programming from introducing Java syntax and object-oriented concepts all the way through designing and building an object-oriented (OO) three-tier Java application using a graphical user interface (GUI) and relational database.

Interest in the object-oriented approach to information system development is skyrocketing, and Java has emerged as a leading OO programming language. Although many Java programming texts are available, most cover introductory and advanced programming techniques, but do not emphasize information systems examples or show more complete solutions requiring an OO approach to systems analysis and design. After teaching OO programming and OO system development courses for several years, we concluded that although CIS and MIS students need to learn OO programming concepts and techniques, they also need to learn how to develop complete business information systems that solve real world problems. That's why we decided to write this book: to provide CIS and MIS students and practitioners with an OO development book designed just for them.

The text presents OO application development by following an iterative approach to systems analysis, design, and implementation. Object-oriented models and techniques based on the Unified Modeling Language (UML) are used throughout, and all Java programming examples and exercises are based on the three-tier design approach. After introducing a business case study, use cases are developed, a class diagram is drawn, problem domain classes are designed and implemented, GUI classes are designed and implemented, and data access classes that interact with a relational database are designed and implemented. Finally, a portion of the business application is ported to the Web. Along the way, readers become immersed in the OO approach to system development as they build their Java programming skills.

THE INTENDED AUDIENCE

Most university degree programs offering CIS and MIS degrees have responded to OO development by covering object-oriented Java programming and object-oriented development in a variety of ways. We designed this text to be flexible enough to accommodate many situations. Students who have completed an introductory programming concepts course (the programming language does not matter) can use this book in an introductory OO development course. This text introduces the Java programming language, OO concepts and terminology, three-tier design, UML, and iterative development. When students later take analysis and design and database management courses, they will have experience with the complete OO development process.

This text can also be used in an advanced development course where the students have had an introductory Java programming course that did not emphasize business system development and OO development. The introductory OO concepts (Chapters 1 and 4) and the Java syntax (Chapters 2 and 3) can be skimmed. More time can then be spent on OO analysis and design and UML. More advanced readers can move rapidly through the book and complete a more elaborate business system project.

Some readers have already studied UML and the object-oriented approach in an analysis and design course. The text is still appropriate for these readers as less time can be spent on the OO analysis and design and more on implementation. This text shows readers with UML experience how the OO models are actually implemented—something students and practitioners really appreciate. Therefore, this text can provide a capstone experience for many readers.

THE APPROACH

Many useful features are built into the text to provide a comprehensive learning experience. Some of the features are important to the OO analysis and design focus of the text. The text uses:

- **Business information system examples**: The analysis, design, and programming examples emphasize business problems of interest to CIS and MIS students.

- **Unified Modeling Language (UML)**: UML models are used extensively to describe system requirements for examples, including use case diagrams, class diagrams, and sequence diagrams. Then the models are used to guide the design and implementation of the system examples.

- **Iterative development**: A realistic iterative approach to development is emphasized throughout the text. The organization of the text is based on an iterative approach that leaves readers with a clear view of how analysis, design, and implementation flow during an iteration.

- **Three-tier design**: The OO design approach uses three-tier design, which divides the system into separate tiers for the GUI, the problem domain classes, and the data access classes. The organization of the text is based on the three-tier view, and each iteration addresses all three tiers.

- **Design for Java applications and for Web-based development**: The approach used for analysis and design is applicable to Java applications and to Web-based Java development.

- **The Bradshaw Marina case study**: An integrated case study is used throughout the text. The case has moderate complexity to provide readers with the experience of seeing a system project conceived, modeled using UML, and constructed following an iterative, three-tier design approach.

OVERVIEW OF THIS BOOK

The text organizes 17 chapters into five parts. A more complete overview of the text is provided in Chapter 1. The five parts include:

- Part 1: Object-Orientation and Java Fundamentals

- Part 2: Defining Problem Domain Classes

- Part 3: Defining GUI Classes

- Part 4: Defining Data Access Classes

- Part 5: Deploying the Three-Tier Application

The major outcome for an OO programming course using this text is to provide a firm foundation for the entire OO development process. The three-tier design approach is emphasized throughout, so that user interface classes, problem domain classes, and data access classes will remain distinct from the beginning. UML is used to show a model of many examples.

Chapter 1 provides an overview of key OO concepts and Java fundamentals. The Bradshaw Marina case study is used to illustrate the concepts and UML models. In keeping with iterative development and three-tier design, the text begins by modeling problem domain classes. The problem domain classes are then implemented and tested. Next, the graphical user interface (GUI) classes are added as the front end that interacts with problem domain classes. Data access classes are then added that allow data to be stored in a relational database. Finally, the three tiers are combined into a complete system module. Standalone Java applications are emphasized in most of the text, but the final chapter shows how to port some of the Bradshaw Marina application to the Web.

By the end of the text, students will have implemented key parts of a working system as shown in the examples, including Java applications and Web-based applications. Hands-on exercises and chapter projects provide opportunities for students to implement additional parts of the system in parallel with the examples.

Each chapter in *Object-Oriented Application Development Using Java* includes the following elements to enhance the learning experience:

- **Chapter Objectives**: Each chapter begins with a list of the important concepts to be mastered within the chapter. This list provides you with a quick reference to the contents of the chapter as well as a useful study aid.

- **Color Coding**: Java code is shown in full color as it would appear in many integrated development environments. The Java keywords, comments, and string literals are color coded by the IDE to increase readability.

 Hands-on Exercises: As new concepts are presented in each chapter, step-by-step instructions allow you to actively apply the concepts you are learning. In each chapter, you pause to review important concepts, and can perform the exercises in class or as homework problems.

- **Chapter Examples**: Several related Java examples are presented and fully explained in each chapter to demonstrate chapter concepts. All the code for the chapter examples is provided on the CD included with the book.

- **Chapter Summaries**: Each chapter's text is followed by a summary of chapter concepts. These summaries provide a helpful way to recap and revisit the ideas covered in each chapter.

- **Review Questions**: End-of-chapter assessment begins with a set of approximately 15-20 review questions that reinforce the main ideas introduced in each chapter. These questions ensure that you have mastered the concepts and understand the information you have learned.

- **Discussion Questions**: Several discussion questions that can be used for class discussion or homework assignments are included for every chapter.

- **Projects**: End-of-chapter projects provide challenging development experiences related to the chapter concepts.

TEACHING TOOLS

The following supplemental materials are available when this book is used in a classroom setting. All of the teaching tools available with this book are provided to the instructor on a single CD.

Electronic Instructor's Manual. The Instructor's Manual that accompanies this textbook includes:

- Additional instructional material to assist in class preparation, including suggestions for lecture topics.

- Solutions to all end-of-chapter materials, including the Review Questions, Discussion Questions, and Projects.

ExamView®

This textbook is accompanied by ExamView, a powerful testing software package that allows instructors to create and administer printed, computer (LAN-based), and Internet exams. ExamView includes hundreds of questions that correspond to the topics covered in this text, enabling students to generate detailed study guides that include page references for further review. The computer-based and Internet testing components allow students to take exams at their computers, and also save the instructor time by grading each exam automatically.

PowerPoint Presentations. This book comes with Microsoft PowerPoint slides for each chapter. These are included as a teaching aid for classroom presentation, to make available to students on the network for chapter review, or to be printed for classroom distribution. Instructors can add their own slides for additional topics they introduce to the class.

Source Code Files. Source code files, containing all of the code necessary for steps within the chapters and the Projects, are provided through the Course Technology Web site at **www.course.com**, and are also available on the Teaching Tools CD-ROM.

Solution Files. Solutions to end-of chapter questions, Hands-on Exercises, and Projects are provided on the Teaching Tools CD-ROM and may also be found on the Course Technology Web site at **www.course.com**. The solutions are password protected.

ABOUT THE AUTHORS

E. Reed Doke is a clinical professor of information systems and associate director for the Information Technology Research Center in the Walton College of Business at the University of Arkansas, Fayetteville. He holds BS and MBA degrees from Drury University and received his Ph.D. in management and computer information systems from the University of Arkansas. Dr. Doke worked for several years as a software developer and information systems manager prior to joining academia and continues to assist firms deal with systems development problems. He has published five books and numerous articles focusing on software design and Object-oriented development.

John W. Satzinger holds a Ph.D. in MIS from the Claremont Graduate University and is an associate professor of CIS at Southwest Missouri State University. Dr. Satzinger was previously on the faculty of Cal Poly Pomona and the University of Georgia and has focused on object-oriented development for over a decade. He has written dozens of articles on user interface design, group work, and system development. His most recent books include *Systems Analysis and Design in a Changing World* and *The Object Oriented Approach: Concepts, Systems Development, and Modeling with UML* (2nd Edition), both published by Course Technology.

Susan Rebstock Williams is an associate professor of information systems at Georgia Southern University. She received a BS in math and computer science as well as an MBA from Southwest Missouri State University, and earned a Ph.D. in information systems from Oklahoma State University. Dr. Williams has thirteen years of experience as a programmer, analyst, and information systems manager. She has conducted corporate training programs in Java and OO development, and continues to work with businesses needing assistance in these and other areas of software development. Dr. Williams has published numerous articles, and is currently pursuing research interests in OO database management systems and Web development issues.

THE COURSE TECHNOLOGY OBJECT-ORIENTED APPLICATION DEVELOPMENT SERIES

The original vision proposed to Course Technology by Reed Doke and John Satzinger is a series of texts on OO development that each includes a different OO language. Each text is based on the same iterative, three-tier OO model and uses the same Bradshaw Marina case study. The series begins with this Java text, but it will also include texts using Visual Basic .NET and Visual C# .NET. Reed Doke and John Satzinger are the series editors for the Object-Oriented Application Development Series at Course Technology.

ACKNOWLEDGEMENTS

Completing a text like this requires the dedication and hard work of many people. The first challenge was to explain to Course Technology that this book was not just another Java programming book—it is about the entire OO system development process. As such, the design, writing, exercises, figures, reviews, editing, and final production of the book did not fit the usual programming book style guide. Even our proposal to use color for the Java code examples required reinventing many aspects of the production process.

As usual at Course Technology, we were fortunate to find interested, excited, and future-oriented people to work with who quickly recognized what we wanted to accomplish with this text. The Senior Editor, Jennifer Muroff, provided a productive working environment for us, with just enough flexibility yet with just enough schedule rigor to keep us on track. She assembled and coordinated a great editorial and production team. First and foremost on that team was Developmental Editor Lisa Ruffolo. Lisa really understood where we were going with this text, and her contributions have been substantial. Lisa understands both programming and writing, giving her the skills to both identify errors and to make valuable suggestions. If you like something specific about this text, it was probably Lisa's idea.

Production Editor Jennifer Goguen had to deal with everything from UML diagram standards, color-coded program examples, fairly elaborate chapter examples in need of quality assurance testing, and a schedule that ended up submitting many chapters out of sequence. Thanks, Jennifer, for making it happen. Many others were also involved in the production of this text, including copy editors, quality assurance testers, graphic artists, and proofreaders. We also want to thank Associate Product Manager Janet Aras for her support and hard work on the instructor's resource kit (IRK).

We want to thank the students in CIS 550 at Southwest Missouri State University for working on the Bradshaw Marina case study and for classroom testing many of the chapters and examples in this text. Jonathan Rigden helped to develop many of the solutions to hands-on exercises and projects.

We would also like to thank our families for being so understanding about all of the time we had to invest in this project. Sorry. It did get out of hand. Now we know.

Last but not least we want to acknowledge and thank the team of reviewers who stood by us from the beginning and helped to see this project through. Their contributions were always insightful and useful. It would be impossible to produce a book like this without interested and knowledgeable reviewers. We were very fortunate. The reviewers were:

Samuel Abraham, Siena Heights University; Richard Baldwin, Austin Community College; Louise Darcey, Texas A&M University; Bill C. Hardgrave, University of Arkansas; and Nick Ourusoff, University of Maine, Augusta.

Dedications

To Eleanor Kay Doke — ERD

To JoAnn, Brian, and Kevin — JWS

To Richard, Josh, Mom and Dad — SRW

TECHNICAL REQUIREMENTS

TO THE USER

Source Code Files

To complete the steps and projects in this book, you will need source code files that have been created for this book. These files are included on the CD that comes with this book. You also can obtain the files electronically from the Course Technology Web site by connecting to **www.course.com**, and then searching for this book title.

Each chapter in this book has its own set of source code files that you use to review the examples and perform the Hands-on Exercises and end-of-chapter Projects. Files for each chapter are stored in a separate folder within the chapter folder. The folder names identify when you need the files. For example, the files for the first example in Chapter 9 are stored in the Chapter09\Example1 folder. Throughout this book, you will be instructed to open files from these folders.

You can use a computer in your school lab or your own computer to complete the chapters, Hands-on Exercises, and Projects in this book.

Using Your Own Computer

To use your own computer to complete the chapters, Hands-on Exercises, and Projects in this book, you will need the following:

- **A 486-level or higher personal computer running Windows 2000 Professional or Windows XP Professional Edition**

- **The Java 2 Software Development Kit (SDK)**. The examples in this text are based on version 1.3 of the Java 2 SDK, which is supplied by Sun Microsystems, Inc. This software, also referred to as the Java Development Kit (JDK), is included on the book's CD.

- **JDK Documentation**. Along with the JDK, Sun Microsystems supplies a collection of HTML files that provide complete documentation on the Java application programming interface (API). This documentation is also included on the book's CD.

- **A Java Integrated Development Environment (IDE)**. (*Optional*) You can use many IDEs for Java with the text. With the exception of Chapter 13, no specific IDE is assumed in the examples. Your instructor will provide information on the IDE to use for your course. You will need to learn the operational aspects of the IDE from your instructor.

- **The Forte IDE**. Forte 3.0, a Java IDE offered by Sun Microsystems, is required for Chapter 13 and is included on the book's CD. Chapter 13 provides a tutorial on Forte, including instructions for installing Forte on your system. Forte is also available for download from the Sun Web site at *http://java.sun.com*.

- **The JavaServer Web Development Kit (JSWDK).** To develop and test the programs in Chapter 17, you need Web server software. Many Java-enabled Web servers (Apache, Tomcat, Jigsaw, iPlanet, etc.) are available. For this book, we have chosen the JavaServer Web Development Kit, developed by Sun Microsystems. The JSWDK provides a simple way to test Java programs that will be deployed on the Web. Instructions for installing the JSWDK are given in Chapter 17.

- **A zip-compatible utility program (such as Winzip).** You will need a zip-compatible utility program (such as Winzip) to install the JDK documentation and to install the data files for Chapter 17.

- **Microsoft Internet Explorer or Netscape Navigator browser software.** You will need either Microsoft Internet Explorer or Netscape Navigator (to run the applets in Chapter 3 and to run the servlets in Chapter 17. If you do not have either program, you can download them for free from *www.netscape.com* or *www.microsoft.com*, respectively.

- **Microsoft Access.** The database applications in this text are based on Microsoft Access 2000 or higher. You will need Access to develop the examples and projects in Chapters 14 through 17.

Installing the JDK

1. Locate the self-extracting file named j2sdk-1_3_1-win.exe on the book's CD.
2. Double-click the file's icon.
3. Follow the instructions the installation program provides. Use the default settings suggested by the installation program.

Installing the JDK Documentation

1. Locate the file named j2sdk-1_3_1-doc.zip on the book's CD.
2. Double-click the file's icon.
3. Extract all files to the root directory of your C: drive, making sure that the option to preserve folder names is checked.

- The JDK and its documentation are also available for download from the Sun Web site at *http://java.sun.com*. The Sun Web site includes a number of other resources that are helpful with Java.

  If you encounter difficulty installing or running the JDK, you can find more information about the system requirements, installation instructions, and troubleshooting tips at the Sun Web site.

Visit Our World Wide Web Site

Additional materials designed especially for you might be available for your course on the World Wide Web. Go to **www.course.com**. Periodically search this site for more details.

TO THE INSTRUCTOR

To complete the chapters in this book, your users must use a set of source code files. These files are included on the Teaching Tools CD-ROM. They also may be obtained electronically through the Course Technology Web site at **www.course.com**. Follow the instructions in the Help file to copy the files to your server or standalone computer. You can view the Help file using a text editor such as WordPad or Notepad. Solutions files for the Hands-on Exercises and Projects may be found on the Instructor's Teaching Tools CD-ROM and also at **www.course.com**.

Once the files are copied, you should instruct your users how to copy the files to their own computers or workstations, including which folder you want them to use.

Course Technology Source Code Files

You are granted a license to copy the source code files to any computer or computer network used by individuals who have purchased this book.

PART 1

Object-Orientation and Java Fundamentals

Object-Oriented System Development

In this chapter you will:

- Learn about the characteristics of object-oriented development
- Understand fundamental object-oriented concepts, including object, class, and instance
- Learn about additional object-oriented concepts, such as attributes, methods, and encapsulation
- See how objects interact through messages and association relationships
- Understand how the concept of inheritance applies to classes of objects
- Learn about the benefits of using object-oriented development
- Preview object-oriented development

Object-oriented information system development involves analysis, design, and implementation of information systems using object–oriented programming languages, technologies, and techniques, and is usually referred to simply as "OO" (pronounced "oh oh") or "the OO approach." But OO often means something different to different information system developers depending upon their background or perspective. For example, to some developers OO means a graphical user interface (GUI) for an otherwise traditional application. To others OO means anything involved with client–server or Web-based systems. Still others say that OO means systems written with an OO programming language such as C++ or Java, regardless of the application.

When developing business systems, OO means using an object–oriented approach to systems analysis **(OOA)**, an object–oriented approach to system design **(OOD)**, and an object–oriented approach to programming **(OOP)** for the entire system development project. OO is not only about a GUI, or client-server relationships, or programming with C++ or Java. Simply learning an OO programming language like Java does not completely involve you in OO. Object-oriented development is a way of thinking, a complete approach to systems analysis, design, and programming.

This text presents an integrated and comprehensive overview of OO system development to introduce information systems students and practitioners to the OO approach. This text emphasizes OO programming using the Java programming language, and it assumes you have some introductory programming background. But experience with OO programming in general or Java programming specifically is not required. Similarly, it is helpful if you have some experience with systems analysis and design techniques and database management, but experience with OOA and OOD is not required.

You might already have read about OO and Java programming, and associate Java with animation and graphics on Web pages. Many Java programming books emphasize animation and graphics, but you also can use Java to develop complete information systems. With this book, you will learn how to develop complete business information systems using the OO approach from start to finish. Most business systems developers, both students and practitioners, want to learn this approach because that is what business organizations want. Therefore, this text provides a foundation in OOA, OOD, and OOP so you can get started with OO information system development using Java.

UNDERSTANDING OO DEVELOPMENT

Object-oriented development is often compared to traditional, procedural development. The **object-oriented approach** to information systems means a system is defined as a collection of objects that work together to accomplish tasks. The objects can carry out actions when asked, and each object maintains its own data. The procedural approach to information systems, on the other hand, means a system is a set of procedures that interact with data. The data are maintained in files separate from the procedures. When the procedure executes, or runs, data files are created or updated. Figure 1-1 shows the difference between object-oriented and procedural development. A procedure accepts an input, processes it, and then updates data in a separate data file. A specific object, however, receives a message and then updates its own internal data. The implications of what seems a simple distinction can actually be significant in terms of analysis, design, and programming, as you will see in the chapters ahead.

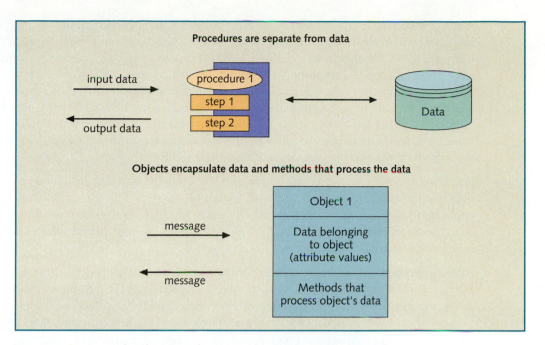

Figure 1-1   Procedural approach versus object-oriented approach

Object-Oriented Programming

Many people think object-oriented development is relatively new, but it dates back several decades. Object-oriented programming started in the 1960s in Norway with the development of the **Simula** programming language, the first language designed for running computer simulations. In the 1960s and now, programming problems that involve simulations require a different approach from procedural programming because simulations involve objects such as ships and planes or customers waiting in lines for bank tellers. Therefore, defining types of objects that maintain their own data values and giving them the ability to behave independently is a useful way for a simulation program to work.

For example, in a bank simulation, one type of object is a customer, and all customers can enter the bank, get in a line, wait in line, and advance to the next position in line. A teller line might be another type of object, able to add customers and move customers through the line to the teller. Before running the simulation, probabilities are set for the expected number of customers that enter the bank per hour and the expected time it takes for a teller to serve each customer. When the simulation runs, customers enter the bank, get in the shortest line, and advance through the line based on numbers randomly generated from probability distributions. Because each object (customers and lines) can behave and interact with other objects, the simulation can be run under many different assumptions to determine the maximum length of a teller line and the longest wait a customer might have. Outcomes of the simulation are used to make decisions about the number of tellers to have on duty at different times of the day.

A major milestone in the history of OO was the development of the **SmallTalk** programming language by Alan Kay and associates at the Xerox Palo Alto Research Center (Xerox PARC) in the early 1970s. SmallTalk was the first general-purpose object-oriented programming language. Kay envisioned a revolutionary computing environment where the user would interact directly with objects on the screen of a notebook-sized computer called the Dynabook. In the late 1960s, a notebook-sized computer seemed impossible—recall that Hal the computer in the 1967 film *2001: A Space Odyssey* was large enough to fill half of the spaceship. Because the electronics and hardware needed to build a notebook computer did not yet exist, Kay focused on the software programming environment that might run the machine.

SmallTalk was the software environment, and Kay designed it to define objects in an application that interact with the user and with other objects. SmallTalk was initially used for GUI applications, similar to those popularized by the Apple Macintosh computer almost a decade later. SmallTalk has since been used for developing business information systems that include business application objects.

Additional object-oriented programming languages have been developed, including Objective-C, Eiffel, and most notably **C++**. C++ is an object-oriented extension to the C procedural language, so when C++ was first introduced, many procedural programmers were already familiar with its syntax. This helped make C++ a leading object-oriented language, although it is not purely object-oriented, because programmers can still use C++ to write procedural programs if they want to. Many special-purpose OO languages have also been developed, such as an object-oriented version of COBOL designed to appeal to business programmers. Figure 1-2 lists some of the object-oriented programming languages in use by the 1990s.

In 1995, Sun Microsystems introduced **Java** as a pure OO language with a syntax similar to C++ and other features that make it ideal for Internet applications, such as the ability to download programs (applets) from the Internet that can run on any computer platform. Microsoft immediately released a version of Java called J++ and has recently introduced a similar language called C# to compete directly with Java. Because Java is a pure OO language and can be used to develop applications on any platform, including Web-based applications, it is an excellent choice for learning OO development and for developing OO systems.

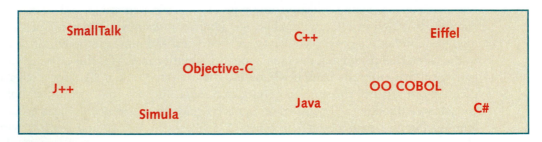

Figure 1-2   Some object-oriented programming languages

Object-Oriented Analysis and Design

You learned earlier that OO development is not only about OO programming. Figure 1-3 shows how object–oriented analysis, design, and programming are related.

As interest in OO development grew in the early 1980s, systems designers needed object–oriented analysis and object–oriented design techniques to help them develop systems. Early OOA and OOD techniques emerged in the late 1980s. Several key procedural system development methodologists turned their attention to OO analysis and design techniques. Ed Yourdon, for example, was instrumental in developing structured analysis and structured design techniques. James Martin is credited with creating the information engineering development techniques in an attempt to improve structured analysis and design. Both Yourdon and Martin went on to write books on OOA and OOD. Other people proposed OOA and OOD techniques based on their work in the industry, including Grady Booch, James Rumbaugh, and Ivar Jacobson. Booch, Rumbaugh, and Jacobson eventually joined forces to define what is now the standard object–oriented analysis and design modeling notation called the **Unified Modeling Language (UML)**.

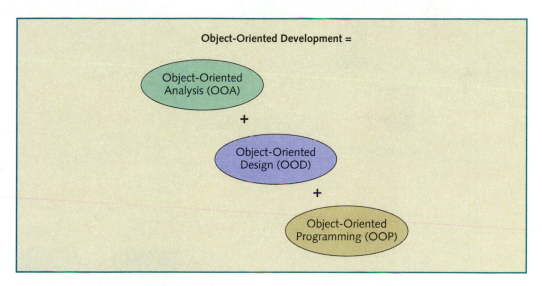

Figure 1-3   Object-oriented development

This text shows you how to interpret and create UML models as you learn about OO development. UML uses a **model–driven approach** to analysis and design, meaning that as a developer, you create graphical models of the system requirements and the system design. Diagrams with symbols such as rectangles, lines, ovals, and squares show what the system is required to accomplish and how a system component should be built. Standard use of these symbols on UML diagrams makes it easier for system developers to communicate with each other during development. Traditional structured analysis and design and information engineering also use a model–driven approach. They create graphical models, such as data flow diagrams (DFDs), entity-relationship diagrams (ERDs), and structure charts during system development. However, in OO development with UML, you create different types of models. OOA and OOD use **class diagrams**, **use case diagrams**, **sequence diagrams**, and **statecharts**, as shown in Figure 1–4. Relying on these models to analyze and build systems defines the OO approach as model-driven.

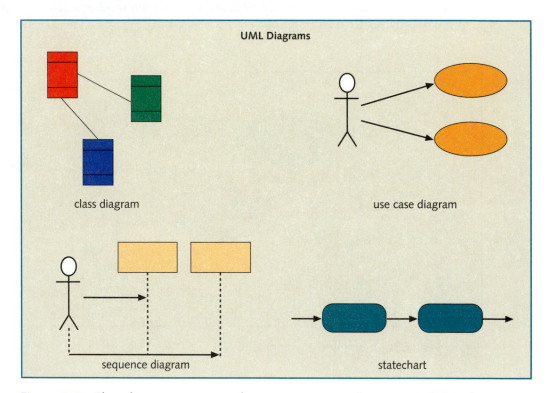

Figure 1-4 Class diagrams, use case diagrams, sequence diagrams, and statecharts

However, OOA and OOD require more than modeling notation. The system development life cycle (SDLC) is a project management framework that defines project phases and activities within phases that are completed when developing a system. The phases typically are named planning, analysis, design, implementation, and support. The SDLC was first created for traditional system development, but it also applies to OO development. In addition to building a system in these phases, OO developers usually follow an iterative approach to analysis, design, and implementation. Iteration means repeating a process or task, so an iterative approach to development means that you complete some analysis, some design, and some implementation, and then complete more analysis, more design, and more implementation.

Techniques such as prototyping and joint application development (JAD) are also usually part of OO development. Prototyping means creating a working model of one or more parts of a system to give users a chance to see and evaluate something concrete. During JAD sessions, key system stakeholders and decision makers work together to define system requirements and designs in a short period of time. Project management, interviewing and data collection, user interface design, testing, and conversion techniques, among others, are required when using OO development, as they are in traditional system development. So, even though the OO approach is different from procedural programming in terms of what a system is and how it works, using the SDLC approach and other project management techniques means that OOA and OOD have much in common with more traditional information system development.

UNDERSTANDING OBJECT-ORIENTED CONCEPTS

As discussed previously, object-oriented development assumes a system is a collection of objects that interact to accomplish tasks. To understand and discuss this development method, you should be familiar with the key concepts that apply to objects and OO, shown in Figure 1-5. These concepts are briefly introduced in this section, and are explained and demonstrated more completely throughout the book.

Figure 1-5   Key OO concepts

Objects, Attributes, and Methods

An **object** in a computer system is like an object in the real world—it is a thing that has attributes and behaviors. A computer system can have many types of objects, such as GUI objects that make up the user interface to the system and problem domain objects that are the focus of the application. For example a **GUI object** such as a button or label has **attributes**, which are characteristics of an object that have values: the size, shape, color, location, and caption of the button. A form or window has attributes, such as height and width, border style, and background color. These GUI objects also have behaviors, or **methods**, which describe what an object can do. For example, a button can be clicked, a label can display text, and a form or window can change size and appear or disappear. Figure 1-6 lists some GUI objects with their attributes and methods.

GUI Objects	Attributes	Methods
Button	size, shape, color, location, caption	click, enable, disable, hide, show
Label	size, shape, color, location, text	set text, get text, hide, show
Form	width, height, border style, background color	change size, minimize, maximize, appear, disappear

Figure 1-6   Attributes and methods of GUI objects

GUI objects are the easiest to understand because users (and developers) can see them and interact with them directly. But OO systems contain other types of objects, called **problem domain objects**, which are specific to a business application. For example, a business system that processes orders includes customer objects, order objects, and product objects. Like GUI objects, problem domain objects also have attributes and methods, as shown in Figure 1-7. The attributes are much like the attributes of data entities in ERDs used in structured analysis and information engineering: Each customer has a name, address, and phone number, for example. But in OO, these objects also have methods, as do GUI objects, giving problem domain objects the ability to perform tasks. For example, the methods of each customer include the ability to set the name and address, give the values of the name and address, and add a new order for the customer. The methods of an order might be to set an order date, calculate an order amount, and add a product to an order.

Problem Domain Objects	Attributes	Methods
Customer	name, address, phone number	set name, set address, add new order for customer
Order	order number, date, amount	set order date, calculate order, amount, add product to order, schedule order shipment
Product	product number, description, price	add to order, set description, get price

Figure 1-7   Attributes and methods in problem domain objects

Object Interactions and Messages

Objects interact by sending **messages** to each other, asking another object to invoke, or carry out, one of its methods. In other words, a customer object representing a customer named Bill gets a message to add a new order for itself. The order, once added, will then calculate the order amount and accomplish other tasks. Objects interacting by sending messages to carry out tasks is the main concept of OOA and OOD.

Figure 1–8 shows an order–processing system (containing Customer Bill) as a collection of interacting objects. The user interacts with GUI objects. The GUI objects interact with problem domain objects by sending messages.

The order-processing system works as follows:

1. The user types information about a product in a text box, and then clicks the button. The click results in a message to the button.

2. The button knows that when it is clicked, it should request that Customer Bill add a new order, so the button sends the message to Customer Bill, a problem domain object representing a customer.

3. Customer Bill knows how to add a new order because that is a method all customers have. To add an order, Customer Bill sends a message to create an order object.

4. The new order object assigns itself an order number (Order 143) and then asks the text box for its text, which the text box supplies. Order 143 uses the text to identify the products the user entered for the order.

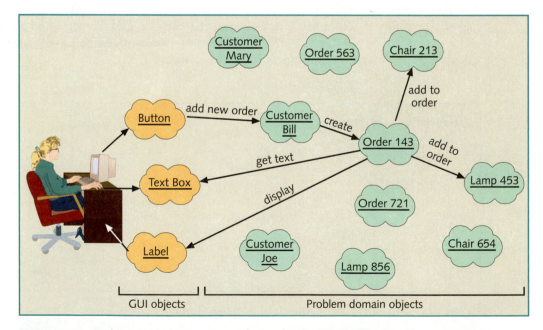

5. Order 143 sends an add-to-order message to each product asking it to add itself to the order, in this case a message to Chair 213 and to Lamp 453.

6. Chair 213 and Lamp 453 add themselves to the order and supply information about their price and availability.

7. Order 143 completes the task by calculating the order amount and sending a message to the label asking it to display information about the completed order to the user.

Encapsulation and Information Hiding

The objects Customer Bill and Order 143 each have attributes and methods, giving them the ability to respond to messages. **Encapsulation** means that an object has attributes and methods combined into one unit, as do objects Customer Bob and Order 143. By combining attributes and methods, you do not need to know the internal structure of the object to send messages to it. You only need to know what an object can do for you. Encapsulation hides the internal structure of objects, also protecting them from corruption. This is what is meant by **information hiding** in OO, another key concept.

Each object also has a unique **identity**, meaning you can find it, or refer to it, and send it a message. You need to know an object's identity before you can ask the object to do something for you, such as creating a new order. The object's identity is usually stored as a memory address. The system uses a specific object like Customer Bill over a period time, so there must be some mechanism for keeping it available. **Persistent objects** are those that are defined as available for use over time. If a system uses thousands of customer objects, each with its own orders, the system must be able to remember all of them.

Classes, Instances, and Associations

An order-processing system has many customer objects, one for each real-world customer (see Figure 1-9). All of the customer objects are *classified* as a type of thing—a customer—so in OO development, you refer to the Customer class when you are talking about all of the customer objects. The **class** defines what all objects of the class represent. When you are talking about computer programming and objects, you can refer to the objects as **instances** of the class. When an object is created for the class, it is common to say the class is *instantiated* (making an instance of a class). Therefore, the terms "instance" and "object" are often used interchangeably.

You have seen that objects interact by sending messages, but they also maintain **association relationships** among themselves. A customer object maintains associations with order objects that apply to the customer, for example, so the customer object can find and inquire about its orders—a customer places an order. Each order object is associated with products—an order includes a product (see Figure 1-10). Object associations are conceptually similar to relationships in an ERD, except each object is responsible for maintaining its relationships with other objects.

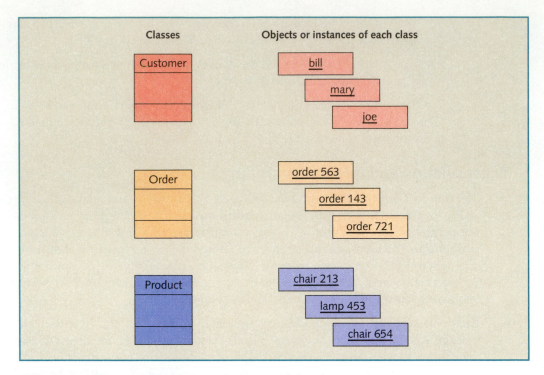

Figure 1-9   Class versus objects or instances of the class

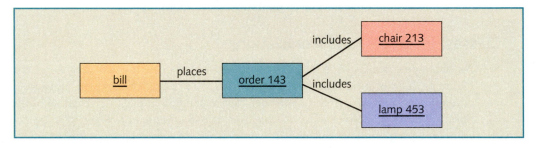

Figure 1-10   Associating objects with other objects

Some association relationships are one-to-one, such as when one order is associated with one customer, and some associations are one-to-many, such as when one customer places many orders. UML refers to the number of associations as the **multiplicity** of the association. Those familiar with ERDs use the term **cardinality** for the same concept.

Inheritance and Polymorphism

Probably the most often used concept when discussing OO is **inheritance**, where one class of objects takes on characteristics of another class and extends them. For example, an object belonging to the Customer class might also be something more general, such as a person. Therefore, if the Person class is already defined, the Customer class can be defined by extending the Person class to take on more specific attributes and methods required of a customer.

For example, the Person class might have attributes for name and address. The Customer class is a special type of person with additional attributes for shipping address and credit card information. Similarly, a sales clerk object is also a person, so the Sales Clerk class can also be defined by extending the Person class. For example, a sales clerk has additional attributes for job title and pay rate. The Person class is a **superclass** and both Customer and Sales Clerk are **subclasses**. This relationship is shown in Figure 1-11.

Classifying objects helps to identify special types of problem domain objects, providing more specific information about the requirements for the system. The result of extending general classes into more specific subclasses is referred to as a **generalization/specialization hierarchy**, sometimes called an **inheritance hierarchy**.

Attributes are not the only characteristics inherited from a superclass. Subclasses also inherit methods and association relationships. A final key concept that is related to generalization/specialization hierarchies and inheritance of methods is **polymorphism**, which means "many forms." In OO, polymorphism refers to the way different objects can respond in their own way to the same message. For example, a dialog box, a network connection, and a document might each receive a message to close. Each knows how to close and will do so in its own way when asked. The sender of the message does not need to know what type of object it is or how it does it; the sender only needs to know that the object responds to the *close* message. Classes are polymorphic if their instances can respond to the same message.

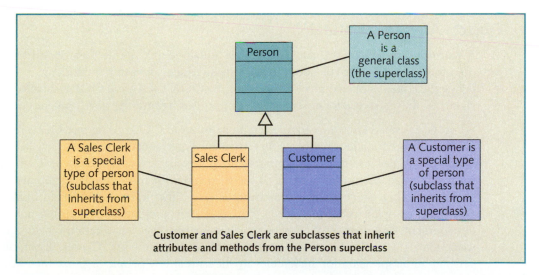

Figure 1-11   Superclass and subclass

For example, a bank has several types of bank accounts, including money market accounts and passbook accounts. Both types of accounts calculate interest, but they follow different rules for interest. The sender of the message *calculateInterest* does not need to know what type of account it is, only that it will calculate interest when asked (see Figure 1-12). This greatly simplifies processing when all bank account objects can be sent the same message and the job is done correctly and completely by each object.

It might seem that you have many OO concepts to learn. As you read through this text and complete Java programming assignments, you will master the subtleties of these OO concepts.

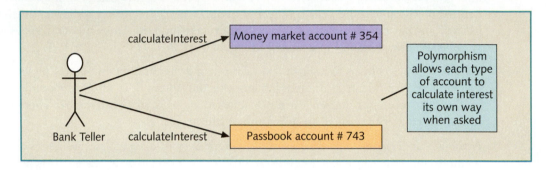

Figure 1-12   Polymorphism for two different types of bank accounts

RECOGNIZING THE BENEFITS OF OO DEVELOPMENT

The object-oriented approach was originally found to be useful in computer simulations and for graphical user interfaces, but why is it being used in more conventional information system development? The two main reasons are the benefits of naturalness and reuse.

Objects Are More Natural

Naturalness refers to the fact that people usually think about their world in terms of objects, so when people talk about their work and discuss system requirements, it is natural to define the classes of objects involved. Additionally, OOA, OOD, and OOP all involve modeling classes of objects, so the focus remains on objects throughout the development process.

Some experienced system developers continue to avoid OO, arguing that OO is really not as natural as procedural programming. In fact, many experienced developers have had difficulty learning OO. Because procedural programming was the first approach to programming they learned, it might seem more natural to them now. But for most people, including those new to programming, procedural programming is very difficult. Few people can think through and write complex procedural code. For most new programmers learning about system development, OO does seem fairly natural. In addition, object orientation is natural to system users. They can easily discuss the objects involved in their work. Classes, classification, and generalization/specialization hierarchies are the natural way people organize their knowledge.

Classes of Objects Can Be Reused

In addition to naturalness, the ability to reuse classes and objects is another benefit of object-oriented development. **Reuse** means that classes and objects can be invented once and used many times. Once a developer defines a class, such as the Customer class, it can be reused in many other systems that have customer objects. If the new system has a special type of customer, the existing Customer class can be extended to a new subclass by inheriting all that a customer is, and then adding the new characteristics. Classes can be reused in this manner during analysis, design, or programming.

When programming, you do not have to see the source code for the class that is being reused, even if you are defining a new class that inherits from it. This simplifies development. Object-oriented programming languages like Java come with class libraries that contain predefined classes most programmers need. In Java, these are called "packages." For example, GUI classes such as buttons, labels, text fields, and check boxes come in one Java package. As a programmer, you do not need to create these classes from scratch. Instead, you use the class to create objects you need for your GUI. Other packages also contain useful classes, such as those to connect to databases or networks and those to hold collections of objects.

LEARNING OO DEVELOPMENT

This book provides a comprehensive guide to OO system development, including OOA, OOD, and OOP. You will use object-oriented programming to learn and practice OO concepts, so it may look like a programming text to you. But keep in mind the distinction between learning a language and learning OO system development as you work through the text. Learning OO development is *more* than only learning Java.

To emphasize this distinction, this section provides a roadmap for the organization of the text.

Introducing Three-Tier Design

As you will see, the book is organized according to an approach to OO development called **three-tier design**. Three-tier design requires that the collection of objects that interact in an OO system are separated into three categories of classes—problem domain classes, GUI classes, and data access classes. As discussed previously, problem domain classes are the classes of objects specific to the business application, such as the Customer class, Order class, and Product class. GUI classes define the objects that make up the user interface to the application, such as buttons, labels, lists, and text boxes. The third category includes data access classes, which work with the database management system to store information about objects for later use.

Three-tier design requires that OO system developers define three categories of classes when designing and building the system. First, the developers identify and specify the problem domain classes. Once these are specified, the developers define how GUI classes will be used to allow the user to interact with the problem domain classes. Finally, they specify data access classes to allow problem domain classes to interact with the database. Once all three tiers are completed, they are ready to work together as a complete system.

The core of this book is organized according to the three tiers of OO development. To understand OO development using Java, you first need to understand basic OO concepts and the basics of Java language syntax. Part 1 introduces OO development and Java. Parts 2 through 5 follow the process of OO development based on the three-tier design approach: problem domain classes, GUI classes, and data access classes. Problem domain classes are covered first because they are the focus during OOA. OOD involves adding GUI classes that users interact with and data access classes to allow object persistence using a database. Adding GUI classes is covered in Part 3, adding data access classes is covered in Part 4, and the three tiers are combined into the completed system in Part 5. Each of the five parts is described in more detail below.

Part 1: Object-Orientation and Java Fundamentals

Part 1 covers OO concepts and introduces the Java programming language. This first chapter sets the stage for OO development and defines the key OO concepts and benefits. Chapters 2 and 3 turn to Java, examining Java fundamentals first in Chapter 2. As with any other programming language, you first need to learn the basic syntax and rules. Java uses variables, computations, and structured programming constructs such as statements, decisions, loops, and arrays. If you have had an introductory course in Java, you might skim or skip Chapter 2.

Chapter 3 introduces Java programming using classes supplied in Java class libraries. This approach provides an object-oriented view of Java, and begins to show the power of interacting with object instances and methods and the benefits of reuse. Supplied classes discussed include String, Date, Calendar, and Vector. An additional supplied class is the Applet class. An Applet is a special Java program that can be downloaded from the Internet and run from a Web page using a browser. Using these classes demonstrates how inheritance and instantiation (making an instance of a class) actually work. The rest of the text focuses on business systems and more complete Java applications.

Chapter 4 introduces OOA and OOD concepts and describes the business case study that is used throughout the text—Bradshaw Marina. Chapter 4 also covers the UML models used during OOA and OOD, including the use case diagram, class diagram, and sequence diagram. These diagrams are used throughout the text to show the value of taking a model-driven approach to development. The models show what the system is used for, what classes are involved, and what messages are sent from object to object. The Java code written to implement the system is based on the details in the models.

Part 2: Defining Problem Domain Classes

Part 2 shows how to use Java to create new problem domain classes that are specific to the business system being developed. In Bradshaw Marina, these classes include boats, docks, and slips. Chapter 5 demonstrates how to create a problem domain class with a few attributes and methods. An approach to testing new classes is introduced where tester programs are written to send messages to instantiate classes and to invoke methods of instances. Chapter 6 continues the discussion of problem domain classes, adding data validation and introducing Java's approach to handling errors—throwing exceptions. Method overloading and more on custom methods are also covered.

Chapters 7 and 8 introduce generalization/specialization and inheritance for problem domain classes. In the Bradshaw Marina system, sailboats and powerboats are subclasses of boat. Adding subclasses and overriding superclass methods are two important concepts you will explore in these chapters. Interfaces, custom exceptions, and examples of polymorphism are also covered.

Chapter 9 shows how to implement association relationships among classes. You will investigate one-to-one associations, including situations where one object needs to know about another object to send it a message. For example, a boat is kept in a slip (one-to-one association). You might ask a slip to tell you what boat is contained in it, requiring a slip to ask a boat for information. The chapter extends the example to one-to-many associations, where a dock has many slips. Now you can ask a dock for a list of all slips and information on the boat in each slip.

Part 3: Defining GUI Classes

Part 3 describes how to create graphical user interface classes that the user can interact with. The GUI classes in turn interact with problem domain classes. Chapter 10 describes the event model for Java that is used to recognize user actions. Then you use built-in Java Swing classes to create the GUI. Chapter 11 describes how to create a GUI window that can interact with problem domain objects for Bradshaw Marina. Chapter 12 extends the example to include a main menu and multiple GUI windows for Bradshaw. Up to this point, you create the GUI components by writing Java code to make sure you understand how the code works. Chapter 13 demonstrates how you can use an integrated development environment (IDE) to visually develop the GUI components of the system.

Part 4: Defining Data Access Classes

Part 4 covers the third tier—data access classes. Data access classes are used to manage database interactions and achieve object persistence. Chapter 14 shows examples of using files, relational databases, and object serialization to achieve object persistence. Object serialization and object-oriented database management systems might be the future of data access classes, but for now, you work with relational databases for this purpose. Therefore, Chapter 15 explores relational database management and structured query language (SQL) for data access classes in more detail.

Part 5: Deploying the Three-Tier Application

Part 5 shows how GUI classes, problem domain classes, and data access classes function together as three tiers to create a complete client-server system. The emphasis in this text is on business systems, and you'll see how the complete OO development process comes together in the Bradshaw Marina examples in Chapter 16. Finally, Chapter 17 demonstrates Web-based technologies and shows you how to deploy the Bradshaw Marina examples on the Web using HTML and Java servlets.

Once you have completed this text, you will understand how all three tiers are designed and implemented using Java to create a complete business system, from OOA to OOD to OOP, including deployment on the Web.

Summary

- Object-oriented information system development includes object-oriented analysis (OOA), object-oriented design (OOD), and object-oriented programming (OOP).

- Object-oriented (OO) systems are viewed as collections of interacting objects that accomplish tasks, and the first OO programming began in the 1960s with the Simula language. SmallTalk, C++, and most recently Java are examples of OO languages.

- The OO development process includes much more than just programming. A model-driven approach using Unified Modeling Language (UML) diagrams defines requirements and designs prior to programming. Other system development principles and techniques are also used in OO development.

- Key object-oriented concepts include objects, classes, instances, messages, encapsulation and information hiding, association relationships, inheritance, and polymorphism.

- The benefits of OO development include naturalness and reuse. Classes and objects are a natural way for people to think about the world. Once classes are defined, they can be reused in other systems.

- This text is organized into five parts following the three-tier design approach to OO development. The three tiers include problem domain classes, GUI classes, and data access classes.

- Part 1 of this text provides an introduction to OO and to Java, Part 2 emphasizes defining and programming problem domain classes, Part 3 emphasizes adding a graphical user interface (GUI) to the system, Part 4 emphasizes adding data access classes to allow object persistence using a database management system, and Part 5 combines the three tiers—GUI classes, problem domain classes, and data access classes—into a finished system, and demonstrates how to deploy the application on the Web.

Key Terms

association relationships	Java	persistent object
attribute	message	polymorphism
C++	method	problem domain object
cardinality	model-driven approach	reuse
class	multiplicity	sequence diagram
class diagram	naturalness	Simula
encapsulation	object	SmallTalk
generalization/specialization hierarchy	object-oriented analysis (OOA)	statechart
GUI object	object-oriented approach	subclass
identity	object-oriented design (OOD)	superclass
information hiding	object-oriented information system development	three-tier design
inheritance	object-oriented programming (OOP)	Unified Modeling Language (UML)
inheritance hierarchy		use case diagram
instance		

Review Questions

1. The analysis, design, and implementation of information systems using object–oriented programming languages, technologies, and techniques is called:

    a. object-oriented development

    b. procedural development

    c. inheritance

    d. information engineering

2. OO development includes which of the following?

    a. only OOA and OOP

    b. only OOD and OOP

    c. OOA, OOD, and OOP

    d. structured analysis and design

3. Which of the following is NOT an example of an OO programming language?

a. SmallTalk

b. Pascal

c. C++

d. Java

4. The first pure general-purpose OO language was:

a. SmallTalk

b. Pascal

c. C++

d. Java

5. UML is an acronym for:

a. Uniform Model Limitations

b. Unknown Marketing Lingo

c. Unified Modeling Language

d. Uninformed Machine Location

6. A model-driven approach to development is used for:

a. traditional, procedural development only

b. object-oriented development only

c. small hobby systems

d. both traditional and OO development

7. Which of the following is NOT a technique used in both traditional and OO development?

a. project management

b. interviewing

c. program testing

d. class diagramming

8. Which of the following is NOT a diagram defined by UML?

a. entity-relationship diagram

b. class diagram

c. use case diagram

d. sequence diagram

9. An object–oriented system is defined as:

   a. a collection of interacting objects that accomplish tasks

   b. classes and procedures that are separate from data

   c. data flow applications that process inputs into outputs

   d. any system designed for the Internet

10. A thing that has attributes and behaviors is called a(n):

    a. scenario

    b. use case

    c. object

    d. method

11. A characteristic of an object that takes on a value is called a(n):

    a. class

    b. use case

    c. object

    d. attribute

12. What an object is capable of doing in terms of behavior is called a(n):

    a. class

    b. use case

    c. object

    d. method

13. Objects that make up the user interface to the system are called:

    a. problem domain objects

    b. data access objects

    c. GUI objects

    d. visual objects

14. Objects that are specific to the business application are called:

    a. problem domain objects

    b. data access objects

    c. GUI objects

    d. visual objects

15. A request asking an object to invoke, or carry out, one of its methods is called a(n):

    a. command

    b. invocation

    c. attribution

    d. message

16. Encapsulation hides the internal structure of objects and protects them from corruption. This is referred to as:

    a. information hiding

    b. polymorphism

    c. inheritance

    d. generalization/specialization

17. Each object has a unique address, meaning you can find it, or refer to it, and send it a message. This is referred to as the:

    a. object key

    b. class identifier

    c. index value

    d. object identity

18. Persistent objects are those that:

    a. are available to use over time

    b. never give up when sending a message

    c. are usually important enough to be given priority

    d. make up the user interface

19. A class and an object are:

    a. different because a class is an instance and an object is a category

    b. the same because a class is the same as an object

    c. different because a class is like an instance and an object is like an association

    d. different because a class is a type of thing and an object is a specific instance

20. Which of the following is an association relationship?

    a. A customer is a special type of person.

    b. A person has an attribute called name.

    c. A customer enrolls in a credit program.

    d. A credit program is a special type of account.

21. The number of associations possible between classes of objects is called:

    a. polymorphism

    b. multiplicity

    c. relationships

    d. methods

22. An example of a superclass of the class Car is:

    a. motor vehicle

    b. sports car

    c. sport utility vehicle

    d. truck

23. An example of a subclass of the class Truck is:

    a. motor vehicle

    b. sports car

    c. station wagon

    d. dump truck

24. Polymorphism means that a blender and a washing machine:

    a. are both tangible objects

    b. can both be told to spin

    c. are types of household appliances

    d. are problem domain objects for a retail store

25. The two benefits of OO development are:

    a. naturalness and reuse

    b. methods and messages

    c. association and generalization/specialization

    d. clients and servers

26. Three-tier design divides the system into the following categories of classes:

    a. GUI classes, database classes, operating system classes

    b. problem domain classes, operating system classes, GUI classes

    c. problem domain classes, GUI classes, data access classes

    d. GUI classes, procedural classes, data access classes

Discussion Questions

1. This chapter (and the whole book) argues that OO development is much more than programming. List and discuss at least four of the system development activities and tasks that do not directly involve programming. Is OO development any different in this regard than traditional development? Discuss.

2. OO is not new, but it has taken a while to catch on with business systems development. Discuss some of the reasons for this. Are there still some factors holding back OO development? Discuss.

Projects

1. Talk with some of your colleagues and friends about procedural programming versus OO programming. Develop a list of at least five specific issues about both approaches that seem natural or unnatural.

2. Review the key features of Visual Basic, which is considered to be partly OO and partly procedural. What specific aspects of VB are object–oriented and which are more traditional?

3. Problem domain classes are a key part of OOA. What are some of the key problem domain classes that would apply to a system for scheduling courses at a university? Expand at least two of these classes into generalization/specialization hierarchies, with a superclass and subclasses.

4. In Project 3, you listed problem domain classes for a system for scheduling courses at a university. What are at least three association relationships between the problem domain classes?

5. Consider the GUI classes that make up one finished GUI form in a Windows system. The GUI form contains many specific GUI objects. List as many of these GUI classes as you can. What are some generalization/specialization hierarchies of GUI classes? What are some association relationships among these classes found on a typical GUI form?

CHAPTER

2

Java Programming Fundamentals

In this chapter you will:

♦ Learn about the Java programming language
♦ Define a Java class
♦ Declare variables and constants
♦ Write computational statements
♦ Write decision-making statements
♦ Write loops
♦ Declare and access arrays

Chapter 1 introduced you to object-oriented systems development, basic OO concepts, and the OO vocabulary. You learned about OO and its brief history. In this chapter, you will learn the fundamentals of the Java programming language.

This book assumes that you are familiar with the basics of some programming language. Although Java requires that you learn a new syntax, many of the Java statements will likely seem familiar to you. For example, the if-then-else syntax and the looping statements while and do are similar in many programming languages.

This chapter shows you how to declare variables; write computational statements, decision-making statements, and loops; and declare and access arrays. After completing this chapter, you will understand basic Java syntax and identify how Java is different from other languages. You should be able to design and write simple Java classes. This chapter focuses on presenting the fundamentals of programming in Java, while Chapter 3 explores Java as an object-oriented language and provides a reference for Java syntax.

INTRODUCING JAVA

First released in mid–1995, Java is a relatively young language, yet in this short period it has achieved popularity and widespread acceptance. Developed by Sun Microsystems, Java was designed to be a powerful, full-featured, object-oriented development language that was easy to learn and use on any computing platform. In addition, Java was designed to support the development of applications for networked environments.

Java's power comes, in part, from its large, useful library of classes containing hundreds of prewritten classes. These classes provide methods to accomplish tasks ranging from simple number formatting to establishing network connections and accessing relational databases. Many of these supplied classes and their methods are illustrated in this and subsequent chapters.

Java is object-oriented, which means it implements the OO concepts you learned about in Chapter 1: class, instance, method, attribute, encapsulation, inheritance, and polymorphism. By adopting the OO model, Java encourages good software design that can dramatically reduce debugging and maintenance chores. Chapter 3 discusses the OO aspects of Java in more detail.

Java's simplicity is achieved by using a set of **keywords** that is smaller than in most other languages. Keywords have special meaning in a programming language and are used in writing statements. Languages such as COBOL and Visual Basic have hundreds of keywords, but Java has only 48, which are listed in Table 2-1. In this book, and in many Java editors, Java's keywords are shown in blue, such as `if` and `for`. In Table 2-1, the keywords in bold are defined in this chapter. Note that **const** and **goto** are not currently used.

Table 2-1   Java Keywords

abstract	**boolean**	**break**	**byte**
case	catch	**char**	**class**
const	continue	**default**	**do**
double	**else**	extends	**final**
finally	**float**	For	goto
If	implements	**import**	instanceof
int	interface	**long**	native
new	**package**	private	protected
public	**return**	**short**	**static**
strictfp	super	**switch**	synchronized
this	throw	throws	transient
try	**void**	volatile	**while**

Java's portability means that programs can be written and compiled once and then run on many different processors and operating systems. Portability is important for Internet applications because Java programs, called Applets and illustrated in Chapter 3, are often downloaded from a server to a client system for execution. The downloaded code must be able to run on a variety of computing platforms without recompiling. If you access the World Wide Web, you have almost certainly downloaded and executed Java Applets, although you probably did not notice.

Java's portability is achieved by using **bytecode** and an **interpreter**. Bytecode is produced when you compile a Java program. Java bytecode then executes under the control of an interpreter designed specifically for each type of computing platform. This interpreter is called the **Java Virtual Machine** (**JVM**). The combination of bytecode and a JVM means that you can write a Java program without knowing what type of computing platform it will be using. For example, you can write the program on a Microsoft Windows system, but then have it execute on a Sun workstation using the UNIX operating system.

Figure 2-1 shows how Java bytecode is produced. The program you write is called a source file and the filename has a .java extension, as in HelloWorldWideWeb.java. When the source file is compiled, a bytecode file is produced. The bytecode filename has a class extension, as in HelloWorldWideWeb.class. The bytecode file is executed by a JVM.

You can compile Java source code files from the command line if you have the **Java Development Kit** (**JDK**) installed on your computer. The JDK consists of the Java compiler, hundreds of prewritten classes, and the JVM. The most recent version of the JDK can be downloaded for free from the Sun Web site at *http://java.sun.com*.

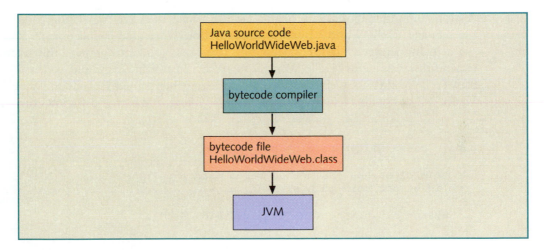

Figure 2-1   Compiling Java

Table 2-2 Integrated Development Environment Software

Vendor	Product	URL
Allaire	Kawa	*www.allaire.com*
Borland	Jbuilder	*www.borland.com*
Helios Software	TextPad	*www.textpad.com*
IBM	Visual Age	*www.ibm.com*
Oracle	JDeveloper	*www.oracle.com*
RealJ	RealJ	*www.realj.com*
Sun Microsystems	Forte	*java.sun.com*
Symantec	Visual Café	*www.symantec.com*

You also can use one of several excellent **Integrated Development Environments (IDEs)** to develop OO software with Java. These IDEs improve development productivity by providing sophisticated editors that interact with the JDK. The editors provide various tools, including color-coding to indicate the parts of a Java program. In addition, powerful debugging and graphical development tools are provided. Table 2-2 lists several Java IDE vendors, the products they offer, and where to find information about these products on the Web. All of the Java examples you see in this book were written and tested using RealJ. Chapter 13 illustrates in some detail how to use Sun Microsystem's Forte.

BUILDING A JAVA CLASS

A programming tradition is to begin learning a new language by writing code to display the message "Hello World". Because Java is an object-oriented language, each source code file actually defines a class. For your first Java class, you can continue this tradition but expand the message to "Hello World Wide Web". In this first example, you will name the class HelloWorldWideWeb and store the code in a file named HelloWorldWideWeb.java. Figure 2-2 shows the HelloWorldWideWeb.java listing, and Figure 2-3 shows the output.

```
public class HelloWorldWideWeb
{
 // this class has one method named main
 public static void main(String[] args)
 {
    System.out.println("Hello World Wide Web");
 }
}
```

Figure 2-2 HelloWorldWideWeb.java listing

```
Hello World Wide Web
```

Figure 2-3   HelloWorldWideWeb output

Take a look at the class listing in Figure 2-2 and shown in the following code. The first line is called a **class header** because it describes the class contained in the source code file. Note that the keywords **public** and **class** are shown in blue.

```
public class HelloWorldWideWeb
```

The keyword **public** indicates that this class has public accessibility, meaning anyone can use it. The keyword **class** indicates that this line of code is a class header, and **HelloWorldWideWeb** establishes the class name.

The color-coding here is important. The dark blue words are Java keywords (**public**) and the black words (**HelloWorldWideWeb**) are **identifiers**. A Java identifier is the name of a class, method, or variable. Java's rules for identifiers are, like many things in Java, quite simple.

- They can be any length you choose.

- They can include any character except a space.

- They must begin with a letter of the alphabet, a dollar sign ($), or the underscore character (_).

Java uses the open curly brace ({) and closed curly brace (}) to delineate a **block of code**. All code in a Java class is enclosed as a single block of code, which itself can contain additional blocks. In the code shown in Figure 2-2, the block begins with the first open curly brace and ends with the last closed curly brace, which are highlighted in the following code:

```
{
    // this class has one method named main
    public static void main(String[] args)
    {
    System.out.println("Hello World Wide Web");
    }

}
```

Java uses code blocks to group statements. Later you will see how Java uses code blocks for methods, loops, and if statements. Note that the HelloWorldWideWeb.java code has a second set of open and closed curly braces defining a block of code within the first block. This second code block is for a method that is explained in the following paragraphs.

Java is case sensitive. For example, Java distinguishes between public and Public and between class and Class (in both of these cases, the lowercase version is the correct keyword). If you have been writing in a language that is not case sensitive, be especially careful when typing Java code.

Also, the compiler does not require you to indent code, but good programming practice encourages indentation as shown in the examples in this text. The compiler also lets you extend a statement over more than one line—no line continuation character is required. (Note, however, that you cannot break a line in the middle of a string literal—a value enclosed within double quotes. To do so, you must use the concatenation operator described in the next section.)

In the HelloWorldWideWeb code, a comment line follows the class header and open curly brace. You use comment lines to add explanation to your code which the compiler ignores. A Java comment begins with a double forward slash `//` and can be on a line by itself or at the end of a line of code. Java has two other forms of comment statements. The first, called a multiline comment, begins with `/*` and ends with `*/`. The second, called a documentation comment, also can extend over multiple lines. However, it begins with `/**` and ends with `*/`. This text, and many Java editors, show Java comments in green. Normally there are comment lines at the beginning of each source code file to provide internal documentation for the class. Sometimes, as in HelloWorldWideWeb, a comment is also written at the beginning of methods, as in the following code:

```
// this class has one method named main
```

The Java code in a class generally consists of variable definitions and one or more methods. The HelloWorldWideWeb example has no variables, but it does have a single method named main. Recall that a method is invoked to do some processing, to provide a service.

Whenever a class has a method named main, like HelloWorldWideWeb, this method is automatically invoked when the class file is loaded into memory; the main method is what executes. This means that when the HelloWorldWideWeb.class file is loaded into memory, the main method begins running.

Methods begin with a **method header**, which is similar to the class header shown earlier. The following code starts with a method header.

```
public static void main(String[] args)
```

A method header is written to identify the method and describe some of its characteristics. Note that in this header, **public**, **static**, and **void** are keywords. These keywords and the syntax of the method header will be explained later in Chapter 3 and in Part 2. For now, understand that public means that any other program can invoke this method: The method has public accessibility. Static means that this method is not associated with an instance, and void means that the method does not return a value.

This main method contains a single statement that is executed to display your message.

```
System.out.println("Hello World Wide Web");
```

This statement, like many you will see in Java, invokes another method to do the real work of displaying the message. `System.out` is an object that provides methods to accomplish various tasks. One of these methods, `println`, displays text that is passed to it. In this example, the information that is contained in parentheses, called an **argument**, is sent to the `println` method, which then displays it.

Because the argument is included between quotation marks (`"Hello World Wide Web"`), Java recognizes it as a character string **literal**. A literal is what you call a value defined within a statement. Notice that this literal is shown in light blue. This color is used for character string literals throughout the book.

After the argument comes a semicolon, indicating the end of the statement. All Java statements end with a semicolon.

Hands-on Exercise 1

1. All of the Java examples, including HelloWorldWideWeb.java, are included on the CD distributed with this book. You should take a few minutes now to locate HelloWorldWideWeb.java in a subfolder named Examples in the Chapter2 folder (Chapter2\Examples).

2. Create a folder on your system named Chapter2Exercise1 and copy HelloWorldWideWeb.java to this folder.

3. Compile and run HelloWorldWideWeb.java using the software recommended by your instructor.

4. Modify the HelloWorldWideWeb.java code to display your name on one line, and your course name and section on a second line.

USING JAVA VARIABLES AND DATA TYPES

You declare a variable to contain data. A variable is the name of a place in memory that can contain data. For example, you can write the following statement to add two values together.

```
a = b + c;
```

In this example, a, b, and c are variables. They are the names of memory locations that contain data. For example, if variable b contains the number 2 and c contains the number 4, then after this statement is executed, a contains the number 6. Figure 2-4 shows these three variables after the statement is executed.

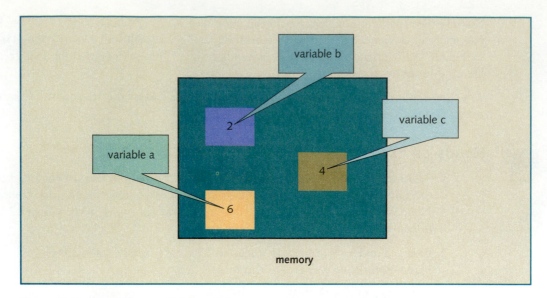

Figure 2-4   Variables containing data

All variables have a data type, name, and value. Each of these characteristics is defined in the following list:

- **Data type**. The data type specifies the kind of data the variable can contain. Unlike some languages, Java is particular about data types. For example, you cannot store a number containing a decimal point into a variable that is expecting only integer values. The specific data types are described in the next section.

- **Name**. A variable name is an identifier you create to refer to the variable.

- **Value**. Every variable refers to a memory location that contains data. You can specify this value. If you do not assign a value to the variable, then Java assigns a default value. Numeric variables are initialized to zero, the character variable is initialized to **null**, and the Boolean variable is initialized to false. Null is a value meaning nothing.

Declaring and Initializing Variables

Before you can declare a variable, you must specify the data type the variable will use. Java has eight **primitive data types**, shown in Table 2-3. These are called primitive data types to distinguish them from more complex data types, such as class names, which are discussed in Chapter 3.

Table 2-3   Java Primitive Data Types

	Type	Range of Values	Size
Numeric with no decimals	1. int	+ or – 2.1 trillion	4 bytes
	2. short	+ or – 32,000	2 bytes
	3. long	+ or – 9 E18	8 bytes
	4. byte	+ or – 127	1 byte
Numeric with decimals	5. double	+ or – 1.79 E308	8 bytes, 15 decimals
	6. float	+ or – 3.4 E38	4 bytes, 7 decimals
Other	7. boolean	true or false	
	8. char	any character	2 bytes

You use the first four data types to contain numeric data without decimals (**int**, **short**, **long**, and **byte**). You use the next two data types to contain numeric data with decimals (**double** and **float**). The primitive data type **boolean** contains only one of two possible values: **true** or **false**. Many Java editors, and this book, show these values in blue; however, Boolean values are technically constants, not keywords.

You use the primitive data type **char** for variables that contain a single character of text. To show text of more than one character, you use the String class, explored in a later section and in Chapter 3. The following examples focus on the **char**, **int**, **double**, and **boolean** data types and their use.

To declare a Java variable, you write the data type followed by the name you want to use. Remember that each Java statement ends with a semicolon.

```
char c;
int i;
double d;
boolean b;
```

Next, you can add code to initialize the variables, assigning each a value. The following statements assign the character value A to variable **c**, the integer value 1 to **i**, the value 2.5 to **d**, and the value **true** to **b**. Notice that the character literal **'A'** uses single quotes. Double quotes are used for a string of characters.

```
c = 'A';
i = 1;
d = 2.5;
b = true;
```

You also can write code to both declare and initialize the variable in one statement. To do so, you use an equal sign, called the **assignment operator**. This operator assigns the value on the right side of the equal sign to the variable named on the left side. For example, the following statements declare the variables as before, and then initialize them to the values indicated:

```
char c = 'A';
int i = 1;
double d = 2.5;
boolean b = true;
```

Java assumes that a numeric literal without decimals, such as 1, is the data type **int**. If you write a numeric literal with decimals, such as 1.1, Java assumes the data type is **double**. Normally, this does not cause problems, unless you are trying to initialize a **float** variable with a literal. You then must write "F" after the literal value to tell Java that it is a **float** data type value instead of **double**, as in the following example:

```
float f = 1.2F;
```

You can declare several variables of the same data type in one statement. For example, if x, y, and z will be data type **double**, you can declare them as in the following code:

```
double x, y, z;
```

In general, you use variables to hold data. You declare variables by writing the data type followed by the name you select for the variable. You can either initialize a variable when it is declared or later using an assignment statement.

Changing Data Types

Review the primitive data types listed in Table 2-3, and note that the six numeric data types have different capacities. For example, a variable with data type **byte** can hold a maximum value of only 127, yet data type **int** has a maximum value of 2.1 trillion. Similarly, data type **float** has a capacity of 3.4 E38, but **double** has a capacity of 1.79 E308, significantly more.

When you write an arithmetic expression such as a = b + c, Java assumes that the data types of all the variables in the expression are the same. If they are not, Java internally promotes those having a lesser capacity to the largest capacity data type used in the expression. In the example a = b + c, assume that variables a and c are data type **int** but that b is data type **double** declared and initialized with the following code:

```
int a;
double b = 3;
int c = 5;
a = b + c;
```

Because variables b and c have different data types, Java internally promotes variable c, which is data type **int**, to data type **double**, and then completes the addition. The result now has a data type of **double**. However, after the addition, Java attempts to assign the result to variable a, which is data type **int**. Because data type **int** has a much smaller capacity than **double**, the compiler generates an error stating that a loss of precision may result from the statement. This means that you might lose important digits in the resulting value.

2

You can override the compiler's objection using a technique called **casting**. To cast a value to another data type, you write the desired data type in parentheses to the left of the variable containing the value. For example, you can cast the contents of variable b from **double** to **int** by rewriting the addition statement as follows:

```
a = (int) b +  c;
```

The cast operation (**int**) converts the contents of variable b from data type **double** to data type **int**, and then completes the addition and assigns the result to variable a. Variable b is not actually changed; its contents are temporarily given the **int** data type for the computation. Note that you are assuming responsibility for any loss of precision in this operation. The Java compiler has warned you of the potential error, and by using the cast you have accepted this potential error.

Using Constants

It is often useful to declare a **constant**—a variable with a value that does not change. You use constants to contain values such as a company name, tax identification number, or phone number that does not change, or changes rarely.

The code to declare a constant is identical to what you use to declare a variable, but with the keyword **final** written in front of the data type, as in the following code. However, constants must be initialized in the same statement that declares them. By convention, you capitalize constant names. If the name consists of more than one word, you also separate the words with the underscore character. For example, to declare a constant for a sales tax rate of 7.5%, you write:

```
final double SALES_TAX_RATE = 7.5;
```

This code declares a variable named **SALES_TAX_RATE** data type **double**, initializes it to 7.5, and makes it **final**, meaning the value cannot be changed.

Using Reference Variables

You have seen that Java variables hold data. Actually, Java has two kinds of variables: **primitive variables** and **reference variables**. Until now you have studied primitive variables. A primitive variable is declared with one of the eight primitive data types and actually contains the data you put there.

In contrast, a reference variable uses a class name as a data type and refers to or points to an instance of that class. A reference variable does not actually contain the data; instead, it refers to an instance of a class that contains the data. For example, you may have noticed that string data, a collection of characters, is not one of the eight Java primitive data types. Instead, string data is contained in an instance of the String class, one of the Java supplied classes.

In the last section of this chapter, you will learn about Java arrays. Arrays contain data and are accessed using a reference variable.

You declare a String reference variable, just as you declared primitive variables, by first specifying the data type, which is the class name String, followed by the variable name you want to use. You can declare a reference variable **s** with data type String by writing the following code:

```
String s;
```

This code creates a variable named **s**, but does not initialize it to a value. It does not yet point to a String instance. In fact, it doesn't point anywhere and has a null value. You can assign a value to a String variable just as you assign a value to a primitive variable. The following code assigns the characters **"Hello Again "** to the String variable named s:

```
s = "Hello Again";
```

You also can declare a String reference variable and assign a value to it in one step, as you did with primitive variables:

```
String s = "Hello Again";
```

Earlier, you declared a primitive **char** variable named **c** by writing the following code:

```
char c = 'A';
```

Then in this section, you saw how to declare a String reference variable by writing the following code:

```
String s = "Hello Again";
```

Note that variable **c** is a primitive *containing* the character value **'A'** while variable **s** is a reference *pointing to* an instance of the String class that contains **"Hello Again"**. Figure 2-5 shows this distinction graphically.

Figure 2-5 shows that variable **c** actually contains **'A'**, but that variable **s** points or refers to an instance of the String class that contains **"Hello Again "**. (Again, note that the character literal uses single quotes, but that the string literal uses double quotes.)

The distinction between primitive and reference variables becomes especially important when you want to compare values. Also, you can use reference variables to invoke methods for the instances to which they refer. Chapter 3 explores these ideas in greater detail and illustrates how to invoke methods in the String class.

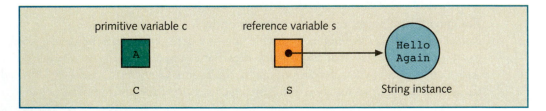

Figure 2-5   Contrasting primitive and reference variables

Creating a Java Class to Demonstrate Variables

A Java class that demonstrates declaring variables and constants called VariableDemo.java is listed in Figure 2-6.

As in HelloWorldWideWeb, the VariableDemo class begins with a class header, an open curly brace, the main method header, and then another open curly brace to begin the main method. The main method includes the code that declares and initializes four primitive variables, one primitive constant, and one String reference variable.

Once the variables are declared and values are assigned, you add statements to display their values.

```
System.out.println("c = " + c);
System.out.println("i = " + i);
System.out.println("c = " + d);
System.out.println("b = " + b);
System.out.println("SALES_TAX_RATE = " + SALES_TAX_RATE);
System.out.println("s = " + s);
```

These statements invoke the method println in the System.out object. Invoking a method means that you send it a message asking it to execute. To write a statement that invokes a method, you write a reference to the class or object (`System.out`) followed by a period or dot, and then add the method name you want to use (`println`).

```
public class VariableDemo
{
   public static void main(String[] args)
   {
      // declare variables & initialize them
      char c = 'A';
      int i = 1;
      double d = 2.5;
      boolean b = true;
      final double SALES_TAX_RATE = 7.5;
      String s = "Hello Again";
      // display variable contents
      System.out.println("c = " + c);
      System.out.println("i = " + i);
      System.out.println("c = " + d);
      System.out.println("b = " + b);
      System.out.println("SALES_TAX_RATE = " + SALES_TAX_RATE);
      System.out.println("s = " + s);
   }
}
```

Figure 2-6   VariableDemo.java listing

```
c = A
i = 1
c = 2.5
b = true
SALES_TAX_RATE = 7.5
s = Hello Again
```

Figure 2-7   Output of VariableDemo.java

Often when you invoke a method you send it one or more values, called arguments, enclosed in parentheses. For example, the first statement above sends the following argument:

```
("c = " + c)
```

The value `"c = "` is simply a String literal and the + sign used here is the **concatenation operator**, which joins the literal with the contents of the variable **c** for display. The concatenation operator automatically converts numeric or Boolean values to string values before the println method is invoked.

The output from VariableDemo.java is shown in Figure 2-7.

Hands-on Exercise 2

1. Create a folder named Chapter2Exercise2 on your system.

2. Locate VariableDemo.java in the folder named Chapter2\Examples on the book's CD, and then copy it to the Chapter2Exercise2 folder you created in Step 1.

3. Compile and run VariableDemo.java using the software recommended by your instructor.

4. Add code to VariableDemo.java to declare and initialize primitive variables for data types **short**, **long**, **byte**, and **float**. Then add code to display the contents of these variables. Remember that Java assumes a data type **float** for literal values with decimal positions, and data type **int** for literal values without decimal positions.

5. Add code to assign the contents of your **float** variable to your **long** variable. Remember that this assignment requires a cast.

COMPUTING WITH JAVA

Java uses the familiar **arithmetic operators** for addition, subtraction, multiplication, and division (+, -, *, /) that are used in other programming languages. Similarly, Java employs parentheses to group parts of an expression and establish precedence according to standard algebraic rules. In addition, Java uses a **remainder operator** (%), also called the **modulus operator**, to produce a remainder resulting from the division of two integers. These arithmetic operators are listed in Table 2–4.

Note that these arithmetic operators do not include exponentiation. The Math class, one of Java's supplied classes, has methods to accomplish exponentiation, rounding, and numerous other tasks. Table 2–5 lists some of the Math class methods.

To invoke one of these methods, you write the name of the class (Math), a period, the name of the method, and then any arguments required. The Math class returns the resulting value after doing the computation. For example, the following statement computes the square root of 10:

```
double answer = Math.sqrt(10)
```

When this statement is executed, four things happen:

1. A variable named **answer** with data type **double** is created.

2. The sqrt method in the Math class is invoked and the argument 10 is passed to it.

3. The sqrt method computes the square root of the argument and returns it.

4. The value returned is assigned to the variable **answer**.

Table 2-4 Java Arithmetic Operators

Operator	Description	Example	Result
+	addition	11 + 2	13
–	subtraction	11 –2	9
*	multiplication	11 * 2	22
/	division	11 / 2	5
%	remainder	11 % 2	1

Table 2-5 Selected Math Class Methods

Method	Description
abs(x)	Returns the absolute value of x
max(x,y)	Returns the greater of x,y
min(x,y)	Returns the smaller of x,y
pow(x,y)	Returns the value of x raised to the power of y
random()	Returns a random number between 0 and 1
round(x)	Returns the closest integer value to x
sqrt(x)	Returns the square root of x

```java
public class ComputationDemo
{
    public static void main(String[] args)
    {
        // illustrate arithmetic operators
        int a = 11;
        int b = 2;
        int c = 4;
        System.out.println("a = " + a);
        System.out.println("b = " + b);
        System.out.println("c = " + c);
        System.out.println("a + b = " + (a + b));
        System.out.println("a - b = " + (a - b));
        System.out.println("a * b = " + (a * b));
        System.out.println("integer division a / b = " + (a / b));
        // cast a & b to double before divide
        System.out.println("double division a / b =
            " + (double) a / (double) b);
        System.out.println("a % b = " + (a % b));
        // illustrate Math class methods
        System.out.println("c to b power = " + Math.pow(c,b));
        System.out.println("square root of c = " + Math.sqrt(c));
    }
}
```

Figure 2-8 ComputationDemo.java listing

The Java class listed in Figure 2-8, ComputationDemo.java, demonstrates the use of the arithmetic operators and two of the methods in the Math class.

Similar to previous examples, this class has a single method named main that begins executing when the class is loaded into memory. The main method begins with code that declares and initializes, and then displays three primitive variables named a, b, and c, all data type int.

Next comes three statements invoking the println method to display the result of computational expressions involving variables a and b. The argument format in these statements is different from what you have seen in previous examples because these arguments actually contain arithmetic expressions that compute values. For example, the argument in the first statement is (`"a + b = " + (a + b)`). First, Java computes the sum (`a + b`), concatenates this result with the string literal `"a + b = "`, and then passes the concatenated string to the println method, which then displays it.

Next is a statement illustrating integer division.

```java
System.out.println("integer division a / b = " + (a / b));
```

Variable `a` contains 11 and `b` contains 2, so the correct result is 5.5. However, because the variables in this statement are both data type **int**, the result of the computation is also **int**, and the displayed result is the **int** value 5—the decimal part of the answer is truncated. To retain the decimal part of the answer, you must cast both variables to either data type **double** or **float**. The following example uses data type **double**. This statement includes a cast to double **(double)** written to the left of **a** and **b** in the arithmetic expression. This cast converts the contents of both variables to data type **double** to perform the computation. Because the contents of both variables are now temporarily data type **double**, the result of the division is also **double** and the decimal position is retained.

```
System.out.println("double a / b = " + (double) a /
(double) b);
```

The next statement illustrates remainder or modulus division.

```
System.out.println("a % b = " + (a % b));
```

This statement divides the contents of **a** (11) by the contents of **b** (2) and produces the remainder (11 divided by 2 is 5 with a remainder of 1).

The final two statements in ComputationDemo.java demonstrate using two of the methods in the Math class.

```
System.out.println("c to b power = " + Math.pow(c,b));
System.out.println("square root of c = " + Math.sqrt(c));
```

The first of these invokes the pow method, which will raise the contents of variable **c** (4) to the power of the contents of variable **b** (2). The second statement invokes the sqrt method, which will compute and return the square root of variable **c**.

The output of this code is shown in Figure 2-9.

```
a = 11
b = 2
c = 4
a + b = 13
a - b = 9
a * b = 22
integer division a / b = 5
double division a / b = 5.5
a % b = 1
c to b power = 16.0
square root of c = 2.0
```

Figure 2-9   ComputationDemo output

Hands-on

Hands-on Exercise 3

1. Create a folder named Chapter2Exercise3 on your system.

2. Locate ComputationDemo.java in the Chapter2\Examples folder on your book's CD, and then copy it to the Chapter2Exercise3 folder you created in Step 1.

3. Compile and run ComputationDemo.java using the software recommended by your instructor.

4. The formula to compute the present value of a future amount is:
   presentValue = futureAmount / (1 + annualInterestRate) raised to the yearsInFuture power.
   a. Declare and populate the following variables (choose your data types carefully):
   presentValue = 0
   futureValue = 1000
   annualInterestRate = .085
   yearsInFuture = 10
   b. Add statements to ComputationDemo.java to compute and display your presentValue. You will need to use the pow method in the Math class to do exponentiation. Note that pow accepts and returns data type **double**.

In addition to the algebraic operators, Java has special operators for writing shortcut code. The **increment** (++) and **decrement** (--) operators, as their names suggest, either add one to or subtract one from a variable. To illustrate, the following two statements produce the same result:

```
i = i + 1;   // add 1 to i
```

and

```
++i;         // add 1 to i
```

Similarly, to decrement you can write:

```
i = i - 1;   // subtract 1 from i
```

or

```
--i;         // subtract 1 from i
```

Note also that ++ or -- can go before or after the variable. However, the placement of these operators can make a difference in an assignment statement. If the operator is before the variable, it increments or decrements before any assignment is made. For example, the first line in the following code increments the variable i and then assigns the value to j, so i and j have the same value. The second line, however, assigns the value of i to j first, and then increments j, so they have different values.

```
j = ++i;   // i and j have the same value
j = i++;   // i and j have a different value
```

Java also supports the use of the assignment operator (=) together with the arithmetic operators (+, -, *, /) to create **assignment operators**. For example, if you want to add five to a variable named `total`, you could write either one of the following statements:

```
total = total + 5;
total += 5;
```

WRITING DECISION-MAKING STATEMENTS

Often, when you are writing business applications, you will want to determine whether a condition is true, and then take some action based on that determination. For example, in a credit card processing application, you may want to see whether the card's credit limit has been reached or exceeded, and if so, reject the charge. You write decision-making statements to evaluate conditions and execute statements based on that evaluation.

Java provides three ways to write decision-making statements: the **if** statement, the **switch** statement, and the **conditional operator**. The Java **if** statement, similar to if statements used in other programming languages, evaluates an expression and then executes one block of code (containing one or more statements) if the expression is true and another code block if the expression is false. The Java **switch** statement, similar to the select statement used in some other languages, is like a multiple-path if statement. It evaluates a variable for multiple values, and then executes one of several code blocks, depending on the contents of the variable being evaluated. The conditional operator is really a shortcut version of the if statement. All three of these are illustrated in the following sections.

Writing if Statements

The Java **if** statement interrogates a logical expression enclosed in parentheses and determines whether the expression is true or false. An expression often compares two values using **logical operators** to see if they are equal or if one is less than the other. In the credit card processing example mentioned earlier, to see if the credit card balance is greater than the credit limit, the expression is (creditCardBalance >= creditLimit). Additional examples of expressions are (examScore > passingScore), (studentAge < 21), and (studentId = scholarshipId). A logical expression can be replaced by a Boolean variable. Table 2-6 lists the Java logical operators.

Table 2-6 Java Logical Operators

Operator	Description
&&	And
==	equal to
>	greater than
>=	greater than or equal to
<	less than
<=	less than or equal to
!	Not
!=	not equal to
||	Or

 Note that unlike other languages, the Java *equal to* operator is two equal signs (==), not one (=), but the *not equal to* operator is !=, instead of !==. Further, unlike other languages, Java does not use <> to mean *not equal to*.

The Java **if** statement has two forms. The first evaluates an expression and then executes a block of code if the expression is true. The second form, called an if-else statement, evaluates an expression, executes one block of code if the expression is true, and executes a second block of code if it is false. The logic of these two forms is shown in Figures 2-10 and 2-11.

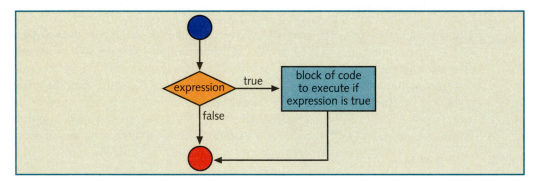

Figure 2-10 if statement logic

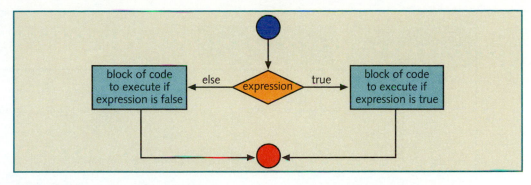

Figure 2-11   if-else statement logic

The format of the two statements is indicated in Figures 2-12 and 2-13.

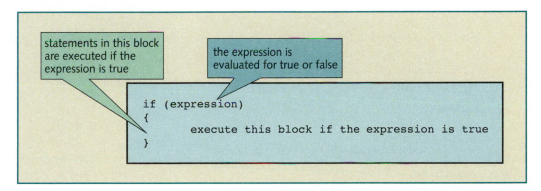

Figure 2-12   if statement format

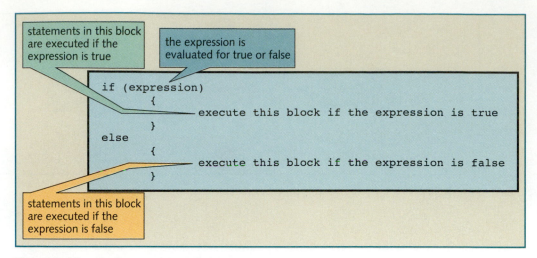

statements in this block
are executed if the
expression is true

the expression is
evaluated for true or false

```
if (expression)
    {
                        execute this block if the expression is true
    }
else
    {
                        execute this block if the expression is false
    }
```

statements in this block
are executed if the
expression is false

Figure 2-13   if-else statement format

The Java class listed in Figure 2–14, IfDemo.java, demonstrates both forms of the if statement.

```java
public class IfDemo
{
    public static void main(String[] args)
    {
        int i = 1;
        // simple if
        if (i < 10)
        {
            System.out.println("i < 10");
        }
        if (i > 0)
            System.out.println("i > 0");

        // if using a block of code
        if (i == 1)
        {
            System.out.println("i equals 1");
            System.out.println("Use a code block to");
            System.out.println("execute more than 1 statement");
        }

        // if - else
        if (i == 2)
            System.out.println("i equals 2");
        else
            { // a block contains multiple statements
                System.out.println("i does not equal 2");
                System.out.println("We can execute more");
```

```
            System.out.println("than one statement in");
            System.out.println("an if");
         }

      // compound logical expressions
      if (i == 1 || i == 2)
         System.out.println("i equals 1 or 2");
      if (i > 0 && i < 3 )              //
         System.out.println("i is > 0 and < 3");

      // nested if can replace compound logical expressions
      if (i > 0)
         if (i < 3)
            System.out.println("i is > 0 and < 3");

      // conditional operator
      int j = (i == 1)? 5: 6;
         System.out.println("i equals " + i);
   }
}
```

Figure 2-14   IfDemo.java listing

This class, similar to the previous examples, has a main method that begins executing when the class is loaded into memory. The main method begins with a statement declaring an integer variable named i, initializing its value to 1.

```
   int i = 1;
```

Next is an **if** statement that evaluates the expression (i < 10). If the expression is true, the println method is invoked to display the literal "i < 10". Notice that the expression being evaluated is written within parentheses immediately following the **if** keyword. If there is only one statement in the **if** block, you can omit the curly braces, as in the next two examples. However, if you have more than one statement in the **if** block, create a code block using curly braces. Note also that each statement ends with a semicolon.

```
   if (i < 10)
      {
         System.out.println("i < 10");
      }
```

Next is an **if** statement evaluating the expression (i > 10). If the expression is true, the println method is invoked to display the literal "i > 0". Note that this **if** statement does not use open and closed braces. In other words, the statement to be executed if the expression is true is not contained in a block of code. Java assumes that if you omit open and closed braces, you want to execute a single statement if the expression is true. However, if you want to execute more than one statement, place the statements within a code block as in the second if statement.

```java
if (i > 0)
   System.out.println("i > 0");

if (i == 1)
   {
       System.out.println("i equals 1");
       System.out.println("Use a code block to");
       System.out.println("execute more than 1 statement");
   }
```

Java does not include an "end if" keyword, so you must use proper indenting and white space according to convention to make the code easy to read and the logic easy to interpret. For example, in the previous code, the expression is written on the first line, and then the statement that executes if the expression is true is indented and placed on a second line. If used, the keyword **else** is on a line by itself aligned with if, followed by the statements to be executed, which are also indented.

The next example illustrates an if-else statement. Here the expression being evaluated is (i == 2). Because this expression is determined to be false, the code block following the else is executed.

```java
// an if - else example
if (i == 2)
   System.out.println("i equals 2");
else
   {  // a block contains multiple statements
      System.out.println("i does not equal 2");
      System.out.println("We can execute more");
      System.out.println("than one statement in");
      System.out.println("an if");
   }
```

A **compound expression** consists of two expressions joined using the logical operators OR (||) and AND (&&). The compound expression in the next example (i == 1 || i == 2) reads: "does variable i contain the value 1 or the value 2?" Because i does contain 1, this compound expression is true. The second statement contains the expression (i > 0 && i < 3), which is interpreted as: "does the variable i contain a value that is greater than 0 and less than 3?" Again, because i contains 1, this compound expression is also true.

```java
// compound logical expressions
if (i == 1 || i == 2)
    System.out.println("i equals 1 or 2");
if (i > 0 && i < 3 )       //
    System.out.println("i is > 0 and < 3");
```

A **nested if** statement is an if statement written inside another if statement. Often you can replace a compound expression with a nested if. The following nested if example produces the same result as the preceding example using a compound expression. Notice that the second and third lines are indented to improve readability.

```
// nested if can replace compound logical expressions
if (i > 0)
   if (i < 3)
     System.out.println("i is > 0 and < 3");
```

Using the Conditional Operator

The `conditional operator` (`?`) provides a shortcut to writing an if-else statement. Use the conditional operator to replace a simple if-else statement. The general structure of this statement is as follows:

variable = expression ? *value*1 : *value*2;

The expression is evaluated and if true, the variable is assigned `value1`. If the expression is false, `value2` is assigned.

Consider the following if-else statement:

```
int j;
if (i == 1)
   j = 5;
else
   j = 6;
```

After this statement is executed, if `i` contains 1, `j` will be assigned 5; otherwise, it will be assigned 6. You can use Java's conditional operator to do exactly the same thing, but using only one line of code:

```
// conditional operator
int j = (i == 1)? 5: 6;
```

Figure 2-15 shows the output from IfDemo.

```
i < 10
i > 0
i equals 1
Use a code block to
execute more than 1 statement
i does not equal 2
We can execute more
than one statement in
an if
i equals 1 or 2
i is > 0 and < 3
i is > 0 and < 3
i equals 1
```

Figure 2-15   IfDemo output

Hands-on Exercise 4

1. Create a folder named Chapter2Exercise4 on your system.

2. Locate IfDemo.java in the Chapter2\Examples folder on the book's CD, and then copy it to the Chapter2Exercise4 folder you created in Step 1.

3. Compile and run IfDemo.java using the software recommended by your instructor. Verify that your output is the same as that shown in Figure 2-15.

4. Add code to IfDemo.java to assign and display a letter grade based on an exam score using the following list. Write the code using if-else statements. Test your statements using a score from each category to ensure that your logic is correct.

Exam Score	Letter Grade
> =90	A
> =80 && < 90	B
> =70 && < 80	C
> =60 && < 70	D
< 60	F

Writing switch Statements

Java implements the case structure with a statement called **switch**. The Java switch acts like a multiple-way if statement by transferring control to one of several statements or blocks, depending on the value of a variable. Use a switch statement when you want to make a decision where there are more than two values you want evaluate.

For example, assume you have a variable `i` that can contain the values 1, 2, 3, or any other value. To test for these four possibilities using if statements, you would have to write a nested if. Note how the indentation in the following code improves readability:

```java
if (i == 1)
  System.out.println("i equals 1");
else
  if (i == 2)
    System.out.println("i equals 2");
  else
    if (i == 3)
      System.out.println("i equals 3");
    else
      System.out.println("i doesn't equal 1, 2, or 3 ");
```

You can simplify this code by using the following switch statement:

```java
switch (i)
{
  case 1: System.out.println("i equals 1");
    break;
  case 2: System.out.println("i equals 2");
    break;
  case 3: System.out.println("i equals 3");
    break;
  default: System.out.println("i doesn't equal 1, 2, or 3 ");
}
```

The basic structure of the switch statement begins with the keyword **switch** followed a variable name in parentheses, and then by one or more case statements contained in a code block. In this example, the variable `i` is being evaluated. Each case statement evaluates the contents of variable `i` for the value specified. The default statement is executed if none of the previous case statements have been executed. The keyword break is written after each case to prevent subsequent statements within the switch from being executed.

Although **switch** can sometimes help you write simpler code by replacing lengthy nested if statements, it does have two important restrictions. First, each case evaluates a single variable for equality only. You cannot test less than or greater than expressions with **switch** statements. Second, the variable being evaluated must be data type **char**, **byte**, **short**, or **int**. None of the other data types can be used.

In summary, switch is an important decision-making tool that you can use to replace nested if statements to simplify your code. However, be aware of its length and data type restrictions.

WRITING LOOPS

Assume that you want to display the integer numbers 1 through 3. One technique is to write three statements displaying these values:

```
System.out.println(1);
System.out.println(2);
System.out.println(3);
```

However, this method is time-consuming if you want to display the numbers 1 through 100, for example. An alternative technique is to write a loop. Loops are powerful programming tools that provide for the repeated execution of one or more statements until a terminating condition occurs. You can write loops to sum values, count things, and as you will see later in this chapter, access arrays. You write Java loops using one of three keywords: **while**, **do**, or **for** (discussed in detail in the following sections).

Writing while Loops

The following code shows a loop to display the numbers 1 through 3:

```
int i = 1;        // declare & initialize loop counter variable
while(i <= 3)     // loop while i is < = 3
{
    System.out.println("while loop - i = " + i);
    i = i + 1;    // increment loop counter
}
```

This loop, called a while loop, begins with a statement declaring an integer variable named i and initializing it to 1. Variable i is called a **loop counter** because it counts the number of times the loop is executed. Next comes the keyword **while** followed by a logical expression in parentheses. The body of the loop containing two statements is contained in the code block. The while loop continues executing the statements in the code block as long as the expression is true. When the expression becomes false, the loop terminates.

In this example, the loop body consists of two statements. The first displays the string literal **"while loop - i = "** concatenated with the contents of variable i. The second statement increments i. Note that you could have used the increment operator i++ instead of writing i = i + 1.

The first time this loop executes, i contains 1, which is displayed, and then i is incremented. The second time the loop executes, i contains 2, which is displayed, and then i is again incremented. The loop continues to the third iteration. At the beginning of the third iteration, i contains 3, which is displayed, and then i is incremented to 4. Next, the while expression becomes false and the loop terminates.

Note how easy it is to modify this loop to display the integer values between 1 and 1000. You simply change the expression to (i <= 1000).

Incidentally, you can easily write an infinite loop in Java. An infinite loop is a loop that never terminates, at least not without outside intervention. Java assumes a single statement loop if you omit the open and closed braces from the block of code. The following code creates an infinite loop:

```
int i = 1;
while(i <= 5)
   System.out.println(i);
   i++;   // this statement is not part of the loop
```

The increment statement is never executed because it is not a part of the loop, even though it is indented correctly. Because i is not incremented, its value remains 1 and the while expression remains true. Remember, the Java compiler ignores indentation. You only use indentation to make your code more readable and understandable.

In general, programming languages provide two kinds of loops: the **pre-test loop** and the **post-test loop**. The pre-test loop tests the terminating condition at the beginning of the loop, and the post-test loop checks at the end. Figure 2-16 maps the logic of these two loop structures. The post-test loop always executes the statements in the body of the loop. In contrast, if the loop terminating condition is initially true, the pre-test loop exits the loop without executing the statements in the loop body. You will use a post-test loop when you want the statements in the loop to execute at least once. Use a pre-test loop when you want to exit the loop without executing any of the loop statements if conditions warrant. The **while** and **for** loops are pre-test, and **do** loops are post-test.

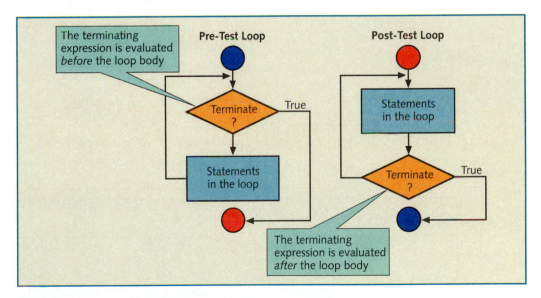

Figure 2-16   Loop structures

Writing do Loops

In the previous section, you saw how to write a while loop to display the integers 1 through 3. You can do the same thing using a do loop, sometimes called a do–while loop. The following code displays 1, 2, and 3 just as the while loop did in the previous example.

```java
int j = 1;
do
{
   System.out.println("do loop: j = " + j);
   j++;                        // use the increment operator
} while(j <= 3);   // don't forget the semicolon here
```

Note the similarities between this code and the earlier while loop code. The first statement declares and initializes a loop counter named j. Next, you write the keyword **do**, followed by a code block containing the statements you want to execute each time the loop repeats. These statements are identical to those in the while loop, except that this loop uses a loop counter named j instead of i. At the end of the loop, you write the keyword **while** followed by an expression, and end it with a semicolon. Don't forget this semicolon, or you will get a compiler error. Figure 2-17 contrasts while and do loops.

As you can see from the previous examples, while loops and do loops can produce identical results. However, recall that while loops use pre-test logic and do loops use post-test logic. You use a do loop when you want to force the execution of the statements in the loop body at least once. You use a while loop when you do not want to force this execution.

The following code illustrates the distinction between pre-test and post-test loop logic:

```java
j = 1;
while(j > 3)   // expression is initially false
{
   System.out.println("while loop executed");
}
do
{
   System.out.println("do loop executed");
}while(j > 3);   // expression is initially false
```

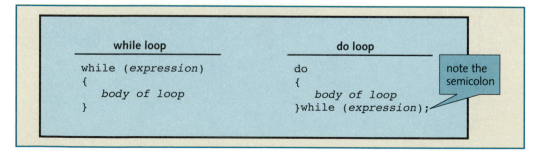

Figure 2-17   Contrasting while and do loops

The first statement initializes variable j to 1. Next comes a while loop with the expression (j > 3), which is initially false. Because a while loop evaluates the expression at the beginning of the loop, the statement within the loop is never executed.

The second loop is a do loop, which uses post-test logic. This means that the expression (j > 3) is evaluated at the end of the loop. Even though the expression is initially false, the statement in the do loop executes once before the loop terminates.

In summary, use a do loop when you want to force the execution of the statements in the loop body at least once, regardless of the expression's evaluation. Use a while loop when you do not want to force this execution.

Writing for Loops

The for loop is similar to the while loop in that it uses pre-test logic; it evaluates the terminating expression at the beginning of the loop. However, the for loop allows you to include loop counter initialization and incrementing code as a part of the **for** statement, which simplifies and shortens your code. To illustrate, the following for loop displays the numbers 1, 2, and 3, similar to the previous while and do loop examples.

```
for(int k = 1; k <= 3; k++)
{
    System.out.println("for loop: k = " + k);
}
```

As you can see, the for loop requires less code than while or do loops because you can include the code to initialize, test, and increment the loop counter in a single line.

Figure 2-18 shows what each part of the statement does.

Note that previously you have written the println statement and the open and closed braces on separate lines. When you have a single statement in a block, you can shorten and simplify the code by writing the entire block on a single line, as in the following code. This makes the for loop code shorter still.

```
{   System.out.println( "k = " + k);   }
```

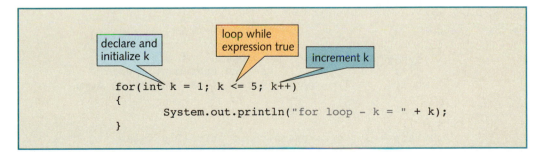

Figure 2-18   for loop

Writing Nested Loops

Sometimes you may want to write a loop within, a loop which is called a **nested loop**. Nested loops are particularly useful when processing data arranged in rows and columns. You can use an outer loop to move across columns and an inner loop to access each row.

You can construct nested loops using any combination of while, do, or for loops, although for loops generally will reduce the number of lines of code. The following illustrates a for loop within another for loop. The outer loop uses a loop counter named m and the inner loop uses a loop counter named n.

```
for(int m = 1; m <= 2 ; m++)     // outer loop begins
{
   for(int n = 1; n <= 3 ; n++)  // inner loop begins
      {System.out.println("nested loop: m = " + m + ", n = "
      + n);}
}
```

In this example, the outer loop executes twice, and each time it executes, the inner loop executes three times. In other words, while variable m contains 1, variable n will be incremented from 1 to 2 and then 3. For each iteration of the inner loop, the contents of both variables are displayed. The println method is invoked a total of six times.

All of the above examples are contained in LoopDemo.java, listed in Figure 2-19. The output from this code is shown in Figure 2-20.

```
public class LoopDemo
{
   public static void main(String[] args)
   {
   // while loop
   int i = 1;  // declare & initialize loop counter variable
   while(i <= 3)  // loop while i is < = 3
   {
      System.out.println("while loop: i = " + i);
      i = i + 1;  // increment loop counter
   }
   // do loop
   int j = 1;
   do
   {
      System.out.println("do loop: j = " + j);
      j++;                 // use the increment operator
   } while(j <= 3);  // don't forget the semicolon here

   // pre-test & post-test compared
   j = 1;
   while(j > 3)  // expression is initially false
   {
      System.out.println("while loop executed");
   }
```

```
do
{
  System.out.println("do loop executed");
}while(j > 3);  // expression is initially false


// for loop
for(int k = 1; k <= 3; k++)
{
  System.out.println("for loop: k = " + k);
}

// nested loop
for(int m = 1; m <= 2 ; m++)     // outer loop begins
{
  for(int n = 1; n <= 3 ; n++)   // inner loop begins
    {System.out.println("nested loop: m = " + m + ", n = " + n);}
}
  }
}
```

Figure 2-19   LoopDemo.java listing

```
while loop: i = 1
while loop: i = 2
while loop: i = 3
do loop: j = 1
do loop: j = 2
do loop: j = 3
do loop executed
for loop: k = 1
for loop: k = 2
for loop: k = 3
nested loop: m = 1, n = 1
nested loop: m = 1, n = 2
nested loop: m = 1, n = 3
nested loop: m = 2, n = 1
nested loop: m = 2, n = 2
nested loop: m = 2, n = 3
```

Figure 2-20   LoopDemo output

Hands-on Exercise 5

1. Create a folder named Chapter2Exercise5 on your system.

2. Locate LoopDemo.java in the Chapter2\Examples folder on the book's CD, and then copy it to the Chapter2Exercise5 folder you created in Step 1.

3. Compile and run LoopDemo.java using the software recommended by your instructor. Verify that your output is the same as that shown in Figure 2-20.

4. Add statements to LoopDemo that will use a for loop to display the even integers 10, 8, 6, 4, and 2.

DECLARING AND ACCESSING ARRAYS

Like most other languages, Java lets you declare arrays to create a group of several variables *with the same data type*. Arrays consist of elements and each element behaves like a variable, except that all of the array elements must have the same data type.

Array elements, like all variables, can contain either primitive data or they can be reference variables. Recall that reference variables point to instances of a class, or as you will shortly see, to an array. The next chapter describes reference variables in more detail and includes several examples.

Java arrays can be either one dimensional or multidimensional. A **one-dimensional array** consists of elements arranged in a single row. Conceptually, a **two-dimensional array** has *both* rows and columns, and a **three-dimensional array** is like a cube, with rows, columns, and pages. However, Java implements multidimensional arrays as arrays of arrays; therefore, you are not restricted by rectangles and cubes. Both one- and two-dimensional arrays are illustrated in the following sections.

Using One-Dimensional Arrays

If you need to have five integer values, such as test scores from an exam, you could declare and use five **int** variables, as in the following code:

```
int testScore1 = 75;
int testScore2 = 80;
int testScore3 = 70;
int testScore4 = 85;
int testScore5 = 90;
```

An alternative is to use a one-dimensional array. To declare a five-element array with integer elements, you could write the following line of code:

```
int testScores[] = new int[5];
```

This code declares an array reference variable **testScores**, and then creates an array instance containing five elements, each with data type **int**. The **new** keyword is used to create a new array instance.

You can access the individual elements of the array by writing the array reference variable followed by the index value of the element enclosed in brackets. In the five-element array example above, the first element can be accessed by writing `testScores[0]`, the second element by `testScores[1]`, and so forth. Note that index values begin with 0, instead of 1.

The code to initialize the array elements is similar to that code used previously to initialize the variables. The following code assigns the value 75 to the first array element (index value 0), 80 to the second, and so on.

```
testScores[0] = 75;
testScores[1] = 80;
testScores[2] = 70;
testScores[3] = 85;
testScores[4] = 90;
```

If you wish, you can declare and populate the array using a single statement, as shown below. This code is noticeably shorter and works well with smaller arrays.

```
int testScores[] = {75, 80, 70, 85, 90};
```

Note that `testScores` is a reference variable. It points or refers to an array instance containing five integer elements containing the values shown in Figure 2-21. The array instance has an attribute named length that contains the number of elements in the array, which in this example is five. You will see how this attribute is used in an upcoming example.

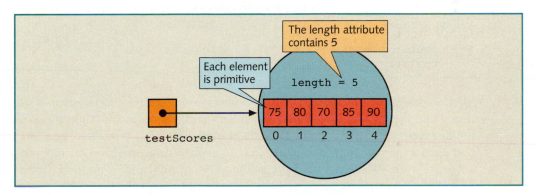

Figure 2-21   A five-element `int` array

You write statements to display the contents of each array element similar to the way you display the contents of individual variables. The following statements display the contents of each element of the `testScores` array. Notice that these statements are quite similar to each other; the only difference is the literal value and the index value.

```
System.out.println("test score 1 = " + testScores[0]);
System.out.println("test score 2 = " + testScores[1]);
System.out.println("test score 3 = " + testScores[2]);
System.out.println("test score 4 = " + testScores[3]);
System.out.println("test score 5 = " + testScores[4]);
```

Assume that you want to compute the average of the values stored in **testScores**. Logically, you first compute the sum of the elements, and then divide by five. One technique is to write five addition statements, and then divide, as in the following code:

```
double average = 0;
average = average + testScores[0];
average = average + testScores[1];
average = average + testScores[2];
average = average + testScores[3];
average = average + testScores[4];
average = average / 5;
System.out.println("average score is " + average);
```

Notice that the five addition statements are identical *except for the index value.* The first index value is 0, the second is 1, and so forth. This suggests that you can write a loop to do the computation instead of writing numerous addition statements. A loop is especially appropriate when working with larger arrays. You can certainly write five statements to compute the sum of an array with five elements; however, it is impractical to write 100 statements to compute the sum of an array having 100 elements.

To illustrate, you can write a **for** loop to compute the sum of the array contents, as in the following code:

```
double average = 0;
for(int i = 0; i < 5; i++)
    {average += testScores[i];}
```

Here the addition statement, which now uses the **+=** assignment operator, is executed five times. The first time it is executed, the index variable **i** contains 0 and therefore points to the first element of **testScores**. On the second iteration, **i** contains 1, pointing to the second element, and so forth. Note that you can easily change this loop to compute the sum of an array with 100 elements by changing the terminating expression from **i < 5** to **i < 100**. After the loop, you can write a statement to divide by five to compute the average.

Figure 2-21 showed you that a Java array is an instance with the attribute **length** containing the number of array elements. The array **testScores** has five elements; therefore, **length** contains 5 and you can substitute it for 5 in the loop. Using the length attribute eliminates the need to change the loop code if the number of array elements is changed. The following code will work for an array of any size:

```
for(int i = 0; i < testScores.length; i++)
    {average += testScores[i];}
```

A Java class named ArrayDemo.java showing these array examples is listed in Figure 2-22, and the output is shown in Figure 2-23.

```java
public class ArrayDemo
{
    public static void main(String[] args)
    {   // declare an int array with 5 elements
        int testScores[] = new int [5];

        // populate the elements
        testScores[0] = 75;
        testScores[1] = 80;
        testScores[2] = 70;
        testScores[3] = 85;
        testScores[4] = 90;

        // display the element contents
        System.out.println("test score 1 = " + testScores[0]);
        System.out.println("test score 2 = " + testScores[1]);
        System.out.println("test score 3 = " + testScores[2]);
        System.out.println("test score 4 = " + testScores[3]);
        System.out.println("test score 5 = " + testScores[4]);

        // compute average using length attribute
        double average = 0;
        for(int i = 0; i < testScores.length; i++)
            {average += testScores[i];}
        average = average / 5;
        System.out.println("average score is " + average);
    }
}
```

Figure 2-22   ArrayDemo.java listing

```
test score 1 = 75
test score 2 = 80
test score 3 = 70
test score 4 = 85
test score 5 = 90
average score is 80.0
```

Figure 2-23   ArrayDemo output

Hands-on Exercise 6

1. Create a folder named Chapter2Exercise6 on your system.

2. Locate ArrayDemo.java in the Chapter2\Examples folder on the book's CD, and then copy it to the Chapter2Exercise6 folder you created in Step 1.

3. Compile and run ArrayDemo.java using the software recommended by your instructor. Verify that your output is the same as that shown in Figure 2-23.

4. Add code to ArrayDemo.java to iterate the testScores array using a for loop to determine and display the letter grade for each exam, using the following list. Write the code using nested if statements.

Exam Score	Letter Grade
> =90	A
> =80 && < 90	B
>=70 && < 80	C
>=60 && < 70	D
< 60	F

Using Multidimensional Arrays

In addition to one-dimensional arrays, Java supports multidimensional arrays. Recall that conceptually, a two-dimensional array is like a table, with rows and columns, and a three-dimensional array is like a cube, with rows, columns, and pages. Each dimension has its own set of brackets when you declare it. Java supports as many dimensions as you care to write, but generally you will work with either one- or two-dimensional arrays.

You can expand the previous test scores example to use a two-dimensional array with five rows and two columns. The two columns represent the two tests and the five rows represent the five students, as shown in Table 2-7. The first column contains the same values as the previous one-dimensional array, testScores.

Table 2-7   A Table of Test Scores

	Test 1	Test 2
Student 1	75	80
Student 2	80	90
Student 3	70	60
Student 4	85	95
Student 5	90	100

You declare a two-dimensional array using two sets of brackets. The first set is used for the row and the second for the column. The following code declares an array named `testScoreTable` with five rows and two columns:

```
int testScoreTable[][] = new int [5][2];
```

Populate this array using the same technique used with the one-dimensional array earlier.

```
// populate the elements in column 1
testScoreTable[0][0] = 75;
testScoreTable[1][0] = 80;
testScoreTable[2][0] = 70;
testScoreTable[3][0] = 85;
testScoreTable[4][0] = 90;
// populate the elements in column 2
testScoreTable[0][1] = 80;
testScoreTable[1][1] = 90;
testScoreTable[2][1] = 60;
testScoreTable[3][1] = 95;
testScoreTable[4][1] = 100;
```

Java implements multidimensional arrays by creating an array of arrays. The two-dimensional array structure for the testScoreTable example is shown graphically in Figure 2-24.

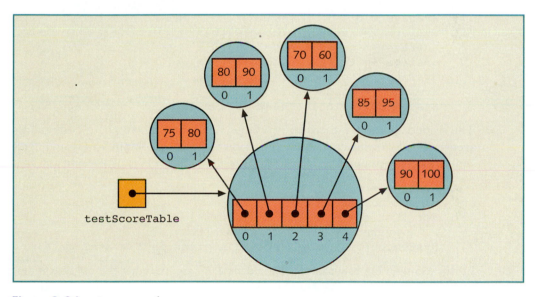

Figure 2-24   An array of arrays

The reference variable `testScoreTable` points to the array instance containing five elements, one for each row. Each of these elements, in turn, is a reference to a second array instance containing two elements, one for each column. You should note that there are actually six array instances shown. Each of them contains elements and each has a length attribute. Because each row of a two-dimensional array is actually a separate array object, each row does not have to be the same length. In other words, you can create a two-dimensional array where the first row has two elements, the second row five elements, and so forth. Although you will usually work with two-dimensional arrays having rows of the same length, Java gives you the option of having rows with different lengths.

In this example, each column represents a separate test. Column 1 contains the scores for test 1, and column 2 contains the scores for test 2. There are three distinct approaches you may take to compute the average for each test. First, you can write individual statements to compute the sum of each column, and then compute its average. Second, you can write two loops, one to sum and compute the average for each column. Or, you can write a nested loop, a loop within a loop, to sum the two columns and compute their average.

The following code illustrates the first approach by computing the sum of column 1, and then its average. Notice that these computation statements use the assignment operator `+=`, which sums `average` and the `testScoreTable` element, and then assigns the result to `average`. Also, notice that the column index remains 0, but that the row index goes from 0 to 4. You would need to write similar code to compute the average for the second column.

```
average = 0;
average += testScoreTable[0][0];
average += testScoreTable[1][0];
average += testScoreTable[2][0];
average += testScoreTable[3][0];
average += testScoreTable[4][0];
System.out.println("test  1 average is " + average/5);
```

The second approach is to write two loops, one for each column, to compute the sum and average. The following code illustrates a loop for the first column. You would need to write a similar loop for column 2.

```
average = 0;
// sum column 1
for (int row = 0; row < 5; row++)
    { average += testScoreTable[row][0];}
System.out.println("test  1 average is " + average/5);
```

In this example the row index is named `row`. Again, note that the column index remains a constant 0 throughout the execution of this loop, but that `row` is incremented with each iteration.

The third solution to compute the average score for each test is to write a nested loop. In this example, there will be an outer loop that will iterate twice, once for each column. The inner loop will iterate five times *for each iteration* of the outer loop.

```
double average;

// outer loop goes across the columns
for(int col = 0; col < 2; col++)
{
    average = 0;
    // inner loop goes down the rows
    for(int row = 0; row < 5; row++)
        {average += testScoreTable[row][col];}
    // end of inner loop

    // compute the column average
    average = average / 5;
    System.out.println("test " + (col + 1) + " average is " +
    average);

}   // end of outer loop
```

This example begins by declaring the variable **average**, which will contain the computation results. Next is the code for the outer loop, which will execute twice, once for each column. The outer loop counter here is named **col** and is used as the column index. The first time the loop executes, **col** will contain 0, and the second time it will contain 1.

The first statement within the outer loop initializes **average** to zero. The outer loop executes twice, once for each column. After its first iteration, **average** will contain the average of the first column. It must be reset to zero before the computation for the second column begins.

The inner loop comes next and uses a loop counter named **row**, which is used as the row index. The inner loop executes five times, once for each row. The single statement within the inner loop simply adds the contents of the array element indexed by **row** and **col** to the variable **average**.

```
average += testScoreTable[row][col];
```

After the inner loop iterates five times, **average** contains the column total. Next comes a statement to divide the total by five to compute the average. Following that, the last statement in the outer loop displays the average.

```
average = average / 5;
System.out.println("test " + (col + 1) + " average is " +
average);
```

Figure 2-25 lists TwoDimArrayDemo.java, and its output is shown in Figure 2-26.

```java
public class TwoDimArrayDemo
{
    public static void main(String[] args)
    {
        // declare an int array with 5 rows & 2 columns
        int testScoreTable[][] = new int [5][2];

        // populate the elements in column 1
        testScoreTable[0][0] = 75;
        testScoreTable[1][0] = 80;
        testScoreTable[2][0] = 70;
        testScoreTable[3][0] = 85;
        testScoreTable[4][0] = 90;
        // populate the elements in column 2
        testScoreTable[0][1] = 80;
        testScoreTable[1][1] = 90;
        testScoreTable[2][1] = 60;
        testScoreTable[3][1] = 95;
        testScoreTable[4][1] = 100;

        // compute the average test score using nested for loop
        double average;
        // outer loop goes across the columns
        for(int col = 0; col < 2; col++)
        {
            average = 0;
            // inner loop goes down the rows
            for(int row = 0; row < 5; row++)
                {average += testScoreTable[row][col];}
            // compute the column average
            average = average / 5;
            System.out.println("test " + (col + 1) + " average is " +
            average);
        }   // end of outer loop
    }
}
```

Figure 2-25   TwoDimArrayDemo.java listing

test 1 average score is 80.0
test 2 average score is 85.0

Figure 2-26   TwoDimArrayDemo output

2

Hands-on Exercise 7

1. Create a folder named Chapter2Exercise7 on your system.

2. Locate TwoDimArrayDemo.java in the Chapter2\Examples folder on the book's CD, and then copy it to the Chapter2Exercise7 folder you created in Step 1.

3. Compile and run TwoDimArrayDemo.java using the software recommended by your instructor. Verify that your output is the same as that shown in Figure 2-26.

4. Add code to display a letter grade for each student for each exam using the grade-assignment logic from Hands-on Exercise 6. In addition to the letter grade, display the exam number (column number + 1) and the student number (row number + 1).

Summary

- Java is a relatively young language, developed by Sun Microsystems and first released in mid-1995. Java was designed to be a powerful, full-featured, object-oriented development language that was easy to learn and use and was independent of computing platforms. Because of these and other features, it has achieved enormous popularity and widespread acceptance.

- The Java Development Kit (JDK) comes with a class library containing hundreds of prewritten classes with methods to accomplish various tasks, ranging from simple number formatting to establishing network connections and accessing relational databases.

- Java's simplicity is achieved by having a much smaller set of keywords than most other languages. Keywords have special meaning within a programming language and are used in writing statements. Java has only 48 keywords, compared to hundreds for many other languages.

- Java's portability is achieved by using bytecode and an interpreter. Bytecode is produced when you compile a Java program. Java bytecode then executes under the control of an interpreter designed specifically for each type of computing platform. This interpreter is called the Java Virtual Machine (JVM).

- Java classes begin with a header line used to identify the class. The Java code inside a class usually consists of variable definitions and one or more methods.

- Methods also begin with a header line written to identify the method and to describe some of its characteristics.

- A Java identifier is the name of a class, method, or variable.

- Java uses the open curly brace (`{`) and closed curly brace (`}`) to delineate a block of code. All code in a Java class is enclosed as one single block of code, which itself usually contains additional blocks. Java uses code blocks to group statements for methods, loops, and if statements.

- Java is case sensitive. For example, Java distinguishes between public and Public and between class and Class (in both of these cases, the lowercase version is the correct keyword). If you have been writing in a language that is not case sensitive, be especially careful when typing Java code.

- A Java comment begins with a double forward slash `//` and can be on a line by itself or at the end of a line of code. Multiline comments begin with `/*` and end with `*/`.

- If a class has a method named main, this method is automatically invoked when the class file is loaded into memory; the main method is what executes.

- You declare a variable to name a place in memory that can contain data. All variables have a data type, name, and value.

- Java has eight primitive data types. These are called primitive data types to distinguish them from more complex data types, such as class names, which are discussed in Chapter 3.

- To declare a Java variable, you write the data type followed by the name you want to use. You can declare several variables of the same data type in one statement.

- The equal sign (=) is called the assignment operator. This operator assigns the value on the right side of the equal sign to the variable named on the left side.

- You can temporarily change the data type of the value contained in a variable using a cast. To cast a value to another data type, you write the desired data type in parentheses to the left of the variable containing the value.

- The code to declare a constant is identical to the code you use to declare a variable, but with the keyword **final** written in front of the data type. However, constants must be initialized in the same statement that declares them.

- Java has two kinds of variables: primitive variables and reference variables. A primitive variable is a variable declared with one of the eight primitive data types, and it actually contains the data you put there. In contrast, a reference variable uses a class name as a data type and refers to or points to an instance of that class. A reference variable does not actually contain the data; instead, it refers to an instance of a class that contains the data.

- The concatenation operator (`+`) joins two string values together.

2

- Java uses the familiar arithmetic operators for addition, subtraction, multiplication, and division (**+**, **−**, *****, **/**).

- Java uses a remainder operator (**%**), sometimes called the modulus operator, to produce a remainder resulting from the division of two integers.

- The Math class, one of Java's supplied classes, has methods to accomplish exponentiation, rounding, and numerous other tasks.

- The increment (**++**) and decrement (**−−**) operators, as their names suggest, either add one to or subtract one from a variable.

- Java supports the use of the assignment operator (**=**) together with the arithmetic operators (**+, −, *, /**) to create assignment operators.

- Java provides three ways to write decision-making statements: the **if**, the **switch**, and the conditional operator. The conditional operator is really a shortcut to writing an if-else statement.

- The Java if statement interrogates a logical expression enclosed in parentheses and determines whether the expression is true or false. An expression often compares two values using logical operators to see if they are equal or if one is less than the other.

- The Java if statement has two forms. The first format evaluates an expression and then executes a block of code if the expression is true. The second form, called an if-else statement, evaluates an expression, executes one block of code if the expression is true, or executes a second block of code if it is false.

- A nested if is an if statement written inside another if statement.

- A compound expression consists of two expressions joined using the logical operators OR (**||**) and AND (**&&**).

- Unlike some other languages, the Java *equal to* operator is two equal signs (**==**), not one (**=**), but the *not equal to* operator is **!=**, instead of **!==**. Further, unlike several other languages, Java does not use **<>** to mean *not equal to*.

- Java implements the case structure with a statement called **switch**. The Java switch statement acts like a multiple-way if statement by transferring control to one of several statements or blocks, depending on the value of an expression.

- You write Java loops using one of three keywords: **while**, **do**, or **for**. There are two kinds of loops: the pre-test loop and the post-test loop. The pre-test loop tests the terminating condition at the beginning of the loop, and the post-test loop checks at the end. Basically, while loops and for loops are pre-test, and do loops are post-test.

- A nested loop is a loop within a loop.

- A one-dimensional array consists of elements arranged in a single row, a two-dimensional array has both rows and columns, and a three-dimensional array is like a cube, with rows, columns, and pages.

- You access the individual elements of the array by writing the array reference variable followed by the index value of the element enclosed in brackets.

- The array instance has an attribute named length that contains the number of elements in the array.

Key Terms

argument	identifier	nested if
arithmetic operators	increment operator	nested loop
assignment operator	Integrated Development Environment (IDE)	null
assignment operators		one-dimensional array
block of code	interpreter	post-test loop
bytecode	Java Development Kit (JDK)	pre-test loop
casting	Java Virtual Machine (JVM)	primitive data type
class header	keyword	primitive variable
compound expression	literal	reference variable
concatenation operator	logical operators	remainder operator
conditional operator	loop counter	three-dimensional array
constant	method header	two-dimensional array
decrement operator	modulus operator	

Review Questions

1. What is bytecode? What is its benefit?

2. What is the JVM? What does it do?

3. When you see two filenames such as Demo.java and Demo.class, what do the extensions class and java indicate?

4. What is an IDE?

5. What is a Java identifier? What are the rules for creating one?

6. What is the purpose of a block of code?

7. What is a Java keyword?

8. What is a primitive variable?

9. What is the error in the statement: `float` d = 2.5;?

10. How can you tell if an identifier is a constant?

11. What does null mean?

12. What is an argument?

13. Explain the difference between Java's use of single and double quotes.

14. What is the `main` method?

15. What does the keyword `new` do?

16. What is the Java conditional operator?

17. Explain the difference between the divide and the remainder operators.

18. What are the limitations of `switch`?

19. What are the two types of loops? How does Java implement each of these?

20. What is an index?

Discussion Questions

1. Discuss the advantages of using methods instead of built-in functions.

2. What impact does using methods have on the number of keywords a language requires?

3. Explain why portability may be lost if you use a Java compiler that produces executable code.

4. Why do you think Java has three separate statements to write loops? Is it not simpler to use just one, such as the for loop?

5. Can you think of any benefit to Java's approach to changing data types? Would it be easier to allow you to assign values from one data type to another without forcing you to write an explicit cast?

Projects

1. Assume a bank account begins with a balance of $100 and earns interest at an annual rate of 5%. The interest is computed at the end of each year using the following formula:

   ```
   newBalance = previousBalance * (1 + interestRate)
   ```

   Write a Java class named ComputeInterest to compute and display this account balance at the end of each year for a five-year period. Do not use loops for Project 1.

2. Repeat Project 1 using a while loop, a do loop, and a for loop. Which loop do you believe is more appropriate for this problem?

3. The following table contains quarterly sales figures for five departments.

	Quarter 1	Quarter 2	Quarter 3	Quarter 4	Total
Department 1	750	660	910	800	
Department 2	800	700	950	900	
Department 3	700	600	750	600	
Department 4	850	800	1000	950	
Department 5	900	800	960	980	
Total					

Design and write a Java class named SalesAnalysis that will:

   a. Declare a two-dimensional integer array named sales. Populate the first four columns using the above data.

   b. Write a loop to compute and populate the total column. Within the loop, display each department total as it is computed.

   c. Write a loop to compute and populate the total row. Within the loop, display each quarter's total as it is computed.

4. Continue with Project 3 by writing a nested loop that will compute and display:

   a. The percentage of total sales made by each department for each quarter and overall.

   b. The percentage of total sales made each quarter.

3

Java Programming With Supplied Classes

In this chapter you will:

♦ Learn about some of the packages and classes supplied with the JDK
♦ Use the String class and its methods
♦ Declare and access a String array
♦ Use the Vector class
♦ Use the Calendar and Date classes
♦ Use the data wrapper classes
♦ Write and execute an applet
♦ Control font and color

Chapter 2 presented Java fundamentals, including an overview of the Java language and its syntax. You saw how to declare and initialize variables and how to write computational statements. In addition, you learned about writing loops, how to code decision-making statements, and how to declare and work with arrays.

You saw that the Java syntax is straightforward, and that the language consists of only 48 keywords. Much of this simplicity is accomplished by using methods in predefined classes that are part of the Java Development Kit (JDK). This chapter focuses on working with some of these supplied classes. You begin by learning more about the String class and how to create and access a String array.

This chapter introduces the Vector class and illustrates how you can use it like a dynamically resizable array. You will learn how to work with dates using the Calendar and Date classes. This chapter also introduces the data wrapper classes, which enable primitive data types to be treated as object instances. The chapter then illustrates how to convert primitive data to wrapper instances and then back to primitive, how to convert String to wrapper and back, and how to convert String data to primitive and back. You finish by developing an applet version of the HelloWorldWideWeb application and then expand it to invoke methods in the Graphics class that enable you to control color and font.

After completing this chapter, you will understand the importance of the supplied classes and be able to use methods in several of them. In Part 3, you begin developing your own classes, the building blocks of object-oriented applications.

USING THE PACKAGES AND CLASSES SUPPLIED WITH JAVA

The **Java Development Kit (JDK)** consists of approximately 75 **packages** containing hundreds of predefined classes and their methods. A Java package is a group of related classes, similar to a class library. You use the keyword **import** to give the Java compiler access to classes contained in specific packages. You can also use the keyword **package** to assign classes to a package. Table 3-1 lists selected packages and shows a few of the classes within each package.

The first four of these packages—`java.lang`, `java.util`, `java.applet`, and `java.text`—are used in this chapter. While `java.lang` is automatically imported by the Java compiler, if you want to access the methods or attributes of classes in any of the other packages, you must write the keyword **import** followed by the list of packages you need. If you omit the import statement, the Java compiler will be unable to locate the class and error messages will result. Note that the package names are lowercase.

Table 3-1   Selected Packages and Classes

Package Name	Selected Classes	Discussed in Chapter
`java.lang`	String wrapper classes Math	3
`java.util`	Calendar Date Vector	3
`java.applet`	Applet	3
`java.text`	DateFormat	3
`java.awt`	Graphics Button Label TextField	3, 11, 12
`javax.swing`	JButton JLabel JTextField	10, 11, 12
`java.io`	InputStream OutputStream	14
`java.sql`	Connection Statement ResultSet	14, 15

Further `java.awt` and `javax.swing` are used in Part 3, which deals with developing GUI classes, `java.io` is illustrated in Chapter 14, and `java.sql` is used in accessing relational database data in Chapter 15.

USING THE STRING CLASS

3

As in many other languages, a Java string is a collection of characters. Java, however, stores string data in instances of the String class, a member of the `java.lang` package. You saw in the previous chapter that you can declare a String instance using code similar to that used to declare a primitive value:

```
String s = "Hello Again";
```

Another way to create an instance of the String class is to use the keyword **new**. This is called **instantiating a class** and means you are creating a new instance of the class. To create a String instance using the **new** keyword, you write:

```
String s = new String("Hello Again");
```

This statement tells Java to first create a new reference variable **s**, create an instance of the String class, store the string value `"Hello Again"` in this instance, and finally assign the location of the new instance to the variable **s**. Using the data type String means that **s** will point to or refer to a String instance.

Object-oriented programming involves instantiating numerous classes, as you will see throughout this text, and using the **new** keyword is the preferred way to instantiate the String class, because it reminds you that you are instantiating a class, not declaring a primitive.

As a class, String has several useful methods. Table 3-2 lists selected methods in the String class. Notice that some of the methods are invoked using a reference variable (**s** in these examples), but that the valueOf method is invoked by specifying the class name, String.

Java has two types of methods: **class methods** and **instance methods**. Instance methods are associated with a specific instance, while class methods are not. You use the class name to invoke a class method, but use a reference variable to invoke an instance method. The instance variable points to the instance for which you are invoking the method. Class methods contain the keyword **static** in their headers. If **static** is omitted, the default is an instance or nonstatic method. Sometime class methods are called **static methods** and instance methods are called **nonstatic methods**.

Table 3-2 Selected String Methods

Method Name	Description
s.charAt(i)	Returns the character in the String instance s at index i (relative to zero)
s.equals(s1)	Compares values character by character in String instances s and s1 and returns either true or false
s.length()	Returns the number of characters in String instance s
s.substring(i,j)	Returns a new String instance containing the string of characters in instance s beginning at index i and ending at j (relative to zero)
s.toUpperCase()	Returns a new String instance containing the contents of instance s converted to uppercase
s.toLowerCase()	Returns a new String instance containing the contents of instance s converted to lowercase
String.valueOf(x)	Returns a String instance containing the primitive in x

To illustrate the differences between class and instance methods, suppose you want to know the number of characters in a string. The String class includes a length method precisely for this purpose: The question is how to invoke this method. A Java reference book will tell you that this method has the following method signature:

```
public int length()
```

This is an instance method because its signature does not contain the keyword **static**. It returns the number of characters in a *specific string instance.* Here you invoke the length method by writing the instance reference variable followed by the method name.

```
// invoke an instance method: length
String s = new String("Hello Again");
System.out.println("length of s is " + s.length());
```

The first statement creates the String instance containing "Hello Again" with **s** referencing the instance, as shown in Figure 3-1. The second statement invokes the length method for the instance referenced by **s**, and then concatenates the value returned with the string literal **"length of s is "**. The resulting string is then passed to the println method.

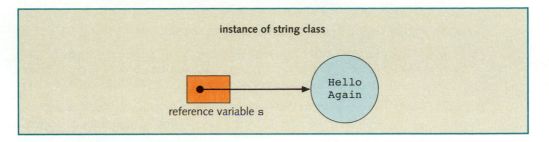

instance of string class

reference variable s

Hello
Again

3

Figure 3-1   A String instance

length of s is 11

Incidentally, a common error for Java programmers is to attempt to invoke an instance method using a reference variable that has not yet been initialized. In other words, the variable contains a null value and *does not point to an instance*; therefore, Java cannot invoke the method you request. When you make this error, Java terminates the execution of your code and displays a message stating that you have a NullPointerException. When you get this message, look for the statement containing the reference variable that caused the error, and then add the code needed to initialize the reference variable.

You specify a class name to invoke a static method. For example, if you want to convert an integer variable to a String instance, you would write the following code:

```java
// invoke a class method – valueOf
int i = 5;
String iString = String.valueOf(i);
System.out.println("value of iString is " + iString);
```

Here your first statement declares the primitive `i` and then initializes it to 5. The next statement declares the String reference variable `iString`, and then invokes the static method valueOf, passing it the variable `i`. The valueOf method creates a new String instance containing the value 5, and `iString` is assigned a pointer to this instance. The last statement concatenates the literal `"value of iString is "` with the contents of the String instance referenced by `iString`, and then passes the resulting value to println. The output from these statements is:

value of iString is 5

In this final example, you write code to illustrate two additional String instance methods: charAt and toUpperCase. The charAt method returns a single character from a string at the index you specify. Note that Java index values begin at 0, not 1. Here, when you specify an index value of 6, the method returns the seventh character in the string.

```
// illustrate additional String instance methods
System.out.println("character at index 6 is " + s.charAt(6));
System.out.println("uppercase is " + s.toUpperCase());
```

String values in Java are **immutable**—they cannot be changed. Methods such as toUpper-Case actually create and return a new String instance. The signature for toUpperCase is:

```
public String toUpperCase()
```

The output from these two methods is:

```
character at index 6 is A
uppercase is HELLO AGAIN
```

Figure 3-2 lists the code in StringDemo, and Figure 3-3 shows its output.

```
public class StringDemo
{
    public static void main(String[] args)
    {
        //  invoke an instance method: length
        String s = new String("Hello Again");
        System.out.println("length of s is " + s.length());

        //  convert primitive to String: valueOf class method
        int i = 5;
        String iString = String.valueOf(i);
        System.out.println("value of iString is " + iString);

        //  illustrate additional String instance methods
        System.out.println("character at index 6 is " + s.charAt(6));
        System.out.println("uppercase is " + s.toUpperCase());
    }
}
```

Figure 3-2   StringDemo.java listing

```
length of s is 11
value of iString is 5
character at index 6 is A
uppercase is HELLO AGAIN
```

Figure 3-3   StringDemo output

Hands-on Exercise 1

1. Create a folder named Chapter3Exercise1 on your system.

2. Locate StringDemo.java in the folder named Chapter3\Examples on the book's CD and then copy it to the Chapter3Exercise1 folder you created in Step 1.

3. Compile and run StringDemo.java using the software recommended by your instructor. Verify that your output is the same as that shown in Figure 3-3.

4. Add the following statements to the beginning of the main method in StringDemo.java:

```
String myInfo = null;

System.out.println("My name is " + myInfo.toUpperCase());
```

5. Recompile and run StringDemo.java with these new statements. You will encounter the NullPointerException message described earlier.

6. Correct the statement:

```
String myInfo = null;
```

to

```
String myInfo ="***";
```

Type your name and course number in place of ***.

7. Recompile and run StringDemo.java with this corrected statement.

CREATING A STRING ARRAY

In Chapter 2 you created an array of integer elements with the statement:

```
int testScores[] = new int[5];
```

This code declares the array reference variable **testScores**, creates an array instance consisting of five elements, each of data type **int**, and then points **testScores** to the array. You then can access a specific element using an index.

The code to create a String array is similar:

```
// declare an array with 4 elements data type String
String stringArray[] = new String[4];
```

This statement declares an array reference variable **stringArray**, creates an Array instance containing four elements, each of which is a reference variable whose data type is String, and then points **stringArray** to the array instance. Note that the elements of the **testScores** array are primitive variables of data type **int**. However, the elements of **stringArray** are reference variables of data type String.

Next you write statements to create four String instances and populate the array elements with references to these instances. Figure 3-4 shows the array and String instances.

```
stringArray[0] = new String("Hello");
stringArray[1] = new String("World");
stringArray[2] = new String("Wide");
stringArray[3] = new String("Web");
```

The **stringArray** variable is a reference variable that points to the array instance. The array instance contains four elements, each of which is a reference variable pointing to a String instance. The four String instances contain the values shown. The attribute named **length** contains the number of array elements.

Just like an array of primitives, you can access a specific element using the index of that element. For example, if you want to display each of the String values here, you write the following code:

```
// display each String value
System.out.println(stringArray[0]);
System.out.println(stringArray[1]);
System.out.println(stringArray[2]);
System.out.println(stringArray[3]);
```

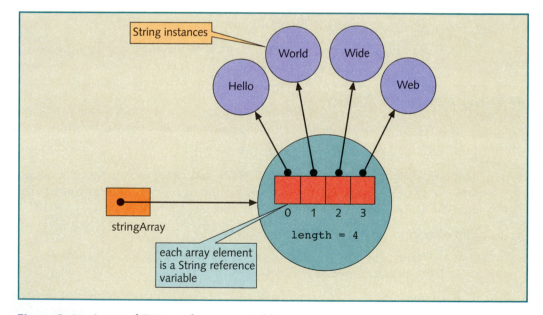

Figure 3-4   Array of String reference variables

Of course, instead of writing a separate statement for each element, you can write a loop to display the values:

```
// display the values using a loop
for(int i = 0; i < stringArray.length; i++)
    { System.out.println(stringArray[i]);}
```

Note that this code uses the `length` attribute to test for the end of the array. You should distinguish between the `length` *attribute* of an array instance and the length *method* of the String class. To illustrate, you can display the number of elements in the array using the `length` attribute:

```
// display the number of array elements
System.out.println(stringArray.length);
```

This statement will display the number of elements, 4. However, if you want to display the number of characters in one of the String instances, you invoke the length method for that instance. Here, you invoke length for the fourth String instance (index 3), which contains "Web." The value displayed by this code is 3.

```
// display the number of characters in Web
System.out.println(stringArray[3].length());
```

You can invoke additional String methods for the String instances referenced by the array elements. For example, to invoke toUpperCase for the String instance referenced by the first array element, you write:

```
// invoke toUpperCase for the first String instance
System.out.println(stringArray[0].toUpperCase());
```

You can also search for a specific value in an array. For example, suppose you want to search **stringArray** for the value "Web." You begin by creating a String instance referenced by the variable **searchValue** containing the value you want to find, as in the following code:

```
// search for the value "Web"
String searchValue = "Web";
```

You next declare an index `i` and initialize it to 0. You also declare a boolean variable named **found** and initialize it to **false** (found will later be set to **true** when you find the value you are seeking).

```
int i = 0;
boolean found = false;
```

You then write a while loop that iterates as long as the index is less than the number of array elements (`i < stringArray.length`) and (`&&`) the boolean variable `found` remains not true (`!found`). Within the loop you write a single if statement that invokes the equals method for the **searchValue** instance to see if its contents match the instance referenced by the array element indexed by `i`. If the instance contents match, `found` is set to **true** to terminate the loop. However, if the contents do not match, the index is incremented and, if the index remains less than the number of array elements, the loop continues.

```java
// loop begins
while(i < stringArray.length && !found)
{
    if (searchValue.equals(stringArray[i]))
        found = true;
    else
        i++;
}
```

Note that in the if statement here you must use the String instance method equals, instead of the equal operator (==), because the elements of **stringArray** are reference variables and not primitive variables. In other words, the elements *point to* String instances; they do not *contain* the string values. String also has a method named equalsIgnoreCase, which, as its name implies, works like the equals method except that the case of the data being examined is ignored.

Following the loop, you can interrogate **found** to see if a matching value was detected, and display an appropriate message.

```java
if (found)
    System.out.println("found " + searchValue);
else
    System.out.println("did not find "+ searchValue);
```

The complete code for StringArrayDemo.java is shown in Figure 3-5, with the output in Figure 3-6.

```java
public class StringArrayDemo
{
    public static void main(String[] args)
    {
        //  declare an array with 4 elements data type String
        String stringArray[] = new String[4];
        //  create String instances and initialize the array elements
        stringArray[0] = new String("Hello");
        stringArray[1] = new String("World");
        stringArray[2] = new String("Wide");
        stringArray[3] = new String("Web");

        //  display the values using a loop
        for(int i = 0; i < stringArray.length; i++)
            { System.out.println(stringArray[i]);}
        //  display the number of array elements
        System.out.println(stringArray.length + " elements");

        //  display the number of characters in Web
        System.out.println("Web length is " + stringArray[3].length());

        //  invoke toUpperCase for the first String instance
        System.out.println(stringArray[0].toUpperCase());
```

```
      //  search for the value "Web"
      String searchValue = "Web";
      int i = 0;
      boolean found = false;
      //  loop begins
      while(i < stringArray.length && !found)
      {
          if (searchValue.equals(stringArray[i]))
              found = true;
          else
              i++;
      }
      if (found)
          System.out.println("found " + searchValue);
      else
          System.out.println("did not find "+ searchValue);
   }
}
```

Figure 3-5   StringArrayDemo.java listing

Hello
World
Wide
Web
4 elements
Web length is 3
HELLO
found Web

Figure 3-6   StringArrayDemo.java output

Hands-on Exercise 2

1. Create a folder named Chapter3Exercise2 on your system.

2. Locate StringArrayDemo.java in the folder named Chapter3Examples on the book's CD and then copy it to the Chapter3\Exercise2 folder you created in Step 1.

3. Compile and run StringArrayDemo.java using the software recommended by your instructor. Verify that your output is the same as that shown in Figure 3-6.

4. Add a loop to the end of the main method in StringArrayDemo.java to display the array elements in reverse order. Your output should read Web, Wide, World, and Hello.

5. Recompile and run StringArrayDemo.java with these new statements.

USING THE VECTOR CLASS

As you have seen, array elements are actually variables. As such, they may be either primitive or reference variables, depending on how you declare the array. In Chapter 2 you created an array of primitive elements, and in the previous section you saw how to create an array of String reference elements. As powerful as they are, however, arrays have a significant limitation: They are fixed in size. It is extremely difficult to change the number of array elements as your code is executing.

You use the Vector class—a member of the `java.util` package, which you must import—to create an array that is dynamically resizable. This means that you can change the number of elements of a vector *while your code is executing.* The Vector class also provides several useful methods, some of which are illustrated in this section. The Vector class has one limitation, however: You cannot create a Vector instance containing primitive elements. All of a vector's elements must contain references to instances; they cannot contain primitive values. Later in this chapter you will learn to work with data wrapper classes to create instances that contain primitive data to overcome this restriction. Table 3-3 lists several commonly used Vector methods and a brief description.

Table 3-3   Selected Vector Methods

Method Name	Description
add(o)	Places a reference to the object instance o into the next available vector element
capacity()	Returns the total number of vector elements
contains(o)	Searches for an element referencing the object instance o; returns true or false
get(i)	Returns the contents of the element at index i
indexOf(o)	Returns the index of the element referencing object instance o if it exists; returns −1 if not
remove(i)	Sets the contents of the element at index i to null
size()	Returns the number of populated elements

In order to use the Vector class, you first create a Vector instance. The following code declares the reference variable **aVector** and creates a Vector instance containing three elements. As you will see shortly, when you add more than three elements, the Vector instance will automatically increase its size. Note that the following code uses parentheses, not brackets, when specifying the number of Vector elements, because you are actually passing the number 3 to the Vector constructor:

```
// declare a vector instance with 3 elements
Vector aVector = new Vector(3);
```

Next you write code to create four instances of String, just like before.

```
// create String instances
String s1 = new String("Hello");
String s2 = new String("World");
String s3 = new String("Wide");
String s4 = new String("Web");
```

You then invoke the Vector instance method **add** to populate the first two elements.

```
// populate the first two elements
aVector.add(s1);
aVector.add(s2);
```

Note that you can create the String instance and populate a vector element using a single statement. The following statement creates the String instance and passes its reference to the add method, which stores the reference in the next available element of the vector. This approach eliminates the need for the additional String reference variable.

```
aVector.add(new String("Hello");
```

Next you invoke the capacity method to display the total number of vector elements, and then you invoke the size method to display the number of *populated* elements. In this example, **aVector** now has three elements, two of which are populated. Therefore, the first statement displays 3 and the second, 2.

```
System.out.println("number of elements = " + aVector.
capacity());
System.out.println(aVector.size() + " are populated");
```

Vector has a built-in search method, **contains**. This method iterates the Vector instance, searching for an element that references the object instance specified. In this example, the method looks for an element referencing the string literal **"Hello"**. The following code will display true, because the first Vector instance does, in fact, reference the string literal **"Hello"**:

```
// search for "Hello"
System.out.println(aVector.contains("Hello"));
```

Next, you add the last two String instances from the previous code to the vector. When the fourth element is added, the number of elements increases automatically.

```
// add two more elements
aVector.add(s3);
aVector.add(s4);
```

Finally, you write a loop to display the contents of the String instances referenced by the vector elements. This code is similar to the code in the previous section that displayed the String instances referenced by the array. The previous array code was:

```
// display the values using a loop
for(int i = 0; i < stringArray.length; i++)
    { System.out.println(stringArray[i]);}
```

The code to iterate the vector and display the String instances is:

```
// loop to display contents
for(int i = 0; i < aVector.size(); i++)
    { System.out.println(aVector.get(i));}
```

There are two differences between the array and vector code. First, the array loop executes while `i < stringArray.length` and the vector loop continues while `i < aVector.size()`. Note that `length` is an attribute but `size()` invokes a method.

The second difference is in the code to retrieve the string data. The array code simply retrieves `stringArray[i]`, but the Vector loop invokes the get method, which returns the string reference. The listing for VectorDemo.java is shown in Figure 3-7, and the output is shown in Figure 3-8. Notice that the class includes a statement to import `java.util.Vector`.

```java
import java.util.Vector;
public class VectorDemo
{
    public static void main(String[] args)
    {
        //  declare a Vector instance with 3 elements
        Vector aVector = new Vector(3);
        //  create String instances
        String s1 = new String("Hello");
        String s2 = new String("World");
        String s3 = new String("Wide");
        String s4 = new String("Web");

        //  populate the first two elements
        aVector.add(s1);
        aVector.add(s2);

        System.out.println("number of elements = " + aVector.capacity());
        System.out.println(aVector.size() + " are populated");

        //  search for "Hello"
        System.out.println(aVector.contains("Hello"));

        //  populate two more elements
        aVector.add(s3);
        aVector.add(s4);

        //  loop to display contents
        for(int i = 0; i < aVector.size(); i++)
            { System.out.println(aVector.get(i));}

    }
}
```

Figure 3-7   VectorDemo.java listing

```
number of elements = 3
2 are populated
true
Hello
World
Wide
Web
```

Figure 3-8   VectorDemo output

Hands-on Exercise 3

1. Create a folder named Chapter3Exercise3 on your system.

2. Locate VectorDemo.java in the folder named Chapter3\Examples on the book's CD and then copy it to the Chapter3Exercise3 folder you created in Step 1.

3. Compile and run VectorDemo.java using the software recommended by your instructor. Verify that your output is the same as that shown in Figure 3-8.

4. Add a loop to the end of the main method in VectorDemo.java to display the contents of the String instances referenced by the vector elements in reverse order. Your output should read Web, Wide, World, and Hello.

5. Recompile and run VectorDemo.java with these new statements.

WORKING WITH DATES

Often, while developing systems, you need to work with dates. For example, many systems deal with today's date, due date, order date, employment date, expiration date, and so forth. Java provides classes with methods that let you retrieve the current system date, format date values, perform arithmetic on date fields, and compare date values. These methods are illustrated in this section.

You use three classes when working with date values: Calendar, Date, and DateFormat. Calendar contains methods and constants, a Date instance contains the actual date value, and a DateFormat instance provides several date formats for display purposes. Calendar and Date are in the `java.util` package, and DateFormat is in `java.text`. The following code begins with import statements for these packages so the Java compiler can access methods and attributes in these classes:

```
import java.util.*;
import java.text.*;
```

Note that the import statement you used in VectorDemo.java was:

```
import java.util.Vector;
```

Next, you create a Calendar instance and then invoke its `getTime` method to obtain an instance of Date containing the current system date. Note that you obtain instances of both Calendar and Date, but you do not use the `new` keyword. You will often encounter methods that return instances, such as in this example. Following the execution of this code, you will have a Calendar instance referenced by `aCalendar` and a Date instance referenced by `today` that contains today's system date.

```
// create a Calendar instance
Calendar aCalendar = Calendar.getInstance();
//  use Calendar instance to return Date instance
Date today = aCalendar.getTime();
```

There may be times when you need to perform arithmetic on a date value—for example, to determine the date for a month from today or a year from today. The Calendar class has an instance method named add that will add a value to the month, day, or year, depending on the arguments that are passed to it. The first argument is a Calendar constant indicating to which part of the date you want to add (month, day, or year), and the second argument is the value you want added. The following code adds one to the current month and year, and creates a new Date instance named `aYearAndMonthLater` containing the new date value.

```
// illustrate arithmetic - add 1 to MONTH and YEAR
aCalendar.add(Calendar.MONTH, 1);
aCalendar.add(Calendar.YEAR, 1);
Date aYearAndMonthLater = aCalendar.getTime();
```

You can also create a Date instance containing a specific date. The following example creates a Date instance for December 15, 1998. The first statement invokes the Calendar instance method named set and passes its arguments for year, month, and day. This example uses the Calendar constant `Calendar.DECEMBER`.

```
// create a specific date
aCalendar.set(1998, Calendar.DECEMBER, 15);
Date eleanorsBirthday = aCalendar.getTime();
```

You use the DateFormat class to provide various display formats for dates. For example, you can display a date as February 20, 2003, Feb 20, 2003, or 2/20/03. The following code illustrates the creation of DateFormat instances for each format. To obtain a format instance, you invoke the class method `getDateInstance`, passing an argument indicating which format you want to use. This class has constants named `LONG`, `MEDIUM`, and `SHORT` that are used to specify the format you want to create.

```
// get DateFormat instances in various formats
DateFormat longFormat = DateFormat.getDateInstance(DateFormat.LONG);
DateFormat mediumFormat =
DateFormat.getDateInstance(DateFormat.MEDIUM);
DateFormat shortFormat =
DateFormat.getDateInstance (DateFormat.SHORT);
```

Next, you invoke the format method, passing it a Date instance you want formatted. This method returns a String containing the date in the desired format. The following statements illustrate these various formats.

```
// display dates using various formats
System.out.println("long format: today is " +
    longFormat.format(today));
System.out.println("medium format: today is " +
    mediumFormat.format(today));
System.out.println("short format: today is " +
    shortFormat.format(today));
System.out.println("A year and month later is " +
    longFormat.format(aYearAndMonthLater));
System.out.println("Eleanor's birthday is " +
    mediumFormat.format(eleanorsBirthday));
```

The Date class also has two useful instance methods to compare the values contained in two Date instances. The method named after returns **true** if the date argument is *after* the Date instance; otherwise, it returns false. Similarly, the method named before returns **true** if the argument is *before* the Date instance, and returns **false** if it is not. In the example, **today** is February 20, 2003 and **aYearAndMonthLater** is March 20, 2004. The following code illustrates the use of the date comparison methods.

```
// illustrate date comparison
if (aYearAndMonthLater.after(today))
    System.out.println("aYearAndMonthLater is after today");
if (today.before(aYearAndMonthLater))
    System.out.println("today is before aYearAndMonthLater");
```

Figure 3-9 shows the complete listing of DateDemo.java, and Figure 3-10 shows its output.

```
import java.util.*;
import java.text.*;

public class DateDemo
{
    public static void main(String[] args)
    {
        // create a Calendar instance
        Calendar aCalendar = Calendar.getInstance();

        // get today's date
        Date today = aCalendar.getTime();

        // illustrate arithmetic - add 1 to MONTH and YEAR
        aCalendar.add(Calendar.MONTH, 1);
```

```
        aCalendar.add(Calendar.YEAR, 1);
        Date aYearAndMonthLater = aCalendar.getTime();

        // create a specific date
        aCalendar.set(1998, Calendar.DECEMBER, 15);
        Date eleanorsBirthday = aCalendar.getTime();

        // get DateFormat instances in each format
        DateFormat longFormat =
DateFormat.getDateInstance(DateFormat.LONG);
        DateFormat mediumFormat =
DateFormat.getDateInstance(DateFormat.MEDIUM);
        DateFormat shortFormat =
DateFormat.getDateInstance(DateFormat.SHORT);

        // display dates using various formats
        System.out.println("long format: today is " +
longFormat.format(today));
        System.out.println("medium format: today is " +
mediumFormat.format(today));
        System.out.println("short format: today is " +
shortFormat.format(today));
        System.out.println("A year and month later is " +
longFormat.format(aYearAndMonthLater));
        System.out.println("Eleanor's birthday is " +
mediumFormat.format(eleanorsBirthday));

        // illustrate date comparison
        if (aYearAndMonthLater.after(today))
           System.out.println("aYearAndMonthLater is after today");
        if (today.before(aYearAndMonthLater))
              System.out.println("today is before
aYearAndMonthLater");
    }
}
```

Figure 3-9   DateDemo.java listing

long format: today is February 20, 2003

medium format: today is Feb 20, 2003

short format: today is 2/20/03

A year and month later is March 20, 2004

Eleanor's birthday is Dec 15, 1998

aYearAndMonthLater is after today

today is before aYearAndMonthLater

Figure 3-10   DateDemo output

Hands-on Exercise 4

1. Create a folder named Chapter3Exercise4 on your system.

2. Locate DateDemo.java in the folder named Chapter3\Examples on the book's CD and then copy it to the Chapter3Exercise4 folder you created in Step 1.

3. Compile and run DateDemo.java using the software recommended by your instructor. Verify that your output is the same as that shown in Figure 3-10.

4. Add statements to the beginning of the main method in DateDemo.java to:
   a. Create a Date instance named myBirthday populated with your date of birth.
   b. Display your birth date in all three formats.

5. Recompile and run DateDemo.java with these new statements.

USING WRAPPER CLASSES

Each of the eight primitive data types—**int**, **double**, **boolean**, and so on—has a corresponding class called a **data wrapper** class. These wrapper classes, except for Integer, are named the same as their primitive counterpart, with the first letter of their name capitalized: Boolean, Byte, Character, Double, Float, Integer, Long, and Short. These classes reside in the **java.lang** package. The primary purpose of these wrapper classes is to contain primitive data *inside* an object instance. In addition, these classes provide several useful methods for converting one data type to another.

You will encounter situations when developing systems where you must use an object instance instead of a primitive data type. For example, you saw earlier that the elements of a vector cannot contain primitive data. If you need to store primitive data in a Vector instance, you first create a wrapper instance containing the data and then store its reference in the Vector instance.

The Java wrapper classes have methods to convert their instance values to primitives or to String instances. The following sections describe how to create wrapper instances from primitive variables and then how to convert the instance contents back to primitive data. You also learn how to invoke wrapper methods to convert string data to primitive and then how to change it back to string. Finally, you learn how to create wrapper instances from string data and then how to change them back to string.

Converting Primitive to Wrapper and Back

You can place a primitive value into a wrapper instance by instantiating the appropriate wrapper class using the primitive variable as the argument. The following example first declares and initializes a **double** primitive, creates an instance of Double by passing the primitive variable as an argument to the constructor, and then displays the contents of **doubleWrapper**.

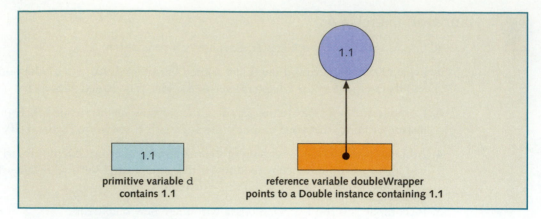

Figure 3-11   A primitive variable and a wrapper instance

```
// declare a primitive
double d = 1.1;
//  create wrapper instance from primitive
Double doubleWrapper = new Double(d);
```

The wrapper instance referenced by **doubleWrapper** now contains the double value 1.1. The wrapper classes once again emphasize the difference between a *primitive variable*, which contains data, and a *reference variable*, which points to an instance containing the data. Figure 3-11 shows the primitive variable named **d** which *contains* the value 1.1 and the reference variable named **doubleWrapper** which *points to* the Double instance containing 1.1.

You can also convert the contents of a wrapper instance to its primitive counterpart. Each wrapper class has an instance method named *xxx*Value (where *xxx* is the primitive data type) that will retrieve the value stored in the wrapper instance and assign it to a primitive variable. For example, use intValue to retrieve the value stored in an Integer instance. The following code invokes **doubleValue** to retrieve the contents of **doubleWrapper** and assign the value to **doublePrimitive**.

```
// assign wrapper contents to primitive: xxxValue instance method
double doublePrimitive = doubleWrapper.doubleValue();
```

Converting String to Primitive and Back

There are times when you will want to convert a numeric value to a string and vice versa. As you will see in Part 3, when developing GUI classes, numeric data that is entered on a GUI screen is actually in string format, and you must convert it to primitive in order to use it in computations. Similarly, numeric data to be displayed on a GUI must be converted to string to be displayed correctly.

The wrapper classes have class methods named parse*xxx* (where *xxx* is the primitive data type) to assign the numeric contents of String instances to primitive variables. For example, use parseDouble to retrieve the contents of a String instance and convert it to data type **double**. The parse*xxx* methods are static, which means you invoke them using the class name instead of a reference variable name. In the following code, you first create a String instance containing 2.2, and then invoke parseDouble to return a **double** primitive value.

```
// assign contents of String instance to primitive
String secondString = new String("2.2");
doublePrimitive = Double.parseDouble(secondString);
```

The wrappers also have a toString method that creates a String instance containing the primitive value passed to it. Next you invoke this method to create a String instance containing the primitive value stored in **doublePrimitive**.

```
// create a String from a primitive: toString class method
String thirdString = Double.toString(doublePrimitive);
```

Converting String to Wrapper and Back

If you want to convert the contents of a String instance directly to a wrapper instance, you can use static wrapper methods named valueOf to accomplish this task. The following code first creates a String instance containing 3.3, and then invokes the Double static method valueOf, which creates a Double instance and stores the contents of the String instance, 3.3, into it.

```
// create wrapper from a String: valueOf class method
String fourthString = new String("3.3");
doubleWrapper = Double.valueOf(fourthString);
```

If needed, you can also convert a wrapper instance to String. The following statements invoke the wrapper method toString to create a String instance from the wrapper instance referenced by **doubleWrapper**.

```
// create a String from wrapper: toString instance method
String fifthString = doubleWrapper.toString();
System.out.println("wrapper to String is " + fifthString);
```

The listing of WrapperDemo.java is shown in Figure 3-12, and the output is shown in Figure 3-13.

```
public class WrapperDemo
{
    public static void main(String[] args)
    {
        // declare a primitive
        double d = 1.1;
        // create wrapper instance from primitive
        Double doubleWrapper = new Double(d);
```

```java
System.out.println("double to wrapper is " + doubleWrapper);
// assign wrapper contents to primitive
double doublePrimitive = doubleWrapper.doubleValue();
System.out.println("wrapper to double  is " +
doublePrimitive);

// assign contents of String instance to primitive
String firstString= new String("2.2");
doublePrimitive = Double.parseDouble(firstString);
System.out.println("String to primitive is " +
doublePrimitive);
// create a String from a primitive: toString class method
String secondString = Double.toString(doublePrimitive);
System.out.println("primitive to String is " + secondString);

// create wrapper from a String: valueOf class method
String thirdString = new String("3.3");
doubleWrapper = Double.valueOf(thirdString);
System.out.println("String to wrapper is " + doubleWrapper);
// create a String from wrapper: toString instance method
String fourthString = doubleWrapper.toString();
System.out.println("wrapper to String is " + fourthString);
    }
}
```

Figure 3-12   WrapperDemo.java listing

> double to wrapper is 1.1
>
> wrapper to double is 1.1
>
> String to primitive is 2.2
>
> primitive to String is 2.2
>
> String to wrapper is 3.3
>
> wrapper to String is 3.3

Figure 3-13   WrapperDemo output

Hands-on Exercise 5

1. Create a folder named Chapter3Exercise5 on your system.

2. Locate WrapperDemo.java in the folder named Chapter3\Examples on the book's CD and then copy it to the Chapter3Exercise5 folder you created in Step 1.

3. Compile and run WrapperDemo.java using the software recommended by your instructor. Verify that your output is the same as that shown in Figure 3-13.

4. Add statements to the beginning of the main method in WrapperDemo.java to:
   a. Create a float primitive named aFloatPrimitive containing 123.456.
   b. Declare aFloatWrapper from aFloatPrimitive.

    c. Create a String instance named aString populated using aFloatWrapper.

    d. Create a float primitive named secondFloatPrimitive using aString.

    e. Create a float wrapper named secondFloatWrapper using aString.

    f. Write statements to display the contents of these five variables.

5. Recompile and run WrapperDemo.java with these new statements.

USING THE APPLET CLASS

An applet is a Java program that is executed by the JVM embedded in another program, generally a Web browser. Applets are typically downloaded to a client system for execution. Because of security concerns, applets cannot access files on the client system or initiate communication links with other systems on the network. Usually applets are displayed as part of a graphical user interface.

Writing a Simple Applet

You can begin by writing AppletDemo1, which will display "Hello World Wide Web," just like the application in Chapter 2, except here you use an applet instead of an application. First, you import the Graphics class from the `java.awt` package and the Applet class from the `java.applet` package. You import Graphics because you will invoke its methods to draw figures and text on the visible panel, and you import Applet because it will be the super class of the applet.

```
import java.awt.Graphics;
import java.applet.Applet;
```

The Applet class is a subclass of Panel. A Panel instance is like a GUI window without a title bar. When you write an applet, such as AppletDemo1 in the following example, you make it a subclass of Applet and therefore a subclass of Panel. This class hierarchy is shown in the class diagram in Figure 3-14.

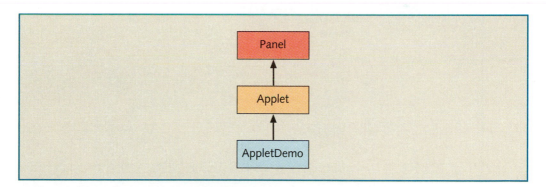

Figure 3-14   Class hierarchy for AppletDemo

Next, write the class header, which is similar to those you have seen before. You specify a **public** class and assign the name AppletDemo1. The keyword **extends**, followed by **Applet**, makes AppletDemo1 a subclass of the Applet class. This means that it inherits numerous methods from Applet and Panel.

public class AppletDemo1 **extends** Applet

To run the applet, the JVM in your Web browser does the following:

1. Loads the applet into memory.

2. Instantiates it, thus creating a panel instance.

3. Makes the panel instance visible.

4. Calls a special method named paint.

For this example, you write a single method, named paint, with the following header:

public void paint(Graphics g)

The method paint is a special method that JVM (running inside a browser) calls after the applet is loaded, instantiated, and displayed. As you can see, the method receives a reference variable for an instance of the Graphics class from the JVM **(Graphics g)**. In this first example, you write only one statement that invokes the Graphics method named drawString to display a string on the panel being displayed.

```
// display the string data
g.drawString("Hello World Wide Web", 20, 30);
```

This method, as its name suggests, is used to display (or more correctly, draw) string data in graphics mode. The argument you send the method consists of the value you want to display, followed by the X and Y coordinates of the upper-left point where the data will appear. The panel uses an X,Y coordinate system; however, the origin (X = 0, Y = 0) is at the upper-left corner of the panel with X increasing to the right and Y increasing down as shown in Figure 3-15. The units used here are pixels.

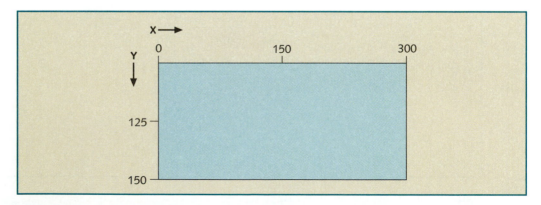

Figure 3-15   Coordinate system for AppletDemo1

AppletDemo1.java is listed in Figure 3-16, and the output is shown in Figure 3-17.

Because the JVM will execute this applet in a browser, you must create a small HTML file to tell the browser about the applet. The HTML code simply specifies the name of the applet bytecode file, which for this example will be AppletDemo1.class, and the size of the panel you want to display, in pixels. A typical display screen is 600 pixels wide and 800 pixels high. The panel in this example is 300 pixels wide and 150 pixels high.

Hands-on Exercise 6

1. Create a folder named Chapter3Exercise6 on your system.

2. Locate AppletDemo1.java in the folder named Chapter3\Examples on the book's CD and then copy it to the Chapter3Exercise6 folder you created in Step 1.

3. Using text editor software recommended by your instructor, create the following HTML file. Enter the following code exactly as shown and save it as Applet-Demo1.html in your folder named Chapter3Exercise6:

```
<APPLET
CODE = "AppletDemo1.class"
WIDTH = 300 HEIGHT = 150>
</APPLET>
```

4. Compile Applet1Demo.java using the software recommended by your instructor.

5. Launch a browser, such as Microsoft Internet Explorer, and then open the Applet Demo1.html file you created in Step 3. The bytecode file named Applet Demo1.class is then loaded, AppletDemo1 is instantiated, and displayed, and the paint method is invoked.

6. Verify that your output is the same as that shown in Figure 3-17.

```java
import java.awt.Graphics;
import java.applet.Applet;

public class AppletDemo1 extends Applet
{
    public void paint(Graphics g)
    {
        //  display the string data
        g.drawString("Hello World Wide Web", 20, 30);
    }
}
```

Figure 3-16 AppletDemo1.java listing

Hello World Wide Web

Figure 3-17   AppletDemo1.java output

Controlling Color and Font

In this section, you learn how to write a second applet named AppletDemo2 by adding code to AppletDemo1 to change the font being displayed, work with color, and draw some figures. The java.awt package includes the Font and Color classes that you use to set the color and font for the text and figures you want to display. AppletDemo2 also needs access to the Graphics and Applet classes; therefore, you will need to import all of these.

```
import java.awt.Graphics;
import java.awt.Font;
import java.awt.Color;
import java.applet.Applet;
```

Often, Java programmers make all classes in a package available by writing an "*" instead of a specific class name. Instead of writing the three separate import statements for the java.awt package, you can write a single line:

```
import java.awt.*;
```

The "*" is called a **wildcard character,** which gives the compiler access to all of the classes in the java.awt package.

The class header here is identical to AppletDemo1 except that the class name is now Applet-Demo2.

```
public class AppletDemo2 extends Applet
```

You also need to change the class name in the HTML file to AppletDemo2.class and the HTML filename to AppletDemo2.html.

```
<APPLET
    CODE = "AppletDemo2.class"
    WIDTH = 300
    HEIGHT = 150>
</APPLET>
```

AppletDemo2 will display "Hello World Wide Web," just as in the application created in Chapter 2, except it will use color and an enhanced font. The first statement invokes the Graphics instance method setColor to use red. The argument passed (Color.red) is a constant in the Color class. Color also has constants **Color.blue, Color.green, Color.yellow**, and so forth.

```
g.setColor(Color.red);
```

You next create an instance of the Font class with arguments specifying the font name, style, and size. Then you invoke the Graphics method setFont and pass the reference to the newly created Font instance.

```
Font f = new Font("TimesRoman", Font.ITALIC,28);
g. setFont(f);
```

You could also combine these two into a single statement. This creates the Font instance, and then passes it to the setFont method. In this code, however, you no longer will have a reference to the Font instance.

```
g. setFont(new Font("TimesRoman", Font.ITALIC,28));
```

The drawstring method is used exactly as before; however, because you have now set the color and font, the string data will appear as red, 28 point, Times Roman italic font.

```
// display the string data
g.drawString("Hello World Wide Web", 20, 30);
```

Next, you set the color to blue and invoke the Graphics instance method fillOval to draw a circle. The arguments you pass are the X and Y coordinates of the upper-left corner of a rectangle around the oval, followed by the oval height and width. Since height and width are equal in this example, and you set the color to blue, you will see a blue circle.

```
// set color to blue and draw a circle
g.setColor(Color.blue);
g.fillOval(50,50,50,50);
```

The last example sets the color to green and draws a rectangle. Again, the arguments are the X and Y coordinates of the upper-left corner followed by height and width.

```
// set color to green and draw a rectangle
g.setColor(Color.green);
g.fillRect(150,50,75,75);
```

Table 3-4 lists selected methods in the Graphics class.

The listing for AppletDemo2 is displayed in Figure 3-18, and the output is shown in Figure 3-19.

Table 3-4   Selected Graphics Methods

Method Name	Description
drawLine(x1,y1,x2,y2)	Draws from x1,y1 to x2,y2
drawRect(x, y, width, height)	Draws rectangle
fillRect(x, y, width, height)	Draws and fills with color
drawOval(x, y, width, height)	Draws oval with x,y upper-left point if width = height, then draws a circle
fillOval(x, y, width, height)	Draws and fills with color

```java
import java.awt.*;
import java.applet.Applet;

public class AppletDemo2 extends Applet
{
   public void paint(Graphics g)
   {
      //  set color to red and font to 28 point Times Roman
          italic
      g.setColor(Color.red);
      Font f = new Font("TimesRoman", Font.ITALIC,28);
      g. setFont(f);
      //  display the string data
      g.drawString("Hello World Wide Web", 20, 30);
      //  set color to blue and draw a circle
      g.setColor(Color.blue);
      g.fillOval(50,50,50,50);
      //  set color to green and draw a rectangle
      g.setColor(Color.green);
      g.fillRect(150,50,75,75);
   }
}
```

Figure 3-18   AppletDemo2.java listing

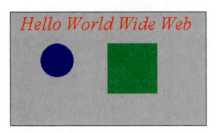

Figure 3-19   AppletDemo2 output

Hands-on Exercise 7

1. Create a folder named Chapter3Exercise7 on your system.

2. Locate AppletDemo2.java in the folder named Chapter3\Examples on the book's CD and then copy it to the Chapter3Exercise7 folder you created in Step 1.

3. Copy the AppletDemo1.html file from your Chapter3Exercise6 folder to your Chapter3Exercise7 folder. Rename this file AppletDemo2.html.

4. Using text editor software recommended by your instructor, change the class name in AppletDemo2.html from "AppletDemo1.class" to "AppletDemo2.class".

5. Compile AppletDemo2.java using the software recommended by your instructor.

6. Launch a browser, such as Microsoft Internet Explorer, and then open the Applet-Demo2.html file. The bytecode file named AppletDemo2.class is then loaded, AppletDemo2 is instantiated, and displayed, and the paint method is invoked.

7. Verify that your output is the same as that shown in Figure 3-19.

3

Summary

- A Java package is a library of related classes. Use the **import** statement to make classes in the various packages available to the Java compiler. The Java Development Kit consists of approximately 75 packages containing hundreds of predefined classes and their methods.

- Java string data is contained in an instance of the String class. This class contains several useful methods to manipulate string data. String values in Java are immutable: They cannot be changed.

- Java has two types of methods: class (or static) methods and instance (or non-static) methods. Instance methods are associated with a specific instance, while class methods are not. You invoke an instance method using a reference variable that points to the instance. You invoke class methods using the class name.

- The **length** attribute of an array instance indicates the number of array elements. The length method of the String class returns the number of characters in the string.

- The Vector class is like a dynamically resizable array; however, all of a vector's elements must contain references to instances; they cannot contain primitive values.

- You use three classes when working with date values: Calendar, Date, and DateFormat. Calendar contains methods and constants, a Date instance will contain an actual date value, and a DateFormat instance provides several date formats for display purposes. You use methods in Date and Calendar to perform computation and comparison of date values. Methods in DateFormat return formatted date values in a String instance.

- Each of the eight primitive data types has a corresponding class called a data wrapper. These classes contain primitive data *inside* an object instance. You can convert the contents of wrapper instances to primitive values using methods within the wrapper classes.

- An applet is a Java program that is executed by the JVM imbedded in another program such as a Web browser. Typically it is downloaded to a client system for execution and, for security reasons, is prevented from accessing files and establishing communication links from the client system.

- Applet is a subclass of Panel, which is like a GUI window without a title bar. You make your applets subclasses of Applet, and thus of Panel. When the browser instantiates and displays the applet, the applet becomes a visible panel on the display screen.

- If an applet is to be executed by the JVM within a browser, you must create an HTML file to tell the browser the name of your applet bytecode file and the size of the panel you want to display.

- The method paint is a special method that the JVM (running inside a browser) calls when the applet is loaded. The method receives a reference variable for an instance of the Graphics class from the JVM, which lets you invoke Graphics methods to set color and font and to draw figures on the display.

Key Terms

class method	instantiate a class	static method
data wrapper	Java Development Kit (JDK)	wildcard character
immutable	nonstatic method	
instance method	package	

Review Questions

1. The Java Development Kit consists of approximately _____ packages.
   a. 10
   b. 1000
   c. 75
   d. 200

3

2. The Java compiler automatically imports the _____ package.

   a. `java.io`

   b. `java.util`

   c. `java.awt`

   d. `java.lang`

3. Java uses double quotes to indicate you are writing:

   a. a String literal

   b. a **char** literal

   c. something to display

   d. an expression

4. The term "instantiating a class" means:

   a. erasing the variables within the class

   b. creating variables inside the class

   c. creating an instance of the class

   d. invoking an instance method of the class

5. Class methods are also called:

   a. static methods

   b. default methods

   c. instance methods

   d. special methods

6. The correct statement to invoke the String valueOf method for primitive variable **i** is:

   a. `aString.valueOf(i);`

   b. `String.valueOf(i);`

   c. `iString.valueOf(i);`

   d. `aString.valueOf();`

7. The index of the first character of a String value is:

   a. 1

   b. 0

   c. the value you specify when you declare the String

   d. 2

8. The String valueOf method converts:

a. primitive to String

b. String to primitive

c. wrapper to String

d. String to wrapper

9. The wrapper method you use to convert a double wrapper instance to a double primitive is:

a. parseDouble

b. convertDouble

c. doubleValue

d. toString

10. The wrapper method you use to convert a String to a wrapper instance is:

a. parseDouble

b. valueOf

c. doubleValue

d. toWrapper

11. Each element in a String array is:

a. a primitive variable

b. null

c. a reference variable

d. It depends on the data type you specify.

12. To obtain the number of elements in a String array named **sArray**, you would write:

a. `sArray.length()`

b. `sArray.length`

c. `String.length()`

d. `StringArray.length`

13. String values in Java:

a. cannot be changed

b. are a primitive data type

c. can be either primitive or reference

d. cannot be placed into an array

3

14. The elements of a vector:
    a. can contain only object references
    b. can contain only primitive values
    c. begin with an index value of 1
    d. must be data type array

15. The Vector method that returns the number of elements is:
    a. size
    b. numberOfElements
    c. capacity
    d. There is no such method.

16. Applet is a subclass of:
    a. Window
    b. GUI
    c. awt
    d. Panel

17. What does the Graphics method drawString do?
    a. Draws a wavy line.
    b. Draws a circle.
    c. Draws characters.
    d. There is no such method.

18. Where is X = 0, Y = 0 on a Panel instance?
    a. lower left
    b. upper left
    c. upper right
    d. lower right

19. What is `Color.red`?
    a. a method
    b. an attribute
    c. a constant
    d. an exception

20. An applet:

a. cannot read a file

b. establishes a communications link

c. A and B

d. neither A nor B

Discussion Questions

1. List several benefits of using methods instead of built-in functions.

2. String instances are immutable. What implications does this have for the methods such as subString and toUpperCase that return a String instance?

3. Explain why using the **new** keyword is the preferred way to instantiate a String.

4. It appears that you could always use a vector instead of an array. Why would you ever use an array?

5. The Date class does not have an **equals** method. Can you think of a way to use the **before** and **after** methods to determine if two date values are the same?

Projects

1. Rewrite ArrayDemo.java from Chapter 2 using a vector.

2. Using the drawString method, write an applet named Chapter3Project2.java that will display both your name and today's date in long format. Select a color and font that you prefer to use.

3. Create a four-row, three-column String array containing the following data. Then write code to display the contents of each row with appropriate labels.

4. Redesign and rewrite Project 3 using a Vector with four elements, one for each row. Each Vector element will contain a reference for a three-element table with one element for each column (flight, gate, and destination).

5. Table 3-5 illustrates a String array graphically. Draw an illustration of the two-dimensional String array in Project 3.

3

Table 3-5   Airline Departure Information

Flight	Destination	Gate
TWA 7401	St. Louis	C33
AA 431	Dallas	D8
Delta 94	Atlanta	A12
United 155	Chicago	B4

CHAPTER

4

Object-Oriented Analysis and Design in a Nutshell

In this chapter you will:

♦ Learn how logical and physical models and iterative and incremental development concepts are used in OOA and OOD

♦ Understand the need for the Unified Modeling Language (UML) and model-driven development

♦ Create and interpret a UML use case diagram, class diagram, and sequence diagram

♦ Understand how the three-tier design approach is used in OOA and OOD

♦ Learn how UML diagrams are developed for a business system development project

You have explored object-oriented concepts and object-oriented programming with Java. As discussed in Chapter 1, object-oriented application development is much broader than OO programming. As with any system development project, OO development requires a thorough understanding of the problem the system is supposed to solve. Before you start programming and testing, identify what functions the system must perform, and carefully design the architecture of the new system. In short, before you can program, you must complete system analysis and design activities for a system development project.

This chapter briefly reviews analysis and design concepts and activities used with OO development. It begins by discussing object-oriented analysis and object-oriented design, including iterative and incremental approaches to development. It then introduces the Unified Modeling Language (UML) to illustrate model-driven development, emphasizing the use case diagram, class diagram, and sequence diagram. It also examines the three-tier design approach to illustrate the transition from OOA to OOD. Finally, it introduces the Bradshaw Marina case study, which is used for examples throughout this text.

The Java programming concepts and techniques that are presented in the remaining sections of the text all follow from the three-tier design approach, and all programming examples are based on the Bradshaw Marina case study and the models described in this chapter.

UNDERSTANDING OOA AND OOD

As in any approach to development, **system analysis** means to study, understand, and define the requirements for the system. **System requirements** define what the system needs to accomplish for the users in business terms. These requirements are usually described using diagrams, or models. A **model** depicts some aspect of the real world—in this case, some aspect of the required system. You need a collection of models to describe all aspects of the system requirements because any given model usually highlights only a part.

The models created during system analysis are often called **logical models** because they show what is required in the system independent of the technology used to implement it. Models created during system design are often called **physical models** because they show how to implement and integrate system components using specific technology. **System design** means to create physical models rather than logical models.

Creating logical models of the system requirements during analysis and then physical models during design is referred to as **model-driven development**. As discussed in Chapter 1, traditional procedural development creates requirements models such as the data flow diagram to show inputs, outputs, and processes, and the entity-relationship diagram (ERD) to show the details about stored data. Traditional design models include structure charts and relational database schemas.

Models created using OO development are different from the traditional models, however, because OO needs to depict, or model, different constructs. Rather than modeling data and processes separately, for example, OO development requires models that define classes of objects and that depict object interactions. OO models and notation are based on UML, discussed in detail in the following section. These models include the use case diagram, class diagram, and sequence diagram, among others.

Because OO development focuses on classes of objects beginning with analysis and continuing through design and programming, it works very well with an iterative approach to development (discussed in Chapter 1). Iterative development means that you analyze then design, and then program to address part of the system requirements. Then you repeat the cycle to address additional requirements. In other words, you only complete some analysis before beginning design, and only complete some design before programming (see Figure 4-1).

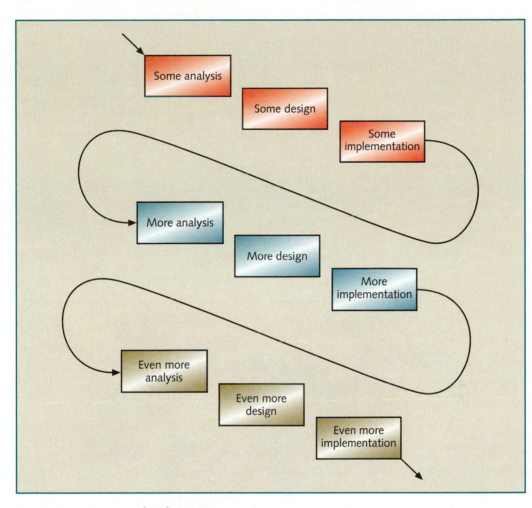

Figure 4-1   Iterative development

Iterative development contrasts with a more traditional approach referred to as the **waterfall method**, where analysis was completed before design could start, and design was completed before programming could start. As with model-driven development, the traditional approach now also uses iterative development extensively. However, iterative development works more smoothly or seamlessly with OO because each iteration involves refining classes or adding more classes.

Incremental development means some of the system is completed and put into operation before the entire system is finished. The most important subsystems might be completed first, for example. Later, additional subsystems are added as they are completed. Incremental development is also used extensively with OO development. Iterative development and incremental development work well together. Several iterations might be required to finish the first subsystem that is released into production, for example, and then additional iterations are required to finish and then integrate the second subsystem.

An increasingly popular approach to development is the **spiral model**, shown in Figure 4–2. To emphasize the iterative nature of development, the project appears in Figure 4–2 as a spiral starting in the middle and working its way out. Each project has its own set of problems, or risks, so the developers should first identify the greatest risks to the success of the project and focus on them in the first iterations. The development team completes analysis, design, prototyping, and evaluation tasks for each iteration, starting in the middle of the spiral. The next iteration then builds on the first iteration.

Object-oriented development also requires other traditional system development tools and techniques as discussed in Chapter 1: project planning, project management, feasibility assessment, management reviews, user involvement, joint application development, prototyping, unit and system testing, and conversion. In other words, most of the key concepts, tools, and techniques covered in any analysis and design course still apply to OO development.

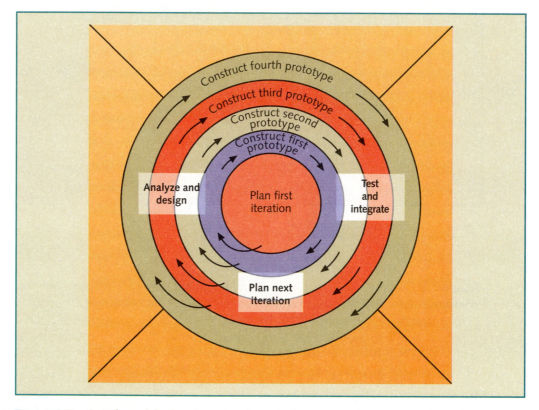

Figure 4-2 Spiral model of system development

4

UNDERSTANDING THE UNIFIED MODELING LANGUAGE

Object-oriented development requires a collection of models that depict system requirements and designs. UML defines a standard set of constructs and diagrams that you can use to model OO systems. Prior to 1996, developers used a variety of OO modeling notations, which made it difficult for project teams to communicate with each other. A standard modeling approach was clearly needed. Of the many people involved in developing OO modeling notations, three key developers joined forces to define and set the standard: Grady Booch, James Rumbaugh, and Ivar Jacobson, all of Rational Software (*www.rational.com*). Their set of diagrams and diagramming notations became the Unified Modeling Language that is now accepted as the standard by the Object Management Group (OMG), an industry association dedicated to improving OO development practices. The use case diagram, the class diagram, and the sequence diagram are three types of diagrams they developed to model OO systems.

You can find complete information on UML and all of the diagrams and constructs at *www.rational.com*. Also explore the many books that summarize UML and explain its subtleties and specific details, including *The Unified Modeling Language User Guide* (1999) by Booch, Rumbaugh, and Jacobson.

Creating and Interpreting the Use Case Diagram

The first step in system modeling is to define the main system functions—what the system must allow the user to do. Each system function is called a **use case**. For example, in a system that processes orders, recording a sale is a required system function and therefore a use case. Breaking down the system into a list of use cases allows the developers to divide up the work and focus on specific system functions. Typically, each iteration of the analysis–design–program cycle addresses a few use cases at a time. This approach is similar to the one used in traditional system development because structured analysis also begins with functional decomposition to identify system activities, and system activities are similar to use cases.

The use case diagram shows two key concepts: the use case and the actor. The **actor** is the person or entity using the system. An example of a use case diagram is shown in Figure 4-3.

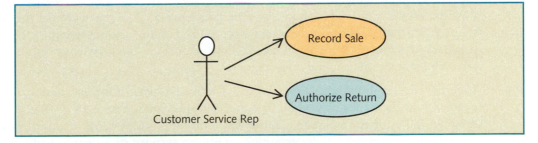

Figure 4-3   An example of a UML use case diagram

Here one actor, a customer service representative, needs the system for two use cases: record a sale and authorize a return. The actor is shown as a stick figure. A line with an arrow connects the actor to each use case. The use case is shown as an oval. An actor does not have to be a person. It can also represent a subsystem or device that provides inputs or receives outputs.

How does the developer identify use cases? One approach is to identify *events* the system must respond to, as in the traditional structured approach to development. Three types of events can affect a system: external events, temporal events, and state events. An **external event** is something that happens outside of the system that requires the system to respond, as when a customer buys a product or returns a product. When a customer buys a product, the system use case is to record a sale. When the customer wants to return a product, the use case is to authorize a return.

Each use case can be documented as a series of steps followed when the user interacts with the system to complete the task. Sometimes the main steps have several variations, called **scenarios**. For example, the steps followed when a sale is recorded for a new customer might be different from the steps followed when a sale is recorded for an existing customer. Examples of external events, use cases, and scenarios are shown in Figure 4-4.

A **temporal event** occurs at a specific point in time, such as at the end of each day or at the end of each month. For example, monthly bills or statements, late notices, paychecks, and daily or monthly reports are produced based on a schedule. These events also should lead to use cases and perhaps multiple scenarios. Less user interaction is required to implement use cases based on temporal events, but they produce important system outputs. A **state event** occurs when the state of an object changes requiring system processing. For example, inventory levels dropping below the reorder point would require a reorder use case, or a student's GPA falling below a required level would require a GPA warning notification use case.

The process of identifying and documenting use cases involves extensive interaction with users. Users typically find external events to be a useful way to think about the system they use. Some users might first name or describe a use case if they are thinking of what they use the system for. If so, you should be sure to document the event that triggers it. The user might focus on many specific scenarios. If so, you should be sure to combine them appropriately into one use case and document the event that triggers it. Try to keep the users focused on events first, however, because temporal and state events might not be obvious, and some external events might trigger use cases that do not involve all users.

As you and your development team identify the use cases, you draw the use case diagrams. One use case diagram might show all of the use cases and all of the actors for the system. If the system is large, you might draw one use case diagram for each subsystem. Other use case diagrams might focus on particular actors, showing only use cases involving the actors. These are useful when reviewing use cases with users.

Each use case needs to be documented and described in detail. One way to document a use case is to list the steps followed by the actor and the system. The steps involve interactions between the actor and the system, much like a dialog or script. UML defines an additional diagram that can be used to document use cases—an **activity diagram**. Sometimes a dialog or activity diagram is created for each scenario for a use case. The amount of detail and the number of diagrams depend upon the complexity of the use case.

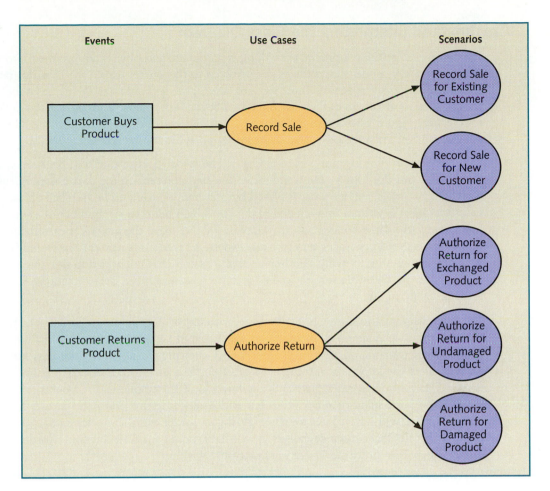

Figure 4-4   Events, use cases, and scenarios

Hands-on Exercise 1

1. Consider a system with these use cases: add new course, schedule course section, register student, assign instructor, produce class list, and record grades. There are two actors: department head and instructor. Draw a use case diagram showing the use cases and the actors, making assumptions about which actor is the user for each use case.

2. Consider a system for a video rental store that responds to these external events: customer wants to become a member, member wants to rent videos, and member returns videos. Name the use case for the system corresponding to each event. Assume processing might differ if a new member was formerly a member, if a member wants to rent videos when the member has unreturned videos, and if a returned video is overdue. List all the scenarios that might apply to each use case.

Creating and Interpreting the Class Diagram

In object–oriented development, everything is an object, and objects are grouped into classes. Therefore, a key model shows the classes involved in the system, called the class diagram. The class symbol is a rectangle with three sections (see Figure 4–5). Include the name of the class in the top section, attributes of the class in the middle section, and methods of the class in the bottom section. Figure 4–5 shows a class named Customer with the attributes of name, address, and phone number. The methods are addCustomer, updateCustomer, and addToOrder.

Another class in the diagram is named Order. The association relationship between the Customer class and the Order class is shown with a line connecting the two classes. A customer places many orders, and an order is placed by only one customer. The number of associations between classes is written on each end of the line. UML refers to the number of associations as multiplicity (the same concept as cardinality in ERDs). Here the asterisk means many, so 0..* means that a customer places zero to many orders. A mandatory relationship would be shown as 1..*, meaning one to many. This implies that a customer is not added to the system until he or she places an order. Be sure to read association relationships in both directions, from left to right and right to left.

The class diagram also shows generalization/specialization hierarchies (inheritance). Figure 4–6 expands the class diagram to include two subclasses of Order: MailOrder and PhoneOrder. The triangle symbol on the line below Order indicates it has subclasses. A PhoneOrder inherits all of the attributes and methods of Order, but includes additional attributes for the name of the phone representative and the duration of the phone call. A MailOrder does not include the same additional attributes but it does include the postmark date. A MailOrder instance, then, will have values for three attributes (order number, order date, and postmark date). A PhoneOrder instance, however, will have values for four attributes (order number, order date, phone order clerk, and call duration).

Figure 4-5   Class diagram example (Customer and Order)

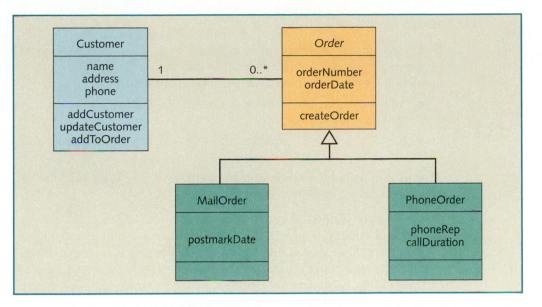

Figure 4-6 Class diagram extended to show generalization/specialization (inheritance)

Note that the name of the Order class is in italics, which indicates it is an **abstract class**. You do not create objects for an abstract class; it only serves to allow subclasses to inherit from it. Therefore, any order must be either a mail order or a phone order in this example. Note also that all orders must be associated with a customer. Both mail orders and phone orders inherit the requirement for an association as well as the attributes and methods.

You will see many examples of class diagrams in this text. Class diagrams are usually created in parallel with the identification of use cases. For example, use case descriptions often mention specific classes with which the actor interacts, revealing classes to add to the class diagram. Sometimes you identify more classes when talking with users, revealing additional use cases that need to be documented. Remember that the process followed is iterative.

Class diagrams also evolve during analysis and design to become more detailed. Initial class diagrams might only show key attributes and custom methods. As the model evolves, more attributes are added, more methods are added, and more details about each attribute and method are included. You learned above that OO development works very well with iterative development. One reason is the use of the class diagram in both analysis and design, adding to it as the project progresses. Then, OO programming means writing statements to define the classes. Classes remain the focus throughout.

Many additional diagram symbols and conventions for class diagrams are not discussed here. UML provides details to handle any interaction or object that might ever appear in a model. The examples in this text address the basic class diagram constructs—classes, association relationships, and inheritance—that are important to business systems.

Hands-on Exercise 2

1. Extend the class diagram shown in Figure 4-6 to show the following additional classes and association relationships. Be sure to include important attributes and show multiplicity for both directions of each association:

   ■ All Orders contain one or more Order Lines with an attribute for quantity of the item on the order line.

   ■ Each Order Line is associated with a Product with a product ID, description, and price.

   ■ A Phone Order, but not a Mail Order, is associated with a Customer Service Representative with an employee ID and name.

2. In Chapter 1, Projects 3 and 4, you listed some of the key problem domain classes and association relationships that would apply to a system for scheduling courses at a university. Your answer probably included classes such as Student, Professor, Course, Course Section, Department, and College. Draw a class diagram showing these classes and association relationships. Include some attributes for each class and indicate multiplicity for all association relationships.

Creating and Interpreting a Sequence Diagram

The sequence diagram shows interactions between the actor and the objects in the system, usually for one use case or scenario. Therefore, the sequence diagram is another way to describe each use case. Because an OO system is a collection of interacting objects, the sequence diagram highlights this interactivity and is often referred to as a **dynamic model**. The class diagram does not highlight object interactions, so it is often referred to as a **static model**.

The actor is shown as a stick figure, as on the use case diagram. Objects are shown as rectangles. The vertical lines below the actor and the objects are called **lifelines** and represent a sequence of time. The lifeline is shown as either a dashed line or a narrow box. The narrow box represents a period of time when it is an **active object**—that is, when it is executing or controlling part of the interaction. The horizontal arrows represent messages sent or received in sequence. A data item returned in response to a message is shown as a dashed line.

Figure 4-7 shows an example of a sequence diagram for the scenario discussed earlier: "Record Sale for Existing Customer".

The actor, the customer service representative, sends a message asking the Order class to create a new order object, named anOrder. The message points directly to the rectangle representing the new order. The new order object is immediately active (the lifeline below it is a narrow box), and it sends a message to the existing customer object named aCustomer asking it to add itself to the new order. The message from anOrder to aCustomer goes to the lifeline because it is an existing customer that has been created previously. When the message is received, aCustomer becomes active. The customer object returns information about the customer that the order object needs to finish its processing and become inactive. Finally, the new order object returns information about the new order to the customer service representative and becomes inactive.

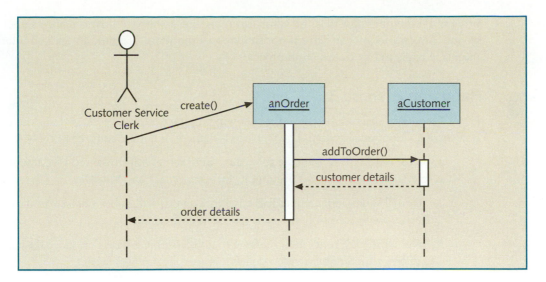

Figure 4-7 Sequence diagram for scenario "Record Sale for Existing Customer"

There are several ways to name objects in a sequence diagram. Object names are always underlined and begin with a lowercase letter; class names are always capitalized. Figure 4-7 uses generic object names to clarify what the class is. For example, anOrder is a name for a generic order object. It begins with a lowercase letter and includes the name of the class for clarity. Similarly, aCustomer is the name used for a generic customer object. Another approach is to include the name of the class after the name of the object separated by a colon. Using this approach, objects in Figure 4-7 would be named anOrder:Order or aCustomer:Customer (all underlined in the diagram). This approach is much clearer when the name of the object is very specific, for example, apollo13:Spacecraft, lisa:Editor, or susan:Professor.

If a class name only is used in a sequence diagram (not underlined), it means a class rather than an object is involved in the interaction. Classes can have static methods and static attributes that might be used in a use case or scenario. For example, the main method of the classes you developed in Chapters 2 and 3 is a static method.

Message names are written above the message line. The create message to anOrder is a general action that results in creating an object. It is implemented in different ways depending upon the OO development tool. Other messages are calls to invoke a method. For example, addToOrder() is a method of the Customer class, invoked by the message addToOrder() from the object anOrder. A name representing the return value is written on the dashed message line—customer details returned by aCustomer and order details returned by anOrder.

Standards vary for how and when sequence diagrams are used. Sometimes sequence diagrams are developed early in the development process to document use cases or scenarios. As with class diagrams, you can draw them at first with little detail, and then add more detail later. Sometimes developers prefer to create sequence diagrams later in the development process. Remember also that the actor can represent a subsystem or a device rather than a person. Also, sometimes an actor is not shown on a sequence diagram. Instead, all interactions might be triggered by a class or an object.

Hands-on Exercise 3

Draw a sequence diagram based on the following interactions between a video store clerk and objects in a video rental system. The scenario is named "Rent Video to Existing Member":

1. Actor sends create message to create a new rental object named aRental, and the create message includes arguments for memberID and videoID.

2. aRental sends addMemberToRental message to a member object based on memberID, named aMember, which returns member details.

3. aRental sends a rentVideo message to a video object based on videoID, named aVideo, which returns video details.

4. aRental returns all rental details to the actor.

Using Three-Tier Design in OO Development

The UML diagrams discussed in the previous section are used in both OO analysis and OO design. This is different from the structured approach where structured analysis uses DFDs and ERDs, and structured design uses structure charts. This is one of the benefits of OO development—the same modeling constructs are used throughout the system development life cycle.

A useful way to look at the distinction between OOA and OOD is based on the *three-tier design* approach introduced in Chapter 1. The three tiers include graphical user interface (GUI) classes, problem domain classes, and data access classes. Three-tier design requires that OO system developers separate three categories of classes when designing and building the system. First, you will identify and specify the problem domain classes, the classes of objects that involve the users' work. Once these are specified, you will define how GUI classes will be used to allow the user to interact with the problem domain classes. Finally, you specify data access classes that allow problem domain classes to interact with the database. Once all three tiers are completed, they are ready to work together as a complete system.

Figure 4-8 shows the three tiers in a simple order-processing system similar to an example in Chapter 1. The user interacts with a graphical user interface usually made up of windows that contain GUI objects such as menus, buttons, text boxes, and labels. The user clicks a mouse and presses keys to get the system to respond. The user does not directly interact with problem domain objects; rather, the GUI objects interact with problem domain objects based on the actions of the user. By separating the user interface classes from the problem domain classes, you are able to focus on the problem domain classes independent of the user interface.

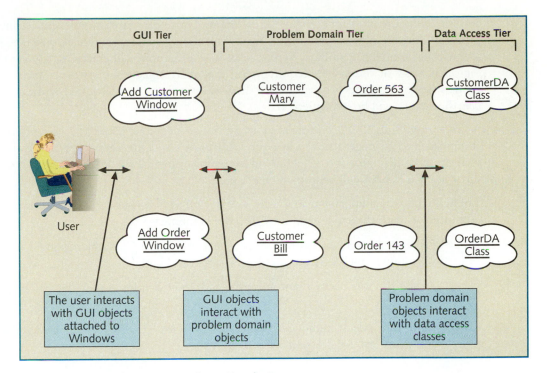

Figure 4-8   The three tiers in three-tier design

When a new problem domain object is created, some database management function is required to make the object persistent—that is, able to be used over time. The processing required to store information about objects to make them persistent is also kept separate from the problem domain classes by defining a separate data access class for each problem domain class to handle the data storage details. There are many ways to store data about objects (as you will see in Chapter 14), and by separating the data storage details from the problem domain classes, you are able to focus on problem domain classes independent of the database.

Separating GUI classes, problem domain classes, and data access classes supports the objective of creating loosely coupled system components. Loosely coupled components are beneficial because you can modify a component with minimal effects on other components. For example, changing the database management system used for the system would only require changing the data access classes, not the GUI classes or problem domain classes. Similarly, changing the user interface would not require changing the data access classes. The three-tier design approach, therefore, makes it easier to maintain and enhance the system. Additionally, independent components are easier to reuse, a major objective of OO development.

Three-tier design also provides a framework for defining OOA and OOD. The class diagram examples above show problem domain classes Customer and Order. OOA involves identifying and modeling the problem domain classes. The sequence diagram example above shows only problem domain objects instantiated from the classes—anOrder and aCustomer. As you identify and model the problem domain classes and the object interactions, you are creating logical models of the system requirements, the main objective of systems analysis. These models are logical models because they show what processing is required without showing *how* the system will be implemented.

As you move into OOD, you need to make design decisions about the user interface and about database management. Adding the GUI classes and the data access classes begins to turn the class diagrams and sequence diagrams into physical models because they begin to show *how* the system will be implemented.

The sequence diagram shown in Figure 4-9 is a physical model because it shows how the user interacts with the system and how the system interacts with a database:

1. The user types information about a new order on a GUI object named addOrder-Window, which contains text boxes, labels, and buttons.

2. Then the user clicks a button on the addOrderWindow to ask the system to add the order.

3. The addOrderWindow GUI object sends a create message to the Order class to create a new order object, named anOrder.

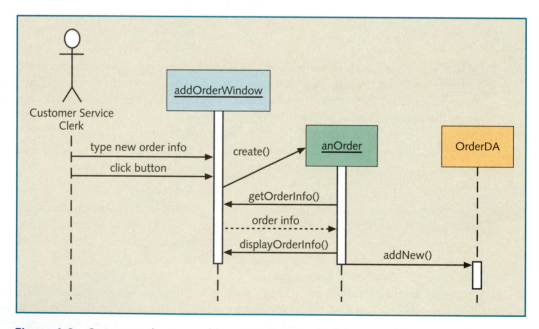

Figure 4-9 Sequence diagram adding GUI object and data access class

4. The new order object asks the GUI object for the order information, invoking the getOrderInfo method defined for the GUI, and the GUI object returns the information previously typed by the user.

5. The order object completes its processing and sends a message to the GUI asking it to display the new order details for the user to review, invoking the GUI's method displayOrderInfo.

6. Finally, the order object sends a message to the Order data access class (OrderDA) asking it to add the new order to the database. The Order data access class takes care of all database interaction required to store the new order.

Three-tier design works well with iterative and incremental development. Each iteration might address a few of the system use cases. First, you define and model problem domain classes important to the use cases. Then you create a sequence diagram for each use case or scenario showing only problem domain objects. You might begin to write OO code to define the problem domain classes and begin to conduct problem domain class testing.

You can also begin to define required GUI classes for each use case or scenario. Each sequence diagram can be expanded to include the GUI classes. The GUI classes can be tested and then integrated with the problem domain classes (and tested again). Prototypes for the first iteration are now available for users to evaluate.

As you develop the OO code to implement the GUI classes, you might begin to write a data access class for each problem domain class to handle database management. Data access classes also can be added to the sequence diagrams. Next, the data access classes are tested and then integrated with the problem domain classes (and tested again). Finally, the GUI classes, problem domain classes, and data access classes are ready to work together for the first iteration.

The next iteration repeats the process for a few more of the use cases. Note that three-tier design works well with iterative development because you can move easily from analysis to design to programming during each iteration, always building upon the models as you go. Prototypes are available early for users to evaluate, and system components remain as independent as possible.

The organization of this book follows the three-tier design approach. Part 2, starting with the next chapter, discusses problem domain classes and programming them with Java. Part 3 discusses GUI classes, programming them with Java, and making them interact with users and Java problem domain classes. Part 4 discusses data access classes and making them interact with problem domain classes. Then all three tiers are tied together into one application with GUI, problem domain, and data access classes functioning together in Part 5, including a Web-based development example. That is how object-oriented business systems are typically developed.

Hands-on Exercise 4

You completed a sequence diagram for a scenario named "Rent Video to Existing Member" in Hands-on Exercise 3. Expand your sequence diagram to include a GUI object named rentVideoWindow and a data access class named RentalDA. RentalDA can store information about the rental in the database when asked by a rental problem domain object using the message addNewRental.

INTRODUCING THE BRADSHAW MARINA CASE STUDY

The Bradshaw Marina case study is used throughout this text to demonstrate OO development principles and practices. The examples used for Java programming are based on this case. This section describes Bradshaw Marina and its need for a computer system. Some UML diagrams are presented to explain the system requirements. Additional diagrams are presented in later chapters that cover specific OO development issues using Java.

When a business determines it needs a computer system, it works with a team of developers to design and develop the system. One of the first tasks for the development team is to analyze the business and identify the functions the system will perform. The following section describes Bradshaw Marina and defines the system it wants to automate. Next, the development team begins object-oriented analysis to identify the use cases and scenarios required, creating use case diagrams. Then the development team identifies required problem domain classes and creates the class diagram. Finally, the team develops sequence diagrams to model object interactions. In the Bradshaw Marina case study, you are a member of the development team.

Exploring the Background of Bradshaw Marina

Bradshaw Marina is a privately owned corporation that rents boat slips and provides boat services on Clinton Lake, a large inland lake located in the midwestern United States. The lake was constructed in the 1970s primarily to provide flood control and generate limited amounts of electrical power. The U.S. Army Corps of Engineers manages the lake and restricts construction near its shores, creating an ideal natural wildlife habitat in addition to providing a beautiful parklike setting for boaters. Bradshaw is the largest of the three marinas on the lake. The three marinas accommodate approximately 600 boats in slips: 450 sailboats and 150 powerboats. Bradshaw's boat population is around 350 sailboats and 75 powerboats, although it has plans to expand these capacities.

Bradshaw Marina would like to have an automated system to track its customers, the slips it leases, and the boats in the slips. Initially, the system will simply maintain basic information for customers, slips, and boats, and perform basic day-to-day business tasks. These tasks include creating a lease, computing the lease amount for a slip, and assigning a boat to a slip. The marina also wants to use the system to search for information, such as vacant slips and slips leased to a specific customer.

Bradshaw eventually wants to enhance the system so it can add boat service records, which will help track tasks such as hauling the boat, painting the bottom, or working on the engine. Later, it will want to add billing features to the system and be able to use the system to generate bills for both slip leases and boat services, record payments, send late notices, and produce accounts receivable and other accounting reports. For now, Bradshaw wants the new system to include information on customers, slips, and boats.

Identifying Bradshaw Use Cases and Scenarios

The first step in the OOA process is identifying use cases that fall within the scope of the system. The main events of interest involve customers—when a customer leases a slip, when a customer buys a new boat, and so on. Because these events involve customers, boats, and slips, the use cases also focus on customers, boats, and slips. Your development team initially spends a lot of time talking with Bradshaw staff about the events involving customers that result in use cases.

For example, use cases involving customers might include add new customer and maintain customer information. A new customer is added when he or she leases a slip, and customer information is maintained whenever a customer changes address or phone number. Similarly, use cases involving leases include lease slip, renew slip lease, and transfer lease. Use cases involving boats include add new boat and maintain boat information. In addition, the system should maintain information about slips and the docks that contain slips. Finally, the system will need to process queries and reports. You work with other members of the development team to create the use case diagram indicating these use cases, which is shown in Figure 4-10.

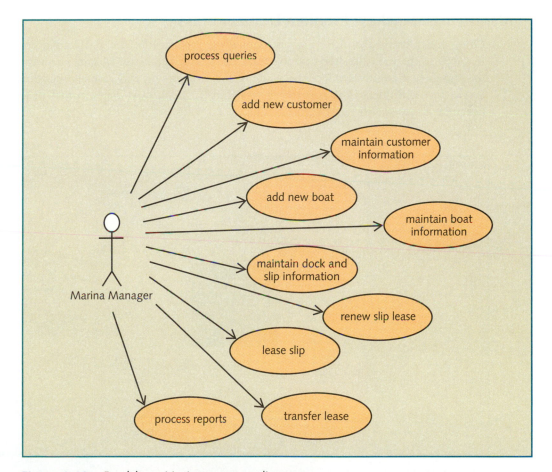

Figure 4-10   Bradshaw Marina use case diagram

Several scenarios could be associated with each use case, so you and your team might decide to divide up the list of use cases and work separately on scenarios. For example, the lease slip use case might have many scenarios you will want to discuss further with Bradshaw. Marina One scenario might be leasing a slip to an existing customer, and another scenario might be leasing a slip to a new customer. Further, another scenario might be leasing an annual slip to a customer, and another might be leasing a daily slip to a customer.

Scenarios can become very specific. It might take several attempts to create a comprehensive and mutually exclusive list of scenarios for the more important use cases. For example, given the situations involving existing customers, new customers, annual slip leases, and daily slip leases, the scenarios for one use case might be finalized as follows:

- Lease annual slip to existing customer
- Lease annual slip to new customer
- Lease daily slip to existing customer
- Lease daily slip to new customer

Identifying Bradshaw Problem Domain Classes

Once you identify the use cases and scenarios, you explore the problem domain classes involved in the use cases. You and the team meet with Bradshaw Marina again to ask about the things that are involved in the work of the marina—in this case the customers, boats, leases, slips, and docks. The first step is to begin an initial class diagram that includes these potential classes, as shown in Figure 4-11.

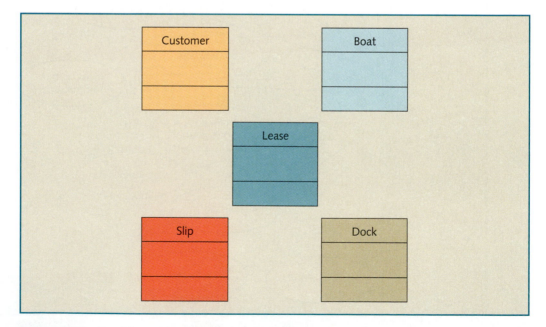

Figure 4-11   Bradshaw Marina initial class diagram

One of the first questions your team asks is about docks and slips. Sometimes the users talk about docks and sometimes they talk about slips. What exactly is a dock? What exactly is a slip? Sometimes you will find that users might be using two terms for the same concept. Other times you will find that user terms take on very specific meanings that you will need to understand. Remember, the problem domain classes reflect detailed user knowledge about their work. Your task is learning as much about the users' work as possible. Is a slip a special type of dock (generalization/specialization hierarchy)? Or is it something else?

It turns out (after quite a few explanations and sketches) that Bradshaw Marina defines a dock as an entire floating structure that boat owners walk on to get to their boats (see Figure 4–12). A slip, on the other hand, is defined as one space on a dock where a boat can be tied up. That is what a customer leases. Therefore, a slip is not a special kind of dock; it is something separate that is associated with a dock. This is just one example of the importance of learning about the users and their work.

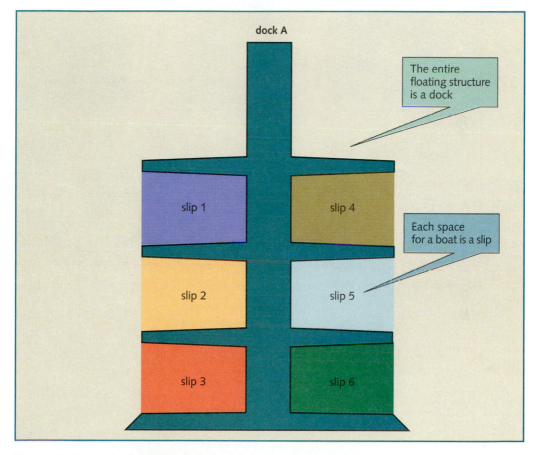

Figure 4-12   A dock contains slips

As you continue to look more closely at the initial classes, you see that you need more specialized information about boats, slips, and leases in the system. For example, Bradshaw has two types of boats: sailboats and powerboats. Bradshaw also has two types of slips: regular and covered. Finally, Bradshaw provides two types of leases: an annual lease and a daily lease. You refine the classes to show the generalization/specialization hierarchies that will require inheritance, as in Figure 4-13.

Because a boat must be either a sailboat or a powerboat, the Boat class is an abstract class (shown in italics), meaning it is only used for inheritance. The Lease class is also an abstract class because any lease must be a daily lease or an annual lease. A slip, on the other hand, might be a regular slip or a covered slip. A covered slip is a special type of regular slip; therefore, the Slip class is a concrete class (not abstract).

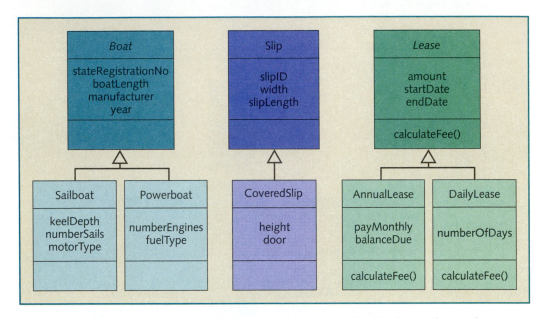

Figure 4-13   Refined classes showing generalization/specialization hierarchies (inheritance)

As you continue modeling problem domain classes, you begin to list the more specific pieces of information about each class—the attributes. You determine that all boats have a state registration number, length, manufacturer, and model year. Sailboats have additional attributes: a keel depth, number of sails, and motor type. Powerboats have different additional attributes: number of engines and fuel type. The reason the Sailboat and Powerboat subclasses are included is because of the different mix of attributes.

You find that slips are identified with a slip number. Bradshaw has slips in various widths and lengths. Some slips are covered, and the cover height is needed. Some covered slips have a door that can be closed to protect the boat. Sailboats cannot use the covered slips because of their mast height.

4

All leases are required to store an amount for the lease, a start date, and an end date, so these are attributes of the Lease class. Annual leases can be paid for monthly, and the balance due needs to be tracked. Daily leases must be paid in advance, so there is no need to store a balance due. The number of days of the daily lease is required, however. The amount for an annual lease and a daily lease are calculated differently. The annual lease amount is based on the slip width, but the daily lease amount is based on the number of days. Therefore, the calculateFee method is different for each lease and is shown as a method of each subclass to highlight this difference.

Once these details are finalized for boats, slips, and leases, the other classes—Customer and Dock—are considered. The complete class diagram showing all problem domain classes is shown in Figure 4-14. Docks are identified by a letter (A, B, C, etc.) and by location (North Cove, South Shore, and so forth). Some docks have electrical service and some have water. Customers are boat owners that lease slips from the marina. The system should maintain standard customer information including name, address, and telephone number.

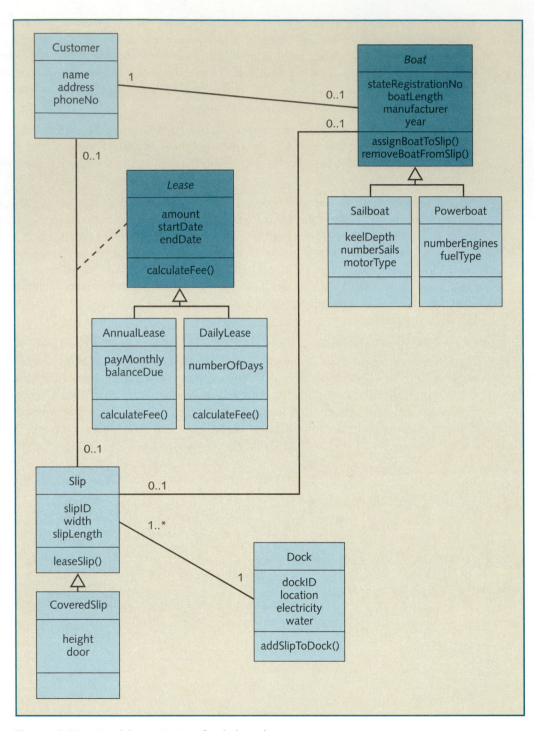

Figure 4-14   Bradshaw Marina final class diagram

Additional methods are included for Slip, Boat, and Dock. Not all methods are included on the class diagram, particularly during the early stages of OOA, but important methods are often included. The Slip class is responsible for leasing itself, so it has a method named leaseSlip. A boat is assigned to a slip or removed from a slip, so it has two methods listed. A dock contains slips, so it has a method named addSlipToDock.

You complete the class diagram by identifying and modeling the association relationship among classes. You already recognized that a dock contains slips and a slip is contained on a dock, for example. The line between Slip and Dock represents the association. Multiplicity is recorded on both ends of the line—a dock contains one or more (1..*) slips. A slip is contained in one and only one (1) dock.

There are other association relationships. A boat is optionally assigned to a slip and each slip optionally contains one boat (multiplicity is represented on both ends as an optional association, written as 0..1). It is therefore possible for Bradshaw to have information about a boat even if it is not assigned to a slip. A customer optionally owns one boat, but a boat must be owned by one and only one customer. Therefore, a customer can lease a slip even if a boat is not yet owned, but there is no reason for Bradshaw to maintain information for a boat without an owner. The multiplicity constraints define information about the business policies of users.

A final association relationship is between slip and customer. A customer optionally leases a slip and a slip is optionally leased by a customer. But this association is really more complex. In fact, the Lease class defined previously exists as a byproduct of the association between customer and slip, so Lease is called an **association class** and is attached to the association line with a dashed line. Association classes are much like associative data entities in ERDs. They are very common in business systems, and associative classes are implemented much like any other class. The notation helps to identify that the association class exists only because of the association.

Creating a Bradshaw Sequence Diagram

The development team already indicated some methods on the class diagram for Bradshaw Marina, as shown earlier in Figure 4-14. For example, the Boat class has a method assignBoatToSlip, the Slip class has a method leaseSlip, and the Lease class has a method calculateFee. These methods result from exploring scenarios and documenting them with sequence diagrams. These three methods, for example, are required by the scenario "Lease Annual Slip to Existing Customer", one of four scenarios identified for the use case lease slip. The sequence diagram showing this scenario is in Figure 4-15. You should create a sequence diagram for each scenario of each use case, but only one example is shown here.

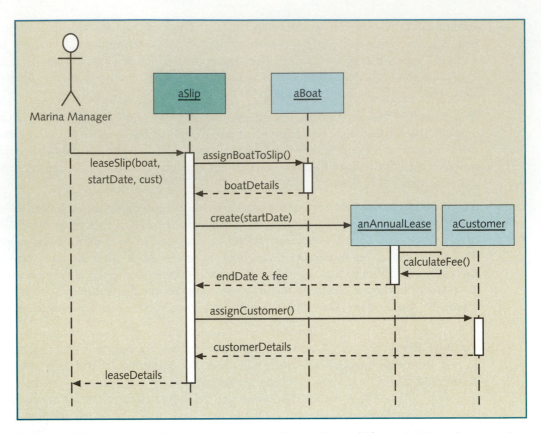

Figure 4-15 Sequence diagram for scenario "Lease Annual Slip to Existing Customer"

In this scenario, the actor is the marina manager. To lease a slip, the actor sends the leaseSlip message to the specific slip object (aSlip), supplying identifying information about the boat, the start date, and the customer. The leaseSlip method of aSlip interacts with other objects to complete the scenario.

The slip sends the assignBoatToSlip message to the boat, for example, which returns boat details. Next, the slip asks the AnnualLease class to create a new lease object, supplying the start date. The new lease object (anAnnualLease) invokes its own method, calculateFee, shown as a message to itself on the activated lifeline, and then it returns the end date and fee to the slip. Next, aSlip sends a message to the customer object asking it to assign itself to the lease, and the customer object returns customer details. Finally, the slip returns all of the lease information to the actor—boat details, lease details, and customer details.

This sequence diagram is a logical model showing only problem domain objects. As you move from OOA to OOD, you will expand the diagram to show the GUI objects the actor interacts with and the data access classes that handle interaction with the database. You will see many sequence diagrams in this text that illustrate Java code examples.

But now that you have documented the use cases, scenarios, problem domain classes, and some of the object interactions, you are also ready to begin writing some OO program code to define the problem domain classes for Bradshaw Marina. And that is what you will learn how to do beginning with the next chapter.

As you continue with this text, you will learn how to implement generalization/specialization hierarchies, association relationships, GUI classes, and data access classes so you can complete the Bradshaw Marina system, including porting the application to the Web.

4

Summary

- Systems analysis means to study, understand, and define the requirements for the system. System requirements define what a system needs to accomplish for the users in business terms using a collection of models.

- Model-driven development means creating logical and physical models during analysis and design to show what is required and how it will be implemented.

- Iterative development, in contrast to the waterfall method, means that analysis, design, and programming go on in parallel, with the process repeated several times until the project is done. Incremental development means part of the system is put to use first before the rest is finished. The spiral model is a newer approach to showing iteration on a system project.

- The Unified Modeling Language (UML) defines a standard set of models and constructs that can be used to model OO systems. Three UML diagrams are emphasized in this text: the use case diagram, class diagram, and sequence diagram.

- The use case diagram shows all of the system functions, called use cases, carried out by a user, called an actor. Use cases are defined by looking for events to which the system is required to respond—external events, temporal events, or state events. Each use case might be described by several, more specific scenarios.

- The class diagram shows the classes of objects that interact in the system, including generalization/specialization hierarchies and association relationships.

- The sequence diagram shows the messages that the actor sends to objects and that objects send to each other during a use case or a more specific scenario.

- The three-tier design approach divides classes of objects into GUI classes used for the user interface, problem domain classes used in the users' work, and data access classes used to interact with the database management system. Three-tier design helps separate concerns of OOA and OOD, but more importantly it results in a client-server architecture that is easier to deploy and maintain.

- Bradshaw Marina is a case study used throughout this text. Bradshaw rents boat slips to customers on Clinton Lake and needs a system to track customers, boats, slips, and leases. The use case diagram, class diagram, and one of the many sequence diagrams that form the basis for the design and programming examples in this text were introduced in this chapter.

Key Terms

abstract class	lifeline	static model
active object	logical model	system analysis
activity diagram	model	system design
actor	model-driven development	system requirements
association class	physical model	temporal event
dynamic model	scenario	use case
external event	spiral model	waterfall method
incremental development	state event	

Review Questions

1. A model is:

a. always a physical object shown in three dimensions

b. a representation of some aspect of the real world

c. only created for simple "toy" systems

d. only useful for classroom examples

2. In OO development, a model is:
   a. something created but only during OOD
   b. something created during both OOA and OOD
   c. rarely used to depict system requirements
   d. always a physical model

3. Systems analysis means to:
   a. define what the system needs to accomplish for users in business terms
   b. create programs using OO technology that users will like
   c. create models showing how the various system components will be implemented with specific technology
   d. only develop systems using OO development techniques

4. System design means to:
   a. define what the system needs to accomplish for users in business terms
   b. create programs using OO technology that users will like
   c. create models showing how the various system components will be implemented with specific technology
   d. only develop systems using OO development techniques

5. Creating logical models of the system requirements during analysis and then physical models during design is the idea behind:
   a. iterative development
   b. model–driven development
   c. incremental development
   d. spiral development

6. Some of the system is completed and put into operation before the entire system is finished when using:
   a. iterative development
   b. model–driven development
   c. incremental development
   d. spiral development

4

7. To emphasize the iterative nature of development, the project is shown as a spiral starting in the middle and working its way out when using:

   a. iterative development

   b. model–driven development

   c. incremental development

   d. spiral development

8. Grady Booch, James Rumbaugh, and Ivar Jacobson are responsible for defining and standardizing:

   a. structured analysis and design

   b. the Unified Modeling Language (UML)

   c. the spiral model

   d. OOA and OOD

9. The UML diagram that shows the system users and system functions is called the:

   a. use case diagram

   b. class diagram

   c. sequence diagram

   d. activity diagram

10. The UML diagram that shows the classes of objects involved in the system is called the:

    a. use case diagram

    b. class diagram

    c. sequence diagram

    d. activity diagram

11. The UML diagram that shows how objects interact is called the:

    a. use case diagram

    b. class diagram

    c. sequence diagram

    d. activity diagram

12. There are many other UML diagrams that are not shown in this chapter, including the:

    a. use case diagram

    b. class diagram

    c. sequence diagram

    d. activity diagram

13. The class diagram is an example of a:

    a. narrative model

    b. dynamic model

    c. traditional development model

    d. static model

14. The sequence diagram is an example of a:

    a. narrative model

    b. dynamic model

    c. traditional development model

    d. static model

15. In a class diagram, the lines that are drawn to connect two classes represent a(n):

    a. attribute

    b. method

    c. association relationship

    d. lifeline

16. Which of the following represents optional one-to-one multiplicity?

    a. 0..*

    b. 1..*

    c. 0..1

    d. 1

17. Which of the following represents mandatory one-to-many multiplicity?

    a. 0..**

    b. 1..*

    c. 0..1

    d. 1

18. On a class diagram, the symbol representing a generalization/specialization hierarchy is:

    a. a dashed line

    b. a triangle pointing to the superclass

    c. a diamond on one end of the association line

    d. indicated by the attributes listed in the class symbol

4

19. On a sequence diagram, an activated object is represented as:

a. a dashed lifeline

b. a stick figure

c. a rectangle with the name capitalized and not underlined

d. a narrow box on the lifeline

20. On a sequence diagram, an actor is represented as:

a. a dashed lifeline

b. a stick figure

c. a rectangle with the name capitalized and not underlined

d. a narrow box on the lifeline

21. The tiers in three-tier design include all of the following EXCEPT:

a. the operating system tier

b. the GUI tier

c. the problem domain tier

d. the data access tier

22. In three-tier design, the first tier considered is:

a. the operating system tier

b. the GUI tier

c. the problem domain tier

d. the data access tier

Discussion Questions

1. What is the difference between a logical model and a physical model? Describe how a sequence diagram can be either a logical or a physical model. Can a class diagram also be either? What would make a class diagram more physical?

2. OO development works well with iteration and incremental development. Discuss some of the reasons why this is true.

3. Without UML, it would be difficult for system developers to communicate about their work on a system project. Discuss why this is so.

4. The Bradshaw Marina case study describes initial system requirements, some additional functions they want to add in the future, and even more functions they want to include eventually. Discuss how you might use incremental development to approach all of Bradshaw's needs.

Projects

1. Given a system with six use cases, list the specific steps to be followed based on the three-tier design approach for developing the system assuming you plan to have three iterations addressing two use cases each. Be as specific as possible in terms of diagrams drawn and programming completed.

2. The Bradshaw Marina case study describes: 1) initial system requirements, 2) some additional functions they want to add in the future, and 3) even more functions they want to include eventually (see Discussion Question 4 above). List at least three use cases for the functions desired in the second phase of the project. List at least four use cases desired for the third phase of the project.

3. Consider the additional Bradshaw Marina requirements for recording boat service for customers. What additional problem domain class would you add to the class diagram? What are the association relationships between this class and other classes? Might this class be expanded to a generalization/specialization hierarchy? If so, what are some potential subclasses? Are there any other problem domain classes you might add? Draw the complete class diagram for Bradshaw that includes all existing classes plus one or more new classes.

4. Figure 4-15 shows a sequence diagram for Bradshaw scenario "Lease Annual Slip to Existing Customer". Draw a similar sequence diagram for the scenario "Lease Annual Slip to New Customer".

PART 2

Defining Problem Domain Classes

5

Writing a Problem Domain Class Definition

In this chapter you will:

♦ Write a class definition
♦ Define attributes
♦ Write methods
♦ Create an instance
♦ Write a tester class
♦ Invoke methods
♦ Work with multiple instances
♦ Write a constructor method

In Part 1 you learned that OO systems employ the three-tier design model consisting of three categories of classes: GUI classes, which provide the user interface for data input and display; problem domain (PD) classes, which model the essential business entities; and data access (DA) classes, which provide for data storage and retrieval services. Here in Part 2 you will learn how to write class definitions for the PD classes using Java. You will work with the GUI classes in Part 3 and the DA classes in Part 4.

You read about Bradshaw Marina in the previous chapter. You will use this case to illustrate the development of an OO system throughout the remainder of this book. This case involves only a few PD classes, yet provides examples of all of the OO concepts you read about in Part 1.

In this chapter you will see how to design and write a class definition for Customer. This definition will include attributes and methods to store and retrieve the attribute values. To test your Customer class definition, you will write a second class named TesterOne to create instances of Customer. TesterOne then tests the methods that access the attribute values.

After you complete this chapter, you will know how to design and code a class definition containing attributes and methods for a simple PD class. You will also be able to design and code a tester class to create instances and invoke methods.

NAMING CONVENTIONS

Recall from Chapters 2 and 3 that Java programmers have adopted a style for writing identifiers, which are the names you assign to classes, class definitions, attributes, and methods:

- Class names start with a capital letter. Examples of class names are Customer and Boat.

- Attribute names begin with a lowercase character, but subsequent words comprising the name are capitalized. Examples of attribute names are address and phoneNo.

- Method names begin with a lowercase character, subsequent words are capitalized, and they usually contain a verb describing what the method does using an imperative form with the verb first and then the noun. Examples of method names are getPhoneNo, setAddress, and computeLease.

DEVELOPING A PD CLASS DEFINITION

Recall that the Bradshaw Marina system has several PD classes such as Customer, Boat, Slip, and Dock and that they have interactions and relationships—a Customer *owns* a Boat, a Boat *is assigned to* a Slip, and a Customer *leases* a Slip, for example. Some of the classes have inheritance relationships. Both Sailboat and Powerboat are *subclasses* of Boat. A Sailboat *is a* Boat, and a Powerboat *is a* Boat.

You begin developing the marina's system by writing a class definition for each of the PD classes. These class definitions are based on *some of* the features of their real-world counterparts. You saw earlier that you model an object's characteristics by defining attributes and you model the behavior by writing methods. In other words, each class definition will contain the attributes and methods that make the objects behave as they need to in the system.

A **class definition** is what you call the Java code you write to represent a class. You begin developing the Bradshaw Marina system by first writing a definition for the Customer class. This class, representing all of the marina's customers, is shown in Figure 5-1. You will design and write class definitions for some of the marina's additional PD classes in later chapters.

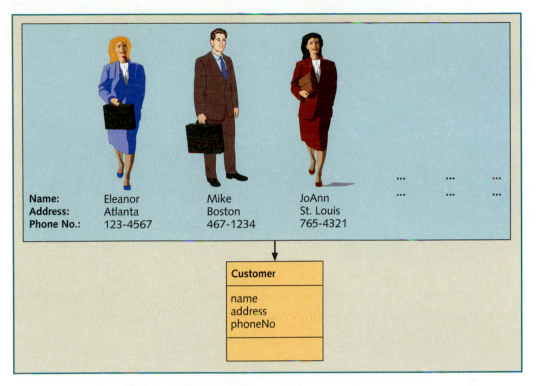

Figure 5-1   The Customer class represents customers

This class has attributes for the customer's name, address, and telephone number as outlined in the case description. (Refer to the Bradshaw Marina case study in Chapter 4.) You will declare these attributes in the class definition you write. In addition, you will write methods to create a new Customer instance, assign values to the attributes, and then retrieve attribute values from the Customer instance.

Class Definition Structure

The structure of a class definition consists of a **class header** followed by attribute definitions and then method code. A class header is a line of code that identifies the class and some of its characteristics. You learned in Chapter 2 that a block of code appears between open and closed curly braces. Here, the entire class definition is contained between open and closed braces. Figure 5–2 illustrates the structure of a Java class definition.

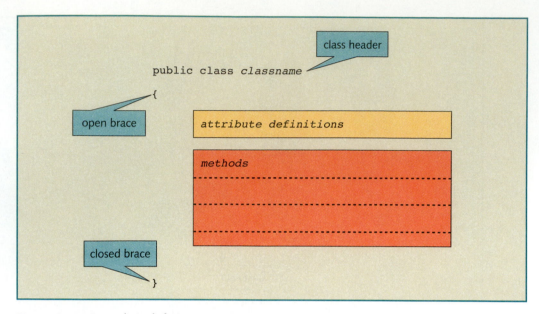

Figure 5-2   Java class definition structure

The class header for the Customer definition is:

> **public class** Customer

Many Java editors show keywords in color; in this book, Java keywords are in blue Courier. The keyword **public** indicates this class has public accessibility, meaning anyone can use it. The keyword **class** indicates this line of code is a class header, and **Customer** establishes the class name. You recall from Chapter 2 that Java is case sensitive. Java sees **Customer** and **customer** as two different names.

Defining Attributes

The Customer class diagram shows three attributes: name, address, and phone number. You define attributes by declaring variables for each one. Recall from Chapter 2 that you declare a variable by writing its data type followed by its name and ending with a semicolon. You use the String data type to define the Customer attributes as:

```
// attribute definitions
private String name;
private String address;
private String phoneNo;
```

When defining attributes, you can specify the **accessibility** of a variable as public, private, or protected. The keyword **public** allows any class to access the variable directly, while **private** prohibits direct access and the variable is accessible only from within the class where it is defined. The keyword **protected** allows both subclasses and classes within the same package to have direct access. If you omit the accessibility specification, Java uses a default (called "package access") that permits classes within the same package direct access. If you want to have package access, omit the accessibility specification.

You choose the accessibility depending upon the type of variable being declared. Public is generally used for constants needing access by other classes. In Chapter 1 you read about encapsulation, which hides the internal structure of attributes from other objects. When defining attributes in class definitions, you use the keyword **private** to restrict access by other classes. This restriction implements the notion of encapsulation and data hiding by preventing others from accessing the data directly. However, you will later provide **accessor methods** that can be invoked to access the attribute values.

Writing Methods

Problem domain classes do not function alone. Instead, their methods provide services to other objects in a system. You saw earlier that in OO systems objects interact in much the same way as real-world objects interact. This interaction is simulated when one object sends a message to another object to invoke a method. One way of viewing this interaction between objects is to apply the basic client-server model, as shown in Figure 5-3. The object sending the message becomes the **client object**, while the object receiving the message becomes the **server object**.

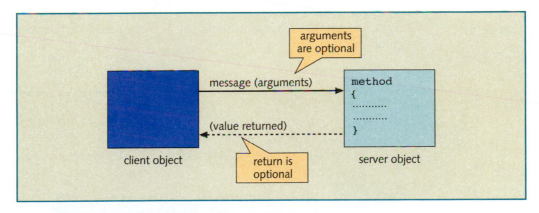

Figure 5-3   Client-server interaction

The client sends a message invoking a server method, perhaps sending along values in the form of arguments. The server method performs the requested task, and may return a value to the client. In Chapter 3, for example, you wrote statements invoking methods in several of the Java supplied classes, such as Math and String. Applying this client-server model to those examples, your statements were client code invoking server methods in the supplied classes.

Method definitions begin with a **method header** followed by statements placed in a block of code. This structure is shown in Figure 5-4.

Notice that the method header shown in Figure 5-4 contains four parts:

1. *accessibility* — The accessibility (public, private, or protected) for a method is the same as that described earlier for variables. Generally, you assign public accessibility to methods because you want other objects to invoke them.

2. *data type* — You want some methods to send a value back to the client object while others you do not. If a method returns a value, you write the data type of the value being returned (int, double, String, etc.). If no value is to be returned, you write the keyword **void**.

3. *method name* — You saw earlier that method names begin with a lowercase character, subsequent words are capitalized, and they usually contain a verb describing what the method does using an imperative form with the verb first and then the noun. Examples of method names are computerServiceCharge and recordPayment.

4. *parameter list* — **Arguments** are passed into **parameters**. The parameter list consists of variable declarations you write so the method can receive arguments being sent from client objects. If values are sent to the method, Java insists that the data types of the argument variables be compatible with the parameter variables. For example, you cannot pass an argument with data type **int** into a parameter variable with data type **String**. If no argument is being passed to the method, then the parameter list is empty parentheses.

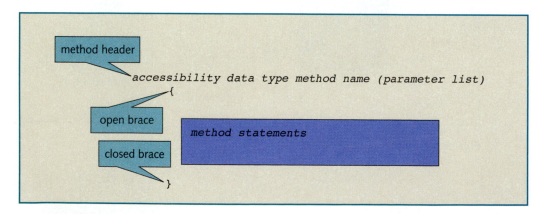

Figure 5-4 Java method structure

The class definition for Customer has three attributes, each with private accessibility, which prevents client objects from accessing them directly. Instead, you write accessor methods that clients can invoke to store and retrieve attribute values.

Accessor methods are often called **standard methods** and are typically not shown on class diagrams because developers assume they are included. In contrast, methods that you write to do other things are called **custom methods** and are shown on class diagrams. The next chapter shows you how to design and write custom methods.

There are two types of accessor methods: those that *get* attribute values and those that *set* attribute values. Accessors that retrieve values are called **get accessor methods** or simply **getters** and are named with the prefix "get" followed by the attribute name; you will write three getter methods named getName, getAddress, and getPhoneNo for the Customer class definition. Similarly, accessor methods that change attribute values are called **set accessor methods** or **setters** and are named with the prefix "set" followed by the attribute name; you will write a setter for each attribute: setName, setAddress, and setPhoneNo. The general format for getters and setters is:

```
// getter format
public attributeDataType getAttributeName()
  { return attributeName; }

// setter format
public void setAttributeName(attributeDataType parameterName)
  { attributeName = parameterName; }
```

The getter method header specifies the data type of the attribute it will return and has a void parameter list. The getter method has a single statement using the keyword **return** to send the contents of the attribute variable to the invoking client object. Methods can return only a single variable value, although it can be a reference variable pointing to an instance, which can contain numerous values. Figure 5-5 lists the three get accessor methods for the Customer class definition.

5

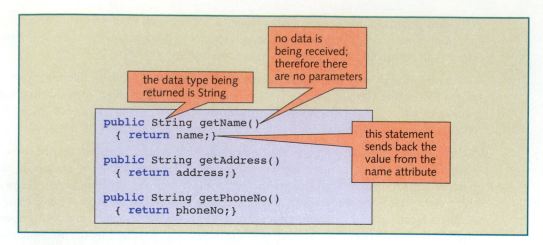

Figure 5-5   Get accessor methods for Customer

Setter methods generally do not return a value; therefore, the setter method header has a **void** return data type. Client objects send setter methods arguments that are used to populate attributes. Therefore, you must declare a parameter variable to receive this argument. Setter methods sometimes have statements to verify that the value it receives is valid. Chapter 6 illustrates setter methods that do data validation. The setters in this chapter will have a single statement that assigns the value received to the attribute variable.

Figure 5-6 lists the three set accessor methods for Customer.

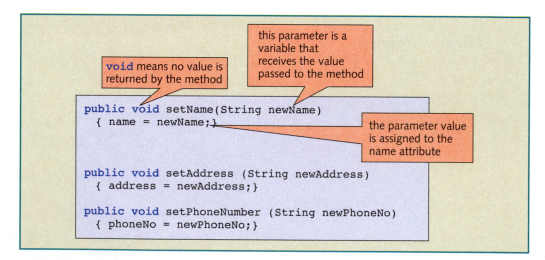

Figure 5-6   Set accessor methods for Customer

You have now completed writing the class definition for Customer that is listed in Figure 5-7. This code defines the three attributes and includes getter and setter methods for each of them.

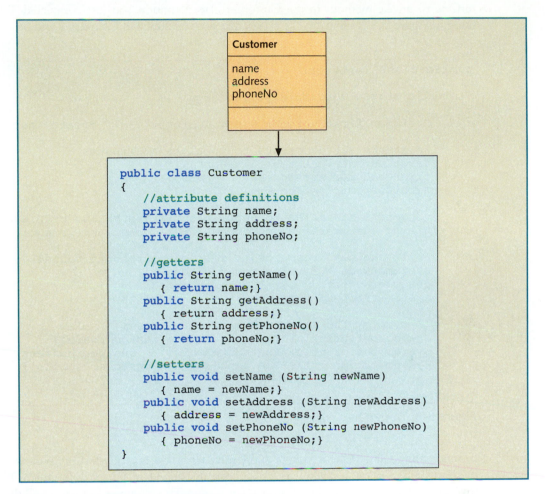

```
Customer

name
address
phoneNo
```

```java
public class Customer
{
    //attribute definitions
    private String name;
    private String address;
    private String phoneNo;

    //getters
    public String getName()
        { return name;}
    public String getAddress()
        { return address;}
    public String getPhoneNo()
        { return phoneNo;}

    //setters
    public void setName (String newName)
        { name = newName;}
    public void setAddress (String newAddress)
        { address = newAddress;}
    public void setPhoneNo (String newPhoneNo)
        { phoneNo = newPhoneNo;}
}
```

Figure 5-7   Customer class definition listing

TESTING A PD CLASS

To simulate the way a client might send messages, you can write a small tester class named TesterOne to invoke methods in the Customer class definition you just completed. TesterOne, listed in Figure 5-8, is similar to the classes that you developed in Chapters 2 and 3.

```java
public class TesterOne
{
    public static void main(String args[])
    {
        Customer firstCustomer = new Customer(); // create instance

        // invoke set accessors to populate attributes
        firstCustomer.setName("Eleanor");
        firstCustomer.setAddress("Atlanta");
        firstCustomer.setPhoneNo("123-4567");

        // define variables to contain attribute values retrieved
        String customerName, customerAddress, customerPhoneNo;

        // invoke get accessors to retrieve attribute values
        customerName = firstCustomer.getName();
        customerAddress = firstCustomer.getAddress();
        customerPhoneNo = firstCustomer.getPhoneNo();

        // display the retrieved attribute values
        System.out.println("The name is " + customerName);
        System.out.println("The address is " + customerAddress);
        System.out.println("The phone is " + customerPhoneNo);
    }
}
```

Figure 5-8   TesterOne.java listing

In this example, TesterOne is a client and Customer is the server. TesterOne will have a single method named main, just like the classes you developed in Chapters 2 and 3. The main method begins execution when TesterOne is loaded. The statements in main will then create a Customer instance, invoke its setter methods to initialize the attributes values for the instance, and then retrieve and display the attribute values by invoking the getter methods.

Creating an Instance

You learned in Chapter 2 that Java has two categories of variables: primitive and reference. Primitive variables use one of the eight primitive data types and actually contain data. Reference variables, on the other hand, use a class name as a data type and contain a memory address that points to or references an instance of a class.

In this example, you will use a variable with data type Customer to reference an instance of the customer class. In Chapter 3 you learned that an instance resides in an area of memory that can contain data and you created instances of several classes such as String. Here you will create an instance of the Customer class you just completed. Then you will invoke instance setter methods to assign the customer's name, address, and phone number.

In Chapter 2 you learned that there are two steps in creating an instance of a class. First, you define a reference variable to reference the instance, and then you use the keyword **new** to actually instantiate the class. For example, you previously created a String instance by writing:

```
String aString = new String("Hello Again");
```

The statement you write to create a Customer instance is similar. First you declare a reference variable named firstCustomer using data type Customer, and then you use the **new** keyword to create the instance.

```
Customer firstCustomer = new Customer();
```

After the class is instantiated, the variable firstCustomer points to the newly created instance, shown in Figure 5-9.

Notice that the attributes for the instance in Figure 5-9 have no values. You next write statements invoking the setter methods to populate the instance attributes. You pass arguments to the setter methods, which assign values to the attributes. Notice that you invoke these methods by specifying the reference variable **firstCustomer**, not the class name Customer. You do this because accessor methods are nonstatic methods associated with individual instances (customers).

```
firstCustomer.setName("Eleanor");
firstCustomer.setAddress("Atlanta");
firstCustomer.setPhoneNo("123-4567");
```

You studied sequence diagrams in the previous chapter and saw how they were used to show interactions between objects in a system. Figure 5-10 contains a sequence diagram showing the communication between TesterOne and Customer to create and populate a Customer instance. Recall that a horizontal line represents a message from one object to another, which means that a client object (TesterOne) is invoking methods in a server object (Customer).

As you can see from Figure 5-10, first, a new Customer instance is created, and then the three setter methods are invoked to populate the attributes. A little later you will learn how to write a special method called a **constructor** to populate instance attributes, which eliminates the statements you write to invoke the setters.

5

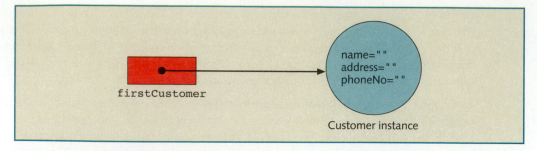

Figure 5-9   A Customer instance

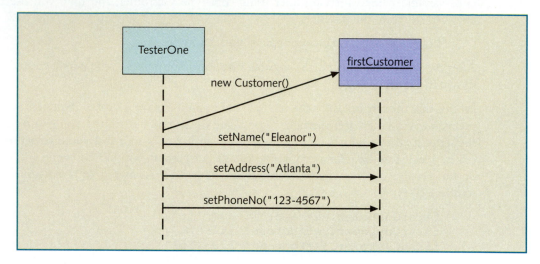

Figure 5-10   Sequence diagram to create and populate a Customer instance

The Customer instance now has values for its attributes, and reflects the structure shown in Figure 5-11.

To verify that the setter methods worked correctly, you can write code to invoke the getters to retrieve the attribute values from the Customer instance and then display them. First, you define three String variables to receive the values to be retrieved.

```
// define variables to contain attribute values retrieved
String customerName, customerAddress, customerPhoneNo;
```

Next, you write statements to invoke the getter methods to retrieve the values stored in the name, address, and phone number attributes for this Customer instance. These statements are shown with explanations in Figure 5-12.

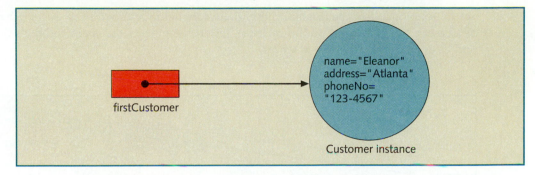

Figure 5-11   Customer instance with attribute values

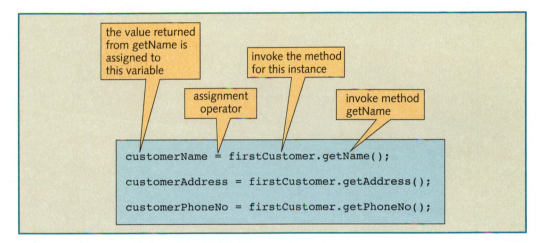

Figure 5-12   Statements invoking Customer getter methods

The final task for TesterOne is to display the attribute values that you just retrieved. Here you use the println method just as it was used earlier in Chapters 2 and 3 to display values. Recall that this method is being invoked for the System.out object. You pass the arguments contained in parentheses to the println method in System.out. The arguments consist of a literal concatenated with the attribute values previously retrieved.

```
// display the retrieved attribute values
System.out.println("The name is " + customerName);
System.out.println("The address is " + customerAddress);
System.out.println("The phone is " + customerPhoneNo);
```

Figure 5-13 contains a sequence diagram showing all of the interaction between TesterOne and Customer and between TesterOne and the System.out object to display the values retrieved. Notice that the diagram shows the values being returned from the getter methods as a dashed horizontal line. In this example, TesterOne remains the client and both Customer and System.out play the role of servers.

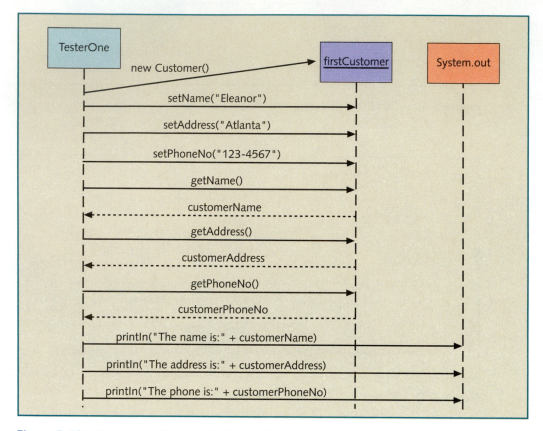

Figure 5-13   Sequence diagram for TesterOne

The output displayed by TesterOne is shown in Figure 5–14. A line is displayed each time the println method is invoked.

The name is Eleanor
The address is Atlanta
The phone is 123-4567

Figure 5-14   TesterOne output

Hands-on Exercise 1

1. Create a folder named Chapter5Exercise1 on your system.

2. Locate Customer.java and TesterOne.java in the folder named Chapter5\Example1 on the book's CD and then copy it to the Chapter5Exercise1 folder you created in Step 1.

3. Compile Customer.java and TesterOne.java, and then run TesterOne using the software recommended by your instructor. Verify that your output is the same as that shown in Figure 5-14.

5

Creating Multiple Instances

In the previous example, the Customer class represented Bradshaw Marina's customers. You wrote a class definition for Customer and used that definition to create a single Customer instance, Eleanor. Bradshaw Marina obviously has many customers, and the Customer class you defined will be used to create and populate numerous instances, as shown in Figure 5-15. This figure shows that the Customer class represents all of the Marina's customers. The class definition was derived from the class diagram, and then the class definition is instantiated as needed. Each customer instance thus represents an individual Marina customer. In this example the customers are Eleanor, Mike and JoAnn.

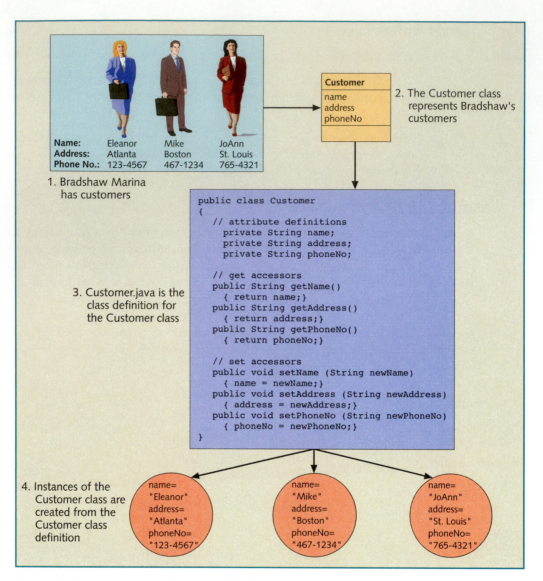

Figure 5-15   Instances of Bradshaw Marina's customers

Next you will write a second tester class named TesterTwo that will create the three instances shown in Figure 5–15 using the same Customer class definition you previously developed. You will then add statements to TesterTwo that will invoke setter methods to populate the attributes for all three Customer instances, and then invoke getter methods to retrieve some of the attribute values. Finally, you will invoke a setter method to change an attribute value for one of the three instances, and then retrieve and display the changed value. TesterTwo is listed in Figure 5–16.

```
public class TesterTwo
{
    public static void main(String args[])
    {
        // define the reference variables
        Customer firstCustomer, secondCustomer, thirdCustomer;

        // define variables to contain attribute values retrieved
        String custName1, custName2, custName3;

        // create the 3 instances
        firstCustomer = new Customer(); // create the first instance
        secondCustomer = new Customer();// create the second instance
        thirdCustomer = new Customer(); // create the third instance

        // invoke setters to populate 1st instance
        firstCustomer.setName("Eleanor");
        firstCustomer.setAddress("Atlanta");
        firstCustomer.setPhoneNo("123-4567");

        // invoke setters to populate 2nd instance
        secondCustomer.setName("Mike");
        secondCustomer.setAddress("Boston");
        secondCustomer.setPhoneNo("467-1234");

        // invoke setters to populate 3rd instance
        thirdCustomer.setName("JoAnn");
        thirdCustomer.setAddress("St. Louis");
        thirdCustomer.setPhoneNo("765-4321");

        // retrieve & display names for all three customers
        custName1 = firstCustomer.getName();
        custName2 = secondCustomer.getName();
        custName3 = thirdCustomer.getName();
        System.out.println("customer 1 name is " + custName1);
        System.out.println("customer 2 name is " + custName2);
        System.out.println("customer 3 name is " + custName3);

        // retrieve & display phone no without using a variable
        System.out.println("3rd phone is " + thirdCustomer.getPhoneNo());

        // change phone no for 3rd customer & redisplay
        thirdCustomer.setPhoneNo("818-1000");
        System.out.println("changed 3rd phone is " +
thirdCustomer.getPhoneNo());
    }
}
```

Figure 5-16   TesterTwo.java listing

TesterOne used a single reference variable named firstCustomer with a data type of Customer to reference the single instance that you created. Here you will create three instances; therefore, you need to define two additional reference variables. You can name these secondCustomer and thirdCustomer, as shown in the following code:

```
// define the reference variables
Customer firstCustomer, secondCustomer, thirdCustomer;
```

You wrote one statement in TesterOne to create the Customer instance:

```
firstCustomer = new Customer(); // create the first instance
```

To create the two additional instances in this example, you can write similar statements:

```
secondCustomer = new Customer();// create the second instance
thirdCustomer = new Customer(); // create the third instance
```

In the previous example, you wrote three statements to invoke setters to populate the attributes for the first customer:

```
// invoke setters to populate 1st instance
firstCustomer.setName("Eleanor");
firstCustomer.setAddress("Atlanta");
firstCustomer.setPhoneNo("123-4567");
```

In TesterTwo, you can add similar statements to populate the additional two instances, as shown in the following code:

```
// invoke setters to populate 2nd instance
secondCustomer.setName("Mike");
secondCustomer.setAddress("Boston");
secondCustomer.setPhoneNo("467-1234");

// invoke setters to populate 3rd instance
thirdCustomer.setName("JoAnn");
thirdCustomer.setAddress("St. Louis");
thirdCustomer.setPhoneNo("765-4321");
```

Note that TesterTwo creates three separate Customer instances, each with its own identity, its own attribute values, and the ability to respond to messages. For example, when you ask secondCustomer to set its name to "Mike," its setName method is invoked and the name attribute *for the second Customer instance* is assigned the value "Mike."

Next you can write statements to retrieve each customer's name. Again, note that the following code uses the reference variable firstCustomer to invoke getName for the first instance, and uses secondCustomer and thirdCustomer to invoke getName for the second and third instances, respectively. First, you define variables to hold the name values returned by the getName methods, as shown in the following code:

```
// define variables to contain attribute values retrieved
String custName1, custName2, custName3;
```

Next you add code to retrieve the names for all three customers, and then display each of the names.

```
// retrieve & display names for all three customers
custName1 = firstCustomer.getName();
custName2 = secondCustomer.getName();
custName3 = thirdCustomer.getName();
System.out.println("customer 1 name is " + custName1);
System.out.println("customer 2 name is " + custName2);
System.out.println("customer 3 name is " + custName3);
```

Next you retrieve and display the phone number for the third customer. This time, however, the retrieved value is not assigned to a variable before displaying it. Instead, the argument for the println method invokes the getPhoneNo method for thirdCustomer. When the value for name is returned, instead of assigning it to a variable, it is simply passed as an argument to the println method where it is displayed.

```
// retrieve & display phone no without using a variable
System.out.println("3rd phone is " + thirdCustomer.getPhoneNo());
```

You have learned how to invoke setter methods to populate an instance. You also can use set-ter methods to change attribute values. You can write the following code to change JoAnn's phone number to 818-1000, and then retrieve and display the number again to verify that it was changed:

```
// change phone no for 3rd customer & redisplay
thirdCustomer.setPhoneNo("818-1000");
System.out.println("changed 3rd phone is " +
thirdCustomer.getPhoneNo());
```

The output from TesterTwo is shown in Figure 5-17. The first three lines display the three customer names followed by the third customer's phone number. The last line displays the updated phone number.

Hands-on Exercise 2

1. Create a folder named Chapter5Exercise2 on your system.

2. Locate Customer.java and TesterTwo.java in the folder named Chapter5\Example2 on the book's CD and then copy it to Chapter5Exercise2 folder you created in Step 1.

3. Compile Customer.java and TesterTwo.java, and then run TesterTwo using the software recommended by your instructor. Verify that your output is the same as that shown in Figure 5-17.

4. Using TesterTwo as a guide, write a new tester class named ExerciseTwoTester.java that will:
   a. Create a Customer instance using *your* name, address, and phone number.
   b. Retrieve and display the name, address, and phone number attributes.
   c. Change your phone number to 123-4567 and then retrieve and display it.

5. Compile and run ExerciseTwoTester to verify that it works correctly.

customer 1 name is Eleanor
customer 2 name is Mike
customer 3 name is JoAnn
3rd phone is 765-4321
changed 3rd phone is 818-1000

Figure 5-17   TesterTwo output

WRITING A CONSTRUCTOR METHOD

In the previous sections, you saw how to create Customer instances and invoke the setter methods to populate the attributes. Although this approach works, you can simplify it by adding a constructor method to your Customer class definition. A constructor method is a special method that is automatically invoked whenever you create an instance of a class using the keyword **new**. The constructor is unique in that it has the same name as the class and it lacks a return data type because it cannot return a value. Actually, even if you do not write a constructor, Java creates a **default constructor** that doesn't do anything. The default constructor consists of only a header and an empty code block. The default constructor for Customer would appear:

```
public Customer()
  { }
```

You can write your own constructor, called a **parameterized constructor** because it has a parameter list, to receive arguments to populate the instance attributes. You want the constructor method for Customer to receive arguments for the three attributes: name, address, and phone number. The constructor will then invoke the setter methods to populate the attributes. The parameterized constructor for Customer appears:

```
// constructor with parameters
public Customer(String aName, String anAddress, String aPhoneNo)
{
    // invoke set accessors to populate attributes
    setName(aName);
    setAddress(anAddress);
    setPhoneNo(aPhoneNo);
}
```

You give this constructor method public access, omit a return type, and name it Customer. The parameter list consists of variable declarations named aName, anAddress, and aPhoneNo that will receive attribute values for the three Customer attributes. The body of the constructor method invokes the set accessor methods, passing the parameter variables that contain the attribute values that were received.

An alternative design is to have the constructor assign the values directly to the attribute variables instead of invoking the setter methods as in the following example:

```
public Customer(String aName, String anAddress, String aPhoneNo)
{
    // populate attributes directly
    name = aName;
    address = anAddress;
    phoneNo = aPhoneNo;
}
```

In the next chapter, you will learn how to add data validation code to the setter methods to ensure that only valid data is stored. When the setters have data validation statements, it is important that the constructor invoke the setters to populate attributes so that data validation is performed.

Next, you write TesterThree to test the constructor method you added to your Customer class definition. Having the parameterized constructor simplifies the code you write for TesterThree. You can begin as you did in TesterTwo by declaring reference variables for the three Customer instances you will create:

```
// define the reference variables
Customer firstCustomer, secondCustomer, thirdCustomer;
```

Next, you can write the statements to create the three instances; however, this time you pass the attribute values as arguments to the constructor method that is invoked as part of the instance creation process. You do not have to invoke the individual setter methods from TesterThree because the constructor in Customer now does this for you.

```
// create three Customer instances with attribute values
firstCustomer = new Customer("Eleanor", "Atlanta", "123-4567");
secondCustomer = new Customer("Mike", "Boston", "467-1234");
thirdCustomer = new Customer("JoAnn", "St. Louis", "765-4321");
```

Finally, as before, you invoke the get accessor methods to retrieve the attribute values, and then display them. As the comment below indicates, you retrieve and display the values without using variables to store the retrieved values. You invoke the getters within the println argument list, and then pass the values returned by the get accessor methods directly to the println method.

```
// retrieve & display names for customers without using variables
System.out.println("customer 1 name is " + firstCustomer.getName());
System.out.println("customer 2 name is " + secondCustomer.getName());
System.out.println("customer 3 name is " + thirdCustomer.getName());
```

The complete listing of TesterThree is shown in Figure 5-18, and the output is shown in Figure 5-19.

5

```
public class TesterThree
{
   public static void main(String args[])
   {
      // define the reference variables
      Customer firstCustomer, secondCustomer, thirdCustomer;

      // create three Customer instances with attribute values
      firstCustomer = new Customer("Eleanor", "Atlanta", "123-4567");
      secondCustomer = new Customer("Mike", "Boston", "467-1234");
      thirdCustomer = new Customer("JoAnn", "St. Louis", "765-4321");

      // retrieve & display names for all three customers without using
variables
      System.out.println("customer 1 name is " + firstCustomer.getName());
      System.out.println("customer 2 name is " + secondCustomer.getName());
      System.out.println("customer 3 name is " + thirdCustomer.getName());
   }
}
```

Figure 5-18   TesterThree.java listing

customer 1 name is Eleanor

customer 2 name is Mike

customer 3 name is JoAnn

Figure 5-19   TesterThree output

Hands-on Exercise 3

1. Create a folder named Chapter5Exercise3 on your system.

2. Locate Customer.java and TesterThree.java in the folder named Chapter5\Example3 on the book's CD and then copy it to the Chapter5Exercise3 folder you created in Step 1.

3. Compile Customer.java and TesterThree.java, and then run TesterThree using the software recommended by your instructor. Verify that your output is the same as that shown in Figure 5-19.

4. Copy your tester class ExerciseTwoTester.java from your folder named Chapter5Exercise2 to your folder named Chapter5Exercise3 that you created in Step 1.

5. Change the name of the copy of ExerciseTwoTester.java in your Chapter5Exercise3 folder to ExerciseThreeTester.java. Remember to change both the class name and the filename.

6. Modify ExerciseThreeTester.java to use Customer.java with the parameterized constructor. Verify that it works and produces the same output as before.

To summarize, you use a class definition to create instances. You write a class definition by first declaring private variables to represent the attributes. Then you write getter and setter methods for each attribute. You invoke getters to retrieve attribute values, and you invoke setters to store attribute values.

Constructor methods are automatically invoked when you instantiate the class. They have the same name as the class you are defining, and their headers do not return a value. You write a parameterized constructor method to receive arguments used to populate the attributes.

WRITING A TELLABOUTSELF METHOD

5

In previous examples, the tester classes invoked the individual customer getter methods to retrieve attribute values. Although this approach works, it can require you to write lengthy client code, especially when the PD class has many attributes. More importantly, if attributes in the PD class are added, removed, or have their data type changed, client statements that invoke the getter methods may also require changes. In a functioning system, numerous clients request attribute values, and making changes to the PD attributes could force you to make changes in several other classes. Good design suggests that you insulate changes in one class from outside classes to reduce maintenance requirements.

An alternative to invoking individual getter methods is to write a single PD method that you invoke to retrieve all of the attribute values for an instance. An appropriate name for this method is tellAboutSelf, and it will retrieve all of the attribute values, place them in a String instance, and then return the String instance to the invoking client. You want tellAboutSelf to have public accessibility and a return data type of String. The method header for tellAbout-Self will therefore be:

```
public String tellAboutSelf()
```

This method for the Customer class has only three statements. The first statement declares a String variable named `info` to contain the attribute values. The second statement invokes the three getter statements, concatenating the values returned with descriptive literals, assigning the result to the String instance referenced by `info`. The last statement returns the `info` variable to the invoking client method.

```
public String tellAboutSelf()
{
    String info;
    info = "Customer name = "
            + getName() + ", Address = "
            + getAddress() + ", Phone Number = "
            + getPhoneNo();
    return info;
}
```

```java
public class TesterFour
{
    public static void main(String args[])
    {
        // define the reference variables
        Customer firstCustomer, secondCustomer, thirdCustomer;

        // create three Customer instances with attribute values
        firstCustomer = new Customer("Eleanor", "Atlanta", "123-4567");
        secondCustomer = new Customer("Mike", "Boston", "467-1234");
        thirdCustomer = new Customer("JoAnn", "St. Louis", "765-4321");

        // invoke tellAboutSelf for all three customers & display
        System.out.println(firstCustomer.tellAboutSelf());
        System.out.println(secondCustomer.tellAboutSelf());
        System.out.println(thirdCustomer.tellAboutSelf());
    }
}
```

Figure 5-20 TesterFour.java listing

Next, you can write TesterFour, listed in Figure 5-20, to create three Customer instances as before. But now you will invoke tellAboutSelf for each Customer instance to obtain attribute values instead of invoking the individual getter methods. Similar to TesterThree, you invoke tellAboutSelf within the argument for println. The output from TesterFour is shown in Figure 5-21.

Customer name = Eleanor, Address = Atlanta, Phone Number = 123-4567
Customer name = Mike, Address = Boston, Phone Number = 467-1234
Customer name = JoAnn, Address = St. Louis, Phone Number = 765-4321

Figure 5-21 TesterFour output

Hands-on Exercise 4

1. Create a folder named Chapter5Exercise4 on your system.

2. Locate Customer.java and TesterFour.java in the folder named Chapter5\Example4 on the book's CD and then copy it to the Chapter5Exercise4 folder you created in Step 1.

3. Compile Customer.java and TesterFour.java, and then run TesterFour using the software recommended by your instructor. Verify that your output is the same as that shown in Figure 5-21.

4. Copy ExerciseThreeTester.java from your folder Chapter5Exercise3 to your folder Chapter5Exercise4, renaming the copy ExerciseFourTester.java and the class name to Exercise4Tester.

5. Modify the tellAboutSelf method in Customer.java to use a single statement instead of three.

6. Modify ExerciseFourTester.java to use Customer.java with tellAboutSelf.

7. Verify that your changes work properly and produce the correct output.

Summary

- Java programmers have adopted naming conventions for classes, methods, and variables. Class names are capitalized while variable and method names begin with a lowercase letter. When a name consists of more than one word, subsequent words are capitalized. Method names generally contain a verb describing what the method does. These naming conventions facilitate the identification of these items.

- Problem domain classes represent real-world objects you want to represent in a system. Problem domain class definitions are written for each PD class.

- A class definition consists of a class header followed by variable definitions for attributes, then methods. The attribute definitions are variables that are created and populated for each instance created for the class.

- Accessor methods are written to provide access to the attribute values: Set accessors, called setters, store values; get accessors, also known as getters, retrieve them. Accessor methods are often called standard methods and are not generally shown on class diagrams.

- Applying the client-server model, methods function as servers by providing services to client objects. Client objects invoke server methods to perform tasks. Clients can send data to a method in the form of arguments. The method being invoked receives the argument(s) into one or more parameter variables, which are declared in the method header. Methods can return a single variable, either primitive or reference, to the client object.

- A special method called a constructor is automatically invoked whenever you instantiate a class. The constructor has no return data type and has the same name as its class. If you do not write a constructor, Java uses a default constructor containing no code. You can write a parameterized constructor to receive values to populate the instance attributes.

- You can write a custom method named tellAboutSelf to retrieve all instance attribute values and return them in a string.

Key Terms

accessibility	constructor	parameter
accessor method	custom method	parameterized constructor
argument	default constructor	standard method
class definition	get accessor method	set accessor method
class header	getter	setter
client object	method header	server object

Review Questions

1. What is a class definition?

2. What is an identifier?

3. What are the conventions for writing an identifier?

4. What is a primitive variable?

5. What is a reference variable?

6. What does a getter do?

7. What does a setter do?

8. Explain attribute accessibility.

9. Explain method accessibility.

10. Distinguish between an argument and a parameter.

11. What is a standard method?

12. Why do getters generally have an empty parameter list?

13. Why do setters generally have a return data type of `void`?

14. What causes a constructor method to be invoked?

15. How are constructor methods named?

16. What is a default constructor?

17. What is a parameterized constructor?

Discussion Questions

1. Why would you not need accessor methods if the attributes were given public access?

2. Explain how a method can return multiple values, even though only a single variable can be returned.

3. What is the benefit of having the constructor invoke setters to populate attributes instead of assigning the attribute values directly?

4. List the ways that using a tellAboutSelf method can reduce maintenance.

5. Assume that you have two Customer instances. The first is referenced by a variable named `cashCustomer` and the second by a variable named `anotherCustomer`. What will be the result of executing the following statement:

```
Customer anotherCustomer = cashCustomer;
```

Projects

1. Assume that you are developing a system that has a problem domain class named Employee that represents all of a firm's employees. Attributes you want to include are employee name (data type String), date employed (data type Date), and annual salary (data type `double`).

   a. Write a class definition for Employee. Include standard methods, a parameterized constructor, and a tellAboutSelf method.

   b. Write statements in tellAboutSelf to format dates employed in short form.

   c. Write a tester class that creates three employees and then invokes tellAboutSelf for all three instances displaying the result. Name the tester class Project1Tester.

   d. Compile and test your classes to verify they are working correctly.

2. Using TesterFour from this chapter as a guide, design and write a tester class named Project2Tester that creates three customer instances; however, the references are to be placed in a three-element array. Note that you will use data type Customer for the array elements.

   a. Name your array reference variable customers.

   b. Use data type Customer for the array elements.

   c. Use Customer.java from Chapter5Example4 that has the tellAboutSelf method.

   d. Write a loop in Project2Tester that iterates the array to display information for all three customer instances using tellAboutSelf.

3. Figure 5-11 depicts a reference variable named firstCustomer pointing to a populated Customer instance. Draw a similar diagram showing the array reference variable, the array, and the three customer instances in Project 2.

More About Problem Domain Classes

In Chapter 5, you learned how to write a definition for the Customer problem domain class. You first declared private variables for each attribute, and then wrote setter methods to store attribute values and getter methods to retrieve them. You then wrote a parameterized constructor to accept arguments that were used to populate the attribute variables. You also developed a method named tellAboutSelf that returned a String instance containing the attribute values formatted for display. Finally, you wrote several tester classes that functioned as clients to create Customer instances and invoke their methods.

In this chapter, you continue working with problem domain classes by writing a class definition for another of Bradshaw Marina's classes, Slip. In the previous chapter, you worked with standard methods. In this chapter, you will develop a custom method named leaseSlip which will calculate the lease fee for a slip.

In Chapter 3, you learned how to display dates in various formats. In this chapter, you will learn how to use methods in the NumberFormat and DecimalFormat classes to format numeric output for improved readability and appearance.

In the previous chapters, you read about static methods and variables. In this chapter, you will see how to declare static variables and write static methods for your Slip class definition.

The technique of overloading methods is explained and illustrated using the Slip constructor and the custom method leaseSlip. Finally, you will add data validation logic for two of Slip's setter methods to verify that the arguments passed to the method are valid. You will learn how to create and throw an exception to signal the client that invalid data has been detected and rejected.

After completing this chapter, you will be more familiar with writing problem domain classes and you will understand when and how to use static variables and methods. You will have seen how to design and write custom methods and how to format output to create more attractive displays. Finally, you will have developed some experience in writing overloaded methods and will have been introduced to exceptions.

WRITING A DEFINITION FOR THE SLIP CLASS

The system you are developing for Bradshaw Marina was introduced in Chapter 4, which also described its various problem domain classes, including Customer and Slip. In Chapter 5, you developed the class definition for Customer. In this chapter, you will write a definition for the Slip class to extend your understanding of problem domain class definitions. Recall that the Slip class has three attributes: slipId, width, and slipLength, plus the custom method leaseSlip as shown in the class diagram in Figure 6-1.

The class definition for Slip follows the same basic structure you used for writing the Customer class definition in Chapter 5. You begin with the class header, followed by an open curly brace.

```
public class Slip
{
```

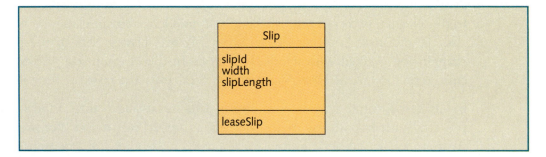

Figure 6-1   Class diagram for the Slip class

Next, you write the attribute definition statements. Here, you assign slipId and width data type **int**, and slipLength data type **double**. Note that you want these definitions to once again have private accessibility to encapsulate the attribute values. This keeps other objects from retrieving or changing the attribute values, except through accessor methods.

```
private int slipId;
private int width;
private double slipLength;
```

Next you write a parameterized constructor because you want to automatically populate the three attributes whenever an instance of the Slip class is created. Remember that when you use the keyword **new** to instantiate a class, the class constructor is automatically invoked. When you instantiate the Slip class, you will pass arguments for the three attributes: slipId, width, and slipLength. Therefore, in the constructor header, you declare three parameter variables to receive these arguments:

```
public Slip(int anId, int aWidth, double aSlipLength)
```

Note that the data types for these parameter variables match the data types for the attributes. In general, argument data types must be **assignment compatible** with parameter data types. This means that the argument variable must be able to be assigned to the parameter variable. For example, you cannot assign an argument with a **double** data type to a parameter with an **int** data type, but you could assign an **int** data type to a **double** data type.

Next, you write statements to populate the Slip attributes. Similar to the parameterized constructor you wrote for the Customer class in Chapter 5, these statements invoke the setter methods to populate the attributes. You have the constructor invoke setter methods to populate the attributes instead of directly assigning the values to avoid redundant code. A little later you will add data validation statements to two setters. If the constructor does not invoke these setters, it must also contain the data validation statements, which results in duplicate code. A better design is to always have the constructor invoke setters. This means the setter is the only method directly assigning values to attribute variables.

```
{
    // invoke setters to populate attributes
    setSlipId(anId);
    setWidth(aWidth);
    setSlipLength(aSlipLength);
}
```

Next, write the standard setter and getter methods for Slip.

```
// setter methods
public void setSlipId(int anId)
    { slipId = anId;}
public void setWidth(int aWidth)
    { width = aWidth;}
public void setSlipLength(double aSlipLength)
    { slipLength = aSlipLength;}
```

```
// getter methods
public int getSlipId()
    { return slipId;}
public int getWidth()
    { return width;}
public double getSlipLength()
    { return slipLength;}
```

The final step for this version of the Slip class definition is to write a tellAboutSelf method. Recall that in Chapter 5 you wrote a tellAboutSelf method for Customer. That method invoked the three getter methods getName, getAddress, and getPhoneNo, concatenated the values returned with descriptive literals, and then returned a string containing the concatenated result.

Similarly, tellAboutSelf for the Slip class will invoke its three getters, concatenate the returned values with descriptive literals, and then return the result.

```
public String tellAboutSelf()
{
    String info;

    info = "Slip: Id = "
            + getSlipId() + ", Width = "
            + getWidth() + ", Length = "
            + getSlipLength();
    return info;
}
```

These tellAboutSelf methods are excellent examples of polymorphism. You have two methods with the same name, residing in different classes, that behave differently. When you invoke tellAboutSelf for Customer, you get the customer's name, address, and telephone number. However, when you invoke tellAboutSelf for Slip, you obtain the slip's ID, width, and length. These are called **polymorphic methods**.

The complete Slip class definition is listed in Figure 6-2.

```
public class Slip
{
   // attributes
   private int slipId;
   private int width;
   private double slipLength;

   // constructor with 3 parameters
   public Slip(int anId, int aWidth, double aSlipLength)
   {
      // invoke setters to populate attributes
      setSlipId(anId);
      setWidth(aWidth);
      setSlipLength(aSlipLength);
```

```
      }

      // setter methods
      public void setSlipId(int anId)
          { slipId = anId;}
      public void setWidth(int aWidth)
          { width = aWidth;}
      public void setSlipLength(double aSlipLength)
          { slipLength = aSlipLength;}

      // getter methods
      public int getSlipId()
          { return slipId;}
      public int getWidth()
          { return width;}
      public double getSlipLength()
          { return slipLength;}

      // custom method tellAboutSelf
      public String tellAboutSelf()
      {
          String info;

          info = "Slip: Id = "
                  + getSlipId() + ", Width = "
                  + getWidth() + ", Length = "
                  + getSlipLength();
          return info;

      }
}
```

Figure 6-2   Slip class definition

In Chapter 5, you wrote several tester classes that invoked methods in your Customer class definition to ensure that the code was correct. Here, you also write a tester class named TesterOne, but this time you will invoke methods in the Slip class definition. You write statements to create three Slip instances and then invoke tellAboutSelf for each instance to retrieve and display the attribute values.

Similar to the tester classes you wrote in Chapter 5, TesterOne has a single method, main, that is automatically invoked by the JVM when TesterOne is loaded into memory.

```
      public class TesterOne
      {
          public static void main(String args[])
          {
```

The main method of TesterOne begins with a statement declaring a three-element array named slips to hold references for the three Slip instances that will be created.

```
      Slip slips[] = new Slip[3];
```

Next, you write three statements to create the three Slip instances using literals as arguments passed to the Slip constructor for slipId, width, and slipLength, respectively. References for the three instances are placed into the three array elements.

```
// create 3 Slip instances
slips[0] = new Slip(1, 10, 20);
slips[1] = new Slip(2, 12, 25);
slips[2] = new Slip(3, 14, 30);
```

Next you write a loop to invoke tellAboutSelf to retrieve and display attribute values for all three Slip instances. Note that this loop uses the array length attribute; therefore, it will work without modification for an array of any size.

```
for(int i = 0; i < slips.length; i++)
    {System.out.println(slips[i].tellAboutSelf());}
```

The argument for the println method first invokes tellAboutSelf to retrieve the slip information, and then passes this to the println method of the System.out object for display. Note that System is the name of a class, and out is a reference variable that refers to an instance of the PrintStream class. System.out then is a reference variable pointing to a PrintStream instance. The PrintStream class is also used later in Chapter 14.

Chapter 4 introduced the UML sequence diagram and illustrated how it depicts the interaction between objects in a system. In the preceding statements, TesterOne interacts with three Slip instances and the System.out object. Figure 6–3 shows a sequence diagram for this interaction.

The five rectangles at the top of the diagram represent the objects TesterOne, the instances of Slip (referenced by slips[0], slips[1], slips[2]), and the System.out object. First, TesterOne creates the three Slip instances populating the slips array with their references. The first element points to the first Slip instance, the second element to the second instance, and so on. TesterOne then invokes tellAboutSelf for the Slip instance referenced by slips[0]. Next, tellAboutSelf invokes the three getter methods for the first Slip instance and then returns the String instance referenced by info to TesterOne. TesterOne then invokes the println method in System.out, passing the String instance referenced by info. Similarly, TesterOne invokes tellAboutSelf for the second and third slips, passing the results returned to println each time.

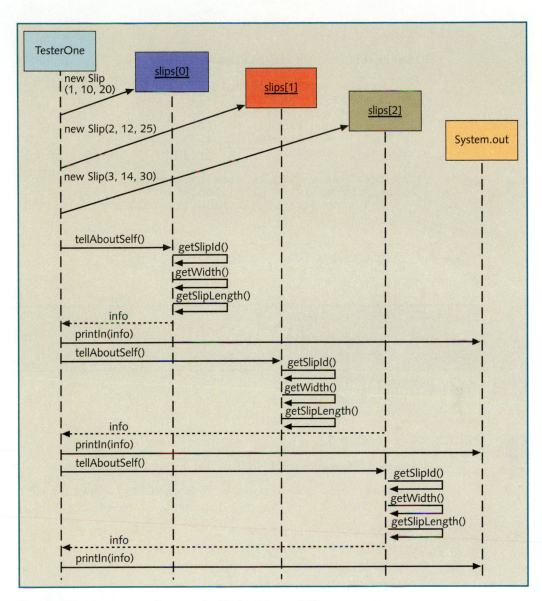

Figure 6-3   Sequence diagram for TesterOne and Slip

TesterOne is listed in Figure 6–4, and its output is shown in Figure 6–5.

```java
public class TesterOne
{
    public static void main(String args[])
    {
        // create an array to hold three Slip references
        Slip slips[] = new Slip[3];
        // create 3 Slip instances
        slips[0]= new Slip(1, 10, 20);
        slips[1]= new Slip(2, 12, 25);
        slips[2]= new Slip(3, 14, 30);

        // retrieve & display attribute values
        for(int i = 0; i < slips.length; i++)
            {System.out.println(slips[i].tellAboutSelf());}
    }
}
```

Figure 6-4   TesterOne.java listing

Slip: Id = 1, Width = 10, Length = 20.0
Slip: Id = 2, Width = 12, Length = 25.0
Slip: Id = 3, Width = 14, Length = 30.0

Figure 6-5   TesterOne.java output

Hands-on Exercise 1

1. Create a folder named Chapter6Exercise1 on your system.

2. Locate TesterOne.java and Slip.java on the book's CD in a folder named Chapter6\Example1, and then copy them to the Chapter6Exercise1 folder you created in Step 1.

3. Compile TesterOne.java and Slip.java, and run TesterOne.java using the software suggested by your instructor. Verify that your output is the same as that shown in Figure 6-5.

4. Modify TesterOne to expand the slips array to five elements and then create two additional Slip instances, adding their references to the new elements of the array:

ID	Width	Length
4	15	30
5	20	35

5. Modify TesterOne to retrieve and display information for all five Slip instances by invoking tellAboutSelf.

WRITING CUSTOM METHODS

So far, you have seen examples of accessor methods such as getId, setWidth, and so forth. These are called standard methods because most problem domain classes have them. This section introduces you to **custom methods**. Custom methods are methods written to do some processing. In contrast, accessor methods are written to store and retrieve values.

The custom method you will write here is named leaseSlip, and in this chapter it computes the lease fee for a slip. This method is expanded in later chapters to link the slip to a Customer and Lease instance.

Bradshaw Marina computes a slip lease fee based on the width of a slip, as shown in Table 6-1. As you can see from the table, fees range from $800 to $1500 depending on the slip's width. Slip length is not considered when determining the fee because generally the length of a slip is proportional to its width. In other words, the wider a slip, the greater its length.

Like all methods, this one begins with a method header. It will have public accessibility because it can be invoked by any object. Because it will compute and return the lease fee, which will be a dollar amount, you will use **double** for the return data type.

        public double leaseSlip()

To compute the lease fee, you could use either a series of if statements or a switch. The following code uses a switch block. The first statement declares a double variable named fee, which will contain the computed lease fee amount. Next, the switch statement tests the contents of the width attribute and then assigns a value to fee based on the contents. Each case statement concludes with **break** to prevent subsequent statements in the switch from being executed.

Table 6-1   Lease Fee Computation

Slip Width	Annual Lease Fee
10	$800
12	$900
14	$1100
16	$1500

```
        double fee;
        switch(width)
        {
            case 10: fee = 800;
            break;
            case 12: fee = 900;
            break;
            case 14: fee = 1100;
            break;
            case 16: fee = 1500;
            break;
            default: fee = 0;
        }
        return fee;
```

The switch block terminates with a closed curly brace. Notice that the preceding code includes the default case, which assigns a value of zero to fee if the width of the slip is not 10, 12, 14, or 16. The last statement in the method returns the computed value to the invoking method. Figure 6-6 lists this revised Slip class definition containing the leaseSlip method.

```
// Chapter 6
// illustrate a PD class with a custom method leaseSlip

public class Slip
{
    // attributes
    private int slipId;
    private int width;
    private double slipLength;

    // constructor with 3 parameters
    public Slip(int anId, int aWidth, double aSlipLength)
    {
        // invoke accessors to populate attributes
        setSlipId(anId);
        setWidth(aWidth);
        setSlipLength(aSlipLength);
    }

// custom method to lease a Slip
public double leaseSlip()
{
    double fee;
    switch(width)
    {
        case 10: fee = 800;
        break;
        case 12: fee = 900;
        break;
        case 14: fee = 1100;
        break;
        case 16: fee = 1500;
```

```
            break;
            default: fee = 0;
        }
        return fee;
}

// set accessor methods
public void setSlipId(int anId)
        {slipId = anId;}
public void setWidth(int aWidth)
        { width = aWidth;}
public void setSlipLength(double aSlipLength)
        { slipLength = aSlipLength;}

// get accessor methods
public int getSlipId()
        { return slipId;}
public int getWidth()
        { return width;}
public double getSlipLength()
        { return slipLength;}

// tellAboutSelf
public String tellAboutSelf()
{
    String info;

    info = "Slip: Id = "
            + getSlipId() + ", Width = "
            + getWidth() + ", Length = "
            + getSlipLength();
    return info;
  }
}
```

Figure 6-6   Slip class definition with leaseSlip method

Next, write a new tester class named Tester Two. Similar to TesterOne, begin by writing statements to declare a three-element array using data type Slip and then create three Slip instances.

```
// create an array to hold three Slip references
Slip slips[] = new Slip[3];
// create 3 Slip instances
slips[0]= new Slip(1, 10, 20);
slips[1]= new Slip(2, 12, 25);
slips[2]= new Slip(3, 14, 30);
```

Next, write a loop that is similar to the one you wrote in TesterOne, but here you invoke the leaseSlip method for each Slip instance and then display the fee that the method computes and returns. The first statement inside the loop invokes leaseSlip for the Slip instance referenced by the array element indexed by the loop variable i. This loop executes three times: the first time i contains 0, the second 1, and the last 2.

The second line of code does several things. First, within the argument for println, the string literal "Fee is" is concatenated with fee returned by leaseSlip in the prior statement. This result is then concatenated with a second literal "for slip" and the slip's ID, which is returned by the getSlipId method. This entire result is then passed to println, where it is displayed.

```java
// compute & display lease fee for each slip instance
for(int i = 0; i < slips.length; i++)
{
    double fee = slips[i].leaseSlip();
    System.out.println("Fee is " + fee + " for slip " + slips[i]
.getSlipId());
}
```

TesterTwo is listed in Figure 6-7, and its output is shown in Figure 6-8.

```java
public class TesterTwo
{
    public static void main(String args[])
    {
        // create an array to hold three Slip references
        Slip slips[] = new Slip[3];
        // create 3 Slip instances
        slips[0]= new Slip(1, 10, 20);
        slips[1]= new Slip(2, 12, 25);
        slips[2]= new Slip(3, 14, 30);

        // compute & display lease fee for each slip instance
        for(int i = 0; i < slips.length; i++)
        {
            double fee = slips[i].leaseSlip();
            System.out.println("Fee is " + fee + " for slip " +
slips[i].getSlipId());
        }
    }
}
```

Figure 6-7   TesterTwo.java listing

```
Fee is 800.0 for slip 1
Fee is 900.0 for slip 2
Fee is 1100.0 for slip 3
```

Figure 6-8   TesterTwo.java output

Hands-on Exercise 2

1. Create a folder named Chapter6Exercise2 on your system.

2. Locate TesterTwo.java and Slip.java on the book's CD in a folder named Chapter6\Example2, and then copy them to the Chapter6Exercise2 folder you created in Step 1.

3. Compile TesterTwo.java and Slip.java, and run TesterTwo.java using the software recommended by your instructor. Verify that your output is the same as that shown in Figure 6-8.

4. Rewrite the fee computation in the leaseSlip method in Slip.java using if statements. Recompile Slip.java and run TesterTwo again to verify that your output is the same as Figure 6-8.

FORMATTING OUTPUT

The dollar amount displayed earlier for the lease fee had no dollar sign or comma, and was displayed with a single decimal position. You can dramatically improve the appearance of numerical data by using methods in the NumberFormat and DecimalFormat classes, members of the java.text package. You can also embed special characters such as tab and new line into data being displayed to control its appearance.

Using NumberFormat and DecimalFormat Classes

The NumberFormat class provides methods to format numerical data as currency with commas, dollar signs, and decimal points. NumberFormat also provides other methods, including those to format currency for various countries. In this section, you create TesterThree to learn three different ways to format the lease fees previously calculated.

Both NumberFormat and DecimalFormat are members of the java.text package, which means you must write an import statement at the beginning of the TesterThree definition. You can use the wildcard "*" to indicate that you want access to multiple classes in the java.text package. If you wanted, you could write two import statements here, one for each class.

```
import java.text.*;
```

TesterThree begins by creating a Slip instance.

```
// create a Slip instance
Slip aSlip = new Slip(3, 14, 30);
```

Next comes a statement to calculate the lease fee for the new slip and assign the value returned to a double variable named fee. The Slip instance is referenced by aSlip.

```
// compute lease fee
double fee = aSlip.leaseSlip();
```

You use two steps to format numerical data as currency. First, you invoke the getCurrencyInstance method in the NumberFormat class to obtain a NumberFormat instance, and then invoke the format method for the instance obtained. The following code illustrates these steps. The first statement invokes the getCurrencyInstance method in the NumberFormat class storing the instance reference in the variable `currencyFormat`. The second statement then invokes the format method for this instance, passing it the lease fee that was previously computed for the slip. This method returns a String instance with the fee formatted as currency with a dollar sign and two decimal positions. This string is then concatenated with the literal "Currency:" and the result passed to the println method for display. The lease fee for this slip is 1100; displayed in currency format, it appears as: $1,100.00.

```
// illustrate currency format
NumberFormat currencyFormat = NumberFormat.getCurrencyInstance();
System.out.println("Currency: " + currencyFormat.format(fee));
```

You use the DecimalFormat class to format numbers with commas and a decimal, but without the dollar sign. Similar to the previous NumberFormat example, you follow two steps to use DecimalFormat. First, you create an instance of DecimalFormat using the keyword **new**, and then you invoke the format method for that instance.

Note that you invoked the NumberFormat method getCurrencyInstance to obtain a NumberFormat instance, but you use the keyword **new** to create an instance of DecimalFormat. NumberFormat has a constructor, but it is much simpler to use getCurrencyInstance to produce an instance that will format numbers as currency.

When you instantiate DecimalFormat, you pass a **format mask** to its constructor. This mask determines how the number will be displayed. The mask you will use is:

```
"##,##0.00"
```

The pound (#) character reserves a position for a number to be displayed, but blanks out any leading zeros. The comma indicates that if there are significant digits to the left, the comma will be displayed. The last four characters in the mask are 0.00, indicating that you want to have one position displayed to the left of the decimal, a decimal point, and then two positions to the right of the decimal point. The character "0" forces a character to display, even if its value is zero.

After creating the DecimalFormat instance, you invoke its format method to format the argument according to the mask you used, and return a String instance containing the formatted data. The following code instantiates DecimalFormat and then invokes the format for the fee. The output displayed is 1,100.00.

```
// illustrate DecimalFormat
DecimalFormat decimalFormat = new DecimalFormat("##,##0.00");
System.out.println("Decimal: " + decimalFormat.format(fee));
```

Using Escape Sequences

Computer systems use special characters such as tab and new line to help format data being displayed or printed. You place these characters into the data being displayed or printed. However, because these characters do not appear on the keyboard, you must enter them using the backslash character (\) followed by a second character such as "t" for tab or "n" for new line. This format is called an **escape sequence**.

You may also use an escape sequence to insert a character that cannot easily be included as output. For example, if you want to display a double quote within a string of characters, you need to use an escape sequence. Table 6-2 lists selected escape sequences.

The following examples use escape sequences placed in a string literal being passed to the println method. The first statement illustrates using a tab by including "\t" in the middle of the literal. It displays "Before tab" at the beginning of the line, tabs to the right, and then displays "after tab."

The second statement illustrates the new line escape sequence. The output displays "Before new line," spaces up one line, and then displays "after new line" on the new line.

The last statement shows how to display a double quote inside a character string.

```
System.out.println("Before tab \t after tab");
System.out.println("Before new line \n after new line");
System.out.println("Display double quote \" ");
```

TesterThree is listed in Figure 6-9, and its output is shown in Figure 6-10.

Table 6-2   Selected Escape Sequences

Escape Sequence	Character Represented
\t	tab
\f	new page
\n	new line
\r	carriage return
\b	backspace
\'	single quote
\"	double quote
\\	backslash

```java
import java.text.*;
public class TesterThree
{
    public static void main(String args[])
    {
        // create a Slip instance
        Slip aSlip = new Slip(3, 14, 30);

        // compute lease fee
        double fee = aSlip.leaseSlip();

        // illustrate currency format
        NumberFormat currencyFormat = NumberFormat.getCurrencyInstance();
        System.out.println("Currency: " + currencyFormat.format(fee));

        // illustrate DecimalFormat
        DecimalFormat decimalFormat = new DecimalFormat("##,##0.00");
        System.out.println("Decimal: " + decimalFormat.format(fee));

        // illustrate number format
        NumberFormat noDollarFormat = NumberFormat.getInstance();
        System.out.println("number: " + noDollarFormat.format(fee));

        // illustrate escape sequences
        System.out.println("Before tab \t after tab");
        System.out.println("Before new line \n after new line");
        System.out.println("Display double quote \" ");
    }
}
```

Figure 6-9   TesterThree.java listing

```
Currency: $1,100.00
Decimal: 1,100.00
number: 1,100
Before tab    after tab
Before new line
after new line
Display double quote "
```

Figure 6-10   TesterThree.java output

USING STATIC VARIABLES AND METHODS

You previously saw how to declare and use **instance variables** and **instance methods**. When you instantiate a class, the new instance receives a copy of all instance variables and methods. For example, each Slip instance created in the previous section had its own copy of the attribute variables slipId, width, and slipLength. Similarly, the accessor methods and custom methods such as leaseSlip are used for each individual instance. To avoid redundancy, Java does not actually create separate copies of these instance methods; however, it appears that instance methods "belong" to each instance.

In this section, you will learn about **class variables** and **class methods**. Class variables and methods are *shared* by all instances of the class—each instance does not have its own copy. The keyword **static** is used to declare class variables and class methods. If you omit static, then Java uses the default **nonstatic**. Nonstatic is another term used for instance variables and methods. When you instantiate a class, the instance gets copies of all nonstatic variables and access to all nonstatic methods, but it *does not* get a copy of static variables and methods.

To illustrate the use of static variables and methods, assume that the Bradshaw Marina system needs to keep track of the total number of slips. You can do this by declaring a static variable in the Slip class. The following statement declares this variable, named numberOfSlips, and initializes it to zero. Use private accessibility here because numberOfSlips will be accessed only by methods within the Slip class.

```
private static int numberOfSlips = 0;
```

To know the number of slips in the marina, each time a new slip is created numberOfSlips should be incremented. Add the following statement to the Slip constructor to increment numberOfSlips each time a Slip instance is created.

```
numberOfSlips++;
```

Next, write a getter method to return the contents of numberOfSlips. Note that you make this a static method because it is not associated with an individual instance, although you could make it nonstatic if you wished. Because it is static, you will invoke it using the class name. If it were nonstatic, you would invoke it using a reference variable pointing to an instance of Slip.

```
public static int getNumberOfSlips()
     { return numberOfSlips;}
```

The revised Slip class definition is listed in Figure 6-11.

```
public class Slip
{
    // attributes
    private int slipId;
    private int width;
    private double slipLength;
```

6

```
   // static attribute variable
   private static int numberOfSlips = 0;

   // constructor with 3 parameters
   public Slip(int anId, int aWidth, double aSlipLength)
   {
   // invoke setters to populate attributes

      setSlipId(anId);
      setWidth(aWidth);
      setSlipLength(aSlipLength);
      numberOfSlips++;
   }

   // custom method to lease a Slip
   public double leaseSlip()
   {
      double fee;
      switch(width)
      {
          case 10: fee = 800;
          break;
          case 12: fee = 900;
          break;
          case 14: fee = 1100;
          break;
          case 16: fee = 1500;
          break;
          default: fee = 0;
      }
      return fee;
   }

// setters
public void setSlipId(int anId)
   {slipId = anId;}
public void setWidth(int aWidth)
   { width = aWidth;}
public void setSlipLength(double aSlipLength)
   { slipLength = aSlipLength;}

// getters
public int getSlipId()
   { return slipId;}
public int getWidth()
   { return width;}
public double getSlipLength()
   { return slipLength;}

// static method
public static int getNumberOfSlips()
   { return numberOfSlips;}

// tellAboutSelf
```

```
public String tellAboutSelf()
{
    String info;

    info = "Slip: Id = "
           + getSlipId() + ", Width = "
           + getWidth() + ", Length = "
           + getSlipLength();
    return info;
}
}
```

Figure 6-11   Slip class definition with static variable and method

Write TesterFour to declare an array and create Slip instances as before. Following the creation of each Slip instance, retrieve and display the number of slip attributes. You invoke the static method getNumberOfSlips by writing the class name, a period, and the method name.

```
System.out.println("Number of slips " + Slip.getNumberOfSlips());
```

This statement invokes getNumberOfSlips, concatenates the value returned with the descriptive literal, and then passes this result to the println method.

You also can substitute an instance reference variable for the class name, because the JVM knows to which class an instance belongs, and simply interprets the instance reference variable as the appropriate class name.

```
// retrieve & display numberOfSlips using reference variable
System.out.println("Number of slips (ref var) " +
slips[0].getNumberOfSlips());
```

This statement produces the same results as the previous one, even though you use the reference variable slips[0]. The Java compiler knows that the instance referenced by slips[0] is a member of the Slip class and therefore invokes the class method getNumberOfSlips.

```
System.out.println("Number of slips" +
firstSlip.getNumberOfSlips());
```

The complete listing of TesterFour.java is listed in Figure 6-12, and its output is shown in Figure 6-13.

```
public class TesterFour
{
    public static void main(String args[])
    {
        // create an array to hold three Slip references
        Slip slips[] = new Slip[3];
        // create 3 Slip instances & display numberOfSlips for each
        slips[0]= new Slip(1, 10, 20);
        System.out.println("Number of slips " +
Slip.getNumberOfSlips());
```

```
        slips[1]= new Slip(2, 12, 25);
        System.out.println("Number of slips " +
Slip.getNumberOfSlips());
        slips[2]= new Slip(3, 14, 30);
        System.out.println("Number of slips " +
Slip.getNumberOfSlips());

        // retrieve & display numberOfSlips using reference variable
        System.out.println("Number of slips (ref var) " +
slips[0].getNumberOfSlips());
    }
}
```

Figure 6-12   TesterFour.java listing

```
Number of slips 1
Number of slips 2
Number of slips 3
Number of slips (ref var) 3
```

Figure 6-13   TesterFour.java output

Overloading Methods

In Part 1 of this book, you learned about method signatures. A **method signature** consists of the method name and its parameter list. Java identifies a method *not only by its name*, but by its signature as well. Therefore, within a class definition, you can write several methods with the same name, but as long as their signature parameter lists differ, Java sees them as unique methods. A method within the same class having the same name as another, but with a different parameter list, is called an **overloaded method**.

Do not confuse overloaded methods with **overridden methods** or polymorphism. You override a method by writing a method with the *same signature* as an *inherited* method. When you override a method, you are, in effect, replacing the inherited method.

A polymorphic method exists when you have a method in one class with the same signature as a method *in a second class*. As you learned in Chapter 2, polymorphism permits different objects to respond in their own way to the same message.

In contrast, an overloaded method has the same name as another method in the class, but a different parameter list. In this section, you develop an overloaded constructor and then overload a custom method. Overridden and polymorphic methods are illustrated in subsequent chapters.

Overloading a Constructor

You may frequently need to use multiple constructors, each having a different parameter list. For example, assume that the majority of the slips at Bradshaw Marina are 12 feet wide and 25 feet long, but a few have different widths and lengths. However, the current Slip constructor requires three arguments: slipId, width, and slipLength.

You can simplify the code required to create a new slip by writing a second Slip constructor having only the single parameter for slipId, and then include statements to assign the default values of 12 and 25 to width and slipLength, respectively. Using these default values eliminates the need to pass them when creating slips 12 feet wide and 25 feet long.

To further simplify your code, you can use static constants for the default width and length values. The following code, added to the Slip class definition, creates these two constants. Note that these are static and final with private accessibility. They are static because they are to be shared by all Slip instances, they are final because their value should not be changed, and they are private because they will be accessed only by methods within the Slip class. Notice that you follow the Java style by using uppercase identifiers containing the underscore character to separate words within the identifier.

```
private static final int DEFAULT_WIDTH = 12;
private static final int DEFAULT_SLIP_LENGTH = 25;
```

The second constructor method header appears the same as the original, except that it has only a single parameter to receive the slip ID value. This constructor method has a single statement that invokes the original constructor, passing the ID plus the default width and length values as arguments. You use the keyword **this** without specifying a method name to invoke the constructor for this class.

```
public Slip(int anId)
  { this(anId,DEFAULT_WIDTH,DEFAULT_SLIP_LENGTH);}
```

TesterFive illustrates the creation of Slip instances invoking both constructors. Recall that Java determines which constructor to invoke by the argument list. If the argument consists of three values, the original constructor with three parameters is executed. If the argument consists of a single value, the new constructor having one parameter is invoked. In other words, the number of arguments determines which constructor is executed: Remember, Java identifies a method by its signature as well as its name.

The first statement in TesterFive creates a Slip instance by passing three arguments, which causes the original constructor with three parameters to be invoked.

```
Slip firstSlip = new Slip(1, 10, 20);
```

The next statement passes the single argument for slipId, which invokes the second constructor. The second Slip instance is then created using the default values for width and length.

```
Slip secondSlip = new Slip(2);
```

The next two statements invoke tellAboutSelf for each Slip instance and display the result.

```
System.out.println(firstSlip.tellAboutSelf());
System.out.println(secondSlip.tellAboutSelf());
```

The output displayed is:

```
Slip: Id = 1, Width = 10, Length = 20.0
Slip: Id = 2, Width = 12, Length = 25.0
```

Overloading a Custom Method

In addition to the constructor, you can overload any method. Assume that Bradshaw Marina, under certain conditions, permits a discounted lease fee. You can include the discounted fee feature by simply writing a second version of the leaseSlip method that accepts a value for the discount as a percentage. This new method will overload the original leaseSlip method developed earlier. Slip will now have two leaseSlip methods, but they will have different signatures. The original leaseSlip has an empty parameter list, but the second has a parameter variable for the discount.

This method consists of three statements to compute and return the discounted lease fee. The first invokes the original leaseSlip method, which computes and returns the lease fee, but without the desired discount. The second statement computes the discounted lease fee, and the third statement returns the fee to the invoking method. Note that you use the keyword **this** to invoke leaseSlip for "this" Slip instance. You could have omitted **this** because it is the default; however, writing it helps make your code clear.

```java
public double leaseSlip(double aDiscountPercent)
{
    double fee = this.leaseSlip();
    double discountedFee = fee * (100 - aDiscountPercent)/100;
    return discountedFee ;
}
```

Next, you can add statements to TesterFour to invoke both the original and the new leaseSlip methods. Java executes the appropriate method, depending on the argument list. If no argument is passed, then the original leaseSlip method is invoked. However, if an argument is coded, then the overloaded method is executed.

```java
System.out.println("Slip 1 fee is " + firstSlip.leaseSlip());
System.out.println("with 10% discount is " +
firstSlip.leaseSlip(10));

System.out.println("Slip 2 fee is " + secondSlip.leaseSlip());
System.out.println("with 20% discount is " +
secondSlip.leaseSlip(20));
```

The updated Slip class definition with the overloaded constructor and leaseSlip methods is listed in Figure 6-14, TesterFive.java is listed in Figure 6-15, and its output is shown in Figure 6-16.

```java
public class Slip
{
    // attributes
    private int slipId;
    private int width;
    private double slipLength;

    // static constants for default attribute values
    private static final int DEFAULT_WIDTH = 12;
    private static final int DEFAULT_SLIP_LENGTH = 25;

    // static attribute variable
    private static int numberOfSlips = 0;

    // constructor with 3 parameters
    public Slip(int anId, int aWidth, double aSlipLength)
    {
        // invoke setters to populate attributes
        setSlipId(anId);
        setWidth(aWidth);
        setSlipLength(aSlipLength);
        numberOfSlips++;
    }

    // constructor with 1 parameter
    public Slip(int anId)
    {   // invoke 3-parameter constructor
        this(anId,DEFAULT_WIDTH,DEFAULT_SLIP_LENGTH);
    }

    // custom method to lease a Slip
    public double leaseSlip()
    {
        double fee;
        switch(width)
        {
            case 10: fee = 800;
            break;
            case 12: fee = 900;
            break;
            case 14: fee = 1100;
            break;
            case 16: fee = 1500;
            break;
            default: fee = 0;
        }
        return fee;
    }
}
```

6

```java
// override leaseSlip
public double leaseSlip(double aDiscountPercent)
{
    double fee = this.leaseSlip();
    double discountedFee = fee * (100 - aDiscountPercent)/100;
    return discountedFee ;
}

// setter methods
public void setSlipId(int anId)
    {slipId = anId;}
public void setWidth(int aWidth)
    { width = aWidth;}
public void setSlipLength(double aSlipLength)
    { slipLength = aSlipLength;}

// getter methods
public int getSlipId()
    { return slipId;}
public int getWidth()
    { return width;}
public double getSlipLength()
    { return slipLength;}

// static method
public static int getNumberOfSlips()
    { return numberOfSlips;}

// tellAboutSelf
public String tellAboutSelf()
{
    String info;

    info = "Slip: Id = "
            + getSlipId() + ", Width = "
            + getWidth() + ", Length = "
            + getSlipLength();
    return info;
}
}
```

Figure 6-14   Slip class definition with overloaded methods

```java
public class TesterFive
{
    public static void main(String args[])
    {
        // create 2 Slip instances using different constructors
        // first use original constructor passing 3 arguments
        Slip firstSlip = new Slip(1, 10, 20);

        // next, use 2nd constructor passing only 1 argument
        Slip secondSlip = new Slip(2);
```

```
      // retrieve & display info for both slips
      System.out.println(firstSlip.tellAboutSelf());
      System.out.println(secondSlip.tellAboutSelf());

      System.out.println("Slip 1 fee is " + firstSlip.leaseSlip());
      System.out.println("with 10% discount is " +
firstSlip.leaseSlip(10));
      System.out.println("Slip 2 fee is " +
secondSlip.leaseSlip());
      System.out.println("with 20% discount is " +
secondSlip.leaseSlip(20));
   }
}
```

Figure 6-15   TesterFive.java listing

6

Slip: Id = 1, Width = 10, Length = 20.0

Slip: Id = 2, Width = 12, Length = 25.0

Slip 1 fee is 800.0

with 10% discount is 720.0

Slip 2 fee is 900.0

with 20% discount is 720.0

Figure 6-16   TesterFive.java output

Hands-on Exercise 3

1. Create a folder named Chapter6Exercise3 on your system.

2. Locate TesterFive.java and Slip.java on the book's CD in a folder named Chapter6\Example3, and then copy them to the Chapter6Exercise3 folder you created in Step 1.

3. Compile TesterFive.java and Slip.java, and run TesterFive.java using the software recommended by your instructor. Verify that your output is the same as that shown in Figure 6-16.

4. Rewrite the overloaded leaseSlip method to use a single statement by omitting the variable fee.

5. Add a third constructor to Slip to accept arguments for slipId and width, but use the default slipLength of 25.

6. Add statements to TesterFive to invoke the constructor you added in Step 5.

7. Recompile TesterFive.java and Slip.java, and run TesterFive.java using the software recommended by your instructor. Verify that the output produced by your new statements is correct.

WORKING WITH EXCEPTIONS

Java uses exceptions to notify you of errors, problems, and other unusual conditions that may occur while your system is running. An **exception**, like almost everything in Java, is an object instance. More specifically, it is an instance of the Throwable class or one of its subclasses.

In Part 1, you saw that OO processing often uses the client-server model. A client invokes a method in a server, perhaps passing along arguments. The server performs its assigned task and may return a value to the invoking client. The server uses exceptions to inform the client of a problem. Perhaps the client sent an inappropriate or invalid argument, or perhaps because of some other condition, the server cannot complete its normal processing.

When such unusual situations arise, the server can create an Exception instance containing information about the situation. The server then sends the Exception instance to the invoking client. Of course, the client must be prepared to receive the exception and take appropriate action.

Java uses five keywords to deal with exceptions: **try**, **catch**, **finally**, **throw**, and **throws**. The first three of these, **try**, **catch**, and **finally**, are used by the client, while the last two, **throw** and **throws**, are used by the server. The following paragraphs illustrate the use of these keywords in adding data validation to the Slip class. Figure 6-17 illustrates the interaction between client and server methods dealing with exceptions.

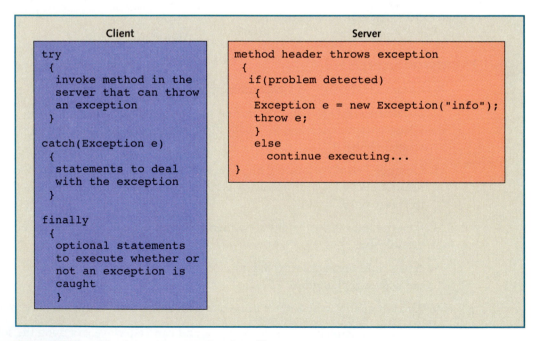

Figure 6-17   Client-server exception handling

Whenever a client invokes a method that may create and throw an exception, the invoking code is placed in a **try block**. The server method indicates that it *may* throw an exception by including the keyword **throws** in its header. Then, if a situation warranting an exception is detected, the server method creates an Exception instance, and sends it to the invoking client using the keyword **throw**. The client *catches* the Exception instance in a **catch block** and executes statements to deal with the exception. The **finally block** is optional but, if included, will execute regardless of whether an exception is caught.

Data Validation for slipId

Slips are attached to a dock, and Bradshaw Marina will never have more than 50 slips connected to a dock. You should therefore add data validation logic to the setSlipId setter method to verify that values passed to it are in the range of 1 through 50. You can add code in this method to create and throw an exception instance if a value outside this valid range is detected. The keyword **throw** sends the Exception instance to the invoking client method.

If a method is to create and throw an exception, then its header must contain the keyword **throws** followed by the class name of the instance it may throw. The following example uses an existing Java class named Exception. In subsequent chapters, you will learn how to write your own custom Exception classes.

The expanded setSlipId header appears as:

```
public void setSlipId(int anId) throws Exception
```

You can then add logic to the method to see if the parameter value received is within the valid range. If the value is outside the acceptable range, instantiate Exception and then throw the instance to the invoking method. The code to instantiate this class uses the keyword **new**. Here, you can pass a string literal describing the error to the Exception constructor. Notice that instead of writing the number 50 in the if statement, you can add the constant MAXIMUM_NUMBER_OF_SLIPS to the Slip class. Similarly, you concatenate MAXIMUM_NUMBER_OF_SLIPS with the descriptive literal. Using this constant eliminates the need to change the code if Bradshaw Marina decides to change the maximum number of slips. All you would need to change is the value in the statement where you define the constant.

If the parameter value is within the acceptable range, the else clause populates the slipId attribute.

```
public void setSlipId(int anId) throws Exception
{   // reject slip Id if < 0 or > maximum
    if (anId < 1 || anId > MAXIMUM_NUMBER_OF_SLIPS)
        {
            Exception e = new Exception("Slip ID not between
            1 & " + MAXIMUM_NUMBER_OF_SLIPS);
            throw e;
```

```
            }
        else
            slipId = anId;
    }
```

Data Validation for Width

Next, add code to the setWidth method to verify that the width parameter is one of the valid width values: 10, 12, 14, or 16. Recall that these values are used in computing the lease fee and therefore must be correct. First, store the valid width values in an integer array named **VALID_SLIP_WIDTHS** by adding the following code to the Slip class definition. This constant is also private, static, and final.

```
private static final int VALID_SLIP_WIDTHS[] = {10,12,14,16};
```

Next, add throws Exception to the setWidth header because it will create and throw an exception instance if an invalid width value is received.

```
public void setWidth(int aWidth)throws Exception
```

The validation logic will iterate the array, seeking a match between the parameter value received and an array value. If a matching value is found, the parameter is valid. However, if the end of the array is reached without finding a matching value, then the parameter contains an invalid value and you will create and throw an exception.

Similar to the array iteration loops you studied in Chapter 2, you first declare a boolean variable named validWidth and initialize it to false. You then code a for loop that will continue until it reaches the end of the array or finds a matching width value. Within the loop body is a single if statement that tests for a match between the parameter value (aWidth) and the array element (VALID_SLIP_WIDTHS[i]). If a match is found, validWidth is set to true, which terminates the loop.

```
boolean validWidth = false;
for(int i = 0; i < VALID_SLIP_WIDTHS.length && !validWidth; i++)
    {
        if(aWidth == VALID_SLIP_WIDTHS[i])
            validWidth = true;
    }
```

Following the loop is another if statement to test validWidth. If it is true, you populate the width attribute with the parameter value. If validWidth is not true, however, you create and throw an instance of Exception containing a message describing the problem.

```
if(validWidth )
    width = aWidth;
else
    {
        Exception e = new Exception("Invalid Slip Width");
        throw e;
    }
```

Note that in this example the setter methods are actually invoked by the constructor. Because the setter methods may throw an exception, their headers must include **throws** `Exception`. This means that if a setter throws an exception to the constructor, the constructor will automatically throw it to the invoking client method, which requires that the constructors include **throws** `Exception` in their headers. Of course, you could instead add try and catch blocks to the constructors and have them explicitly throw the exception if it is caught.

The complete Slip class definition containing the setter methods with data validation is listed in Figure 6-18.

```java
public class Slip
{
    // attributes
    private int slipId;
    private int width;
    private double slipLength;

    // static attribute variable
    private static int numberOfSlips = 0;

    // static constants for default attribute values
    private static final int DEFAULT_WIDTH = 12;
    private static final int DEFAULT_SLIP_LENGTH = 25;

    // static constants for data validation
    private static final int MAXIMUM_NUMBER_OF_SLIPS = 50;
    private static final int VALID_SLIP_WIDTHS[] = {10,12,14,16};

    // constructor with 3 parameters
    public Slip(int anId, int aWidth, double aSlipLength)throws
    Exception
    {
        // invoke setters to populate attributes
        setSlipId(anId);
        setWidth(aWidth);
        setSlipLength(aSlipLength);
        numberOfSlips++;
    }

    // constructor with 1 parameter
    public Slip(int anId)throws Exception
    {   // invoke 3-parameter constructor
        this(anId,DEFAULT_WIDTH,DEFAULT_SLIP_LENGTH);
    }

    // custom method to lease a Slip
    public double leaseSlip()
    {
        double fee;
        switch(width)
        {
```

6

```
            case 10: fee = 800;
            break;
            case 12: fee = 900;
            break;
            case 14: fee = 1100;
            break;
            case 16: fee = 1500;
            break;
            default: fee = 0;
            }
        return fee;
    }

    // override leaseSlip
    public double leaseSlip(double aDiscountPercent)
    {
        double fee = this.leaseSlip();
        double discountedFee = fee * (100 - aDiscountPercent)/100;
        return discountedFee ;
    }

    // setter methods
    public void setSlipId(int anId) throws Exception
    {   // reject slip Id if < 0 or > maximum
        if (anId < 1 || anId > MAXIMUM_NUMBER_OF_SLIPS)
            {
                Exception e = new Exception("Slip ID not between 1
                & " + MAXIMUM_NUMBER_OF_SLIPS);
                throw e;
            }
         else
            slipId = anId;
    }

    public void setWidth(int aWidth)throws Exception
    {
        boolean validWidth = false;
        for(int i = 0; i < VALID_SLIP_WIDTHS.length &&
        !validWidth;i++)
        {
            if(aWidth == VALID_SLIP_WIDTHS[i])
                validWidth = true;
        }
        if(validWidth)
        width = aWidth;ß
        else
            {

            Exception e = new Exception("Invalid Slip Width");
            throw e;
        }
    }

public void setSlipLength(double aSlipLength)
    { slipLength = aSlipLength;}
```

```java
// getter methods
public int getSlipId()
    { return slipId;}
public int getWidth()
    { return width;}
public double getSlipLength()
    { return slipLength;}

// static method
public static int getNumberOfSlips()
    { return numberOfSlips;}

// tellAboutSelf
public String tellAboutSelf()
{
    String info;

    info = "Slip: Id = "
            + getSlipId() + ", Width = "
            + getWidth() + ", Length = "
            + getSlipLength();
    return info;
    }
}
```

Figure 6-18   Slip class definition with data validation

Catching Exceptions

Exceptions are thrown by server methods invoked by clients. In this example, Slip is the server with methods that will create and throw an exception if either an invalid slip ID or width is detected. In this example, TesterSix is the client that will test the data validation code in Slip.

Whenever you write code that invokes a method containing throws in its header, the invoking code must be prepared to catch the exception; otherwise, the JVM will terminate processing if an exception is thrown and not caught. The first step in catching an exception is to place the invoking statement in a try block, as shown below and in Figure 6-19. A try block begins with the keyword **try** followed by a block of code containing the invoking statement or statements. The following code first declares a Slip reference variable named firstSlip initialized to null, followed by a try block containing the statement instantiating Slip:

```java
Slip firstSlip = null;
try     // force exception with invalid slip Id
{
    firstSlip = new Slip(150, 10, 25);
    System.out.println(firstSlip.tellAboutSelf());
}
catch (Exception n) // display exception message
{ System.out.println(n); }
```

Note that the try block contains two statements. If the first statement causes an exception to be thrown, the second is not executed. Instead, execution begins at the following catch block.

Incidentally, you do not declare the Slip reference variable within the try block because its scope would have been limited *to that block*. Because you want to use this reference variable outside the try block, declare it outside the block.

The statement that instantiates Slip invokes its constructor and passes arguments for slipId, width, and slipLength. Recall that the constructor invokes the setter methods to populate the attributes. Therefore, when you instantiate the class and the constructor is invoked, it invokes setSlipId, which contains code to throw an exception if an invalid setSlipId is detected. The previous example deliberately passes an invalid value (150), which causes the setter to create and throw an exception.

Notice that the Slip constructor calls setSlipId, which throws an exception, but that the constructor does *not* catch the exception. In this example, the constructor is not required to deal with the exception because you added **throws** Exception to the constructor header, meaning that the constructor automatically rethrows an exception that was originally thrown by a method it invokes. If necessary, you could include code in the constructor to catch the exception, and then simply throw it again, and it would be caught by the method that invoked the constructor.

Following the try block in TesterSix, you can write a catch block to receive and deal with the exception thrown by setSlipId. Similar to a method header, the catch block must specify a parameter variable to receive a reference to the Exception instance. The parameter variable must indicate the data type, which in this example is the class name Exception. Within the catch block is a statement invoking println to display the message contained in the Exception instance.

```
catch (Exception n) // display exception message
{ System.out.println(n); }
```

Next, add statements to TesterSix to test the validation code that was added to setWidth. Again, attempt to create a new Slip instance within a try block. Pass the first constructor a width value of 15, which is invalid.

```
try  // force exception with invalid width
{
    firstSlip = new Slip(1, 15, 25);
    System.out.println(firstSlip.tellAboutSelf());
}
```

Next, write a catch block to catch the exception that will be thrown.

```
catch (Exception n) // display exception message
    { System.out.println(n); }
```

The keyword **finally** is used to add a block of code after a try block to contain code that you want executed *whether or not an exception was caught*. TesterSix includes finally blocks to illustrate their use.

Figure 6-19 lists TesterSix.java, and its output is shown in Figure 6-20.

```
public class TesterSix
{
   public static void main(String args[])
   {
      Slip firstSlip = null;
      try     // force exception with invalid slip Id
      {
          firstSlip = new Slip(150, 10, 25);
          System.out.println(firstSlip.tellAboutSelf());
       }
       catch (Exception n) // display exception message
       { System.out.println(n); }

       try     // force exception with invalid width
       {
          firstSlip = new Slip(1, 15, 25);
          System.out.println(firstSlip.tellAboutSelf());
       }
       catch (Exception n) // display exception message
          { System.out.println(n); }
       finally
          {System.out.println("finally block is always executed");}

       try     // create a slip using valid id & width
       {
          firstSlip = new Slip(2, 10, 25);
          System.out.println(firstSlip.tellAboutSelf());
       }
       catch (Exception n)
          { System.out.println(n); }
       finally
          {System.out.println("finally block is always executed");}
   }
}
```

Figure 6-19   TesterSix.java listing

```
java.lang.Exception: Slip ID not between 1 & 50
java.lang.Exception: Invalid Slip Width
finally block is always executed
Slip: Id = 2, Width = 10, Length = 25.0
finally block is always executed
```

Figure 6-20   TesterSix.java output

Hands-on Exercise 4

1. Create a folder named Chapter6Exercise4 on your system.

2. Locate TesterSix.java and Slip.java on the book's CD in a folder named Chapter6\Example4, and then copy it to the Chapter6Exercise4 folder you created in Step 1.

3. Compile TesterSix.java and Slip.java, and run TesterSix.java using the software recommended by your instructor. Verify that your output is the same as that shown in Figure 6-20.

4. Add statements to the Slip constructor to catch the exceptions thrown by setSlipId and setWidth, and then rethrow the exception using the **throw** keyword. Test your code to verify that you get the same output as before.

5. Add statements to the setSlipLength method in Slip to verify that the length value received is between 20 and 40, inclusive. Use appropriately named constants for these minimum and maximum values. Add try-catch statements to TesterSix to test your new data validation code.

Summary

- Accessor methods are called standard metho ds because most problem domain classes have them, but they are generally not shown on class diagrams. Custom methods are methods you write to do some processing and are included in class diagrams.

- You use methods in the NumberFormat and DecimalFormat classes (members of the java.text package) to format numerical data for display. You can also embed special characters, called escape sequences, into data being displayed to alter the output. An escape sequence consists of the backslash character (\) followed by other characters such as "n" for new line and "t" for tab.

- The keyword **static** is used to declare class variables and methods. Static variables and methods are associated with classes instead of individual instances. When you instantiate a class, the new instance is given a copy of all instance variables and access to instance methods, but the new instance does *not* get a copy of static variables and methods.

- You invoke static methods by writing the class name, a period, and the method name. Nonstatic methods are invoked by writing an instance reference variable, a period, and the method name. You can also invoke class methods using an instance reference variable.

- A method signature consists of the method name and its parameter list. Java identifies a method by its entire signature, not only by its name. A method with the same name as another in that same class, but with a different parameter list (a different signature), is called an overloaded method.

- Java uses exceptions to notify you of errors, problems, and other unusual conditions that may occur while your system is running. An exception is an instance of the Throwable class or one of its subclasses.

- Java uses five keywords when dealing with exceptions: **try**, **catch**, **finally**, **throw**, and **throws**. The first three of these, **try**, **catch**, and **finally**, are used by client methods, while the last two, **throw** and **throws**, are used by server methods.

- If a method is to create and throw an exception, then its header must contain the keyword **throws** followed by the class name of the instance it may throw.

- Whenever you write code that invokes a method containing **throws** in its header, you must be prepared to catch the exception; otherwise, the JVM will terminate processing if an exception is thrown and not caught.

6

Key Terms

assignment compatible	exception	nonstatic
catch block	finally block	overloaded method
class method	format mask	overridden method
class variable	instance method	polymorphic method
custom method	instance variable	try block
escape sequence	method signature	

Review Questions

1. Concatenate means:

a. to separate items in a string

b. to subtract numeric items

c. to join items together

d. to display things

2. Static variables:

a. are never populated

b. are seldom replicated

c. only one copy exists

d. are also called instance variables

3. A static method:

a. may be invoked by referencing the class name

b. may be invoked by referencing the instance name

c. both a and b

d. neither a nor b

4. Static final variables are also called:

a. constants

b. instance constants

c. free variables

d. none of the above

5. The keyword `this`:

a. is invalid

b. refers to the class and all of its static values

c. refers to the instance attributes

d. refers to the instance whose method is executing

6. The NumberFormat and DecimalFormat classes are members of which package:

a. java.text

b. java.lang

c. java.system

d. java.format

7. An escape sequence:

a. consists of a backward slash "\" followed by other characters

b. consists of a forward slash "/" followed by other characters

c. consists of an asterisk "*" followed by other characters

d. none of the above

8. A method's signature is:

   a. its name

   b. its header

   c. its name and parameter list

   d. its arguments

9. An overloaded method:

   a. cannot be invoked

   b. is a method with too many statements

   c. has the same parameter list as another method, but a different name

   d. has the same name as another method, but a different parameter list

10. Which of the following can be overloaded?

   a. a constructor

   b. accessor methods

   c. custom methods

   d. all of the above

11. An exception is:

   a. an instance

   b. an attribute

   c. a method

   d. none of the above

12. The keyword `throws`:

   a. sends an exception to the invoking method

   b. must be in the header of a method sending an exception

   c. is used together with the keyword `return`

   d. is invalid

13. A method that can receive an exception:

   a. will generally terminate

   b. must catch the exception using a catch block

   c. both a and b

   d. neither a nor b

6

14. A finally block:

   a. is part of a switch

   b. will always be executed

   c. will be executed only if an exception is detected

   d. is invalid—the keyword is final

15. The NumberFormat class is used to:

   a. concatenate data

   b. change the data types of variables

   c. format numerical data

   d. There is no such class.

Discussion Questions

1. In this chapter, the Slip constructor methods invoke setter methods to populate the attributes. What problems are created if instead you write assignment statements in the constructors to populate the attributes?

2. What are the benefits of having the one-parameter constructor invoke the three-parameter constructor? What changes would you need to make to the one-parameter constructor if it did not invoke the three-parameter constructor?

3. What problems would be created if you accidentally made the three Slip attributes static?

4. TesterThree used the single import directive: import java.text.*;
   what benefit might you have by writing two separate imports, one for NumberFormat and a second for DecimalFormat?

   ```
   import java.text.NumberFormat;
   import java.text.DecimalFormat;
   ```

5. Can you replace the following with a *single* statement?

   ```
   NumberFormat currencyFormat = NumberFormat.getCurrencyInstance();
   String feeToDisplay = currencyFormat.format(fee);
   System.out.println("Currency format is: " + feeToDisplay);
   ```

   What are the benefits of doing this? Are there disadvantages?

Projects

1. Assume Bradshaw Marina has added a dock containing 30 slips, all the same size: 12 feet wide and 30 feet long. The ID for the first slip is 1, the second 2, and so forth through 30.

   a. Create a folder on your system named Chapter6Project1.

   b. Locate TesterFive.java and Slip.java on the book's CD in a folder named Chapter6\Example3, and then copy it to the Chapter6Project1 folder you created in Step a.

   c. Change the name TesterFive.java to Project1Tester.java. Remember to change both the file name and the class name in the class header.

   d. Add statements to Project1Tester that will create the 30 Slip instances described above. Place the Slip references into an array.

   e. Add a loop to Project1Tester to invoke tellAboutSelf for all 30 of these new Slip instances.

2. Using Chapter6\Example3 as a guide:

   a. Create a folder on your system named Chapter6Project2.

   b. Locate TesterFive.java and Slip.java on the book's CD in a folder named Chapter6\Example3, and then copy it to the Chapter6Project2 folder you created in Step a.

   c. Change the name TesterFive.java to Project2Tester.java. Remember to change both the file name and the class name in the class header.

   d. Add a nonstatic method named getFormattedFee to Slip. This method will receive no argument, invoke leaseSlip to compute the fee, format the fee as currency, and return a string containing the formatted fee.

   e. Add a second nonstatic method to overload the method you added in Step d. This second method will receive a discount percent as an argument, invoke the second leaseSlip that receives a discount percent argument, format the fee as currency, and return a string containing the formatted fee.

   f. Add statements to Project2Tester that will verify that both of your new methods are working properly.

3. Using Chapter6\Example3 as a guide:

   a. Create a folder on your system named Chapter6Project3.

   b. Locate TesterFive.java and Slip.java on the book's CD in a folder named Chapter6\Example3, and then copy them to the Chapter6Project3 folder you created in Step a.

c. Change the name TesterFive.java to Project3Tester.java. Remember to change both the file name and the class name in the class header.

d. Add a static method named formatFee to Slip. This method will receive a fee as an argument, format the fee as currency, and return a string containing the formatted fee.

e. Add statements to Project3Tester that will verify that your new methods are working properly.

4. Projects 2 and 3 above accomplish the same result. Is one designed better than the other? Why?

Generalization/Specialization and Inheritance

In this chapter you will:

♦ Create generalization/specialization hierarchies by using the **extends** keyword to implement inheritance with problem domain classes

♦ Invoke the superclass constructor when writing a subclass constructor

♦ Use the **abstract** and **final** keywords with Java superclasses

♦ Override superclass methods in subclasses

♦ Learn how polymorphism works with Java subclasses

♦ Learn the implications of **protected** and **private** access in superclasses

In Chapters 5 and 6, you learned how to create and test Java problem domain classes, and you created two problem domain classes for Bradshaw Marina: Customer and Slip. Recall that the Bradshaw Marina case presented in Chapter 4 showed a generalization/specialization hierarchy for types of boats. This chapter shows how to create the superclass Boat and then create and test two subclasses that inherit attributes and methods of Boat—Sailboat and Powerboat.

Inheritance is a powerful mechanism in object-oriented programming because it lets you easily extend an existing class to simplify development and testing and to facilitate reuse. When you use inheritance, you work with the Java keyword **extends** to extend a superclass.

Once you implement the superclass Boat and the subclasses Sailboat and Powerboat, you can demonstrate polymorphism by having sailboat instances and powerboat instances respond to the tellAboutSelf method in their own way. This can be accomplished by overriding superclass methods with new methods in subclasses that have the same signature as the method in the superclass.

Other Java programming concepts that apply to inheritance are also demonstrated in this chapter, including the keywords and concepts of **abstract** classes, **final** classes, and **protected** access.

IMPLEMENTING THE BOAT GENERALIZATION/SPECIALIZATION HIERARCHY

In Chapter 4, you included the Boat class on the class diagram for Bradshaw Marina because Bradshaw needs to store information about all boats in the marina, including values for attributes such as a boat's state registration number, length, manufacturer, and model year. Figure 7-1 shows the Boat class from the Bradshaw Marina class diagram. The Java source code for the Boat class is shown in Figure 7-2.

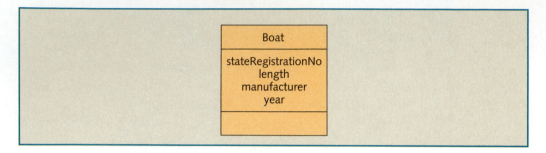

Figure 7-1   The Boat class

```java
// Boat -- an initial Boat class (not abstract)

public class Boat
{
    // attributes
    private String stateRegistrationNo;
    private double length;
    private String manufacturer;
    private int year;

    // constructor
    public Boat(String aStateRegistrationNo, double aLength,
                String aManufacturer, int aYear)
    {
        setStateRegistrationNo(aStateRegistrationNo);
        setLength(aLength);
        setManufacturer(aManufacturer);
        setYear(aYear);
    }

    // set accessor methods
    public void setStateRegistrationNo(String aStateRegistrationNo)
        { stateRegistrationNo = aStateRegistrationNo; }
    public void setLength(double aLength)
        { length = aLength; }
    public void setManufacturer(String aManufacturer)
        { manufacturer = aManufacturer; }
```

```
public void setYear(int aYear)
   {  year = aYear; }

// get accessor methods
public String getStateRegistrationNo()
   {  return stateRegistrationNo; }
public double getLength()
   {  return length; }
public String getManufacturer()
   {  return manufacturer; }
public int getYear()
   {  return year; }
}
```

Figure 7-2   Initial Boat class definition

You write the Boat class header and the four boat attributes as follows:

```
public class Boat
{
   // attributes
   private String stateRegistrationNo;
   private double length;
   private String manufacturer;
   private int year;
```

The Boat class constructor accepts values for all four attributes:

```
// constructor
public Boat(String aStateRegistrationNo, double aLength,
            String aManufacturer, int aYear)
```

The Boat class includes eight standard accessor methods: four setter methods and four getter methods. The constructor invokes the four setter accessor methods as in previous examples. Note that the accessor methods do not include validation in this example to keep it brief (you will add validation in Hands–on Exercise 1).

Testing the Boat Superclass

Figure 7-3 shows a tester program named TesterOne to test the Boat class. It creates three boat instances, and then retrieves information about each boat. The output for TesterOne is shown in Figure 7-4.

```java
// TesterOne to test initial Boat class (not abstract)

public class TesterOne
{
    public static void main(String args[])
    {
    // create three boats
    Boat firstBoat = new Boat("MO34561", 28, "Tartan", 1998);
    Boat secondBoat = new Boat("MO45678", 27, "S2 Yachts", 1994);
    Boat thirdBoat = new Boat("MO56789", 30, "Catalina", 2001);

    // retrieve information about the boats
    System.out.println("Boat 1 information is: "
        + firstBoat.getStateRegistrationNo() + " "
        + firstBoat.getLength() + " "
        + firstBoat.getManufacturer() + " "
        + firstBoat.getYear());

    System.out.println("Boat 2 information is: "
        + secondBoat.getStateRegistrationNo() + " "
        + secondBoat.getLength() + " "
        + secondBoat.getManufacturer() + " "
        + secondBoat.getYear());

    System.out.println("Boat 3 information is: "
        + thirdBoat.getStateRegistrationNo() + " "
        + thirdBoat.getLength() + " "
        + thirdBoat.getManufacturer() + " "
        + thirdBoat.getYear());
    }
}
```

Figure 7-3   TesterOne to test initial Boat class

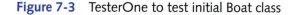

Boat 1 information is: MO34561 28.0 Tartan 1998
Boat 2 information is: MO45678 27.0 S2 Yachts 1994
Boat 3 information is: MO56789 30.0 Catalina 2001

Figure 7-4   TesterOne output

Information about each boat is retrieved by TesterOne using standard accessor methods. The sequence diagram that shows how the tester program interacts with Boat is shown in Figure 7–5. Note that the sequence diagram shows only one instance created by TesterOne. Boat is now ready to use as a superclass.

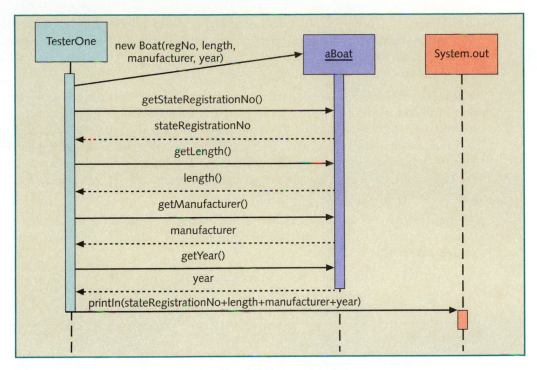

Figure 7-5 Sequence diagram for TesterOne

Hands-on Exercise 1

1. Locate Boat.java and TesterOne on the book's CD in the folder named Example1 in Chapter7, and then compile it and run it using the software suggested by your instructor.

2. Note that there is no validation for the setter methods. Add reasonable validation statements in each setter method. For example, registration number should be at least seven characters, manufacturer should be at least two characters, year should be between 1950 and 2003, and length should be between 10 and 100. If the value is not valid, set the value to a default value. No exceptions are required. Write a tester program that creates boats with invalid values to test that the validation sets values to defaults as planned.

Using the Extends Keyword to Create the Sailboat Subclass

The class diagram for the Bradshaw Marina system shows that there are special types of boats, and each special type of boat has attributes that all boats share plus additional attributes. For example, a sailboat has a keel depth (sometimes called draft), a number of sails, and a motor type (none, inboard, or outboard). A powerboat does not have sails and its keel depth is unimportant. However, a powerboat might have several engines, and you should know the number of engines and their fuel type (gas or diesel). The generalization/specialization hierarchy from the Bradshaw Marina class diagram that shows special types of boats is reproduced in Figure 7-6.

Recall that a generalization/specialization hierarchy means that a general superclass includes attributes and methods that are shared by specialized subclasses. Instances of the subclasses inherit the attributes and methods of the superclass, and they include additional attributes and methods. The Boat class, with four attributes and eight accessor methods, is the superclass. Sailboat, with three additional attributes, and Powerboat, with two additional attributes, are two subclasses. Recall that the triangle symbol pointing to the Boat class in Figure 7-6 means Boat is the superclass on the class diagram.

To implement a subclass with Java, use the **extends** keyword in the class header to indicate which class the new class is extending. For example, to define the Sailboat class as a subclass of Boat, the header would be:

```
public class Sailboat extends Boat
```

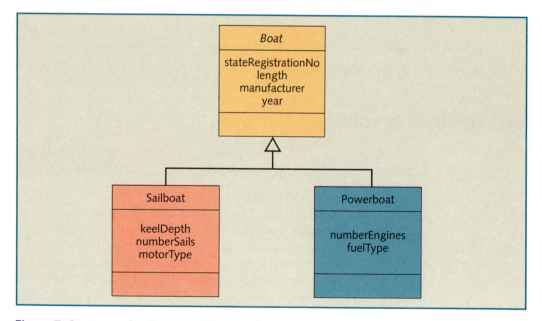

Figure 7-6 Generalization/specialization hierarchy for Boat classes

The rest of the class definition would include any attributes and any methods *in addition to* those inherited from the superclass. You do not have to list or define the inherited attributes or methods in the subclass. For example, you add the additional attributes to the Sailboat class as follows:

```
// additional attributes beyond those inherited from Boat
private double keelDepth;
private int noSails;
private String motorType;
```

The Sailboat class includes six accessor methods, two for each additional attribute. The Java source code for the Sailboat class is shown in Figure 7-7. As with any public class, the source code for the Sailboat class is included in a separate file with the same name as the class. It is not included in the Boat source code file.

```
// Sailboat -- A subclass of abstract class Boat

public class Sailboat extends Boat
{
    // additional attributes beyond those inherited from Boat
    private double keelDepth;
    private int noSails;
    private String motorType;

    // constructor
    public Sailboat(String aStateRegistrationNo, double aLength,
                    String aManufacturer, int aYear, double aKeelDepth,
                    int aNoSails, String aMotorType)
    {
        // invoke super class constructor
        super(aStateRegistrationNo, aLength, aManufacturer, aYear);

        // set subclass attribute values
        setKeelDepth(aKeelDepth);
        setNoSails(aNoSails);
        setMotorType(aMotorType);
    }

    // set accessor methods
    public void setKeelDepth(double aKeelDepth)
    {   keelDepth = aKeelDepth; }
    public void setNoSails(int aNoSails)
    {   noSails = aNoSails; }
    public void setMotorType(String aMotorType)
    {   motorType = aMotorType; }
```

```
// get accessor methods
public double getKeelDepth()
{   return keelDepth; }
public int getNoSails()
{   return noSails; }
public String getMotorType()
{   return motorType; }
}
```

Figure 7-7   Sailboat class definition

You can write one or more constructors for the subclass. The constructor shown in Figure 7-7 accepts seven parameters, four for the attributes defined in the Boat superclass and three additional attributes for those defined in the Sailboat subclass:

```
// constructor
public Sailboat(String aStateRegistrationNo, double aLength,
                String aManufacturer, int aYear, double
                aKeelDepth,
                int aNoSails, String aMotorType)
```

The Sailboat constructor uses the **super** keyword to invoke the constructor of the Boat superclass, passing it the four arguments the Boat class expects: registration number, length, manufacturer, and year. This way, the Boat constructor can complete any processing it provides to populate its private attributes. If the superclass constructor is not explicitly invoked by the subclass, the superclass default constructor is automatically invoked. Be careful, though, because if the superclass has a parameterized constructor that replaces the default constructor and the parameterized constructor is *not explicitly invoked* by the subclass constructor, an error will occur. Invoking the superclass constructor must be the first statement in the subclass constructor. This statement must use the **super** keyword like a method name, with arguments passed to the superclass in parentheses:

```
// invoke super class constructor
super(aStateRegistrationNo, aLength, aManufacturer, aYear);
```

When the Boat constructor is finished executing, control returns to the Sailboat constructor where the three remaining attribute values are set using the Sailboat set accessor methods:

```
// set subclass attribute values
setKeelDepth(aKeelDepth);
setNoSails(aNoSails);
setMotorType(aMotorType);
```

When the Sailboat constructor executes, it creates a Sailboat instance that has 14 standard accessor methods and values for seven attributes. A tester program can create one or more sailboat instances and invoke any of the 14 methods, and the tester program does not need to worry about whether inheritance is involved. Each Sailboat instance behaves as one unit that encapsulates attribute values and methods. The tester program does not need to know structure of the original generalization/specialization hierarchy to use the Sailboat class.

Inheritance is a powerful technique because you as programmer do not need to know how the Boat class is written to extend it. You do not need access to the source code. As with any class in Java, you only need the constructor signature and any required method signatures. Then you can extend the class as required.

Testing the Sailboat Subclass

A tester program is shown in Figure 7-8 with the output in Figure 7-9. Three Sailboat references and three Sailboat instances are created with seven arguments each—the registration number, length, manufacturer, model year, keel depth, number of sails, and motor type:

```java
// create three sailboats (7 arguments)
Sailboat firstBoat = new Sailboat("MO34561", 28, "Tartan",
                        1998, 4.11, 2, "Inboard Diesel");
Sailboat secondBoat = new Sailboat("MO45678", 27, "S2 Yachts",
                        1994, 3.9, 4,"Outboard Gas");
Sailboat thirdBoat = new Sailboat("MO56789", 30, "Catalina",
                        2001, 5.5, 3,"Inboard Diesel");
```

```java
// TesterTwoA -- to test Sailboat subclass

public class TesterTwoA
{
    public static void main(String args[])
    {

    // create three sailboats (7 arguments)
    Sailboat firstBoat = new Sailboat("MO34561", 28, "Tartan",
                            1998, 4.11, 2, "Inboard Diesel");
    Sailboat secondBoat = new Sailboat("MO45678", 27, "S2 Yachts",
                            1994, 3.9, 4, "Outboard Gas");
    Sailboat thirdBoat = new Sailboat("MO56789", 30, "Catalina",
                            2001, 5.5, 3, "Inboard Diesel");

    // retrieve information about the sailboats
    System.out.println("Boat 1 information is: "
        + firstBoat.getStateRegistrationNo() + " "
        + firstBoat.getLength() + " "
        + firstBoat.getManufacturer() + " "
        + firstBoat.getYear() + " "
        + firstBoat.getKeelDepth() + " "
        + firstBoat.getNoSails() + " "
        + firstBoat.getMotorType());

    System.out.println("Boat 2 information is: "
        + secondBoat.getStateRegistrationNo() + " "
        + secondBoat.getLength() + " "
        + secondBoat.getManufacturer() + " "
        + secondBoat.getYear() + " "
        + secondBoat.getKeelDepth() + " "
        + secondBoat.getNoSails() + " "
        + secondBoat.getMotorType());
```

7

```
        System.out.println("Boat 3 information is: "
          + thirdBoat.getStateRegistrationNo() + " "
          + thirdBoat.getLength() + " "
          + thirdBoat.getManufacturer() + " "
          + thirdBoat.getYear() + " "
          + thirdBoat.getKeelDepth() + " "
          + thirdBoat.getNoSails() + " "
          + thirdBoat.getMotorType());
    }
}
```

Figure 7-8   TesterTwoA to test Sailboat class

Boat 1 information is: MO34561 28.0 Tartan 1998 4.11 2 Inboard Diesel

Boat 2 information is: MO45678 27.0 S2 Yachts 1994 3.9 4 Outboard Gas

Boat 3 information is: MO56789 30.0 Catalina 2001 5.5 3 Inboard Diesel

Figure 7-9   TesterTwoA output

The sequence diagram for TesterTwoA is shown in Figure 7-10.

After you create the sailboat instances, you can use any of the getter methods to get information about the sailboats; it does not matter if the method is in Boat or in Sailboat. To get information about the sailboat referenced by firstBoat, the following statements are included:

```
        // retrieve information about the sailboats
        System.out.println("Boat 1 information is: "
          + firstBoat.getStateRegistrationNo() + " "
          + firstBoat.getLength() + " "
          + firstBoat.getManufacturer() + " "
          + firstBoat.getYear() + " "
          + firstBoat.getKeelDepth() + " "
          + firstBoat.getNoSails() + " "
          + firstBoat.getMotorType());
```

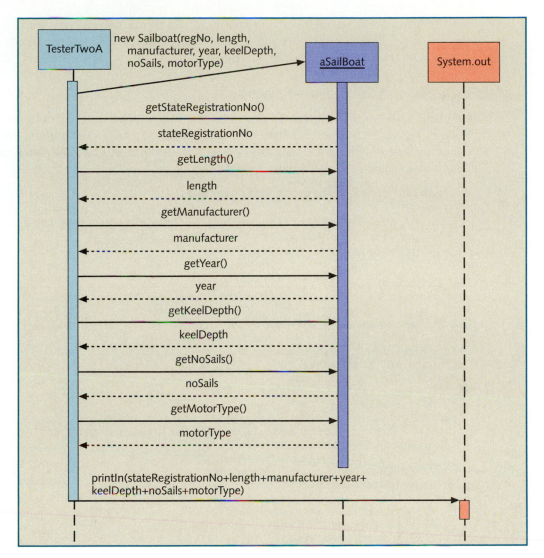

Figure 7-10   Sequence diagram for TesterTwoA

Hands-on Exercise 2A

1. Locate Boat.java, Sailboat.java, and TesterTwoA.java on the book's CD in the folder named Example2 in Chapter7, and then compile and run them using the software suggested by your instructor.

2. Copy the Boat.java source code file you created for Hands-on Exercise 1 to replace Boat.java in Example2, and then compile it. Recompile Sailboat.java and TesterTwoA.java, and then run TesterTwoA to verify that it still works correctly with all of the changes you made to the Boat class.

3. Write a tester program called TesterTwoC.java that creates sailboats with invalid values similar to the tester you wrote in Hands-on Exercise 1 to test that the validation sets values to defaults as planned.

Adding a Second Subclass—Powerboat

Powerboat is the second subclass of Boat. The Java source code for the Powerboat class is shown in Figure 7-11. Note that Powerboat also extends the Boat class, and the Powerboat class can be added without affecting the Sailboat class or the Boat class. The class header and definition of attributes for Powerboat are as follows:

```java
public class Powerboat extends Boat
{
    // additional attributes beyond those inherited from Boat
    private int noEngines;
    private String fuelType;
```

```java
// Powerboat -- a subclass of abstract class Boat

public class Powerboat extends Boat
{
    // additional attributes beyond those inherited from Boat
    private int noEngines;
    private String fuelType;

    // constructor
    public Powerboat(String aStateRegistrationNo, double aLength,
                    String aManufacturer, int aYear, int aNoEngines,
                    String aFuelType)
    {
        // invoke super class constructor
        super(aStateRegistrationNo, aLength, aManufacturer, aYear);

        // set subclass attribute values
        setNoEngines(aNoEngines);
        setFuelType(aFuelType);
    }

    // set accessor methods
    public void setNoEngines(int aNoEngines)
    {   noEngines = aNoEngines; }
    public void setFuelType(String aFuelType)
    {   fuelType = aFuelType; }

    // get accessor methods
    public int getNoEngines()
    {   return noEngines; }
    public String getFuelType()
    {   return fuelType; }
}
```

Figure 7-11   Powerboat class definition

The constructor for Powerboat expects six parameters, four required by Boat plus two additional attributes for Powerboat. Similar to the Sailboat constructor, the Powerboat constructor also invokes the superclass constructor, passing the four arguments expected by the Boat class. Then the two remaining attributes are assigned using the setter methods of Powerboat:

```java
// constructor
public Powerboat(String aStateRegistrationNo, double aLength,
                 String aManufacturer, int aYear, int aNoEngines,
                 String aFuelType)
{
    // invoke super class constructor
    super(aStateRegistrationNo, aLength, aManufacturer, aYear);

    // set subclass attribute values
    setNoEngines(aNoEngines);
    setFuelType(aFuelType);
}
```

Now that you have created two subclasses of Boat, you can use both classes as needed. For example, a tester program can create a few sailboats and a few powerboats, and get back information from any of the boats. Figure 7-12 shows the tester program named TesterTwoB that creates both types of boats. The output for the tester program is shown in Figure 7-13, and the sequence diagram is shown in Figure 7-14. The Java code in the tester program that creates the four boats is as follows:

```java
// create two sailboats (7 arguments)
Sailboat firstBoat = new Sailboat("MO34561", 28, "Tartan",
                         1998, 4.11, 2, "Inboard Diesel");
Sailboat secondBoat = new Sailboat("MO45678", 27, "S2 Yachts",
                         1994, 3.9, 4, "Outboard Gas");

// create two powerboats (6 arguments)
Powerboat thirdBoat = new Powerboat("MO67891", 30, "Bayliner",
                         2001, 2, "Gas");
Powerboat fourthBoat = new Powerboat("MO78910", 27,
                         "Slickcraft", 1995, 1, "Gas");
```

```java
// TesterTwoB -- to test both Sailboat and Powerboat subclasses

public class TesterTwoB
{
    public static void main(String args[])
    {
    // create two sailboats (7 arguments)
    Sailboat firstBoat = new Sailboat("MO34561", 28, "Tartan",
                             1998, 4.11, 2, "Inboard Diesel");
    Sailboat secondBoat = new Sailboat("MO45678", 27, "S2 Yachts",
                             1994, 3.9, 4,"Outboard Gas");
```

7

```
// create two powerboats (6 arguments)
Powerboat thirdBoat = new Powerboat("MO67891", 30, "Bayliner",
                        2001, 2, "Gas");
Powerboat fourthBoat = new Powerboat("MO78910", 27, "Slickcraft",
                        1995, 1, "Gas");

// get information about two sailboats (7 attributes)
System.out.println("This boat is a " + firstBoat.toString()
    + firstBoat.getStateRegistrationNo() + " "
    + firstBoat.getLength() + " "
    + firstBoat.getManufacturer() + " "
    + firstBoat.getYear() + " "
    + firstBoat.getKeelDepth() + " "
    + firstBoat.getNoSails() + " "
    + firstBoat.getMotorType());

System.out.println("This boat is a " + secondBoat.toString()
    + secondBoat.getStateRegistrationNo() + " "
    + secondBoat.getLength() + " "
    + secondBoat.getManufacturer() + " "
    + secondBoat.getYear() + " "
    + secondBoat.getKeelDepth() + " "
    + secondBoat.getNoSails() + " "
    + secondBoat.getMotorType());

// get information about two powerboats (six attributes)
System.out.println("This boat is a " + thirdBoat.toString()
    + thirdBoat.getStateRegistrationNo() + " "
    + thirdBoat.getLength() + " "
    + thirdBoat.getManufacturer() + " "
    + thirdBoat.getYear() + " "
    + thirdBoat.getNoEngines() + " "
    + thirdBoat.getFuelType());

System.out.println("This boat is a " + fourthBoat.toString()
    + fourthBoat.getStateRegistrationNo() + " "
    + fourthBoat.getLength() + " "
    + fourthBoat.getManufacturer() + " "
    + fourthBoat.getYear() + " "
    + fourthBoat.getNoEngines() + " "
    + fourthBoat.getFuelType());
    }
}
```

Figure 7-12   TesterTwoB to test both Sailboat and Powerboat

This boat is a Sailboat@256a7cMO34561 28.0 Tartan 1998 4.11 2 Inboard Diesel
This boat is a Sailboat@310d42MO45678 27.0 S2 Yachts 1994 3.9 4 Outboard Gas
This boat is a Powerboat@5d87b2MO67891 30.0 Bayliner 2001 2 Gas
This boat is a Powerboat@77d134MO78910 27.0 Slickcraft 1995 1 Gas

Figure 7-13 TesterTwoB output

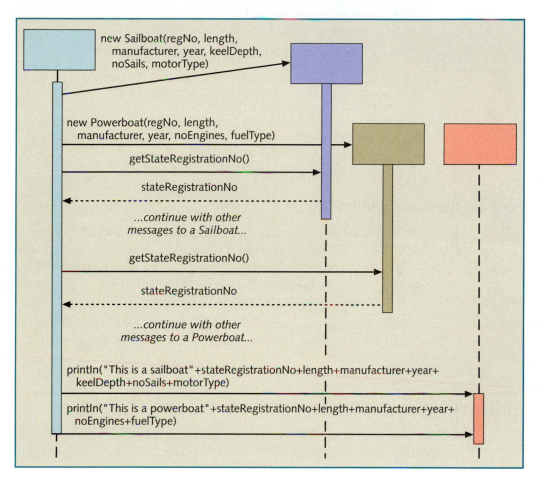

Figure 7-14 Sequence diagram for TesterTwoB

Once the boats are created, you can invoke the four getter methods inherited from the Boat class for either the sailboats or the powerboats. However, the sailboats have three additional getter methods that powerboats do not have. Powerboats have two additional getter methods that sailboats do not have. The toString method is used here to return the name of the class. Getting information about the first boat (a sailboat) uses all seven getter methods encapsulated in Sailboat:

```
System.out.println("This boat is a " + firstBoat.toString()
    + firstBoat.getStateRegistrationNo() + " "
    + firstBoat.getLength() + " "
    + firstBoat.getManufacturer() + " "
    + firstBoat.getYear() + " "
    + firstBoat.getKeelDepth() + " "
    + firstBoat.getNoSails() + " "
    + firstBoat.getMotorType());
```

Getting information about the third boat (a powerboat) uses six methods:

```
System.out.println("This boat is a " + thirdBoat.toString()
    + thirdBoat.getStateRegistrationNo() + " "
    + thirdBoat.getLength() + " "
    + thirdBoat.getManufacturer() + " "
    + thirdBoat.getYear() + " "
    + thirdBoat.getNoEngines() + " "
    + thirdBoat.getFuelType());
```

Hands-on Exercise 2B

1. Locate Powerboat.java and TesterTwoB.java on the book's CD in the folder named Example2 in Chapter7, and then compile them using the software suggested by your instructor. Note that you need the compiled Boat (the one you modified to include simple validation) to compile Powerboat.java. You need the compiled Sailboat to compile and run TesterTwoB.java.

2. Modify the tester program you wrote for Hands-on Exercise 2A to test the validation inherited from Boat by Sailboat and by Powerboat. Name the file TesterTwoD.java.

UNDERSTANDING ABSTRACT AND FINAL CLASSES

The Boat and Sailboat examples earlier demonstrated the Boat class, the Sailboat class, and the Powerboat class. First, Boat instances were created, and then Sailboat and Powerboat instances were created. These are all examples of **concrete classes**—classes that can be instantiated. Notice that a concrete class can have subclasses.

Using Abstract Classes

You can create a class that is not intended to be instantiated. Instead, the class is only used to extend into subclasses. This is called an *abstract* class, as discussed in Chapter 4. For example, Bradshaw Marina only leases slips for sailboats and powerboats, and a boat must be one type or the other. Boat instances alone will never be created (except to be tested, as in Hands-on Exercise 1). On the class diagram, an abstract class is shown with its class name in italics.

The **abstract** keyword is used in the class header to declare an abstract class with Java. To make the Boat class abstract, the header would read:

> **public abstract class** Boat

The Sailboat and Powerboat classes can extend the Boat exactly as above. But if the Boat class is abstract, the tester program that creates boats (refer to TesterOne, shown earlier in Figure 7-3) would not run correctly. Instead, the Boat class would throw an InstantiationError exception. Therefore, never try to instantiate an abstract class; always extend it and then instantiate the subclass. The benefit of having the Boat superclass is that different types of boats can extend it; you do not have to rewrite code common to all boats. Use abstract classes to facilitate reuse.

Using Final Classes

The previous examples show that classes are easy to extend, and that you do not need to have the source code for a class to extend it. Sometimes a class is created that should *not* be extended. For example, consider a class in a payroll program named Paycheck. The Paycheck class might have a method for calculating the pay amount. If the Paycheck class could be extended, you could add a method that changes the amount of the paycheck, bypassing validation and other controls that have been designed into the payroll system. Therefore, it might be desirable for security purposes to restrict the ability to extend a class.

The **final** keyword is used to declare that a class cannot be extended. For example, if Bradshaw Marina did not want the Powerboat class to be extended, the class header would be:

> **public final class** Powerboat

Many of the Java core classes are final and cannot be extended, including wrapper classes such as Integer, Double, and Boolean. The String class is also final. When a class is final, performance is improved because the JVM does not have to look for subclass methods that might override superclass methods at run time. The JVM knows that final classes do not have subclasses.

Recall that the **final** keyword is also used to declare constants with values that cannot be changed. Methods can also be declared final so they cannot be overridden by a subclass. So the keyword **final** simply means "cannot be changed."

Hands-on Exercise 2C

1. Return to the original Boat class and TesterOne in Hands-on Exercise 1. Change the Boat class so it is abstract and recompile it. Run TesterOne. What happens?

2. Return to the Boat, Sailboat, and Powerboat classes, and TesterTwoA and TesterTwoB in Hands-on Exercises 2A and 2B. Change the Boat class so it is abstract and recompile all files. What happens when you run TesterTwoA and TesterTwoB?

3. Again return to the Boat, Sailboat, and Powerboat classes in Hands-on Exercises 2A and 2B. Change the Boat class to final and recompile all files. What happens?

OVERRIDING A SUPERCLASS METHOD

A powerful capability of a subclass is to override a method contained in its superclass. **Method overriding** occurs when the method in the subclass will be invoked instead of the method in the superclass if both methods have the same signature. Recall that a method's signature consists of its name, return type, and parameter list. For example, the signature of the Sailboat method setNoSails with one **int** parameter is:

```
void setNoSails(int)
```

Overriding a method allows the subclass not only to extend the superclass but also to modify the behavior of the superclass. Method overriding is different from method overloading (discussed in Chapter 6). Overloading means that two or more methods in the same class have the same name but a different return type or parameter list. Overriding means methods in both the superclass and the subclass have the same signature (the same name, return type, and parameter list).

Adding and Overriding the tellAboutSelf Method

You can use method overriding by adding a tellAboutSelf method to the Boat class and then overriding it in the Sailboat class. The tellAboutSelf method was shown as a custom method added to the Slip class in Chapter 6. You can add a tellAboutSelf method to classes to make it easier to get information about an instance of the class, including the Boat class. You can then override the Boat method in the Sailboat class to allow the Sailboat class to tell about itself in its own way. The tellAboutSelf method for Boat is coded as follows, shown completely in Figure 7–15:

```
public String tellAboutSelf()
{
   // returns values of attributes as one string (Boat class)
   String boatDetails;
   boatDetails = " "
   + stateRegistrationNo + " "
   + length + " "
   + manufacturer + " "
   + year;
   return boatDetails;
}
```

```
// Boat -- abstract Boat class with tellAboutSelf method

public abstract class Boat
{
    // attributes
    private String stateRegistrationNo;
    private double length;
    private String manufacturer;
    private int year;

    // constructor
    public Boat(String aStateRegistrationNo, double aLength,
                String aManufacturer, int aYear)
    {
        setStateRegistrationNo(aStateRegistrationNo);
        setLength(aLength);
        setManufacturer(aManufacturer);
        setYear(aYear);
    }

    // custom method
    public String tellAboutSelf()
    {
        // returns values of attributes as one string
        String boatDetails;
        boatDetails = " "
        + stateRegistrationNo + " "
        + length + " "
        + manufacturer + " "
        + year;
        return boatDetails;
    }

    // set accessor methods
    public void setStateRegistrationNo(String aStateRegistrationNo)
        {  stateRegistrationNo = aStateRegistrationNo; }
    public void setLength(double aLength)
        {  length = aLength; }
    public void setManufacturer(String aManufacturer)
        {  manufacturer = aManufacturer; }
    public void setYear(int aYear)
        {  year = aYear; }

    // get accessor methods
    public String getStateRegistrationNo()
        {  return stateRegistrationNo; }
    public double getLength()
        {  return length; }
    public String getManufacturer()
        {  return manufacturer; }
    public int getYear()
        {  return year; }
}
```

Figure 7-15 Abstract Boat class with tellAboutSelf method

If the Boat class is a concrete class, the tellAboutSelf method would return information about the registration number, length, manufacturer, and model year of the boat. If Boat has a Sailboat subclass, the tellAboutSelf method defined in the Boat class would return the first four attributes of the sailboat. But how can you find the other sailboat details?

Overriding the method is accomplished by using the same tellAboutSelf method signature in the subclass Sailboat. The statements in the subclass method control what the system does when a sailboat is asked to tell about itself. The superclass method in Boat is ignored (overridden). The tellAboutSelf method written for Sailboat, shown in Figure 7-16, is written as follows:

```
// custom method overrides superclass method
    public String tellAboutSelf()
    {
        // invokes four superclass get methods
        String allDetails;
        allDetails = "This is a sailboat "
        + getStateRegistrationNo() + " "    // invoke Boat method
        + getLength() + " "                 // invoke Boat method
        + getManufacturer() + " "           // invoke Boat method
        + getYear() + " "                   // invoke Boat method
        + keelDepth + " "
        + noSails + " "
        + motorType;
        return allDetails;
    }
```

```
// Sailboat -- a subclass of abstract class Boat that
// overrides tellAboutSelf method in superclass

public class Sailboat extends Boat
{
    // additional attributes beyond those inherited from Boat
    private double keelDepth;
    private int noSails;
    private String motorType;

    // constructor
    public Sailboat(String aStateRegistrationNo, double aLength,
                String aManufacturer, int aYear, double aKeelDepth,
                int aNoSails, String aMotorType)
    {
        // invoke super class constructor
        super(aStateRegistrationNo, aLength, aManufacturer, aYear);

        // set subclass attribute values
        setKeelDepth(aKeelDepth);
        setNoSails(aNoSails);
        setMotorType(aMotorType);
    }
```

```
        // custom method overrides superclass method
        public String tellAboutSelf()
        {
            // invokes four superclass get methods
            String allDetails;
            allDetails = "This is a sailboat "
            + getStateRegistrationNo() + " "      // invoke Boat method
            + getLength() + " "                    // invoke Boat method
            + getManufacturer() + " "              // invoke Boat method
            + getYear() + " "                      // invoke Boat method
            + keelDepth + " "
            + noSails + " "
            + motorType;
            return allDetails;
        }
        // set accessor methods
        public void setKeelDepth(double aKeelDepth)
        {   keelDepth = aKeelDepth; }
        public void setNoSails(int aNoSails)
        {   noSails = aNoSails; }
        public void setMotorType(String aMotorType)
        {   motorType = aMotorType; }

        // get accessor methods
        public double getKeelDepth()
        {   return keelDepth; }
        public int getNoSails()
        {   return noSails; }
        public String getMotorType()
        {   return motorType; }
}
```

Figure 7-16   Sailboat class that overrides the tellAboutSelf method

TesterThreeA in Figure 7-17 shows how to test the tellAboutSelf method. Two sailboats are created. Then output is produced by asking each instance to tell about itself, shown in Figure 7-18.

```
// TesterThreeA -- demonstrates overriding using tellAboutSelf()
// method for Sailboat

public class TesterThreeA
{
    public static void main(String args[])
    {
    // create two sailboats (7 arguments)
    Sailboat firstBoat = new Sailboat("MO34561", 28, "Tartan",
                        1998, 4.11, 2, "Inboard Diesel");
    Sailboat secondBoat = new Sailboat("MO45678", 27, "S2 Yachts",
                        1994, 3.9, 4, "Outboard Gas");
```

```
        // get information about sailboats using tellAboutSelf method
        System.out.println(firstBoat.tellAboutSelf());
        System.out.println(secondBoat.tellAboutSelf());
    }
}
```

Figure 7-17   TesterThreeA to test tellAboutSelf method

This is a sailboat MO34561 28.0 Tartan 1998 4.11 2 Inboard Diesel
This is a sailboat MO45678 27.0 S2 Yachts 1994 3.9 4 Outboard Gas

Figure 7-18   TesterThreeA output

Hands-on Exercise 3A

1. Locate Boat.java, Sailboat.java, and TesterThreeA.java on the book's CD in the folder named Example3 in Chapter7, and then compile it and run it using the software suggested by your instructor.

2. Add a new subclass of Sailboat named CruisingSailboat with a constructor and accessor methods. One additional attribute of CruisingSailboat stores the name of the life raft manufacturer. Include a tellAboutSelf method that overrides the Sailboat method and provides information on all attributes of CruisingSailboat. Write a tester program based on TesterThreeA to verify.

3. You probably had to copy and paste code from Sailboat to CruisingSailboat. Does this sound like a good idea from a maintenance perspective? Explain. See the next section for a solution.

Overriding and Invoking a Superclass Method

Sometimes you might want to override a method by extending what the method does. For example, the Boat tellAboutSelf method already includes statements that return values for four attributes all boats have. The Sailboat tellAboutSelf method replicates this code when it overrides the method.

Figure 7-19 shows another way to override the tellAboutSelf method, demonstrated in the Powerboat class. When the Powerboat tellAboutSelf method is used, it invokes the superclass method using the **super** keyword like an object reference, using the "object reference *dot* method name" syntax. For example, in the statement **super.tellAboutSelf()**, **super** refers to the superclass and tellAboutSelf is the superclass method invoked. That way the statements in the superclass method are executed first, returning information to the subclass method. Then the subclass method continues executing statements specific to the sailboat. The returned allDetails string will contain information about all six of the Powerboat attributes:

```
// custom method overrides but invokes superclass method
public String tellAboutSelf()
{
   // invokes superclass method when overriding then adds to it
   String allDetails;
   allDetails = "This is a powerboat "
   + super.tellAboutSelf() + " "
   + noEngines + " "
   + fuelType;
   return allDetails;
}
```

```
// Powerboat -- a subclass of abstract class Boat that
// overrides but also invokes superclass tellAboutSelf method

public class Powerboat extends Boat
{
   // additional attributes beyond those inherited from Boat
   private int noEngines;
   private String fuelType;

   // constructor
   public Powerboat(String aStateRegistrationNo, double aLength,
                String aManufacturer, int aYear, int aNoEngines,
                String aFuelType)
   {
      // invoke super class constructor
      super(aStateRegistrationNo, aLength, aManufacturer, aYear);

      // set subclass attribute values
      setNoEngines(aNoEngines);
      setFuelType(aFuelType);
   }

   // custom method overrides but invokes superclass method
   public String tellAboutSelf()
   {
      // invokes superclass method when overriding then adds to it
      String allDetails;
      allDetails = "This is a powerboat "
      + super.tellAboutSelf() + " "
      + noEngines + " "
      + fuelType;
      return allDetails;
   }
}
```

```
    // set accessor methods
    public void setNoEngines(int aNoEngines)
    {  noEngines = aNoEngines; }
    public void setFuelType(String aFuelType)
    {  fuelType = aFuelType; }

    // get accessor methods
    public int getNoEngines()
    {  return noEngines; }
    public String getFuelType()
    {  return fuelType; }
}
```

Figure 7-19 Powerboat class that overrides and invokes tellAboutSelf method

Testing Two Method-Overriding Approaches

A tester program that demonstrates method overriding in both Sailboat and Powerboat (named TesterThreeB) is shown in Figure 7-20. First, four boats are created. Next, the tellAboutSelf method is invoked for each boat.

```
// TesterThreeB -- demonstrates overriding using tellAboutSelf()
// method with both Sailboat and Powerboat subclasses

public class TesterThreeB
{
    public static void main(String args[])
    {
    // create two sailboats (7 arguments)
    Sailboat firstBoat = new Sailboat("MO34561", 28, "Tartan",
                            1998, 4.11, 2, "Inboard Diesel");
    Sailboat secondBoat = new Sailboat("MO45678", 27, "S2 Yachts",
                            1994, 3.9, 4, "Outboard Gas");

    // create two powerboats (6 arguments)
    Powerboat thirdBoat = new Powerboat("MO67891", 30, "Bayliner",
                            2001, 2, "Gas");
    Powerboat fourthBoat = new Powerboat("MO78910", 27, "Slickcraft",
                            1995, 1, "Gas");

    // get information about sailboats using tellAboutSelf method
    System.out.println(firstBoat.tellAboutSelf());
    System.out.println(secondBoat.tellAboutSelf());

    // get information about powerboats using tellAboutSelf method
    System.out.println(thirdBoat.tellAboutSelf());
    System.out.println(fourthBoat.tellAboutSelf());

    }
}
```

Figure 7-20 TesterThreeB to test two approaches to method overriding

This is a sailboat MO34561 28.0 Tartan 1998 4.11 2 Inboard Diesel
This is a sailboat MO45678 27.0 S2 Yachts 1994 3.9 4 Outboard Gas
This is a powerboat MO67891 30.0 Bayliner 2001 2 Gas
This is a powerboat MO78910 27.0 Slickcraft 1995 1 Gas

Figure 7-21   TesterThreeB output

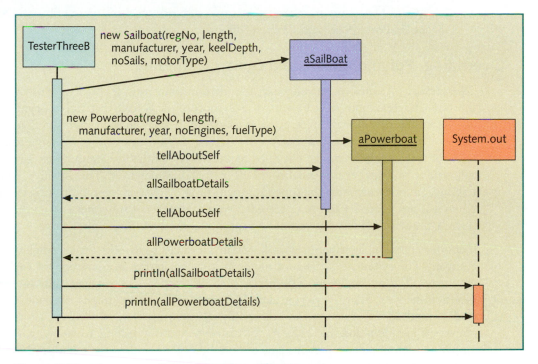

Figure 7-22   Sequence diagram for TesterThreeB

The output produced is shown in Figure 7-21, with all seven attributes listed for the sailboats and all six attributes listed for the powerboats. The sequence diagram for TesterThreeB is shown in Figure 7-22. Note how simple the interaction is now that each boat takes responsibility for telling about itself.

Hands-on Exercise 3B

1. Locate Powerboat.java and TesterThreeB.java on the book's CD in the folder named Example3 in Chapter7. Compile them and run TesterThreeB using the software suggested by your instructor. Note that Boat and Sailboat from Hands-on Exercise 3A must be included for Powerboat to compile and for TesterThreeB to compile and run.

2. Modify Sailboat so its tellAboutSelf method invokes the superclass method, then extends it as done in Powerboat. Run TesterThreeA to verify that the modified Sailboat class works correctly (the tester that tests Sailboat only). Run TesterThreeB to verify that it works correctly with Sailboat and Powerboat.

3. You created a CruisingSailboat class in Hands-on Exercise 3A. Modify it so its tellAboutSelf method invokes its superclass method. Run the tester program you created in Hands-on Exercise 3A to verify that the modified CruisingSailboat class works correctly.

4. Write a tester program that creates two instances of three types of boats—Sailboats, Powerboats, and CruisingSailboats.

Overriding, Polymorphism, and Dynamic Binding

The previous method-overriding example demonstrates one form of polymorphism and shows a clear example of a benefit of polymorphism. Recall that polymorphism means objects of different classes can respond to the same message in their own way. Each subclass has its own way of telling about itself. As long as you know that the superclass has a tellAboutSelf method, you do not need to keep track of the specific subclass involved. You can send a message to the instance asking it to tell about itself. The instance will always respond, either by invoking the superclass method or by overriding it. Processing is simplified when it is not necessary to test to see what type of instance it is before sending the message. Instead, the responsibility for responding appropriately is left to the instance.

Consider an example where a payroll system produces paychecks for all employees in the company. The system uses different methods to calculate the pay amount for each type of employee. If the Employee class has a method named calculatePay, subclasses such as HourlyEmployee, SalaryEmployee, and ManagementEmployee might override the calculatePay method and calculate pay differently. The payroll system needs to go through all employee instances and ask each to calculatePay without having to know what type of employee each instance represents. The responsibility for handling the calculation is delegated to the instance, simplifying the processing required by the system. System maintenance is also simplified, because as new types of employees are added, or as pay calculations are changed for one type of employee, the change does not necessarily affect the rest of the system.

Java uses **dynamic binding** to resolve which method to invoke when the system runs and finds more than one method with the same name in a generalization/specialization hierarchy for a class. Making the decision at run time provides flexibility when adding new subclasses that override superclass methods. For example, if a new type of powerboat is added (perhaps a personal watercraft) with its own tellAboutSelf method, any applications that interact with boats can invoke the new tellAboutSelf method as long as the object reference used was a personal watercraft.

UNDERSTANDING PRIVATE VERSUS PROTECTED ACCESS

The previous Boat class examples include attributes that are all declared as **`private`**, as described in Chapter 5. Private access means no other object can directly read or modify the value of the attribute. Instead, other objects must use the methods of the class to get or set values. This is what encapsulation and information hiding mean. By making the attributes private, you protect the integrity of the values of the attributes. No values can be changed without following validation procedures included in the set accessor methods. Similarly, no values can be retrieved unless a public getter method has been included for the attribute.

Private access also limits the ability of an instance of the subclass to directly access attributes defined by the superclass. This is ordinarily appropriate because any method of the subclass that needs the value of an attribute defined in the superclass can invoke the get accessor method to get the value. Notice the tellAboutSelf method in Sailboat shown earlier in Figure 7-16. The values of the attributes in Boat are accessed using the Boat get accessor methods, as shown again in the following code:

```
// custom method overrides superclass method
  public String tellAboutSelf()
  {
    // invokes four superclass get methods
    String allDetails;
    allDetails = "This is a sailboat "
    + getStateRegistrationNo() + " "     // invoke Boat method
    + getLength() + " "                  // invoke Boat method
    + getManufacturer() + " "            // invoke Boat method
    + getYear() + " "                    // invoke Boat method
    + keelDepth + " "
    + noSails + " "
    + motorType;
    return allDetails;
  }
```

You can declare the attributes of a superclass so they can be accessed directly by methods in the subclass. **Protected access** means that attribute values can be directly accessed by subclasses (as well as by other classes in the package). For example, Boat attributes can be changed to protected access using the **`protected`** keyword:

```
// attributes (changed to protected access)
protected String stateRegistrationNo;
protected double length;
protected String manufacturer;
protected int year;
```

The Sailboat tellAboutSelf method can then be changed to directly access the values of the attributes as follows:

```
// custom method overrides superclass method
public String tellAboutSelf()
{
    // directly access superclass attributes
    // because they are protected rather than private
    String allDetails;
    allDetails = "This is a sailboat "
    + stateRegistrationNo + " "   // direct access Boat attribute
    + length + " "                // direct access Boat attribute
    + manufacturer + " "          // direct access Boat attribute
    + year + " "                  // direct access Boat attribute
    + keelDepth + " "
    + noSails + " "
    + motorType;
    return allDetails;
}
```

Note that the first four attribute values are defined in the Boat class. The last three are defined in the Sailboat class (and remain private rather than protected). A tester program that creates a sailboat using the revised Boat and Sailboat classes and invokes its tellAboutSelf method will work as expected. You will implement and test this example in Hands-on Exercise 3C.

Although you can declare attributes as public using the **public** keyword, meaning that any object can directly access the value, avoid this technique because it violates encapsulation and information hiding. Similarly, you can restrict access to objects in the same package if no access qualifier is included, but you should also avoid this technique. In fact, protected access actually does allow direct access to any class in the same package, as with package access, so use protected access with care. The only real difference between package and protected access applies when a subclass is part of a different package. A protected attribute in the superclass could be accessed by the subclass, but a package access attribute could not.

Note that a String variable named allDetails is declared in the tellAboutSelf method. As discussed in Chapter 2, allDetails is a *local variable* that is accessible only to statements within the method, and it exists only as long as the method is executing. Local variables cannot be protected or public.

You also can declare methods as protected or private. Private methods can only be invoked from a method within the class. Not even subclass methods can invoke a private method of its superclass. Protected methods, however, can be invoked by a method in a subclass.

Hands-on Exercise 3C

1. Return to the Boat.java, Sailboat.java, Powerboat.java, and TesterThreeB.java you completed for Hands-on Exercise 3B. Modify the Sailboat tellAboutSelf method as shown in the previous example so the method directly accesses attribute values of the Boat class. What happens when you try to compile the class?

2. Modify Boat so the attributes are protected rather than private. Compile Boat and recompile Sailboat and Powerboat. Use TesterThreeB to verify that protected access in Boat allows direct access to the values in Sailboat.

Summary

- Generalization/specialization hierarchies show superclasses and subclasses, and subclasses inherit characteristics of the superclass.

- Inheritance in Java allows you to easily create subclasses by extending the capabilities of another class.

- The subclass inherits the attributes and the methods of the superclass.

- In Java, the **extends** keyword is used in the subclass header to indicate the superclass that a subclass extends, as in **public class** `Sailboat extends Boat`.

- The subclass constructor invokes the superclass constructor using the **super** keyword much like a method name with arguments: **super(**`arguments`**)**.

- You can add a subclass to a superclass without affecting other subclasses. A subclass can also have its own subclasses.

- An **abstract** class is a class that is not instantiated. It exists only to serve as a superclass for one or more concrete subclasses that can be instantiated.

- A **final** class is a class that cannot be extended, either for security reasons or for efficiency.

- Method overriding means that a method in a subclass with the same name and signature as a method in the superclass will be invoked in place of the superclass method. A method can override and then invoke the superclass method to extend rather than completely replace the method using the **super** keyword as a reference much like an object reference: **super**`.methodName()`.

- Method overriding in Java allows one form of polymorphism where instances can respond to messages in their own way, without the requester needing to know the subclass of the instance. Dynamic binding allows this flexibility where at run time the decision about what method to invoke is made.

- Private access for attributes means not even subclass methods can directly access the values of the attributes, but **protected** access allows direct access by subclass methods.

7

Key Terms

In the following list, the key terms printed in blue are Java keywords.

abstract	**final**	protected access
concrete class	method overriding	**public**
dynamic binding	**private**	**super**
extends	**protected**	

Review Questions

1. Consider the terms superclass and subclass. In a generalization/specialization hierarchy, which is general and which is special?

2. Explain how inheritance applies in generalization/specialization. What is inherited by the subclass?

3. Sketch an example of how a generalization/specialization hierarchy is shown on a class diagram for a superclass named Car and a subclass named SportsCar.

4. What symbol indicates inheritance between two classes on a class diagram?

5. What Java keyword is used to allow one class to inherit from another class?

6. Write the class header for the SportsCar class that inherits from Car.

7. Write the class header for a class named Car that is abstract.

8. What would happen if your tester program included the statement
   `Car aCar = new Car(aMake, aModel)` if Car is an abstract class?

9. What is the difference between concrete and abstract classes?

10. Where is the statement `super(aValue)` written in a subclass?

11. What happens if you do not specifically invoke the superclass constructor in the subclass constructor?

12. What is the difference between method overloading and method overriding?

13. Explain how method overriding allows polymorphism. Give an example.

14. Assume you have Car and SportsCar classes as described earlier and Car is not abstract. Write statements for a tester program that instantiate one car and one sports car where the constructor of Car accepts make and model as parameters and Sports-Car adds the top speed.

15. Write the statement that would invoke the superclass method after overriding it for a method named calculateFee().

16. What is a final class and what are two reasons for declaring a class final?

17. Write the class header for a class named Paycheck that is abstract.

18. Write the class header for a class named HourlyPaycheck that extends Paycheck and is final.

19. How is a final class similar to final variables and final methods?

20. What is the effect of using protected rather than private access to attributes in a superclass?

Discussion Questions

1. Much is said about the importance of inheritance in object-oriented programming. Discuss several specific ways that inheritance makes OO development easier from the standpoint of the programmer.

2. Some programmers say inheritance is not really that important when modeling problem domain classes for business systems compared to the importance of association relationships between classes. Discuss how generalization/specialization (involving inheritance) is different from association relationships between classes. Debate the following statement: Inheritance is "convenient" while association relationships are "essential" in business systems.

Projects

1. Write an additional subclass for Boat named Rowboat. A few specific attributes might apply to a rowboat, specifically type of material (wood, fiberglass, or inflatable) and oar type (paddles, wood oars, or metal oars). Include accessor methods for the new class, a tellAboutSelf method that overrides then invokes the superclass method, and a tester program that tests the class. Draw a sequence diagram for the tester program.

2. Consider a special type of boat named PersonalWatercraft. Should it be a subclass of Boat or Powerboat? Discuss. Draw the generalization/specialization hierarchy for all types of boats in this chapter based on your decision, including CruisingSailboat and Rowboat discussed previously.

3. Assume PersonalWatercraft is a subclass of Powerboat (this does not imply that it should be for Project 2). What additional attributes might be applicable to Personal-Watercraft? Create the Java class using at least two additional attributes and add accessor methods. Include a parameterized constructor that accepts values for all PersonalWatercraft attributes. Write a tester class to test the new class by instantiating a few personal watercraft and a few powerboats. Explain why Powerboat does not have to be and should not be changed to an abstract class.

4. Considering PersonalWatercraft in Project 3, explain what happens when the PersonalWatercraft constructor invokes the superclass constructor. Trace all statements that are executed from beginning to end by listing them.

5. Add a tellAboutSelf method to the PersonalWatercraft class that overrides then invokes the Powerboat tellAboutSelf method. Explain what happens when the Personal-Watercraft tellAboutSelf method is invoked. Trace all statements that are executed.

Additional Inheritance Concepts and Techniques

In this chapter you will:

- ◆ Learn how to require a subclass to override a superclass method by including an abstract method in the superclass
- ◆ Create a Java interface and use an interface to require a class to implement methods
- ◆ Create and use custom exceptions that provide detailed information about an error by extending the Exception class
- ◆ Learn how all Java classes implicitly extend the Object class

Chapter 7 introduced techniques for implementing inheritance by creating subclasses with Java. This chapter continues discussing inheritance concepts and techniques. Several techniques can be used to require classes to include methods to ensure that all instances can respond to the same message. First, you will learn how to use an abstract method in a superclass to require that a subclass implement a method. Second, you will explore interfaces as a Java construct that can also require classes to implement methods. Next, you will see how to use inheritance to extend any nonfinal classes. For example, you can create custom exceptions by extending the built-in Java Exception class. Finally, the Object class is discussed as the superclass of all classes. The problem domain classes you create for Bradshaw Marina all implicitly extend Object, and Object methods are inherited by all of the classes.

INTRODUCING THE INITIAL LEASE CLASS

For the Bradshaw Marina case described in Chapter 4, the class diagram includes three generalization/specialization hierarchies that require inheritance: Boat, Slip, and Lease. Chapter 7 used the Boat hierarchy as an example. This chapter uses the Lease hierarchy as an example to demonstrate additional inheritance concepts. One reason this example is explained in detail is because it includes the first problem domain classes that contain attributes that hold references to other objects rather than to primitive variables or String references. The problem domain classes for the Lease hierarchy have attributes that are references to Date instances. Business systems use dates extensively, so you also must understand how to use them. Date and Calendar classes were introduced in Chapter 3.

The Lease hierarchy is shown in the class diagram in Figure 8-1. Lease now has two subclasses: AnnualLease and DailyLease.

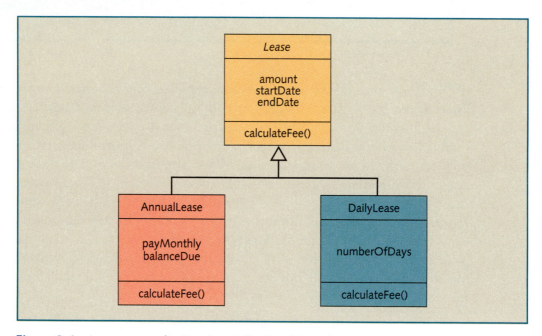

Figure 8-1   Lease generalization/specialization hierarchy

```
// Lease — an initial Lease class with
// Date instances as attributes

import java.util.*; // for Date class
public class Lease
{
    // attributes
    private double amount;
    private Date startDate;
    private Date endDate;

    // constructor
    public Lease(Date aStartDate)
    {
        setStartDate(aStartDate);
        setEndDate(null);
        setAmount(0);
    }

    // set accessor methods
    public void setAmount(double anAmount)
    { amount = anAmount; }
    public void setStartDate(Date aStartDate)
    { startDate = aStartDate; }
    public void setEndDate(Date anEndDate)
    { endDate = anEndDate; }

    // get accessor methods
    public double getAmount()
    { return amount; }
    public Date getStartDate()
    { return startDate; }
    public Date getEndDate()
    { return endDate; }
}
```

Figure 8-2   The initial Lease class definition

The initial Lease class definition is shown in Figure 8-2. Lease has attributes for amount, start date, and end date. The initial Lease class is not abstract, so you can test it with a tester program before writing any subclasses. Later, you will change it to an abstract class. The Lease class has two Date attributes, so you use the **import** keyword to import the Date class from java.util package, as you learned in Chapter 3. The import statement and class header are:

```
import java.util.*; // for Date class
public class Lease
```

You then declare the three attributes all leases have, including two reference variables for dates:

```
// attributes
private double amount;
private Date startDate;
private Date endDate;
```

The constructor accepts one parameter—a reference to a Date instance for the start date of the lease. The end date is set to null and the amount of the lease is set to zero:

```
// constructor
   public Lease(Date aStartDate)
   {
      setStartDate(aStartDate);
      setEndDate(null);
      setAmount(0);
   }
```

With this design, subclasses will set the end date and the amount of the lease, although the superclass includes methods for setting and getting these values.

A tester program that tests the Lease class is shown in Figure 8-3.

```
// TesterOne to test initial Lease class
// with various start dates

import java.util.*; //for Date and Calendar classes
public class TesterOne
{
   public static void main(String args[])
   {
   // create a Calendar instance set to the current date
   Calendar aCalendar = Calendar.getInstance();

   // set the calendar to a specific date and assign to date1
   aCalendar.set(2003, Calendar.FEBRUARY, 4);
   Date date1 = aCalendar.getTime();

   // add one month to the calendar and assign to date2
   aCalendar.add(Calendar.MONTH, 1);
   Date date2 = aCalendar.getTime();

   // add 10 days to the calendar and assign to date3
   aCalendar.add(Calendar.DATE, 10);
   Date date3 = aCalendar.getTime();

   // create three leases
   Lease firstLease = new Lease(date1);
   Lease secondLease = new Lease(date2);
   Lease thirdLease = new Lease(date3);

   // retrieve information about the Leases
   System.out.println("Lease 1 information is: "
      + firstLease.getAmount() + " "
      + firstLease.getStartDate() + " "
      + firstLease.getEndDate());

   System.out.println("Lease 2 information is: "
      + secondLease.getAmount() + " "
      + secondLease.getStartDate() + " "
      + secondLease.getEndDate());
```

```
        System.out.println("Lease 3 information is: "
            + thirdLease.getAmount() + " "
            + thirdLease.getStartDate() + " "
            + thirdLease.getEndDate());
    }
}
```

Figure 8-3   TesterOne source code

Because start dates are required by the constructor, the tester program creates three dates using a Calendar instance, as discussed in Chapter 3. Several ways to set the calendar are shown in the tester program for review. A Calendar instance is created and set to the current date by default. To set the date for the calendar to a specific date, use the Calendar set method, and then assign the date to a date reference (date1) using the getTime method. Use the Calendar add method to add one month to the calendar, which is assigned to date2. Finally, use the add method to add ten days to the calendar, which is assigned to date3:

```
// create a Calendar instance set to the current date
Calendar aCalendar = Calendar.getInstance();

// set the calendar to a specific date and assign to date1
aCalendar.set(2003, Calendar.FEBRUARY, 4);
Date date1 = aCalendar.getTime();

// add one month to the calendar and assign to date2
aCalendar.add(Calendar.MONTH, 1);
Date date2 = aCalendar.getTime();

// add 10 days to the calendar and assign to date3
aCalendar.add(Calendar.DATE, 10);
Date date3 = aCalendar.getTime();
```

Next, three leases are created and information about each lease is retrieved using the get accessor methods, as shown earlier in Figure 8-3. Although the Lease class will be changed to abstract, this tester is used to test the Lease class before continuing with the subclasses. The output is shown in Figure 8-4. Note that the amount is zero and the end date is null because Lease does not set them. Subclasses will set those values.

Lease 1 information is: 0.0 Tue Feb 04 17:34:05 CST 2003 null

Lease 2 information is: 0.0 Tue Mar 04 17:34:05 CST 2003 null

Lease 3 information is: 0.0 Fri Mar 14 17:34:05 CST 2003 null

Figure 8-4   Output of TesterOne

ADDING AN ABSTRACT METHOD TO LEASE

Sometimes it is desirable to require that all subclasses include a method. For example, all Lease subclasses need a calculateFee method because the subclasses are responsible for determining the lease amount. Requiring all subclasses to have a method is also necessary for polymorphism. If a lease does not have a calculateFee method, then an error could occur if a Lease instance without the method is asked to calculate the fee.

One way you can require that a subclass include, or implement, a method is to declare the method as abstract in the superclass. An **abstract method** is a method without any statements, and if a class has an abstract method, the class must also be abstract. A revised Lease class that is abstract and contains an abstract method named calculateFee is shown in Figure 8-5.

```java
// Lease -- an abstract Lease class to extend that also
// includes abstract method calculateFee

import java.util.*; // for Date and Calendar classes
public abstract class Lease
{
    // attributes
    private double amount;
    private Date startDate;
    private Date endDate;

    // constructor
    public Lease(Date aStartDate)
    {
        setStartDate(aStartDate);
        setEndDate(null);
        setAmount(0);
    }

    // abstract method subclasses must override
    public abstract double calculateFee(int aLength);

    // set accessor methods
    public void setAmount(double anAmount)
    { amount = anAmount; }
    public void setStartDate(Date aStartDate)
    { startDate = aStartDate; }
    public void setEndDate(Date anEndDate)
    { endDate = anEndDate; }

    // get accessor methods
    public double getAmount()
    { return amount; }
    public Date getStartDate()
    { return startDate; }
    public Date getEndDate()
    { return endDate; }
}
```

Figure 8-5 Abstract Lease class with abstract method

An abstract method can have a return type, and it can list parameters. The abstract method is declared as in the following code. Note that the method header includes the **abstract** keyword, includes no statements, and ends with a semicolon.

```
// abstract method subclasses must override
public abstract double calculateFee(int aLength);
```

If you do not change the Lease header to include the **abstract** keyword, you will receive a compile error stating that Lease must be declared abstract. If Lease is declared abstract, running the tester program shown in Figure 8-3 will result in an InstantiationError exception.

Hands-on Exercise 1

1. Locate Lease.java and TesterOne.java on the book's CD in the folder named Example1 in the Chapter8 folder, and compile and run them using the software suggested by your instructor.

2. Experiment by creating some dates to use as start dates for TesterOne. Create three dates using the Calendar add method, one by adding to the year, one by adding to the month, and one by adding to the date. Create three more dates using the Calendar set method. Use these six new dates in a revised TesterOne to instantiate six leases.

3. Change the Lease class to add the abstract calculateFee method as shown in Figure 8-5 and recompile. You should get a compile error because Lease.java is not an abstract class.

4. Change the Lease class to be abstract and then compile it. It should compile correctly. Run TesterOne and you will get an InstantiationError exception because the abstract Lease class cannot be instantiated.

IMPLEMENTING THE ANNUALLEASE SUBCLASS

The class diagram in Figure 8-1 shows two Lease subclasses: AnnualLease and DailyLease. AnnualLease includes the attributes balanceDue and payMonthly. The balanceDue attribute refers to the amount of the annual lease that remains unpaid. The payMonthly attribute is a Boolean value that indicates whether monthly payments will be made for the annual lease. If the lease is paid monthly, the balance due is initially set to eleven-twelfths of the lease amount, which assumes the first month is paid up front.

The class definition for the AnnualLease class is shown in Figure 8-6. Although the class adds only two attributes, the constructor and some of the methods are more complex. You import the java.util package to make the Date and Calendar classes available. Note that both the subclass and the superclass must import the package because they both use Date and Calendar classes.

```java
// AnnualLease -- subclass of Lease overrides abstract
// method calculateFee.

import java.util.*;
public class AnnualLease extends Lease
{
    // attribute in addition to those inherited from Lease
    private double balanceDue;
    private boolean payMonthly;

    // constructor
    public AnnualLease(Date aStartDate,
            int aSlipWidth, boolean isPayMonthly)
    {
        // invoke superclass constructor
        super(aStartDate);
        // use calendar to add 1 year to start date
        Calendar aCalendar = Calendar.getInstance();
        aCalendar.setTime(aStartDate);
        aCalendar.add(Calendar.YEAR, 1);
        // invoke superclass method to set end date
        setEndDate(aCalendar.getTime());
        // invoke superclass setAmount method after getting
        // fee amount from calculateFee method
        setAmount(calculateFee(aSlipWidth));
        // invoke AnnualLease methods
        setPayMonthly(isPayMonthly);
        if (payMonthly)
            setBalanceDue(getAmount() - getAmount()/12);
        else
            setBalanceDue(0);
    }
    // custom method calculateFee
    // overrides abstract method in Lease
    public double calculateFee(int aWidth)
    {
        double fee;
        switch(aWidth)
        {
            case 10: fee = 800;
            break;
            case 12: fee = 900;
            break;
            case 14: fee = 1100;
            break;
            case 16: fee = 1500;
            break;
            default: fee = 0;
        }
        return fee;
    }
```

```
    // set accessor methods
    public void setPayMonthly(boolean isPayMonthly)
    {   payMonthly = isPayMonthly; }
    public void setBalanceDue(double anAmount)
    {   balanceDue = anAmount; }

    // get accessor methods
    public boolean getPayMonthly()
    {   return payMonthly; }
    public double getBalanceDue()
    {   return balanceDue; }
}
```

Figure 8-6 AnnualLease class definition with calculateFee method

Be sure to include the **extends** keyword in the class header to extend the Lease class:

```
    import java.util.*;
    public class AnnualLease extends Lease
```

The constructor accepts three parameters: the start date, the slip width, and the payMonthly Boolean value. The slip width value is needed to calculate the amount of the annual lease, although the slip width is not retained by the instance. This is the first example in this text that includes a parameter for the constructor that is not set as an attribute value. The payMonthly value is needed to calculate the balance due and is retained as an attribute value.

```
    // constructor
    public AnnualLease(Date aStartDate,
            int aSlipWidth, boolean isPayMonthly)
```

The constructor block contains 11 statements, plus comments included to explain each step. The first statement invokes the superclass constructor using the start date as an argument. The Lease constructor assigns the start date, sets the end date to null, and sets the amount to zero, as discussed earlier.

```
    // invoke superclass constructor
    super(aStartDate);
```

Control then returns to the AnnualLease constructor, and the end date is calculated by adding one to the year of the start date, first by creating a Calendar instance, setting it to the start date, and then adding one year to the Calendar instance. The superclass setEndDate method is then invoked and passed the revised value of the Calendar instance:

```
    // use calendar to add 1 year to start date
    Calendar aCalendar = Calendar.getInstance();
    aCalendar.setTime(aStartDate);
    aCalendar.add(Calendar.YEAR, 1);
    // invoke superclass method to set end date
    setEndDate(aCalendar.getTime());
```

The next statement of the constructor also invokes a superclass method, this time the setAmount method. But the amount is calculated first by invoking the calculateFee method of AnnualLease, and the amount returned is immediately passed as an argument to setAmount. The calculateFee method will be discussed in more detail later in this chapter.

```
// invoke superclass setAmount method after getting
// fee amount from calculateFee method
setAmount(calculateFee(aSlipWidth));
```

The final statements assign the payMonthly attribute value and then assign the balanceDue attribute value. The balanceDue value is determined by the Boolean payMonthly value using an if block. If the lease is paid monthly, the balance due is eleven-twelfths of the lease amount; otherwise, the amount due is zero:

```
// invoke AnnualLease methods
setPayMonthly(isPayMonthly);
if (payMonthly)
    setBalanceDue(getAmount() - getAmount()/12);
else
    setBalanceDue(0);
```

The Slip class demonstrated in Chapter 6 includes a method named leaseSlip. This method calculated the fee for a lease based on the width of the slip to simplify the example. In the complete Bradshaw Marina system, the Lease subclasses calculate the lease amount. Therefore, the calculateFee method is now required in all Lease subclasses, and this is why the abstract method was added to the Lease class. The lease amount is calculated the same way as in the slip example, using the width in a switch block and returning the fee:

```
// custom method calculateFee
// overrides abstract method in Lease
public double calculateFee(int aWidth)
{
    double fee;
    switch(aWidth)
    {
        case 10: fee = 800;
        break;
        case 12: fee = 900;
        break;
        case 14: fee = 1100;
        break;
        case 16: fee = 1500;
        break;
        default: fee = 0;
    }
    return fee;
}
```

IMPLEMENTING THE DAILYLEASE SUBCLASS

The other Lease subclass is DailyLease, where a customer leases a slip for a short time, anywhere from a few days to several months. The DailyLease class definition is shown in Figure 8-7. A daily lease has one additional attribute—the number of days of the lease. This value is calculated based on the start date and end date. There are no monthly payments or balance due for a daily lease.

```java
// DailyLease -- subclass of Lease overrides abstract
// method calculateFee

import java.util.*;
public class DailyLease extends Lease
{
    // attribute in addition to those inherited from Lease
    private int numberOfDays;

    // constructor
    public DailyLease(Date aStartDate, Date anEndDate,
                        int aSlipWidth)
    {
        // invoke superclass constructor
        super(aStartDate);
        // use calendar to get day of year of start date
        Calendar aCalendar = Calendar.getInstance();
        aCalendar.setTime(aStartDate);
        int day1 = aCalendar.get(Calendar.DAY_OF_YEAR);
        // use calendar to get day of year of end date
        aCalendar.setTime(anEndDate);
        int day2 = aCalendar.get(Calendar.DAY_OF_YEAR);
        // set number of days
        setNumberOfDays(day2 - day1);
        // invoke superclass method to set end date
        setEndDate(anEndDate);
        // invoke superclass method to set amount after
        // getting fee amount from calculateFee method
        setAmount(calculateFee(aSlipWidth));
    }
    // custom method calculateFee
    // overrides abstract method in Lease
    //(different from method in AnnualLease)
    public double calculateFee(int aWidth)
    {
        double fee;
        switch(aWidth)
        {
```

8

```
            case 10: fee = 20 * getNumberOfDays();
            break;
            case 12: fee = 25 * getNumberOfDays();
            break;
            case 14: fee = 30 * getNumberOfDays();
            break;
            case 16: fee = 35 * getNumberOfDays();
            break;
            default: fee = 0;
        }
        return fee;
    }

    // set accessor method
    public void setNumberOfDays(int aNumberOfDays)
    {   numberOfDays = aNumberOfDays; }
    // get accessor method
    public int getNumberOfDays()
    {   return numberOfDays; }
}
```

Figure 8-7   DailyLease class definition with calculateFee method

As with AnnualLease, DailyLease imports the java.util package and extends the Lease class:

```
import java.util.*;
public class DailyLease extends Lease
{
    // attribute in addition to those inherited from Lease
    private int numberOfDays;
```

The DailyLease constructor expects three parameters; the start date, end date, and slip width. Although AnnualLease calculates the end date based on the start date, DailyLease calculates the number of days based on the start date and the end date:

```
// constructor
public DailyLease(Date aStartDate, Date anEndDate,
                       int aSlipWidth)
```

The constructor first invokes the superclass constructor passing the start date as an argument. Then a Calendar instance is created and set to the start date, and the day of the year is assigned to a variable:

```
// invoke superclass constructor
super(aStartDate);
// use calendar to get day of year for start date
Calendar aCalendar = Calendar.getInstance();
aCalendar.setTime(aStartDate);
int day1 = aCalendar.get(Calendar.DAY_OF_YEAR);
```

Next, the end date is used to get the day of the year, and the number of days is calculated based on the two numbers:

```
// use calendar to get day of year of end date
aCalendar.setTime(anEndDate);
int day2 = aCalendar.get(Calendar.DAY_OF_YEAR);
// set number of days
setNumberOfDays(day2 - day1);
```

The final statements of the DailyLease constructor invoke superclass methods to set the end date and the lease amount:

```
// invoke superclass method to set amount after
// getting fee amount from calculateFee method
setAmount(calculateFee(aSlipWidth));
```

The calculateFee method overrides the superclass abstract method, and the amount is calculated based on the slip width and the number of days of the lease. Slip width is passed as an argument from the constructor but is not retained. Number of days is calculated and set by the constructor. Note that even though the number of days is used in the calculation, it is not passed as an argument because the value is an attribute of the DailyLease class. All calculate-Fee methods have the same method signature.

```
// custom method calculateFee
// overrides abstract method in Lease
//(different from method in AnnualLease)
public double calculateFee(int aWidth)
{
    double fee;
    switch(aWidth)
    {
        case 10: fee = 20 * getNumberOfDays();
        break;
        case 12: fee = 25 * getNumberOfDays();
        break;
        case 14: fee = 30 * getNumberOfDays();
        break;
        case 16: fee = 35 * getNumberOfDays();
        break;
        default: fee = 0;
    }
    return fee;
}
```

8

TESTING THE ANNUALLEASE AND DAILYLEASE CLASSES

Now that you have two Lease subclasses, you can test them using the tester program shown in Figure 8–8.

```java
// TesterTwo to test AnnualLease and DailyLease subclasses
import java.util.*;
public class TesterTwo
{
    public static void main(String args[])
    {
    // create and set three dates from calendar
    Calendar aCalendar = Calendar.getInstance();
    aCalendar.set(2003, Calendar.AUGUST, 28);
    Date date1 = aCalendar.getTime();
    aCalendar.set(2003, Calendar.SEPTEMBER, 3);
    Date date2 = aCalendar.getTime();
    aCalendar.set(2003, Calendar.SEPTEMBER, 7);
    Date date3 = aCalendar.getTime();

    // create two AnnualLeases
    AnnualLease firstLease = new AnnualLease(date1, 14, true);
    AnnualLease secondLease = new AnnualLease(date2, 16, false);
    // create two DailyLeases
    DailyLease thirdLease = new DailyLease(date1, date2, 14);
    DailyLease fourthLease = new DailyLease(date2, date3, 16);

    // retrieve information about the Annual Leases
    System.out.println("AnnualLease 1 information is: \n"
        + firstLease.getAmount() + " "
        + firstLease.getStartDate() + " "
        + firstLease.getEndDate() + " "
        + firstLease.getBalanceDue() + " "
        + firstLease.getPayMonthly());

    System.out.println("AnnualLease 2 information is: \n"
        + secondLease.getAmount() + " "
        + secondLease.getStartDate() + " "
        + secondLease.getEndDate() + " "
        + secondLease.getBalanceDue() + " "
        + secondLease.getPayMonthly());

    // retrieve information about daily leases
    System.out.println("DailyLease 1 information is: \n"
        + thirdLease.getAmount() + " "
        + thirdLease.getStartDate() + " "
        + thirdLease.getEndDate() + " "
        + thirdLease.getNumberOfDays());
```

```
System.out.println("DailyLease 2 information is: \n"
    + fourthLease.getAmount() + " "
    + fourthLease.getStartDate() + " "
    + fourthLease.getEndDate() + " "
    + fourthLease.getNumberOfDays());
    }
}
```

Figure 8-8　TesterTwo to test AnnualLease and DailyLease

AnnualLease 1 information is:

1100.0 Thu Aug 28 11:58:16 CDT 2003 Sat Aug 28 11:58:16 CDT 2004 1008.334 true

AnnualLease 2 information is:

1500.0 Wed Sep 03 11:58:16 CDT 2003 Fri Sep 03 11:58:16 CDT 2004 0.0 false

DailyLease 1 information is:

180.0 Thu Aug 28 11:58:16 CDT 2003 Wed Sep 03 11:58:16 CDT 2003 6

DailyLease 2 information is:

140.0 Wed Sep 03 11:58:16 CDT 2003 Sun Sep 07 11:58:16 CDT 2003 4

Figure 8-9　TesterTwo output

To test the program, TesterTwo first creates three dates to use for the leases. Next, it instantiates two annual leases and two daily leases using the dates. Annual leases accept a start date, a slip width, and a Boolean value representing whether monthly payments are being made. Daily leases accept a start date, an end date, and a slip width.

```
// create two AnnualLeases
AnnualLease firstLease = new AnnualLease(date1, 14, true);
AnnualLease secondLease = new AnnualLease(date2, 16, false);

// create two DailyLeases
DailyLease thirdLease = new DailyLease(date1, date2, 14);
DailyLease fourthLease = new DailyLease(date2, date3, 16);
```

The first lease begins August 28th for a slip 14 feet wide and does require monthly payments. The second annual lease begins September 3rd for a 16-foot slip and does not require monthly payments. The third lease is a daily lease beginning August 28th and ending September 3rd for a 14-foot slip. The fourth lease is a daily lease for a 16-foot slip beginning September 3rd and ending September 7th.

The tester program retrieves information about each lease, getting five values for each annual lease and four values for each daily lease. The output shown in Figure 8-9 is as expected, showing for the first lease (an annual lease) an amount of 1100.0, a start date of Thu Aug 28 2003, an end date one year later Sat Aug 28 2004, and a balance due of 1008.334 since the value of payMonthly is true. The third lease (a daily lease) has an amount of 180.0, starts Thu Aug 28 2003, ends Wed Sep 03 2003, and is for six days.

Hands-on Exercise 2

1. Locate Lease.java, AnnualLease.java, DailyLease.java, and TesterTwo.java on the book's CD in the folder named Example2 in the Chapter8 folder, and compile the Lease classes and TesterTwo, and then run TesterTwo using the software suggested by your instructor.

2. Temporarily remove the calculateFee method from the AnnualLease class by surrounding it by begin comment and end comment symbols (/* and */). Try to recompile AnnualLease now that it does not include the method. What happens? Remove the comment symbols so AnnualLease does compile correctly.

3. Recall the tellAboutSelf method examples in Chapter 7. Add an abstract tellAboutSelf method to Lease that returns a string. Note that an abstract method cannot contain statements. Add tellAboutSelf methods to AnnualLease and DailyLease that override (but do not invoke) the abstract Lease tellAboutSelf method. Revise TesterTwo so it uses tellAboutSelf in place of the individual getter methods.

UNDERSTANDING AND USING JAVA INTERFACES

Adding an abstract method to the Lease superclass is one way to require that subclasses override the method. Requiring a method in a class is often desirable when you want to assure all users of the class (mainly programmers developing systems that use the class) that all instances can invoke the method. Otherwise, sending a message invoking a method that is not included in the instance will result in an error.

Another approach to requiring methods in classes is to define an interface. An **interface** is a Java component that defines abstract methods and constants that must be included by classes that use the interface. The concept is simple: Knowing how to use something means *knowing how to interface with it.* You interface with a car by using a steering wheel, gas pedal, and brake pedal. You expect all cars to have these controls. It is desirable to standardize how to interface with something. If you were asked whether you know how to drive a Mars Rover, you might respond by saying, "Yes, if it has the usual car interface—a steering wheel and pedals."

In OO systems, you use or control object instances by sending them messages based on method signatures. The methods an instance can respond to can be defined as the *interface* to the instance. If you want to assure the programmer that an instance has a defined set of methods, you can define a Java interface and declare that the class *implements* the methods required by the interface. Now the programmer knows what the instances of the class are capable of doing.

Component-based development refers to the fact that components interact in a system using a well-defined interface but might be built using a variety of technologies. As long as you know how to interface with the component, it can be used in the system. It is not necessary to know the technology used or the internal structure of the component. Java interfaces are an approach to defining how Java components can be used, and therefore play an important role in developing component-based systems.

Java interfaces are also often explained in the context of inheritance, where classes that implement an interface are said to "inherit" the methods. Because a Java class can extend only one superclass but can implement one or more interfaces, it is often said that interfaces allow Java subclasses a form of **multiple inheritance**, the ability to "inherit" from more than one class.

Multiple inheritance means that a subclass is part of two or more generalization/specialization hierarchies. Consider the Mars Rover mentioned earlier. It is a special type of motor vehicle, inheriting all of the characteristics of a motor vehicle. But it might also be considered a special type of spacecraft, or a special type of robot. It often becomes difficult to decide what to use as the superclass and what should and should not be inherited. When a programming environment must deal with multiple inheritance, it is difficult for the compiler to reconcile issues such as which attributes to inherit and which methods to override.

Some OO programming languages (C++, for example) allow you to implement multiple inheritance. The designers of Java deliberately decided *not* to allow multiple inheritance because of the complexity it can introduce. Interfaces are therefore described as an alternate way to implement multiple inheritance with Java. But you might find it more useful to think of interfaces as a way of defining how components can interact with each other.

Creating a Java Interface

You create a Java interface much like a class—using a header and including abstract methods that must be included in any class that implements the interface. In the lease example, all subclasses are expected to include a method named calculateFee. Therefore, you can create an interface requiring the inclusion of the calculateFee method, named LeaseInterface, instead of including the abstract method in Lease. An interface name begins with a capital letter by convention, and using the word "interface" in the name helps to identify it as an interface rather than a class.

An interface is written in a source code file and then compiled just like a class. The header for LeaseInterface uses the **interface** keyword in place of class, followed by the interface name.

```
public interface LeaseInterface
```

The source code filename is the same as the interface name. The source code file extension is .java and the compiled file extension is .class.

The interface definition contains abstract methods, declared the same as the abstract method earlier in the Lease class:

```
// method all lease subclasses must include
public abstract double calculateFee(int aWidth);
```

8

The complete LeaseInterface definition is shown in Figure 8-10. Once the interface is written and compiled, any class can implement it. Note that this interface only has one abstract method. Interfaces often have a long list of methods. Additionally, many interfaces are included with Java, and some of these will be used with GUI classes beginning in Chapter 10.

```
// Interface to use with Lease classes
// that requires calculateFee method

public interface LeaseInterface
{
    // method all lease subclasses must include
    public abstract double calculateFee(int aWidth);

}
```

Figure 8-10   The LeaseInterface definition

The AnnualLease class can implement the LeaseInterface by using the **implements** keyword in the class header along with the interface name. AnnualLease still extends Lease. The complete class header would be rewritten as:

    public class AnnualLease **extends** Lease **implements** LeaseInterface

You can now remove the abstract method named calculateFee from the Lease class as the interface requires that the calculateFee method be included in AnnualLease.

Hands-on Exercise 3

1. Return to the Lease classes and TesterTwo you started in Hands-on Exercise 2, found again in the folder named Example3 in the Chapter8 folder. Compile the Lease classes and TesterTwo and then run TesterTwo. You will modify these files to create the interface examples shown earlier.

2. Add a file named LeaseInterface.java as shown above and compile it. Modify the Lease class by removing the abstract calculateFee method. Modify the AnnualLease class so it implements LeaseInterface. Modify the DailyLease class so it implements LeaseInterface. Run the original version of TesterTwo to test your modified Lease classes.

Implementing More Than One Interface

Java classes can implement more than one interface, and an interface can include abstract final variables (constants). Including constants with values is another way that interfaces can allow inheritance. All classes that implement the interface have the constants available just as if they were defined within the class. The following example illustrates how a class can implement multiple interfaces and how an interface can include constants.

Bradshaw Marina decided that all problem domain classes should implement an interface that requires the tellAboutSelf method. This way, the programmers can always be sure all instances can respond to the tellAboutSelf message. The header for the interface named CompanyInterface is as follows:

```
public interface CompanyInterface
```

Define the abstract method tellAboutSelf next:

```
// all classes must implement this method
public abstract String tellAboutSelf();
```

The Bradshaw Marina system also requires constants in many places that contain the company name and address. Declare three static final variables and assign them values in CompanyInterface:

```
// constants with values all classes might need
public static final String COMPANY_NAME =
          "Bradshaw Marina";
public static final String COMPANY_ADDRESS =
          "PO Box 101 Lake Clinton";
public static final String COMPANY_PHONE =
          "(419) 555-8765";
```

The complete CompanyInterface definition is shown in Figure 8-11. Other constants might be included in the CompanyInterface. If the system ultimately will be sold as a software package for marinas that are similar to Bradshaw, the package could be tailored to the customer by changing the values of the constants.

You can use the DailyLease class to see how to use two interfaces with one subclass. Multiple interface names are separated by commas following the **implements** keyword in the header. The class header can continue to a second line if necessary, as shown in the revised header as follows:

```
public class DailyLease extends Lease implements
        LeaseInterface, CompanyInterface
```

Add the tellAboutSelf method to DailyLease as it is now required by the interface. In this example, the method returns information about Bradshaw Marina to demonstrate that DailyLease instances have access to the values of the constants included in the CompanyInterface:

```
// required by CompanyInterface
// not complete but tests constants in interface
public String tellAboutSelf()
{
   return "This is a daily lease for " + numberOfDays +
   " days for company " + COMPANY_NAME +
   " located at " + COMPANY_ADDRESS;
}
```

```
// Interface to use for all Bradshaw PD classes
// Requires tellAboutSelf method
// Plus constants for basic company information

public interface CompanyInterface
{
    // all classes must implement this method
    public abstract String tellAboutSelf();

    // constants with values all classes might need
    public static final String COMPANY_NAME =
                "Bradshaw Marina";
public static final String COMPANY_ADDRESS =
                "PO Box 101 Lake Clinton";
public static final String COMPANY_PHONE =
                "(419) 555-8765";
}
```

Figure 8-11 The CompanyInterface definition

The complete revised class definition for DailyLease is shown in Figure 8-12.

```
// DailyLease — subclass of Lease class implements two interfaces

import java.util.*;
public class DailyLease extends Lease implements
      LeaseInterface, CompanyInterface
{
    // attributes in addition to those inherited from Lease
    private int numberOfDays;

    // constructor
    public DailyLease(Date aStartDate, Date anEndDate, int aSlipWidth)
    {
        // invoke superclass constructor
        super(aStartDate);
        // use calendar to compute and set number of days
        Calendar aCalendar = Calendar.getInstance();
        aCalendar.setTime(aStartDate);
        int day1 = aCalendar.get(Calendar.DAY_OF_YEAR);
        aCalendar.setTime(anEndDate);
        int day2 = aCalendar.get(Calendar.DAY_OF_YEAR);
        setNumberOfDays(day2 - day1);
        // invoke superclass method to set end date
        setEndDate(anEndDate);
        // invoke superclass method after getting fee amount
        setAmount(calculateFee(aSlipWidth));
    }
    // custom method calculateFee
    // required by LeaseInterface
    public double calculateFee(int aWidth)
    {
```

```java
        double fee;
        switch(aWidth)
        {
            case 10: fee = 20 * getNumberOfDays();
            break;
            case 12: fee = 25 * getNumberOfDays();
            break;
            case 14: fee = 30 * getNumberOfDays();
            break;
            case 16: fee = 35 * getNumberOfDays();
            break;
            default: fee = 0;
        }
        return fee;
    }

    // method required by  CompanyInterface
    // not complete but tests constants in interface
    public String tellAboutSelf()
    {
        return "This is a daily lease for " + numberOfDays +
        " days for company " + COMPANY_NAME +
        " located at " + COMPANY_ADDRESS;
    }
    // set accessor method
    public void setNumberOfDays(int aNumberOfDays)
    {   numberOfDays = aNumberOfDays; }

    // get accessor method
    public int getNumberOfDays()
    {   return numberOfDays; }

}
```

Figure 8-12   DailyLease that implements two interfaces

Testing the Complete Interface Example

Figure 8-13 shows the source code for TesterThree that tests AnnualLease with one interface and DailyLease with two interfaces. It creates two annual leases and two daily leases as in TesterTwo. This time, the tellAboutSelf method is invoked in the daily leases and returns information about Bradshaw Marina and the lease.

```
// TesterThree to test AnnualLease and DailyLease
// with LeaseInterface and CompanyInterface

import java.util.*;
public class TesterThree
{
    public static void main(String args[])
    {
    // create three dates from calendar
    Calendar aCalendar = Calendar.getInstance();
    aCalendar.set(2003, Calendar.AUGUST, 28);
    Date date1 = aCalendar.getTime();
    aCalendar.set(2003, Calendar.SEPTEMBER, 3);
    Date date2 = aCalendar.getTime();
    aCalendar.set(2003, Calendar.SEPTEMBER, 7);
    Date date3 = aCalendar.getTime();

    // create two AnnualLeases
    AnnualLease firstLease = new AnnualLease(date1, 14, true);
    AnnualLease secondLease = new AnnualLease(date2, 16, false);

    // create two DailyLeases
    DailyLease thirdLease = new DailyLease(date1, date2, 14);
    DailyLease fourthLease = new DailyLease(date2, date3, 16);

    // retrieve information about the Annual Leases
    System.out.println("AnnualLease 1 information is: \n"
        + firstLease.getAmount() + " "
        + firstLease.getStartDate() + " "
        + firstLease.getEndDate() + " "
        + firstLease.getBalanceDue() + " "
        + firstLease.getPayMonthly());

    System.out.println("AnnualLease 2 information is: \n"
        + secondLease.getAmount() + " "
        + secondLease.getStartDate() + " "
        + secondLease.getEndDate() + " "
        + secondLease.getBalanceDue() + " "
        + secondLease.getPayMonthly());

    // test tellAboutSelf method of DailyLease
    System.out.println(thirdLease.tellAboutSelf());
    System.out.println(fourthLease.tellAboutSelf());

    }
}
```

Figure 8-13   TesterThree to test AnnualLease and DailyLease that implement interfaces

AnnualLease 1 information is:

1100.0 Thu Aug 28 12:15:28 CDT 2003 Sat Aug 28 12:15:28 CDT 2004 1008.334 true

AnnualLease 2 information is:

1500.0 Wed Sep 03 12:15:28 CDT 2003 Fri Sep 03 12:15:28 CDT 2004 0.0 false

This is a daily lease for 6 days for company Bradshaw Marina located at PO Box 101 Lake Clinton

This is a daily lease for 4 days for company Bradshaw Marina located at PO Box 101 Lake Clinton

Figure 8-14   Output of TesterThree

The output of TesterThree is shown in Figure 8-14.

Hands-on Exercise 4

1. Locate Lease.java, AnnualLease.java, DailyLease.java, LeaseInterface.java, Company-Interface.java, and TesterThree.java on the book's CD in the folder named Example4 in the Chapter8 folder, and compile them using the software suggested by your instructor. Start with the classes in the folder rather than with the classes you modified in Hands-on Exercise 3. Run TesterThree.

2. The tellAboutSelf method should include more information than shown in DailyLease. Complete the method so it includes all daily lease information (refer to your solution for Hands-on Exercise 2 or rewrite the Lease tellAboutSelf method so it is not abstract), but retains Bradshaw Marina's company information. Run TesterThree to verify that the new tellAboutSelf method works correctly.

3. Add a tellAboutSelf method to AnnualLease and change AnnualLease so it also implements CompanyInterface. Change TesterThree so it uses the tellAboutSelf method of AnnualLease rather than getter methods.

4. Recall the additional dates you created in Hands-on Exercise 1. Copy the code that creates them into TesterThree and use them to create at least two additional annual leases and two additional daily leases.

USING CUSTOM EXCEPTIONS

Problem domain classes are not the only Java classes that can be extended using inheritance. Any Java class, including those supplied with Java, that are not declared final can be extended. One example where extending a built-in class is desirable is a **custom exception**, an exception that is written specifically for an application.

You learned how to use Java exceptions in Chapter 6. The Slip instance throws an exception if data values are not valid. It is often helpful to include more specific information about an error when throwing an exception. You can define a custom exception to provide information about why the error occurred. To do so, you define a new class that extends the Exception class. Add attributes you want to remember for the custom exception. Add or override methods that you want the custom exception to invoke.

Defining the LeasePaymentException

Consider the AnnualLease class. Annual leases allow customers to make monthly payments after providing an initial payment. To record the monthly payments, you must add another method to AnnualLease, and the method must validate the payment amount. If the payment is invalid, an exception must be thrown to ensure that the sender corrects any error. Therefore, you can define a custom exception that can be thrown by the method.

For the Bradshaw Marina system, create an exception named LeasePaymentException by defining a class that extends the Exception class. The class definition is shown in Figure 8-15.

```
// LeasePaymentException -- a custom Exception

public class LeasePaymentException extends Exception
{
    // attributes for custom exception
    double paymentAmount;    // the amount of the payment attempted
    AnnualLease theLease;    // reference to the lease involved
    String exceptionMessage;// text of the message

    // constructor: when instantiated by Lease instance, accepts
    // the amount and reference to the lease
    public LeasePaymentException(double anAmount, AnnualLease aLease)
    {
        // invoke superclass constructor
        super("this is a custom LeasePaymentException \n");
        // assign lease reference and amount to attributes
        theLease = aLease;
        paymentAmount = anAmount;
        // construct message by asking the lease for date and balance
        exceptionMessage = " for lease starting " +
                        theLease.getStartDate() +
                        "\n with amount due " +
                        theLease.getBalanceDue() +
                        " but payment made of " + anAmount;
    }
    // override toString method of Exception to provide
    // more complete information about the exception
    public String toString()
    {
        return super.toString() + exceptionMessage;
    }

    // accessor methods can be included to return
    // specific exception information if desired
}
```

Figure 8-15 LeasePaymentException class definition

The class definition includes three attributes that will hold values for the amount of the invalid payment, a reference to the lease receiving the payment, and the message containing more specific information about what occurred.

```
public class LeasePaymentException extends Exception
{
    // attributes for custom exception
    double paymentAmount;   // the amount of the payment attempted
    AnnualLease theLease;   // reference to the lease involved
    String exceptionMessage;// text of the message
```

The lease reference variable included as an attribute illustrates an important OO programming concept. Attributes of instances can contain references to other instances, as with the Date instances used earlier in this chapter. This time, the reference is to a problem domain class defined for the Bradshaw Marina system. In examples in the next chapter, you will continue to learn about the benefits of including reference variables as attributes when you implement association relationships among instances. Here, an instance of a LeasePaymentException is associated with an instance of AnnualLease.

The LeasePaymentException has a parameterized constructor that accepts values for the amount of the invalid payment and the reference to the AnnualLease instance. The constructor first invokes the superclass constructor (of the Exception class), passing a string that the constructor expects. Then, values are assigned for all attributes, including the exceptionMessage string that includes specific values obtained directly from the AnnualLease instance:

```
public LeasePaymentException(double anAmount, AnnualLease aLease)
{
    // invoke superclass constructor
    super("this is a custom LeasePaymentException \n");
    // assign lease reference and amount to attributes
    theLease = aLease;
    paymentAmount = anAmount;
    // construct message by asking the lease for date and balance
    exceptionMessage = " for lease starting " +
                        theLease.getStartDate() +
                        "\n with amount due " +
                        theLease.getBalanceDue() +
                        " but payment made of " + anAmount;

}
```

Recall that the Exception class includes the toString method that retrieves information about the exception. The toString method is a method all classes have (see the section on the Object class later in this chapter), and Exception has its own version of toString that returns any message passed to its constructor. You saw this in the exception examples in Chapter 6.

The LeasePaymentException class overrides the Exception toString method to provide more specific information. It first invokes the superclass toString, which returns the string **"this is a custom LeasePaymentException \n"**, and then it adds the additional string referenced by the exceptionMessage attribute:

```
// override toString method of Exception to provide
// more complete information about the exception
public String toString()
{
    return super.toString() + exceptionMessage;
}
```

The sequence diagram in Figure 8-16 shows the interaction between LeasePaymentException and AnnualLease. Note that the new LeasePaymentException identifies which annual lease is involved and asks it for information that is then stored in the exceptionMessage string. This string is later returned to the method that catches the exception.

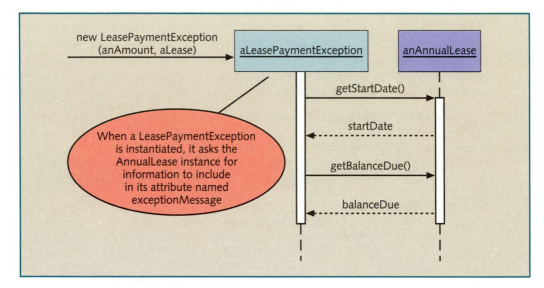

Figure 8-16   Partial sequence diagram showing LeasePaymentException and AnnualLease interacting in the constructor

Throwing a Custom Exception

The LeasePaymentException was designed for use by the AnnualLease class. A custom method for AnnualLease can be added to the class to record a payment, named recordLease-Payment, which expects to receive the amount of the payment. The recordLeasePayment method throws LeasePaymentException if the payment amount is not valid. Therefore, the method is declared using the **throws** keyword:

```
public void recordLeasePayment(double anAmount)
      throws LeasePaymentException
```

The method includes simple validation to determine whether the payment is less than or equal to the amount due. If the payment amount is greater than the amount due, an exception is thrown. First, a LeasePaymentException reference is declared and a new LeasePaymentException is instantiated and assigned to the reference. The arguments passed to the new exception include the invalid amount and a reference to the lease throwing the exception, using the keyword **this**. Next, the exception is thrown:

```
LeasePaymentException e = new
      LeasePaymentException(anAmount, this);
throw e;
```

If the amount is valid, the amount is subtracted from the balance due using the Java subtraction operator. The complete recordLeasePayment method is as follows:

```
// record lease payment
public void recordLeasePayment(double anAmount)
   throws LeasePaymentException
{
   if (anAmount > balanceDue)
   {
      LeasePaymentException e =
                new LeasePaymentException(anAmount, this);
      throw e;
   }
   else
   {
      balanceDue -= anAmount;
   }
}
```

The complete class definition for AnnualLease that throws the exception is shown in Figure 8-17.

```
// AnnualLease -- subclass of Lease with recordLeasePayment
// method, throws LeasePaymentException

import java.util.*;
public class AnnualLease extends Lease
{
   // attributes in addition to those inherited from Lease
   private double balanceDue;
   private boolean payMonthly;
```

8

```java
// constructor
public AnnualLease(Date aStartDate,
        int aSlipWidth, boolean isPayMonthly)
{
   // invoke superclass constructor
   super(aStartDate);
   // use calendar to add 1 year to start date
   Calendar aCalendar = Calendar.getInstance();
   aCalendar.setTime(aStartDate);
   aCalendar.add(Calendar.YEAR, 1);
   // invoke superclass method to set end date
   setEndDate(aCalendar.getTime());
   // invoke superclass method after getting fee amount
   setAmount(calculateFee(aSlipWidth));
   // invoke AnnualLease methods
   setPayMonthly(isPayMonthly);
   if (payMonthly)
      setBalanceDue(getAmount() - getAmount()/12);
   else
      setBalanceDue(0);
}

// record lease payment
public void recordLeasePayment(double anAmount)
   throws LeasePaymentException
{
   if (anAmount > balanceDue)
   {
      LeasePaymentException e =
              new LeasePaymentException(anAmount, this);
      throw e;
   }
   else
   {
      balanceDue -= anAmount;
   }
}

// custom method calculateFee
public double calculateFee(int aWidth)
{
   double fee;
   switch(aWidth)
   {
      case 10: fee = 800;
      break;
      case 12: fee = 900;
      break;
      case 14: fee = 1100;
      break;
      case 16: fee = 1500;
      break;
      default: fee = 0;
   }
```

```
        return fee;
    }

    // set accessor methods
    public void setPayMonthly(boolean isPayMonthly)
    {   payMonthly = isPayMonthly; }
    public void setBalanceDue(double anAmount)
    {   balanceDue = anAmount; }

    // get accessor methods
    public boolean getPayMonthly()
    {   return payMonthly; }
    public double getBalanceDue()
    {   return balanceDue; }
}
```

Figure 8-17   AnnualLease with recordPaymentMethod that throws a LeasePaymentException

Testing the LeasePaymentException

TesterFour tests the LeasePaymentException and the revised AnnualLease class with the recordLeasePayment method that throws the exception. TesterFour is shown in Figure 8-18.

```
// TesterFour to test AnnualLease with custom exception

import java.util.*;
public class TesterFour
{
    public static void main(String args[])
    {
        // create a date from calendar
        Calendar aCalendar = Calendar.getInstance();
        aCalendar.set(2003, Calendar.AUGUST, 28);
        Date date1 = aCalendar.getTime();

        // create an AnnualLease with monthly payments
        AnnualLease firstLease = new AnnualLease(date1, 14, true);

        // record a lease payment that exceeds balance due that
        // causes the lease to throw an exception
        try
        {
            firstLease.recordLeasePayment(1200.00);
        }
        catch(LeasePaymentException e)
        {
            System.out.println(e.toString());
        }
    }
}
```

Figure 8-18   TesterFour to test AnnualLease and the LeasePaymentException

LeasePaymentException: this is a custom LeasePaymentException
for lease starting Thu Aug 28 19:46:20 CDT 2003
with amount due 1008.3333333333334 but payment made of 1200.0

Figure 8-19   TesterFour output

The output for TesterFour is shown in Figure 8-19.

TesterFour instantiates and tests just one annual lease. It uses a try-catch block to attempt to record a payment for the lease. The annual lease costs $1,200.00 based on a slip width of 14 feet. Because payMonthly is true, the balance due is $1,008.33. A payment of $1,200 is attempted, which should result in an exception. Note the exception message includes these details.

A sequence diagram of the interaction for TesterFour is shown in Figure 8-20.

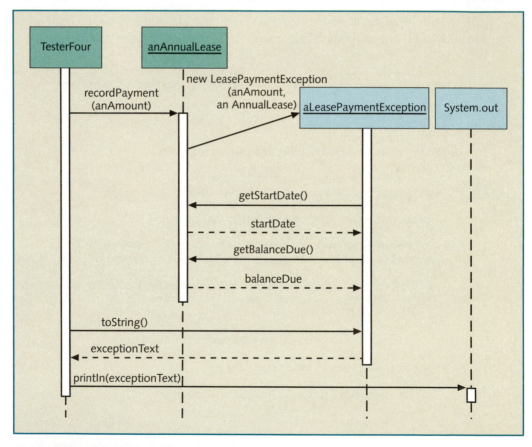

Figure 8-20   Sequence diagram showing TesterFour interaction with AnnualLease that throws LeasePaymentException

Hands-on Exercise 5

1. Locate Lease.java, AnnualLease.java, LeasePaymentException.java, and TesterFour.java on the book's CD in the folder named Example5 in the Chapter8 folder, and compile them using the software suggested by your instructor. Run TesterFour.

2. Experiment with TesterFour to create a variety of annual leases and attempt making valid and invalid payments. What happens when a lease with "payMonthly = false" has a payment? Does the string returned by the exception still make sense?

Handling Payments as a Batch

When testing new classes, particularly when testing validation and exceptions, it is often useful to create a batch-processing tester application. Batch processing takes a collection of transactions and processes them one after the other. If the transaction is completed successfully, a success message is displayed. If the transaction results in an exception, an exception message is displayed but the application continues processing until the batch is completed.

A tester program that can process both valid and invalid lease payment transactions without terminating is shown as TesterFive in Figure 8-21.

```java
// TesterFive to test AnnualLease with custom exception
// for batch of multiple payment transactions

import java.util.*;
public class TesterFive
{
    public static void main(String args[])
    {
    // create three dates from calendar
    Calendar aCalendar = Calendar.getInstance();
    aCalendar.set(2003, Calendar.AUGUST, 28);
    Date date1 = aCalendar.getTime();
    aCalendar.set(2003, Calendar.SEPTEMBER, 3);
    Date date2 = aCalendar.getTime();
    aCalendar.set(2003, Calendar.SEPTEMBER, 7);
    Date date3 = aCalendar.getTime();

    // create three AnnualLeases with monthly payments
    AnnualLease firstLease = new AnnualLease(date1, 14, true);
    AnnualLease secondLease = new AnnualLease(date2, 16, true);
    AnnualLease thirdLease = new AnnualLease(date3, 12, true);

    // invoke processPayment method of TesterFive to process
    // a batch of payments
    System.out.println("Processing three payments:");
    processPayment(firstLease, 200);     // a valid payment
    processPayment(secondLease, 2000);   // an invalid payment
    processPayment(thirdLease, 400);     // a valid payment
```

8

```
    }

    // private method of TesterFive to process batch of payments
    private static void processPayment(AnnualLease aLease,
                                       double aPayment)
    {
        try
        {
            // invoke method of the lease referenced in aLease
            aLease.recordLeasePayment(aPayment);
            System.out.println("Payment transaction successful " +
                               "for lease " +
                               aLease.getStartDate().toString());
        }
        catch(LeasePaymentException e)
        {
            // show LeasePaymentException if caught
            System.out.println(e.toString());
        }
        catch(Exception e)
        {
            // show any other Exception if caught
            System.out.println(e.toString());
        }
    }
}
```

Figure 8-21   TesterFive to process a batch of payments with exceptions

```
Processing three payments:
Payment transaction successful for lease Thu Aug 28 19:55:16 CDT 2003
LeasePaymentException: this is a custom LeasePaymentException
 for lease starting Wed Sep 03 19:55:16 CDT 2003
 with amount due 1375.0 but payment made of 2000.0
Payment transaction successful for lease Sun Sep 07 19:55:16 CDT 2003
```

Figure 8-22   TesterFive output

The output of TesterFive is shown in Figure 8-22.

TesterFive first instantiates three annual leases, all with monthly payments:

```
// create three AnnualLeases with monthly payments
AnnualLease firstLease = new AnnualLease(date1, 14, true);
AnnualLease secondLease = new AnnualLease(date2, 16, true);
AnnualLease thirdLease = new AnnualLease(date3, 12, true);
```

To process payments for each annual lease, you can include a static method in the tester program to process payments. In this example, the method is named processPayment, and its parameters are a reference to an annual lease to which the payment applies and the amount of the payment. Note that it must be a static method because it is invoked by the static main method. The method header is:

```
// private method of TesterFive to process batch of payments
private static void processPayment(AnnualLease aLease,
                                   double aPayment)
```

The body of the method includes try-catch blocks that first invoke the recordLeasePayment method of the AnnualLease instance, passing the amount of the payment. If the AnnualLease instance throws a LeasePaymentException, the first catch block catches it and displays the exception information by invoking the toString method. Other corrective action might be taken if this represented a batch-processing application. Note that there is a second catch block. Should another type of exception be thrown, the second more generic catch block would catch it and handle it differently from the first catch block. In this example, both catch blocks simply display information. The complete processPayment method is shown in the following code:

```
// private method of TesterFive to process batch of payments
private static void processPayment(AnnualLease aLease,
                                   double aPayment)
{
    try
    {
        // invoke method of the lease referenced in aLease
        aLease.recordLeasePayment(aPayment);
        System.out.println("Payment transaction successful " +
                           "for lease " +
                           aLease.getStartDate().toString());
    }
    catch(LeasePaymentException e)
    {
        // show LeasePaymentException if caught
        System.out.println(e.toString());
    }
    catch(Exception e)
    {
        // show any other Exception if caught
        System.out.println(e.toString());
    }
}
```

TesterFive includes three payments, one for each annual lease. The first payment is valid, the second payment is invalid, and the third is valid:

```
// invoke processPayment method of TesterFive to process
// a batch of payments
System.out.println("Processing three payments:");
processPayment(firstLease, 200);      // a valid payment
processPayment(secondLease, 2000);    // an invalid payment
processPayment(thirdLease, 400);      // a valid payment
```

The output produced displays messages indicating a successful transaction for the first payment, a LeasePaymentException for the second payment, and a successful transaction for the third payment.

Hands-on Exercise 6

1. Locate TesterFive.java on the book's CD in the folder named Example5 in the Chapter8 folder (along with files you used for Hands-on Exercise 5), and compile it using the software suggested by your instructor. Run TesterFive.

2. Modify TesterFive so that more than one valid payment is made for one of the leases. Note whether the balance due decreases correctly. Continue adding payments until a payment becomes invalid. Verify that LeasePaymentException is thrown correctly.

3. To test any software thoroughly, you should create a variety of test cases and list the expected output of each test case. Then when you run the test, you can verify that the output matches the expected output. Create a list of test cases for leases and one or more payments and record the expected output. Modify TesterFive to include the test cases and run it to verify.

UNDERSTANDING THE OBJECT CLASS AND INHERITANCE

You have created a number of problem domain classes for Bradshaw Marina, and implemented subclasses by using the **extends** keyword. Subclasses inherit the functionality you included in the superclass. But how did the superclass gain the functionality it has? The answer is that all classes in Java extend one common superclass named the Object class.

The Object class defines basic functionality that any other class of objects needs in Java. All built-in Java class hierarchies have Object as the common ancestor. But any problem domain class you define also extends Object, although it is done implicitly for you. Therefore, it is useful to understand the Object class and its methods.

One method you have worked with already is the toString method. All classes inherit toString from the Object class. By default, toString returns a string representation of the name of the class and a hexadecimal representation of its address. Many classes override the toString method to provide more specific information. The Exception class toString method is one example you have used. Many developers override toString in problem domain classes so it functions much like the tellAboutSelf method you have used for Bradshaw Marina.

Additional methods of the Object class are clone, equals, finalize, getClass, hashCode, notify, notifyAll, and wait. Method signatures and descriptions are shown in Table 8-1.

Problem domain classes you create can include the code that extends Object in the class header if they do not extend some other class:

```
public abstract class Lease extends Object
```

AnnualLease and DailyLease extend Lease, so they could not directly extend Object, but they both inherit Object methods as well as Lease methods. An annual lease referenced by the variable aLease could invoke the toString method:

```
String myString = aLease.toString();
```

Recall that the equals method was used to compare two string instances in Chapter 3. Additionally, you can use the equals method to compare two Lease references to determine whether they refer to the same lease:

```
boolean areTheyIdentical = aLease.equals(anotherLease);
```

Table 8-1   Methods of the Object Class

Method	Signature	Notes
clone	protected Object clone()	Creates and returns a copy of this object
equals	public boolean equals(Object obj)	Indicates whether some other object is "equal to" this one
finalize	protected void finalize()	Called by the garbage collector on an object when garbage collection determines that there are no more references to the object
getClass	public final Class getClass()	Returns the run-time class of an object
hashCode	public int hashCode()	Returns a hash code value for the object
notify	public final void notify()	Wakes up a single thread that is waiting on this object's monitor
notifyAll	public final void notifyAll()	Wakes up all threads that are waiting on this object's monitor
wait	public final void wait(long timeout)	Causes current thread to wait until either another thread invokes the notify() method or the notifyAll() method for this object, or a specified amount of time has elapsed
toString	public String toString()	Returns a string representation of the object

8

Summary

- The Lease generalization/specialization hierarchy is another example of inheritance in the Bradshaw Marina case study.

- AnnualLease and DailyLease both have their own ways of calculating the lease fee, and there are several ways to require that a method be included in a class to assure that all instances will respond to the same message.

- If you want to require that all subclasses include a method, you can include an abstract method in a superclass. An abstract method cannot contain any code and must end with a semicolon. Only an abstract class can include an abstract method.

- An interface is a Java component that you can use to require that classes contain methods. An interface defines how to interact, or *interface*, with an instance by defining methods that can be invoked. An interface can also define available constants. In component-based development, you create system components with well-defined interfaces to allow components to interact.

- The **interface** keyword is used in the interface header to define an interface, which is created in a java source code file and compiled like a class. The **implements** keyword is used in the class header to define the interfaces for a class.

- Because an interface defines methods to include, it can also be thought of as a way to implement multiple inheritance in Java, where a class inherits from more than one parent. But interfaces do not include methods to inherit; they only define abstract methods that must be included in a class that implements the interface.

- You can use the **extends** keyword to define classes that inherit from built-in Java classes, such as to extend the Exception class into a custom exception. Any class that is not final can be extended. Custom exceptions are helpful when you need to provide detailed information following an exception.

- In Java, the Object class is the superclass of all classes, and problem domain classes such as Boat and Lease implicitly extend the Object class. Object class methods are inherited by all classes.

Key Terms

abstract method	custom exception	interface
component-based development	implements	multiple inheritance

Review Questions

1. What keyword defines a method in a superclass that must be included in a subclass?

2. Write the complete method header for an abstract method named getCustomer–Name that returns a string.

3. What symbol is required after the abstract method header?

4. If a class includes an abstract method, can the class itself be instantiated? Explain.

5. What other approach can be used to require that a class include specific methods?

6. Write the interface header for an interface named BoatInterface.

7. What keyword indicates that a class implements an interface?

8. Write the class header for the Sailboat class that implements the BoatInterface.

9. What methods might be included in the BoatInterface? What constants might be included?

10. Write the statement to declare an integer constant for the BoatInterface named MAX_LENGTH.

11. Write the class header for the Sailboat class that implements the BoatInterface and the CompanyInterface.

12. Explain what classes can be extended other than problem domain classes you create.

13. Explain why custom exceptions are important for business systems.

14. Write a class header for a custom exception named LeaseCreationException.

15. Assume LeaseCreationException is thrown by the constructor of the Lease class. Write the header for the Lease constructor.

16. Assume the LeaseCreationException is caught by a try-catch block in a tester program that instantiates a daily lease. Write the complete try-catch block that catches the exception and displays the message.

17. Write a class header that shows the Boat class explicitly extending the Object class.

18. Write a class header for the Boat class that extends the Object class and implements the BoatInterface and the CompanyInterface.

8

Discussion Questions

1. Why would it be desirable to require that specific methods be included in any subclass that extents a class? In other words, why include abstract methods or implement interfaces?

2. In what ways is an interface important for component-based development? In what ways is an interface like inheritance?

3. In the Lease classes, must calculateFee be public rather than private? Note that the method does not assign an amount; it just calculates and returns it based on the width. Discuss when public versus private access is advisable.

Projects

1. Consider an additional lease type named OneDayLease. This lease has the same end date as start date and the lease fee is a flat fee rather than based on slip width. There are no attributes in addition to the Lease class attributes. Create the OneDayLease as a subclass of Lease, implementing the LeaseInterface and the CompanyInterface. Write a tester program to test the class.

2. Return to the examples in Chapter 7 for Boat classes that include tellAboutSelf methods. Revise the Boat classes to implement CompanyInterface and update the tellAboutSelf methods so Bradshaw Marina information is included in the string returned by tellAboutSelf. Write a tester program to test the classes.

3. Recall the validation added to the Boat class in Hands-on Exercise 1 in Chapter 7. Take your solution and create a custom exception named BoatException to throw if any of the values are invalid. Write a batch-processing tester program to test valid and invalid values.

4. A chapter example showed a custom exception used with annual leases. All Lease classes use start dates and end dates. Consider how a custom exception might be used for all Lease classes that accept dates. For example, you might validate the dates to be within a reasonable range (this year and next year, for example). You might validate that an end date supplied for a daily lease is after the start date. Design and implement a custom exception to use for invalid lease dates and modify the Lease classes so they throw the exception. Write a batch-processing tester program to test a variety of valid and invalid dates for daily and annual leases.

CHAPTER

9

Implementing Association Relationships

In this chapter you will:

- ◆ Review Bradshaw Marina's class diagram
- ◆ Implement association relationships with one-to-one multiplicity between Java classes
- ◆ Navigate from one instance to another when there is a one-to-one association
- ◆ Learn how to use the Vector class to create association relationships with one-to-many multiplicity between Java classes
- ◆ Navigate one-to-many association relationships using methods of the Vector class
- ◆ Learn how to create and use an association class with Java

In Chapters 7 and 8 you learned how to implement generalization/specialization hierarchies that provide inheritance relationships from a superclass to a subclass. The class diagram shows these generalization/specialization hierarchies. But a class diagram also shows *association relationships* between classes, and these relationships are important to business information systems. Lines between classes on a class diagram that can be described by verb phrases are the association relationships. For example, the Bradshaw Marina system requires several association relationships between classes: a customer *owns* a boat and a boat *is assigned to* a slip. For Bradshaw Marina managers, knowing this information is as important as knowing the name and address of the customer and the manufacturer and length of the boat; association relationships model key requirements for a business information system.

This chapter shows how to use Java to implement association relationships between classes. Once you have implemented a one-to-one association relationship, you will learn how to navigate from one instance to another. For example, you can navigate instances to find information about the customer who owns a boat. You will also explore one-to-many association relationships to find information about each slip that is part of a dock. Finally, you will learn how to create and use an association class—the Lease class that was introduced in Chapter 8.

REVIEWING BRADSHAW MARINA'S CLASS DIAGRAM

In Chapter 4 you learned about the information system requirements for Bradshaw Marina. The Bradshaw Marina class diagram shows the problem domain classes that the system needs. This class diagram is shown again in Figure 9-1. The classes introduced so far include Customer, Slip (including subclass), Boat (including subclasses), and Lease (including subclasses). The class diagram also shows how instances of the classes are associated, or connected, to each other. It is important to know, for example, what boat is assigned to a slip and what customer owns the boat. Association relationships on the class diagram indicate that the system requires information about these associations.

Association relationships are shown on the class diagram as lines connecting classes. These associations connect instances of a class with instances of another class. The numbers written on the line at both ends indicate the multiplicity of the association (recall that 1..1 means one-to-one and 1..* means one-to-many). Using association relationships in a class diagram, you can navigate from instance to instance following the association. For example, if you have a Customer instance, you can find the Boat instance associated with the customer. Once you have the Boat instance, you can find the Slip instance for the boat.

Business information systems usually have many association relationships. In fact, these association relationships are often more important than generalization/specialization hierarchies in business systems because they indicate important requirements that must be remembered or stored by the system. The Bradshaw class diagram shows the following association relationships, all of which define information that the Bradshaw Marina system needs to track:

- A customer owns a boat

- A boat is owned by a customer

- A boat is assigned to a slip

- A slip contains a boat

- A dock contains many slips

- A slip is attached to a dock

- A slip is leased to a customer (Lease is an association class)

- A customer leases a slip (Lease is an association class)

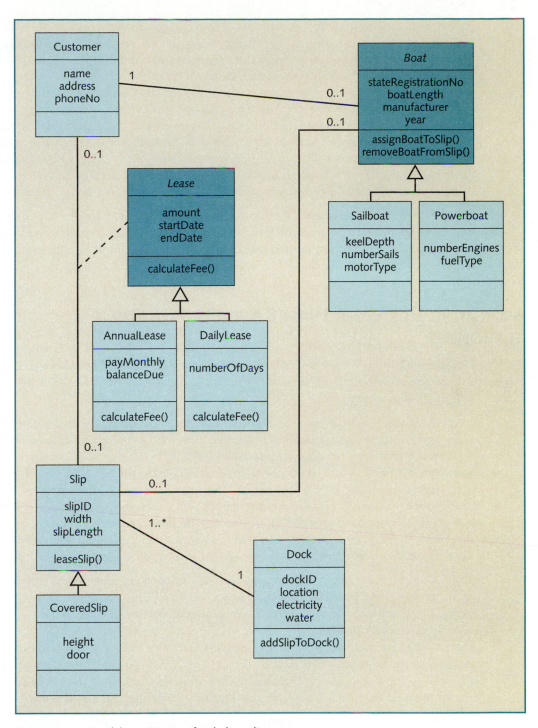

Figure 9-1 Bradshaw Marina final class diagram

9

Association relationships are sometimes shown as *aggregation relationships* or *composition relationships* on the class diagram. (A diamond symbol on one end of the association line indicates aggregation or composition.) An aggregation relationship is a strong association where one instance "contains" the other, such as a town that contains shopping centers or schools. A composition relationship is also a strong association where one instance is composed of or "part of" another, such as walls that are part of a building. You implement aggregation and composition relationships using the same techniques as the association relationships demonstrated in this chapter. Some analysts do not include them at all during analysis, and the Bradshaw Marina class diagram does not show them. Other analysts, however, might use a composition relationship between a dock and its slips (a dock is composed of slips) if they feel it helps convey more information about the nature of the association.

The Lease class is an example of an *association class* that exists because of the relationship between Slip and Customer, as discussed in Chapter 4. It is shown as a class connected by a dashed line to an association between Slip and Customer. You implement an association class like any other class with Java and then associate it with other classes.

ASSOCIATING CUSTOMER WITH BOAT: ONE-TO-ONE ASSOCIATION RELATIONSHIP

Chapter 5 introduced the Customer class and Chapter 7 introduced the Boat class, including Sailboat and Powerboat subclasses. Customer and Boat have an association relationship: a customer owns a boat.

Note that the line on the class diagram represents *two* relationships between Customer and Boat, one for each "direction." First, a customer *owns* a boat, and second, a boat *is owned by* a customer. The system developer must carefully define each "direction" of the relationship, and each "direction" of the relationship must be handled separately with Java. For example, each "direction" of the relationship might differ on whether it is mandatory or optional. A boat must be owned by a customer (mandatory relationship between Boat and Customer), but a customer might be included in the system who does not own a boat (optional relationship between Customer and Boat). In other associations, the multiplicity is different in each direction. For example, a dock contains many slips, but a slip is part of only one dock.

To implement an association relationship in Java, you use a reference variable as an attribute of a class. Figure 9-2 reviews how a reference variable points to an actual instance; in this example, a Customer reference variable points to a Customer instance and a Boat reference variable points to a Boat instance. Therefore, if you add a reference variable for a Customer instance as an attribute in the Boat class, each Boat instance can point to a Customer instance and invoke the customer's methods. If you add a reference variable for a Boat instance as an attribute in the Customer class, each Customer instance can point to a Boat instance and invoke the boat's methods. That is how association relationships are implemented with Java.

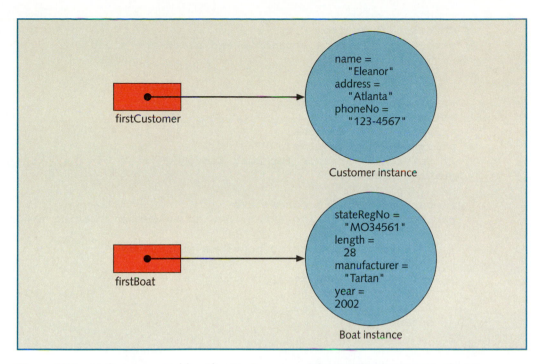

Figure 9-2   Reference variables (firstCustomer and firstBoat) point to actual instances (customer named Eleanor and boat number MO34561)

The tester programs you have written up to this point include reference variables that are used to point to instances and invoke their methods. You have also seen String and Date reference variables used as attributes of classes for Bradshaw Marina examples in this text. A string, such as the name of the boat manufacturer, is an instance of the String class that the manufacturer attribute of Boat points to. A date, such as the start date of a lease, is an instance of the Date class to which the startDate attribute of Lease points.

This chapter introduces nothing new about the concept of reference variables as attributes. What is new is the use of reference variables to implement association relationships. The examples in this chapter will be easy for you to follow if you understand the difference between a reference variable and an instance.

Modifying the Customer Class

Recall that the Customer class includes attributes for name, address, and phone number. To implement a one-to-one association relationship with the Boat class, simply add an attribute to Customer that holds a reference to a boat. The Customer class definition that includes the association relationship is shown in Figure 9-3. The list of attributes to the Customer class now include three strings plus a Boat reference variable named boat.

```java
// Customer class from Chapter 5
// with Boat reference attribute and accessors added

public class Customer
{
    // attribute definitions
    private String name;
    private String address;
    private String phoneNo;
    // reference variable for Boat instance
    private Boat boat;

    // constructor with parameters
    public Customer(String aName, String anAddress, String aPhoneNo)
    {
        // invoke accessors to populate attributes
        setName(aName);
        setAddress(anAddress);
        setPhoneNo(aPhoneNo);
        // initially no Boat
        setBoat(null);
    }

    // get accessors
    public String getName()
        { return name;}
    public String getAddress()
        { return address;}
    public String getPhoneNo()
        { return phoneNo;}
    public Boat getBoat()
        { return boat;}

    // set accessors
    public void setName(String newName)
        { name = newName;}
    public void setAddress(String newAddress)
        { address = newAddress;}
    public void setPhoneNo(String newPhoneNo)
        { phoneNo = newPhoneNo;}
    public void setBoat(Boat aBoat)
        { boat = aBoat;}
}
```

Figure 9-3   Modified Customer class definition

Note that the Boat reference variable points to a Boat instance; it is not a value representing the boat ID number or some other value used as a key or identifier to a boat. Key values or identifiers are used to implement relationships in relational databases, as when a foreign key is included in a table so it can be joined to another table. The reference variable, on the other hand, points directly to the Boat instance.

Accessor methods are also added to the Customer class, one to set the Boat reference variable and one to get the Boat reference variable. The setter method accepts a Boat reference as a parameter and assigns the reference to the attribute:

```
public void setBoat(Boat aBoat)
    { boat = aBoat;}
```

The getter method returns the reference. Note that the return type is aBoat.

```
public Boat getBoat()
    { return boat;}
```

The constructor is unchanged except that it sets the Boat reference variable to **null**. After the Customer instance is created, the Boat reference can be set as required using the setBoat method.

TesterOneA, shown in Figure 9-4, tests the modified Customer class. Note that the Boat class has not been changed; TesterOneA only tests one direction of the relationship: A Customer owns a boat.

9

```
// TesterOneA - associate Customer with Boat
// Customer class is modified but not Boat class

public class TesterOneA
{
    public static void main(String args[])
    {
        // create a Customer instance
        Customer firstCustomer = new
                Customer("Eleanor", "Atlanta", "123-4567");

        // create a Boat instance
        Boat firstBoat = new Boat("M034561", 28, "Tartan", 2002);

        // set the Boat for the Customer
        firstCustomer.setBoat(firstBoat);

        // you can get the Boat reference from Customer
        // then use it to get Boat information
        Boat aBoat = firstCustomer.getBoat();
        System.out.println("Customer boat information is "
                + aBoat.getStateRegistrationNo() + " "
                + aBoat.getManufacturer() + " "
                + aBoat.getLength() + " "
                + aBoat.getYear());
```

```
        // you can also verify Customer to Boat association
        // by navigating directly, asking Customer for its Boat
        // reference then using it with Boat accessor
        System.out.println("Again, customer boat information is "
                + firstCustomer.getBoat().getStateRegistrationNo() + " "
                + firstCustomer.getBoat().getManufacturer() + " "
                + firstCustomer.getBoat().getLength() + " "
                + firstCustomer.getBoat().getYear());
    }
}
```

Figure 9-4   TesterOneA source code

Figure 9-5 shows the sequence diagram that illustrates the interaction in TesterOneA, and Figure 9-6 shows the output of TesterOneA.

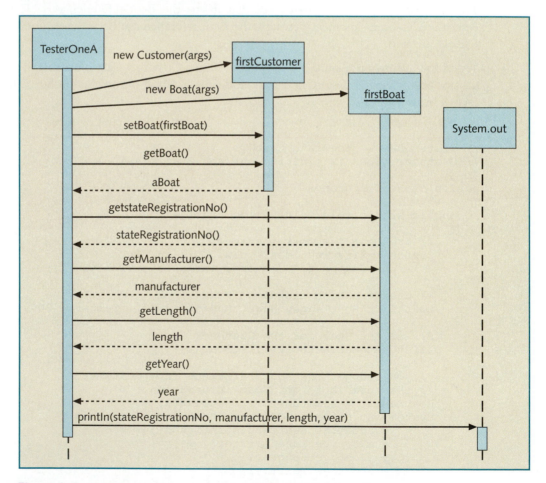

Figure 9-5   Sequence diagram showing TesterOneA interaction

First, you instantiate a customer and a boat using the following code:

```
// create a Customer instance
Customer firstCustomer = new
                Customer("Eleanor", "Atlanta", "123-4567");

// create a Boat instance
Boat firstBoat = new Boat("MO34561", 28, "Tartan", 2002);
```

Next, invoke the setBoat method of Customer using the Boat reference firstBoat:

```
// set the Boat for the customer
firstCustomer.setBoat(firstBoat);
```

Now that the customer has a value for its Boat reference, the tester program can get the Boat reference from the customer and use the Boat reference to get information about the boat:

```
Boat aBoat = firstCustomer.getBoat();
System.out.println("Customer boat information is "
        + aBoat.getStateRegistrationNo() + " "
        + aBoat.getManufacturer() + " "
        + aBoat.getLength() + " "
        + aBoat.getYear());
```

A more powerful approach to navigating association relationships is to invoke a series of methods in one statement. Consider the following statement:

```
firstCustomer.getBoat().getStateRegistrationNo()
```

The statement should be read from left to right. First, the Customer instance assigned to the reference variable firstCustomer receives a message to invoke its getBoat method. The Customer instance returns a reference to the boat. Next, the returned Boat reference replaces the first part of the statement, so the Boat instance receives a message to invoke its getStateRegistrationNo method, which returns the state registration number as a string. The following series of statements in TesterOneA directly navigates from the customer to the boat each time boat information is required, obtaining the same result as shown above:

```
System.out.println("Again, customer boat information is "
        + firstCustomer.getBoat().getStateRegistrationNo() + " "
        + firstCustomer.getBoat().getManufacturer() + " "
        + firstCustomer.getBoat().getLength() + " "
        + firstCustomer.getBoat().getYear());
```

> Customer boat information is MO34561 Tartan 28.0 2002
>
> Again, customer boat information is MO34561 Tartan 28.0 2002

Figure 9-6 Output of TesterOneA

Modifying the Boat Class

Up to this point, the Boat class has not been modified, but the Customer class now implements the one-to-one association relationship with Boat. A Boat instance, however, has no way of knowing about the customer. In other words, only one direction of the relationship has been implemented, from Customer to Boat. The Boat class can also be modified by adding a Customer reference variable as an attribute along with two accessor methods. That way, the other direction of the relationship can be implemented: A boat *is owned by* a customer. The modified Boat class definition is shown in Figure 9-7.

```java
// Concrete Boat class from Chapter 7
// with Customer reference attribute and accessors
// plus custom method assignBoatToCustomer

public class Boat
{
    // attributes
    private String stateRegistrationNo;
    private double length;
    private String manufacturer;
    private int year;

    // reference variable points to a Customer instance
    private Customer customer;

    // constructor
    public Boat(String aStateRegistrationNo, double aLength,
            String aManufacturer, int aYear)
    {
        setStateRegistrationNo(aStateRegistrationNo);
        setLength(aLength);
        setManufacturer(aManufacturer);
        setYear(aYear);
        // initially no Customer for this boat
        setCustomer(null);
    }

    // custom method to assign a Boat to a Customer
    public void assignBoatToCustomer(Customer aCustomer)
    {
        setCustomer(aCustomer); // point Boat to the Customer instance
        customer.setBoat(this); // point Customer to this Boat
    }

    // set accessor methods
    public void setStateRegistrationNo(String aStateRegistrationNo)
        { stateRegistrationNo = aStateRegistrationNo; }
    public void setLength(double aLength)
        { length = aLength;}
    public void setManufacturer(String aManufacturer)
        { manufacturer = aManufacturer; }
    public void setYear(int aYear)
        {  year = aYear;   }
```

```
      public void setCustomer(Customer aCustomer)
         {   customer = aCustomer;   }

      // get accessor methods
      public String getStateRegistrationNo()
         { return stateRegistrationNo; }
      public double getLength()
         { return length; }
      public String getManufacturer()
         { return manufacturer; }
      public int getYear()
         { return year; }
      public Customer getCustomer()
         { return customer; }
}
```

Figure 9-7   Modified Boat class definition

This code also includes one additional change to the Boat class: A custom method named assignBoatToCustomer is added. This method accomplishes more than the setter method setCustomer. It does invoke the setCustomer method, but it also asks the customer to set its boat attribute to **this** boat. In other words, the assignBoatToCustomer method establishes the association relationship in both directions:

```
// custom method to assign a Boat to a Customer
   public void assignBoatToCustomer(Customer aCustomer)
   {
       setCustomer(aCustomer); // point Boat to the Customer instance
       customer.setBoat(this); // point Customer to this Boat
   }
```

TesterOneB shown in Figure 9-8 tests both Customer and Boat by creating a Customer instance and a Boat instance. Then the boat's assignBoatToCustomer method is invoked.

```
// TesterOneB - associate Boat with Customer

public class TesterOneB
{
   public static void main(String args[])
   {
       // create a Customer instance
       Customer firstCustomer = new
               Customer("Eleanor", "Atlanta", "123-4567");

       // create a Boat instance
       Boat firstBoat = new Boat("MO34561", 28, "Tartan", 2002);

       // assign the Boat to the Customer
       firstBoat.assignBoatToCustomer(firstCustomer);
```

```
// verify Boat to Customer association:
// ask boat for its Customer reference
// then use it with Customer accessor
System.out.println("Boat owner information is "
        + firstBoat.getCustomer().getName() + " "
        + firstBoat.getCustomer().getAddress() + " "
        + firstBoat.getCustomer().getPhoneNo());

// verify Customer to Boat association:
// ask Customer for its Boat reference
// then use it with Boat accessor
System.out.println("Customer boat information is "
        + firstCustomer.getBoat().getStateRegistrationNo() + " "
        + firstCustomer.getBoat().getManufacturer() + " "
        + firstCustomer.getBoat().getLength() + " "
        + firstCustomer.getBoat().getYear());
    }
}
```

Figure 9-8   TesterOneB source code

Because the assignBoatToCustomer method establishes the association relationship in both directions, TesterOneB can verify both directions. The following code uses the direct navigation approach to get customer information for the boat.

```
System.out.println("Boat owner information is "
        + firstBoat.getCustomer().getName() + " "
        + firstBoat.getCustomer().getAddress() + " "
        + firstBoat.getCustomer().getPhoneNo());
```

Then the code shown previously in TesterOneA gets boat information from the customer:

```
System.out.println("Customer boat information is "
        + firstCustomer.getBoat().getStateRegistrationNo() + " "
        + firstCustomer.getBoat().getManufacturer() + " "
        + firstCustomer.getBoat().getLength() + " "
        + firstCustomer.getBoat().getYear());
```

The output of TesterOneB is shown in Figure 9-9.

Boat owner information is Eleanor Atlanta 123-4567

Customer boat information is MO34561 Tartan 28.0 2002

Figure 9-9   Output of TesterOneB

Hands-on Exercise 1

1. Locate Customer.java, Boat.java, and TesterOneA.java on the book's CD in the folder named Example1 in the Chapter9 folder, and compile and run it using the software suggested by your instructor.

2. Modify TesterOneA to instantiate some additional customers and boats, associate customers with boats, and then verify that the associations work correctly.

3. Note that Boat.java includes the changes introduced in this section, but TesterOneA does not require the changes. TesterOneB, however, does require the changes. Compile and run TesterOneB with Customer and Boat.

4. Modify TesterOneB to instantiate the additional customers and boats you added to TesterOneA previously, and then verify that the associations work correctly in both directions.

ADDING CAPABILITY TO THE BOAT CLASS

The customer and boat examples earlier establish both directions of the association relationship. You can use additional techniques to increase the functionality of classes that have association relationships. For example, Bradshaw Marina does not want to keep information about a boat if its owner is not a customer. Therefore, when a Boat is instantiated, it could require a Customer reference as a parameter in the constructor. That way, the relationship between Boat and Customer becomes mandatory instead of optional. The header for the constructor for Boat becomes:

```
// constructor (adding customer reference)
    public Boat(String aStateRegistrationNo, double aLength,
            String aManufacturer, int aYear, Customer aCustomer)
```

The code in the constructor sets values for all attributes and then invokes the assignBoatToCustomer method, which sets the customer attribute of the boat and asks the customer to set its boat attribute.

```
    {
        setStateRegistrationNo(aStateRegistrationNo);
        setLength(aLength);
        setManufacturer(aManufacturer);
        setYear(aYear);
        // association between boat and customer done here
        assignBoatToCustomer(aCustomer);
```

An additional modification to Boat is a new tellAboutSelf method. Because the association between Boat and Customer is mandatory, the tellAboutSelf method can return information about the boat (as shown previously), and it can also get information about the customer who owns the boat and return that information, too. The string reference named customerDetails refers to information that the Boat instance gets directly from the Customer instance.

```java
// tellAboutSelf method returning Boat and Customer information
public String tellAboutSelf()
{
    String boatDetails = "I am a Boat" +
        " state reg number " + getStateRegistrationNo() +
        " length " + getLength() +
        " Manufacturer " + getManufacturer() +
        " Year " + getYear();
    String customerDetails = "\n and Owner is " + customer.getName() +
        " living in " + customer.getAddress() +
        " with phone " + customer.getPhoneNo();
    return boatDetails + customerDetails;
}
```

Figure 9-10 shows a sequence diagram that illustrates how the tellAboutSelf method works. You will have a chance to modify the Boat class to include the new constructor and the tellAboutSelf method in Hands-on Exercise 2.

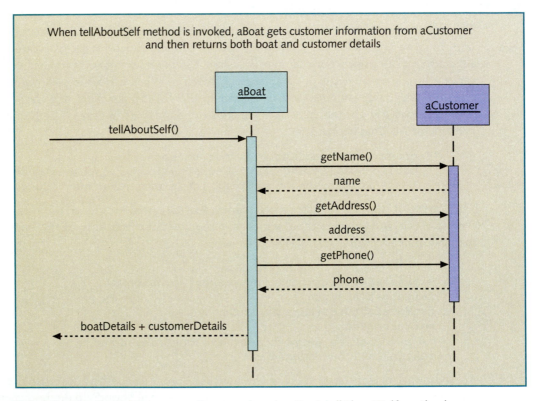

Figure 9-10   Partial sequence diagram showing Boat tellAboutSelf method

TesterTwo, shown in Figure 9-11, tests the new Boat class. The tester program is greatly simplified because of the Boat tellAboutSelf method. Two customers and two boats are instantiated, and Customer references are passed to the Boat constructor, which establishes the association between each customer and boat in both directions. Next, each boat is asked to tell about itself, resulting in output with complete information about the boat and its owner.

```java
// TesterTwo - associate Boat with Customer
// use tellAboutSelf to get boat and customer details

public class TesterTwo
{
    public static void main(String args[])
    {
    // create several customers
    Customer firstCustomer = new
            Customer("Eleanor", "Atlanta", "123-4567");
    Customer secondCustomer = new
            Customer("JoAnn", "St Louis", "987-6543");

    // create boats passing customer references
    Boat firstBoat = new
        Boat("MO34561", 28, "Tartan", 2002, firstCustomer);
    Boat secondBoat = new
            Boat("MO98765", 32, "Catalina", 2001, secondCustomer);

    // use Boat tellAboutSelf method to get back details
    System.out.println(firstBoat.tellAboutSelf());
    System.out.println(secondBoat.tellAboutSelf());
    }
}
```

Figure 9-11   TesterTwo source code

Figure 9-12 shows the sequence diagram for TesterTwo. The output of the TesterTwo source code is shown in Figure 9-13.

9

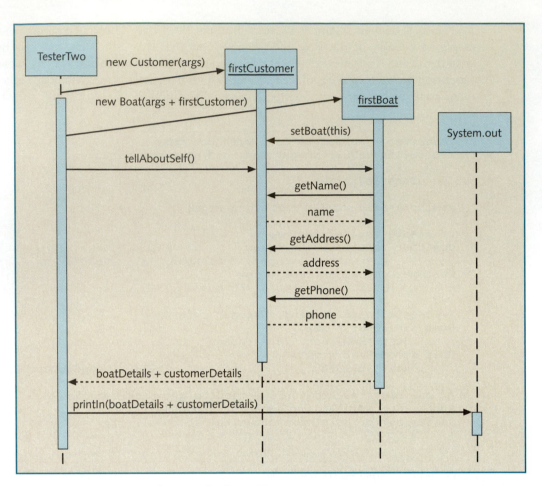

Figure 9-12   Sequence diagram for TesterTwo

I am a Boat state reg number MO34561 length 28.0 Manufacturer Tartan Year 2002
and Owner is Eleanor living in Atlanta with phone 123-4567
I am a Boat state reg number MO98765 length 32.0 Manufacturer Catalina Year 2001
and Owner is JoAnn living in St Louis with phone 987-6543

Figure 9-13   Output of TesterTwo

Hands-on Exercise 2

1. Locate Customer.java and TesterTwo.java on the book's CD in the folder named
   Example2 in the Chapter9 folder. Copy Boat.java from your Hands-on Exercise 1

solution and modify it as shown in this section. Compile and run the example using the software suggested by your instructor.

2. Modify Customer by adding a tellAboutSelf method that returns information about the customer's boat. Remember that a customer is not required to have a boat, so include an if statement to test whether the boat attribute is **null** before attempting to get boat information.

3. Write a tester program that tests the Customer tellAboutSelf method with a customer who has a boat and with a customer who does not have a boat.

ASSOCIATING DOCK AND SLIP: A ONE-TO-MANY ASSOCIATION RELATIONSHIP

The Slip class was introduced in Chapter 6, and Slip has an association relationship with Dock, as seen in Figure 9-1. The relationship goes in two directions: a slip is attached to a dock and a dock contains many slips. The association relationship between Slip and Dock is one-to-one, so it is implemented the same way as the Customer and Boat relationships you worked with in the previous section. However, the association relationship between Dock and Slip is one-to-many, indicated by the 1..* notation on the association line, so a different approach is required.

Implementing a one-to-many association relationship requires that a Dock instance have reference variables for more than one slip. You can use the Vector class (introduced in Chapter 3) to instantiate a container that can hold many reference variables, so you can use a Vector in the Dock class to hold many Slip reference variables. You can use methods of the Vector class to add Slip references and get Slip references.

Introducing the Dock Class

The class definition for Dock is shown in Figure 9-14. The Dock class has four attributes: an ID number, a location, plus two Boolean variables indicating whether the dock has electricity and water.

```java
// Dock class to illustrate 1 to many association with Slip

import java.util.*;
public class Dock
{
    // attributes
    private int id;
    private String location;
    private boolean electricity;
    private boolean water;

    // implement slip association with Vector class
    private Vector slips;
```

```java
// constructor
public Dock(int anId, String aLocation,
            boolean anElectricity, boolean aWater)
{
    setId(anId);
    setLocation(aLocation);
    setElectricity(anElectricity);
    setWater(aWater);
    Slips = new Vector(10); // start with Vector for 10 slips
}

// custom method addSlipToDock
public void addSlipToDock(Slip aSlip)
{
    slips.addElement(aSlip); // connect dock to slip (1..*)
    aSlip.setDock(this);     // connect slip to dock (1..1)
}
// custom method to return vector of slips
public Vector getSlips()
    { return slips;}

// set accessor methods
public void setId(int anId)
    { id = anId;}
public void setLocation(String aLocation)
    { location = aLocation;}
public void setElectricity(boolean anElectricity)
    { electricity = anElectricity;}
public void setWater(boolean aWater)
    { water = aWater;}
// get accessor methods
public int getId()
    { return id;}
public String getLocation()
    { return location;}
public boolean getElectricity()
    { return electricity;}
public boolean getWater()
    { return water;}
}
```

Figure 9-14 The Dock class definition

A fifth attribute that implements the one-to-many association relationship is a Vector named slips.

```java
// attributes
private int id;
private String location;
private boolean electricity;
private boolean water;

// implement slip association with Vector class
private Vector slips;
```

The constructor for Dock sets values for the four attributes. Then it instantiates a new Vector that can hold ten reference variables, and assigns the new Vector to the reference variable named slips.

```
slips = new Vector(10); // start with Vector for 10 slips
```

A method is added to Dock that returns the reference variable named slips much like any other getter method. Note that the type returned is a Vector.

```
// custom method to return vector of slips
public Vector getSlips()
    { return slips;}
```

To add a slip to the dock, a custom method is added named addSlipToDock. The method uses the Vector addElement method to add a slip reference to the slips Vector. Next, the slip is asked to set its dock reference variable (see the following Slip class definition). The complete addSlipToDock method is as follows:

```
// custom method addSlipToDock
    public void addSlipToDock(Slip aSlip)
    {
        slips.addElement(aSlip);    // connect dock to slip (1..*)
        aSlip.setDock(this);        // connect slip to dock (1..1)
    }
```

Associating the Slip Class With Dock

The Slip class was introduced in Chapter 6, and many features were added to it, including constants and exceptions for validation. A simplified version of the Slip class is used in this example. Slip is modified much like Boat to implement a mandatory one–to–one association relationship. First, a Dock reference variable is added as an attribute of Slip. Standard accessor methods for the Dock reference attribute are also added. Next, the constructor is modified to expect a Dock reference parameter. Therefore, when a slip is instantiated, it must be associated with a dock. A statement in the constructor also asks the dock to add the slip to the dock, so the association is established in both directions:

```
// constructor with 3 parameters plus Dock reference
public Slip(int aNo, int aWidth, double aSlipLength, Dock aDock)
{
    // invoke accessors to populate attributes
    setNo(aNo);
    setWidth(aWidth);
    setSlipLength(aSlipLength);
    // assign slip to an existing dock
    setDock(aDock);
    // tell dock to associate with this slip
    dock.addSlipToDock(this);
```

The Slip class definition is shown in Figure 9-15 and includes additional modifications. First, because a slip is assigned to a boat, a Boat reference variable is also added as an attribute. Additionally, accessor methods for the Boat reference attribute are included. Therefore, a slip is associated with a dock, and a slip is associated with a boat.

9

```java
// Slip with Boat reference and accessors
// and Dock reference variable and accessors

public class Slip
{
   // attributes
   private int no;
   private int width;
   private double slipLength;
   private Boat boat;
   private Dock dock;

   // constructor with 3 parameters plus dock reference
   public Slip(int aNo, int aWidth, double aSlipLength, Dock aDock)
   {
      // invoke accessors to populate attributes
      setNo(aNo);
      setWidth(aWidth);
      setSlipLength(aSlipLength);
      // assign slip to an existing dock
      setDock(aDock);
      // tell dock to associate with this slip
      dock.addSlipToDock(this);
      // initially no boat in slip
      setBoat(null);
   }

   // set accessor methods
   public void setNo(int aNo)
      { no = aNo; }
   public void setWidth(int aWidth)
      { width = aWidth; }
   public void setSlipLength(double aSlipLength)
      { slipLength = aSlipLength;}
   public void setBoat(Boat aBoat)
      { boat = aBoat;}
   public void setDock(Dock aDock)
      { dock = aDock; }

   // get accessor methods
   public int getNo()
      { return no;}
   public int getWidth()
      { return width;}
   public double getSlipLength()
      { return slipLength;}
   public Boat getBoat()
      { return boat; }
   public Dock getDock()
      { return dock; }
}
```

Figure 9-15 The Slip class definition

Testing the 'Dock Contains Slips' Association Relationship

TesterThreeA tests the Dock and Slip association relationships without including boats. The source code is shown in Figure 9-16.

```java
// TesterThreeA
// Dock has Slips (ignores Boat and Customer for now)

import java.util.*;
public class TesterThreeA
{
    public static void main(String args[])
    {
        // declare Dock and Slip reference variables
        Dock firstDock;
        Slip firstSlip;
        Slip secondSlip;
        Slip thirdSlip;

        // create a Dock instance
        firstDock = new Dock(1, "Main Cove", true, false);

        // create three Slip instances for the Dock
        firstSlip = new Slip(1, 10, 20, firstDock);
        secondSlip = new Slip(2, 12, 25, firstDock);
        thirdSlip = new Slip(3, 14, 25, firstDock);

        // verify Dock to Slip association (1 to many):
        // first get the Vector of slips from the Dock
        Vector slips = firstDock.getSlips();
        // next use Vector size method to get number of slips
        System.out.println("Dock 1 has " + slips.size() + " slips");
        // iterate through Vector to get information on each slip
        for(int i = 0; i < slips.size(); i++)
        {
            // get slip reference variable from slips Vector of Dock
            Slip aSlip = (Slip) slips.elementAt(i);
            // verify slip information
            System.out.println("  Slip number " + aSlip.getNo()
            + " has width of " + aSlip.getWidth()
            + " has length of " + aSlip.getSlipLength());
        }

        // verify slip to dock association (1:1)
        System.out.println("First slip is on Dock "
        +    firstSlip.getDock().getId()
        + " with location " + firstSlip.getDock().getLocation()
        + " with electricity " + firstSlip.getDock().getElectricity()
        + " and water " + firstSlip.getDock().getWater());
    }
}
```

Figure 9-16   TesterThreeA source code

First, one dock and three slip reference variables are declared. Then one dock and three slips are instantiated. Each slip is passed the same dock reference, so all three slips are associated with the dock and the dock is associated with each slip.

```
// declare Dock and Slip reference variables
Dock firstDock;
Slip firstSlip;
Slip secondSlip;
Slip thirdSlip;

// create a Dock instance
firstDock = new Dock(1, "Main Cove", true, false);

// create three Slip instances for the Dock
firstSlip = new Slip(1, 10, 20, firstDock);
secondSlip = new Slip(2, 12, 25, firstDock);
thirdSlip = new Slip(3, 14, 25, firstDock);
```

Now the tester program can test the associations in both directions. First, the one-to-many association is tested by asking the dock for its Vector of slips, and the number of slips can be verified by using the Vector size method:

```
// verify Dock to Slip association (1 to many):
// first get the Vector of slips from the Dock
Vector slips = firstDock.getSlips();
// next use Vector size method to get number of slips
System.out.println("Dock 1 has " + slips.size() + " slips");
```

Once the tester program has the Vector of slips, each slip can be accessed using a for loop that repeats based on the size of the slips Vector:

```
for(int i = 0; i < slips.size(); i++)
```

Inside the for loop, each element from the slips Vector is retrieved using the elementAt method and the for loop index i. When retrieving a reference variable from a Vector, the element must be cast back to its original type, in this case to a Slip reference. Then the Slip reference is assigned to a Slip variable named aSlip.

```
Slip aSlip = (Slip) slips.elementAt(i);
```

Finally, the Slip reference variable is used to get information about the slip. Because these statements are inside a for loop, information about each slip associated with the dock is displayed. The complete for loop follows:

```
for(int i = 0; i < slips.size(); i++)
{
    // get slip reference variable from slips Vector of Dock
    Slip aSlip = (Slip) slips.elementAt(i);
    // verify Slip information
    System.out.println(" Slip number " + aSlip.getNo()
    + " has width of " + aSlip.getWidth()
    + " has length of " + aSlip.getSlipLength());
}
```

The output up to this point shows a dock with three slips, and information about each slip is listed.

The final section of TesterThreeA tests the association between Slip and Dock, a one-to-one association. The direct navigation approach is used to get the Dock reference from Slip and then to get dock information.

```
// verify slip to dock association (1:1)
System.out.println("First slip is on Dock "
+    firstSlip.getDock().getId()
+ " with location " + firstSlip.getDock().getLocation()
+ " with electricity " + firstSlip.getDock().getElectricity()
+ " and water " + firstSlip.getDock().getWater());
```

The output is shown in Figure 9-17.

First slip is on Dock 1 with location Main Cove with electricity true and water false
Dock 1 has 3 slips
    Slip number 1 has width of 10 has length of 20.0
    Slip number 2 has width of 12 has length of 25.0
    Slip number 3 has width of 14 has length of 25.0

Figure 9-17   Output of TesterThreeA

Adding the Boat and Customer Classes to the Example

The Slip class definition includes a Boat reference attribute and accessor methods, so the Slip class is ready to associate a Slip instance with a boat. Boat can now be modified to associate with a Slip. First, add a Slip reference attribute and accessor methods to Boat. Then add a method to Boat named assignBoatToSlip. A boat does not have to be assigned to a Slip initially, so the constructor sets the Slip reference attribute to **null**. (See the Boat class definition in Figure 9-18.

```
// Boat class (not abstract) with Customer reference variable
// and Customer parameter in constructor, tellAboutSelf method,
// Slip reference variable, and assignBoatToSlip method

public class Boat
{
    // attributes
    private String stateRegistrationNo;
    private double length;
    private String manufacturer;
    private int year;
```

9

```java
// reference variable points to a Customer instance
private Customer customer;
// reference variable points to a Slip instance
private Slip slip;

// constructor (adding Customer reference)
public Boat(String aStateRegistrationNo, double aLength,
            String aManufacturer, int aYear, Customer aCustomer)
{
   setStateRegistrationNo(aStateRegistrationNo);
   setLength(aLength);
   setManufacturer(aManufacturer);
   setYear(aYear);
   // association between boat and customer done here
   assignBoatToCustomer(aCustomer);
   setSlip(null); // boat not in slip yet
}
// custom method to assign a Boat to a Customer
public void assignBoatToCustomer(Customer aCustomer)
{
   setCustomer(aCustomer);
   Customer.setBoat(this);
}
// custom method to assign a Boat to a Slip
public void assignBoatToSlip(Slip aSlip)
{
   setSlip(aSlip);
   Slip.setBoat(this);
}
// tellAboutSelf method returning Boat and Customer information
public String tellAboutSelf()
{
   String boatDetails = "I am a Boat" +
    " state reg number " + getStateRegistrationNo() +
    " length " + getLength() +
    " Manufacturer " + getManufacturer() +
    " Year " + getYear();
   String customerDetails = "\n and Owner is " +
      customer.getName() +
    " living in " + customer.getAddress() +
    " with phone " + customer.getPhoneNo();
   return boatDetails + customerDetails;
}

// set accessor methods
public void setStateRegistrationNo(String aStateRegistrationNo)
   { stateRegistrationNo = aStateRegistrationNo; }
public void setLength(double aLength)
   { length = aLength;}
public void setManufacturer(String aManufacturer)
   { manufacturer = aManufacturer; }
public void setYear(int aYear)
   { year = aYear;  }
public void setCustomer(Customer aCustomer)
   { customer = aCustomer;  }
public void setSlip(Slip aSlip)
   { slip = aSlip; }
```

```
    // get accessor methods
    public String getStateRegistrationNo()
        { return stateRegistrationNo; }
    public double getLength()
        { return length; }
    public String getManufacturer()
        { return manufacturer; }
    public int getYear()
        { return year; }
    public Customer getCustomer()
        { return customer; }
    public Slip getSlip()
        { return slip; }
}
```

Figure 9-18   Boat class definition that associates with Slip

The Boat class already is designed to associate with a customer, so this example can also include the Customer class without any modification. Now the power of the association relationships becomes apparent. If you have a Customer reference, you can navigate to find the customer's boat, its slip, and its dock. Similarly, if you have a Dock reference, you can find each slip and navigate to the slip's boat and to the customer who owns it.

TesterThreeB, shown in Figure 9-19, provides a comprehensive test of these associations.

```
// TesterThreeB
// Dock has Slips with Boat and Customer

import java.util.*;
public class TesterThreeB
{
    public static void main(String args[])
        {
        // declare reference variables
        Dock firstDock;
        Slip firstSlip;
        Slip secondSlip;
        Customer firstCustomer;
        Customer secondCustomer;
        Boat firstBoat;
        Boat secondBoat;

        // create a Dock instance
        firstDock = new Dock(1, "Main Cove", true, false);

        // create two Slip instances for the Dock
        firstSlip = new Slip(1, 10, 20, firstDock);
        secondSlip = new Slip(2, 12, 25, firstDock);
```

9

```
// create two Customer instances
firstCustomer = new
      Customer("Eleanor", "Atlanta", "123-4567");
secondCustomer = new
      Customer("JoAnn", "St Louis", "987-6543");

// create Boats passing Customer references
firstBoat = new
      Boat("MO34561", 28, "Tartan", 2002, firstCustomer);
secondBoat = new
      Boat("MO98765", 32, "Catalina", 2001, secondCustomer);

// assign the Boats to the Slips
firstBoat.assignBoatToSlip(firstSlip);
secondBoat.assignBoatToSlip(secondSlip);

// verify Customer to Boat to Slip to Dock
System.out.println("Information for customer "
    + firstCustomer.getName()
    + "\n Boat is " + firstCustomer.getBoat().getManufacturer()
    + "\n Slip is " + firstCustomer.getBoat().getSlip().getNo()
    + "\n Dock is "
    + firstCustomer.getBoat().getSlip().getDock().getId());

// verify Dock to Slip to Boat association (1 to many):
// first get the Vector of slips from the Dock
Vector slips = firstDock.getSlips();
// next use Vector size method to get number of slips
System.out.println("Dock 1 has " + slips.size() + " slips");
// iterate through Vector to get information on each Slip
for(int i = 0; i < slips.size(); i++)
{
   Slip aSlip = (Slip) slips.elementAt(i);
   // verify Slip to Boat to Customer
   System.out.println(" Slip number " + aSlip.getNo()
   + " has width of " + aSlip.getWidth()
   + " has length of " + aSlip.getSlipLength()
   + "\n containing " + aSlip.getBoat().tellAboutSelf());
   }
  }
}
```

Figure 9-19   TesterThreeB source code

Figure 9-20 shows a sequence diagram of the interactions. First, reference variables are declared for a dock, two slips, two customers, and two boats. Next, the dock and two slips are instantiated. The association is completed in both directions by the Slip constructor. Next, two customers and two boats are instantiated, and the association is completed in both directions by the Boat constructor. Finally, each boat is assigned to a slip using the assignBoatToSlip method, which completes the association in both directions.

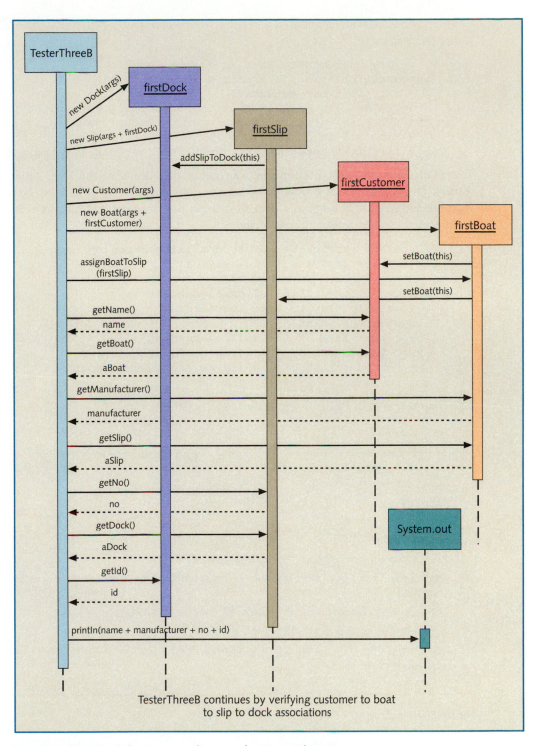

Figure 9-20   Partial sequence diagram for TesterThreeB

Once all associations are established, a customer reference can be used to navigate all the way to the Dock instance:

```
// verify Customer to Boat to Slip to Dock
System.out.println("Information for customer "
    + firstCustomer.getName()
    + "\n Boat is " + firstCustomer.getBoat().getManufacturer()
    + "\n Slip is " + firstCustomer.getBoat().getSlip().getNo()
    + "\n Dock is "
    + firstCustomer.getBoat().getSlip().getDock().getId());
```

TesterThreeB continues by testing the association from dock to the slips, boats, and customers. The Vector of slips is obtained from the dock and used in a for loop. Note that the Boat tellAboutSelf method gets information about the customer and returns it. You can also get specific customer information directly.

```
// iterate through Vector to get information on each Slip
for(int i = 0; i < slips.size(); i++)
{
    Slip aSlip = (Slip) slips.elementAt(i);
    // verify Slip to Boat to Customer
    System.out.println(" Slip number " + aSlip.getNo()
    + " has width of " + aSlip.getWidth()
    + " has length of " + aSlip.getSlipLength()
    + "\n containing " + aSlip.getBoat().tellAboutSelf());
}
```

The output shown in Figure 9-21 verifies all associations.

Information for customer Eleanor

    Boat is Tartan

    Slip is 1

    Dock is 1

Dock 1 has 2 slips

    Slip number 1 has width of 10 has length of 20.0

    containing I am a Boat state reg number MO34561 length 28.0 Manufacturer Tartan Year 2002

    and Owner is Eleanor living in Atlanta with phone 123-4567

    Slip number 2 has width of 12 has length of 25.0

    containing I am a Boat state reg number MO98765 length 32.0 Manufacturer Catalina Year 2001

    and Owner is JoAnn living in St Louis with phone 987-6543

Figure 9-21   Output of TesterThreeB

Hands-on Exercise 3

1. Locate Customer.java, Boat.java, Slip.java, Dock.java, TesterThreeA.java, and TesterThreeB.java on the book's CD in the folder named Example3 in the Chapter9 folder. Compile and run TesterThreeA and TesterThreeB using the software suggested by your instructor.

2. Modify TesterThreeB to add an additional dock and some slips, and then add some customers and boats for the slips. Verify that all associations work correctly.

3. Add a tellAboutSelf method to Slip that gets information about its boat and the boat's owner. If no boat is assigned to the slip, have the string indicate that the slip is available. (*Hint*: If Boat has a tellAboutSelf method that returns customer information, can you have Slip invoke that method?) Write a tester program to test all associations using the Slip tellAboutSelf method.

4. Add a tellAboutSelf method to Dock that gets information about each slip, its boat, and its owner (if a boat is in the slip). (*Hint*: Include a for loop in the Dock tellAboutSelf method.) Write a tester program to test all associations using the Dock tellAboutSelf method.

9

CREATING AND USING AN ASSOCIATION CLASS—LEASE

The Lease generalization/specialization hierarchy, which includes subclasses named Annual-Lease and DailyLease, was described in Chapter 8. The Lease class hierarchy is an association class in the Bradshaw Marina class diagram, meaning that a lease is much like an association between a customer and a slip, but with attributes for start date, end date, amount of lease, and so on. The notation in the partial class diagram shown in Figure 9-22 includes a dashed line attaching Lease to the association relationship between Customer and Slip.

The association between Customer and Slip is one-to-one, so the dashed line attaching Lease to this relationship means that there is one lease between each customer and slip. Often, association classes like Lease result from many-to-many associations, where a customer has many leases and a slip has many leases over a period of time.

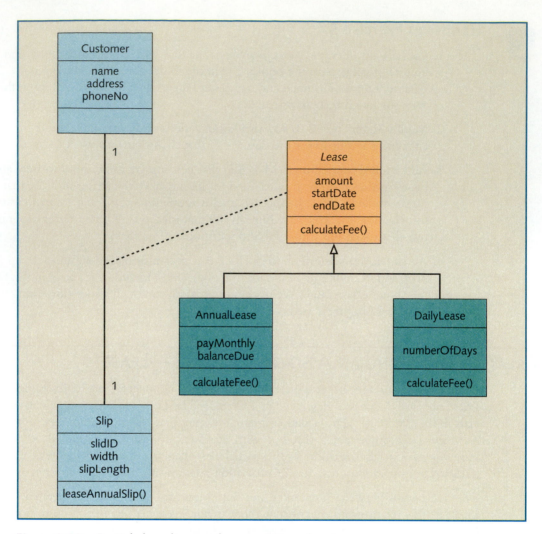

Figure 9-22 Partial class diagram for association class Lease

The example in this section involves five problem domain classes. The Lease superclass is modified to include a Slip reference attribute and a Customer reference attribute. Accessor methods are also included. No other changes have been made to the Lease class, introduced in Chapter 8 (see Figure 9-23). The Lease superclass can remain an abstract class. Note also that AnnualLease is a subclass of Lease, and it inherits the association between Lease and Slip and between Lease and Customer. This example includes no changes to the AnnualLease class even though an AnnualLease instance will be associated with a slip and a customer.

```java
// Abstract initial Lease class to extend with abstract method
// plus Slip and Customer reference attributes and accessors

import java.util.*; // for Date and Calendar classes
public abstract class Lease
{
   // attributes
   private double amount;
   private Date startDate;
   private Date endDate;
   // references to customer and to slip
   Customer customer;
   Slip slip;

   // constructor
   public Lease(Date aStartDate)

   {
      setStartDate(aStartDate);
      setEndDate(null);
      setAmount(0);
      // no customer or slip yet
      setCustomer(null);
      setSlip(null);
   }

   // abstract method subclasses must override
   public abstract double calculateFee(int aLength);

   // set accessor methods
   public void setAmount(double anAmount)
      { amount = anAmount; }
   public void setStartDate(Date aStartDate)
      { startDate = aStartDate; }
   public void setEndDate(Date anEndDate)
      { endDate = anEndDate; }
   public void setCustomer(Customer aCustomer)
      { customer = aCustomer; }
   public void setSlip(Slip aSlip)
      { slip = aSlip; }

   // get accessor methods
   public double getAmount()
      { return amount; }
   public Date getStartDate()
      { return startDate; }
   public Date getEndDate()
      { return endDate; }
   public Customer getCustomer()
      { return customer; }
   public Slip getSlip()
      { return slip; }
}
```

Figure 9-23   Modified Lease class definition

This example also uses the Boat class from the last section and associates it with Customer and with Slip. Boat is not directly associated with Lease, so the class definition does not have to change. The Customer class from earlier in this chapter does have an association with Lease, so you must change it by adding a Lease reference attribute along with accessor methods.

The Slip class requires more modification because it needs a custom method that creates a Lease instance and associates it with a customer and with a slip (see Figure 9-24). To change the Slip class, you first add a Lease reference attribute along with accessor methods. Because AnnualLease and DailyLease have constructors with different parameters, you include a method for creating an annual lease named leaseAnnualSlip, as in the following code. The parameters for this method include a customer reference, the start date, and the Boolean indicating whether monthly payments will be made.

```java
// custom method leaseSlip creates AnnualLease instance
// note: slip takes responsibility for much processing
public void leaseAnnualSlip(Customer aCustomer, Date aStartDate,
                    boolean isPayMonthly)
```

Figure 9-24 shows the completed Slip class definition after modification.

```java
// Slip with Lease reference
// plus leaseAnnualSlip method that does
// much processing to create an AnnualLease

import java.util.*;
public class Slip
{
   // attributes
   private int no;
   private int width;
   private double slipLength;
   private Boat boat;
   private Lease lease;

   // constructor with 3 parameters
   public Slip(int aNo, int aWidth, double aSlipLength)
   {
      // invoke accessors to populate attributes
      setNo(aNo);
      setWidth(aWidth);
      vsetSlipLength(aSlipLength);
      setBoat(null); // initially no boat is assigned to this slip
      setLease(null);// initially no lease for this slip
   }

   // custom method leaseSlip creates AnnualLease instance
   // note: slip takes responsibility for much processing
   public void leaseAnnualSlip(Customer aCustomer, Date aStartDate,
                       boolean isPayMonthly)
   {
      // create AnnualLease instance and assign it to lease
      // which is an attribute of this slip
      lease = new AnnualLease(aStartDate, width, isPayMonthly);
```

```
        // tell lease to set its slip to this slip
        lease.setSlip(this);
        // tell lease to set its customer
        lease.setCustomer(aCustomer);
        // tell customer to set its lease
        aCustomer.setLease(lease);
    }

    // set accessor methods
    public void setNo(int aNo)
        { no = aNo; }
    public void setWidth(int aWidth)
        { width = aWidth; }
    public void setSlipLength(double aSlipLength)
        { slipLength = aSlipLength;}
    public void setBoat(Boat aBoat)
        { boat = aBoat;}
    public void setLease(Lease aLease)
        { lease = aLease;}

    // get accessor methods
    public int getNo()
        { return no;}
    public int getWidth()
        { return width;}
    public double getSlipLength()
        { return slipLength;}
    public Boat getBoat()
        { return boat; }
    public Lease getLease()
        { return lease; }
}
```

Figure 9-24   Modified Slip class definition

The leaseAnnualSlip method first instantiates AnnualLease, assigning the returned reference
to a Lease reference. The complete AnnualLease class definition is shown in Chapter 8. Note
that you can assign a reference to a subclass to a reference variable of the superclass, as shown
in the following code:

```
    public void leaseAnnualSlip(Customer aCustomer, Date aStartDate,
                        boolean isPayMonthly)
    {
        // create AnnualLease instance and assign it to lease
        // which is an attribute of this slip
        lease = new AnnualLease(aStartDate, width, isPayMonthly);
        // tell lease to set its slip to this slip
        lease.setSlip(this);
        // tell lease to set its customer
        lease.setCustomer(aCustomer);
        // tell customer to set its lease
        aCustomer.setLease(lease);
    }
```

The start date and width of the slip are passed to AnnualLease, which invokes the superclass constructor to assign the start date, calculates the lease amount based on slip width, assigns the end date, and sets the balance due if there are to be monthly payments. The next statement asks the lease to set its slip reference. Then it asks the lease to set its customer reference. Finally, it asks the customer to set its lease reference.

Now that Slip, Lease, and Customer are modified, and Boat and AnnualLease are included without modification, TesterFour can test the classes. Figure 9-25 shows a sequence diagram that illustrates these interactions between Slip, AnnualLease, and Customer in TesterFour.

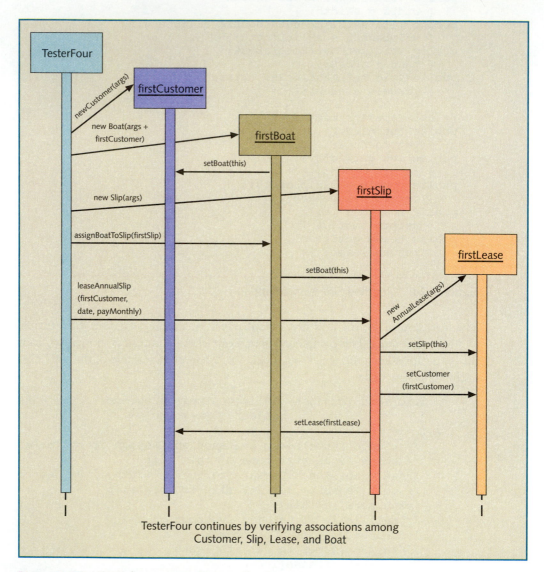

Figure 9-25 Partial sequence diagram for TesterFour

The source code for TesterFour is shown in Figure 9-26, and the output it produces is shown in Figure 9-27.

```java
// TesterFour to test leaseAnnualSlip method of Slip
// that creates AnnualLease and associates everything

import java.util.*;
public class TesterFour
{
   public static void main(String args[])
   {
   // create and set a date from calendar
   Calendar aCalendar = Calendar.getInstance();
   aCalendar.set(2003, Calendar.AUGUST, 28);
   Date date1 = aCalendar.getTime();

   Customer firstCustomer;
   Boat firstBoat;
   Slip firstSlip;
   Lease firstLease;

   // create a Customer instance
   firstCustomer = new Customer("Eleanor", "Atlanta", "123-4567");
   // create a Boat instance for customer
   firstBoat = new Boat("MO3456", 28,"Tartan", 2002, firstCustomer);
   // create a Slip instance
   firstSlip = new Slip(1, 12, 20);

   // assign the Boat to the Slip
   firstBoat.assignBoatToSlip(firstSlip);

   // lease this Slip to Customer (slip creates new annual lease)
   firstSlip.leaseAnnualSlip(firstCustomer, date1, true);

   // get new AnnualLease reference from Slip
   firstLease = firstSlip.getLease();

   // verify Boat to Customer association
   System.out.print(firstBoat.getCustomer().getName() + " owns ");
   // verify Customer to Boat association
   System.out.println(firstCustomer.getBoat().getManufacturer()
           + " " " + firstCustomer.getBoat().getLength());

   // verify Slip to Boat association
   System.out.print("Boat " +
        firstSlip.getBoat().getStateRegistrationNo());
   // verify Boat to Slip association
   System.out.println(" is assigned to Slip no " +
        firstBoat.getSlip().getNo());

   // verify Customer to Lease to Slip
   System.out.print(firstCustomer.getName() +
        " has leased slip no ");
```

9

```
System.out.println(firstCustomer.getLease().getSlip().getNo());
System.out.println("The lease amount is " +
    firstCustomer.getLease().getAmount());

// verify Slip to Lease to Customer
System.out.print("Slip number " + firstSlip.getNo() +
    " is leased to ");
System.out.println(firstSlip.getLease().getCustomer().getName());
System.out.println("The lease amount is " +
    firstSlip.getLease().getAmount());

// verify Slip to Boat to Customer to Lease and back to Slip!!!
System.out.println("Starting with slip 1 navigating to slip " +
  firstSlip.getBoat().getCustomer().getLease().getSlip().getNo());

  }
}
```

Figure 9-26   TesterFour source code

TesterFour first creates a Date to use as the start date, and then declares reference variables for a customer, boat, slip, and lease which will be assigned an AnnualLease reference. Next, Customer, Boat, and Slip are instantiated and the boat is assigned to a slip:

```
// create a Customer instance
firstCustomer = new Customer("Eleanor", "Atlanta", "123-4567");
// create a Boat instance for customer
firstBoat = new Boat("MO3456", 28,"Tartan", 2002, firstCustomer);
// create a Slip instance
firstSlip = new Slip(1, 12, 20);

// assign the Boat to the Slip
firstBoat.assignBoatToSlip(firstSlip);
```

```
Eleanor owns Tartan 28.0
Boat MO3456 is assigned to Slip no 1
Eleanor has leased slip no 1
The lease amount is 900.0
Slip number 1 is leased to Eleanor
The lease amount is 900.0
Starting with slip 1 navigating to slip 1
```

Figure 9-27   TesterFour output

Now that all instances are created and associated, the slip can be leased:

```
// lease this Slip to Customer (slip creates new annual lease)
firstSlip.leaseAnnualSlip(firstCustomer, date1, true);
```

The leaseAnnualSlip method instantiates AnnualLease and establishes the associations between Slip and Lease and Customer and Lease.

All associations can now be verified, including:

- Verifying Boat to Customer
- Verifying Customer to Boat
- Verifying Slip to Boat
- Verifying Boat to Slip
- Verifying Customer to Lease to Slip
- Verifying Slip to Lease to Customer

Finally, associations are navigated from Slip to Boat to Customer to Lease and back to Slip, completing a full circle. This statement accomplishes the final test:

```
// verify Slip to Boat to Customer to Lease and back to Slip!!!
System.out.println("Starting with slip 1 navigating to slip " +
    firstSlip.getBoat().getCustomer().getLease().getSlip().getNo());
```

All output produced by TesterFour is shown in Figure 9-27.

Hands-on Exercise 4

1. Locate Customer.java, Boat.java, Slip.java, Lease.java, AnnualLease.java, and TesterFour.java on the book's CD in the folder named Example4 in the Chapter9 folder. Compile and run the example using the software suggested by your instructor.

2. Add additional customers, boats, and slips to the tester program and test all associations.

3. Add the DailyLease class (from Chapter 8) to the example. Note that you do not need to modify DailyLease, but you do need to add a leaseDailySlip method to Slip that is similar to the leaseAnnualSlip method. Modify TesterFour so it creates daily leases instead of annual leases.

4. Add Dock to the example. Note that Dock already associates with Slip. However, note that the version of the Slip class in the Example4 folder no longer has a reference to Dock, so you will need to add the reference and accessor methods back into Slip that were included in the previous hands-on exercise. Modify TesterFour from Step 3 above so it includes Dock. The output should show information about a dock, including each slip, its boat, the boat's customer, and the lease.

Summary

- Association relationships show an important part of the requirements for a business information system and are shown on the class diagram as lines connecting classes. Association relationship examples in the Bradshaw Marina class diagram include: A customer owns a boat, a boat is assigned to a slip, a slip is part of a dock, and so forth.

- Association relationships are implemented in two directions that must be considered separately. For example, one direction indicates that a customer optionally owns a boat, and the other direction indicates that a boat must be owned by one and only one customer. In other words, some association relationships are optional and others are mandatory. Additionally, some have one-to-one multiplicity and some have one-to-many multiplicity. For example, a slip is part of one dock but a dock contains many slips.

- One-to-one association relationships are implemented in Java by including a reference variable as an attribute in one class that points to an instance of another class. Accessor methods are also included that set or get the reference variable.

- One-to-many association relationships are implemented using a Vector that contains a collection of reference variables. For example, a Vector named slips is included as an attribute of Dock, and slips contains a collection of Slip references. Accessor methods use methods of the Vector class to add and retrieve reference variables.

- Association relationships can be navigated directly by writing one statement with multiple method calls that are executed from left to right. For example, the statement `aBoat.getSlip().getDock().getLocation()` will get the location of a dock by asking the boat for its slip reference, which is used to get the dock reference, which is used to get the dock location.

- An association class on the class diagram is created much like any other class with Java. The association class exists because of a relationship between two classes, such as a Lease between Slip and Customer.

Review Questions

1. Describe the two directions of an association relationship between a Car and an Owner?

2. Give an example of an optional relationship—for example, between a Person and a Pet. Can one direction be optional and one direction be mandatory?

3. Give an example of a mandatory relationship, such as between a Mother and a Child. Can both directions be mandatory?

4. Give an example of a composition relationship.

5. Give an example of an aggregation relationship.

6. In your own words, describe how an association relationship is implemented using Java.

7. How are one-to-one association relationships implemented differently from one-to-many association relationships?

8. Write a statement that declares an attribute of Pet used to associate with one Person.

9. Write the header for a constructor for the Pet class with parameters for name, breed, and a Person reference variable to associate with.

10. Write a statement that declares a Vector in Person to hold a collection of Pet references.

11. Write a complete accessor method for Pet named setPerson assuming the Pet can have only one Person.

12. Write a complete method for Pet named assignPetToPerson that establishes the association in both directions.

13. Write statements for a short tester program that instantiates Person and Pet and then displays information about the Person by navigating from the Pet (based on your code written for Review Questions 8 through 12).

14. Modify the short tester program you wrote for Review Question 13 to instantiate several Pets for the Person, and then display information about each Pet by navigating from the Person. (*Hint*: Use a for loop with the Vector of pets.)

15. Consider the Mother and Child classes mentioned in Review Question 3. Write the statements to declare a mother attribute in Child and a children Vector in Mother.

16. Write a complete method for Child named assignChildToMother that establishes the associations in both directions.

17. Write statements for a short tester program that instantiates Mother and Child based on your code written for Review Question 16, and then displays information about the Mother by navigating from a Child.

9

18. Modify the short tester program you wrote for Review Question 17 to instantiate several children and a mother, and then display information about each Child by navigating from the Mother. (*Hint*: Use a for loop with the Vector of children.)

19. Consider a set of classes that are associated together in this sequence: House, Street, City, State, Country, Continent, and Planet. Assume standard accessor methods are used, such as getHouse, getStreet, etc., which return reference variables to associated instances. Write a Java statement that navigates from a house to get the name of the planet where the house is located.

Discussion Questions

1. Why are association relationships so important in business information systems? Can you imagine a business system without generalization/specialization hierarchies? Can you imagine a business system without association relationships? Discuss.

2. Because association relationships have two directions, a boat might know what slip it is assigned to, but a slip might not know what boat is assigned to it. When would it be desirable to implement one direction of the relationship but not the other? Discuss what might be accomplished by controlling association relationships.

3. This chapter showed one-to-one and one-to-many association relationships in Java. Can you use Java to directly implement many-to-many relationships? If so, explain how you would do so.

4. Relational databases also implement association relationships, but they use foreign keys instead of reference variables. Discuss the key differences between using object references as attributes and using foreign keys in relational databases.

Projects

1. In the Review Questions, you worked with a Person and Pet example. Implement the example as a Java project. Make sure your tester program tests the associations in both directions.

2. In the Review Questions, you worked with a Mother and Child example. Implement the example as a Java project. Make sure your tester program tests the associations in both directions.

3. Bradshaw Marina eventually wants to include boat service records in their system. Revise the Bradshaw Marina class diagram to include a BoatServiceRecord class that is associated with Boat. Each boat might have zero or more services, and each service applies to one boat. The attributes of BoatServiceRecord are invoice number, service date, service type, and total charges. Create a project that includes the BoatServiceRecord class plus Boat and Customer. Include the capability to associate the customer with the boat. Include a method in Boat named recordBoatService that instantiates BoatServiceRecord. Write a tester program to test the project.

4. In the Review Questions, you worked with a house, street, city, state, country, continent, and planet example. Draw the solution as a class diagram with attributes, including multiplicity between classes. Implement the example as a Java project. Make sure your tester program includes at least two instances of each class and tests the associations in both directions.

9

PART 3

Defining GUI Classes

10

Writing Graphical User Interfaces

Part 2 (Chapters 5–9) dealt with problem domain classes. You learned how to write PD class definitions consisting of attributes and methods, and how to create association and inheritance relationships among PD classes. Here in Part 3 (Chapters 10–13), you will learn how to develop graphical user interface (GUI) classes. You provide a graphical user interface so that users can both enter and display data. This chapter introduces the fundamentals, and Chapters 11 and 12 show you how to develop GUI classes for Bradshaw Marina. Chapter 13 illustrates the use of an Integrated Development Environment (IDE) to develop GUI screens.

All of the visible GUI components, and some invisible ones as well, are instances of the supplied Java GUI classes. For example, if you want to open a GUI window, you write your own class that extends the Frame class, instantiate it, and invoke an inherited method named setVisible to make it visible. If you want to include a push button, you instantiate the Button class and invoke a method to place that instance on your GUI window.

There are two distinct sets of GUI classes: the original AWT (Abstract Windowing Toolkit) classes and the new and improved Swing classes. Both AWT and Swing have classes to create controls such as windows, push buttons, text fields, and menus. In fact, several of the Swing classes extend AWT classes. This chapter illustrates both AWT and Swing classes.

Users create events by performing actions such as clicking a button or pressing a key on the keyboard. In this chapter you will learn more about events and how to interact with the user by writing code that responds to these events.

After completing this chapter, you will be able to write GUI class definitions using buttons, labels, text fields, panels, and menus. You will know how to use layout managers to help you position GUI components on the screen. You also will understand how to write methods to handle events and how to convert an application to an applet.

UNDERSTANDING JAVA'S GUI CLASSES

Figure 10-1 shows a GUI window containing additional GUI components. The window is called a frame and is an instance of the Frame class. The frame shown in Figure 10-1 consists of two panel instances. A panel is an invisible frame used to hold other components. In the top panel are instances of Label and TextField, and in the bottom panel are three button instances.

Java has two distinct sets of GUI classes. The original Java GUI classes, generally referred to as AWT, are in the java.awt package. The Swing classes, in the javax.swing package, were released with Java 2 and have capabilities beyond the AWT classes. The Swing classes have names similar to the AWT classes, but begin with the letter J (JButton, JApplet, JLabel, etc.). Both AWT and Swing have classes to create controls such as windows, push buttons, text fields, and menus. In fact, several of the Swing classes extend AWT classes. All of the graphical components you see on a Java GUI window are instances of classes in either the java.awt or javax.swing packages.

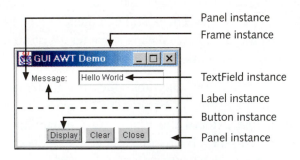

Figure 10-1   A frame with GUI components

Table 10-1   Description of Selected AWT GUI Classes

Component	Description
Applet	The superclass of all applets
Button	Push button; click causes event
Component	The superclass of all GUI classes
Container	A component that can contain other components
Frame	A GUI window with a title bar
Label	Used to display but not input text
Panel	An invisible container
TextField	Used to display and input text
Window	The superclass of Frame

Table 10-1 briefly describes selected AWT classes. The classes in bold are illustrated in this chapter.

The style and appearance of GUI components are called their **look and feel**. The AWT classes are tied to the local platform's GUI features and adopt the local platform's look and feel. In other words, if your GUI is running on a Windows platform, the windows, dialog boxes, buttons, and other components adopt the Windows GUI style and appearance. However, if your GUI runs on a Sun workstation, its appearance follows the style for that platform.

In contrast, when using the Swing GUI components, you have the option of using the local platform's GUI style or a standard look and feel (called "metal") that is common to all platforms. The Swing examples in this book use the metal look and feel. Figure 10-18, later in the chapter, is similar to Figure 10-1 but uses the metal look and feel, as do all of the Swing GUI examples.

The GUI classes, both AWT and Swing, take advantage of inheritance. You can see from Figure 10-2 that all of the GUI classes are subclasses of Component. In fact, Component contains many important methods that are inherited by its subclasses. You can explore the documentation files that come with the JDK to learn more about the GUI classes and their methods.

10

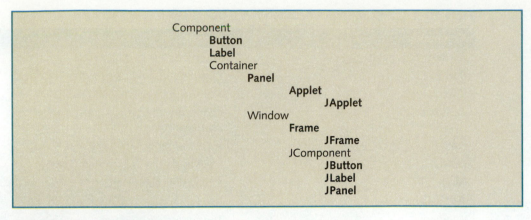

Figure 10-2   Hierarchy of selected AWT and Swing GUI classes

In Figure 10-2, classes in bold are illustrated in Chapter 10. Applet is in the java.applet package.

Using AWT Classes

The class definition for a GUI generally follows the structure you used for problem domain class definitions. However, one conceptual difference is that you create an instance of your GUI and *make it visible*: You can see the instance that was created from your GUI class definition. This means that you will write statements to instantiate all of the GUI components (such as push buttons, labels, and text fields) that you want to have on your window, and then write statements to add them to the window.

Creating a Window With a Button

The first example of a GUI class definition is named AWTFrameWithAButton, and it consists of a frame containing a button. As shown in Figure 10-2, Frame's inheritance hierarchy is Window, Container, and Component. This means that Frame, and therefore your GUI class, inherits methods from all three of these superclasses. AWTFrameWithAButton will use the AWT classes Frame and Button; therefore, the first statement imports classes from the java.awt package. Instead of writing a single import statement using the asterisk (*) wildcard character, you could write two individual statements indicating the specific classes you want to import.

```
import java.awt.*;
```

This class will actually be a subclass of Frame; therefore, its class header must extend the Frame class.

```
public class AWTFrameWithAButton extends Frame
```

This class will have only two methods: main and constructor. As you learned in previous chapters, the main method is automatically invoked by the JVM when the class is loaded into memory. In this example, main simply creates an instance of AWTFrameWithAButton that automatically invokes the constructor.

```
public static void main(String args[])
   { // create instance of Frame
     AWTFrameWithAButton frameWithButton = new AWTFrameWithAButton();
   }
```

The constructor method in AWTFrameWithAButton accomplishes five tasks:

1. Creates an instance of Button with the caption "Close."

   ```
   Button closeButton = new Button("Close");
   ```

2. Adds the button instance to the frame. The add method is inherited from Component.

   ```
   this.add(closeButton);
   ```

3. Establishes the frame size. The setSize method is inherited from Component.

   ```
   this.setSize(300,150);
   ```

4. Places a title on the frame. The setTitle method is inherited from Frame.

   ```
   this.setTitle("AWT Frame With A Button");
   ```

5. Makes the frame visible. The setVisible method is inherited from Component.

   ```
   this.setVisible(true);
   ```

The statements in Steps 2 through 5 all use the reference **this** because the methods being invoked are for this instance—the instance of AWTFrameWithAButton that was just created. However, because **this** is implied, you can omit it if you wish. The frame displayed by AWTFrameWithAButton is shown in Figure 10-3.

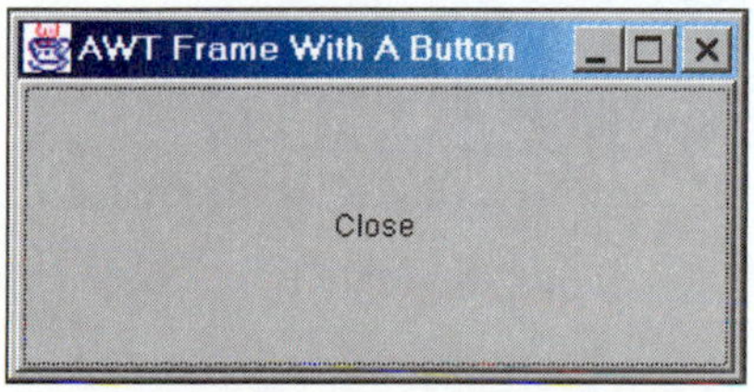

Figure 10-3 A frame with a button

This frame has a couple of problems. First, the button has expanded to fill the entire frame space, which gives it a strange appearance. The second problem is one you can't detect from looking at Figure 10-3; when you click the button, nothing happens. This GUI does not respond to the button click event. In the following sections, you will see how to use layout manager classes to help control the size and location of components you place on a frame, and how to make the GUI respond to events.

Using Layout Managers

The AWT includes several classes called **layout managers**, which determine how components are positioned on containers such as frames and panels. Generally you will not specify screen coordinates like you did in Chapter 6, but you will work with layout managers to position your components. Java provides several layout managers; however, the most frequently used are FlowLayout, BorderLayout, and GridLayout. To use a layout manager, you first instantiate the manager you want to use, and then invoke the setLayout method, passing it a reference for the layout manager you want to use. The setLayout method, like many others, is inherited from the Container class.

If you do not specify which layout manager to use, Java uses BorderLayout for frames and FlowLayout for panels. The previous AWTFrameWithAButton example uses the default BorderLayout. BorderLayout has five regions, named north, south, east, west, and center, as shown in Figure 10-4.

Components placed on a container using the BorderLayout manager *expand to fill the space available.* That's why the button in Figure 10-3 is so large: It expanded to fill the frame space. You saw in the previous example that you invoke the add method to place components on a frame. If you are using BorderLayout, you can pass the add method an argument to specify in which region you want the component to be placed. Several of the following examples use BorderLayout.

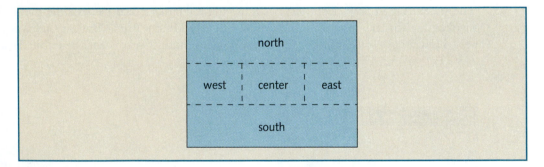

Figure 10-4   BorderLayout regions

The FlowLayout manager simply places components onto the frame as you add them, left to right. Unlike the BorderLayout manager, however, components added using FlowLayout do not expand to fill the entire space. Instead, they retain their normal size.

The GridLayout manager arranges the container into a grid consisting of rows and columns. When you instantiate GridLayout, you specify the number of rows and columns you want to have. Then, when you add components to the container, they are placed one after the other in row and column sequence. Similar to BorderLayout, components expand to fill the space available when using GridLayout.

The following statement instantiates FlowLayout and then invokes the setLayout method for the frame to make FlowLayout its manager.

```
this.setLayout(new FlowLayout());
```

Figure 10-5 shows that the button is now its normal size. However, this GUI still does not respond to someone clicking the button. You will learn in the next sections how to deal with this click event.

Handling Java Events

Users interact with GUI screens by entering data and clicking components such as buttons and menus. An event is a signal that the user has taken some action, such as clicking a button. An event is also an instance of a class, such as MouseEvent, WindowEvent, or ActionEvent. The event instance is created as the result of the user's action. Your GUI class needs to be able to respond to events.

The GUI you see in Figure 10-5 actually consists of two instances: an instance of the Button class referenced by the variable **closeButton** and an instance of AWTFrameWithAButton, which is a subclass of Frame and is referenced by the keyword **this**. When you click a GUI component, such as a button, the button instance is called the **event source**. In this example, you want AWTFrameWithAButton to respond to the button click event, which makes it an **event listener**. This relationship is shown graphically in Figure 10-6.

Figure 10-5   A frame with a button using FlowLayout

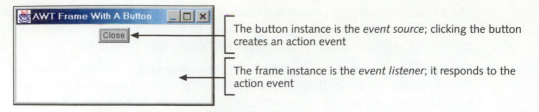

Figure 10-6   Button event source and frame event listener

The event listener wants the event source to notify it when the event source detects an event. The event listener **registers** with the event source by invoking a method in the event source. Button events are called **action events** and their registration method is named addActionListener. The statement to register AWTFrameWithAButton as an event listener with `closeButton` is:

```
closeButton.addActionListener(this);
```

The argument passed to addActionListener is `this`, which references the instance of AWTFrameWithAButton (the event listener).

The next step is to write a method to handle the event. For button events, this method is named actionPerformed. When the button detects a click event, it invokes actionPerformed for instances that have registered as event listeners. The next three sections illustrate three different techniques for handling events.

Implementing Interfaces

You learned about interfaces in Chapter 8. An interface is like a class, except that its methods are abstract. In addition, although you can extend only one class, you can implement multiple interfaces. When you implement an interface, you must override all of its methods. One approach to handling events is to implement the appropriate interface for the event, and then write methods to override the interface's methods and deal with the event or events.

The interface you use for button clicks is named ActionListener and has one abstract method, named actionPerformed. To implement this interface, you add the implements clause to the AWTFrameWithAButton class header.

```
public class AWTFrameWithAButton extends Frame implements
ActionListener
```

Now AWTFrameWithAButton extends the Frame class and implements the ActionListener interface. Next you add a statement to the constructor to register AWTFrameWithAButton as an event listener with `closeButton`.

```
closeButton.addActionListener(this);
```

You will need to import both the ActionListener interface and ActionEvent class from the java.awt.event package. You can write either two separate import statements or one statement using the wildcard character.

```
import java.awt.event.*;
```

Next, you write the actionPerformed method, overriding the abstract method in the Action-Listener interface, to deal with the event. The method signature requires a parameter variable to receive a reference to the ActionEvent instance. In this example, nothing is done with the event instance; however, you must still write the parameter variable, because it is specified in the abstract method's header.

```
public void actionPerformed(ActionEvent e)
```

You want to terminate processing when the Close button is clicked. One way to stop execution is to invoke the exit method in the System class.

```
{ System.exit(0);}
```

At this point, AWTFrameWithAButton responds to the button click event, but it does not respond to a click on the window close icon, which triggers a window closing event. The interface you implement to respond to window events is named WindowListener, so you add WindowListener to the implements clause of the class header for AWTFrameWithAButton. This class now extends Frame and implements *two* interfaces.

```
public class AWTFrameWithAButton extends Frame implements
ActionListener, WindowListener
```

In the previous example, you invoked the button's addActionListener method to register the frame instance as a listener for button events. Similarly, you must now invoke the frame's addWindowListener method to register the frame as a listener for frame events. Note that for window events, the frame instance is both the event source and the event listener. The following statement illustrates this code and the relationship is shown graphically in Figure 10-7.

```
this.addWindowListener(this);
```

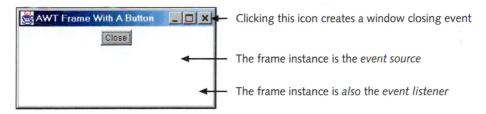

Clicking this icon creates a window closing event

The frame instance is the *event source*

The frame instance is *also* the *event listener*

Figure 10-7   Frame event source and frame event listener

The WindowListener interface has seven abstract methods, and you must override all of them, even though window closing is the only event to which you want to respond. The code for these seven methods is:

```java
public void windowClosing(WindowEvent event)
    { shutDown(); }
public void windowClosed(WindowEvent event){}
public void windowDeiconified(WindowEvent event){}
public void windowIconified(WindowEvent event){}
public void windowActivated(WindowEvent event){}
public void windowDeactivated(WindowEvent event){}
public void windowOpened(WindowEvent event){}
```

Notice that only the windowClosing method actually performs a task (it invokes the shut-Down method described below). Although the other six methods contain no code (they are null), you are required to write them because you implemented the WindowListener interface, and when you implement an interface, you must override all of its abstract methods. In the next two sections, you will learn how to avoid writing these null methods.

Because both the actionPerformed and the windowClosing methods terminate processing, you should add a method named shutDown which terminates processing. You invoke shut-Down from both actionPerformed and windowClosing, which eliminates having duplicate code in these two methods.

```java
public void shutDown()
    { System.exit(0);}
```

The complete listing of AWTFrameWithAButton is shown in Figure 10-8.

```java
// illustrate event handling using listener interfaces
import java.awt.*;
import java.awt.event.*;

public class AWTFrameWithAButton extends Frame implements
ActionListener, WindowListener
{
   public static void main(String args[])
   {   // create instance of Frame
       AWTFrameWithAButton frameWithButton = new AWTFrameWithAButton();
   }

   // constructor
   public AWTFrameWithAButton()
   {  // create instance of Button
      Button closeButton = new Button("Close");
      // set FlowLayout as the layout manager
      this.setLayout(new FlowLayout());
      // place Button on Frame instance
      this.add(closeButton);
      // establish size, create title & make it visible
      this.setSize(300,150);
      this.setTitle("AWT Frame With A Button");
```

```
        this.setVisible(true);
        // register frame as listener for button event
        closeButton.addActionListener(this);
        // register frame as listener for frame event
        this.addWindowListener(this);

    }
    // actionPerformed is invoked when closeButton is clicked
    public void actionPerformed(ActionEvent e)
        { shutDown(); }

    //  The following 7 methods are required because we implemented
WindowListener
    // windowClosing invoked when window closed
    public void windowClosing(WindowEvent event)
        { shutDown(); }

    public void windowClosed(WindowEvent event){}
    public void windowDeiconified(WindowEvent event){}
    public void windowIconified(WindowEvent event){}
    public void windowActivated(WindowEvent event){}
    public void windowDeactivated(WindowEvent event){}
    public void windowOpened(WindowEvent event){}

    // terminate
    public void shutDown()
    {
        this.dispose();
        System.exit(0);
    }
}
```

Figure 10-8   AWTFrameWithAButton.java listing

Hands-on Exercise 1

1. Create a folder named Chapter10Exercise1 on your system.

2. Locate AWTFrameWithAButton.java in the folder named Chapter10\Example1 on the book's CD and then copy it to the Chapter10Exercise1 folder you created in Step 1.

3. Compile AWTFrameWithAButton.java and then run it using the software recommended by your instructor. Verify that your GUI appears and behaves correctly.

4. The method windowIconified is invoked when you minimize a window by clicking the minimize icon in the title bar. Add statements to this method to display a message when the window is minimized. Recompile and test your modifications.

10

Extending Adapter Classes

A second way of dealing with events is to use an **adapter class**. An adapter class is a supplied class that implements a listener interface and then overrides all of the interface methods with null methods. For example, WindowAdapter, a member of the java.awt.event package, implements the WindowListener interface and overrides all seven of the interface's abstract methods. The benefit of using WindowAdapter is that you do not have to override the seven window event handler methods like you did in the previous section.

The WindowAdapter methods, however, are null; they contain no code. This means that if you want your GUI class to respond to window events, then you must override the methods corresponding to those events. For example, if you want to terminate when the window is closed, then you need to override the windowClosing method.

You use WindowAdapter by extending it in your GUI class. In other words, your class becomes a subclass of WindowAdapter and it inherits the seven adapter methods. This means that your class does not have to implement WindowListener nor does it have to include its seven abstract methods. Instead, you write only the methods you need. Specifically, to respond to the window closing event, you need write only the windowClosing method.

Extending an adapter creates a slight complexity, however. In the previous example, AWTFrameWithAButton extended Frame. Because you cannot extend *two* classes, AWTFrameWithAButton cannot extend both Frame and WindowAdapter.

One solution is to create two separate classes: AWTFrameWithAButton plus a small second class you can name WindowCloser. AWTFrameWithAButton will extend Frame, and WindowCloser will extend WindowAdapter, as shown in Figure 10-9.

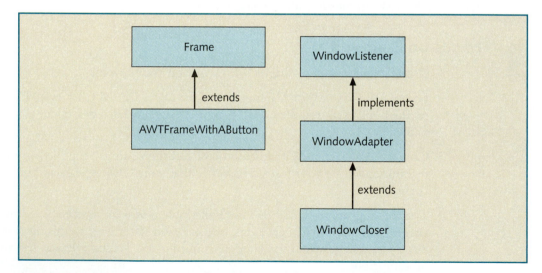

Figure 10-9   Class diagram for AWTFrameWithAButton and WindowCloser

When you use this approach, WindowCloser becomes the listener for window events and will contain the event handler method windowClosing. WindowCloser will have only two methods: windowClosing and a constructor. AWTFrameWithAButton's constructor will instantiate WindowCloser, thereby invoking its constructor, and pass it a reference to the frame instance. Then when the window closing icon is clicked, the windowClosing method in WindowCloser is invoked and it, in turn, invokes shutDown in AWTFrameWithAButton.

The statements you add to the AWTFrameWithAButton constructor to instantiate WindowCloser and register it as a listener for window events are:

```
WindowCloser eventHandler = new WindowCloser(this);
this.addWindowListener(eventHandler);
```

Note that addWindowListener is being invoked for the frame instance because it is the event source. Also note that the argument passed to the WindowCloser constructor is a reference to the frame instance, the instance of AWTFrameWithAButton.

Java permits you to create a source file containing more than one class, but only one of the classes may be public. In this example, the source file is named AWTFrameWithAButton.java and the public class is AWTFrameWithAButton. You can add the WindowCloser class to this file, provided that its accessibility is not public. The code for WindowCloser is:

```
// WindowCloser is a subclass of WindowAdapter
class WindowCloser extends WindowAdapter
{
    AWTFrameWithAButton frameToClose;
    // constructor populates reference to frame instance

    public WindowCloser(AWTFrameWithAButton frame)
    { frameToClose = frame;}

    // windowClosing is invoked when window closed
    // this method overrides windowClosing in WindowAdapter
    public void windowClosing(WindowEvent event)
    { frameToClose.shutDown();    }
}
```

10

WindowCloser extends WindowAdapter and has two methods: a constructor and the event handling method windowClosing. When AWTFrameWithAButton instantiates WindowCloser, it passes a reference to the AWTFrameWithAButton instance. The WindowCloser constructor receives this reference into the parameter variable named frame and uses it to populate the reference variable frameToClose, which has a data type AWTFrameWithAButton.

Then when the close window icon on the frame is clicked, a window closing event is triggered and the windowClosing method in WindowCloser is invoked. The windowClosing method then invokes shutDown for the AWTFrameWithAButton instance, which terminates execution.

The frame and button appear and behave exactly as in the previous example. The listing for AWTFrameWithAButton and WindowCloser is shown in Figure 10-10.

```java
// illustrate event handling using an adapter class

import java.awt.*;
import java.awt.event.*;
public class AWTFrameWithAButton extends Frame implements
ActionListener
{
    public static void main(String args[])
    {   // create instance of Frame
        AWTFrameWithAButton frameWithButton = new AWTFrameWithAButton();
    }

    // constructor
    public AWTFrameWithAButton()
    {   // create instance of Button
        Button closeButton = new Button("Close");
        // set FlowLayout as the layout manager
        this.setLayout(new FlowLayout());
        // place Button on Frame instance
        this.add(closeButton);
        // establish size, create title & make it visible
        this.setSize(300,150);
        this.setTitle("AWT Frame With A Button");
        this.setVisible(true);
        // register frame as listener for button event
        closeButton.addActionListener(this);

        // create instance of WindowCloser
        WindowCloser eventHandler = new WindowCloser(this);

        // register WindowCloser as listener for frame event
        this.addWindowListener(eventHandler);
    }

    // actionPerformed is invoked when closeButton is clicked
    public void actionPerformed(ActionEvent e)
        { shutDown(); }

    public void shutDown()
    {
        this.dispose();
        System.exit(0);   // terminate
    }
}
```

```
// WindowCloser is a subclass of WindowAdapter
class WindowCloser extends WindowAdapter
{
    AWTFrameWithAButton frameToClose;
    // constructor populates reference to frame instance
    public WindowCloser(AWTFrameWithAButton frame)
    { frameToClose = frame;}

    // windowClosing is invoked when window closed
    // this method overrides windowClosing in WindowAdapter
    public void windowClosing(WindowEvent event)
    { frameToClose.shutDown();    }
}
```

Figure 10-10   AWTFrameWithAButton.java with WindowCloser listing

The benefit of using an adapter class here is that the window event handling code is removed from AWTFrameWithAButton. You have eliminated the need to write all seven window event handling methods, even though you wanted to use only one of them. The disadvantage is that you must write the new class (WindowCloser) and instantiate it from AWTFrameWithAButton.

Hands-on Exercise 2

1. Create a folder named Chapter10Exercise2 on your system.

2. Locate AWTFrameWithAButton.java in the Chapter10\Example2 folder on the book's CD and then copy it to the Chapter10Exercise2 folder you created in Step 1.

3. Compile AWTFrameWithAButton.java and then run it using the software recommended by your instructor. Verify that your GUI appears and behaves correctly.

4. windowIconified is invoked when you minimize a window by clicking the minimize icon in the title bar. Modify WindowCloser to include windowIconified and have it display a message when the window is minimized. Recompile and test your modifications.

Creating Inner Classes

A third way of dealing with events is to use an **anonymous inner class**. An inner class is a class that you define inside of another class. An anonymous inner class is an inner class you write without giving it a name. You can use an anonymous inner class to simplify the code needed to handle events, especially window events.

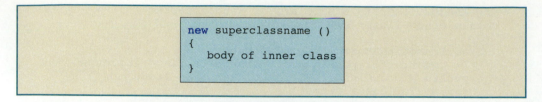

Figure 10-11   Expanded keyword **new** used with anonymous inner classes

Inner classes, just like other (outer) classes, can extend a class and implement interfaces. However, an important benefit of using an inner class is that it can extend a *different* class from its outer class. This means that you can have your outer class extend Frame and have your inner class extend an adapter class, such as WindowAdapter in this example. The inner class will be the event listener for window events.

The code to create an inner class uses an expanded form of the **new** keyword, as shown in Figure 10-11.

The code to create the inner class is combined with the code to register the anonymous inner class with the frame instance as a listener for window events.

```
this.addWindowListener
    (   // begin inner class definition
        new WindowAdapter() // superclass is WindowAdapter
        {
            public void windowClosing(WindowEvent event)
                {shutDown();}
        }// end of inner class definition
    );
```

The relationship between AWTFrameWithAButton, the WindowListener interface, WindowAdapter, and the anonymous inner class is shown in Figure 10-12. The superclass of AWTFrameWithAButton is Frame and the superclass of the anonymous inner class is WindowAdapter. WindowAdapter in turn implements the WindowListener interface. Because the anonymous inner class is defined within AWTFrameWithAButton, it has complete access to all of the methods, including shutDown, which it invokes in the windowClosing method.

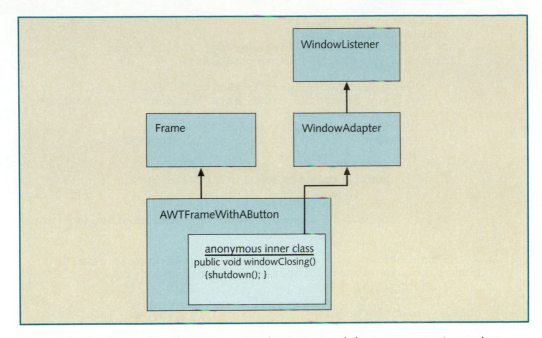

Figure 10-12   Hierarchy of AWTFrameWithAButton and the anonymous inner class

10

The listing of AWTFrameWithAButton with the anonymous inner class is shown in Figure 10-13. In this example, using the inner class appears to be the simplest approach to handling window events.

```java
// illustrate event handling using an anonymous inner class
import java.awt.*;
import java.awt.event.*;
public class AWTFrameWithAButton extends Frame implements
ActionListener
{
    public static void main(String args[])
    {   // create instance of Frame
        AWTFrameWithAButton frameWithButton = new AWTFrameWithAButton();
    }

    // constructor
    public AWTFrameWithAButton()
    {   // create instance of Button
        Button closeButton = new Button("Close");
        // set FlowLayout as the layout manager
        this.setLayout(new FlowLayout());
        // place Button on Frame instance
        this.add(closeButton);
        // establish size, create title & make it visible
        this.setSize(300,150);
```

```
        this.setTitle("AWT Frame With A Button");
        this.setVisible(true);
        // register frame as listener for button event
        closeButton.addActionListener(this);

        // create anonymous inner class to handle window closing event
        // register the inner class as a listener with the frame
        this.addWindowListener
        (    // begin inner class definition
             // superclass of inner class is WindowAdapter
             new WindowAdapter()
             {
                 public void windowClosing(WindowEvent event)
                     {shutDown();} // invoke shutDown in outer class
             }    // end of inner class definition
        );       // end of argument sent to addWindowListener method
    }

    // actionPerformed is invoked when closeButton is clicked
    public void actionPerformed(ActionEvent e)
        { shutDown(); }

    public void shutDown()
    {
      this.dispose();
      System.exit(0);   // terminate
    }
}
```

Figure 10-13   AWTFrameWithAButton.java listing

When you compile a class with an inner class, the compiler produces two class files. If the inner class has a name, its class file name consists of the outer class name concatenated with a dollar sign concatenated with the inner class name. For example, if your outer class is named Outer and the inner class is named Inner, the compiler produces a class file named Outer.class for the outer class and Outer$Inner.class for the inner class.

If the inner class is anonymous, the class file for the inner class has the same name as the outer class concatenated with a dollar sign and a sequence number beginning with 1 for the first inner class, 2 for the second, and so forth. For example, if your outer class is named Outer, the first anonymous inner class file is named Outer$1.class. When AWTFrameWithAButton with its anonymous inner class is compiled, two class files are produced: AWTFrameWithAButton.class and AWTFrameWithAButton$1.class.

To summarize, there are three techniques for dealing with events: implement a listener interface, extend an adaptor class, or use an anonymous inner class. For button events, the simpler approach is to implement the ActionListener interface, because it has only one abstract method that you must override. For window events, unless you intend to include all seven window event handler methods, using an anonymous inner class is generally the simpler technique and is used throughout the remainder of this book.

Hands-on Exercise 3

1. Create a folder named Chapter10Exercise3 on your system.

2. Locate AWTFrameWithAButton.java in the folder named Chapter10\Example3 on the book's CD and then copy it to the Chapter10Exercise3 folder you created in Step 1.

3. Compile AWTFrameWithAButton.java and then run it using the software recommended by your instructor. Verify that your GUI appears and behaves correctly.

4. The method windowIconified is invoked when you minimize a window by clicking the minimize icon in the title bar. Add the windowIconified method to the anonymous inner class and have it display a message when the window is minimized. Recompile and test your modifications.

Using Multiple GUI Components

In the previous section you saw how to create a visible frame and make it respond to button click and window closing events. In this section you will see how to place additional GUI components onto the frame. You will also learn how to work with several buttons and determine which one was clicked. Figure 10-1 showed you a frame with a label, a text field, three buttons, and two panels. You will see in this section how to create that frame.

The class developed in this section, AWTFrameAndComponents, begins just like AWTFrameWithAButton in the previous section, by importing classes from the java.awt and java.awt.event packages. The class header also implements the ActionListener interface. This class continues to use the anonymous inner class to handle the window closing event; therefore, you do not need to implement the WindowListener interface.

```
import java.awt.*;
import java.awt.event.*;

public class AWTFrameAndComponents extends Frame implements
ActionListener
```

Next are statements declaring reference variables for the three button and two TextField instances. These variables require class scope because they are used in more than one method.

```
Button displayButton, clearButton, closeButton;
TextField messageTextField;
```

Next comes the main method containing a single statement to instantiate the frame, which automatically invokes the constructor.

```
public static void main(String args[])
{
// create instance of AWTFrameAndComponents
AWTFrameAndComponents frameAndCompnents = new AWTFrameAndComponents();
}
```

10

The constructor method is responsible for instantiating all of the GUI components, placing them on the frame, registering the buttons and frame as event listeners, and finally making the frame visible. The frame will have seven components; therefore, the first seven statements instantiate them.

```
displayButton = new Button("Display");
clearButton = new Button("Clear");
closeButton = new Button("Close");
Label messageLabel = new Label("Message:");
messageTextField = new TextField(15);
Panel upperPanel = new Panel();
Panel lowerPanel = new Panel();
```

Refer back to Figure 10-1. The upperPanel will contain the Label and TextField instances, and the lowerPanel will hold the three Button instances. Recall that the default layout manager for panels is FlowLayout, which means the components are added left to right and they retain their original size. The code placing the components onto the panels is:

```
upperPanel.add(messageLabel);
upperPanel.add(messageTextField);

lowerPanel.add(displayButton);
lowerPanel.add(clearButton);
lowerPanel.add(closeButton);
```

Next, the two populated panel instances are added to the frame instance. Recall that the default layout manager for Frame is BorderLayout. You want to place the upperPanel in the north region and the lower panel in the south region. You accomplish this by writing statements that invoke the add method for the frame instance (referenced by **this**), and pass the panel reference and the region name as arguments.

```
this.add("North",upperPanel);
this.add("South",lowerPanel);
```

Next, you register the frame instance (**this**) as an event listener for the three buttons by invoking addActionListener for each.

```
displayButton.addActionListener(this);
clearButton.addActionListener(this);
closeButton.addActionListener(this);
```

Then, as in previous examples, the setSize, setTitle, and setVisible methods are invoked.

```
this.setSize(320,150);
this.setTitle("AWT Frame and Components");
this.setVisible(true);
```

The final statements in the constructor create the anonymous inner class to handle the window closing event and are identical to those in the AWTFrameWithAButton constructor.

```
// create anonymous inner class to handle window closing event
// register the inner class as a listener with the frame
this.addWindowListener
(   // begin inner class definition
    new WindowAdapter() // superclass is WindowAdapter
    {
        public void windowClosing(WindowEvent event)
            {shutDown();} // invoke shutDown in outer class
    }// end of inner class definition
); // end of argument sent to addWindowListener method
```

In this example, any one of three buttons can be clicked and you want to take different actions, depending on which one was clicked. For example, if the display button is clicked, you want to display a message, but if the clear button is clicked, you want to clear the message. If the close button is clicked, you want to shut down as you did in previous examples.

When a button is clicked, an ActionEvent is triggered, and the actionPerformed method is invoked for the registered event listener. In other words, actionPerformed is invoked whenever *any* of the buttons are clicked. This means you must add code to determine which button was clicked and then take the appropriate action. When actionPerformed is invoked, it is passed an ActionEvent instance containing information about the triggering event. Among other things, this instance knows who the event source is.

ActionEvent has a method named getSource that will return a reference for the event source—the GUI component that experienced the event. Therefore, you can write a series of if statements to determine which button is experiencing the event. Although you could include the code to display the message, clear the message, and terminate execution within the actionPerformed method, a better technique is to have actionPerformed determine which event occurred and then invoke a separate method to deal with the event. This approach simplifies your design by having one method deal with one task instead of several. The following if statements invoke the getSource method for the ActionEvent instance, and then compare the value returned to a button reference. If the button was the event source, then the appropriate method (displayMessage, clearMessage, or shutDown) is invoked.

```
if(e.getSource() == displayButton)
    displayMessage();
if(e.getSource() == clearButton)
    clearMessage();
if(e.getSource() == closeButton)
  shutDown();
```

10

The displayMessage method places a message in the messageTextField instance. TextField has a method, appropriately named setText, to do this. You pass setText the value that you want displayed. Note that TextField also has a method named getText which retrieves and returns the contents as a String instance.

```java
public void displayMessage()
    { messageTextField.setText("Hello World"); }
```

In a similar manner, clearMessage invokes setText and passes spaces to be displayed, which erases the message.

```java
public void clearMessage()
    { messageTextField.setText("              "); }
```

The shutDown method is exactly the same as in the previous examples. The complete code for AWTFrameAndComponents is listed in Figure 10-14.

```java
// illustrate multiple AWT components

import java.awt.*;
import java.awt.event.*;

public class AWTFrameAndComponents extends Frame implements
ActionListener
{
    // Button & TextField reference variables need class scope
    Button displayButton, clearButton, closeButton;
    TextField messageTextField;

    public static void main(String args[])
    {   // create instance of AWTFrameAndComponents
        AWTFrameAndComponents frameAndComponents = new
AWTFrameAndComponents();
    }

    // constructor
    public AWTFrameAndComponents()
    {   // create Button, Label and TextField instances
        displayButton = new Button("Display");
        clearButton = new Button("Clear");
        closeButton = new Button("Close");
        Label messageLabel = new Label("Message:");
        messageTextField = new TextField(15);
        // create two Panels - default FlowLayout manager
        Panel upperPanel = new Panel();
        Panel lowerPanel = new Panel();
        // add label & textfield to upper panel
        upperPanel.add(messageLabel);
        upperPanel.add(messageTextField);
        // add buttons to lower panel
        lowerPanel.add(displayButton);
        lowerPanel.add(clearButton);
```

```
      lowerPanel.add(closeButton);
      // add panels to frame - frame default is BorderLayout
      this.add("North",upperPanel);
      this.add("South",lowerPanel);
      // register frame as event listener with all buttons
      displayButton.addActionListener(this);
      clearButton.addActionListener(this);
      closeButton.addActionListener(this);
      this.setSize(320,150);
      this.setTitle("AWT Frame and Components");
      this.setVisible(true);

      // create anonymous inner class to handle window closing event
      // register the inner class as a listener with the frame
      this.addWindowListener
      (  // begin inner class definition
         new WindowAdapter() // superclass is WindowAdapter
         {
            public void windowClosing(WindowEvent event)
                {shutDown();} // invoke shutDown in outer class
         }// end of inner class definition
      ); // end of argument sent to addWindowListener method
   }

   // actionPerformed is invoked when a Button is clicked
   public void actionPerformed(ActionEvent e)
   {  // see which button was clicked
      if(e.getSource() == displayButton)
         displayMessage();
      if(e.getSource() == clearButton)
         clearMessage();
      if(e.getSource() == closeButton)
         shutDown();
   }
   public void displayMessage()
      { messageTextField.setText("Hello World"); }
   public void clearMessage()
      { messageTextField.setText("             "); }
   public void shutDown()
      {
         this.dispose();
         System.exit(0);   // terminate
      }
}
```

Figure 10-14 AWTFrameAndComponents.java listing

Hands-on Exercise 4

1. Create a folder named Chapter10Exercise4 on your system.

2. Locate AWTFrameAndComponents.java in the folder named Chapter10\Example4 on the book's CD and then copy it to the Chapter10Exercise4 folder you created in Step 1.

3. Compile AWTFrameAndComponents.java and then run it using the software rec-ommended by your instructor. Verify that your GUI appears and behaves correctly.

4. Add a fourth button named whoButton with the caption "Who?" When whoButton is clicked, invoke a method named displayMyName that will display your name in messageTextField.

5. Recompile and test your modifications.

CONVERTING AN APPLICATION TO AN APPLET

In Chapter 3 you saw how to write a simple applet. An applet is a class you write that extends the Applet class and runs under control of a browser such as Internet Explorer or Netscape Navigator, or the Applet Viewer supplied with Java. In this section you will see how to convert a GUI application such as AWTFrameAndComponents to an applet.

Because an applet executes under control of a browser, you do not write statements to instantiate the applet, make it visible, or terminate its execution; the browser performs all of these tasks for you. Further, AWT applets do not have a title bar, and an HTML statement determines their size. Therefore, you can convert AWTFrameAndComponents to an applet named AWTApplet primarily by using the delete key:

- Delete the main method.
- Delete all references to the close button.
- Delete the anonymous inner class.
- Delete the shutDown method.
- Delete the statement that invokes the setVisible, setSize, and setTitle methods.

Also, because AWTApplet will extend the Applet class, you will need to import the java.applet package.

Applets have a method named init that is invoked when the applet is loaded into memory. You can change the constructor method's name to init and add a void return type. The completed AWTApplet code is listed in Figure 10-15.

```
// illustrate AWT Applet

import java.awt.*;
import java.awt.event.*;
import java.applet.*;

public class AWTApplet extends Applet implements ActionListener
{
    // Button & TextField reference variables need class scope
    Button displayButton, clearButton, closeButton;
    TextField messageTextField;
```

```
// constructor
public void init()
{
    // create Button, Label and TextField instances
    displayButton = new Button("Display");
    clearButton = new Button("Clear");
    Label messageLabel = new Label("Message:");
    messageTextField = new TextField(15);
    // create two Panels - default FlowLayout manager
    Panel upperPanel = new Panel();
    Panel lowerPanel = new Panel();
    // add label & textfield to upper panel
    upperPanel.add(messageLabel);
    upperPanel.add(messageTextField);
    // add buttons to lower panel
    lowerPanel.add(displayButton);
    lowerPanel.add(clearButton);
    // add panels to frame - frame default is BorderLayout
    this.add("North",upperPanel);
    this.add("South",lowerPanel);
    // register frame as listener for button events
    displayButton.addActionListener(this);
    clearButton.addActionListener(this);
}

// actionPerformed is invoked when a Button is clicked
public void actionPerformed(ActionEvent e)
{   // see which button was clicked
    if(e.getSource() == displayButton)
        displayMessage();
    if(e.getSource() == clearButton)
        clearMessage();
}
public void displayMessage()
    { messageTextField.setText("Hello World"); }
public void clearMessage()
    { messageTextField.setText("         "); }
}
```

Figure 10-15 AWTApplet.java listing

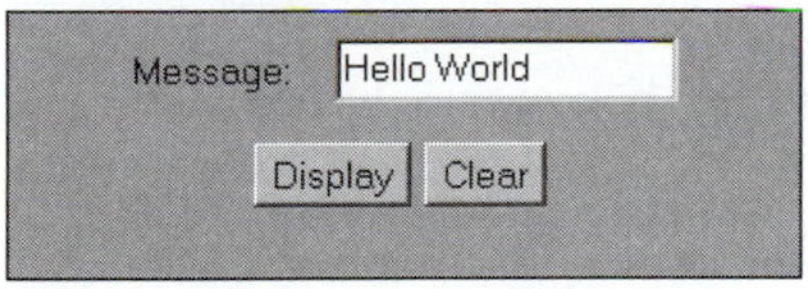

Figure 10-16 AWTApplet output

10

Finally, you will need to write a small HTML file to test AWTApplet. HTML code is used to tell the browser the name of your applet and its size. This HTML file consists of the two statements shown in the following code. The first tells the browser the name of the Applet class file and the size of the applet. The second statement indicates the end of the HTML code. You can run the applet by either opening this HTML file with a browser, or the Applet Viewer program that comes with Java.

```
<APPLET CODE="AWTApplet.class" WIDTH="300" HEIGHT="100">
</APPLET>
```

The output from the applet appears in Figure 10-16. It is quite similar to the output from AWTFrameAndComponents except for the missing close button.

Hands-on Exercise 5

1. Create a folder named Chapter10Exercise5 on your system.

2. Locate AWTApplet.java and AWTApplet.html in the folder named Chapter10\Example5 on the book's CD and then copy them to the Chapter10Exercise5 folder you created in Step 1.

3. Compile AWTApplet.java using the software recommended by your instructor.

4. Run the applet using either a browser or Applet Viewer, verifying that it appears and behaves correctly.

5. Add a third button named whoButton with the caption "Who?" When whoButton is clicked, invoke a method named displayMyName that will display your name in messageTextField.

6. Recompile and test your modifications.

USING SWING CLASSES

The Swing classes are the newer, improved versions of the original AWT classes. Generally you will want to use them instead of the AWT classes when writing GUI classes because of their improved appearance and capability. For example, the Swing applet provides a title bar and drop-down menus.

Figure 10-2 shows the hierarchical relationship between selected Swing classes and their AWT counterparts. Notice that the names of the Swing classes begin with the letter J: JApplet, JFrame, JButton, and so forth. In this section you will see how to replicate AWTFrameAndComponents using Swing classes. In addition, you will learn how to add drop-down menus and write methods that respond to menu click events. You will also see how to take advantage of the improvements added to the JApplet class.

Converting an AWT GUI to Swing

In this section you will see how to modify AWTFrameAndComponents to use the Swing components, creating a new class named SwingFrameAndComponents. The Swing components reside in the javax.swing package; therefore, you will need to import this package.

```
import javax.swing.*;
```

Next, the class header will be changed to the new name, SwingFrameAndComponents, and you will extend JFrame instead of Frame. However, you still implement the ActionListener interface. Because you will continue to use an anonymous inner class to handle window events, you will not implement WindowListener.

```
public class SwingFrameAndComponents extends JFrame implements
ActionListener
```

Next, you will change the class names Button, Label, TextField, and Panel to JButton, JLabel, JTextField, and JPanel. Then you will add a new statement to obtain a reference to the JFrame instance, and use this reference to invoke the add method to add the panel instances to the frame.

```
Container c = this.getContentPane();
c.add("North",upperPanel);
c.add("South",lowerPanel);
```

All of the remaining code stays the same. The output is similar to that generated by AWTFrameAndComponents, and its behavior is identical. The listing for SwingFrame-AndComponents is shown in Figure 10-17. The output is shown in Figure 10-18.

10

```
// illustrate Swing components

import java.awt.*;
import javax.swing.*;
import java.awt.event.*;

public class SwingFrameAndComponents extends JFrame implements
ActionListener
{
    // Button & TextField reference variables need class scope
    JButton displayButton, clearButton, closeButton;
    JTextField messageTextField;

    public static void main(String args[])
    {
        // create instance of SwingFrameAndComponents
        SwingFrameAndComponents frameAndCompnents = new
SwingFrameAndComponents();
    }
```

```java
        // constructor
        public SwingFrameAndComponents()
        {
            // create Button, Label and TextField instances
            displayButton = new JButton("Display");
            clearButton = new JButton("Clear");
            closeButton = new JButton("Close");
            JLabel messageLabel = new JLabel("Message:");
            messageTextField = new JTextField(15);
            // create two Panels - default FlowLayout manager
            JPanel upperPanel = new JPanel();
            JPanel lowerPanel = new JPanel();
            // add label & textfield to upper panel
            upperPanel.add(messageLabel);
            upperPanel.add(messageTextField);
            // add buttons to lower panel
            lowerPanel.add(displayButton);
            lowerPanel.add(clearButton);
            lowerPanel.add(closeButton);
            // add panels to frame - frame default is BorderLayout
            Container c = this.getContentPanel();
            c.add("North",upperPanel);
            c.add("South",lowerPanel);
            // register frame as listener for button events
            displayButton.addActionListener(this);
            clearButton.addActionListener(this);
            closeButton.addActionListener(this);
            this.setSize(320,150);
            this.setTitle("Swing Frame and Components");
            this.setVisible(true);

            // create anonymous inner class to handle window closing event
            // register the inner class as a listener with the frame
            this.addWindowListener
            (   // begin inner class definition
                new WindowAdapter() // superclass is WindowAdapter
                {
                    public void windowClosing(WindowEvent event)
                        {shutDown();} // invoke shutDown in outer class
                }// end of inner class definition
            ); // end of argument sent to addWindowListener method
        }

        // actionPerformed is invoked when a Button is clicked
        public void actionPerformed(ActionEvent e)
        {   // see which button was clicked
            if(e.getSource() == displayButton)
                displayMessage();
            if(e.getSource() == clearButton)
                clearMessage();
            if(e.getSource() == closeButton)
                shutDown();
        }
        public void displayMessage()
            { messageTextField.setText("Hello World"); }
```

```
public void clearMessage()
    { messageTextField.setText("              "); }
// terminate
public void shutDown()

    {

        this.dispose();

        {System.exit(0);  // terminate
    }
```

Figure 10-17 SwingFrameAndComponents.java listing

Figure 10-18 SwingFrameAndComponents output

Hands-on Exercise 6

1. Create a folder named Chapter10Exercise6 on your system.

2. Locate SwingFrameAndComponents.java in the folder named Chapter10\Example6 on the book's CD and then copy it to the Chapter10Exercise6 folder you created in Step 1.

3. Compile and run SwingFrameAndComponents.java using the software recommended by your instructor, verifying that it appears and behaves correctly.

4. Add a fourth button named whoButton with the caption "Who?" When whoButton is clicked, invoke a method named displayMyName that will display your name in messageTextField.

5. Recompile and test your modifications.

Adding Drop-down Menus

You can create and add drop-down menus for both AWT and GUI frames. In this example, you will see how to add menus to a Swing frame. (You use the same approach for an AWT frame.)

A Swing drop-down menu consists of instances of *at least* three classes: JMenuBar, JMenu, and JMenuItem. You can add drop-down menus to a frame by first creating an instance of JMenuBar, then an instance of JMenu, and then JMenuItem. You add the menu item to the menu, add the menu to the menu bar, and finally add the menu bar to the frame instance. Figure 10-19 illustrates a menu bar, two menus, and three menu items.

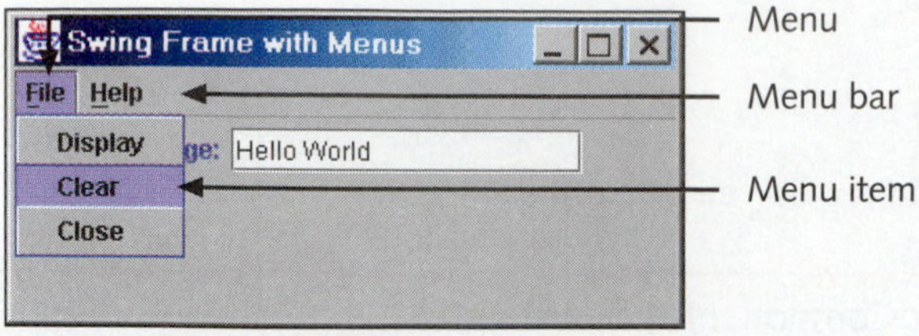

Figure 10-19 SwingFrameWithMenus output

Next you will see how to convert SwingFrameAndComponents to SwingFrameWithMenus. This new class will behave the same as SwingFrameAndComponents, except that a drop-down menu will replace the buttons to display and clear the message and close the frame. You begin by changing the class name to SwingFrameWithMenus and then remove all references to JButton. Next you add a statement to declare references for the three menu items that will replace the three buttons.

```
JMenuItem displayMenu, clearMenu, closeMenu;
```

Next you create an instance of JMenuBar, two instances of Jmenu, and three instances of JMenuItem.

```
JMenuBar menuBar = new JMenuBar();
JMenu fileMenu = new JMenu("File");
JMenu helpMenu = new JMenu("Help");
displayMenu = new JMenuItem("Display");
clearMenu = new JMenuItem("Clear");
closeMenu = new JMenuItem("Close");
```

You can create a **mnemonic key** for each of the menus by invoking Jmenu's setMnemonic method. A mnemonic key is a shortcut to opening a menu and it appears underlined as part of the menu caption. You click the menu to open it or you can press the mnemonic key and the Alt key simultaneously. Note that the mnemonic character is enclosed in *single* quotes.

```
fileMenu.setMnemonic('F');
helpMenu.setMnemonic('H');
```

Next you add statements that invoke methods to add the menu bar to the frame, the two menus to the menu bar, and the three menu items to the File menu.

```
this.setJMenuBar(menuBar);
menuBar.add(fileMenu);
menuBar.add(helpMenu);
fileMenu.add(displayMenu);
fileMenu.add(clearMenu);
fileMenu.add(closeMenu);
```

Next you register the frame as an event listener with the menu items just like you registered with the buttons in the previous example.

```
displayMenu.addActionListener(this);
clearMenu.addActionListener(this);
closeMenu.addActionListener(this);
```

Just like a button click event, a menu item click event invokes the actionPerformed method for registered event listeners. In the previous example, if statements determined which button was clicked. Similarly, in this example, if statements determine which menu item is clicked and invoke the appropriate method.

```
if(e.getSource() == displayMenu)
    displayMessage();
if(e.getSource() == clearMenu)
    clearMessage();
if(e.getSource() == closeMenu)
    shutDown();
```

The complete listing of SwingFrameWithMenus is shown in Figure 10-20.

```
// illustrate Swing menus

import java.awt.*;
import javax.swing.*;
import java.awt.event.*;

public class SwingFrameWithMenus extends JFrame implements
ActionListener
{
    // The GUI reference variables need class scope
    JTextField messageTextField;
    JMenuItem displayMenu, clearMenu, closeMenu;

    public static void main(String args[])
    {
        // create instance of Frame
        SwingFrameWithMenus frame = new SwingFrameWithMenus();
    }
    // constructor
    public SwingFrameWithMenus()
    {
        // create menu bar, menus, & menu items
        JMenuBar menuBar = new JMenuBar();
        JMenu fileMenu = new JMenu("File");
        JMenu helpMenu = new JMenu("Help");
        displayMenu = new JMenuItem("Display");
        clearMenu = new JMenuItem("Clear");
        closeMenu = new JMenuItem("Close");

        fileMenu.setMnemonic('F');
        helpMenu.setMnemonic('H');
```

```java
        this.setJMenuBar(menuBar);      // add bar to frame
        menuBar.add(fileMenu);          // add menus to bar
        menuBar.add(helpMenu);
        fileMenu.add(displayMenu);      // add menu items to menus
        fileMenu.add(clearMenu);
        fileMenu.add(closeMenu);

        // create instances of Label and TextField
        JLabel messageLabel = new JLabel("Message:");
        messageTextField = new JTextField(15);
        // add label & textfield to upper panel
        Container c = this.getContentPanel();
        c.setLayout(new FlowLayout());
        c.add(messageLabel);
        c.add(messageTextField);
        // register frame as listener for menu events
        displayMenu.addActionListener(this);
        clearMenu.addActionListener(this);
        closeMenu.addActionListener(this);
        this.setSize(320,150);
        this.setTitle("Swing Frame with Menus");
        this.setVisible(true);

        // register frame as listener for window event
        // create anonymous inner class to handle window closing event
        this.addWindowListener(new WindowAdapter()
            {
                public void windowClosing(WindowEvent event)
                    {shutDown();}
            }
        );
    }
    // actionPerformed is invoked when a menu item is clicked
    public void actionPerformed(ActionEvent e)
    {   // see which menu item was clicked
        if(e.getSource() == displayMenu)
            displayMessage();
        if(e.getSource() == clearMenu)
            clearMessage();
        if(e.getSource() == closeMenu)
            shutDown();
    }

    public void displayMessage()
        { messageTextField.setText("Hello World"); }
    public void clearMessage()
        { messageTextField.setText("             "); }
    // terminate
    public void shutDown()
        {System.exit(0);}
}
```

Figure 10-20 SwingFrameWithMenus.java listing

Hands-on Exercise 7

1. Create a folder named Chapter10Exercise7 on your system.

2. Locate SwingFrameWithMenus.java in the folder named Chapter10\Example7 on the book's CD and then copy it to the Chapter10Exercise7 folder you created in Step 1.

3. Compile and run SwingFrameWithMenus.java using the software recommended by your instructor, verifying that it appears and behaves correctly.

4. Add a menu item named whoMenu with the caption "Who?" to the Help menu. Use the character "W" as a mnemonic. Add code to invoke a method named displayMyName that will display your name in messageTextField when whoMenu is clicked.

5. Recompile and test your modifications. Remember to test both clicking whoMenu and using the mnemonic key.

Converting a Swing Application to an Applet

You previously saw how to convert an AWT application to an applet. In this section, you follow the same steps to convert a Swing application to a Swing applet. The Swing Applet class, named JApplet, is similar to the AWT Applet class with some refinements. One of those refinements is the provision to add a menu bar and menus.

The steps to convert SwingFrameWithMenus to an applet named SwingApplet are nearly identical to those you used earlier to convert an AWT frame to an applet:

- Extend JApplet instead of JFrame.

- Delete the main method.

- Delete all references to the close menu item.

- Delete the anonymous inner class.

- Delete the shutDown method.

- Delete the statements that invoke the setVisible, setSize, and setTitle methods.

The HTML file is the same as before, except that the class name is now SwingApplet.class and its code specifies SwingApplet.class. The completed SwingApplet.java code is listed in Figure 10–21 and its output is shown in Figure 10–22.

```
// illustrate Swing Applet
import java.awt.*;
import javax.swing.*;
import java.awt.event.*;
```

```java
public class SwingApplet extends JApplet implements ActionListener
{
    // The GUI reference variables need class scope
    JTextField messageTextField;
    JMenuItem displayMenu, clearMenu;

    public void init()
    {
        // create menu bar, menus, & menu items
        JMenuBar menuBar = new JMenuBar();
        JMenu fileMenu = new JMenu("File");
        JMenu helpMenu = new JMenu("Help");
        displayMenu = new JMenuItem("Display");
        clearMenu = new JMenuItem("Clear");

        fileMenu.setMnemonic('F');
        helpMenu.setMnemonic('H');

        this.setJMenuBar(menuBar);      // add bar to frame
        menuBar.add(fileMenu);          // add menus to bar
        menuBar.add(helpMenu);
        fileMenu.add(displayMenu);      // add menu items to menus
        fileMenu.add(clearMenu);

        // create instances of Label and TextField
        JLabel messageLabel = new JLabel("Message:");
        messageTextField = new JTextField(15);
        // add label & textfield to upper panel
        Container c = this.getContentPanel();
        c.setLayout(new FlowLayout());
        c.add(messageLabel);
        c.add(messageTextField);
        // register frame as listener for menu events
        displayMenu.addActionListener(this);
        clearMenu.addActionListener(this);
    }
    // actionPerformed is invoked when a menu item is clicked
    public void actionPerformed(ActionEvent e)
    {   // see which menu item was clicked
        if(e.getSource() == displayMenu)
            displayMessage();
        if(e.getSource() == clearMenu)
            clearMessage();
    }
    public void displayMessage()
        { messageTextField.setText("Hello World"); }
    public void clearMessage()
        { messageTextField.setText("           "); }
}
```

Figure 10-21 SwingApplet.java listing

Figure 10-22 SwingApplet output

Hands-on Exercise 8

1. Create a folder named Chapter10Exercise8 on your system.

2. Locate SwingApplet.java and SwingApplet.html in the folder named Chapter10\Example8 on the book's CD and then copy them to the Chapter10Exercise8 folder you created in Step 1.

3. Compile SwingApplet.java using the software recommended by your instructor.

4. Run SwingApplet.html using either a browser or AppletViewer, verifying that it appears and behaves correctly.

5. Add a menu item named whoMenu with the caption "Who" to the Help menu. Use the character "W" as a mnemonic. Add code to invoke a method named displayMyName that will display your name in messageTextField when whoMenu is clicked.

6. Recompile and test your modifications. Remember to test both clicking whoMenu and using the mnemonic key.

Summary

- All of the graphical components you see on Java GUI windows are instances of classes in either the java.awt or javax.swing packages. The original Java GUI classes, generally referred to as AWT (Abstract Windowing Toolkit), are in the java.awt package. The Swing classes, in the javax.swing package, were released with Java 2 and have capabilities beyond the AWT classes.

- The style and appearance of GUI components are called their look and feel. The AWT classes are tied to the local platform's GUI features and adopt its look and feel. The Swing GUI components have the option of using the local platform's GUI style or using a standard look and feel, called metal, that is common to all platforms.

- Component is the superclass of all GUI classes. Container is the superclass of the GUI classes that can contain other components. Examples of Containers are Panel and Frame.

- A frame instance becomes a visible window. A panel is an invisible frame used to hold other components. Labels display data, and TextFields can both display and input data.

- The AWT includes several classes called layout managers that determine how components are positioned on containers such as frames and panels. There are several layout managers; however, the most frequently used are FlowLayout, BorderLayout, and GridLayout. If you do not specify which layout manager to use, Java uses BorderLayout for frames and FlowLayout for panels.

- Components placed onto a container using BorderLayout expand to fill the space available. FlowLayout simply places components onto a frame as you add them left to right and they retain their normal size. GridLayout arranges the container into a grid consisting of rows and columns.

- Users interact with GUI screens by entering data and clicking on components such as buttons and menus. An event is a signal that the user has taken some action, such as clicking a button. The GUI instance experiencing the event is called the event source. The instance responding to the event is called an event listener.

- There are three techniques to handle events: implement an interface, use an adapter class, or use an inner class. You will usually implement the ActionListener interface for button and menu events and use an anonymous inner class to handle window events.

- The actionPerformed method is invoked whenever a button or menu item is clicked. The windowClosing method is invoked when a window is closed.

- You can create and add drop-down menus for both AWT and GUI frames.

- An applet is a class you write that extends the Applet class and it runs under control of a browser or Applet Viewer. You do not instantiate an applet, make it visible, or terminate its execution; the browser does all of this for you. HTML code is used to tell the browser the name of your applet and its dimensions.

- The Swing Applet class, named JApplet, is similar to the AWT Applet class with some refinements. One of those refinements is the provision to add a menu bar and menus.

Key Terms

action event	event listener	look and feel
adapter class	event source	mnemonic key
anonymous inner class	layout manager	register

Review Questions

1. The Java AWT classes reside in the _____ package.

a. java.awt

b. javax.swing

c. java.package

d. java.awt.gui

2. An instance of the Frame class is also a _____.

a. component

b. container

c. window

d. all of the above

3. Panel is a subclass of _____.

a. Label

b. Container

c. Window

d. all of the above

4. The style and appearance of GUI components are called their _____.

a. charisma

b. public persona

c. look and feel

d. style and look

10

5. You create an instance of the Button class by _____.

   a. invoking its newButton method

   b. invoking its createButton method

   c. invoking its constructor method

   d. invoking its giveMeAButton method

6. The keyword `this` refers to _____.

   a. the new button instance

   b. the new frame instance

   c. the new component instance

   d. the instance whose method is executing

7. The default layout manager for Frame is _____.

   a. GridLayout

   b. BorderLayout

   c. SystemLayout

   d. FlowLayout

8. The default layout manager for Panel is _____.

   a. GridLayout

   b. BorderLayout

   c. SystemLayout

   d. FlowLayout

9. A Java event _____.

   a. is an instance

   b. is the result of the user's action

   c. occurs at an event source

   d. all of the above

10. You may deal with an event by _____.

   a. implementing an interface and overriding its methods

   b. using an adapter class

   c. using an inner class

   d. all of the above

11. The event handler for button clicks is named _____.

    a. actionPerformed

    b. buttonClickEvent

    c. actionTaken

    d. buttonEvent

12. An event source and an event listener _____.

    a. must be the same

    b. may be the same

    c. cannot be the same

    d. none of the above

13. An adapter class _____.

    a. is supplied with Java

    b. is a different class for different types of events

    c. extends an interface

    d. all of the above

14. AWT applets _____.

    a. execute under control of an HTML file

    b. must have a main method

    c. must extend Applet or a subclass of Applet

    d. must have a constructor method

15. Swing applets _____.

    a. must extend JApplet or one of its subclasses

    b. may have menus

    c. may have an init method

    d. all of the above

10

Discussion Questions

1. Why do you think that some of the Swing classes extend AWT classes?

2. Why is there not a window closing method for applets?

3. Use the Java documentation to investigate keyboard events. Is there an adapter class for keyboard events? What interface is implemented? What methods does this interface have?

4. The examples in this chapter that used menus did not use buttons. Could you use buttons and menus together?

5. Several of the Swing classes provide clear advantages to their AWT counterparts. Why do you think people still use AWT classes?

Projects

1. The Bradshaw Marina Customer class has attributes for name, address, and phone number. Using SwingFrameAndComponents.java (Figures 10-17 and 10-18) as a model, design a GUI that a user might use to input information for a new customer. You are to:

   - Place three text fields on the GUI to input name (15 characters), address (15 characters), and phone number (10 characters).

   - Place three labels describing the text fields.

   - Use three buttons:

     Accept: invoke println to display the name, address. and phone number that was entered.

     Clear: erase the contents of your three text fields.

     Close: terminate.

   - Set your frame size to 700, 150 to accommodate your labels and text fields.

     Hint: Use the TextField getText method to retrieve the contents of the TextField instance.

2. Convert your solution from Project 1 to a Swing applet that uses both menus *and* buttons.

11

A GUI Interacting With a Problem Domain Class

In this chapter you will:

♦ Learn more about Java's GUI classes

♦ Write a GUI class that interacts with a PD class

♦ Work with font and color

♦ Use a dialog box

♦ Work with radio buttons, CardLayout layout manager, and lists

♦ Write an Applet that interacts with a PD class

In the previous chapter you learned how to write a GUI class to display a frame containing various GUI components such as labels, text fields, and push buttons, as well as how to write methods to handle events. This chapter continues working with these GUI classes, introduces additional GUI classes, and shows you how to write GUI classes that interact with the problem domain classes, Customer and Boat, that you developed in Part 2. All of the examples in this chapter use Swing components.

This chapter begins by creating a GUI to add a new Bradshaw Marina customer. The GUI accepts customer name, address, and phone number; validates the data; and then creates a Customer instance. You will see how to use the Color and Font classes to create an attractive logo for Bradshaw Marina. You will also learn how to display important messages to the user using a dialog box.

Next you will see how to write a GUI class to find a specific customer, display the selected customer's address and phone number, and update the customer's information. In this example you will work with another application of the Vector class and learn about the JList classes. You will recall from Part 2 that a Vector is similar to an array but is a Java class with useful methods. The JList class is a GUI component that provides you with the ability to display a list of string items, such as customer names, and then select an item from the list.

The final example in this chapter develops a GUI named AddBoat to add a new boat to the system. In Part 2 you developed the Boat class and its two subclasses: Sailboat and Powerboat. The AddBoat GUI deals with all of these and illustrates the use of the CardLayout and RadioButton classes. CardLayout is a layout manager that allows you to dynamically replace a panel being displayed. In this chapter, you use CardLayout to change part of the GUI frame to show powerboat instead of sailboat information. You will also use the RadioButton class to create radio buttons so you can indicate the type of boat—sailboat or powerboat—plus sailboat engine configuration and powerboat fuel type.

After completing this chapter, you will understand how to design and write a GUI class that interacts with a PD class. You will have a better understanding of using color and font, and you will see how to use the new classes introduced here: RadioButton, CardLayout, JList, and Vector. The examples developed in this chapter are also used in Chapter 12, which deals with developing multiple GUI classes to interact with multiple PD classes.

Adding a New Customer

In this section you will see how to develop a GUI class named AddCustomer to input customer attribute values and then create instances of the Customer class you developed in Chapter 5. The GUI frame for adding a new customer is shown in Figure 11-1. The overall frame uses the GridLayout manager with three rows and one column. The first row contains the Bradshaw Marina logo as shown. The second row holds a Panel instance named center-Panel, which also uses GridLayout and is formatted into three rows and two columns. The first column of centerPanel contains three labels and the second contains three text fields. The bottom row contains a Panel instance named lowerPanel, which uses FlowLayout and holds three buttons.

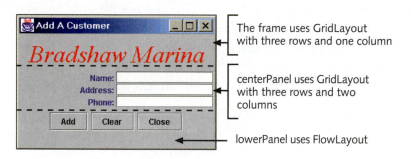

Figure 11-1   Frame to add a new customer

Similar to the SwingFrameAndComponents class you developed in the previous chapter, AddCustomer begins by importing the packages for the classes it uses. The java.awt package has the Font, Color, and various layout manager classes. The GUI Swing components are in javax.swing, and the ActionEvent class and ActionListener interface are in java.awt.event.

```java
import java.awt.*;
import javax.swing.*;
import java.awt.event.*;
```

Next you add four statements to declare reference variables that will be accessed by several methods and therefore require class scope. The first statement declares three reference variables for the JTextField instances used to input the customer name, address, and phone number. The second statement declares three reference variables for the JButton instances, shown in Figure 11-1, which are clicked to add a new customer after the data has been entered, clear the text fields, and close the frame and terminate processing. The third statement declares a Customer reference variable used when creating a new Customer instance, and the last statement declares three String variables, which are used to contain the customer data that is retrieved from the text fields.

```java
JTextField customerNameText, customerAddressText, customerPhoneText;
JButton addButton, clearButton, closeButton;
Customer aCustomer;
String customerName, customerAddress, customerPhone;
```

As with the GUI examples in the previous chapter, the main method here is used only to instantiate AddCustomer. The constructor method is invoked and it, in turn, constructs the frame and all of its GUI components and makes the frame visible.

```java
public static void main(String args[])
{ AddCustomer frame = new AddCustomer(); }
```

The constructor begins with statements that set the frame's layout manager to GridLayout and format it with three rows and one column. Then instances of Panel are created for centerPanel and lowerPanel.

```java
Container c(new = this.getContentPane();
c.setLayout(new GridLayout(3,1));
JPanel centerPanel = new JPanel(new GridLayout(3,2));
JPanel lowerPanel = new JPanel(new FlowLayout());
```

Creating the Logo Panel

Next are the statements that create the logo for Bradshaw Marina. First, an instance of JLabel, named logoLabel, is created to contain the marina's logo. The first statement instantiates JLabel, passing its constructor a blank value and a constant contained in the SwingConstants class, telling the Label instance to center itself. SwingConstants contains a number of useful constants, and you should review this class in the JDK documentation.

11

Next, the foreground color is set to red by invoking the setForeground method and passing it the constant `Color.red`. Then the font is set to Times Roman 36–point italic by invoking the setFont method and passing it the font name (TimesRoman), style, and size. Both set-Foreground and setFont are inherited from Component. Finally, the actual logo is placed into the Label instance using its setText method, and the label is added to the Frame instance. Notice that the setForeground and setFont methods are invoked for the logoLabel instance: This means that the font and color of the other components are not affected.

```
JLabel logoLabel = new JLabel(" ",SwingConstants.CENTER);
logoLabel.setForeground(Color.red);
logoLabel.setFont(new Font("TimesRoman", Font.ITALIC,36));
logoLabel.setText("Bradshaw Marina");
c.add(logoLabel);
```

Creating the Center Panel

The next statements create three instances of TextField, and then the labels and text fields are added to centerPanel. This panel is then added to the Frame instance. In this example, the JLabel constructor is passed two arguments. The first is the caption to be displayed in the label, and the second is a constant that sets the alignment of the caption. The class Swing-Constants contains constants such as LEFT, RIGHT, and CENTER.

```
customerNameText = new JTextField();
customerAddressText = new JTextField();
customerPhoneText = new JTextField();
centerPanel.add(new JLabel("Name: ", SwingConstants.RIGHT));
centerPanel.add(customerNameText);
centerPanel.add(new JLabel("Address: ", SwingConstants.RIGHT));
centerPanel.add(customerAddressText);
centerPanel.add(new JLabel("Phone: ", SwingConstants.RIGHT));
centerPanel.add(customerPhoneText);
c.add(centerPanel);
```

Creating the Lower Panel

Next, three Button instances are created and added to the lower panel. The lower panel containing the three buttons is then added to the Frame instance.

```
addButton = new JButton("Add");
clearButton = new JButton("Clear");
closeButton = new JButton("Close");
lowerPanel.add(addButton);
lowerPanel.add(clearButton);
lowerPanel.add(closeButton);
c.add(lowerPanel);
```

As in the GUI examples in the previous chapter, the next statements register the frame as a listener for button events, set the frame size, add a title, and make it visible.

```java
addButton.addActionListener(this);
clearButton.addActionListener(this);
closeButton.addActionListener(this);

this.setSize(300,200);
this.setTitle("Add A Customer");
this.setVisible(true);
```

Handling Events

This example, just like those in the previous chapter, uses an anonymous inner class to handle the window closing event. In fact, the identical code is used here, so you can copy it from the previous example.

Also, similar to the examples in the previous chapter, the actionPerformed method determines which button was clicked and then invokes the appropriate method to handle the event. This frame includes three push buttons, and they correspond to three events: add a customer, clear the form, or close. The methods for these events are named addCustomer, clearForm, and shutDown.

```java
public void actionPerformed(ActionEvent e)
    {
        // see which button was clicked
        if(e.getSource() == addButton)
            {addCustomer();}
        if(e.getSource() == clearButton)
            {clearForm();}
        if(e.getSource() == closeButton)
            {shutDown();}
    }
```

11

The shutDown method is identical to that in the SwingFrameAndComponents example in the previous chapter. Similarly, the clearForm method simply stores spaces in the text fields.

The addCustomer method retrieves the data from the text fields and uses it to create a Customer instance. The JTextField method getText retrieves the string contents of a text field. The statements to retrieve the contents of the three text fields are:

```java
customerName = customerNameText.getText();
customerAddress = customerAddressText.getText();
customerPhone = customerPhoneText.getText();
```

Using a Dialog Box

If a user clicks the Add button but hasn't entered the customer's name, address, and phone number, you should display a message. However, if the user has entered all the data, you should create the Customer instance.

This example uses a dialog box to indicate that the customer has been added or that data is missing. A dialog box is a small window you create to display a message and request the user to acknowledge the message by clicking an OK button before continuing. The Swing class used to display simple dialog boxes is JOptionPane. You can invoke methods in JOptionPane to display various kinds of dialog messages, including error messages, warning messages, and question messages. Each message displays an icon indicating its type. In addition, you can require a user response ranging from clicking a simple OK button, which is used here, to selecting a Yes, No, or Cancel button. You can also request the user to type a response. To learn more, you should review the JOptionPane class methods in the JDK documentation.

The statement to display a simple dialog box with a message that requires the user to click the OK button to continue is:

```
JOptionPane.showMessageDialog(this, "some message ");
```

The method showMessageDialog is a static method in the JOptionPane class and accepts two arguments. The first is a reference to the Frame instance where the dialog box will be displayed, and the second is the message you want to display. The dialog boxes for missing data and customer added are shown in Figures 11-2 and 11-3. When either dialog box is displayed, the user must click the OK button before processing will continue.

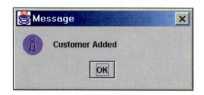

Figure 11-2   Dialog box displayed for missing data

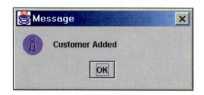

Figure 11-3   Dialog box displayed when customer is added

The missing data dialog box is displayed if any of the customer data is missing. In other words, if the user fails to enter a name, address, or phone number, the dialog box is displayed. The technique used here to detect missing data is to invoke the length method for the String instance containing the data. If this method returns zero, there is no data. If all three data items are entered, the Customer instance is created and the customer added dialog box is displayed.

```java
if(customerName.length() == 0 || customerAddress.length() == 0 ||
customerPhone.length() == 0)
    JOptionPane.showMessageDialog(this, "Please Enter All Data ");
else
{
    aCustomer = new Customer(customerName, customerAddress, customerPhone);
    JOptionPane.showMessageDialog(this, "Customer Added");
    clearForm();
}
```

The listing of AddCustomer.java is shown in Figure 11-4.

```java
// Add Customer GUI
import java.awt.*;              // Font, Color, Layout managers
import javax.swing.*;           // GUI components
import java.awt.event.*;        // ActionEvent, ActionListener
public class AddCustomer extends JFrame implements ActionListener
{
    // variables needing class scope
    JTextField customerNameText, customerAddressText, customerPhoneText;
    JButton addButton, clearButton, closeButton;
    Customer aCustomer;
    String customerName, customerAddress, customerPhone;

    public static void main(String args[])
    {   AddCustomer frame = new AddCustomer(); }

    // constructor
    public AddCustomer()
    {
        Container c = this.getContentPane();
        c.setLayout(new GridLayout(3,1));
        JPanel centerPanel = new JPanel(new GridLayout(3,2));
        JPanel lowerPanel = new JPanel(new FlowLayout());

        // create logo
        JLabel logoLabel = new JLabel(" ",SwingConstants.CENTER);
        logoLabel.setForeground(Color.red);
        logoLabel.setFont(new Font("TimesRoman", Font.ITALIC,36));
        logoLabel.setText("Bradshaw Marina");
        c.add(logoLabel);

        // create TextFields for name, address & phone
        customerNameText = new JTextField();
        customerAddressText = new JTextField();
```

11

```java
        customerPhoneText = new JTextField();
        // add labels and TextFields to the panels
        centerPanel.add(new JLabel("Name: ", SwingConstants.RIGHT));
        centerPanel.add(customerNameText);
        centerPanel.add(new JLabel("Address: ", SwingConstants.RIGHT));
        centerPanel.add(customerAddressText);
        centerPanel.add(new JLabel("Phone: ", SwingConstants.RIGHT));
        centerPanel.add(customerPhoneText);
        c.add(centerPanel);
        // create & add Buttons to bottom panel
        addButton = new JButton("Add");
        clearButton = new JButton("Clear");
        closeButton = new JButton("Close");
        lowerPanel.add(addButton);
        lowerPanel.add(clearButton);
        lowerPanel.add(closeButton);
        c.add(lowerPanel);

        // register frame as listener for button events
        addButton.addActionListener(this);
        clearButton.addActionListener(this);
        closeButton.addActionListener(this);

        this.setSize(300,200);
        this.setTitle("Add A Customer");
        this.setVisible(true);

        // create anonymous inner class to handle window closing event
        this.addWindowListener(new WindowAdapter()
            {
                public void windowClosing(WindowEvent event)
                    {shutDown();}
            }
        );
    }
    // actionPerformed is invoked when a Button is clicked
    public void actionPerformed(ActionEvent e)
    {
        // see which button was clicked
        if(e.getSource() == addButton)
            {addCustomer();}
        if(e.getSource() == clearButton)
            {clearForm();}
        if(e.getSource() == closeButton)
            {shutDown();}
    }
    private void addCustomer()
    {
        customerName = customerNameText.getText();
        customerAddress = customerAddressText.getText();
        customerPhone = customerPhoneText.getText();
```

```
      if(customerName.length() == 0 || customerAddress.length() == 0 ||
customerPhone.length() == 0)
      JOptionPane.showMessageDialog(this, "Please Enter All Data ");
      else
        {
          aCustomer = new Customer(customerName, customerAddress,
customerPhone);
          JOptionPane.showMessageDialog(this, "Customer Added");
          clearForm();
        }

    }
    private void clearForm()
    {
      customerNameText.setText("");
      customerAddressText.setText("");
      customerPhoneText.setText("");
      customerNameText.requestFocus();
    }

    public void shutDown()
        { System.exit(0); }
}
```

Figure 11-4   AddCustomer.java listing

Hands-on Exercise 1

1. Create a folder named Chapter11Exercise1 on your system.

2. Locate AddCustomer.java and Customer.java on the book's CD in a folder named Chapter 11\Example1, and then copy them to the Chapter11Exercise1 folder you created in Step 1.

3. Compile AddCustomer.java and Customer.java, and then run them using the software recommended by your instructor. Verify that your GUI appears and behaves correctly.

4. Convert AddCustomer to an applet by completing the following tasks:
   a. Change the class name to AddCustomerApplet.
   b. Extend JApplet instead of JFrame.
   c. Remove the main method.
   d. Rename the constructor to init with a return type of void.
   e. Remove all references to closeButton, including the shutDown method.
   f. Remove the inner class.
   g. Remove the statements that invoke setTitle, setSize, and setVisible.

5. Write an HTML file named AddCustomerApplet.html, and then compile and test your code. Your applet should behave the same as AddCustomer except for the missing Close button.

FINDING A CUSTOMER

You will sometimes need to search for a specific Bradshaw Marina customer and then display the information for that customer. You will see in this section how to develop a class named FindCustomer to find a customer and then display his or her address and phone number. At this point in the development of the Bradshaw system, you do not yet have a database of customer information. After you create a database in Chapter 15, you can use FindCustomer to retrieve customer records from the database. For now, however, FindCustomer will simulate interaction with a database.

The frame to find a customer is shown in Figure 11-5. Like the AddCustomer frame, this frame is divided into three rows or cells by using GridLayout with three rows and one column.

The three cells indicated in Figure 11-5 include the following:

- The top cell contains the Bradshaw Marina logo.

- The center cell contains a Panel instance named centerPanel, which is divided into two parts using GridLayout with one row and two columns. The left cell of centerPanel contains an instance of JList, which is described in detail in the following section. The right cell of centerPanel contains another panel named centerRightPanel that uses GridLayout to form two rows and one column. These two cells contain JTextField instances, which display the customer's address and phone number.

- The bottom cell contains a Panel instance named lowerPanel, which the FlowLayout uses to position the three Button instances.

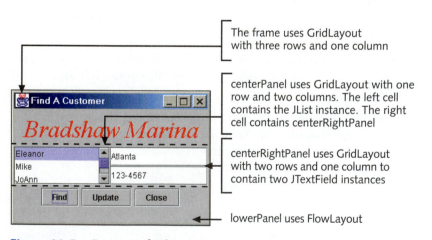

Figure 11-5   Frame to find a customer

Parts of FindCustomer are similar to AddCustomer. For example, FindCustomer imports java.awt, javax.swing, and java.awt.event. However, FindCustomer also imports java.util. Vector because it uses the Vector class to contain customer references and customer names.

```java
import java.awt.*;
import javax.swing.*;
import java.awt.event.*;
import java.util.Vector;
```

In addition to the class scope variables for the text fields and buttons, FindCustomer uses variables for the two Vector instances, customers and customerNames, plus a reference for the JList instance named customerList.

```java
Vector customers, customerNames;
JList customerList;
JTextField customerAddressText, customerPhoneText;
JButton findButton, updateButton, closeButton;
Customer aCustomer;
```

Just like AddCustomer, FindCustomer's main method instantiates the frame that invokes the constructor. This constructor begins with code that sets GridLayout with three rows for the Frame instance, and then creates Panel instances for the center and lower cells. At this point you may want to review Figure 11-5 to see how these statements relate to the figure.

```java
Container c = this.getContentPane();
c.setLayout(new GridLayout(3,1));
JPanel centerPanel = new JPanel(new GridLayout(1,2));
JPanel centerRightPanel = new JPanel(new GridLayout(2,1));
JPanel lowerPanel = new JPanel(new FlowLayout());
```

The code to create the marina's logo and add it to the frame is identical to what you saw earlier in AddCustomer.

```java
JLabel logoLabel = new JLabel(" ",SwingConstants.CENTER);
logoLabel.setForeground(Color.red);
logoLabel.setFont(new Font("TimesRoman", Font.ITALIC,36));
logoLabel.setText("Bradshaw Marina");
c.add(logoLabel);
```

Creating a Vector of Customers

FindCustomer simulates interaction with a database by creating an instance of Vector, creating six customer instances, and then populating the Vector instance with the customer references. A separate method named createCustomers is invoked to actually create and populate the Vector.

The first statement creates the Vector instance. The next six statements create customer instances and invoke the Vector's add method to populate the Vector's elements with references to the customer instances.

```
private void createCustomers()
{
    customers = new Vector();
    customers.add(new Customer("Eleanor", "Atlanta", "123-4567"));
    customers.add(new Customer("Mike", "Boston", "467-1234"));
    customers.add(new Customer("JoAnn", "St. Louis", "765-4321"));
    customers.add(new Customer("Dave", "Atlanta", "321-4567"));
    customers.add(new Customer("Brian", "Boston", "467-1234"));
    customers.add(new Customer("Dan", "St. Louis", "587-4321"));
}
```

Creating a Vector of Customer Names

Next is a statement that creates a second Vector named customerNames, which is populated with customer names and is used later to populate the instance of JList where the customer names are displayed. This Vector is populated using a three-statement for loop that iterates the customers Vector created in the previous code.

- The first statement retrieves the Customer instance from the customer Vector element indexed by i and assigns it to aCustomer. Note that the data type Object retrieved from the Vector must be cast to data type Customer.

- Next the customer getName method is invoked to retrieve the customer's name and assign it to customerName.

- The last statement in the loop invokes the Vector add method to populate the customerNames element indexed by i with the customer name.

```
customerNames = new Vector();
for(int i = 0; i < customers.size(); i++)
    {
        aCustomer = (Customer) customers.get(i);
        String customerName = aCustomer.getName();
        customerNames.add(customerName);
    }
```

Note that you could combine the last two statements.

```
customerNames.add(aCustomer.getName());
```

Using the JList Class

FindCustomer uses the JList class to display a list of customer names as shown in Figure 11-5. When the user selects one of the names and then clicks the Find button, that customer's address and phone number are displayed. Although it is not used here, selecting an item in a list also triggers a ListSelectionEvent, which invokes the event handler method valueChanged. You first must register as an event listener with the JList instance by invoking its registration method addListSelectionListener.

The following statement instantiates JList and passes its constructor a Vector containing references to the names of the six customers created earlier.

```
customerList = new JList(customerNames);
```

JList does not automatically include scroll bars. Here, the list of customer names may extend beyond the visible list window; therefore, you will want to add scroll bars by creating an instance of JScrollPane and pass its constructor the JList reference variable. You can see the scroll bars for the list in Figure 11-5.

```
JScrollPane scrollPaneCustomerList = new JScrollPane(customerList);
```

Adding Text Fields

Next, you create text fields for the customer's address and phone number, add them to centerRightPanel, add centerRightPanel to centerPanel, and finally add centerPanel to the frame. Incidentally, JTextField is used here instead of JLabel because you will want to enter a new address and phone number when updating.

```
customerAddressText = new JTextField("          ");
customerPhoneText = new JTextField("          ");
centerPanel.add(scrollPaneCustomerList);
centerRightPanel.add(customerAddressText);
centerRightPanel.add(customerPhoneText);
centerPanel.add(centerRightPanel);
c.add(centerPanel);
```

The remaining statements in the FindCustomer constructor are the same as those in AddCustomer. They create and add the buttons to lowerPanel, add lowerPanel to the Frame instance, register the frame as an event listener with the three buttons, set the frame's title and size, make it visible, and finally create an anonymous inner class to handle the window closing event.

11

Handling Events

The actionPerformed method is invoked when any of the three buttons are clicked. Similar to previous examples, this method determines which button experienced the event, and then invokes a method to handle the event.

```
public void actionPerformed(ActionEvent e)
{
    if(e.getSource() == findButton)
        {findCustomer();}
    if(e.getSource() == updateButton)
        {updateCustomer();}
    if(e.getSource() == closeButton)
        {shutDown();}
}
```

Finding a Customer

The purpose of the findCustomer method is to determine which customer name is selected on the JList instance customerList, and then retrieve and display that customer's address and phone number. The JList class provides a method named getSelectedIndex, which returns the index of the item selected on the list. Here, you can take advantage of the fact that the customer names in the List instance are in the same sequence as the customer reference variables stored in the customers Vector. In other words, the first customer name belongs to the customer referenced by the first element of customers, the second name matches the second customer, and so forth. This means that after you obtain the index of the selected name, you can use that same index to retrieve the customer reference stored in the customers Vector. Once you have the customer reference, you can invoke the getAddress and getPhoneNumber methods for the Customer instance to retrieve the values and display them in the text fields.

```
private void findCustomer()
{
    int i = customerList.getSelectedIndex();
    aCustomer = (Customer) customers.get(i);
    customerAddressText.setText(aCustomer.getAddress());
    customerPhoneText.setText(aCustomer.getPhoneNo());
}
```

Note that you could combine the first two statements in this method by writing:

```
aCustomer = (Customer) customers.get(customerList.getSelectedIndex());
```

This statement first invokes getSelectedIndex for customerList, and then passes this value to the get method in the Vector instance named customers. The value returned by the get method is cast to data type Customer and then assigned to the reference variable aCustomer.

Updating a Customer

FindCustomer also lets you change a customer's address and phone number. First, you select the customer's name from the list, and then click the Find button to display his or her values. You can enter the new address and phone number values in the text fields, and then click the Update button.

The updateCustomer method is invoked when you click the Update button. This method takes the same approach as findCustomer by invoking getSelectedIndex and using the index of the name to retrieve the customer reference. In this method, however, the values in the text fields are retrieved and then passed to the setAddress and setPhoneNo methods to store the new values for this customer.

```java
private void updateCustomer()
{
    int i = customerList.getSelectedIndex();
    aCustomer = (Customer) customers.get(i);
    aCustomer.setAddress(customerAddressText.getText());
    aCustomer.setPhoneNo(customerPhoneText.getText());
}
```

The shutDown method is identical to what you used in AddCustomer. The complete listing for FindCustomer.java is shown in Figure 11-6.

11

```java
// Find Customer GUI
import java.awt.*;        // Font, Color, Layout managers
import javax.swing.*;     // GUI components
import java.awt.event.*;  // ActionEvent, ActionListener, WindowAdapter
import java.util.Vector;  // Vector
public class FindCustomer extends JFrame implements ActionListener
{
    // variables needing class scope
    Vector customers, customerNames;
    JList customerList;
    JTextField customerAddressText, customerPhoneText;
    JButton findButton, updateButton, closeButton;
    Customer aCustomer;

    public static void main(String args[])
        {FindCustomer frame = new FindCustomer(); }

    // constructor
    public FindCustomer()
    {   // Use GridLayout and 3 panels for the Frame instance
        Container c = this.getContentPane();
        c.setLayout(new GridLayout(3,1));
        JPanel centerPanel = new JPanel(new GridLayout(1,2));
        JPanel centerRightPanel = new JPanel(new GridLayout(2,1));
        JPanel lowerPanel = new JPanel(new FlowLayout());

        // create logo
        JLabel logoLabel = new JLabel(" ",SwingConstants.CENTER);
```

```java
logoLabel.setForeground(Color.red);
logoLabel.setFont(new Font("TimesRoman", Font.ITALIC,36));
logoLabel.setText("Bradshaw Marina");
c.add(logoLabel); // add logo to the Frame

// build JList
this.createCustomers();  // simulate a database of customers
customerNames = new Vector(); // names used for JList
for(int i = 0; i < customers.size(); i++)
    {
        aCustomer = (Customer) customers.get(i);  // get customer
        String customerName = aCustomer.getName();  // get the name
        customerNames.add(customerName);  // add name to vector
    }

customerList = new JList(customerNames); // create the list
// add scroll bars to the list
JScrollPane scrollPaneCustomerList = new JScrollPane(customerList);

// create TextFields for address & phone
customerAddressText = new JTextField("         ");
customerPhoneText = new JTextField("          ");
// add list and TextFields to the panels
centerPanel.add(scrollPaneCustomerList);
centerRightPanel.add(customerAddressText);
centerRightPanel.add(customerPhoneText);
centerPanel.add(centerRightPanel);
c.add(centerPanel); // add center panel to the Frame

// create & add Buttons for bottom panel
findButton = new JButton("Find");
updateButton = new JButton("Update");
closeButton = new JButton("Close");
lowerPanel.add(findButton);
lowerPanel.add(updateButton);
lowerPanel.add(closeButton);
c.add(lowerPanel);

this.setSize(300,200);
this.setTitle("Find A Customer");
this.setVisible(true);

// register frame as listener for button events
findButton.addActionListener(this);
updateButton.addActionListener(this);
closeButton.addActionListener(this);

// create anonymous inner class to handle window closing event
this.addWindowListener(new WindowAdapter()
    {
        public void windowClosing(WindowEvent event)
            {shutDown();}
    }
);
```

```java
}
// actionPerformed is invoked when a Button is clicked
public void actionPerformed(ActionEvent e)
{    // see which button was clicked
    if(e.getSource() == findButton)
        {findCustomer();}
    if(e.getSource() == updateButton)
        {updateCustomer();}
    if(e.getSource() == closeButton)
        {shutDown();}
}
private void findCustomer()
{
    int i = customerList.getSelectedIndex(); // get index of item
    aCustomer = (Customer) customers.get(i); // get customer reference
    customerAddressText.setText(aCustomer.getAddress());
    customerPhoneText.setText(aCustomer.getPhoneNo());
}
private void updateCustomer()
{
    int i = customerList.getSelectedIndex(); // get index of item
    aCustomer = (Customer) customers.get(i); // get customer reference
    aCustomer.setAddress(customerAddressText.getText());
    aCustomer.setPhoneNo(customerPhoneText.getText());
}

public void shutDown()
    { System.exit(0); }

// create customers to simulate a database
private void createCustomers()
{    // create a Vector instance & populate with 6 new customers
    customers = new Vector();
    customers.add(new Customer("Eleanor", "Atlanta", "123-4567"));
    customers.add(new Customer("Mike", "Boston", "467-1234"));
    customers.add(new Customer("JoAnn", "St. Louis", "765-4321"));
    customers.add(new Customer("Dave", "Atlanta", "321-4567"));
    customers.add(new Customer("Brian", "Boston", "467-1234"));
    customers.add(new Customer("Dan", "St. Louis", "587-4321"));
}
}
```

11

Figure 11-6   FindCustomer.java listing

Hands-on Exercise 2

1. Create a folder named Chapter11Exercise2 on your system.

2. Locate FindCustomer.java and Customer.java on the book's CD in a folder named Chapter 11\Example2, and then copy them to the Chapter11Exercise2 folder you created in Step 1.

3. Compile FindCustomer.java and Customer.java, and then run them using the soft-ware recommended by your instructor. Verify that your GUI appears and behaves correctly.

4. Convert FindCustomer to an applet by completing the following tasks:
   a. Change the class name to FindCustomerApplet.
   b. Extend JApplet instead of JFrame.
   c. Remove the main method.
   d. Rename the constructor to init with a return type of void.
   e. Remove all references to closeButton, including the shutDown method.
   f. Remove the inner class.
   g. Remove the statements that invoke setTitle, setSize, and setVisible.

5. Write an HTML file named FindCustomerApplet.html, and then compile and test your code. Your applet should behave the same as FindCustomer except for the missing Close button.

Hands-on Exercise 3

1. Create a folder named Chapter11Exercise3 on your system.

2. Locate FindCustomer.java and Customer.java on the book's CD in a folder named Chapter11\Example2, and then copy them to the Chapter11Exercise3 folder you created in Step 1.

3. Using the examples from the previous chapter as a guide, replace the push buttons with menus.

4. Compile and test FindCustomer.java with your modifications.

Hands-on Exercise 4

1. Create a folder named Chapter11Exercise4 on your system.

2. Locate FindCustomer.java and Customer.java on the book's CD in a folder named Chapter11\Example2, and then copy them to the Chapter11Exercise4 folder you created in Step 1.

3. Modify FindCustomer.java to respond to ListSelectionEvent. Invoke the findCustomer method when the user selects a customer name in the list.
   Hints:
   a. Import javax.swing.event.ListSelectionListener.
   b. Implement the ListSelectionListener interface.
   c. Register the FindCustomer Frame instance as a selection event listener by invoking the JList registration method addListSelectionListener.
   d. Write the event handler method named valueChanged and have it invoke findCustomer if customerList was the event source.

4. Compile and test FindCustomer.java with your modifications.

5. Which technique do you think is a better design: using the find button or using the selection event?

ADDING A BOAT

In this section you will develop a new GUI class named AddBoat that you can use to add a new boat to the marina system. AddBoat will interact with the Boat, Sailboat, and Powerboat classes you developed in Part 2 to create instances of each type of boat. In this section, you will also learn how to use the RadioButton class and the CardLayout layout manager. Radio buttons give you the ability to select from one of several options on a GUI frame. The Card–Layout manager enables you to dynamically replace one panel with another.

You will recall from Part 2 that Boat is the superclass for Sailboat and Powerboat. The class diagram is repeated in Figure 11-7. The attributes of Boat (stateRegNumber, boatLength, manufacturer, and year) are common to both subclasses, while the subclasses contain attributes that are unique to them. For example, Sailboat has keelDepth, numberSails, and motorType, and Powerboat has numberEngines and fuelType.

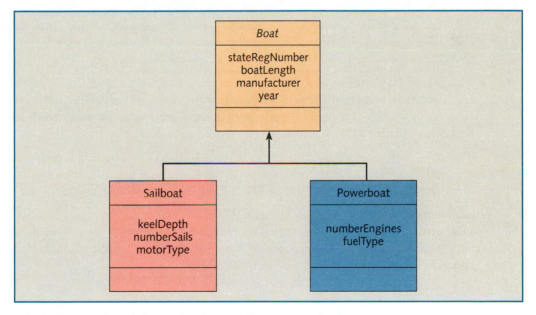

Figure 11-7   Class diagram for Boat, Sailboat, Powerboat

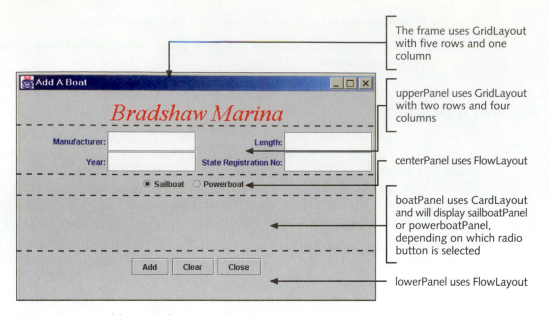

The frame uses GridLayout with five rows and one column

upperPanel uses GridLayout with two rows and four columns

centerPanel uses FlowLayout

boatPanel uses CardLayout and will display sailboatPanel or powerboatPanel, depending on which radio button is selected

lowerPanel uses FlowLayout

Figure 11-8   Add a Boat frame

The Add a Boat frame is shown in Figure 11-8. This example uses the same frame to add both sailboats and powerboats. The overall frame uses GridLayout to create five rows. Similar to AddCustomer, the top row is used for the Bradshaw Marina logo.

The second row consists of a Panel instance named upperPanel, which uses GridLayout to create two rows and four columns that contain the labels and text fields as shown. The text fields in upperPanel are used to input the four attribute values for Boat, which are required for both sailboats and powerboats.

The third row contains a Panel instance named centerPanel, which uses the FlowLayout manager. This panel contains two instances of the RadioButton class. The user will select either the Sailboat or the Powerboat button. The Sailboat button is initially selected as the default.

The fourth row, which is blank in Figure 11-8, contains a Panel instance named boatPanel, which uses the CardLayout manager. This enables you to dynamically change the contents of boatPanel. Here, if the Sailboat radio button is selected, then boatPanel displays the sailboat-Panel shown in Figure 11-9.

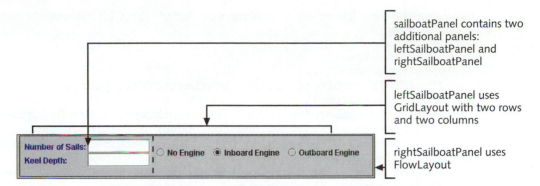

sailboatPanel contains two additional panels: leftSailboatPanel and rightSailboatPanel

leftSailboatPanel uses GridLayout with two rows and two columns

rightSailboatPanel uses FlowLayout

Figure 11-9   sailboatPanel

However, if the Powerboat radio button is selected, then boatPanel displays the powerboat-Panel shown in Figure 11-10.

The sailboatPanel uses the FlowLayout manager and contains two additional panels: leftSail-boatPanel and rightSailboatPanel. The leftSailboatPanel uses GridLayout with two rows and two columns, and the rightSailboatPanel uses FlowLayout. As shown in Figure 11-9, the left-SailboatPanel contains labels and text fields for number of sails and keel depth. The rightSail-boatPanel contains three radio buttons for the three sailboat engine options: none, inboard, or outboard.

The powerboatPanel uses FlowLayout and contains the text field for number of engines and two radio buttons for fuel type, gasoline, or diesel.

As shown earlier in Figure 11-8, the lowerPanel contains three buttons, just like you saw in the AddCustomer frame.

The AddBoat class definition begins with **import** statements for the java.awt, javax.swing, and java.awt.event packages, and the class header extending JFrame.

```
import java.awt.*;
import javax.swing.*;
import java.awt.event.*;
public class AddBoat extends JFrame implements ActionListener
```

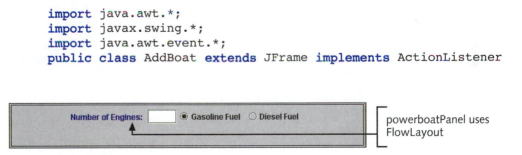

powerboatPanel uses FlowLayout

Figure 11-10   powerboatPanel

Following the class header are statements that declare the GUI reference variables that require class scope.

```
JPanel boatPanel;
CardLayout boatLayout;
JTextField manufacturerText, boatLengthText, yearText,
stateRegistrationText;
JTextField numberOfSailsText, keelDepthText, numberOfEnginesText;
JRadioButton sailboatRadioButton, powerboatRadioButton;
JRadioButton noEngineRadioButton, inboardEngineRadioButton,
outboardEngineRadioButton;
JRadioButton gasolineFuelRadioButton, dieselFuelRadioButton;
JButton addButton, clearButton, closeButton;
```

Next comes the main method whose sole job is to instantiate AddBoat. The constructor actually builds the frame containing the various GUI components.

```
public static void main(String args[])
{   AddBoat frame = new AddBoat(); }
```

Creating Panels

Next come the statements that set GridLayout for the frame and create the various Panel instances.

```
Container c = this.getContentPane();
c.setLayout(new GridLayout(5,1));
JPanel upperPanel = new JPanel(new GridLayout(2,4));
JPanel centerPanel = new JPanel(new FlowLayout());
JPanel sailboatPanel = new JPanel(new FlowLayout());
JPanel powerboatPanel = new JPanel(new FlowLayout());
JPanel lowerPanel = new JPanel(new FlowLayout());
```

Using CardLayout

The next three statements create an instance of CardLayout referenced by a variable named boatLayout, create an instance of JPanel referenced by boatPanel, and then assign CardLayout to boatPanel. This enables the contents of boatPanel to dynamically change from sailboat-Panel to powerboatPanel and back as the class is executing. The construction of these two panels is described shortly.

```
boatLayout = new CardLayout();
boatPanel = new JPanel();
boatPanel.setLayout(boatLayout);
```

Next come the statements to create the Bradshaw Marina logo, which are identical to those in previous examples and are not repeated here. The upperPanel contains the labels and text fields to input the four Boat attribute values: manufacturer, length, year, and state registration. The following statements construct upperPanel and add it to the frame.

```
manufacturerText = new JTextField(15);
boatLengthText= new JTextField(4);
yearText = new JTextField(6);
stateRegistrationText = new JTextField(15);
upperPanel.add(new JLabel("Manufacturer: ", SwingConstants.RIGHT));
upperPanel.add(manufacturerText);
upperPanel.add(new JLabel("Length: ", SwingConstants.RIGHT));
upperPanel.add(boatLengthText);
upperPanel.add(new JLabel("Year: ", SwingConstants.RIGHT));
upperPanel.add(yearText);
upperPanel.add(new JLabel("State Registration No: ",
SwingConstants.RIGHT));
upperPanel.add(stateRegistrationText);
c.add(upperPanel);
```

Using Radio Buttons

The centerPanel contains two radio buttons that allow you to indicate the type of boat: sailboat or powerboat. The statements to create these two RadioButton instances are:

```
sailboatRadioButton = new JRadioButton("Sailboat", true);
powerboatRadioButton = new JRadioButton("Powerboat", false);
```

Two arguments are passed to the RadioButton constructor. The first is the caption you wish to be displayed with the button. The second argument is the button's initial state. A value of **true** means the button is initially selected and **false** means it is not selected. In this example, the Sailboat button is initially selected as the default.

A check box, which is an instance of JCheckBox, is similar to a radio button in that it may be either selected or not. However, check boxes are not associated with a group and any number of check boxes can be selected. Here you want only one item selected, sailboat *or* powerboat; therefore, you use radio buttons.

Creating the sailboatPanel

You saw earlier how to construct boatPanel, which, using CardLayout, will display either sailboatPanel or powerboatPanel. The following code constructs these panels.

The sailboatPanel contains two additional panels, leftSailboatPanel and rightSailboatPanel, as shown earlier in Figure 11-9. The leftSailboatPanel uses GridLayout with two rows and two columns to hold the labels and text fields for number of sails and keel depth. The rightSailboatPanel contains radio buttons for the three sailboat motor configurations: none, inboard,

11

or outboard. Inboard is initially selected as the default because most sailboats at this marina have inboard engines.

First, you write statements to create the left and right Panel instances, the two instances of TextField, and the three instances of RadioButton.

```
JPanel leftSailboatPanel = new JPanel(new GridLayout(2,1));
JPanel rightSailboatPanel = new JPanel(new FlowLayout());
numberOfSailsText = new JTextField(4);
keelDepthText = new JTextField(4);
noEngineRadioButton = new JRadioButton("No Engine", false);
inboardEngineRadioButton = new JRadioButton("Inboard Engine", true);
outboardEngineRadioButton = new JRadioButton("Outboard Engine", false);
```

Next come statements to create a ButtonGroup instance named sailboatEngineGroup, and then add the three radio buttons created previously to the group.

```
ButtonGroup sailboatEngineGroup = new ButtonGroup();
sailboatEngineGroup.add(noEngineRadioButton);
sailboatEngineGroup.add(inboardEngineRadioButton);
sailboatEngineGroup.add(outboardEngineRadioButton);
```

Next, the left and right panels are populated and added to sailboatPanel.

```
leftSailboatPanel.add(new JLabel("Number of Sails: "));
leftSailboatPanel.add(numberOfSailsText);
leftSailboatPanel.add(new JLabel("Keel Depth: "));
leftSailboatPanel.add(keelDepthText);
rightSailboatPanel.add(noEngineRadioButton);
rightSailboatPanel.add(inboardEngineRadioButton);
rightSailboatPanel.add(outboardEngineRadioButton);
sailboatPanel.add(leftSailboatPanel);
sailboatPanel.add(rightSailboatPanel);
```

An important characteristic of radio buttons is that only one button within a group can be selected. When a radio button is selected, its state is true; not selected is false. When you select one radio button, all other buttons in the same group are deselected. You assign individual RadioButton instances to a group by first creating an instance of the ButtonGroup class, and then add the radio buttons to the ButtonGroup instance. The following statements create a ButtonGroup instance named typeOfBoat, and then invoke its add method for sailboatRadioButton and powerboatRadioButton. The Button instances are added to the centerPanel and are, in turn, added to the frame.

```
ButtonGroup typeOfBoat = new ButtonGroup();
typeOfBoat.add(sailboatRadioButton);
typeOfBoat.add(powerboatRadioButton);
centerPanel.add(sailboatRadioButton);
centerPanel.add(powerboatRadioButton);
c.add(centerPanel);
```

Finally, a border is added to the sailboatPanel, and sailboatPanel is added to boatPanel. The class BorderFactory has methods to create various types of borders for panels. You can review these by reading about BorderFactory in the JDK documentation. The example here invokes a method named createLineBorder and passes it the constant Color.black to create a plain black border around the panel. Next the sailboatPanel is added to boatPanel. Remember, boatPanel uses CardLayout and will be able to display either the sailboatPanel or the powerboatPanel.

```
sailboatPanel.setBorder(BorderFactory.createLineBorder(Color.black));

boatPanel.add(sailboatPanel, "sailboat");
```

Creating the powerboatPanel

The powerboatPanel has fewer components than sailboatPanel, as shown earlier in Figure 11-10. As you can see, powerboatPanel uses FlowLayout and contains a label, a text field, and two radio buttons.

The construction of powerboatPanel is straightforward. First, the instances of JTextField, JRadioButton, and ButtonGroup are created, the radio buttons are added to the group and then to the panel, and the label and text field are added to the panel. Then, similar to the statements that constructed sailboatPanel, a border is created and powerboatPanel is added to the boatPanel. This means that boatPanel now contains both sailboatPanel and powerboatPanel, and can display one or the other. The final statement here adds boatPanel to the overall frame.

```
numberOfEnginesText = new JTextField(4);
gasolineFuelRadioButton = new JRadioButton("Gasoline Fuel", true);
dieselFuelRadioButton = new JRadioButton("Diesel Fuel", false);
ButtonGroup powerboatFuelGroup = new ButtonGroup();

powerboatFuelGroup.add(gasolineFuelRadioButton);
powerboatFuelGroup.add(dieselFuelRadioButton);
powerboatPanel.add(new JLabel("Number of Engines: "));
powerboatPanel.add(numberOfEnginesText);
powerboatPanel.add(gasolineFuelRadioButton);
powerboatPanel.add(dieselFuelRadioButton);

powerboatPanel.setBorder(BorderFactory.createLineBorder(Color.black));
boatPanel.add(powerboatPanel, "powerboat");
c.add(boatPanel);
```

The Add, Clear, and Close buttons are identical to those you saw in AddCustomer, and the code to set the size, title, and make the frame visible is also similar.

```
addButton = new JButton("Add");
clearButton = new JButton("Clear");
closeButton = new JButton("Close");
lowerPanel.add(addButton);
```

11

```
lowerPanel.add(clearButton);
lowerPanel.add(closeButton);
c.add(lowerPanel);

this.setSize(550,350);
this.setTitle("Add A Boat");
this.setVisible(true);
```

Registering for Events

The statements that register the Frame instance as an event listener with the Button instances are also identical to those in AddCustomer.

```
addButton.addActionListener(this);
clearButton.addActionListener(this);
closeButton.addActionListener(this);
```

This frame is used to input either sailboat or powerboat information. If the sailboat radio button is selected, boatPanel displays sailboatPanel, and if the powerboat radio button is selected, boatPanel displays powerboatPanel. Clicking a radio button causes it to be selected and triggers an action event, just like clicking a push button. This means you also want to register the frame as an event listener with the two radio buttons. This will cause the event handling method actionPerformed to be invoked when either of the radio buttons or a button is clicked.

```
sailboatRadioButton.addActionListener(this);
powerboatRadioButton.addActionListener(this);
```

A radio button also triggers an ItemEvent when it is either selected or deselected. You can register as an event listener by invoking the radio button registration method addItemListener. The example here, however, uses only ActionEvent.

The final statements in the constructor method create the same anonymous inner class as before to handle the window closing event.

Handling Events

The actionPerformed method begins with similar code to that in AddCustomer that you saw earlier. The first three statements determine which push button was clicked, and then invoke a method to deal with the event. The shutDown method terminates processing as before. The addBoat and clearForm methods are described below.

```
public void actionPerformed(ActionEvent e)
    {
        if(e.getSource() == addButton)
            addBoat();
        if(e.getSource() == clearButton)
            clearForm();
```

```
        if(e.getSource() == closeButton)
            shutDown();
    }
```

The final two statements in actionPerformed determine if sailboatRadioButton or power-boatRadioButton was clicked. Recall that boatPanel employs the CardLayout manager, and that you added both sailboatPanel and powerboatPanel to boatPanel. CardLayout enables you to display either sailboatPanel or powerboatPanel. The CardLayout methods first and last, as their names suggest, enable you to display the first or last panels in the layout. In this example, boatPanel contains only two panels; therefore, the first is sailboatPanel and the last is powerboatPanel. Invoking the method first displays the sailboatPanel and invoking last displays the powerboatPanel. The variable boatLayout references the CardLayout instance.

```
    if(e.getSource() == sailboatRadioButton)
        boatLayout.first(boatPanel);
    if(e.getSource() == powerboatRadioButton)
        boatLayout.last(boatPanel);
```

If sailboatRadioButton is clicked, the first panel, sailboatPanel, is displayed, as shown in Figure 11-11.

FORMATTING

For spaces between text paragraph, DO NOT USE paragraph return.

- Measure from baseline of first line of text to baseline of next line of text. Measure the amount of spec.

- Put cursor in paragraph (or line of text) to be formatted: i.;e., the second line.

- Use "space before" in Paragraph Attributes (Cmd-Shf-F). Put in the amount, hit apply. Guesstimate until correct space *between* is achieved.

REFLOW and FLIPPING RECTO/VERSO

To change Recto to Verso or Verso to Recto, using Master Pages:

- Select All on page, using item tool.

- Shift-click to deselect all paragraphs and headers

- Delete *selected* items (should be everything that is on the original master page.)

- Pull down from the Master Document layout palette the correct recto or verso to the page being changed. Box will turn gray.

- Find the *extra text box* and delete.

11

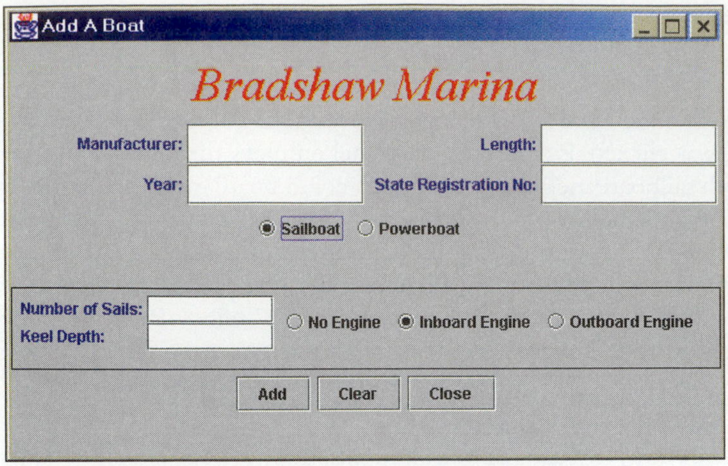

Figure 11-11   Add a sailboat

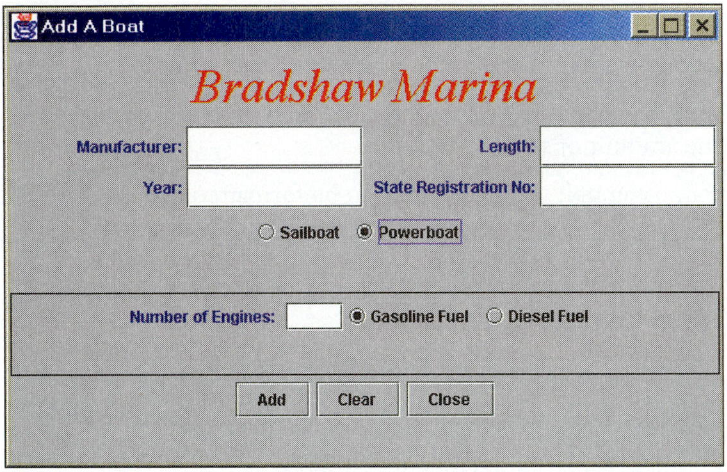

Figure 11-12   Add a powerboat

On the other hand, if powerboatRadioButton is clicked, powerboatPanel is displayed in the boatPanel, as shown in Figure 11-12.

Writing the clearForm Method

The clearForm method here is similar to the one in AddCustomer in that it blanks out all of the text fields by storing spaces in them.

```
manufacturerText.setText("");
```

```
boatLengthText.setText("");
yearText.setText("");
stateRegistrationText.setText("");
numberOfSailsText.setText("");
keelDepthText.setText("");
```

In addition to blanking out the text fields, clearForm also forces a click event on sailboatRadioButton by invoking its doClick method. This causes the actionPerformed method to be invoked, which will display the sailboatPanel on the frame.

```
sailboatRadioButton.doClick();
```

The last two statements in clearForm force a click on inboardEngineRadioButton and set the focus to the manufacturer text field. The doClick method for inboardEngineRadioButton is invoked to select it as the default.

```
inboardEngineRadioButton.doClick();
manufacturerText.requestFocus();
```

Writing the addBoatMethod

The addBoat method is invoked by actionPerformed when the Add button is clicked. This method retrieves the manufacturer, length, year, and registration information from their respective text fields, performs simple data validation of the information, and then invokes either addSailboat or addPowerboat, depending upon which radio button is selected, to complete the process of adding a boat.

A try-catch structure is used here because parseDouble and parseInt are invoked to convert the string data in the length and year text fields to numeric primitive data, and will throw a NumberFormatException if the data is not numeric. If the exception is thrown, then addBoat displays an error message using a dialog box.

If the data is successfully converted to numeric data, the manufacturer and registration information is then retrieved. Next, these string values are tested for zero length, which would indicate the data is missing. If missing data is detected, an error message is displayed in a dialog box. If the data passes these data validation checks, either addSailboat or addPowerboat is invoked, depending upon which radio button is selected. Note that the data items common to both kinds of boats—registration, length, manufacturer, and year—are passed as arguments to these methods.

```
private void addBoat()
{
try
{
   double boatLength = Double.parseDouble(boatLengthText.getText());
   int year = Integer.parseInt(yearText.getText());
   String manufacturer = manufacturerText.getText();
   String stateRegistration = stateRegistrationText.getText();
   if (manufacturer.length() == 0 || stateRegistration.length() == 0)
     JOptionPane.showMessageDialog(this, "Please Enter All Data ");
```

11

```
        else
          {
          if(sailboatRadioButton.isSelected())
             addSailboat(stateRegistration,boatLength,manufacturer,year);
          else
             addPowerboat(stateRegistration,boatLength,manufacturer,year);
          }
      }
    catch(NumberFormatException e)
        {JOptionPane.showMessageDialog(this, "length and year must be
numeric");}
    }
```

Writing the addSailboatMethod

The addSailboat method receives the registration, length, manufacturer, and year into parameter variables, and then retrieves the number of sails and keel depth from the text fields. A try-catch block is once again used because parseDouble and parseInt are invoked to convert the string data into primitive numeric data and these methods will throw an exception if the data is not numeric. If the exception is thrown, an error message is displayed in a dialog box.

After the number of sails and keel depth are retrieved and converted to primitive numeric data, three if statements determine which of the three motor type radio buttons are selected, and the appropriate value is placed into motorType. Finally, a new Sailboat instance is created and a descriptive message is displayed in a dialog box.

```
private void addSailboat(String aStateRegistration,double aBoatLength,String
aManufacturer,int aYear)
{
    String motorType = "";
    try
    {
        int numberOfSails = Integer.parseInt(numberOfSailsText.getText());
        double keelDepth = Double.parseDouble(keelDepthText.getText());
        if(noEngineRadioButton.isSelected())
           motorType = "none";
        if(inboardEngineRadioButton.isSelected())
           motorType = "inboard";
        if(outboardEngineRadioButton.isSelected())
           motorType = "outboard";
        Sailboat aSailboat = new Sailboat(aStateRegistration, aBoatLength,
aManufacturer, aYear, keelDepth, numberOfSails, motorType);
        JOptionPane.showMessageDialog(this,"Sailboat added");
        clearForm();
    }
```

```
    catch(NumberFormatException e)
        {JOptionPane.showMessageDialog(this, "number of sails & keel depth
must be numeric ");}
}
```

Writing the addPowerboatMethod

The addPowerboat method is similar to addSailboat except that numberOfEngines is retrieved and there are only two radio buttons to test: gasolineFuelRadioButton and dieselFuelRadioButton.

```
private void addPowerboat(String aStateRegistration,double aBoatLength,
String aManufacturer,int aYear)
{
    try
    {
      int numberOfEngines = Integer.parseInt(numberOfEnginesText.getText());
      String fuelType = "";
      if(gasolineFuelRadioButton.isSelected())
          fuelType = "gasoline";
      if(dieselFuelRadioButton.isSelected())
          fuelType = "diesel";
      Powerboat aPowerboat = new Powerboat(aStateRegistration, aBoatLength,
aManufacturer, aYear, numberOfEngines, fuelType);
      JOptionPane.showMessageDialog(this,"Powerboat added");
      clearForm();
    }
    catch(NumberFormatException e)
    {JOptionPane.showMessageDialog(this, "number of engines must be
numeric "); }
}
```

The complete listing of AddBoat.java is shown in Figure 11-13.

```
// Add Boat GUI
import java.awt.*;        // Font, Color, Layout managers
import javax.swing.*;     // GUI components
import java.awt.event.*;  // ActionEvent, ActionListener, WindowAdapter

public class AddBoat extends JFrame implements ActionListener
{
    // GUI reference variables needing class scope
    JPanel boatPanel;
```

11

```java
    CardLayout boatLayout;
    JTextField manufacturerText, boatLengthText, yearText,
stateRegistrationText;
    JTextField numberOfSailsText, keelDepthText, numberOfEnginesText;
    JRadioButton sailboatRadioButton, powerboatRadioButton;
    JRadioButton noEngineRadioButton, inboardEngineRadioButton,
outboardEngineRadioButton;
    JRadioButton gasolineFuelRadioButton, dieselFuelRadioButton;
    JButton addButton, clearButton, closeButton;


    public static void main(String args[])
    {   AddBoat frame = new AddBoat(); }

    // constructor
    public AddBoat()
    {   // create the panels
        Container c = this.getContentPane();
        c.setLayout(new GridLayout(5,1));
        JPanel upperPanel = new JPanel(new GridLayout(2,4));
        JPanel centerPanel = new JPanel(new FlowLayout());
        JPanel sailboatPanel = new JPanel(new FlowLayout());
        JPanel powerboatPanel = new JPanel(new FlowLayout());
        JPanel lowerPanel = new JPanel(new FlowLayout());

        // CardLayout permits the dynamic change of panel contents
        boatLayout = new CardLayout();
        boatPanel = new JPanel();
        boatPanel.setLayout(boatLayout);

        // create logo
        JLabel logoLabel = new JLabel(" ",SwingConstants.CENTER);
        logoLabel.setForeground(Color.red);
        logoLabel.setFont(new Font("TimesRoman", Font.ITALIC,36));
        logoLabel.setText("Bradshaw Marina");
        c.add(logoLabel); // add logo to the Frame

        // build upper panel
        manufacturerText = new JTextField(15);
        boatLengthText = new JTextField(4);
        yearText = new JTextField(6);
        stateRegistrationText = new JTextField(15);
        upperPanel.add(new JLabel("Manufacturer: ", SwingConstants.RIGHT));
        upperPanel.add(manufacturerText);
        upperPanel.add(new JLabel("Length: ", SwingConstants.RIGHT));
        upperPanel.add(boatLengthText);
        upperPanel.add(new JLabel("Year: ", SwingConstants.RIGHT));
        upperPanel.add(yearText);
        upperPanel.add(new JLabel("State Registration No: ",
SwingConstants.RIGHT));
        upperPanel.add(stateRegistrationText);
        c.add(upperPanel); // add panel to the Frame

        // build center panel
        // create radio buttons for type of boat - sailboat is default
```

```
        sailboatRadioButton = new JRadioButton("Sailboat", true);
        powerboatRadioButton = new JRadioButton("Powerboat", false);

        // create a ButtonGroup for boat type buttons
        ButtonGroup typeOfBoat = new ButtonGroup();
        typeOfBoat.add(sailboatRadioButton);
        typeOfBoat.add(powerboatRadioButton);

        // add radio buttons to centerPanel
        centerPanel.add(sailboatRadioButton);
        centerPanel.add(powerboatRadioButton);
        c.add(centerPanel); // add center panel to the Frame

        // build sailboat panel
        JPanel leftSailboatPanel = new JPanel(new GridLayout(2,1));
        JPanel rightSailboatPanel = new JPanel(new FlowLayout());
        numberOfSailsText = new JTextField(4);
        keelDepthText = new JTextField(4);
        noEngineRadioButton = new JRadioButton("No Engine", false);
        inboardEngineRadioButton = new JRadioButton("Inboard Engine", true);
        outboardEngineRadioButton = new JRadioButton("Outboard Engine",
false);

        ButtonGroup sailboatEngineGroup = new ButtonGroup();
        sailboatEngineGroup.add(noEngineRadioButton);
        sailboatEngineGroup.add(inboardEngineRadioButton);
        sailboatEngineGroup.add(outboardEngineRadioButton);
        leftSailboatPanel.add(new JLabel("Number of Sails: "));
        leftSailboatPanel.add(numberOfSailsText);
        leftSailboatPanel.add(new JLabel("Keel Depth: "));
        leftSailboatPanel.add(keelDepthText);
        rightSailboatPanel.add(noEngineRadioButton);
        rightSailboatPanel.add(inboardEngineRadioButton);
        rightSailboatPanel.add(outboardEngineRadioButton);
        sailboatPanel.add(leftSailboatPanel);
        sailboatPanel.add(rightSailboatPanel);
        // create border for the panel
        sailboatPanel.setBorder(BorderFactory.createLineBorder(Color.black));
        boatPanel.add(sailboatPanel, "sailboat");

        // build powerboat panel
        numberOfEnginesText = new JTextField(4);
        gasolineFuelRadioButton = new JRadioButton("Gasoline Fuel", true);
        dieselFuelRadioButton = new JRadioButton("Diesel Fuel", false);
        ButtonGroup powerboatFuelGroup = new ButtonGroup();
        powerboatFuelGroup.add(gasolineFuelRadioButton);
        powerboatFuelGroup.add(dieselFuelRadioButton );
        powerboatPanel.add(new JLabel("Number of Engines: "));
        powerboatPanel.add(numberOfEnginesText);
        powerboatPanel.add(gasolineFuelRadioButton);
        powerboatPanel.add(dieselFuelRadioButton);
        powerboatPanel.setBorder(BorderFactory.createLineBorder(Color.black));
        boatPanel.add(powerboatPanel, "powerboat");
        c.add(boatPanel);
```

11

```java
        // create and add Buttons for bottom panel
        addButton = new JButton("Add");
        clearButton = new JButton("Clear");
        closeButton = new JButton("Close");
        lowerPanel.add(addButton);
        lowerPanel.add(clearButton);
        lowerPanel.add(closeButton);
        c.add(lowerPanel); // add lower panel to the Frame

        this.setSize(550,350);
        this.setTitle("Add A Boat");
        this.setVisible(true);

        // register frame as listener for events
        addButton.addActionListener(this);
        clearButton.addActionListener(this);
        closeButton.addActionListener(this);
        sailboatRadioButton.addActionListener(this);
        powerboatRadioButton.addActionListener(this);
        // create anonymous inner class to handle window closing event
        this.addWindowListener(new WindowAdapter()
            {
                public void windowClosing(WindowEvent event)
                    {shutDown();}
            }
        );
    }
// actionPerformed is invoked when a Button is clicked
public void actionPerformed(ActionEvent e)
{
    // see which button was clicked
    if(e.getSource() == addButton)
        addBoat();
    if(e.getSource() == clearButton)
        clearForm();
    if(e.getSource() == closeButton)
        shutDown();
    if(e.getSource() == sailboatRadioButton)
        boatLayout.first(boatPanel); // show sailboat panel
    if(e.getSource() == powerboatRadioButton)
        boatLayout.last(boatPanel);  // show powerboat panel
}

private void addBoat()
{
    try
    {
        double boatLength = Double.parseDouble(boatLengthText.getText());
        int year = Integer.parseInt(yearText.getText());
        String manufacturer = manufacturerText.getText();
        String stateRegistration = stateRegistrationText.getText();

        if (manufacturer.length() == 0 || stateRegistration.length() == 0)
            JOptionPane.showMessageDialog(this, "Please Enter All Data ");
```

```
            else
                {
                    if(sailboatRadioButton.isSelected())
                        addSailboat(stateRegistration, boatLength,
manufacturer,
                            year);
                    else
                        addPowerboat(stateRegistration,
boatLength,manufacturer,
                            year);
                }
        }
        catch(NumberFormatException e)
        {JOptionPane.showMessageDialog(this, "length and year must be
numeric");}
    }
    private void addSailboat(String aStateRegistration,double
aBoatLength,String aManufacturer,int aYear)
    {
        String motorType = "";
        try
        {
            int numberOfSails = Integer.parseInt(numberOfSailsText.getText());
            double keelDepth = Double.parseDouble(keelDepthText.getText());
            if(noEngineRadioButton.isSelected())
                motorType = "none";
            if(inboardEngineRadioButton.isSelected())
                motorType = "inboard";
            if(outboardEngineRadioButton.isSelected())
                motorType = "outboard";
            Sailboat aSailboat = new Sailboat(aStateRegistration, aBoatLength,
                aManufacturer, aYear, keelDepth, numberOfSails, motorType);
            JOptionPane.showMessageDialog(this,"Sailboat added");
            clearForm();
        }
        catch(NumberFormatException e)
        {JOptionPane.showMessageDialog(this, "number of sails & keel depth
must be numeric ");}
    }
    private void addPowerboat(String aStateRegistration,double
        aBoatLength,String aManufacturer,int aYear)
    {
        try
        {
            int numberOfEngines =
                Integer.parseInt(numberOfEnginesText.getText());
            String fuelType = "";
            if(gasolineFuelRadioButton.isSelected())
                fuelType = "gasoline";
            if(dieselFuelRadioButton.isSelected())
                fuelType = "diesel";
            Powerboat aPowerboat = new Powerboat(aStateRegistration,
```

11

```
        aBoatLength, aManufacturer, aYear, numberOfEngines, fuelType);
            JOptionPane.showMessageDialog(this,"Powerboat added");
            clearForm();
        }
        catch(NumberFormatException e)
            {JOptionPane.showMessageDialog(this, "number of engines must be
numeric "); }


    }

    private void clearForm()
    {
        manufacturerText.setText("");
        boatLengthText.setText("");
        yearText.setText("");
        stateRegistrationText.setText("");
        numberOfSailsText.setText("");
        keelDepthText.setText("");
        sailboatRadioButton.doClick();
        inboardEngineRadioButton.doClick();
        manufacturerText.requestFocus();
    }


    public void shutDown()
    {  System.exit(0);   }
}
```

Figure 11-13 AddBoat.java listing

Hands-on Exercise 5

1. Create a folder named Chapter11Exercise5 on your system.

2. Locate AddBoat.java, Boat.java, Sailboat.java, and Powerboat.java on the book's CD in a folder named Chapter11\Example3, and then copy them to the Chapter11Exercise5 folder you created in Step 1.

3. Convert AddBoat by completing the following tasks:
   a. Change the class name to AddBoatApplet.
   b. Extend JApplet instead of JFrame.
   c. Remove the main method.
   d. Rename the constructor to init with a return type of void.
   e. Remove all references to closeButton, including the shutDown method.
   f. Remove the inner class.
   g. Remove the statements that invoke setTitle, setSize, and setVisible.

4. Write an HTML file named AddBoatApplet.html, and then compile and test your code. Your applet should behave the same as AddBoat except for the missing Close button.

Summary

- You invoke the showMessageDialog method in the JOptionPane class to display a dialog box containing a message.

- You can test for missing data in a text field by checking the length of the string data for zero.

- You use JList to display a list of string data contained in a Vector instance. You can add scroll bars by instantiating JScrollPane, passing the JList reference variable to the constructor.

- You select an item in a list by clicking it, which triggers both an ItemEvent and an ActionEvent. The JList method named getSelectedIndex returns the index of the selected item.

- The CardLayout layout manager enables you to dynamically change the contents of a panel. You can add several panels to a Panel instance using CardLayout, and then invoke methods to make any one of them visible.

- You use the RadioButton class to create radio buttons. An important characteristic of a radio button is that only one button within a group can be selected. When you select one radio button, all other buttons in the same group are deselected. You assign individual RadioButton instances to a group by first creating an instance of the ButtonGroup class, and then adding the radio buttons to the ButtonGroup instance.

- You register for radio button events just like you do for push buttons: by invoking their addActionListener method. The event handler method actionPerformed is then invoked whenever a radio button is clicked, either to select or deselect it. You can simulate a radio button click event by invoking a radio button's doClick method. This will trigger event handler methods as if the button was actually clicked.

11

Review Questions

1. The contents of text fields are _____.

   a. string

   b. numeric primitive

   c. either string or numeric primitive

   d. neither string nor numeric primitive

2. The contents of labels are _____.

   a. string

   b. numeric primitive

   c. either string or numeric primitive

   d. neither string nor numeric primitive

3. What is the primary difference between a text field and a label?

a. There really is no difference.

b. You cannot change the label's contents after it has been displayed.

c. You cannot enter data into a label.

d. Labels can display different color and font.

4. The GridLayout layout manager can _____.

a. have the same number of rows as columns

b. have one row and two columns

c. have two rows and one column

d. all of the above

5. `Color.red` refers to _____.

a. a constant in the Color class

b. a method in the Color class

c. an object in the Color class

d. It is invalid.

6. `Font.ITALIC` refers to _____.

a. a constant in the Font class

b. a method in the Font class

c. an object in the Font class

d. It is invalid.

7. `SwingConstants.RIGHT` refers to _____.

a. a constant in the SwingConstants class

b. a method in the SwingConstants class

c. an object in the SwingConstants class

d. It is invalid

8. To display a dialog box, you _____.

a. create an instance of JDialogBox

b. invoke a method in JOptionPane

c. You cannot use a dialog box in Java.

d. none of the above

9. A String instance with zero length means _____ .

    a. You cannot have a string with no length.

    b. there is no data in the string

    c. you will get an exception

    d. you need to instantiate the String

10. A Vector is like an array except _____ .

    a. Vector can contain both primitive and reference variables

    b. Vector can only reference variables

    c. you can sort a Vector

    d. They are the same.

11. The JList class is used to display _____ .

    a. any data type

    b. only string data

    c. only numeric data

    d. all of the above

12. When you click a radio button _____ .

    a. all other buttons in the same group are deselected

    b. an action event occurs

    c. the clicked button is selected

    d. all of the above

13. The argument you pass to the JList constructor to create the data in the list is _____ .

    a. string data

    b. a Vector instance

    c. the data you want displayed in the list

    d. none of the above

14. The doClick event in RadioButton _____ .

    a. triggers an action event for the button

    b. is an instance method

    c. There is no such method.

    d. is a class method

11

15. The ButtonGroup class _____.

   a. create lines around push buttons

   b. create lines around radio buttons

   c. assign radio buttons to a logical group

   d. There is no such class.

Discussion Questions

1. In a subsequent chapter, you will learn how to compose GUI windows using a drag-and-drop technique with an IDE tool. List reasons why you should be able to write Java code such as that presented in this chapter to create GUI, instead of using an IDE with drag-and-drop tools.

2. Describe a design of FindCustomer that would benefit from using the JList ListSelectionEvent whenever a specific customer was selected from the list. Which approach do you think is a better design: using ActionEvent or ListSelectionEvent?

3. The AddBoat design could be altered to use two completely different GUIs: one for sailboats and a second for powerboats. Describe advantages for choosing this design over the one presented in the chapter.

4. If you were assured by Bradshaw Marina that the only possible values for number of engines was 1, 2, or 3, you could use radio buttons for these values instead of a text field. Do you think replacing the text field with radio buttons is a better design? Are there additional text fields that could possibly be replaced with radio buttons?

Projects

1. Write a new subclass of Boat named Rowboat with attributes width and maximumNumberOfPassengers. Include a tellAboutSelf method. Next, write a tester class named RowboatTester to create two rowboats, and then retrieve and display their attributes to ensure that your new Rowboat class is working properly.

2. Expand AddBoat.java from your book's CD folder Chapter11\Example3 to accommodate your new Rowboat class by completing the following tasks:

   a. Add a third radio button named rowboatRadioButton to the centerPanel.

   b. Create a rowBoatPanel similar to powerBoatPanel to be displayed in boatPanel when rowboatRadioButton is selected.

   c. Add a method named addRowBoat to instantiate RowBoat if rowboatRadioButton is selected when addButton is clicked.

11

Designing Multiwindow Applications

In this chapter you will:

- ♦ Design a main menu that displays other windows
- ♦ Instantiate a second window and make it visible
- ♦ Navigate among multiple windows
- ♦ Return to a main menu
- ♦ Navigate a problem domain association relationship

In the previous chapter, you learned how to design GUI classes that interact with problem domain classes. You saw how to develop GUI classes to add a new Bradshaw Marina customer, find an existing customer, and add a boat to the system. This chapter continues working with these same GUI classes and shows you how to design a main menu GUI class that facilitates navigation among multiple windows. Instead of having stand-alone classes to accomplish individual tasks such as adding a customer, finding a customer, and adding a boat, you will see how to begin developing an integrated system using a main menu to launch these classes. Then you will see how to return to the menu. All of the examples in this chapter use Swing components.

The examples in this chapter use Vectors to simulate customer and boat databases, making the examples more robust than the ones used in Chapter 11. Two Vectors are used, one for customers and one for boats. Although Chapters 14 and 15 describe data access classes and database processing in detail, two data access methods are introduced in this chapter: initialize, which performs initialization tasks, and getAll, which returns a Vector of all the customer and/or boat instances.

This chapter begins by showing you how to create a main menu for Bradshaw Marina. This menu has three push buttons: Find a Customer, Add a Customer, and Close. When you click the Find a Customer button, the FindCustomer class you developed in the previous chapter is instantiated and its GUI is displayed. Similarly, when you click Add a Customer, the AddCustomer class from the previous chapter is instantiated and its GUI is displayed. Both AddCustomer and FindCustomer function as before, except that they simulate a customer database. Also, when you click the Close button, you now return to the main menu GUI.

Next you will see how to navigate a problem domain association relationship. You will recall from Chapter 9 that the Customer and Boat classes have an association relationship: a customer owns a boat. You learned how to include reference attributes in Boat and Customer to associate them with each other. In this chapter you will see how to design a GUI class to add a customer and his or her boat together. This is accomplished by linking the AddCustomer GUI to the AddBoat GUI you developed in the previous chapter.

The final example in this chapter shows you how to design a GUI to find a customer and display his or her address, phone number, and boat information using a single GUI class. This example takes advantage of the association relationship between the Customer and Boat classes.

After completing this chapter, you will understand how to design GUIs that navigate among multiple windows. You will also know how to design a GUI that navigates a problem domain association relationship. The examples developed in this chapter are expanded in subsequent chapters, which deal with data access classes and database management systems.

NAVIGATING MULTIPLE WINDOWS

Although you can design the Bradshaw Marina system with separate stand-alone GUI classes for each task, such as AddCustomer, FindCustomer, AddBoat, and so forth, a better approach is to link them by designing a main menu GUI that launches these GUI classes. Linking these GUIs makes it easier for you to go from one task (such as FindCustomer) to a second (such as AddCustomer). The main menu GUI displays push buttons for the available tasks, such as add a customer and find a customer. You click one of these buttons to instantiate and display the appropriate GUI. After completing that task, you click a Close button to return to the main menu. In this section you will see how to simulate a customer database and design and write a main menu GUI.

Simulating a Customer Database

In Part 4 (Chapter 15) you will learn how to design data access classes that use a relational database and then see how to use Java and the Structured Query Language (SQL) to store and retrieve data for Bradshaw Marina. The focus in this chapter, however, is multiple GUI windows; therefore, here you will simulate the interaction with a database by using a Vector of customers and boats. This section describes the simulation of a customer database. The boat database simulation is described in a later section.

You will recall from Part 1 (Chapters 1–4) that OO systems employ a three-tier design consisting of GUI classes, problem domain (PD) classes and data access (DA) classes. As their names suggest, GUI classes provide a graphical interface for the input and display of data, PD classes model the business entities and processes, and DA classes provide data storage and retrieval services. A major advantage of the three-tier design is that classes in each tier can be independent of those in another. For example, neither the GUI nor PD classes need to know how the DA classes store data. They only need to be able to invoke methods to store and retrieve data. Similarly, the DA classes are completely unaware of the GUI classes. This independence can dramatically simplify future maintenance chores because modifications to classes in one tier do not require changes to classes in another tier. To illustrate, because the PD and GUI classes are unaware of how the DA classes store and retrieve data, a change from one type of database to another, for example, will not affect the GUI and PD classes.

Two of the DA methods, initialize and getAll, are introduced here and added to the PD class Customer. The Main Menu GUI invokes these methods but is unaware of their implementation. This means that later you can convert to a real database management system without changing the Main Menu GUI (this point is illustrated later in Chapter 16).

The following list defines the two DA methods and provides code examples:

1. *initialize*: This method performs initialization tasks in preparation for database access. In the examples here, this method creates six customer instances and stores their references into a Vector named customers, which is declared with class scope.

```
public static void initialize()
{
   customers = new Vector();
   Customer aCustomer;
   aCustomer = new Customer("Eleanor", "Atlanta", "123-4567");
   aCustomer = new Customer("Mike", "Boston", "467-1234");
   aCustomer = new Customer("JoAnn", "St. Louis", "765-4321");
   aCustomer = new Customer("Dave", "Atlanta", "321-4567");
   aCustomer = new Customer("Brian", "Los Angeles", "467-1234");
   aCustomer = new Customer("Dan", "Reston", "587-4321");
}
```

A statement is added to the Customer constructor to actually populate the database.

```
public Customer(String aName, String anAddress, String aPhoneNo)
{
   // invoke set accessors to populate attributes
   setName(aName);
   setAddress(anAddress);
   setPhoneNo(aPhoneNo);
   customers.add(this);      // simulate add to dbms
}
```

12

2. *getAll:* This method returns the Vector reference containing references to all instances of the Customer class. Using the getAll method, you can access a specific customer instance by retrieving its reference from the Vector.

```
public static Vector getAll()
{ return customers;}
```

The MainMenu constructor invokes the initialize method to create the Vector of customers, and then AddCustomer and FindCustomer invoke getAll to retrieve the Vector, which gives them access to all of the customer instances.

Because this example is simulating a database, whenever a new customer is created, you want to add it to the Vector of customers. You accomplish this by invoking the Vector's add method and passing it the new customer's reference. The following statement is added to the customer constructor. The reference **this** refers to the customer instance that was just created. The Vector's add method stores the customer reference into the next available element in the Vector.

```
customers.add(this);
```

Designing the Main Menu

The main menu for Bradshaw Marina is shown in Figure 12-1. This frame instance is divided into two rows using GridLayout manager. The top row is used to display the marina's logo, which is identical to the examples in the previous chapter. The bottom row contains a panel named lowerPanel that uses the default FlowLayout manager to place the three buttons left to right. In this figure, the frame is not large enough to accommodate all three buttons on one row, so the third button is placed in the second row as shown. If you increase the size of the frame, then all three buttons will be on one row.

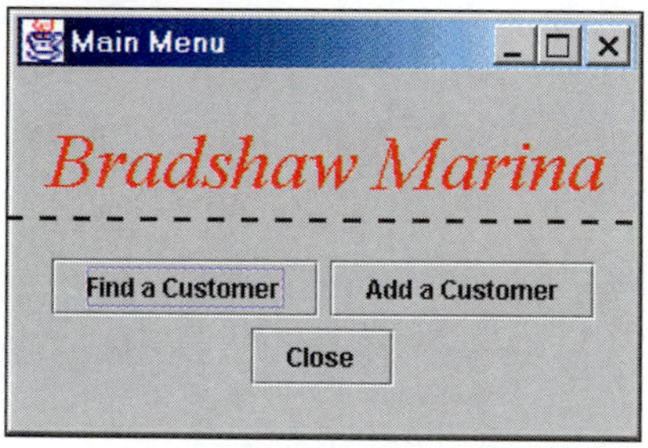

Figure 12-1   Main menu for Bradshaw Marina

The listing of MainMenu.java is shown in Figure 12-2.

```java
// Multiple window navigation - GUI Menu for AddCustomer & FindCustomer
import java.awt.*;        // Font, Color, Layout managers
import javax.swing.*;     // GUI components
import java.awt.event.*;  // ActionEvent, ActionListener, WindowAdapter
public class MainMenu extends JFrame implements ActionListener
{
    // variables needing class scope
    JButton findCustomerButton, addCustomerButton, closeButton;
    public static void main(String args[])
    {   MainMenu frame = new MainMenu(); }

    // constructor
    public MainMenu()
    {
        Container c = this.getContentPane();
        c.setLayout(new GridLayout(2,1));
        JPanel lowerPanel = new JPanel(); // default FlowLayout

        // create logo
        Font defaultFont = c.getFont(); // get font so can restore
        JLabel logoLabel = new JLabel(" ",SwingConstants.CENTER);
        logoLabel.setForeground(Color.red);
        logoLabel.setFont(new Font("TimesRoman", Font.ITALIC,36));
        logoLabel.setText("Bradshaw Marina");
        c.add(logoLabel); // add logo to the Frame

        // create Buttons for bottom panel
        findCustomerButton = new JButton("Find a Customer");
        addCustomerButton = new JButton("Add a Customer");
        closeButton = new JButton("Close");
        // add the buttons
        lowerPanel.add(findCustomerButton);
        lowerPanel.add(addCustomerButton);
        lowerPanel.add(closeButton);
        c.add(lowerPanel); // add lower panel to the Frame

        // register frame as listener for button events
        findCustomerButton.addActionListener(this);
        addCustomerButton.addActionListener(this);
        closeButton.addActionListener(this);

        this.setSize(300,200);
        this.setTitle("Main Menu");
        this.setVisible(true);

        Customer.initialize(); // initialize the pseudo-dbms
```

12

```java
        // create anonymous inner class to handle window closing event
        this.addWindowListener(new WindowAdapter()
            {
                public void windowClosing(WindowEvent event)
                    {shutDown();}
            }
        );
    }
    // actionPerformed is invoked when a Button is clicked
    public void actionPerformed(ActionEvent e)
    {
        // see which button was clicked
        if(e.getSource() == findCustomerButton)
            {findCustomer();}
        if(e.getSource() == addCustomerButton)
            {addCustomer();}
        if(e.getSource() == closeButton)
            {shutDown();}
    }
    private void findCustomer()
    {
        FindCustomer findCustomerFrame = new FindCustomer(this);
        findCustomerFrame.setSize(300,200);
        findCustomerFrame.setTitle("Find A Customer");
        findCustomerFrame.setVisible(true);
        this.setVisible(false);
    }
    private void addCustomer()
    {
        AddCustomer addCustomerFrame = new AddCustomer(this);
        addCustomerFrame.setSize(300,200);
        addCustomerFrame.setTitle("Add A Customer");
        addCustomerFrame.setVisible(true);
        this.setVisible(false);
    }
    public void shutDown()
        {   System.exit(0);   }
}
```

Figure 12-2   MainMenu.java listing

The main method is invoked when the class is loaded into memory and it instantiates the class, which automatically invokes its constructor. The constructor creates and displays the Bradshaw Marina logo, creates the push buttons and adds them to the frame, registers as an event listener for the push button events, and creates an anonymous inner class to handle the window closing event.

The actionPerformed method determines which button was clicked and invokes the appropriate method—findCustomer, addCustomer, or shutDown—to handle the event. The shutDown method is identical to the examples in previous chapters.

The findCustomer method creates and displays the FindCustomer GUI frame and makes the MainMenu frame invisible. It accomplishes this by first instantiating FindCustomer, then invoking its setSize, setTitle, and setVisible methods, and finally invoking MainMenu's setVisible method and passing it an argument of **false**. This means that after you click the Find a Customer button on the MainMenu GUI, the FindCustomer GUI is created and displayed, and the main menu disappears.

```
private void findCustomer()
{
    FindCustomer findCustomerFrame = new FindCustomer(this);
    findCustomerFrame.setSize(300,200);
    findCustomerFrame.setTitle("Find A Customer");
    findCustomerFrame.setVisible(true);
    this.setVisible(false);
}
```

A sequence diagram mapping the interaction between MainMenu, Customer, and FindCustomer is shown in Figure 12-3. As you can see, MainMenu first invokes Customer.initialize to initialize the simulated database. Next, MainMenu creates the FindCustomer frame and makes it visible. When FindCustomer is instantiated, its constructor invokes Customer.getAll to obtain the Vector containing all of the customer references. Finally, MainMenu makes itself invisible.

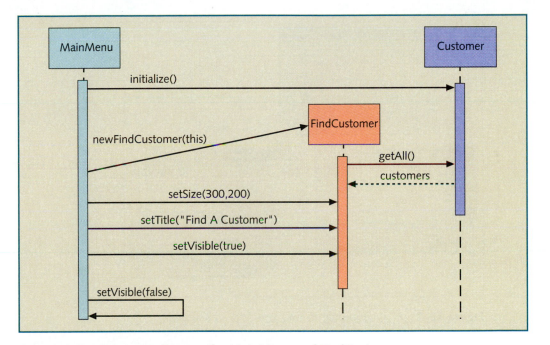

Figure 12-3 Sequence diagram for MainMenu and FindCustomer

In a similar manner, when you click the Add a Customer push button, the AddCustomer GUI frame is created and displayed, and the main menu becomes invisible.

```
private void addCustomer()
{
    AddCustomer addCustomerFrame = new AddCustomer(this);
    addCustomerFrame.setSize(300,200);
    addCustomerFrame.setTitle("Add A Customer");
    addCustomerFrame.setVisible(true);
    this.setVisible(false);
}
```

The sequence of GUI frames to find and add a customer is shown in Figure 12-4. If you click the Find a Customer button on the main menu, the FindCustomer frame appears. You can then select a customer from the list, and his or her address and phone number are displayed. If you click the Close button, the FindCustomer frame disappears and the MainMenu GUI reappears.

If you click the Add a Customer button on the main menu, the AddCustomer frame appears and the main menu closes. You then enter the customer's name, address, and phone number and click the Add button. A dialog box appears, showing a Customer Added message. You click the OK button on the dialog box, and then click the Close button on the AddCustomer frame to return to the main menu.

Figure 12-4   GUI sequence to find and add a customer

Finding a Customer

The FindCustomer GUI frame in this chapter looks exactly like the FindCustomer frame in Chapter 11. Note, however, two important differences in its behavior. First, clicking the Close button in this FindCustomer frame causes the main menu to reappear. Second, FindCustomer can display the new customers you add with AddCustomer. This version of FindCustomer shares the Vector of customers with AddCustomer, which means that the customers you add also store their reference in the customers Vector. This makes the customer information available for display in the list shown on the FindCustomer frame.

The FindCustomer class from the previous chapter is used here with four minor changes:

- Because FindCustomer is now instantiated by MainMenu, its main method is no longer needed and is removed. The original code in the main method that instantiated FindCustomer is now in the findCustomer method in MainMenu.

- When MainMenu instantiates FindCustomer, it passes a reference of itself to the FindCustomer constructor so that FindCustomer can invoke MainMenu's setVisible method.

```
FindCustomer findCustomerFrame = new FindCustomer(this);
```

The FindCustomer constructor then uses this reference to populate a reference variable named parentMenu with data type MainMenu.

```
public FindCustomer(MainMenu menu)
    {
        parentMenu = menu;
```

- The shutDown method in FindCustomer then uses this reference to make the main menu visible by invoking its setVisible method. It invokes the (inherited) dispose method, which destroys the FindCustomer instance. Note that shutDown is invoked by either clicking the Close button or closing the FindCustomer window.

```
public void shutDown()
{
    parentMenu.setVisible(true);
    this.dispose();
}
```

- In the previous chapter, FindCustomer had a method named createCustomers, which was invoked by the constructor. The purpose of this method was to create six customer instances and then populate a Vector with references to these six customer instances. The version of FindCustomer in this chapter simply invokes the Customer class method getAll to obtain the populated Vector.

```
customers = Customer.getAll();
```

12

Adding a Customer

The AddCustomer GUI class from Chapter 11 is also used in this chapter, although it contains the following minor modifications:

- The main method is removed.

- When MainMenu instantiates AddCustomer, it passes a reference of itself to the AddCustomer constructor.

```
AddCustomer addCustomerFrame = new AddCustomer(this);
```

- The shutDown method in AddCustomer is identical to that in FindCustomer. It makes the main menu visible. It then invokes the dispose method, which destroys the AddCustomer instance.

```
public void shutDown()
{
    parentMenu.setVisible(true);
    this.dispose();
}
```

Hands-on Exercise 1

1. Create a folder on your system named Chapter12Exercise1.

2. Locate MainMenu.java, FindCustomer.java, AddCustomer.java, and Customer.java on the book's CD in a folder named Chapter12\Example1, and then copy them to the Chapter12Exercise1 folder you created in Step 1.

3. Compile all the classes in Chapter12Exercise1 and run MainMenu using the software recommended by your instructor.

4. Add a new customer and then find this new customer to make sure the classes are working properly.

NAVIGATING A PD ASSOCIATION RELATIONSHIP

In Part 2 you learned about inheritance and association relationships among PD classes. In Chapter 7 you saw that Boat has two subclasses, Sailboat and Powerboat, and in Chapter 9 you saw that Customer and Boat had a one-to-one association. Figure 12-5 shows a partial class diagram indicating these relationships. Notice that this diagram shows that Customer has a reference attribute for Boat and that Boat has a reference attribute for Customer. The boat instance method assignBoatToCustomer populates both of these attributes, which links the customer and boat instances.

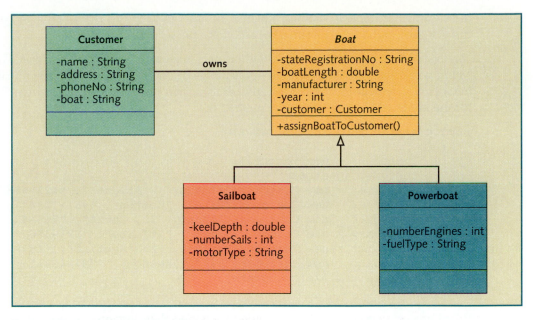

Figure 12-5   Customer and Boat class diagram

In this section, you will see how to use these PD relationships with GUI classes. You will make slight modifications to AddCustomer, FindCustomer, and AddBoat from previous examples to develop a multiwindow system that adds a new customer along with his or her boat, and then links them together. In the next section, you will learn how to use the Customer–Boat association to search for a customer and then display the customer's address and phone number, plus his or her boat information.

Simulating a Customer and Boat Database

In the previous section, you saw how to simulate a customer database using a Vector. You will use the same technique here for boats, and make similar modifications to the Boat class. Previously, in order to simulate a customer database, you added two methods to Customer: initialize and getAll. The initialize method first created six customer instances and then created and populated a Vector with references for these instances. Next, getAll returned a reference to the Vector containing the customer references.

The same approach is used for Boat. An initialize method is added that creates six boat instances—three sailboats and three powerboats—and then creates and populates a Vector containing references to these boat instances. However, in this example, customers own boats. Therefore, this initialize method also invokes assignBoatToCustomer to link each boat to a customer by populating the boat attribute in the customer instance, and by populating the customer attribute in the boat instance. In order to keep this example simple, you assign the first boat to the first customer, the second to the second, and so forth.

The MainMenu class from the previous example is used here *without modification*. The Main-Menu constructor invokes Customer.initialize as before. However, Customer.initialize now has a new statement to invoke Boat.initialize and pass it the Vector of customers. The code for the modified Customer.initialize method is:

```
public static void initialize()
    {
        customers = new Vector();
        Customer aCustomer;
        aCustomer = new Customer("Eleanor", "Atlanta", "123-4567");
        aCustomer = new Customer("Mike", "Boston", "467-1234");
        aCustomer = new Customer("JoAnn", "St. Louis", "765-4321");
        aCustomer = new Customer("Dave", "Atlanta", "321-4567");
        aCustomer = new Customer("Brian", "Los Angeles", "467-1234");
        aCustomer = new Customer("Dan", "Reston", "587-4321");
        Boat.initialize(customers);
    }
```

Boat.initialize first creates a Vector named boats, and then instantiates six boats to populate the Vector:

```
public static void initialize(Vector customers)
    {
        boats = new Vector();
        Customer aCustomer;
        Boat aBoat;
        Sailboat aSailBoat;
        Powerboat aPowerboat;
        aSailBoat = new Sailboat("MO34561", 28, "Tartan", 1998, 2,
4.11,"Diesel");
        aSailBoat = new Sailboat("MO98765", 28, "J-Boat", 1986, 4, 5.0,
"Diesel");
        aSailBoat = new Sailboat("MO12345", 26, "Ranger", 1976, 7, 4.5,
"Outboard");
        aPowerboat = new Powerboat("MO445566", 30, "Bayliner", 2001,
2,"Gas");
        aPowerboat = new Powerboat("MO223344", 24, "Tracker", 1996, 1,
"Gas");
        aPowerboat = new Powerboat("MO457812", 19, "Ranger", 2001,1,
"Gas");
```

Next, Boat.initialize iterates the boat and customer Vectors to link each boat to a customer by invoking assignBoatToCustomer for each boat. In this example, the first boat is assigned to the first customer, the second to the second, and so forth. The first statement in the loop retrieves the customer reference from the customer Vector at index i, and the second statement retrieves the boat reference from the boat Vector, also at index i. Note that you are required to cast the data type for both customer and boat references as they are retrieved from their respective Vectors. The third statement then invokes assignBoatToCustomer for the boat reference just retrieved, and passes the customer reference as an argument. This method populates the customer attribute in the boat instance and the boat attribute in the customer instance, linking the two instances together.

```
for(int i = 0; i < boats.size(); i++)
    {
        aCustomer = (Customer) customers.get(i);
        aBoat = (Boat) boats.get(i);
        aBoat.assignBoatToCustomer(aCustomer);
    }
```

After Boat.initialize completes execution, you have two Vectors: customers (containing six customer references) and boats (containing six boats). Each customer instance now contains a boat attribute that references a boat. Similarly, each boat instance has a customer attribute that references a customer. You can invoke accessor methods to retrieve these attributes, just like you do for the other attributes (name, address, and phone number). You can also invoke Customer.getAll to retrieve the customer Vector and Boat.getAll to retrieve the boat Vector.

Finally, similar to the modification made to the customer constructor, the boat constructor now contains a statement that adds a new boat instance to the boat Vector each time it is invoked. This means that whenever you create a new boat instance, its reference is automatically added to the boat Vector.

```
public Boat(String aStateRegistrationNo, double aLength, String
aManufacturer, int aYear)
    {
        setStateRegistrationNo(aStateRegistrationNo);
        setLength(aLength);
        setManufacturer(aManufacturer);
        setYear(aYear);
        setCustomer(null);// initially no Customer for this boat
        boats.add(this);  // simulate add to DBMS
    }
```

Adding a Customer and Boat

The MainMenu class is identical in both appearance and operation to the previous example from the "Adding a Customer" section. Similarly, FindCustomer is copied without modification from the previous example. The Customer class has a statement added to its constructor that invokes Boat.initialize, which creates the six boat instances and links the six boats to the six customers created in Customer.initialize.

Adding a Customer

In order to add a new customer to the system, you click the Add a Customer button on the main menu, which will then display the AddCustomer frame. The AddCustomer class has two minor modifications from what you saw in the previous example:

- The caption for the Add a Customer push button has been changed from Add a Customer to Add Boat, and its name changed from addButton to addBoatButton.

- The addCustomer method, which is invoked when addBoatButton is clicked, now has statements added to instantiate AddBoat, make it visible, and make the AddCustomer frame invisible.

```
AddBoat addBoatWindow = new AddBoat(this, aCustomer);
addBoatWindow.setSize(550, 350);
addBoatWindow.setTitle("Add a Boat for this Customer");
addBoatWindow.setVisible(true);
this.setVisible(false);
```

Note that two arguments are passed to the AddBoat constructor: `this` and `aCustomer`. The keyword `this` references the AddCustomer instance, which AddBoat uses to return to the AddCustomer frame, and `aCustomer` references the customer instance that was just created. This customer reference is later passed to the boat instance method assignBoatToCustomer to link the boat and customer instances.

Adding a Boat

After you enter the customer name, address, and phone number, you click addBoatButton, which invokes addCustomer to create a customer instance and display the AddBoat frame. The AddBoat class is copied from Chapter 11 with three modifications, which are similar to those you made to AddCustomer earlier in the chapter:

- The main method is removed, because AddBoat is now instantiated and made visible by AddCustomer.

- When AddCustomer instantiates AddBoat, it passes a reference of itself and the newly created customer instance to the AddBoat constructor, which is modified to receive these arguments. AddBoat requires a reference to the AddCustomer instance because when its closeButton is clicked, AddBoat makes the AddCustomer frame visible by invoking its setVisible method. The customer reference is needed by assignBoatToCustomer to link the customer instance to the boat instance being created.

```
public AddBoat(AddCustomer returnToWindow, Customer newCustomer)
```

- The shutDown method in AddBoat is modified to make the AddCustomer frame visible by invoking its setVisible method. It then invokes the inherited dispose method, which destroys the AddBoat instance.

```
public void shutDown()
    {
        addCustomerWindow.setVisible(true);
        this.dispose();
}
```

The GUI sequence to add a new customer and his or her boat is shown in Figure 12-6. From the main menu, you click the Add a Customer & Boat button, which displays the Add-Customer frame. You enter the customer's name, address, and phone number, and click the Add Boat button, which displays the AddBoat frame. Next you enter the boat information, just as you did in the previous chapter, and click the Add Customer & Boat button. The dialog box then appears with the message, "Customer and Boat added."

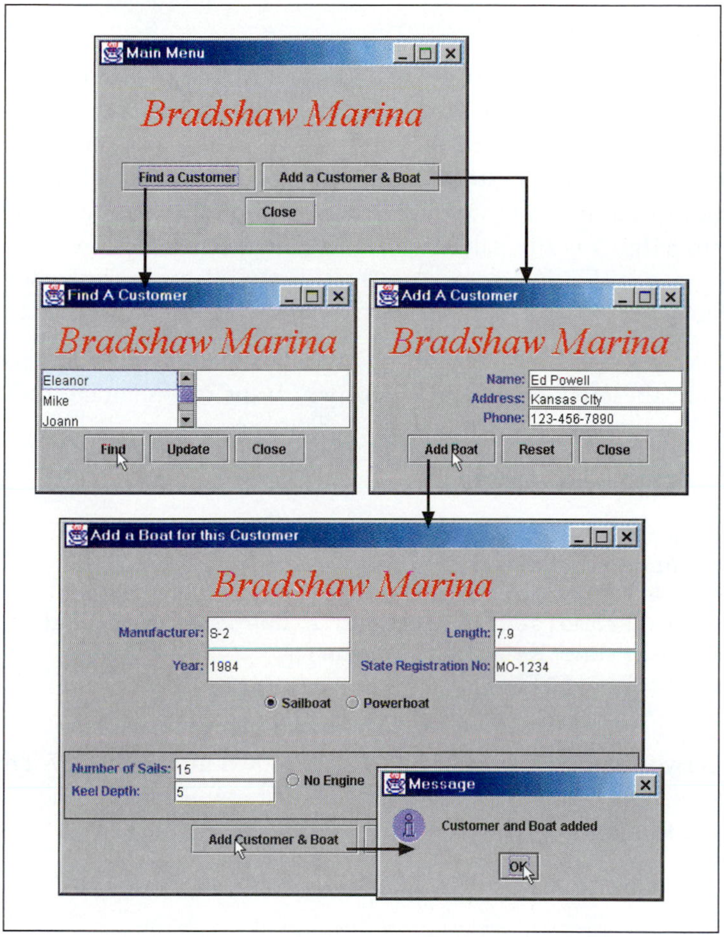

Figure 12-6   GUI sequence to add a customer and boat

Hands-on Exercise 2

1. Create a folder on your system named Chapter12Exercise2.

2. Locate MainMenu.java, FindCustomer.java, AddCustomer.java, Customer.java, AddBoat.java, Boat.java, Sailboat.java, and Powerboat.java on the book's CD in a folder named Chapter12\Example2, and then copy them to the Chapter12Exercise2 folder you created in Step 1.

3. Compile all the classes in Chapter12Exercise2 and run MainMenu using the software recommended by your instructor.

4. Add a new customer and his or her boat, then find this new customer to make sure the classes are working properly.

Finding a Customer and Boat

In the previous chapter, you saw how to use FindCustomer to locate and display a customer's address and phone number. FindCustomer displays a list of customer names, and when you click on a specific name, that customer's address and phone number are displayed. In this chapter, because customers and their boats are linked with an association relationship, you can display a customer's address and phone number plus his or her boat information together on the same frame. In this section, you will see how to develop a new class named FindCustomerAndBoat that displays the customer and boat information together.

You begin by making a slight modification to the findCustomer method in the MainMenu class from the previous section. Here you want to instantiate the new class FindCustomerAndBoat, instead of the previous FindCustomer class.

```
private void findCustomer()
{
    FindCustomerAndBoat findCustomerFrame = new
FindCustomerAndBoat(this);
    findCustomerFrame.setSize(450,225);
    findCustomerFrame.setTitle("Find A Customer and Boat");
    findCustomerFrame.setVisible(true);
    this.setVisible(false);
}
```

The GUI frame displayed by FindCustomerAndBoat is shown in Figure 12-7. The frame is divided into four rows using GridLayout manager. The first row is used for the marina logo just like the previous examples.

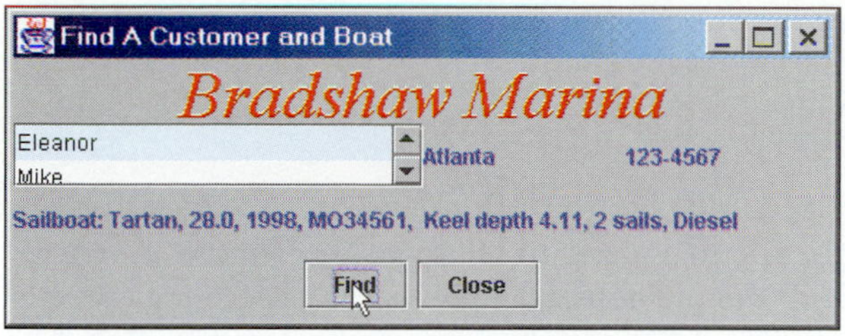

Figure 12-7   FindCustomerAndBoat GUI

The second row contains a panel named centerPanel, which has one row and two columns. The left column of centerPanel will contain a JList instance to display customer names, which is the same as the JList used earlier in FindCustomer. The right column contains a panel named centerRightPanel, which is divided into two columns. The first column holds a label instance to display the customer's address and the second column has a label instance to contain the customer's phone number. Labels are used here instead of text fields because you will not be entering address or phone information. You use text fields whenever you want to enter information.

The third row contains a panel named lowerPanel and uses the default FlowLayout manager to display a string containing the customer's boat information. This string is obtained by invoking Boat's tellAboutSelf method that you studied in Chapter 7. The fourth row also uses FlowLayout to display the two push buttons Find and Close. The following code creates the four rows and formats the last three:

```
Container c = this.getContentPane();
c.setLayout(new GridLayout(4,1));
JPanel centerPanel = new JPanel(new GridLayout(1,2));
JPanel centerRightPanel = new JPanel(new GridLayout(1,2));
JPanel lowerPanel = new JPanel();
```

The code to display the logo and to create and display the list of customer names is identical to what you saw in the FindCustomer class.

Next come the statements to create the JLabel instances for address, phone number, and boat information, add them to the panels, and add the panels to the frame.

```
customerAddressLabel = new JLabel();
customerPhoneLabel = new JLabel();
boatInfoLabel = new JLabel();

centerRightPanel.add(customerAddressLabel);
```

12

```
centerRightPanel.add(customerPhoneLabel);
centerPanel.add(centerRightPanel);
c.add(centerPanel);
c.add(boatInfoLabel);
```

The two push buttons are created, added to the lower panel, and the frame is registered as an event listener for both buttons. The statements to create an anonymous inner class to handle window closing are copied from the previous example.

```
findButton = new JButton("Find");
exitButton = new JButton("Close");
lowerPanel.add(findButton);
lowerPanel.add(exitButton);
c.add(lowerPanel);
findButton.addActionListener(this);
exitButton.addActionListener(this);
```

The actionPerformed method determines which button was clicked and invokes either find-Customer or shutDown.

```
public void actionPerformed(ActionEvent e)
    {
        // see which button was clicked
        if(e.getSource() == findButton)
            {findCustomer();}
        if(e.getSource() == exitButton)
            {shutDown();}
    }
```

The shutDown method makes the main menu visible and disposes of the FindCustomerAnd-Boat frame instance. This method is invoked when either the exitButton is clicked or the window is closed.

```
public void shutDown()
{
    parentMenu.setVisible(true);
    this.dispose();
}
```

The findCustomer method first invokes the getSelectedIndex method for the customerList instance to retrieve the index of the customer name that was selected from the list.

```
private void findCustomer()
{
    int i = customerList.getSelectedIndex();
```

Next, the Vector instance method called get is invoked to retrieve the reference for the customer instance from the customers Vector at index `i`. Note that you must cast the reference value returned by the get method to data type Customer because items stored in a Vector are stored as data type Object. This reference is assigned to the variable aCustomer.

```
aCustomer = (Customer) customers.get(i);
```

Next, the address and phone number accessor methods for the customer instance are invoked. The values returned are used as arguments that are passed to the setText methods, which populate the address and phone number labels.

```
customerAddressLabel.setText(aCustomer.getAddress());
customerPhoneLabel.setText(aCustomer.getPhoneNo());
```

Next, invoking the getBoat accessor method for the customer instance retrieves the reference for this customer's boat.

```
Boat thisBoat = aCustomer.getBoat();
```

The tellAboutSelf method is invoked for the boat instance and the string value returned is used to populate the boatInfoLabel.

```
String BoatInfo = thisBoat.tellAboutSelf();
boatInfoLabel.setText(BoatInfo);
```

Note that you can combine these last three statements into one to reduce the amount of code. The following statement first invokes getBoat to obtain the boat reference, then invokes tellAboutSelf for the boat instance just obtained, and finally invokes setText for the label instance, passing it the string returned by tellAboutSelf.

```
boatInfoLabel.setText(aCustomer.getBoat().tellAboutSelf());
```

12

The tellAboutSelf method used here is an excellent example of polymorphism. Both the Sailboat and Powerboat classes have this method, but when you invoke it here, you don't know whether you are invoking for a sailboat or a powerboat. Although tellAboutSelf in Sailboat is similar to the same method in Powerboat, they are completely different methods that return different values. The method in Sailboat returns the sailboat attribute values, and the one in Powerboat returns the powerboat values.

Note that when you obtain the boat reference used to invoke tellAboutSelf, the reference variable has data type Boat because you do not know if the boat is a sailboat or a powerboat.

Boat, Sailboat, and Powerboat all have the tellAboutSelf method. The methods in Sailboat and Powerboat first invoke tellAboutSelf in the Boat class to obtain the boat attribute values, and then concatenate the string returned with the subclass attribute values obtained by invoking getter methods.

The tellAboutSelf method for Sailboat is shown in the following code. The method first declares two string variables, one to contain the boat's information and a second to hold the sailboat information. The second statement first invokes the Boat tellAboutSelf method by specifying **super.tellAboutSelf()**. The string value returned is then concatenated with the literal **"Sailboat: "**, and the result is stored in boatInfo. The third statement is actually a long statement consisting of four lines that create a string value named sailboatInfo containing descriptive literals concatenated with the results of invoking the sailboat accessor, and then converting the numeric values returned to string by invoking the toString method. The last statement concatenates boatInfo with sailboatInfo and returns the concatenated value.

```
public String tellAboutSelf()
    {
        String boatInfo, sailboatInfo;
        boatInfo = "Sailboat: " + super.tellAboutSelf() + ", ";
        sailboatInfo = " Keel depth "
                    + Double.toString(getKeelDepth()) + ", "
                    + Integer.toString(getNoSails()) + " sails, "
                    + getMotorType();
        return boatInfo + sailboatInfo;
    }
```

The tellAboutSelf method in the Boat superclass is also shown below. It consists of a single statement consisting of four lines. This statement invokes the boat accessor, converts the numeric values to string, concatenates the string values, and then returns the result.

```
public String tellAboutSelf()
    {
        return (getManufacturer() + ", "
                + Double.toString(getBoatLength()) + ", "
                + Integer.toString(getYear()) + ", "
                + getStateRegistrationNo());
    }
```

The GUI relationships are shown in Figure 12-8. Note that the only difference between this figure and Figure 12-6 is that FindCustomer has been replaced with Find Customer and Boat.

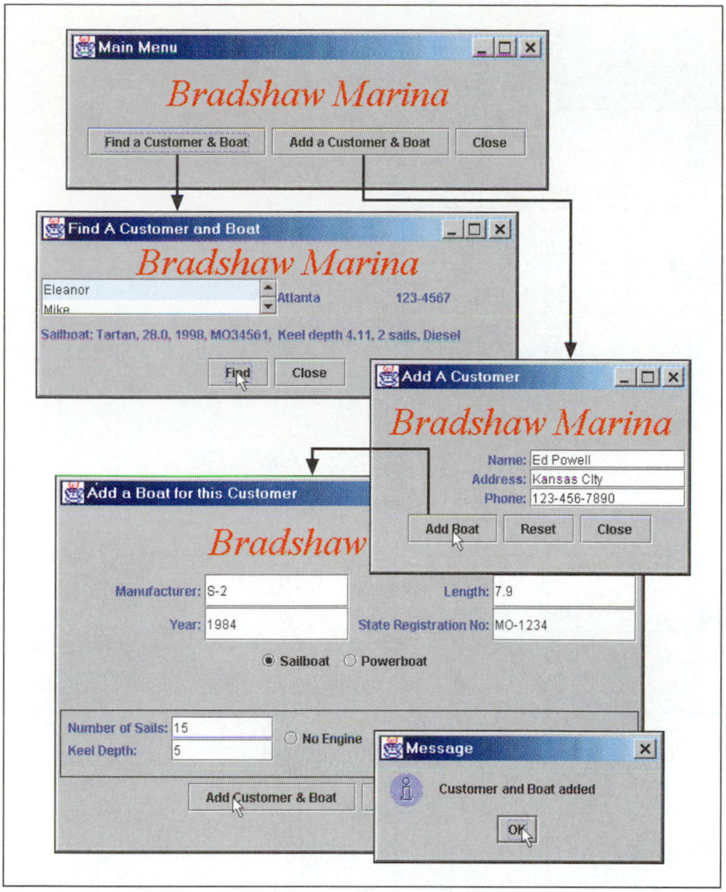

Figure 12-8   GUI sequence to add and find a customer and boat

A sequence diagram mapping the interaction between FindCustomerAndBoat, aBoat, and aCustomer in the findCustomer method is shown in Figure 12-9.

12

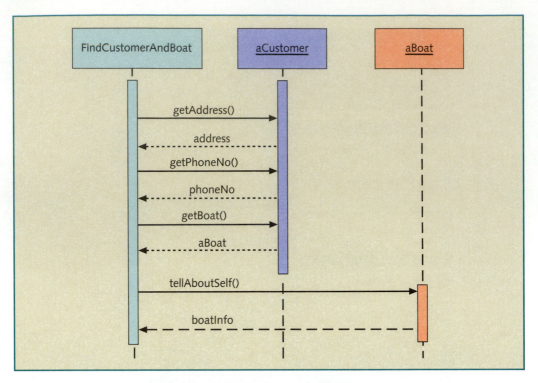

Figure 12-9   Sequence diagram for findCustomer method

Hands-on Exercise 3

1. Create a folder on your system named Chapter12Exercise3.

2. Locate MainMenu.java, FindCustomerAndBoat.java, AddCustomer.java, Customer.java, AddBoat.java, Boat.java, Sailboat.java, and Powerboat.java on the book's CD in a folder named Chapter12\Example3, and then copy them to the Chapter12Exercise3 folder you created in Step 1.

3. Compile all the classes in Chapter12Exercise3 and run MainMenu using the software recommended by your instructor.

4. Add a new customer and his or her boat, then find this new customer to make sure the classes are working properly.

Hands-on Exercise 4

1. Create a folder on your system named Chapter12Exercise4.

2. Locate MainMenu.java, FindCustomerAndBoat.java, AddCustomer.java, Customer.java, AddBoat.java, Boat.java, Sailboat.java, and Powerboat.java on the book's CD in a folder named Chapter12\Example4, and then copy them to the Chapter12Exercise4 folder you created in Step 1.

3. Modify FindCustomerAndBoat.java to respond to a ListSelectionEvent. Invoke the findCustomer method when the user selects a customer name in the list. *Hints*:
   a. Import javax.swing.event.ListSelectionListener.
   b. Implement the ListSelectionListener interface.
   c. Register the FindCustomerAndBoat frame instance as a selection event listener by invoking the JList registration method addListSelectionListener. Remember to pass a reference to the frame as an argument.
   d. Write the event handler method named valueChanged and have it invoke findCustomer.

4. Recompile FindCustomerAndBoat.java and run MainMenu using the software recommended by your instructor.

5. Add a new customer and his or her boat, and then find this new customer to make sure the classes with your modifications are working properly.

12

Summary

- Instead of having stand-alone classes to accomplish individual tasks such as adding a customer, finding a customer, and adding a boat, this chapter illustrates the development of an integrated system using a main menu to launch the individual classes to accomplish the processing tasks.

- This main menu has push buttons that launch other GUIs to accomplish these various tasks. For example, Find a Customer launches FindCustomer, Add a Customer launches AddCustomer, and Close terminates the menu. FindCustomer and AddCustomer from the previous chapter are modified to return to the main menu when their Close button is clicked.

- You can design a GUI class to add a customer and his or her boat together by linking the AddCustomer GUI to the AddBoat GUI from the previous chapter. AddBoat is launched when you click the Add a Boat button on the AddCustomer GUI.

- You can also design a GUI to find a customer, display his or her address and phone number, and display his or her boat information using a single GUI class by using the association relationship between the Customer and Boat classes. You first retrieve the customer instance, and then use the boat reference in that instance to retrieve the boat attribute values. You can invoke tellAboutSelf to retrieve a String instance containing the attribute values.

Review Questions

1. The steps you take to go to another window are to _____.

    a. dispose of the current window and then instantiate and make the other window visible

    b. instantiate and make the other window visible and then dispose of the current window

    c. invoke a method in the other window

    d. none of the above

2. The setVisible method uses the arguments _____.

    a. true and false

    b. yes and no

    c. 0 or 1

    d. none of the above

3. The Data Access method initialize is a(n) _____ method.

    a. instance

    b. dormant

    c. class

    d. none of the above

4. The Data Access method getAll is a(n) _____ method.

    a. instance

    b. dormant

    c. class

    d. none of the above

5. The three tiers in a three-tier design are _____.

    a. GUI, Swing, and PD

    b. GUI, PD, and DA

    c. AWT, GUI, and Swing

    d. none of the above

6. The PD classes _____.

    a. model the business entities and processes

    b. simulate a database

    c. are instantiated by the main menu

    d. none of the above

7. The DA classes _____.

    a. model the business entities and processes

    b. perform data storage and retrieval tasks

    c. are instantiated by the main menu

    d. none of the above

8. The data types of the reference variables contained in a Vector instance are _____.

    a. the same as when you placed them into the Vector

    b. Object

    c. String

    d. none of the above

9. You can pass an instance reference to a(n) _____.

    a. constructor method

    b. class method

    c. instance method

    d. all of the above

10. The getAll method illustrated in this chapter returns a _____.

    a. string instance

    b. customer instance

    c. boat instance

    d. none of the above

12

11. The data type of the boat attribute in the Customer class is _____.

    a. either Sailboat or Powerboat

    b. Object

    c. Boat

    d. none of the above

12. The tellAboutSelf method resides in _____.

    a. Boat

    b. Sailboat

    c. Powerboat

    d. all of the above

13. The getSelectedIndex method is used for a _____.

    a. text field

    b. list

    c. label

    d. none of the above

14. The getBoat method resides in _____.

    a. Customer

    b. Boat

    c. MainMenu

    d. none of the above

15. The Integer.toString method _____.

    a. returns a String value

    b. accepts an int argument

    c. is a class method

    d. all of the above

Discussion Questions

1. Assume that you cannot use Boat as a data type; you must use either Sailboat or Powerboat. Describe the changes you would be required to make to the FindBoatAndCustomer example if you were required to use Boat data types of only Sailboat and Powerboat. *Hint*: Consider adding a typeOfBoat attribute to Boat and/or Customer.

2. The dispose method is invoked in the shutDown method in AddCustomer, FindCustomer, AddBoat, and FindCustomerAndBoat. What do you think will happen if the statements invoking dispose are removed?

3. The designs you saw in this chapter required that the Close button return you to the main menu. Visualize a design that included buttons to bypass the main menu and go directly to another GUI. For example, how would you implement a design that called for direct navigation from the AddBoat GUI to the FindCustomer GUI?

4. At Bradshaw Marina, only a few customers own two boats. List modifications that would be needed to the AddBoat example in this chapter to accommodate this situation. Can you think of a way to handle a customer with two boats *without* making these modifications?

5. The examples in this chapter display a single frame at a time. Under what conditions would you want to have two or more frames visible at the same time? How could you modify the AddCustomer/FindCustomer example at the beginning of the chapter to have the MainMenu, FindCustomer, and AddCustomer GUIs all visible at the same time?

12

Projects

1. In Project 1 at the end of Chapter 11, you wrote a new subclass of Boat named Rowboat with attributes width and maximumNumberOfPassengers with a tellAboutSelf method. Then you expanded AddBoat.java to accommodate this new class. Incorporate the new Rowboat class and the modified AddBoat class to Example 3 shown in Figure 12-8.

2. In Figure 12-4, the design of MainMenu passes a reference of itself when it launches either FindCustomer or AddCustomer. The shutDown method in FindCustomer and AddCustomer then uses this main menu reference to go back to the main menu by invoking its setVisible method.

An alternative design is to launch the FindCustomer and AddCustomer GUIs by instantiating them without passing a reference value, leaving the main menu frame instance visible. The shutDown methods in FindCustomer and AddCustomer will then simply invoke dispose:

```
this.dispose();
```

Modify MainMenu.java, FindCustomer.java and AddCustomer.java to use this alternative design. Note that MainMenu now remains visible.

CHAPTER 13

Using an Integrated Development Environment

In this chapter you will:

♦ Understand Rapid Application Development (RAD)

♦ Explore the role and benefits of an Integrated Development Environment (IDE)

♦ Install the Forte IDE

♦ Tour the Forte IDE and its components

♦ Create, compile, and execute a simple GUI program using the Forte tool set

♦ Use Forte to create a GUI application from the Bradshaw Marina case

♦ Use the Forte debugger to identify and correct program errors

♦ Generate program documentation using the Forte javadoc utility

In the previous chapter, you learned how to write class definitions for complex GUI applications and navigate among problem domain classes. You learned how to work with multiple windows and create a MainMenu class that integrates various functions in a system. You experienced the challenge of developing complex GUI applications and may have devoted many hours to writing these programs using traditional text editors.

In this chapter, you will learn how to use an IDE to speed up and improve the process of writing GUI-intensive applications. You will work through a series of guided tasks instead of Hands-on Exercises, gaining first-hand experience with the features and benefits of an IDE as you create both a simple GUI program and one of the GUI applications from the Bradshaw Marina case.

After completing this chapter, you will be familiar with the basic tools of an IDE and you will understand how the features of an IDE facilitate the development of information systems in a RAD environment. You will understand how to use an IDE to organize and manage a group of related programs. You will know how to use an IDE to create and modify programs using both traditional source editing features and visual GUI editing capabilities. You will know how to work with a powerful debugging facility to find and fix problems within a Java program. Finally, you will understand how to use an IDE to generate program documentation.

UNDERSTANDING RAPID APPLICATION DEVELOPMENT (RAD)

In Chapter 4, you were introduced to the iterative development approach to systems analysis and design, and you learned that this approach is used extensively in object–oriented development. Recall that iterative development means that you perform some analysis, then some design, then some programming to address part of the system requirements, and then the cycle repeats itself to address additional requirements, as shown in Figure 13-1 (reproduced from Figure 4-1).

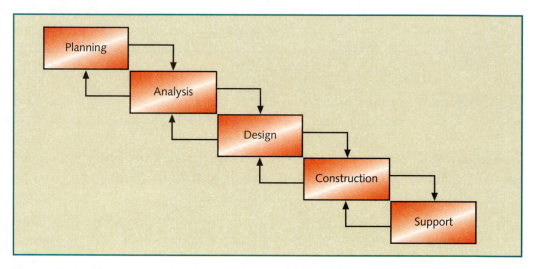

Figure 13-1   The iterative development methodology

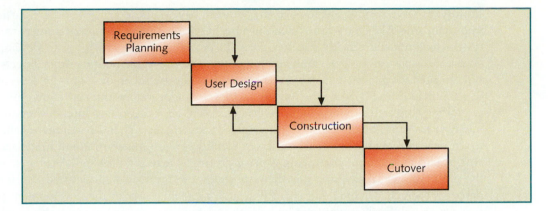

Figure 13-2   The RAD methodology

In contrast to earlier approaches where all of the analysis was completed before design could start, and all of the design was completed before programming could start, the iterative approach enables software developers to respond more rapidly to changing business requirements as a project unfolds. Software development, however, remains labor-intensive, and development cycles often become lengthy. Because windows of opportunity in today's fast-paced business world are short, lengthy development cycles are often unacceptable.

Powerful software development tools now meet the demand for rapid deployment of software systems, leading to new methodologies that compress the development cycle, including RAD. Developers take many different approaches to RAD. However, the general RAD methodology is illustrated in Figure 13-2.

Although RAD is based on the same steps as the iterative approach, it differs in at least two important respects. First, the goal of RAD is to radically reduce the time it takes to develop and implement a system. This requires the use of powerful software development tools, including visual development environments similar to the IDE you will use in this chapter. Secondly, RAD makes extensive use of prototyping, and it is here that IDEs begin to play a powerful role in the development process.

A **prototype** is a model or mock-up of how something will look or act. It depicts the important features of what the final product will look like (or how it will behave), but may or may not have any real functionality. You probably have created prototypes of your own as you have worked your way through this text. For instance, in the previous chapter you created a scaled-down version (or prototype) of a GUI application—a program that looked like a working GUI application when executed, but one that did not yet have the functionality to respond to user-generated events such as button clicks. Although this program was not fully functional, you could use it to see what your application would look like and to identify potential problems with your screen design. As you will discover, you could have used an IDE to quickly create a prototype of this program.

13

Prototypes serve various purposes in the software development process and are particularly important in RAD. One of the main purposes is to allow users and programmers to define system requirements quickly and accurately. In prototyping, the strategy is to develop basic core features first, and get the look and feel of them before implementing other aspects of the system. Reducing what you try to implement at the outset is one strategy for reducing development time. Engaging the users in the development process through rapid prototyping is another. Research supports the idea that successful application development requires user involvement from the outset. Seeing examples of screens, reports, and core functionality early in the development process enables users to identify errors, omissions, and misunderstandings with regard to system requirements. When a prototype reveals a problem, developers modify the prototype repeatedly (and rapidly) until users and developers are satisfied that the basic design is correct. Catching and correcting such problems early in the development process reduces overall development time by helping to ensure that the system being built will meet the needs of the users. Sometimes prototypes evolve into working systems; other times they are discarded. In either case, the ability to generate prototypes quickly is central to RAD.

The RAD approach is used extensively for many kinds of application development projects. IDEs and other computer-based tools that support RAD have been widely adopted in industry. Accordingly, you should know something about RAD and gain some experience using the tools common to an IDE.

EXPLORING THE ROLE AND BENEFITS OF AN IDE

An **Integrated Development Environment (IDE)** is a set of software tools that helps you code, test, and document the programs you write. As you will see, IDEs are helpful in any software development project. However, they are particularly useful in software projects based on a RAD approach. Many organizations rely on software development to create or maintain a competitive advantage in the marketplace. The ability to respond quickly to problems and opportunities can be crucial to the success of a business venture. Because time spent in software development increases the response time, tools such as IDEs that help to reduce development time are valuable, particularly when developing real-world business applications.

IDEs include many tools that support software development tasks. These range from simple text editors to intelligent editors that recognize patterns as you type and can complete code for you as well as visual development tools that generate code based on pictures that you draw. IDEs also make it easy to organize, compile, and execute your programs, and they provide facilities to help you test your programs and isolate errors that keep them from running as you intend. Most IDEs also include features that help you develop program documentation. These tools simplify programming tasks, making your job as a programmer easier and reducing the time it takes to develop working programs.

You can use a variety of Java IDEs to write, compile, and test Java programs. Some of the more popular IDEs were listed in Chapter 2, Table 2-2. This text uses Forte for Java, offered by Sun Microsystems (the creators of Java). The Forte tool set includes:

- Program management tools that let you organize and work with groups of related programs

- A source editor that includes code completion features as well as syntactical formatting (color-coding and code indentation) and standard text editing capabilities

- A visual GUI editor that writes code as you arrange GUI components on the screen

- Tools that compile and run programs with as little as a single button click

- A debugging facility that helps you identify and correct logic errors in your programs

- A documentation generator that produces program documentation from information within your source code

The basic features and benefits of each of these tools are described below and demonstrated throughout this chapter.

Introducing the Benefits of Program Management Tools

Forte uses projects, packages, and filesystems to organize and manage programs you write. A **project** is a mechanism for grouping related programs together so that they are easier to find, manage, and work on. Within Forte, every program that you write is always part of a project. That project may be one you create, or it may be the Forte default project. If you do not specify a project, the Forte default project will be used. Programs in a project do not have to be in the same folder. For example, you could create a project for the Bradshaw Marina case and include all programs for this system, regardless of their folder location.

Organizing your work into projects has several advantages. Within Forte, you can restrict your view to work only with those files in the current project, yet easily add new or existing programs to the project as well as delete programs from the project. When working with a group of related programs, you can compile all the programs in the project with a single command. You can also designate the main project class so that running and debugging the project is easier. Additionally, you can customize settings that control the look and feel of the workspaces on a project-by-project basis so that when you change projects, these settings change as well. Projects are useful when you are working within Forte, but it is important to remember that their structure is not visible to other text editors or to the JVM.

When working in Forte, you will also designate packages and filesystems for the programs you write. For now, you can think of a **package** as the folder that contains your program. A **filesystem** is the hierarchical organization of directories (or folders) that exist above the package level folder. Filesystems control the Java classpath; if you do not correctly designate

13

filesystems, Forte may not be able to compile and execute all the programs in your project. Whether or not you use an IDE, all Java classes (including those you write and those that are supplied with the JDK) are grouped into packages and filesystems, and unlike projects, these structures are visible to the JVM. While you can create packages and filesystems of your own, until you have more experience with these concepts it is best to avoid potential problems by accepting the default values suggested by Forte for these items.

Introducing the Benefits of the Source Editor

The Forte source editing tool provides standard text editing capabilities as well as color-coding and code indentation features. In the Forte source editor, Java keywords appear in blue, comments appear in light gray (rather than green), and string literals appear in magenta (rather than light blue). Although this is a different color-coding scheme than the one used in this text, do not let these differences cause you concern. You will also notice that as you type, the source editor indents for each code block (as defined by curly braces) and properly maintains the indentation level for nested blocks of code. Built-in color-coding and automatic code indentation improve quality by making programs easier to read and maintain.

The Forte source editor also includes code completion features that reduce coding time and lessen the likelihood of syntax errors. The source editor includes a list of common abbreviations. When you type an abbreviation in the list followed by a space, Forte inserts a predefined string. For example, typing `impa` followed by a space generates the text `import java.awt`. In addition to the abbreviations supplied with Forte, you can add new abbreviations of your own. Another feature of the source editor helps you complete lines of code by matching words. As you type, the source editor recognizes partial Java class and method names. Forte suggests possible matches for the class or method name you are typing; to complete the class or method name, you select the appropriate item from a list. Similarly, if you type the first few characters of a word used elsewhere in your program (such as a variable name), Forte will suggest the rest of the word.

You can also use shortcut keys to perform standard editing functions such as positioning the insertion point, selecting text, performing cut/copy/paste operations, and searching through text. See the Forte online documentation for a complete list of Forte abbreviations and shortcut keys.

Introducing the Benefits of the GUI Editor

The GUI editor allows you to select icons representing various GUI components (such as buttons, radio buttons, textfields, and lists), and then arrange them on the screen. As you manipulate these icons, Forte generates the programming statements required to build the screen that you are seeing. As you reposition icons or change their properties, the code is dynamically updated to reflect your changes. You can use layout managers and nested panels to quickly create complex GUI forms, such as the one shown in Figure 13-3.

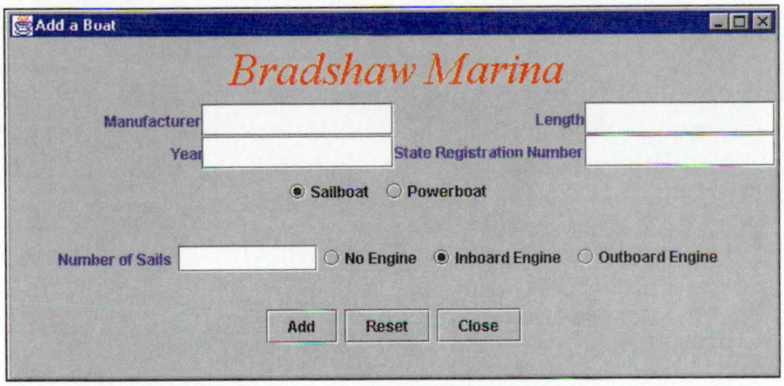

Figure 13-3   A form created with the GUI editor

You can use the GUI editor to attach listeners to components, and then specify the appropriate actions to take in the event handling methods. You can add other customized code to achieve desired functionality. Because the Forte GUI editor is a powerful tool, you need to practice to become proficient. An hour or two of practice time can result in many hours of reduced labor when developing GUI-intensive applications.

Introducing the Benefits of Compilation and Execution Tools

You can compile and execute your programs in Forte with as little as a single button click. Forte displays syntax errors generated by the compiler in the Output window and lets you jump directly from an error message to the line of code that caused the problem. When you execute a program, Forte displays the output in one window and any runtime errors in a separate window, enabling you to see both the output and the error messages at the same time.

Introducing the Benefits of the Debugging Tool

Forte includes a debugging tool (commonly known as a debugger) to help you isolate logic errors in your program. The debugger allows you to set **watch variables** (described later in this chapter) to see how their values change as your program runs. Setting watch variables can help you identify programming errors. You also can set and remove **breakpoints** (also described later in this chapter) so you can step through your program and follow the thread of execution.

Introducing the Benefits of the Documentation Generator

Most IDEs, including Forte, help you create documentation directly from information contained within your source code. Forte generates documentation in HTML. This documentation includes information other programmers need in order to use the public methods in your classes. Producing and accessing this documentation supports code reusability—an important benefit of the object-oriented approach.

INSTALLING THE FORTE IDE

To perform the exercises in this chapter, you must install Forte on your computer. For your convenience, the Community Edition of Forte for Java IDE (Release 3.0) is on the CD that accompanies this text. You also can download Forte free of charge from the Sun Microsystems Web site (*http://java.sun.com*).

Note that Forte requires the runtime environment supplied with the Java 2 Software Development Kit (SDK), Standard Edition, version 1.3.1 (or higher). This is the version used for all of the examples in this text. This version of the Java SDK is also included on the CD that accompanies this text or may be downloaded from the Sun Web site. The Java 2 SDK (version 1.3.1 or higher) must be installed on your computer *prior to* installing Forte. Please also make certain that your machine meets the minimum system requirements as specified in Table 13-1 before installing Forte on your machine. Forte will not run satisfactorily on machines that do not meet these minimum specifications.

To install Forte on your computer:

1. Insert the Forte CD that accompanies this text into your CD drive.

2. Start Windows Explorer and locate the ffj_installers_ce folder on your CD drive.

3. Open the **ffj_installers_ce** folder, open the **Windows** folder, and double-click the **forte_ce_2** file. The Installation Wizard will guide you through the remainder of the installation. You can accept the default folder names and other suggestions made by the wizard.

The Installation Wizard asks you to enter the directory where you will store individual files. Type the path to the folder where you want to store your projects and other files, such as **c:\java projects**, and then click **OK**.

If you used an IDE before installing Forte 3.0, you can import its settings. You can also select the directory where a Web server is installed, if necessary.

When the SetUp Wizard appears, accept the defaults to finish the wizard.

Table 13-1   System Requirements for the Community Edition of Forte for Java (for Microsoft Windows)

System Component	Minimum	Recommended
Hardware system	Pentium II 350 MHz	Pentium III 450 MHz
Memory (RAM)	128 MB	256 MB
Hard disk space	128 MB	256 MB
Disk space for installation	110 MB	110 MB
Runtime environment	Java 2 SDK, Standard Edition, Version 1.3.1 for Windows	

LEARNING THE FORTE BASICS—A QUICK TOUR

This section explains the basic features of Forte and identifies its components.

To start Forte:

1. On the desktop, double-click the **Forte for Java CE** icon. After Forte initializes its workspaces, a welcome window appears.

2. The welcome window includes a tip of the day. Click to clear the **Show Welcome Screen on Startup** check box if you do not want to see the welcome window each time you start Forte. Then click **Close** to close the welcome window.

3. The Forte main window appears, as shown in Figure 13-4. Note that the main window occupies only the upper quarter of the screen. Forte uses the remaining screen area to display other workspaces and windows as needed. The main window is the primary control panel.

4. If any other windows open, such as the Explorer window, the Source Editor, or the Properties window, close or minimize them, as you do not need them now. You will learn more about these windows later.

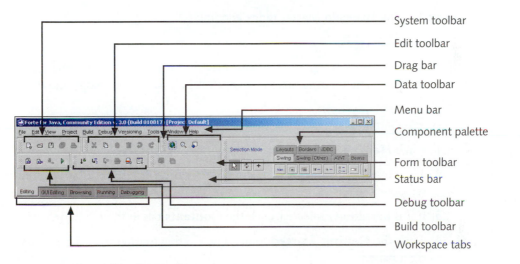

Figure 13-4   The Forte main window

13

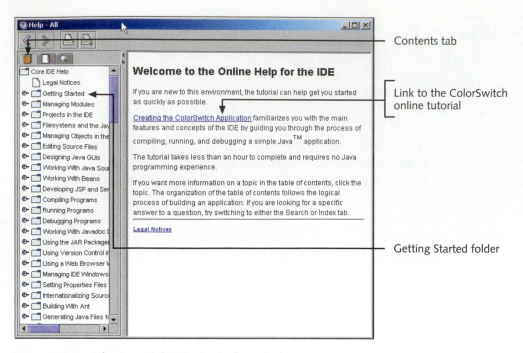

Contents tab

Link to the ColorSwitch online tutorial

Getting Started folder

Figure 13-5   The JavaHelp Master Index window

If this is your first time using an IDE, you may find it helpful to read the materials in the Forte online Help. The Getting Started pages explain Forte terminology and the layout of its workspaces.

To access the Getting Started materials:

1. Click **Help** on the menu bar, and then click **Contents**.

2. The Help window appears, as shown in Figure 13-5. If necessary, maximize this window.

3. If it is not already selected, click the **Contents** tab in the left pane.

4. Click the **Getting Started** folder. The Getting Started material appears in the right pane.

5. Click the links as needed to browse through these materials.

6. When finished, close or minimize the Help window.

You may also find it helpful to work through the first online tutorial—the ColorSwitch application.

To run the online tutorial:

1. If necessary, repeat Steps 1 through 3 above to access the online Help materials.

2. If it is not already selected, click the **Core IDE Help** folder in the left pane.

3. In the right pane, click the **Creating the ColorSwitch Application** link. The tutorial begins.

4. Click the links as needed to complete the tutorial.

5. When finished, close or minimize the Help window.

Understanding the Main Window

As shown in Figure 13-4, the Forte main window includes a menu bar, several toolbars, a component palette, five tabbed workspaces, and a status bar. As with any Windows program, you use the menu bar to select commands to perform tasks, such as opening and closing files, opening and closing projects, compiling, executing and debugging programs, and accessing online Help.

The toolbars provide buttons for many of the most common commands. To learn the name of these buttons, point to a button and wait for the ScreenTip. You can hide or reveal toolbars by right-clicking any empty space on the toolbar and checking or unchecking a toolbar name. You can also change the position of any toolbar by using the drag bar to move it to a new location. The drag bar is the set of double lines that appear on the left edge of the toolbar.

The component palette, located on the right side of the main window, contains tabs that allow you to create GUI applications from AWT, Swing, and other components using a visual editing technique. This means that you can create GUI applications by selecting icons (such as buttons and labels) from the component palette and placing them in the Form Editor. The Form Editor is a window you use to create and edit GUI applications. The component palette also contains tabs that list layout managers and border styles. You will use the component palette and Form Editor extensively in this chapter.

13

Understanding the Workspaces

In the lower-left portion of the main window are five workspace tabs (see Figure 13-4 again). A **workspace** is a collection of windows that support certain types of activities, such as editing or debugging. There are five workspaces in Forte:

- Editing
- GUI Editing
- Browsing
- Running
- Debugging

When you open any of these workspaces, additional windows appear from which you can perform various tasks.

Exploring the Editing Workspace

You can use the Editing workspace to create or modify Java, HTML, or plain text files in the Source Editor window (see Figure 13-6). The Source Editor supports typical text editing operations (such as copy, cut, and paste) as well as the color-coding, indentation, and code completion features mentioned earlier (see Figure 13-7).

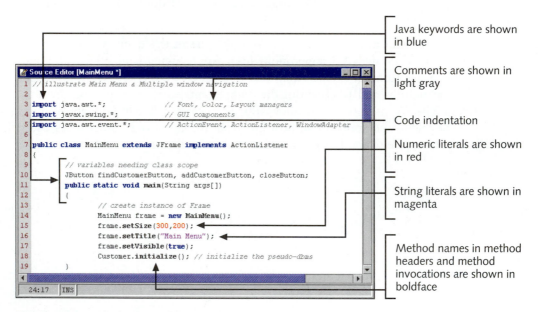

Figure 13-6 The Source Editor window

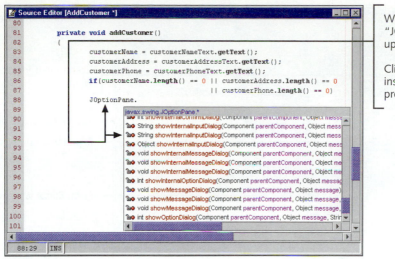

When you type "JOptionPane." this pop-up list appears.

Click a method in the list to insert code into your program.

Figure 13-7 The code completion feature of the Source Editor

You can customize the color-coding, indentation, and code completion features by clicking Tools on the menu bar, clicking Options, and then changing the Editor Settings for the Java Editor.

The Source Editor also includes a word-matching feature that enables you to type the first few characters of a word used in your program (such as a variable name) and have the rest of the word generated for you. If there is more than one possible match, you can press Ctrl+L or Ctrl+K to scroll forward and backward (respectively) through a list of possible matches.

Exploring the GUI Editing Workspace

In the GUI Editing workspace, you create GUI applications using the component palette, Form Editor, and Component Inspector (see Figure 13-8).

If any of these windows are not visible, you can reveal them by clicking View on the menu bar, and then clicking the name of the window you want to see. Figures 13-8 through 13-12 illustrate the windows; you do not need to open them now.

You use the component palette to visually add components to the Form Editor window. As you manipulate components in the GUI Editing workspace, source code generated by the Form Editor appears in the Source Editor window. You use the Component Inspector to adjust the properties of a component (such as the color, font, and text for a label) and to establish event listeners and event handling methods. You can also use the Component Inspector to customize advanced features that define how code is generated.

13

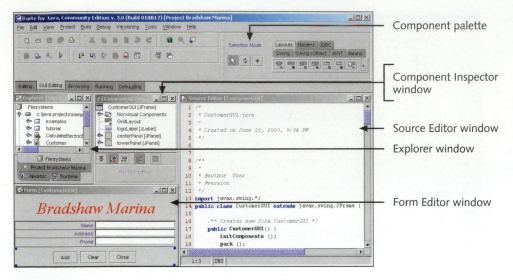

Component palette

Component Inspector window

Source Editor window

Explorer window

Form Editor window

Figure 13-8 Windows in the GUI Editing workspace

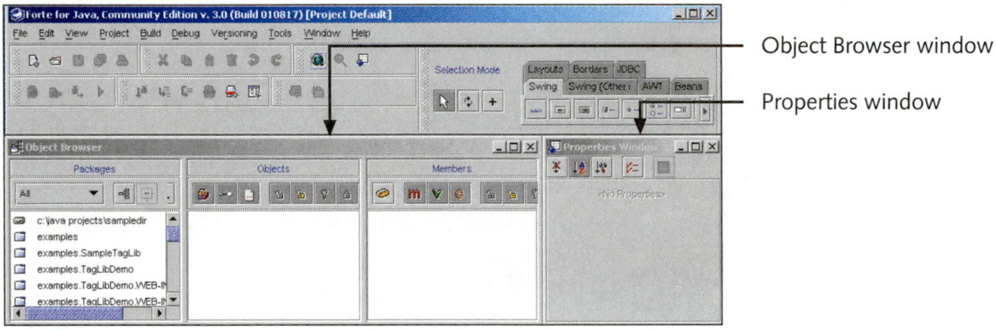

Object Browser window

Properties window

Figure 13-9 Windows in the Browsing workspace

Exploring the Browsing Workspace

The Browsing workspace shows the hierarchy of packages, classes, methods, and variables in your program (see Figure 13-9). Although this is useful, you will not be required to use the Browsing workspace to complete the exercises in this text.

Exploring the Running Workspace

The Running workspace opens when you run your program (see Figure 13-10). Any runtime errors will be displayed in a separate Output window. The Output window also opens when the compiler detects syntax errors. If you double-click a syntax error message in the Output window (syntax errors have a red background), Forte opens the Source Editor window and takes you directly to the line of code where the error occurred. Once your program compiles properly, Forte launches your application.

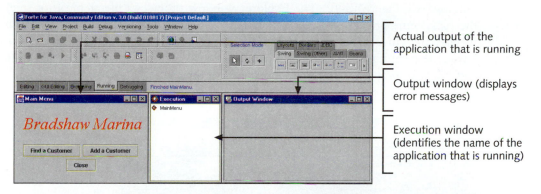

Figure 13-10   Windows in the Running workspace

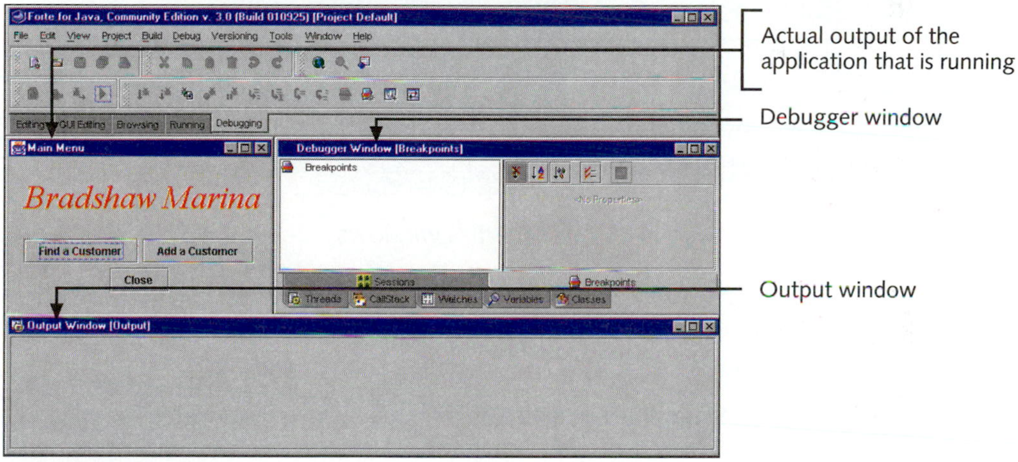

Figure 13-11   Windows in the Debugging workspace

13

Exploring the Debugging Workspace

In the Debugging workspace, you can set breakpoints in your program and watch the values of variables (see Figure 13-11). A **breakpoint** is a flag that tells the debugger to pause execution of your program. You can then examine the values of different variables and step through your program to identify any errors.

Exploring Other Windows and the Status Bar

In addition to these workspaces, Forte also includes the Explorer window and the Properties window (see Figure 13-12). The Explorer window provides a hierarchical (or tree) view of the filesystems, projects, files, and other objects in use. The Filesystems tab and Project tab identify the current filesystem and project. If you accepted the defaults when you installed Forte, the default project will be Project Default. The Properties window displays the names and values of properties for the node selected in the Explorer window.

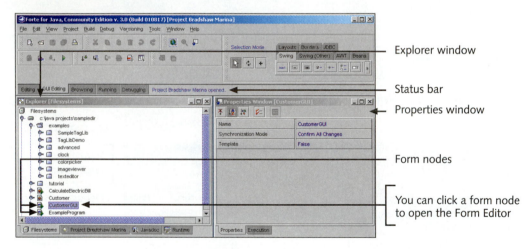

Figure 13-12   The Explorer and Properties windows

In most cases, the windows you need to complete a particular task (such as GUI Editing) open automatically when you click a workspace tab or open a file.

 You can display most of these windows at any time by choosing the window you want to see from the View option on the menu bar. You also can resize or reposition any window at any time.

 If you inadvertently close the Form Editor window, you can open it again by opening the Explorer window and clicking the form node for the form you want to open.

The status bar is in the lower-right portion of the main window. The status bar shows progress information as Forte loads and saves projects, compiles programs, and performs other tasks.

Using Forte to Create a Simple GUI Program

Now that you are familiar with the terminology and layout of the Forte IDE, you can use Forte to create a simple GUI program. This first example program will display the message "Welcome to Forte!" when a button is pressed, as shown in Figure 13-13. Later, you will use Forte to create one of the Bradshaw Marina GUIs from Chapter 11.

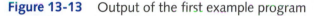

Message appears when button is pressed

Figure 13-13 Output of the first example program

Creating a New File for the Example Program

To create the first example program, your first task is to create a new file within the default project. To do this:

1. Start Forte, if necessary.

2. If the Explorer window is not visible, click **View** on the menu bar, and then click **Explorer** to open the Explorer window.

3. In this example you will use the Forte default project. To verify that the default project is loaded, check to see that the Project tab at the bottom of the Explorer window is labeled Project Default as shown in Figure 13-14.

4. If the default project is not loaded, click **Project** on the menu bar, and then click **Project Manager**. In the Project Manager dialog box, click **Project Default** and click **Open** (see Figure 13-15).

13

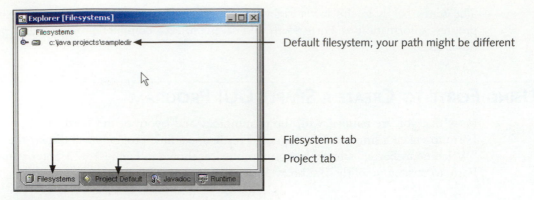

Default filesystem; your path might be different

Filesystems tab

Project tab

Figure 13-14 Identifying the default project in the Explorer window

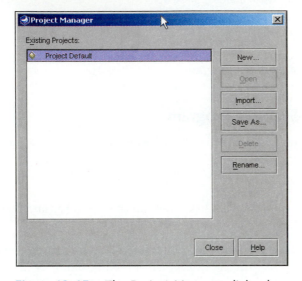

Figure 13-15 The Project Manager dialog box

5. To create a new program, click **File** on the menu bar, and then click **New**. The New From Template Wizard dialog box appears, as shown in Figure 13-16. A template lets you define the kind of program you want to create.

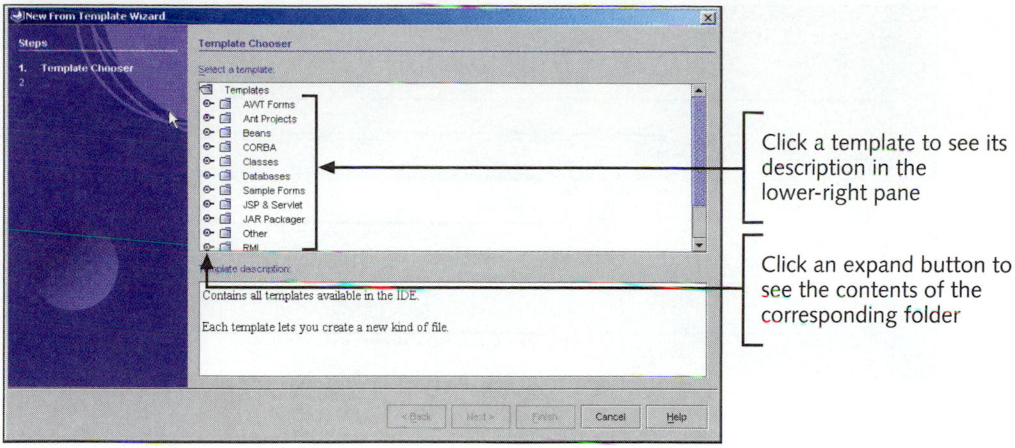

Click a template to see its description in the lower-right pane

Click an expand button to see the contents of the corresponding folder

Figure 13-16 The Template Chooser dialog box

6. To indicate that this program will be a Swing application, click the **expand** button to the left of the Swing Forms folder, and then click **JFrame**. A description of the JFrame component appears in the lower-right pane. Click **Next**.

7. In the Target Location pane, you specify the name of your program and the package to which it will belong. In the Name text box, type **ExampleProgram**. Accept the text in the Package text box to indicate that you want to use the default package. Notice that the Directory text box includes the name of the default filesystem. Click **Finish**. A dialog box appears asking if you want to include this program in the current project.

8. Click **Yes** to add your program to the Forte default project. Forte opens the GUI Editing workspace and the Source Editor, Form Editor, and Component Inspector windows (see Figure 13-17). If these windows do not appear, select the appropriate options from the view menu.

Take a moment to scroll through the Source Editor window and you will see that some code has already been generated for you, as illustrated in Figure 13-18.

13

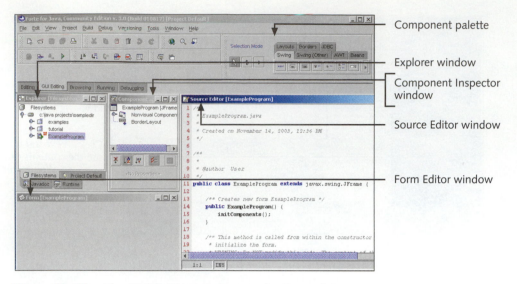

Figure 13-17   The GUI Editing workspace for ExampleProgram

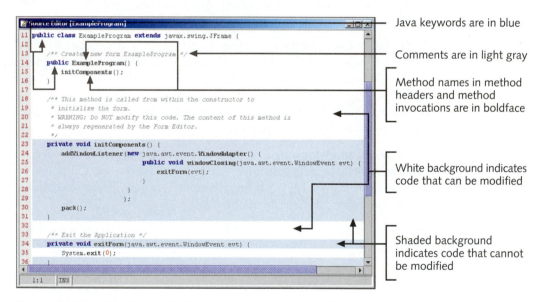

Figure 13-18   The Source Editor window for ExampleProgram

While in the Source Editor, notice the color-coding and indentation. Also note that portions of the generated code appear in a shaded background. This code is guarded by the Form

Editor and is not directly editable. However, you can add or modify code in any of the white areas of the Source Editor window.

Next, examine the Form Editor window, shown in Figure 13–19.

Notice in Figure 13–19 that the Component Inspector contains a BorderLayout node. Recall that BorderLayout is the default layout for JFrame components, and the JFrame template is the one you chose for this program. Your next task is to modify the layout and complete the design of this form.

Component Inspector [ExampleProgram]	
ExampleProgram [JFrame]	
Nonvisual Components	
BorderLayout	
Horizontal Gap	0
Vertical Gap	0
Properties	

Figure 13-19   The Component Inspector window for ExampleProgram

Designing the Form for the Example Program

The example program uses a GridLayout with two rows and one column rather than BorderLayout. The top cell of the grid contains a label, and the bottom cell contains a button.

To change the layout of the form:

1. Click the **Layouts** tab in the component palette, and then click the **GridLayout** button. The Layouts pane and its various buttons are shown in Figure 13-20.

To find out what the icons represent, you can move your mouse slowly over them to reveal the ScreenTips.

2. Click anywhere in the Form Editor window. Notice that the BorderLayout node in the Component Inspector changes to GridLayout.

13

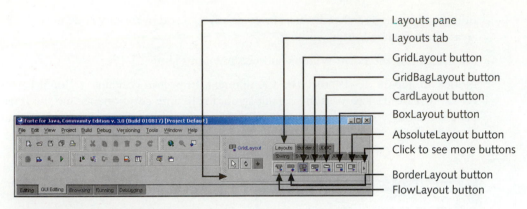

Layouts pane
Layouts tab
GridLayout button
GridBagLayout button
CardLayout button
BoxLayout button
AbsoluteLayout button
Click to see more buttons

BorderLayout button
FlowLayout button

Figure 13-20   The Layouts pane of the component palette

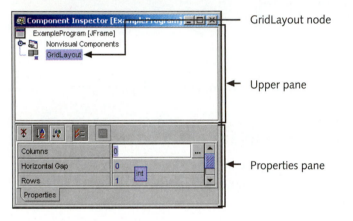

GridLayout node

Upper pane

Properties pane

Figure 13-21   The Component Inspector window for the GridLayout node

3. To change the grid size to one column and two rows, scroll through the upper pane of the Component Inspector until you see the GridLayout node. Click the **GridLayout** node. Its properties are displayed as shown in Figure 13-21.

Remember, you can expand the Component Inspector window to make the properties and their values easier to read.

4. Click the default value **0** for the number of columns, type **1**, and press **Enter**. Click the Rows value and then type **2**. Press **Enter**. Although you cannot see it, the Form Editor now contains a grid with one column and two rows.

You want the program to display a "Welcome to Forte!" message in the upper cell of the grid in response to a button click. The text of this message is created using a label component. The color, font, and style properties of the label text are formatted to achieve the desired effect.

To add a label to the upper cell of the grid and format its properties:

1. Click the Swing tab on the component palette, and then click the JLabel button. The Swing pane and its various buttons are shown in Figure 13-22.

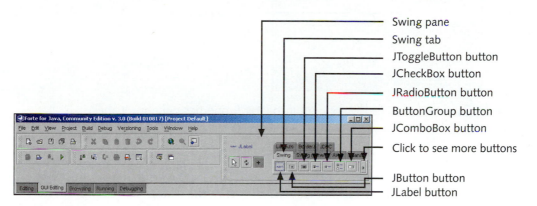

Swing pane
Swing tab
JToggleButton button
JCheckBox button
JRadioButton button
ButtonGroup button
JComboBox button
Click to see more buttons

JButton button
JLabel button

Figure 13-22   The Swing pane of the component palette

2. Click anywhere in the Form Editor window. A label with the text jLabel1 appears in the Form Editor, a corresponding node is added to the Component Inspector, and the properties of this label are displayed in the Properties pane. Note that the source code needed to generate the label is also added in the Source Editor window (see Figure 13-23). If you scroll to the bottom of the Source Editor window, you will also see that a line of code declaring jLabel1 as a variable has also been added.

13

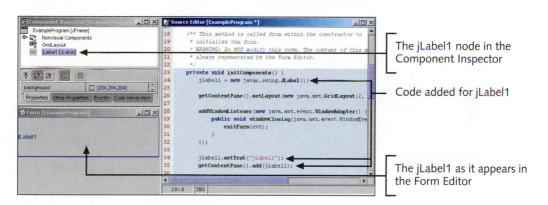

The jLabel1 node in the Component Inspector

Code added for jLabel1

The jLabel1 as it appears in the Form Editor

Figure 13-23   Form Editor and Source Editor windows after adding jLabel1

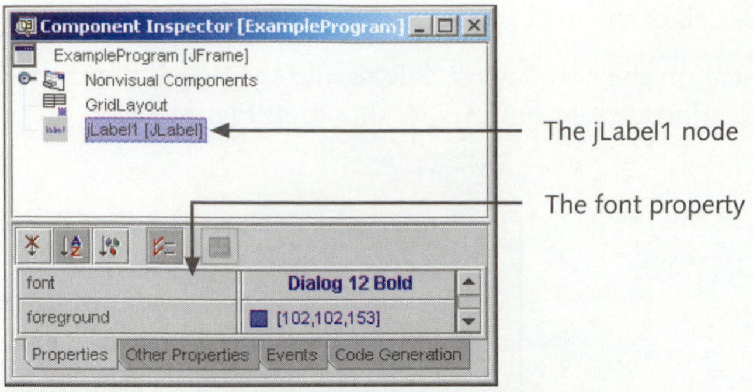

The jLabel1 node

The font property

Figure 13-24   The Component Inspector Properties pane for jLabel1

3. To change the font of the label, scroll through the properties in the Properties pane of the Component Inspector until you see the font property (see Figure 13-24). Click the **font** property, and then click the ellipsis (**...**) button.

4. In the Property Editor dialog box, click **Arial** for the font, click **Bold** for the font style, click **14** for the font size, and then click **OK** (see Figure 13-25).

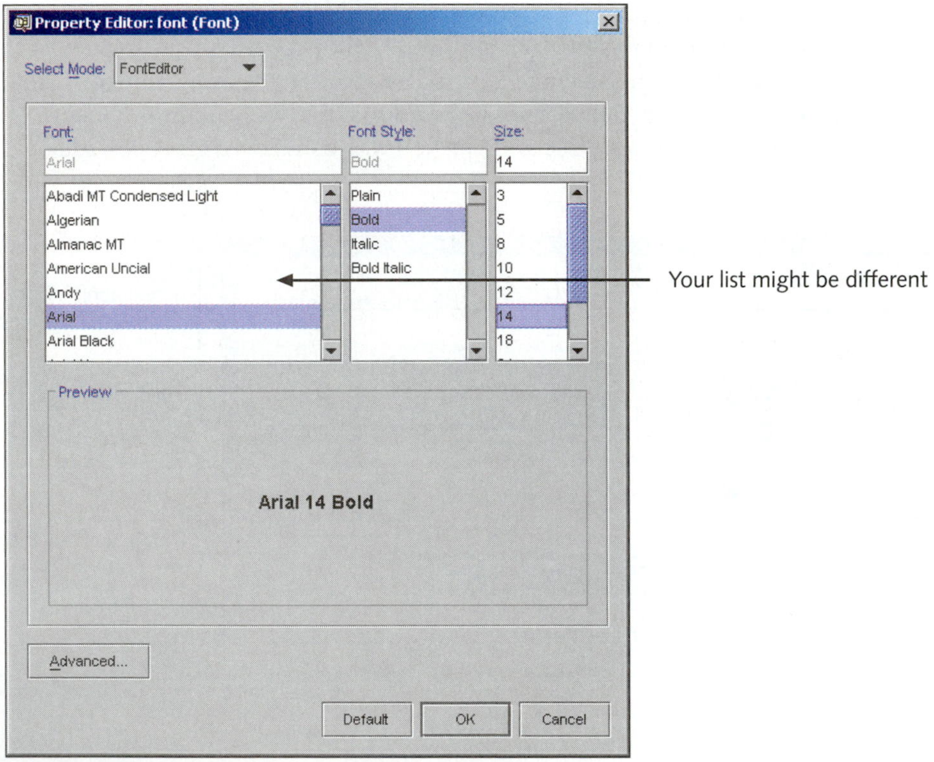

Your list might be different

Figure 13-25   The Property Editor dialog box

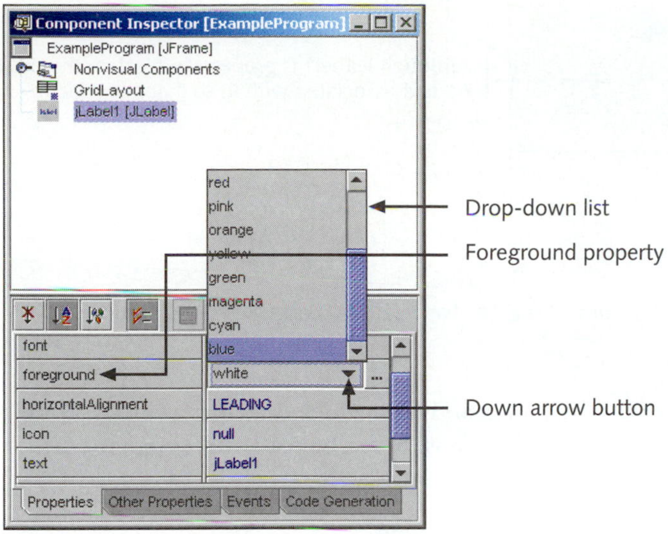

Figure 13-26   Changing the foreground property for jLabel1

5. To change the color of the label, scroll through the Properties pane of the Component Inspector and locate the foreground property. Click the **foreground** property, and then click the **down arrow** button to open the drop-down list. Scroll through the list and click **blue** (see Figure 13-26). Resize the Component Inspector window, if necessary, to see the colors.

6. To center the label, click the **horizontalAlignment** property in the Properties pane of the Component Inspector. Click the **down arrow** button to open the drop-down list, and then click **CENTER**.

7. Although the label is now formatted as you wish it to be, the text of the label still reads "jLabel1." Recall that when a button is pressed, the text of the label is to become "Welcome to Forte!" Until that time, however, the label text should be left blank. To change the text of the label so that it initially appears blank, scroll through the Properties pane of the Component Inspector to locate the text property. Click the **text** property, press **Delete**, and then press **Enter**.

This deletes the text of the label but leaves all your formatting intact, so that when you later set the text of the label to "Welcome to Forte!" the label will be formatted properly. In the Form Editor, the top cell of the grid is now blank (see Figure 13-27).

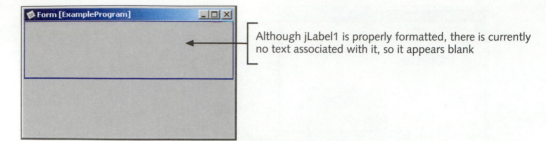

Although jLabel1 is properly formatted, there is currently no text associated with it, so it appears blank

Figure 13-27   Form Editor window after formatting jLabel1

After you change the layout of the form and then add and format a label, you can add a button to the lower cell of the grid. When pressed, this button will change the text of the label to "Welcome to Forte!"

To add a button to the grid and format its properties:

1. Click the **Swing** tab on the component palette, if necessary, and then click the **JButton** button.

2. Click anywhere in the Form Editor. The button is displayed in the lower cell of the grid, a corresponding node is displayed in the Component Inspector, and source code is added to the Source Editor (see Figure 13-28).

Source Editor window

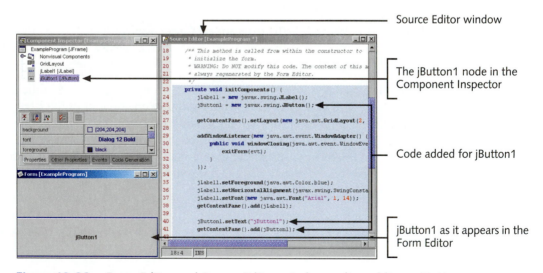

The jButton1 node in the Component Inspector

Code added for jButton1

jButton1 as it appears in the Form Editor

Figure 13-28   Form Editor and Source Editor windows after adding a JButton

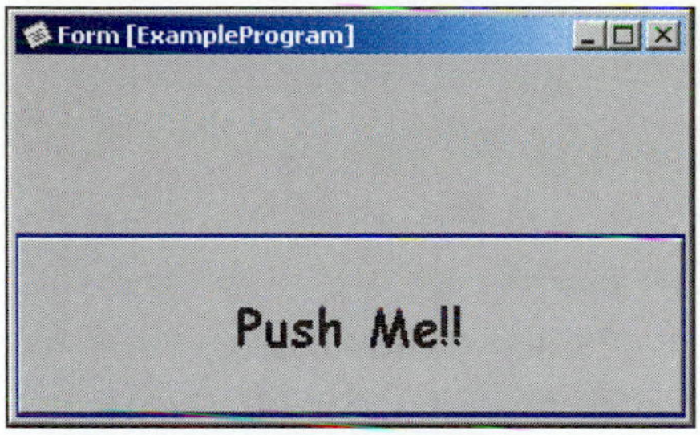

Figure 13-29   The label and button in the Form Editor window

3. In the Properties pane of the Component Inspector, click the **font** property, click the ellipsis (**...**) button, and then change the font to **Comic Sans MS, bold, 24 point**. If you don't have this font on your computer, use a similar sans-serif font. Click **OK**.

4. Scroll down to the text property, click the default value **jButton1**, type **Push Me!!**, and then press **Enter**. The button in the lower cell of the grid now says "Push Me!!" in the font size and style you selected, and the Form Editor window appears similar to Figure 13-29.

Making the Buttons in the Example Program Work

To make your button work, you must associate an event listener and an event handling method with the button. When you do this, Forte will generate some code for you. However, Forte cannot anticipate the unique actions that should be performed once the event handling method is invoked. You will need to add custom code to the event handler so that it will respond in the desired manner.

To associate an event handler with the button:

1. In the upper pane of the Component Inspector window, click the **jButton1** node to select it, if necessary.

2. Click the **Events** tab in the lower pane of the Component Inspector. Click the **actionPerformed** property, and then press **Enter**. The Events tab is shown in Figure 13-30.

13

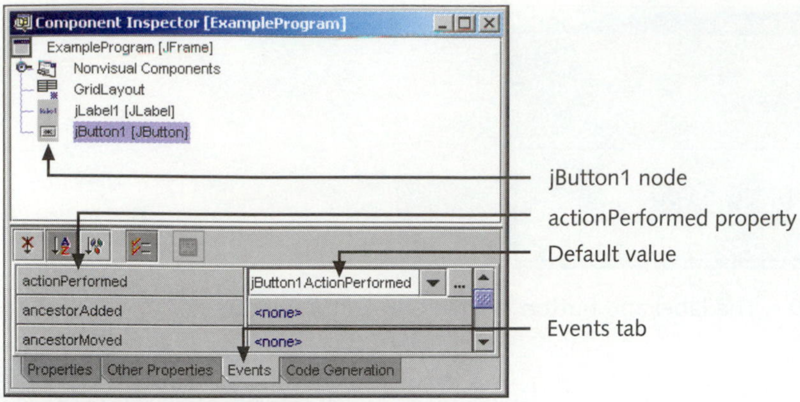

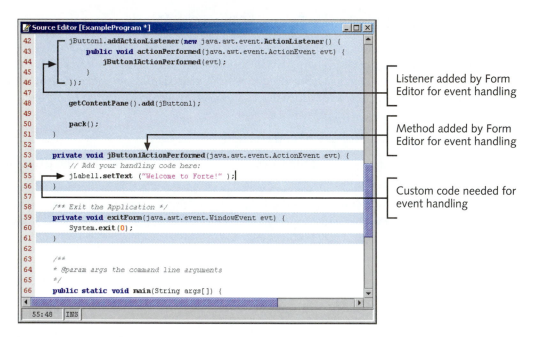

Figure 13-30   The Events tab in the Component Inspector

3. Forte switches to the Source Editor window, where the code to add the listener and an event handling method stub have been added to the source file. To make the button display the "Welcome to Forte!" message when pressed, you must add the custom code shown in Figure 13–31 to the event handler.

Figure 13-31   Adding code to the event handler

4. To add code, position the insertion point at the end of the comment statement that reads **//Add your handling code here:**. Press **Enter**, and add the following line of code:

```
jLabel1.setText ("Welcome to Forte!" );
```

5. To save the file, click **File** on the menu bar, and then click **Save**. You are now ready to compile and execute your program.

Compiling and Executing the Example Program

To compile and execute the program:

1. Click **Build** on the menu bar, and then click **Compile**. If the compilation is successful, the message "Finished ExampleProgram" appears in the status bar of the main window. If there were syntax errors, they appear in red in the Output window. You can double-click a red error message to jump to the line of code that is problematic. Once you have fixed your errors, recompile the program. When the build is successful, you can run the application.

2. To run the program, click **Build** on the menu bar, and then click **Execute**. If there are no execution errors, Forte opens the Running workspace and begins executing the program.

3. Click the **Push Me!!** button. ExampleProgram produces the output shown in Figure 13-13. If there are execution errors, they appear in the Output window.

4. When you are finished, close ExampleProgram, and then click the **GUI Editing** tab in the main window to return to the GUI Editing workspace.

Examining the Code Generated by the GUI Editor

Before you begin the second example, look carefully at the source code that was generated by Forte in the first example. (If you are not continuing the same Forte session from the first example, make sure that the default project is loaded, click the Project Default tab in the Explorer window, and open the ExampleProgram file.)

Did you notice the way that Forte named the variables that were created for your GUI components and event handling method? When you created the label and button components, for example, Forte named these jLabel1 and jButton1. If you add more buttons, Forte would name them jButton2, jButton3, etc. Notice also that the event handling method for your button was named jButton1ActionPerformed (at line 53). Subsequent button handling methods would be named jButton2ActionPerformed, jButton3ActionPerformed, etc. While these names are acceptable to the compiler, they make GUI programs unnecessarily difficult to read and can be hard to keep track of when adding event handling code to your program. As you will see in the next example, you can overcome this difficulty by giving these variables more meaningful names.

13

You may have also noticed that Java classes in the generated source code are referenced by their complete package names. For example, the variable jButton1 is declared at line 73 with the statement:

```
private javax.swing.JButton jButton1;
```

The reason for this is that Forte does not automatically add import statements to the source file. In most of the programs you have written for this book, you have included a statement to import some or all of the classes in the javax.swing package. When you include the import statement, you do not have to supply the full package name in the code. You can add import statements to the program generated by Forte to shorten the amount of code you type when customizing the event handling methods. This, too, will be illustrated shortly.

USING FORTE FOR A BRADSHAW MARINA GUI APPLICATION

Now you can use Forte to create one of the GUI applications for the Bradshaw Marina case. In this example, you will use the GUI Editor to re-create the AddCustomer GUI from Chapter 11 (shown in Figure 13-32).

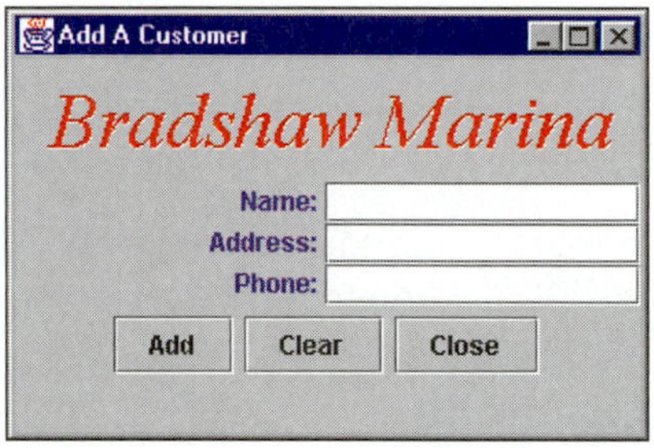

Figure 13-32 The AddCustomer GUI

This time you will create a project to manage the program files that will be needed.

Creating a Project for the Bradshaw Marina GUI Application

Recall that the AddCustomer GUI program from Chapter 11 makes use of the Customer class. Because the application utilizes more than one class, it will be helpful to create a project to manage these program files.

To create a project:

1. Click **Project** on the menu bar, click **Project Manager**, and then click the **New** button. The Create New Project dialog box appears.

2. Delete the current project name, type **Bradshaw Marina**, and then press **Enter**.

The Explorer and Properties windows open, and you are now ready to begin adding programs to the new project.

Creating a New File for the Bradshaw Marina GUI Application

As with the first example program, the AddCustomer GUI program from Chapter 11 is a Swing application based on the JFrame template. To distinguish this application from the original AddCustomer program in Chapter 11, name the new program CustomerGUI.

To create a new file for the GUI program:

1. Click **File** on the menu bar, and then click **New**.

2. As in the first example, this program will also be a Swing application, so click the **expand** button to the left of the Swing Forms option (if it is not already open), and then click **JFrame**, if necessary. Click **Next**.

3. In the Name text box, type **CustomerGUI**, and then click **Finish**, accepting the default in the Package text box. (This program will now be part of the default package.)

4. If Forte asks if you want to include this program in the current project, click **Yes**. Forte switches to the GUI Editing workspace so you can begin designing the form. (Notice that the Explorer window now contains a tab labeled Project Bradshaw Marina.)

Designing the Form for the Bradshaw Marina GUI Application

As before, the Form Editor defaults to the BorderLayout layout manager. The AddCustomer GUI from Chapter 11 utilizes the GridLayout with three rows and one column. Your first step in designing the form is to change the form to GridLayout and add the Bradshaw Marina logo to the upper cell of the grid.

To change the layout of the form and add the logo:

1. Click the **Layouts** tab on the component palette, and then click the **GridLayout** button.

2. Click anywhere in the Form Editor window to apply this layout to the form. Notice that the Component Inspector now contains a GridLayout node (rather than a BorderLayout node).

13

3. Use the Component Inspector to change the grid size to one column and three rows. Recall that to do this, you click the **GridLayout** node in the upper pane of the Component Inspector window, and enter the appropriate values for the **Columns** and **Rows** properties.

4. To add the Bradshaw Marina logo label to the upper cell of the grid, click the **JLabel** button on the Swing pane of the component palette, and then click in the Form Editor window.

5. In the original program in Chapter 11, this label was named logoLabel. To change the name of this label from the default name jLabel1 to logoLabel, right-click the **jLabel1** node in the Component Inspector, and then click **Rename**. In the Rename dialog box, type **logoLabel**, and then click **OK**.

6. Use the Component Inspector to change the font, foreground, horizontal alignment, and text properties of the label to their appropriate values as you did in the first example. To make your form look like the one in Chapter 11, use a 36-point, italic, Times New Roman font, and set the foreground color to red. Set the horizontalAlignment property to **CENTER** and change the text property to **Bradshaw Marina**.

Recall that in the original AddCustomer GUI application in Chapter 11, the center cell of the grid contained an inner panel that also utilized GridLayout. Your next step will be to create this inner panel.

To do this:

1. Click the **CustomerGUI** node in the Component Inspector to select the entire frame.

2. Click the **JPanel** button on the Swing pane of the component palette. (You might have to click the right arrow button in the component palette to scroll the list).

3. Click in the Form Editor. The panel (outlined in blue) is added to the form, a corresponding node named jPanel1 is added to the Component Inspector, and code is added to the source file.

4. In Chapter 11 this panel was named centerPanel. To change the name of this panel from jPanel1 to centerPanel, right-click the **jPanel1** node in the Component Inspector, and then click **Rename**. In the Rename dialog box, type **centerPanel**, and then click **OK**.

Recall that by default JPanel components use FlowLayout, however in this program you want centerPanel to be of the GridLayout type.

To change the layout of centerPanel to GridLayout and set the size of the inner grid:

1. Click the **expand** button to the left of the centerPanel node in the Component Inspector. Right-click the **FlowLayout** subnode that appears directly beneath the centerPanel node. Point to **Set Layout**, and then click GridLayout. Notice that centerPanel now contains a **GridLayout** subnode. See Figure 13-33.

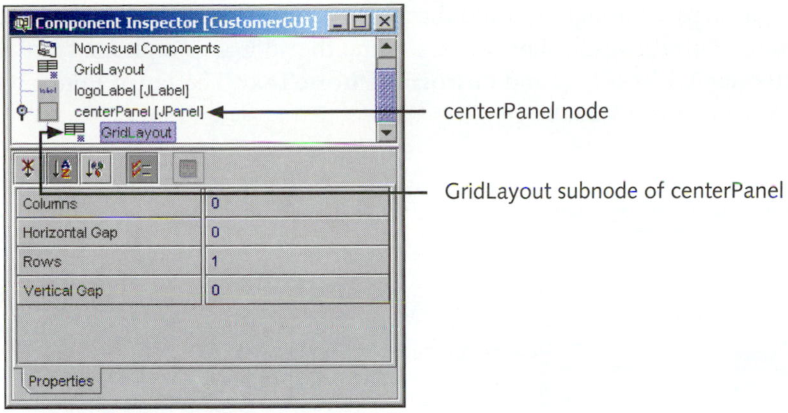

Figure 13-33   The GridLayout subnode of centerPanel

2. To change the number of rows and columns in the grid for centerPanel, click the **GridLayout** subnode of centerPanel. In the Properties pane, change the Columns property to **2** and the Rows property to **3**, and then press **Enter**.

In the AddCustomer GUI, the inner grid contains several labels and textfields. Next, you will add these labels and textfields to the inner grid. Recall that when you use GridLayout, components are added to the grid in order from left to right, top to bottom, so be careful to add labels and textfields in the proper order. If you make a mistake, you can delete a component from the Form Editor by selecting it and pressing the **Delete** key.

To add labels and textfields to the inner grid:

1. To select the centerPanel, click the **centerPanel** node in the Component Inspector.

2. To add the Name label, click the **JLabel** button on the Swing pane of the component palette, and then click inside the center panel in the Form Editor.

3. Use the Component Inspector as you did in the first example to change the text property of the first label to **Name:** and set the horizontalAlignment property to **RIGHT**.

4. Select the centerPanel again by clicking the **centerPanel** node in the Component Inspector.

5. To add the Name textfield, click the **JTextField** button on the Swing pane of the component palette, and then click inside the center panel in the Form Editor.

6. Right-click the **jTextField1** node in the Component Inspector, click **Rename**, and rename this component **customerNameText**. Click **OK**. Scroll down to the text property, delete the default value (leaving it blank), and press **Enter**.

13

7. Repeat Steps 1 through 6 to add the address and phone labels and textfields. In keeping with the original program, rename the address and phone textfields to **customerAddressText** and **customerPhoneText**. The Form Editor will resemble Figure 13-34.

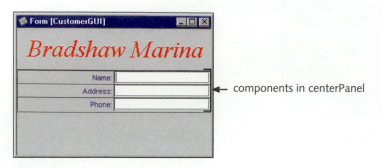

Figure 13-34 The Form Editor with components in centerPanel

You might wonder if the variable names for the labels in the centerPanel should be changed. If you look back at the original program, you will see that labels in the centerPanel were not assigned variable names. Instead, they were added anonymously because their properties were never accessed. If you wish, you can change the default variable names generated by Forte for these labels using the rename procedure, but because these variables are never referenced again, there isn't any real advantage to doing so.

You are now ready to add the buttons that will allow the user to add customers, clear the form, and close the application. You must first add a panel to the lower cell of the grid. This panel will contain the three desired buttons.

To create the lower panel and its buttons:

1. Scroll to the top of the Component Inspector window. Click the **CustomerGUI** node to select the entire frame.

2. Click the **JPanel** button in the Swing pane of the component palette, and then click in the Form Editor. The panel (outlined in blue) is added to the form, a corresponding node named jPanel2 is added to the Component Inspector, and code is added to the source file.

3. Rename the panel to **lowerPanel**.

4. To add a button to the lower panel, click the **JButton** icon in the Swing pane of the component palette, and then click inside the lower panel in the Form Editor.

5. Rename the button to **addButton**.

6. Use the Component Inspector to change the text property of this button to **Add**.

7. Repeat Steps 4 and 5 to add two more JButton components to this lower panel for Clear and Close (renaming them **clearButton** and **closeButton**, respectively). The Form Editor will now similar to Figure 13-35. Your design might look slightly different.

Figure 13-35   The Form Editor with all components added

The final step in designing the form is to set its title. The AddCustomer.java program in Chapter 11 set the title of the JFrame component to "Add a Customer."

To add a title to the form:

1. Scroll to the top of the upper pane in the Component Inspector, and click the **CustomerGUI** node to select it.

2. Click the **Properties** tab in the lower pane of the Component Inspector, scroll to the **title** property, and then change its value to **Add a Customer**.

3. It is a good idea to periodically save your work. Click **File** on the menu bar, and then click **Save** to save the file.

Making the Buttons in the Bradshaw Marina GUI Application Work

Now you will add the code to make your buttons work. The most complex of these buttons is the Add button, which when pressed retrieves the values from the textfields, and checks to see that all values have been entered. If any textfields have been left blank, an error message is displayed. Otherwise, values from the textfields are used to create an instance of the Customer class, a "Customer Added" message is displayed, and the textfields are cleared.

To add code to make the Add button work:

1. Click the **addButton** node in the Component Inspector, if necessary, to select the addButton node.

2. In the Component Inspector, click the **Events** tab, click the **actionPerformed** property, and then press **Enter**. The IDE switches to the Source Editor window.

If you inadvertently clicked the ellipsis (…) button for the actionPerformed property, the Handlers for actionPerformed dialog box opens. Press the **Cancel** button to close this dialog box, and try again.

3. Notice that Forte recognized the new name of your button variable (addButton) and named the event handler method accordingly as addButtonActionPerformed. To complete the event handling method, you must add the following code immediately after the comment **//Add your handling code here:**

```
customerName=customerNameText.getText();
customerAddress=customerAddressText.getText();
customerPhone=customerPhoneText.getText();

if(customerName.length()==0 || customerAddress.length()==0 ||
   customerPhone.length() == 0)
    JOptionPane.showMessageDialog(this, "Please Enter All Data" );
else
{
  aCustomer = new Customer(customerName, customerAddress,
    customerPhone);
  JOptionPane.showMessageDialog(this, "Customer Added" );
  clearButtonActionPerformed(evt);
}
```

The last line of this code deserves explanation. In the Chapter 11 version of this program, this line of code invoked the clearForm method to clear the form upon completion of the add operation. The clearForm method was also called by the single event handling method in the original program when the event listener detected that the Clear button was pressed. As you have noticed, Forte generates separate event handling methods for each component that you set up through the Events tab in the Component Inspector. In the new version of the program, the event handler for the Clear button is named clearButtonActionPerformed, and this is the method that you call to clear the form when the add operation is complete. The method requires a WindowEvent argument, so you include the WindowEvent evt in the parameter list.

Notice also that the statements you added do not use the full package names for Java classes (you used JOptionPane rather than javax.swing.JOptionPane). Also, recognize that the IDE is currently unaware of the string variables (customerName, customerAddress, customerPhone) and customer variable (aCustomer) you used in the code you added to the program. In order for the compiler to handle these properly, you need to add an import statement and variable declaration statements to the program.

To add these statements:

1. Scroll to the top of the program in the Source Editor window, and before the class definition statement, add a statement to import all the classes in the Swing package (i.e., import javax.swing.*;).

2. Scroll to the end of the file in the Source Editor window and insert the following two lines of code immediately after the comment **//End of variables declaration**. (You must insert these lines of code after the comment because the area above the comment is a protected block of code.)

```
String customerName, customerAddress, customerPhone;
Customer aCustomer;
```

Two other button handlers are still needed—one for the Clear button and one for the Close button.

To add the code to make these buttons work:

1. To add an event handler for the Clear button, click the **clearButton** node in the Component Inspector. Click the **Events** tab in the Component Inspector, click the **actionPerformed** property, and then press **Enter**.

2. In the Source Editor window, add the following code immediately after the comment **//Add your handling code here**:

```
customerNameText.setText("");
customerAddressText.setText("");
customerPhoneText.setText("");
customerNameText.requestFocus();
```

3. Repeat Step 1 to add an event handler for the Close button. The event handling code to be added for the Close button is simply:

```
System.exit(0);
```

4. Click **File** on the menu bar, and then click **Save** to save the file.

Compiling and Executing the Bradshaw Marina GUI Application

You are almost ready to compile and execute your program. However, before you can successfully compile this program, the Customer problem domain class will need to be added to your project.

To add the Customer PD class and compile and execute the program:

1. Use Windows Explorer to locate the Customer.java program in the Example2 folder for this chapter on the CD. Copy this file to the folder that contains your CustomerGUI.java program.

2. In Forte, open the **Customer.java** file by clicking **File** on the menu bar, and then clicking **Open File**.

3. If a dialog box opens asking whether Customer.java should be in the default package, click the **Accept** button.

13

The source code will appear in the Source Editor window on a second tabbed pane as shown in Figure 13-36. The CustomerGUI program is still in the Source Editor window on the first tabbed pane.

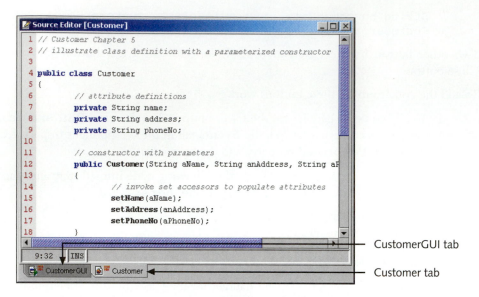

CustomerGUI tab

Customer tab

Figure 13-36 The Source Editor with CustomerGUI and Customer Loaded

4. Click **Tools** on the menu bar, and then click **Add to Project** to add this program to your project.

5. Click the **CustomerGUI** tab to return to that program and compile the CustomerGUI program. If the compilation is successful, the message "Finished CustomerGUI" appears in the status bar of the main window. If there were syntax errors, they appear in the Output window.

 Remember, you can double-click a red error message to jump to the line of code that is problematic. Once you have fixed your errors, recompile the program.

6. When the build is successful, execute the program. It should work just as it did in Chapter 11.

USING THE DEBUGGER

You have seen how to develop GUI programs using the visual editing capabilities of the Forte IDE. In this section, you will learn about Forte's debugging utility and discover how it can help you find and fix logic errors in your programs. A debugging utility, more commonly called a **debugger**, consists of a set of tools that monitor the progress of your program at runtime. You will use the Forte debugger to set breakpoints that allow you to observe the values of variables as your program is executing and to issue special instructions for executing your program one line of code at a time. The Forte debugger has many options, only some of which are discussed in this text. Knowing something about this powerful tool will help you determine what is wrong with your code when it seems to you that your program ought to be working but isn't.

Getting Started with the Debugger

Before you begin using the Forte debugger, understand that a debugger is intended to help you identify errors in your program that occur at runtime. Recall that runtime errors are not the same as syntax errors. Syntax errors are caught by the compiler—not by the debugger. Your program must compile without syntax errors before you will be able to use the debugger.

You will explore some of the basic features of the debugger using a simple GUI application that computes the amount due for an electric bill based upon a beginning and ending meter reading. Although this program is not part of the Bradshaw Marina application, it will help you understand the debugger. The program was developed using the Forte GUI editor and is included on the CD that accompanies this text. Before working with the debugger, it will be helpful to run this program and get a feel for how it works.

To run the CalculateElectricBill.java program:

1. Close any programs currently loaded in Forte by closing the Source Editor window.

2. Use Windows Explorer to locate the **CalculateElectricBill.java** program in the Example3 folder for Chapter 13 on the CD. Copy this file to the folder on your system that represents the default filesystem.

3. If the default project is not already open, click **Project** on the menu bar, and then click **Project Manager**. Click **Project Default** in the list of Existing Projects, and then click the **Open** button.

4. Open the CalculateElectricBill program by clicking **File** on the menu bar, and then clicking **Open File**. In the Open dialog box, navigate to the folder that represents your default filesystem, and open the **CalculateElectricBill.java** file.

5. If a dialog box opens asking whether CalculateElectricBill.java should be in the default package, click the **Accept** button.

6. To add this program to the default project, click **Tools** on the menu bar, and then click **Add to Project**.

13

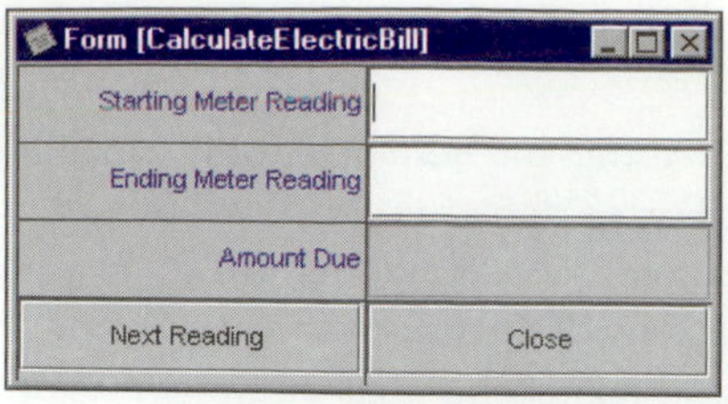

Figure 13-37 The CalculateElectricBill input form

7. Compile and execute the program. The input form shown in Figure 13-37 appears.

8. Enter **200** for the starting meter reading and **500** for the ending meter reading, and then press **Enter**. The program calculates the kilowatt-hours used and multiplies this number by $0.50 to determine the amount due. In this case, the kilowatt-hours used will be 300 (500 – 200) and the amount due will be $150 (300 x $0.50).

9. To enter the next meter reading, press the **Next Reading** button. This clears the textfields and positions the cursor in the Starting Meter Reading textfield.

10. Close the CalculateElectricBill application window and return to the GUI Editing workspace.

You will now use the debugger to set breakpoints and monitor the progress of this program as it executes.

Setting Breakpoints and Establishing Watch Variables

Recall that a breakpoint is a flag in your program that tells the debugger to pause execution of your program. You can set breakpoints using the Debug toolbar or the Debug menu, but the simplest way is to use a series of shortcut keys. For this program, you will set a breakpoint at line 127. (This is the line of code in the meterEndTextActionPerformed method that invokes the setText() method to display the amount due.)

To set a breakpoint:

1. If the Source Editor is not already open, click **View** on the menu bar and then click **Source Editor**. In the Source Editor, locate line 127. This line of code reads:

```
amtDueText.setText("" + amtDue);
```

2. Select this line of code, click **Debug** on the menu bar, then click **Add Break-point**. The Add Breakpoint dialog box appears. Accept the defaults by clicking **OK**. Notice that this line of code now appears in a red background, indicating that the breakpoint has been set. When you run your program in the debugger, activity will temporarily be suspended just before this line of code is executed. While program execution is suspended, you will normally want to see the values of key variables or expressions in the application. Four variables are of interest here: startReading, endReading, kwhUsed, and amtDue. In debugger terminology, variables you are interested in watching are called watch variables, or more simply watches.

3. To set a watch on the startReading variable, select the startReading variable in the Source Editor, right-click the variable, and then click **Add Watch** on the shortcut menu. The Add New Watch dialog box appears as shown in Figure 13-38.

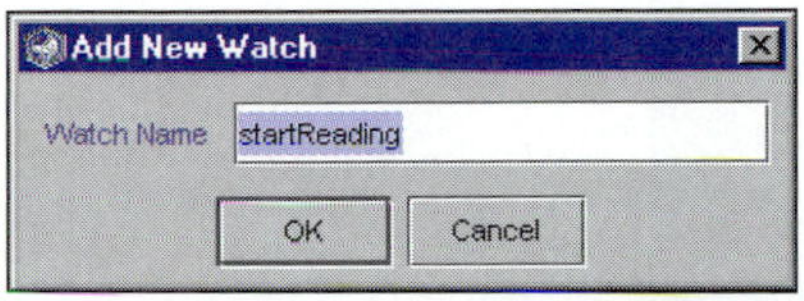

Figure 13-38   The Add New Watch dialog box

4. Click **OK** to establish the watch.

5. Repeat Steps 3 and 4 to add watches on the endReading, kwhUsed, and amtDue variables.

You are now ready to use the debugger to monitor the progress of your program and view the values of your watch variables.

To monitor the watch variables as breakpoints are reached:

1. Start the debugger by clicking **Debug** on the menu bar, and then clicking **Start**.

2. If you have made changes to the source code since the last compilation, Forte will first recompile your program. The IDE then switches to the Debugging workspace, and the Source Editor, Output, and Debugger windows open. (You may wish to resize some of these windows so that they are easier to work with.) The debugger automatically begins executing your program and will continue execution until it reaches a breakpoint. In this program, you have set only one breakpoint, and it occurs *after* the beginning and ending meter readings have been entered.

3. Enter the same meter readings that you did initially (**200** for the starting meter reading and **500** for the ending meter reading) and press **Enter**.

13

4. When the breakpoint is reached, the debugger pauses execution of your program. Notice that the line of code in the Source Editor where the breakpoint occurred now appears with a blue background (rather than red), indicating that this breakpoint has been reached. Also, a message indicating the line at which the breakpoint occurred is displayed in the Output window.

5. Click the **Watches** tab in the Debugger window, if necessary, and you will see the current values of the four watch variables (see Figure 13-39).

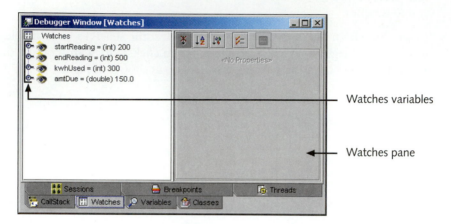

Figure 13-39   The Watches pane of the Debugger window

6. To resume execution of your program, make sure that either the Source Editor or the Debugger window is the active window, and press **Ctrl+F5**. (Pressing **Ctrl+F5** in the Calculate Electric Bill application window will have no effect.) The amount due is displayed in the Amount Due textfield, and the program waits for more input.

7. To enter another set of meter readings, click the **Next Reading** button, and then enter **6599** for a starting meter reading and **8999** for an ending meter reading. Press **Enter**.

8. Again, the debugger suspends execution upon reaching the breakpoint at line 127. Click the **Watches** tab to see the new values of the four watch variables.

9. Make sure that either the Debugger window or Source Editor is the active window, and then press **Ctrl+F5** once more to resume execution of your program. The program displays an amount due of $1200.

Finding and Correcting Program Errors

Next, you will see how the debugger can help you isolate and correct errors in your programs. The CalculateElectricBill program has a hidden error—when non-numeric values are entered for the meter readings, a NumberFormatException error occurs. As you have learned, this runtime error can be easily overcome using a try-catch block.

To force this runtime error to occur and make corrections to the program:

1. Click the **Next Reading** button. Enter a starting meter reading of **A** and an ending meter reading of **B**, and then press **Enter**. The program throws NumberFormatException errors. These errors are listed in the Output window.

2. Close this debugging session by clicking **Debug** on the menu bar, and then clicking **Finish**. Click the **Do not show this dialog box next time** check box, and then click **OK** to close the dialog box.

3. Return to the GUI Editing workspace. In the Source Editor, modify the meterEndTextActionPerformed method to include the try-catch block statements shown in Figure 13-40.

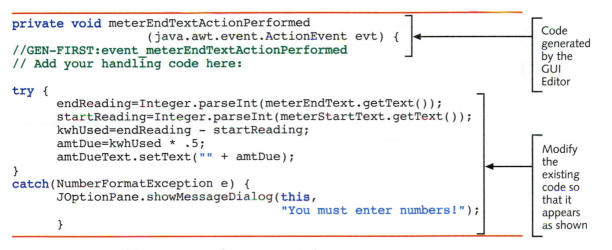

```java
private void meterEndTextActionPerformed
                (java.awt.event.ActionEvent evt) {
//GEN-FIRST:event_meterEndTextActionPerformed
// Add your handling code here:

try {
    endReading=Integer.parseInt(meterEndText.getText());
    startReading=Integer.parseInt(meterStartText.getText());
    kwhUsed=endReading - startReading;
    amtDue=kwhUsed * .5;
    amtDueText.setText("" + amtDue);
}
catch(NumberFormatException e) {
    JOptionPane.showMessageDialog(this,
                        "You must enter numbers!");
    }
```

Code generated by the GUI Editor

Modify the existing code so that it appears as shown

Figure 13-40 Modifications to catch non-numeric data errors

4. Restart the debugger, and enter **A** and **B** once more for the meter readings. The program responds correctly and displays an informative message.

5. When the breakpoint is reached, monitor the status of the watch variables in the Watch tab of the Debugger window. The program responds correctly and issues an informative message to the user.

Remember that you can resume execution by pressing Ctrl+F5 when either the Source Editor or the Debugger window is active.

Although the above modifications solve runtime errors that result from improper data entry, there is another problem with this program. If you have ever looked at your electric meter, you know that it has a limited number of display digits. Assume that electric meters have only four digits. In other words, meter readings will always be a number between 0000 and 9999. When the number of kilowatt-hours used exceeds 9999, the meter rolls over and begins at 0000 again.

To see how the program handles this situation:

1. Click the **Next Reading** button and enter **9990** for a starting meter reading, and **0090** for an ending reading. The program immediately reaches the breakpoint.

2. Click in the Source Editor window to make it the active window, and then press **Ctrl+F5** to resume executing program.

3. Notice that the amount due returned by the program is a negative number. Something is wrong. Although no runtime exceptions were thrown, the program contains a hidden logic error.

By now you have probably surmised that the correct number of kilowatt-hours used is 100 and the amount due is $50. Ten kilowatt-hours were used to cause the meter to roll from 9990 to 0000, and 90 kilowatt-hours have been used since the rollover. However, the program has calculated the kilowatt-hours used incorrectly as 0090 - 9990 = -9900, with a corresponding amount due of -$4,950. To correct the problem, the possibility of a rollover needs to be taken into account in the kilowatt-hours-used computation. To fix this problem:

1. Close this debugging session by clicking **Debug** on the menu bar, and then clicking **Finish**.

2. Return to the GUI Editing workspace and modify the code within the meterEndTextActionPerformed method as shown in Figure 13-41.

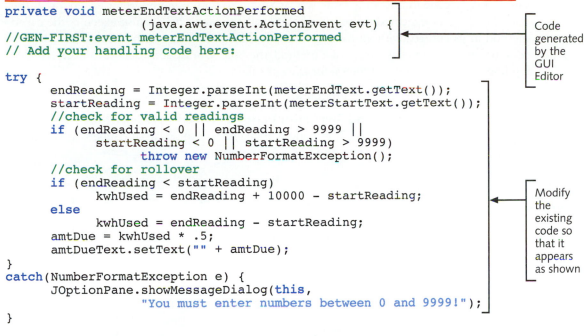

```
private void meterEndTextActionPerformed
                    (java.awt.event.ActionEvent evt) {
//GEN-FIRST:event_meterEndTextActionPerformed
// Add your handling code here:

try {
    endReading = Integer.parseInt(meterEndText.getText());
    startReading = Integer.parseInt(meterStartText.getText());
    //check for valid readings
    if (endReading < 0 || endReading > 9999 ||
        startReading < 0 || startReading > 9999)
            throw new NumberFormatException();
    //check for rollover
    if (endReading < startReading)
        kwhUsed = endReading + 10000 - startReading;
    else
        kwhUsed = endReading - startReading;
    amtDue = kwhUsed * .5;
    amtDueText.setText("" + amtDue);
}
catch(NumberFormatException e) {
    JOptionPane.showMessageDialog(this,
              "You must enter numbers between 0 and 9999!");
}

}//GEN-LAST:event_meterEndTextActionPerformed
```

Code generated by the GUI Editor

Modify the existing code so that it appears as shown

Figure 13-41 Modifications to handle meter rollovers

3. Restart the debugger and try the rollover meter readings again to confirm that the modification you made did indeed fix the rollover problem.

4. Continue to test the program, trying many different kinds of numbers (as well as non-numeric data) to verify that the program now performs correctly in all cases. Monitor the watch variables as the program executes.

5. Stop the debugger.

Stepping Through a Program

Setting breakpoints and watch variables is a common debugging technique and is among the debugging features you are likely to use most often. However, other helpful features involve the ability to single-step through a program, executing one line of source code at a time.

Any time the debugger pauses execution of your program, you can use various "step" options to execute your program one line of code at a time and observe the values of the watch variables at each line of code. The Step Into option executes a single line of code. If that line of code contains a method call, individual statements in the called method will also be executed one at a time each time the Step Into command is carried out. The debugger also has options that allow you to "step over" or "step out of" methods. The Step Over option single-steps

13

through your code in much the same way as Step Into with one important exception. If the line of code to be executed includes a method call, the Step Over option executes the called method in its entirety, without pausing at each instruction in the method. If the next line of code to be executed is itself part of a method, the Step Out option executes all the remaining lines of that method and then returns to its caller.

To begin stepping through your program:

1. Modify the **meterEndTextActionPerformed** method to reflect the changes shown in Figure 13-42. This code will enable you to see what happens as you use the Step Into, Step Over, and Step Out commands.

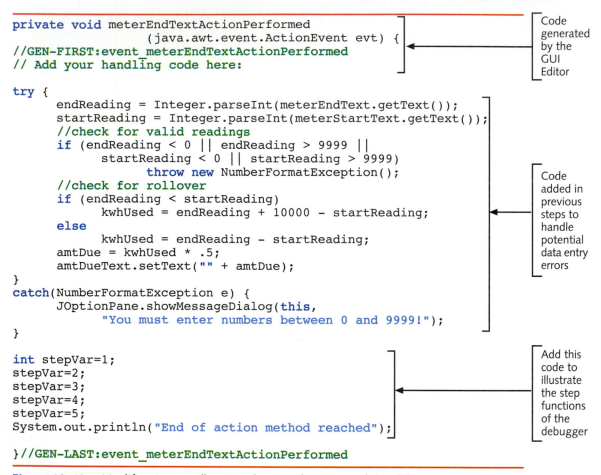

```
private void meterEndTextActionPerformed
                (java.awt.event.ActionEvent evt) {
//GEN-FIRST:event_meterEndTextActionPerformed
// Add your handling code here:

try {
    endReading = Integer.parseInt(meterEndText.getText());
    startReading = Integer.parseInt(meterStartText.getText());
    //check for valid readings
    if (endReading < 0 || endReading > 9999 ||
        startReading < 0 || startReading > 9999)
            throw new NumberFormatException();
    //check for rollover
    if (endReading < startReading)
        kwhUsed = endReading + 10000 - startReading;
    else
        kwhUsed = endReading - startReading;
    amtDue = kwhUsed * .5;
    amtDueText.setText("" + amtDue);
}
catch(NumberFormatException e) {
    JOptionPane.showMessageDialog(this,
        "You must enter numbers between 0 and 9999!");
}

int stepVar=1;
stepVar=2;
stepVar=3;
stepVar=4;
stepVar=5;
System.out.println("End of action method reached");

}//GEN-LAST:event_meterEndTextActionPerformed
```

Code generated by the GUI Editor

Code added in previous steps to handle potential data entry errors

Add this code to illustrate the step functions of the debugger

Figure 13-42 Modifications to illustrate the step functions of the debugger

2. Add a watch on stepVar, and then run the debugger again, entering appropriate values for the starting and ending meter readings.

3. When the breakpoint is reached, the line of code where the breakpoint is set will be highlighted in blue in the Source Editor. This is the line of code that will be executed next. Recall that this line of code invokes the setText() method of the JTextField class. You do not want to single-step through the statements in the setText() method, so click in the Source Editor window to make it the active window, and then press **F8** to "step over" this method call.

4. Notice that the statement after the catch block is now highlighted in blue, indicating that this is the next line of code to be executed. This line of code will set the value of stepVar to 1. Press **F7** to "step into" (or execute) this line of code. Observe the value of stepVar in the Watches pane and the movement of the blue bar in the Source Editor.

5. Press **F7** five more times to single step through the remaining code, observing the value of stepVar in the Watches pane as you go. When the System.out.println() statement is reached, a question dialog box appears. Make sure that the **Step Out** option button is selected, and click **OK**. The message "End of action method reached" appears in the Output window. (If necessary, click **View** on the menu bar, and then click **Output Window** to open the Output window.)

6. Next, you will see how the "step out" option works. Press **Ctrl+F5** to continue debugging. (If necessary, restore the Calculate Electric Bill window to make it visible.) Press the **Next Reading** button and enter a new set of valid meter readings.

7. When the breakpoint is reached, click in the Source Editor window and press **Ctrl+F7** to step out of the current method. Observe that the debugger executes the remaining code but does so without pausing at each line. This is confirmed by the fact that the System.out.println() statement at the end of the method executed a second time displaying its message in the Output window.

8. Make sure that the Source Editor is the active window, press **Ctrl+F5** to continue executing the program, and then end the debugging session.

Exploring Other Debugger Options

The debugger has other useful options you should be aware of. For instance, in addition to pausing execution at a breakpoint, you can instruct the debugger to pause execution at the first line of code in the main method, or to run to the cursor and then pause. You can set watches on expressions as well as variables, and you can set conditional breakpoints to instruct the debugger to pause only when a certain condition is met (for example, to pause when the kilowatt-hours used is less than zero). Similarly, you can set breakpoints on method names, classes, exceptions, and other items. More information can be found in the online Forte documentation. We encourage you to explore these and other debugger capabilities on your own.

GENERATING JAVADOC DOCUMENTATION

The final feature of Forte that you will learn about deals with generating program documentation. If you look closely at the source code generated by the GUI editor, you will notice that some of the block comments look a little different than the block comments you are used to. These comments, which begin with /** and end with */, are called **doc comments**. Like other comments, doc comments explain the purpose of a class, the purpose of a method, and so on. However, doc comments serve a special purpose. They are used by a tool in the Java SDK called the **javadoc utility** to generate HTML pages that contain pertinent information about your classes, methods, variables, and so forth. The resulting documentation is useful to other programmers who use your classes to create programs of their own or who may be asked to maintain yours.

Notice that several of the doc comments generated by the IDE include an @ symbol (such as @author, @version, and @param). The @ character signifies the beginning of a **javadoc tag**. There are a number of different javadoc tags. Each tag identifies a certain kind of information and instructs the javadoc utility to perform special tasks when creating HTML pages from the doc comments. For example, the @param tag is used to identify the name of one argument of a method, followed by a description. The description may contain additional HTML tags. Each javadoc tag must start a new line. Unlike other comments, the position of doc comments within the source code is critical. Doc comments are ignored unless they are placed before declarations. Generally speaking, you put doc comments immediately before the declaration of a class or a method (see Figure 13-43).

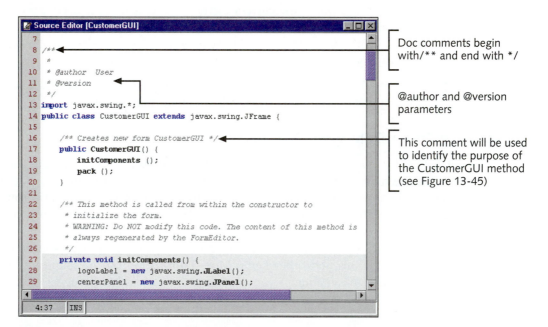

Figure 13-43 Doc comments

Once the doc comments are in place in the source code, you can instruct the Forte IDE to generate the corresponding HTML documentation file.

To experiment briefly with this feature:

1. Open the project containing the CustomerGUI.java program you created with the GUI editor earlier in this chapter. Because this file already contains valid doc comments, you will be able to generate the HTML pages that document its methods.

2. Click the **Filesystems** tab in the Explorer window, and then right-click the **CustomerGUI.java** source file.

3. Point to **Tools**, and then click **Generate Javadoc**.

4. The javadoc utility runs and asks if you want to view the HTML documentation that was generated in a Web browser. Click **Yes**, maximize the Web Browser window, and look through the documentation. Selected portions of this documentation are shown in Figures 13-44, 13-45, and 13-46.

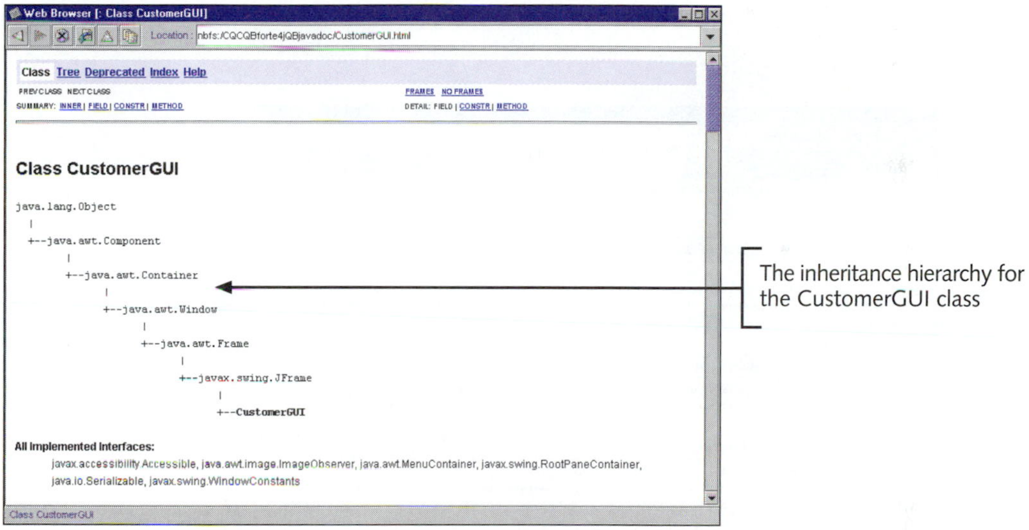

The inheritance hierarchy for the CustomerGUI class

13

Figure 13-44   Documentation generated to show the class structure for the CustomerGUI program

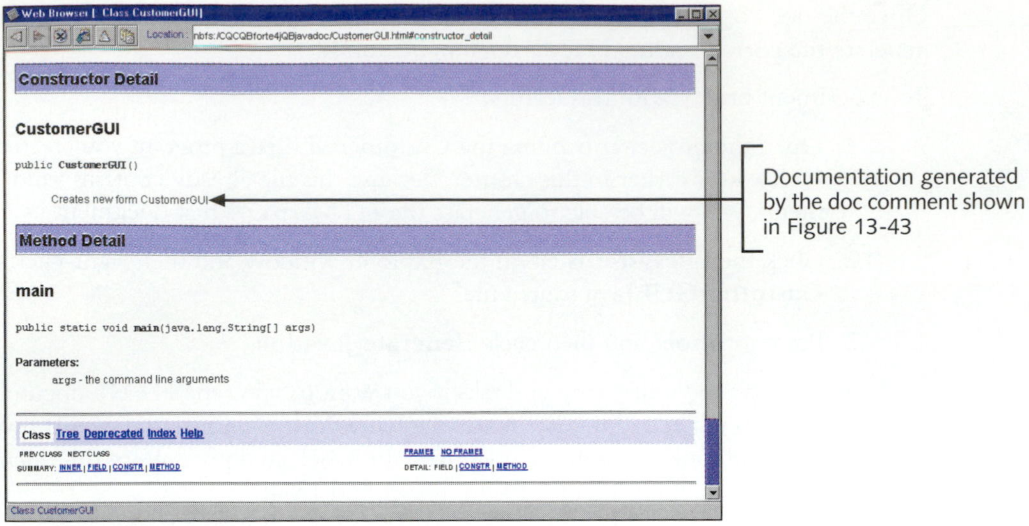

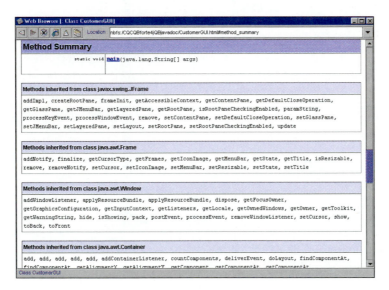

Figure 13-45   Documentation generated for methods defined within the CustomerGUI program

Figure 13-46   Documentation generated to summarize inherited methods used in the CustomerGUI program

You cannot generate javadoc documentation for source files that do not contain valid doc comments. However, you can add doc comments to the source code of any program. You can do this directly by using the source editor, or you can use the Auto Comment feature of the Forte IDE to help you create them. The Forte IDE also has features that let you search the javadoc-generated HTML pages for a specific class, method, field, or other item of interest. For more detailed information on using the IDE to add javadoc comments to source code, refer to the Forte online documentation.

Summary

- Rapid Application Development is an iterative development strategy that compresses the traditional system development life cycle. The goal of RAD is to significantly reduce information system development and implementation time.

- A prototype is a model (or mock-up) of some portion of an information system. The prototyping strategy is to develop core features first, and get the look and feel of them before implementing other features. RAD makes extensive use of prototyping.

- Prototypes are modified iteratively, with feedback from users at each step. This improves communication between programmers and users, shortens the requirements definition portion of the development cycle, and engages users in the development effort.

- An IDE is a set of software tools that helps you code, debug, and test a system as you develop it. IDEs are useful in any software development project, but they are particularly valuable in RAD because of their ability to reduce development time.

- An IDE includes tools that assist you with source editing, GUI editing, program compilation and execution, debugging, documentation, and program organization and management. The Forte IDE supports all these features.

- The source editor within Forte supports color-coding, indentation, and code-completion features.

- The Forte GUI editor is a visual development tool that generates code from pictures that you draw. Code generated by an IDE tends to be slightly longer and may be more difficult to read than code you write yourself, but automatic code generation saves enough time to offset these potential drawbacks.

- Filesystems and packages correspond to the hierarchical organization of the directories (or folders) that you use. A package is the folder that contains your program, or more typically, a set of related programs. A filesystem is the set of folders that exist above the

13

package-level folder. The JVM recognizes these structures, and it is important to specify these items correctly when using Forte.

- Forte uses projects to organize and manage related sets of programs. Project structures are not recognized by the JVM or by other systems software.

- A debugger allows you to monitor the progress of a program at runtime and isolate errors that prevent it from running as intended. Through the Forte debugger, you can set breakpoints and establish watches that enable you to observe the changing values of variables in your program. The debugger also provides features that enable you to single-step through your program.

- A breakpoint is a flag that instructs the debugger to temporarily suspend execution of your program.

- A watch variable is a variable whose value you want to see when the debugger suspends program execution.

- Doc comments begin with /** and end with */, and they often include special tags that begin with the @ sign. The javadoc utility uses these comments to produce program documentation in HTML format. This documentation is useful to other programmers who may use your classes.

- The Forte javadoc utility helps you with the creation and placement of doc comments within your programs. The GUI editor automatically generates doc comments within the programs it creates.

- Using an IDE makes your job as a programmer easier, reduces overall development time, improves program quality, and supports program reuse.

- To use an IDE effectively, you must invest some time learning the tools and features it supports. Time invested in overcoming this learning curve, however, saves a significant amount of time in the long run.

Key Terms

breakpoint	Integrated Development Environment (IDE)	project
debugger		prototype
doc comment	javadoc tag	watch variable
filesystem	javadoc utility	workspace
	package	

Review Questions

1. What is RAD? How does RAD differ from the traditional approach to systems development?

2. What is an IDE? Why is an IDE particularly useful in a RAD environment?

3. What are the major tools in an IDE and what are the features of each?

4. What is a prototype? Why is prototyping important? How does an IDE support prototyping?

5. What is the difference between a source editor and a GUI editor?

6. What does it mean to add a breakpoint and watch variables to a program? How are breakpoints and watch variables useful?

7. What does it mean to single-step through a program? What is the benefit of single-stepping through a program?

8. What is the purpose of doc comments?

9. What are the major benefits of using an IDE? What are the potential drawbacks?

Discussion Questions

1. Now that you have gained some experience using an IDE, describe in your own words how an IDE can improve programmer productivity. Also describe the effect this may have on organizations that rely on rapid information system development to remain competitive.

2. Compare and contrast the following terms: project, package, filesystem.

3. Do you think that code-generation tools like the ones in the IDE you used in this chapter will one day replace the need for programmers? Why or why not?

4. Suppose that when you graduate, the organization you work for considers purchasing an IDE for its programmers to use in the development of a mission-critical information system that must be completed in a short time frame. Your supervisor learns that you have had experience working with a Java IDE and asks for your advice on this matter. Would you recommend that the organization adopt an IDE for this project? Why or why not? What important issues should be considered before making such a purchase?

13

Projects

1. Use the Forte GUI editor to re-create the CalculateElectricBill example. You do not need to include code to check for data entry errors.

2. Use the GUI editor to create a new version of the CalculateElectricBill example in which the Next Reading button and Close button are contained within a single button panel rather than in cells of a grid. Add a Calculate button to the button panel. When pressed, the Calculate button should calculate the amount due.

3. Use the Forte GUI editor to re-create the AddBoat GUI from Chapter 11. (*Hint*: To establish radio button groups, define additional code in the Post-Creation Code property of the radio button elements. This property is found on the Code Generation tab of the Component Inspector.)

PART 4

Defining Data Access Classes

Designing Data Access Classes

In Part 2 you learned how to design and write problem domain (PD) classes. In Part 3 you learned how to design and write GUI classes that interact with the PD classes. Here in Part 4 you will learn to design and write data access (DA) classes that provide data storage and retrieval services. Part 5 shows you how to connect all three tiers of an OO system: GUI, PD, and DA.

Generally, most data is stored in a relational database; however, this chapter introduces you to various approaches that illustrate the benefits of using a DA class. You will learn how to store attribute values in sequential and random access files, and how to store entire instances in a sequential file. You will be introduced to relational database concepts and see how to design a database table containing attribute data, and you will use the Structured Query Language (SQL) to access the data.

After completing this chapter, you will be able to design a DA class that works with sequential files and random access files. You will be able to design and create a relational database, and design a DA class with methods that will store and retrieve items in the database.

MAKING OBJECTS PERSISTENT

The previous chapters ignored the issue of data storage and retrieval. For example, you saw how to create instances of the Customer class, but you did not learn how to make these instances persistent over time. All of the instances you created in earlier chapters disappeared when the system stopped running. Of course, in a real application, you must find a way to store data so it can be retrieved when necessary. In an OO application, you use **object persistence** when you store instances or their attribute values for future retrieval. You make the object instances persist over time; you store them for future access.

There are two approaches to achieving persistence: **attribute storage** and **object storage**. Attribute storage involves retrieving the attribute values from the instance to be made persistent, and then writing these values to a file. Figure 14-1 illustrates the attribute storage technique to make a customer instance persistent.

To make a customer instance persistent, you first invoke the accessor methods to obtain the customer's name, address, and phone number. Then you write these values to a customer data file. You can re-create the customer instance later by reversing the process: First you read the data from the customer data file and then instantiate Customer using the data values from the file to populate the attributes.

Object storage involves writing the entire instance to a file using a technique called **object serialization**. A benefit of object storage is that the instance can be retrieved intact; it is not necessary to re-create it. In contrast, attribute storage requires that you first retrieve the attribute values, and then instantiate the class. This chapter illustrates both attribute and object storage.

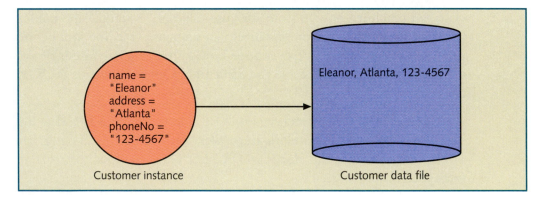

name =
  "Eleanor"
address =
  "Atlanta"
phoneNo =
  "123-4567"

Eleanor, Atlanta, 123-4567

Customer instance   Customer data file

Figure 14-1   Making a customer instance persistent using attribute storage

DESIGNING A DATA ACCESS CLASS

The fundamental purpose of a DA class is to provide methods that store and retrieve data and make instances of a PD class persistent. As you saw in Chapter 4, the three-tier OO design model calls for three categories of classes: GUI classes that provide the user interface for data input and display, PD classes that model the essential business entities, and DA classes that provide for data storage and retrieval. This three-tier model implements client-server architecture that is significantly easier to deploy and maintain.

Data storage and retrieval tasks are placed in a DA class for two reasons. First, data input and output code is isolated from other classes, which can dramatically reduce maintenance. Changes in data storage should have no impact on GUI and PD classes. Similarly, GUI and PD modifications generally will not affect DA classes. Second, the three-tier architecture supports the client-server model where GUI, PD, and DA functions may reside on multiple machines at various sites. Separate classes for each tier make deployment easier in a client-server environment. For details, see Chapter 17 in Part 5.

You further isolate the DA class by requiring that DA methods are invoked only by the PD class. This means that only the PD class is aware of the DA class. The services provided by the DA class appear to be provided by the PD class, thus effectively hiding the DA class from all other classes.

Data Access Methods

Generally you will write a separate DA class for each PD class. In this chapter, for example, you will write a DA class named CustomerDA, which provides data storage and retrieval services for customers. Remember, however, that only the PD class will invoke methods in the DA class. Classes that require data storage and retrieval services must invoke the DA methods in Customer, which in turn invokes the CustomerDA methods. This idea is illustrated in the section "Communicating With a Data Access Class" later in this chapter.

Recall from Chapter 3 that Java has two types of methods: static and nonstatic. Static methods, sometimes called class methods, are not tied to a specific instance. You invoke static methods using the class name. Because you will not have instances of the DA class, all of its methods are static.

Four basic tasks are provided by CustomerDA and thus by Customer: retrieve a customer, store a customer, change a customer's data, and remove a customer. These functions are implemented in the DA class using methods named find, addNew, update, and delete. Although the statements within these DA methods depend on the specific storage implementation, their signatures remain the same. In other words, clients that invoke these methods are unaware of the specific implementations and need only know the method signature. These methods and their headers are described in the following sections. The statements within these methods are described in the implementation sections later in this chapter.

14

Finding a Customer

The find method searches for a specific customer; if it is found, the method returns a reference to the instance. The examples in this section use the customer's phone number as the key, which means that each customer is uniquely identified by telephone number. The find method accepts an argument that contains the phone number of the customer to be retrieved. If the customer is found, then a reference to the customer instance is returned. If the customer is not located, the method creates and throws an instance of the custom exception class NotFoundException. The header for the find method appears as follows:

```
public static Customer find(String phoneNo) throws NotFoundException
```

Adding a Customer

The addNew method adds a customer to the system. This method receives a reference to the new customer instance as an argument and returns no data. Because you do not want to have duplicate customers stored, this method first determines if there is an existing customer with the same phone number as the customer being added. If an existing customer with the same phone number is detected, the addNew method will create and throw an instance of the custom exception class DuplicateException. The header for the addNew method appears as follows:

```
public static void addNew(Customer aCustomer) throws DuplicateException
```

Changing a Customer

In this system, customers can change their address and phone number. The purpose of the update method is to store these changed values. The update method receives the customer reference as an argument, locates the existing customer, and replaces the address and phone number values. If the customer cannot be located, then the update method throws a NotFoundException. This method does not return a value. The header for the update method appears as follows:

```
public static void update(Customer aCustomer) throws NotFoundException
```

Deleting a Customer

The delete method removes a customer from the system. Like update, it first locates the customer whose reference was received as an argument, and then removes it from data storage. Like update, if the customer cannot be located, the delete method throws a NotFoundException. The header for the delete method appears as follows:

```
public static void delete(Customer aCustomer) throws NotFoundException
```

Additional Data Access Methods

The DA classes illustrated in this section have three additional methods: initialize, terminate, and getAll. As their names suggest, initialize performs initialization chores, terminate does termination tasks, and getAll retrieves all members of a class. The initialize and terminate methods receive no arguments and return no data. The actual statements in these methods depend on the specific implementation of the DA class. This chapter illustrates four different implementations, and the details for these methods are described in later sections. The initialize and terminate method headers appear as follows:

```
public static void initialize()
public static void terminate()
```

The getAll method retrieves all customers that are stored in the system and returns their references in a Vector instance. This method takes no arguments. The getAll method header appears as follows:

```
public static Vector getAll()
```

Figure 14-2 recaps the seven DA method headers.

```
public static Customer find(String phoneNo) throws NotFoundException

public static void addNew(Customer aCustomer) throws DuplicateException

public static void update(Customer aCustomer) throws NotFoundException

public static void delete(Customer aCustomer) throws NotFoundException

public static void initialize()

public static void terminate()

public static Vector getAll()
```

Figure 14-2   DA method headers

14

COMMUNICATING WITH A DATA ACCESS CLASS

In the previous section, you saw that the DA methods are invoked only by the corresponding PD class. In this section, the Customer class invokes methods in CustomerDA. Clients must invoke methods in Customer, which in turn invokes the DA methods. This restriction is imposed to isolate the DA class from all but its matching PD class. To the other classes, it appears that the PD class, Customer, is providing data storage and retrieval services for its instances.

To enable Customer to invoke the seven DA methods, you must provide seven corresponding methods in Customer, which are then invoked by clients. The sole purpose of these methods is to act as a buffer between other classes and the DA class. In keeping with the spirit of minimum maintenance, you should design these methods so they will not be sensitive to the data storage method you use. For example, whether you store data using a relational database or a sequential file, you want the seven method headers to remain the same. This feature is demonstrated in the implementation sections later in the chapter.

Finding a Customer

The purpose of the PD find method is to invoke the DA find method. It is a static method, because it is not tied to a specific customer instance. Because the DA method returns a customer reference, you want the PD method to also return the reference. Similarly, because the DA method may throw a NotFoundException, you want the PD find method header to contain a throws clause.

The single statement in the PD find method simply invokes find in CustomerDA, passes it the phone number that was received, and then returns the customer reference value that is returned by the DA method. The PD find method appears as follows:

```
public static Customer find(String phoneNo) throws NotFoundException
   {return CustomerDA.find(phoneNo);}
```

Adding a Customer

The addNew method in the PD class invokes the addNew method in the DA class to store a new customer instance. It is a nonstatic method because it is invoked for the new customer instance being added. The method receives no argument and returns no data. Because the DA addNew method may throw a DuplicateException, you must include a throws clause in the method header. The single statement in the method invokes addNew in CustomerDA, passing it a reference to the new customer instance. The method appears as follows:

```
public void addNew() throws DuplicateException
   {CustomerDA.addNew(this);}
```

Changing a Customer

The PD update method invokes the update method in the DA class. It is a nonstatic method, and because the DA update method throws a NotFoundException, you must specify a throws clause in the PD method header. The method invokes update in CustomerDA, passing a reference to the new customer instance. The method appears as follows:

```
public void update() throws NotFoundException
   {CustomerDA.update(this);}
```

Deleting a Customer

The delete method in the PD class invokes the delete method in the DA class. Like update, its header contains a throws clause and passes a reference of the customer instance being deleted. The method appears as follows:

```
public void delete() throws NotFoundException
   {CustomerDA.delete(this);}
```

Additional Problem Domain Methods

Because the DA classes in the previous section have the additional methods initialize, terminate, and getAll, you must also include them in the PD class. All of these are static methods that simply invoke the corresponding method in the DA class. The getAll method returns a Vector reference. The methods appear as follows:

```java
public static void initialize()
   {CustomerDA.initialize();}

public static void terminate()
   {CustomerDA.terminate();}

public static Vector getAll()
   {return CustomerDA.getAll();}
```

UNDERSTANDING JAVA I/O

Java views data input and output as a flow of bytes, or a **data stream**. This abstraction permits you to focus on data without dealing with specific physical I/O devices. Java uses two different types of data streams: **byte stream** and **character stream**. Data in byte streams uses **Unicode**, a standard character set with two bytes for each character. Unicode accommodates all the characters in major international languages. Character stream data is stored in the default format of the system where the data is stored. Character streams, however, are automatically translated into Unicode when read by Java.

You learned in Chapter 3 that the java.io package contains several classes with various methods to input and output data to files. Table 14-1 lists selected classes in the java.io package and shows the class hierarchy along with brief descriptions. These classes are used in the following implementation sections.

14

Table 14-1 Selected Classes in the java.io Package

Class Name	Description
File	Contains file specification information
Reader	Superclass for character input streams
BufferedReader	readLine method for sequential files
ObjectInputStream	readObject method for object serialization
OutputStream	Superclass for byte output streams
FileOutputStream	
PrintStream	println method for sequential files
ObjectOutputStream	writeObject method for object serialization
RandomAccessFile	readLine and writeBytes methods for random files

You are already familiar with variables and their values. The examples in this chapter use variables to contain customer attributes such as name, address, and phone number. A **record** is a related collection of variables. A customer record would consist of customers' names, addresses, and phone numbers. A **file** consists of a collection of related records. A customer file contains a set of customer records.

The examples in this chapter illustrate three types of file organization: sequential, random access, and database. **Sequential files** contain records that are stored and processed in sequential order. To obtain data stored in the fifth record, for example, you must first read the previous four records. The BufferedReader class provides a method named readLine to input data from a sequential file, and the PrintStream class has a method named println to output sequential data.

In contrast, a **random access file** is organized so you can access a record by specifying its record number. You use the RandomAccessFile class and its readLine and writeBytes methods when working with random files.

A **database** is one or more files organized to help make queries. The data in a **relational database** is organized into tables that can be related to each other. Each table column represents an attribute and each row represents a record. The **Structured Query Language** (**SQL**), introduced later in this chapter and described in more detail in Chapter 15, is a standard set of keywords and statements used to access relational databases. The java.sql package contains classes with methods you will invoke while working with a relational database.

Implementing Persistence With a Sequential File

Attribute storage, which calls for the storage of attribute values, is used in the following examples for both sequential and random access files. The initialize method for both of these file types reads the customer records containing the attribute values for customers, creates a customer instance for each record, and then places the references for these customer instances into a Vector instance. This technique permits the ready access of a particular customer without additional file input or output. Similarly, the terminate method iterates the Vector and writes the attribute values for each customer instance to the file.

The CustomerDA class for the sequential files class begins with import statements for Vector and the java.io package. The java.io package contains all the classes this example needs for file input and output.

```
import java.util.Vector;
import java.io.*;
```

Two variables are declared at the beginning of CustomerDA that will have class scope. The first is a Vector reference variable named customers, which will contain references to all the customer instances. The second, also a reference variable, contains a reference to an instance of the File class. This instance contains the file specification for the sequential file used in this example. As you can see, the name of the sequential file is Customer.dat; the file is on the A drive.

```
static Vector customers;
static File customerFile = new File("A:/Customer.dat");
```

The initialize Method

The purpose of the initialize method is to read the attribute values for all of the customers from the sequential file, create an instance for each customer, and store references for those instances into a Vector. The first statement in the initialize method creates the Vector instance named customers, which will be populated with references to customer instances.

```
customers = new Vector();
```

The remainder of the method is executed only if a customer data file exists. The if statement invokes the exists and length methods for the File instance named customerFile. The file must exist and not have a length of zero before the method will attempt to read data. The test for zero length is necessary because it is possible that there are no records in the file.

```
if(customerFile.exists() && customerFile.length() != 0)
```

The statements that create a BufferedReader instance and invoke its readLine method to read a customer's name, address, and phone number are placed in a try block, because if an I/O error occurs, an exception will be thrown. The statement that instantiates BufferedReader also instantiates FileReader and passes this instance as an argument to the BufferedReader constructor. The argument passed to the FileReader constructor is a reference to the File instance.

```
try
{
BufferedReader in = new BufferedReader(new FileReader(customerFile));
```

Following the BufferedReader instantiation is a statement that declares String variables to contain the customer attribute values. Next comes a do loop that invokes the readLine method to read the customer's name, address, and phone number, create a customer instance, and add the customer reference to the Vector customers. This loop continues until a null value for customer phone number is detected, which means there is no more data.

```
String name, address, phoneNo;
do
{
   name = in.readLine();
   address = in.readLine();
   phoneNo = in.readLine();

   if(name != null)
      customers.addElement(new Customer(name, address, phoneNo));
} while(phoneNo != null);
```

The last part of the initialize method is a catch block that executes if an exception is thrown by any of the statements in the try block.

```
catch (Exception e)
    {System.out.println (e);}
```

The complete initialize method is shown in Figure 14-3.

14

```java
public static void initialize()
{
    customers = new Vector();
    if(customerFile.exists() && customerFile.length() != 0)
    {
        try
        {
            BufferedReader in = new BufferedReader(new FileReader
(customerFile));

            String name, address, phoneNo;
            do
            {
                name = in.readLine();
                address = in.readLine();
                phoneNo = in.readLine();

                if(name != null)
                    customers.addElement(new Customer(name, address,
phoneNo));
            } while(phoneNo != null);

        }

        catch (Exception e)
            {System.out.println (e);}
    }
```

Figure 14-3   CustomerDA initialize method for sequential file storage

The terminate Method

The terminate method is responsible for creating a file that contains attribute values for all the customer instances referenced by the Vector customers. First, the method creates an instance of PrintStream, using an instance of FileOutputStream (and File) as arguments. Next it iterates the customers Vector. For each customer reference, attribute values are obtained by invoking accessor methods; these values are then written to the sequential file by invoking the println method. All of this code is placed within a try block because an I/O error can occur, which would cause an exception to be thrown. The terminate method is shown in Figure 14-4.

```java
public static void terminate()
{
    try
    {
        // create PrintStream for output
        PrintStream out = new PrintStream(new FileOutputStream
(customerFile));

        for(int i = 0; i < customers.size(); i++)
        {
            Customer aCustomer = (Customer) customers.elementAt(i);
```

```
                out.println(aCustomer.getName());
                out.println(aCustomer.getAddress());
                out.println(aCustomer.getPhoneNo());
            }
        }

    catch (Exception e)
        {System.out.println (e);}
}
```

Figure 14-4   CustomerDA terminate method for sequential file storage

The find Method

All of the existing customer instances are referenced by the Vector instance named customers. Therefore, the find method simply iterates the customers Vector, seeking a customer instance with a phone number that matches the value received by the method. If the customer is found, its reference is returned. If no customer is found, a NotFoundException is thrown. The find method is shown in Figure 14-5.

```
public static Customer find(String phoneNo) throws NotFoundException
{
    Customer   aCustomer = null;
    boolean foundIt = false;

    for(int i = 0; i < customers.size() && !foundIt; i++)
    {
        aCustomer = (Customer) customers.elementAt(i);
        if(phoneNo.equals(aCustomer.getPhoneNo()))
            foundIt = true;
    }
    if(foundIt)
        return aCustomer;
    else
        throw (new  NotFoundException("not found "));
}
```

Figure 14-5   CustomerDA find method for sequential file storage

The first statement declares a customer reference variable named **aCustomer** and initializes it to a null value. The second statement declares a boolean variable named **foundIt** and initializes its value to **false**.

Next comes a for loop that iterates customers. The first statement in the loop retrieves a reference to the customer instance at Vector element **i**. Then, an if statement invokes the String equals method to see if there is a matching phone number. If a match is identified, then **foundIt** is set to **true**, which terminates the loop. Note that the loop will also terminate if the end of the Vector instance is reached (loop counter variable **i** becomes equal to the value returned by the size method).

14

At the end of the find method, an if statement interrogates the value of `foundIt`. If the value is true, then a reference to the customer instance is returned; if false, then an instance of Not-FoundException is created and thrown to the invoking method.

The addNew Method

Invoke this method to add a customer to the system. Because all customer references in this example are stored in a Vector, addNew adds the new reference to the Vector after checking for a duplicate phone number (in this example duplicate is assumed to be found). The method is shown in Figure 14-6.

```java
public static void addNew(Customer aCustomer) throws DuplicateException
{
    boolean duplicate = false;

    for(int i = 0; i < customers.size() && !duplicate; i++)
    {
        Customer existingCustomer = (Customer) customers.elementAt(i);
        if(existingCustomer.getPhoneNo().equals(aCustomer.getPhoneNo()))
            duplicate = true;
    }
    if(duplicate)
        throw (new  DuplicateException(" Customer Already Exists "));
    else
        customers.addElement(aCustomer);
}
```

Figure 14-6   CustomerDA addNew method for sequential file storage

The method begins by declaring a boolean variable named **duplicate** and initializing it to **false**. Next, a two-statement for loop searches the customers Vector to determine whether this customer already exists; if it does, a DuplicateException is thrown. The loop terminates whenever a duplicate customer is detected or the end of the Vector is reached.

The first statement within the loop retrieves the customer reference. Note that the retrieved reference must be cast to data type Customer because references contained in a Vector are data type Object. The second statement invokes the String equals method to see if there is a match between the new customer's phone number and the existing customer's number. If a match is found, duplicate is set to **true** and the loop terminates.

The if statement following the loop tests the contents of the duplicate variable. If it is **true**, then an instance of DuplicateException is created and thrown. However, if duplicate contains **false**, a reference for the new customer is added to the Vector.

The update Method

The update method for sequential file storage contains no code because nothing needs to be done. Updates are made to the customer instance by invoking accessor methods (setName, setAddress, setPhoneNo), which change the attribute values for the specified instance. When processing concludes, the terminate method writes the attribute values for all of the instances to a sequential file. The method is shown in Figure 14-7.

```
public static void update(Customer aCustomer) throws NotFoundException
   {}
```

Figure 14-7   CustomerDA update method for sequential file storage

The delete Method

The delete method removes a customer from the system. In a sequential file, you delete a customer by removing the reference for the customer instance from the Vector. The method is shown in Figure 14-8.

```
public static void delete(Customer aCustomer) throws NotFoundException
{
    String phoneNo = aCustomer.getPhoneNo();
    boolean foundIt = false;

    for(int i = 0; i < customers.size() && !foundIt; i++)
    {
        aCustomer = (Customer) customers.elementAt(i);
        if(phoneNo.equals(aCustomer.getPhoneNo()))
            {
                foundIt = true;
                customers.removeElementAt(i);
            }
    }
    if(!foundIt)
        throw (new NotFoundException("not found "));
}
```

Figure 14-8   CustomerDA delete method for sequential file storage

The method begins by invoking the getPhoneNo accessor method to obtain the customer's telephone number. Next, a boolean variable named `foundIt` is declared and initialized to `false`. Then a for loop iterates the Vector, seeking a reference for the customer with a matching telephone number. If a matching customer is found, the reference is removed from the Vector by invoking removeElementAt, passing the index of the reference. If no matching customer is found, then the method throws a NotFoundException.

The getAll Method

The Vector instance named customers contains references to all existing customer instances. The getAll method simply returns a reference to this Vector. The invoking method can then retrieve the desired customer reference from the Vector. The method is shown in Figure 14-9.

14

```
public static Vector getAll()
   {return customers;}
```

Figure 14-9 CustomerDA getAll method for sequential file storage

The DuplicateException and NotFoundException Classes

The DA class uses the DuplicateException and NotFoundException classes to inform the invoking client of a problem. Their design follows that presented in earlier chapters. Figure 14–10 shows these two classes.

```
public class DuplicateException extends Exception
{
   public DuplicateException(String message)
      { super(message);}
}

public class NotFoundException extends Exception
{
   public NotFoundException(String message)
      { super(message);}
}
```

Figure 14-10 DuplicateException and NotFoundException classes

Testing CustomerDA for a Sequential File Implementation

In this section you will write a class named TesterOne to exercise the DA methods you developed in the previous sections. TesterOne will be described in some detail here, because it is used without modification in the random access, object serialization, and relational database examples later in this chapter. This tester class will complete the following tasks:

1. Create two new customer instances.

2. Invoke the initialize method.

3. Invoke addNew to add the two new customers to storage.

4. Retrieve a reference to the first customer by invoking find.

5. Invoke getAll to retrieve references to both customers.

6. Invoke delete for the second customer and verify the deletion.

7. Change the first customer's address and verify the change.

8. Invoke the terminate method.

These tasks are shown graphically in the sequence diagram in Figure 14–11. Note that to reduce clutter, the sequence diagram omits the invocation of accessor and display methods.

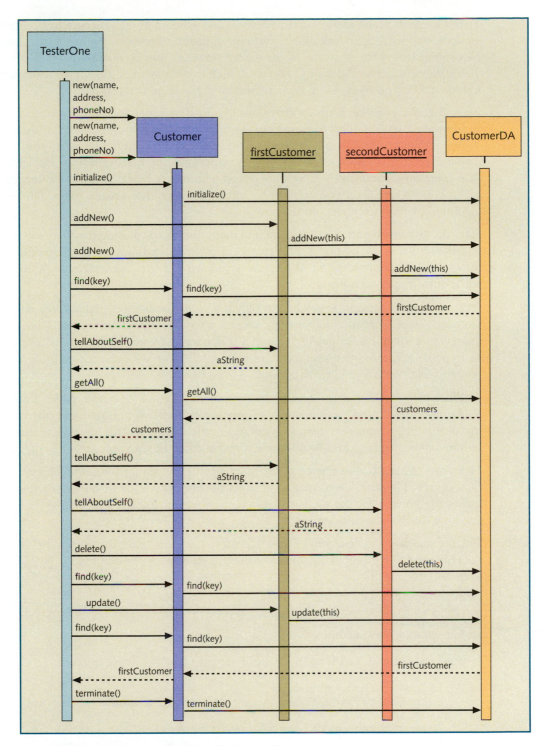

Figure 14-11   Sequence diagram for TesterOne

14

TesterOne first creates two customer instances and stores their references in firstCustomer and secondCustomer, respectively. Next, it invokes initialize to prepare for subsequent processing. Note that TesterOne is aware of the Customer class, but is not aware of CustomerDA. TesterOne invokes methods in Customer, which in turn invokes the appropriate methods in CustomerDA. This relationship is clearly shown in the sequence diagram.

Next, TesterOne invokes addNew twice, once for firstCustomer and once for secondCustomer, to add these two customers to storage. In this example, the customer references are stored in a Vector instance, which is not written to the sequential file until the terminate method is invoked. However, TesterOne is completely unaware of the specific storage implementation. The statements that invoke addNew are placed within a try block because addNew can throw a DuplicateException if you attempt to add a customer that already exists. Customers are identified by their telephone number.

After the two customers are added, the find method is invoked using the first customer's telephone number as an argument. This statement is also placed in a try block because find can throw a NotFoundException. When the reference for the first customer is returned, its tellAboutSelf method is invoked.

Next, the getAll method is invoked to obtain a Vector instance containing references for all customers stored. In this example, there are only two customers: Eleanor and Mike. Following the statement that invokes getAll is a loop that iterates the Vector instance, which was returned to retrieve each customer reference and invoke tellAboutSelf for each of them. The string returned from tellAboutSelf is then displayed.

The delete method is then invoked to remove the second customer, Mike, from storage. Remember that TesterOne is unaware of how the customer is removed, but that after invoking delete, the customer is simply gone. Again, the statement that invokes delete is placed within a try block because a NotFoundException could be thrown.

Next, the address for the first customer is changed by invoking the setAddress method, and then update. The setAddress method changes the attribute value in the instance, and update makes the change for the persistent data somewhere in storage. The change is verified by invoking find for the first customer.

The last statement in TesterOne invokes terminate, which writes the customers' attributes to the sequential file, thus making them persistent. TesterOne is listed in Figure 14-12; its output is shown in Figure 14-13.

```java
import java.util.Vector;
public class TesterOne
{
    public static void main(String args[])
    {
        // create two customers
        Customer firstCustomer = new Customer("Eleanor", "Atlanta",
"123-4567");
        Customer secondCustomer = new Customer("Mike", "Boston", "467-
1234");
        Customer.initialize();
```

```
        try // test addNew
        {
            firstCustomer.addNew();
            secondCustomer.addNew();
            System.out.println("added two customers");
        }
        catch(DuplicateException e)
            {System.out.println(e);}

        try // test find
        {
            firstCustomer = Customer.find("123-4567");
            System.out.println("find " + firstCustomer.tellAboutSelf());
        }
        catch(NotFoundException e)
            {System.out.println(e);}

        // test getAll
        Vector allCustomers = Customer.getAll();
        for(int i = 0; i < allCustomers.size(); i++)
        {   // display attributes for each customer retrieved
            firstCustomer = (Customer) allCustomers.elementAt(i);
            System.out.println("getAll " +
firstCustomer.tellAboutSelf());
        }

        try // test delete
        {   // delete Mike
            secondCustomer.delete();
            System.out.println("delete " +
secondCustomer.tellAboutSelf());
            // try to find the customer just deleted
            secondCustomer = Customer.find("467-1234");
            System.out.println("find " + secondCustomer.tellAboutSelf());
        }
        catch(NotFoundException e)
            {System.out.println(e);}

        try // test update
        {       // change address for Eleanor
            firstCustomer = Customer.find("123-4567");
            firstCustomer.setAddress("Clayton");
            firstCustomer.update();
            // display address after change
            firstCustomer = Customer.find("123-4567");
            System.out.println("update " +
firstCustomer.tellAboutSelf());
        }
        catch(NotFoundException e)
            {System.out.println(e);}

        Customer.terminate();
    }
}
```

Figure 14-12   TesterOne listing

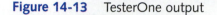

added two customers

find Eleanor, Atlanta, 123-4567

getAll Eleanor, Atlanta, 123-4567

getAll Mike, Boston, 467-1234

delete Mike, Boston, 467-1234

NotFoundException: not found

update Eleanor, Clayton, 123-4567

Figure 14-13   TesterOne output

Hands-on Exercise 1

1. Create a folder named Chapter14Exercise1 on your system.

2. Copy all the Java source files from the Chapter14/Example1 folder on your book's CD to the Chapter14Exercise1 folder on your system. This folder includes Customer.java, CustomerDA.java, DuplicateException.java, NotFoundException.java, and TesterOne.java.

3. Note that CustomerDA will use drive A for the Customer.dat file, unless you alter the File statement at the beginning of the class. If in doubt, ask your instructor where to place the Customer.dat file.

4. Compile these programs using the software recommended by your instructor.

5. Run TesterOne and verify that the program output is as shown in Figure 14-13.

Implementing Persistence With a Random Access File

This section illustrates the benefit of isolating I/O chores in a DA class. Changing the storage implementation from sequential to random access involves changing the file specification to `A:/Customer.ran` and making minor changes to the initialize and terminate methods in CustomerDA. No other classes are affected, and you use the same Customer and Tester classes with no modification. In fact, you will continue to use the Customer and Tester classes from the sequential file example in later sections that describe implementation with object serialization and databases.

The CustomerDA initialize method for sequential file access instantiated BufferedReader. To use a random access file, you instantiate RandomAccessFile instead. This is the only modification required in initialize; the change is shown in boldface in Figure 14-14.

```
public static void initialize()
{
customers = new Vector();
if(customerFile.exists()&& customerFile.length() != 0)
{
    // read all customers in, create instances, populate Vector
    try
    {
        RandomAccessFile in = new RandomAccessFile(customerFile,"r");
        String name = in.readLine();
        String address = in.readLine();
        String phoneNo = in.readLine();
        while(name != null)
        {
            customers.addElement(new Customer(name, address, phoneNo));
            name = in.readLine();
            address = in.readLine();
            phoneNo = in.readLine();
        }
    }
    catch (Exception e)
        {System.out.println (e);}
}
```

Figure 14-14   CustomerDA initialize method for random access file storage

Similarly, the terminate method in CustomerDA for sequential file storage instantiated PrintStream and invoked its println method to output the attribute values. When using a random access file, you instantiate RandomAccessFile and then invoke its writeBytes method to output the attribute values. Figure 14–15 shows the terminate method for a random access file, with the modifications shown in boldface.

```
public static void terminate()
{
    try
    {
        RandomAccessFile out = new RandomAccessFile(customerFile, "rw");

        for(int i = 0; i < customers.size(); i++)
        {
            if(customers.elementAt(i) != null)
            {
                // '\r' is carriage return character used as delimiter
                Customer aCustomer = (Customer) customers.elementAt(i);
                out.writeBytes(aCustomer.getName()+'\r');
                out.writeBytes(aCustomer.getAddress()+'\r');
```

14

```
            out.writeBytes(aCustomer.getPhoneNo()+'\r');
        }
    }
    out.close();
    }
catch (Exception e)
    {System.out.println (e);}
}
```

Figure 14-15   CustomerDA terminate method for random access file storage

As you saw earlier, the only modifications required to switch from sequential file to random file persistence were made to CustomerDA. You use exactly the same Customer and Tester classes, and the output is identical.

Hands-on Exercise 2

1. Create a folder named Chapter14Exercise2 on your system.

2. Copy CustomerDA.java from the Chapter14/Example2 folder on your book's CD to the Chapter14Exercise2 folder on your system.

3. Because the *only* class modified to switch from sequential to random access file storage is CustomerDA.java, you copy Customer.java, DuplicateException.java, NotFoundException.java, and TesterOne.java from your Chapter14Exercise1 folder to your Chapter14Exercise2 folder.

4. Note that CustomerDA will use drive A for the Customer.ran file, unless you alter the File statement at the beginning of the class. If in doubt, ask your instructor where to place Customer.ran.

5. Compile these programs using the software recommended by your instructor. Run TesterOne and verify that the program output is as shown in Figure 14-13.

Implementing Persistence With Object Serialization

When you implement persistence using object serialization, you employ object storage that stores entire instances. This approach contrasts with the attribute storage techniques you saw earlier. With object serialization, you write instances to a file and then read them later. Instances are retrieved intact, so you do not need to re-create them.

Changing from a random access file to object serialization involves changing the file specification to `A:/Customer.obj` and changing the initialize and terminate methods in CustomerDA. No other classes are affected, and as in the previous example, you use the same Customer and Tester classes with no modification.

The CustomerDA initialize method for random file access instantiated RandomAccessFile and invoked its readLine method to read the attribute values. With object serialization, you instantiate ObjectInputStream and invoke its readObject method. This initialize method uses a while loop to read each customer instance from the file and add its reference to the Vector. The loop terminates when the end of the file is reached and the boolean variable `eof` becomes `true`. If end of file is detected while reading objects, the readObject method throws an EndOfFileException, and the catch block for this exception sets `eof` to `true`, which terminates the loop. The CustomerDA initialize method, with modifications for object serialization, is shown in Figure 14-16.

```java
public static void initialize()
{
   customers = new Vector();
   boolean eof = false;      // end of file

   if(customerFile.exists()&& customerFile.length() != 0)
   {
      try
      {
         ObjectInputStream in = new ObjectInputStream(new
FileInputStream (customerFile));
         while(!eof) // loop until end of file
         {
            try
               { customers.addElement(in.readObject()); }
            catch(EOFException e)
               {eof = true;}
         }
      }
      catch (Exception e)
         {System.out.println (e);}
   }
}
```

Figure 14-16   CustomerDA initialize method for object serialization

14

The terminate method in CustomerDA for random access file storage instantiated RandomAccessFile and invoked its writeBytes method to output the attribute values. When using a serialized file, you instantiate ObjectOutputStream and then invoke its writeObject method to output each instance. The method logic is to retrieve each customer reference from the Vector, as in the previous section. Here, however, the writeObject method is invoked to write the instance to the file instead of writing the individual attribute values. Figure 14-17 shows the terminate method with modifications for using object serialization. Notice that after all instances have been written to the file, the ObjectOutputStream close method is invoked. This is necessary to complete the output process.

```java
public static void terminate()
{
    try
    {
        ObjectOutputStream out = new ObjectOutputStream(new FileOutput-
Stream (customerFile));
        for(int i = 0; i < customers.size(); i++)
        {
            if(customers.elementAt(i) != null)
                out.writeObject(customers.elementAt(i)
        }

        out.close();
    }
    catch (Exception e)
        {System.out.println (e);}
}
```

Figure 14-17   CustomerDA terminate method for object serialization

Like the previous two examples, the modifications required for object serialization were made to CustomerDA. Here, however, you must make a minor change to the Customer class by adding the clause **implements** `java.io.Serializable` to the class header. This clause implements the Serializable interface, which then permits customer instances to be stored in a file. You will continue to use the same Tester class as before, and the output is identical.

Hands-on Exercise 3

1. Create a folder named Chapter14Exercise3 on your system.

2. Copy Customer.java and CustomerDA.java from the Chapter14/Example3 folder on your book's CD to the Chapter14Exercise3 folder on your system.

3. You use the same Exception and Tester classes; therefore, copy DuplicateException.java, NotFoundException.java, and TesterOne.java from your Chapter14Exercise1 folder to your Chapter14Exercise3 folder.

4. Note that CustomerDA will use drive A for the Customer.obj file, unless you alter the File statement at the beginning of the class. If in doubt, ask your instructor where to place Customer.obj.

5. Compile these programs using the software recommended by your instructor.

6. Run TesterOne and verify that the program output is as shown in Figure 14–13.

DESIGNING A RELATIONAL DATABASE

A relational database provides tools for you to organize data into tables. Each column represents a field and each row represents a record. Figure 14–18 shows the table used in this example for customers. Each customer is identified by his or her telephone number. A field used to uniquely identify a record is called a **primary key**. Primary keys are described and illustrated more thoroughly in Chapter 15. In the following sections, you will learn how to use the SQL language to access a relational database and then design a CustomerDA class with methods that implement persistence with a database.

The examples in this book use the Microsoft Access relational database software. Two protocols are required to access this database: **Java Database Connectivity (JDBC)** and **Open Database Connectivity (ODBC)**. JDBC is the Sun Microsystems protocol for database connectivity, and ODBC is a protocol that provides methods to the Microsoft Access database. In addition, a driver named JdbcOdbcDriver, which serves as a bridge connecting JDBC and ODBC, is provided with the JDK. When you use other vendors' databases, you use their ODBC drivers.

ODBC requires the database to be registered as a **data source name**. This data source name is then used instead of the actual database.

14

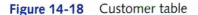

Each column represents an attribute value

Each row represents a customer

CustomerTable : Table		
Name	**Address**	**PhoneNo**
Eleanor	Atlanta	123-4567
Mike	Boston	467-1234

Figure 14-18 Customer table

Hands-on Exercise 4

In this exercise you will copy the customer database to your system and register it as a data source name with ODBC. This step is necessary in order for you to complete Hands-on Exercise 5.

1. Create a folder named Chapter14Exercise4 on your system.

2. Copy the database file named Customers.mdb from the Chapter14/Example4 folder on your book's CD to the Chapter14Exercise4 folder you created in Step 1.

3. Click the **Start** button on the Windows taskbar, point to **Settings**, and then click **Control Panel**.

4. Double-click the **Administrative Tools** icon. Then double-click the **Data Sources (ODBC)** icon. The ODBC Data Source Administrator window appears.

5. On the **User DSN** tab, click **MS Access Database** from the list of data source names, and then click **Add**. The Create New Data Source dialog box appears.

6. Make sure that **Microsoft Access Driver (*.mdb)** is selected, and then click **Finish**. The ODBC Microsoft Access Setup dialog box appears.

7. Enter **Chapter14CustomerDatabase** in the Data Source Name field, and then click the **Select** button.

8. In the right pane of the Select Database window, open the folder on your hard disk that contains the Customers.mdb file.

9. Click **Customers.mdb** in the left pane, and then click **OK**.

10. Click **OK** to close the other ODBC windows, and then close the Control Panel window.

11. To ensure that the database file copied from the CD is not write-protected, check the file properties.
    a. Start Windows Explorer and locate the **Customers.mdb** file.
    b. Right-click **Customers.mdb**, and then click **Properties**.
    c. If the Read-only attribute is checked, uncheck it and click **OK**. Otherwise, click **Cancel**. Close Windows Explorer.

Understanding the Structured Query Language (SQL)

The **Structured Query Language (SQL)** is a popular, standardized language used to access relational databases. This section introduces SQL basics and illustrates four SQL statements. For a more complete discussion, see Chapter 15.

You previously learned that a DA class performs four basic tasks: retrieve a customer, store a customer, change a customer's data, and delete a customer. You also saw that these functions are implemented in the DA class using methods named find, addNew, update, and delete. When you use a relational database, these four methods invoke methods in the Statement class to execute SQL statements.

The find method uses the SQL SELECT statement to retrieve a specific customer's record from the database. The SQL statement to retrieve Eleanor's record is:

```
SELECT Name, Address, PhoneNo FROM CustomerTable
    WHERE PhoneNo = '123-4567'
```

The keyword SELECT is shown here in uppercase; however, SQL is not case-sensitive, so you could write it as `Select` or `select`. The table column names `Name`, `Address`, and `PhoneNo` are listed next because you want to retrieve these values for the customer. `CustomerTable` is the name of the database table to be searched. Within a single database, you can have multiple tables, so you must specify the table from which you want data retrieved. You will work with multiple tables in Chapter 15. The clause `WHERE PhoneNo = '123-4567'` indicates the key of the customer you are seeking. Instead of using a literal value for the telephone number, you could use a variable. Notice that String values are enclosed in single quotes.

The addNew method uses the SQL INSERT statement to add a new customer's record to the database. For example, the following SQL statement will add a customer's record to the database. The variables following the VALUES keyword contain the attribute values for the customer to be added. You could use literal values instead of the name, address, and phoneNumber variables. The SQL keywords are shown in uppercase. Note that you must specify the table and table column names.

```
INSERT INTO CustomerTable (Name, Address, PhoneNo)
    VALUES  (name, address, phoneNumber)
```

The update method employs the SQL UPDATE statement to change the contents of one or more fields in a customer's record. The following SQL statement replaces the customer's name and address with the values contained in the variables.

```
UPDATE CustomerTable SET Name = name, Address = address
WHERE PhoneNo = phoneNumber
```

The delete method executes the SQL DELETE statement, which specifies the key value of the customer to be deleted.

```
DELETE FROM CustomerTable WHERE PhoneNo = phoneNumber
```

Understanding the java.sql Package

The java.sql package contains the classes with methods you invoke when working with relational databases in Java. The four classes you will use in this chapter are listed in Table 14-2 with brief descriptions.

14

Table 14-2   Selected Classes in the java.sql Package

Class Name	Description
DriverManager	getConnection method establishes a connection to the database and returns a connection instance
Connection	createStatement method returns a statement instance, which is used to execute SQL statements
Statement	contains methods that execute SQL statements: executeQuery for SQL INSERT executeUpdate for SQL INSERT, UPDATE, and DELETE
ResultSet	Instance containing data is returned by the Statement method executeQuery. The data contains 0 to n rows of data depending on the specific SQL SELECT that was executed. ResultSet methods next, first, last, and previous point the cursor to a specific row. Methods getInt, getString, etc., retrieve data from a row.

Implementing Persistence With a Database

The previous examples of persistence—sequential file, random access file, and object serialization—had the initialize method read in all the customers and store their references in a Vector. Then the various methods manipulated the customer instances using the Vector. When processing was complete, the terminate method wrote the customers back to a file.

A relational database calls for a different approach. The initialize method establishes a connection to the database, the processing methods find, addNew, update, delete, and getAll access the database directly, and the terminate method severs the database connection to release system resources.

The CustomerDA class for a relational database, in addition to importing Vector and the java.io package, imports the java.sql package.

```
import java.util.Vector;
import java.io.*;
import java.sql.*;
```

Like the previous CustomerDA classes you saw, this one also has two variables declared with class scope. The first is a Vector reference variable named customers, which contains references to all the customer instances. The second, also a reference variable, is a customer reference variable.

```
static Vector customers;
static Customer aCustomer;
```

Next comes a statement that creates a String variable containing the data source name you established in Hands-on Exercise 4, followed by statements that declare reference variables for the Connection and Statement classes, and String variables for the customer name, address, and phone number.

```
// The Data Source name is "Chapter14CustomerDatabase"
static String url = "jdbc:odbc:Chapter14CustomerDatabase";
static Connection aConnection;
static Statement aStatement;

// declare variables for Customer attribute values
static String name;
static String address;
static String phoneNumber;
```

The initialize Method

The purpose of the initialize method in this example is to load the JDBC–ODBC driver and create a connection instance that links to the database. The driver is loaded by invoking the Class method forName, and the connection instance is created by invoking the getConnection method in the DriverManager class. The forName method can throw a ClassNotFoundException and getConnection can throw a SQLException; therefore, the statements that invoke these methods are placed into try blocks and the appropriate catch blocks follow.

The complete initialize method is shown in Figure 14-19.

```
public static void initialize()
{
    try
    {
        // load the jdbc - odbc bridge driver for Windows
        Class.forName("sun.jdbc.odbc.JdbcOdbcDriver");
        // create connection instance
        aConnection = DriverManager.getConnection(url, "", "");
        // create statement object instance for this connection
        aStatement = aConnection.createStatement();
    }
    catch (ClassNotFoundException e)
        {System.out.println(e);}
    catch (SQLException e)
        { System.out.println(e);    }
}
```

Figure 14-19   CustomerDA initialize method for a relational database

14

The terminate Method

The terminate method for a relational database is considerably simpler and shorter than in the previous implementations. Here, terminate simply invokes the close method for both the statement and connection instances. This code is placed within a try block because a SQLException will be thrown if an error is detected. The terminate method is shown in Figure 14-20.

```java
public static void terminate()
{
    try
    {    // close everything
        aStatement.close();
        aConnection.close();
    }
    catch (SQLException e)
        { System.out.println(e); }
}
```

Figure 14-20   CustomerDA terminate method for a relational database

The find Method

The logic of the find method is straightforward. It uses the SQL SELECT statement to retrieve a specific customer's attribute values from the database. These values are returned within an instance of ResultSet whose methods are then invoked to extract the attribute values. A customer instance is then created and returned to the invoking method. If the desired customer is not found, the method throws a NotFoundException. The find method is shown in Figure 14-21.

```java
public static Customer find(String key) throws NotFoundException
{
    aCustomer = null;

    // define the SQL query statement using the phone number key
    String sqlQuery = "SELECT Name, Address, PhoneNo FROM CustomerTable
" + "WHERE PhoneNo = '" + key +"'";

    // execute the SQL query statement
    try
    {
        ResultSet rs = aStatement.executeQuery(sqlQuery);
        // next method sets cursor & returns true if there is data
        boolean gotIt = rs.next();
```

```
   if (gotIt)
   {
       // extract the data
       String name = rs.getString(1);
       String address = rs.getString(2);
       String phoneNumber = rs.getString(3);
       // create Customer instance
       aCustomer = new Customer(name, address, phoneNumber);
   }
   else
   {
       // nothing was retrieved
       throw (new NotFoundException("not found "));
   }
   rs.close();
}

catch (SQLException e)
   { System.out.println(e);}

return aCustomer;
}
```

Figure 14-21   CustomerDA find method for a relational database

The first statement declares a customer reference variable named aCustomer and initializes it to a null value. The second statement declares a String variable containing the SQL SELECT statement. Next the Statement executeQuery method is executed. The argument passed to this method is a String containing the SQL statement. Notice that this method returns an instance of ResultSet. The ResultSet method named next is then invoked to point to the row of data within the ResultSet instance. This method returns a boolean value. If the method returns true, then the getString methods are invoked to extract the customer's name, address, and phone number, and a customer instance is created. However, if the next method returns false, the ResultSet instance contains no data and a NotFoundException is created and thrown. The last line in the method returns the customer reference.

The addNew Method

Invoke this method to add a customer to the system by executing an SQL INSERT statement. The method first invokes the Customer accessor methods to obtain the attribute values, then invokes the find method to see whether this customer already exists. If it does, a DuplicateException is thrown. The statement that invokes the find method is placed in a try block, and if the customer is not a duplicate, a NotFoundException is thrown. The catch block for the NotFoundException invokes the executeUpdate method to execute the SQL INSERT statement. The method is shown in Figure 14-22.

14

```
public static void addNew(Customer aCustomer) throws DuplicateException
{
    // retrieve the customer attribute values
    name = aCustomer.getName();
    address = aCustomer.getAddress();
    phoneNumber = aCustomer.getPhoneNo();

    // create the SQL insert statement using attribute values
    String sqlInsert = "INSERT INTO CustomerTable (Name, Address,
PhoneNo)" +  "VALUES ('" +
                            name        + "', '" +
                            address     + "', '" +
                            phoneNumber + "')";

    // see if this customer already exists in the database
    try
    {
        Customer c = find(phoneNumber);
        throw (new DuplicateException("Customer Exists "));
    }

    // if NotFoundException, add customer to database
    catch(NotFoundException e)
    {
        try
        {
            // execute the SQL update statement
            int result = aStatement.executeUpdate(sqlInsert);
        }
        catch (SQLException ee)
            { System.out.println(ee); }
    }
}
```

Figure 14-22   CustomerDA addNew method for a relational database

The update Method

The update method for a relational database first invokes accessor methods to retrieve the customer's attribute values and then invokes the find method to ensure that the customer record exists. If the customer is not found, the find method throws a NotFoundException and the update method rethrows it to the invoking client method. If the customer's record is found, then the executeUpdate method for the statement instance is invoked to execute the SQL UPDATE statement. The method is shown in Figure 14–23.

```
public static void update(Customer aCustomer) throws NotFoundException
{
    // retrieve the customer attribute values
    phoneNumber = aCustomer.getPhoneNo();
    name = aCustomer.getName();
    address = aCustomer.getAddress();
```

```
// define the SQL query statement using the phone number key
String sqlUpdate = "Update CustomerTable " +
                   " SET Name      = '" + name +"', " +
                   " address    = '" + address +"' " +
                   " WHERE PhoneNo = '" + phoneNumber +"'";
// see if this customer already exists in the database
// NotFoundException is thrown by find method
try
{
    Customer c = Customer.find(phoneNumber);
    // if found, execute the SQL update statement to delete
    int result = aStatement.executeUpdate(sqlUpdate);
}

catch (SQLException ee)
    { System.out.println(ee); }
}
```

Figure 14-23   CustomerDA update method for a relational database

The delete Method

The delete method for a relational database is similar to the update method. First, the Customer accessor method getPhoneNo is invoked to get the customer's phone number. Then the find method is invoked to see if the customer record for this phone number exists. If the customer record does not exist, a NotFoundException is thrown, which is then rethrown by the delete method. If the customer record is found, then the Statement executeUpdate method is invoked to execute the SQL DELETE statement. The method is shown in Figure 14-24.

```
public static void delete(Customer aCustomer) throws NotFoundException
{
    // retrieve the phone no (key)
    phoneNumber = aCustomer.getPhoneNo();

    // create the SQL delete statement
    String sqlDelete = "DELETE FROM CustomerTable " +
                       "WHERE PhoneNo = '" + phoneNumber +"'";

    // see if this customer already exists in the database
    // NotFoundException is thrown by find method
    try
    {
        Customer c = Customer.find(phoneNumber);
        // if found, execute the SQL update statement
        int result = aStatement.executeUpdate(sqlDelete);
    }
    catch (SQLException e)
        { System.out.println(e); }
}
```

Figure 14-24   CustomerDA delete method for a relational database

14

The getAll Method

The getAll method for a relational database illustrates how to work with a ResultSet instance that contains multiple rows of data. Like find, getAll invokes the Statement method execute-Query to execute an SQL SELECT statement. The SQL statement for getAll, however, does not specify a specific customer's phone number, so the attributes for all customers are retrieved and stored in a ResultSet instance. The next method is invoked, pointing the cursor to the first row of data and returning true if data exists; otherwise, it returns false. The if statement is executed; within this statement is a while loop that iterates the rows of the ResultSet instance. Each iteration retrieves a customer's name, address, and phone number, creates a customer instance, and adds the customer's reference to a Vector. After retrieving all rows of the result set, the Vector reference named customers is returned to the invoking method. The getAll method is shown in Figure 14-25.

```java
public static Vector getAll()
{
    // define the SQL query statement
    String sqlQuery= "SELECT Name, Address, PhoneNo FROM CustomerTable";
    try
    {
        // execute the SQL query statement
        ResultSet rs = aStatement.executeQuery(sqlQuery);
        boolean moreData = rs.next();
        if (moreData)
            // next method sets cursor & returns true if there is data
            while (moreData)
            {
                // extract the data
                name = rs.getString(1);
                address = rs.getString(2);
                phoneNumber = rs.getString(3);
                // create Customer instance
                aCustomer = new Customer(name, address, phoneNumber);
                customers.addElement(aCustomer);
                moreData = rs.next();
            }
        rs.close();
    }

    catch (SQLException e)
        { System.out.println(e);}
    return customers;
}
```

Figure 14-25 CustomerDA getAll method for a relational database

Testing CustomerDA for a Database Implementation

You can test the CustomerDA class for the relational database using the same Customer and Tester classes you used in the previous examples. The output is identical to the previous examples.

Hands-on Exercise 5

Note that this exercise uses the data source name you registered in Hands-on Exercise 4. You must complete that exercise before attempting this one.

1. Copy CustomerDA.java from the Chapter14/Example5 folder on your book's CD to the Chapter14Exercise4 folder on your system. Note that you are using the same folder you created in Hands-on Exercise 4.

2. Copy Customer.java, DuplicateException.java, NotFoundException.java, and TesterOne.java from your Chapter14Exercise1 folder to your Chapter14Exercise4 folder.

3. Compile these programs using the software recommended by your instructor.

4. Run TesterOne and verify that the program output is as shown in Figure 14–13.

Note that running TesterOne adds a customer (Eleanor) to the database. If you perform this Hands-on Exercise more than once, open Customers.mdb in the Chapter14\Exercise4 folder and delete the customers from the Customer table.

- -

Summary

- Object persistence means that you store instance data for future retrieval. You can achieve persistence by storing either attribute values or entire instances.

- You design a data access (DA) class to provide methods that store and retrieve data to make instances of PD classes persistent.

- You generally write a separate DA class for each PD class. You communicate with the DA class by invoking its methods from the corresponding PD class. Classes that require data storage and retrieval services must invoke PD methods, which in turn invoke DA methods. This restriction is imposed to isolate the DA class from all but its matching PD class.

- A DA class performs four basic tasks: retrieve, store, change, and delete. These tasks are implemented in the DA class using methods named find, addNew, update, and delete. The DA class also has a getAll method that returns a Vector referencing all PD instances, plus initialize and terminate methods.

14

- Java views data input and output as simply a flow of bytes, or a data stream. This abstraction permits you to focus on data without dealing with physical input/output devices. The java.io package contains classes with methods to input and output data to the various types of files.

- You achieved persistence in this chapter using sequential files, random access files, object serialization, and relational databases. In each case, however, only the DA class is aware of the specific storage technique being used. The same PD and Tester classes were used for each implementation.

- A relational database permits you to organize your data into tables. Each column represents an attribute and each row represents a record. The Structured Query Language (SQL) is a popular, standard language used to access relational databases. The java.sql package contains the classes with methods to invoke when working with relational databases in Java.

Key Terms

attribute storage	Java Database Connectivity (JDBC)	random access file
byte stream		record
character stream	object persistence	relational database
database	object serialization	sequential file
data source name	object storage	Structured Query Language (SQL)
data stream	Open Database Connectivity (ODBC)	Unicode
file	primary key	

Review Questions

1. SQL is a(n) _____.
   a. DBMS
   b. keyword
   c. class
   d. language

2. JDBC is a(n) _____.

   a. DBMS

   b. keyword

   c. protocol

   d. language

3. The package that contains the classes needed for database access is _____.

   a. java.io

   b. java.dbms

   c. java.sql

   d. java.rdbms

4. A relational database table always has _____.

   a. sub-tables

   b. rows and columns

   c. a key field

   d. a relationship with other tables

5. The SQL keyword _____ is used to retrieve data from a relational database.

   a. DELETE

   b. INSERT

   c. FIND

   d. SELECT

6. The DA classes are hidden from _____.

   a. GUI

   b. PD

   c. GUI and PD

   d. all but PD

7. The Statement class _____.

   a. is instantiated by invoking a Connection method

   b. has methods to execute SQL statements

   c. both a and b

   d. There is no such class.

14

8. Java treats I/O _____.

  a. as other languages do

  b. as a stream of bytes

  c. as Unicode

  d. It depends on the physical device.

9. Object serialization is a(n) _____.

  a. RDBMS tool for storing attributes

  b. Java tool for storing object instances

  c. class

  d. language

10. ODBC is a _____.

  a. DBMS

  b. keyword

  c. protocol

  d. language

11. A primary key is _____.

  a. used to identify a record

  b. a special field to sequence data

  c. an attribute of a DBMS instance

  d. part of SQL

12. The Customer class in this chapter _____.

  a. has DA methods

  b. is the only class permitted to invoke CustomerDA methods

  c. is a PD class

  d. all of the above

13. ResultSet is a _____.

  a. class

  b. keyword

  c. DBMS term

  d. language

14. NotFoundException is _____.

    a. a supplied Exception class

    b. a member of the java.exception package

    c. seldom used

    d. none of the above

15. SQLException is _____.

    a. a supplied Exception class

    b. a member of the java.exception package

    c. seldom used

    d. none of the above

Discussion Questions

1. What are the advantages and disadvantages of removing the DA methods from the CustomerPD class and permitting TesterOne to invoke them directly?

2. Do you think you can apply the Customer class from the object serialization example in Hands-on Exercise 3 to the other exercises? Why or why not?

3. Why do you think the getAll method is not used as a surrogate for find? In other words, why can you not remove the find method and instead invoke getAll, then search the Vector for the customer you want? Under what conditions might you want to take this approach?

4. This chapter did not address the use of object databases. Describe how an object database differs from a relational database.

5. Which of the implementations described in this chapter would be the best for Bradshaw Marina? Why?

14

Projects

The Customer class used in the examples in this chapter contained three attributes: name, address, and phone number. Assume that Bradshaw Marina has decided to track each customer's e-mail address.

1. Use Microsoft Access to add this new attribute to the database table. You may wish to create another database file and data source name. Review Hands-on Exercise 4 to see how to create a data source name.

2. Make the necessary modifications to the Customer, CustomerDA, and TesterOne classes used in the relational database example to accommodate this new attribute.

   a. Customer: add the attribute, write getter and setter, update constructor, tellAboutSelf.

   b. TesterOne: modify the statements that instantiate Customer to include e-mail as an argument to the constructor.

   c. CustomerDA: modify addNew, find, and update methods to accommodate the new attribute.

3. Test your modifications.

CHAPTER 15

Creating More Complex Database Applications

In this chapter you will:

♦ Understand the structure and use of multiple tables in a relational database

♦ Create a Java application that retrieves information from more than one table in a relational database

♦ Develop a database application that implements one-to-one relationships on a class diagram

♦ Develop a database application that implements one-to-many relationships on a class diagram

♦ Develop a database application that implements association classes on a class diagram

♦ Understand control-break logic

In the previous chapter, you learned several techniques for implementing object persistence. You were introduced to data access (DA) classes and their methods, and used these to create applications that read and write object attributes to sequential and random files. You learned about object serialization and how you can use it to read and write entire objects. You also learned how to develop applications that access information in a relational database using DA methods and SQL statements to retrieve, insert, update, and delete rows within a relational table.

The concepts you learned in the previous chapter provide a good foundation for developing more complex database applications. So far, however, you have worked with a relational database that contains only a single table. In practice, relational databases often include tens, hundreds, and in some cases even thousands of tables. One of the advantages of a relational database over other forms of persistence is that a relational database can easily combine information from different tables to answer questions that a business owner or manager might have. For example, while it is helpful to retrieve a list of all customers in a database or the name and address of the customer with a particular phone number, just think how much more helpful it would be to get a list of all customers and the state registration numbers of the boats they own.

In this chapter you will develop relational database applications that involve multiple tables. First, you will learn how to implement the one-to-one relationship between Customer and Boat on the Bradshaw Marina class diagram. Next, you will see how to implement the one-to-many relationship between Dock and Slip. Finally, you will learn how to implement the more complex Lease association class.

IMPLEMENTING A ONE-TO-ONE RELATIONSHIP IN A DATABASE APPLICATION

In Chapter 9 you reviewed the Bradshaw Marina class diagram. This diagram, reproduced in Figure 15-1, shows the problem domain classes the Bradshaw system needs. For now, concentrate only on the relationships between Customer and Boat. Recall that these relationships are mandatory one-to-one relationships in both directions. That is, a customer always owns exactly one boat, and a boat always belongs to exactly one customer.

In Chapter 9 you learned how to implement the one-to-one relationships between instances of these two classes, and how to navigate from one instance to another when object persistence is not required. You will now see how to implement this one-to-one association using a relational database to achieve object persistence.

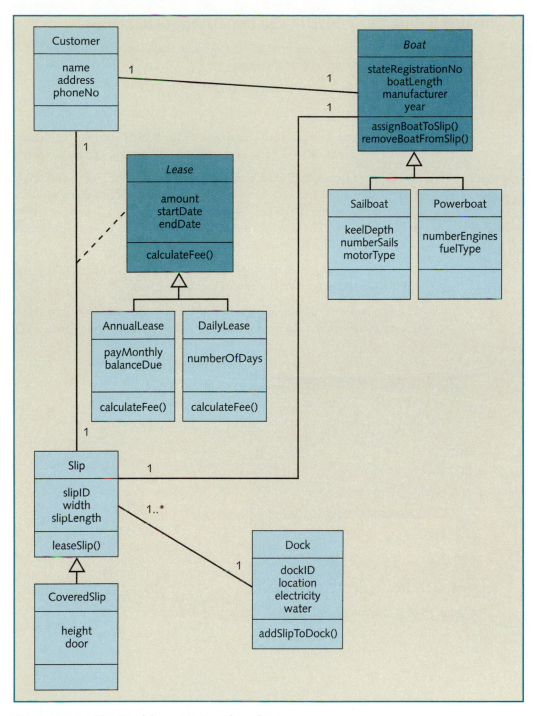

Figure 15-1   The Bradshaw Marina class diagram

Understanding the Tables in CustomerAndBoatDatabase

To develop the Java applications that use a relational database, you must first understand the structure of the tables that will be involved.

To examine the structures of the database tables:

1. Create a Chapter15Example1 folder on your system.

2. Locate **CustomerAndBoatDatabase.mdb** in the Example1 folder for this chapter on the book's CD, and copy it to the folder you created in Step 1.

3. To open CustomerAndBoatDatabase, start Microsoft Access. If you are using Access 2000, the Microsoft Access dialog box opens. If not already selected, click **Open an existing file**. Click **More Files**, and then click **OK**. See Figure 15-2. (If you are using Access 2002, click **More Files** in the Open a file section of the New File task pane.)

4. In the Open dialog box, navigate to the Chapter15Example1 folder and then double-click **CustomerAndBoatDatabase.mdb**.

5. The CustomerAndBoatDatabase window opens. This window lists the tables in this database—BoatTable and CustomerTable—as shown in Figure 15-3.

Figure 15-2 Opening a database in Microsoft Access

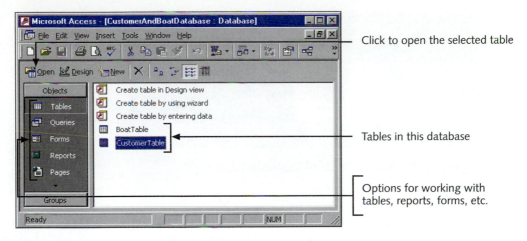

Figure 15-3 The CustomerAndBoatDatabase window

6. To view the contents of BoatTable, click **BoatTable**, and then click the **Open** button. The BoatTable window appears. Notice that it contains five fields (or columns)—StateRegistrationNo, BoatLength, Manufacturer, Year, and CustomerPhoneNo—as shown in Figure 15-4.

7. To open CustomerTable, click **CustomerTable**, then click the **Open** button. Notice that this table includes three fields—CustomerName, Address, and PhoneNo—as shown in Figure 15-5.

StateRegistrationNo	BoatLength	Manufacturer	Year	CustomerPhoneNo
MO12345	26	Ranger	1976	765-4321
MO223344	24	Tracker	1996	467-1234
MO34561	35	Tartan	1998	123-4567
MO457812	19	Ranger	2001	587-4321
MO54321	30	Bayliner	2001	321-4567
MO98765	28	J-Boat	1986	467-1122

Figure 15-4 The contents of BoatTable

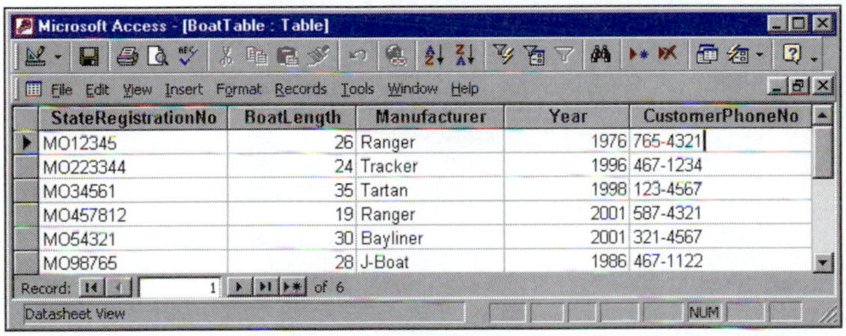

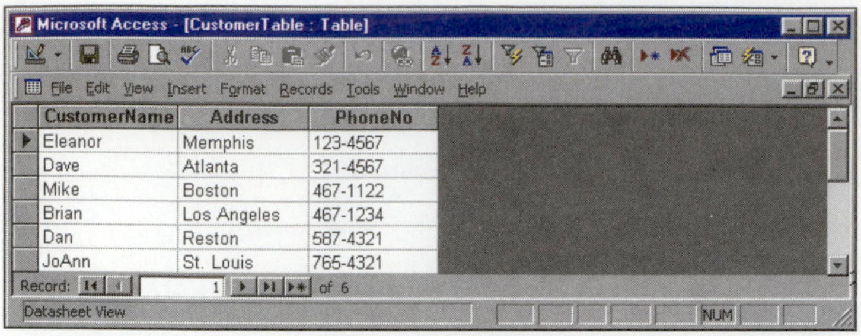

CustomerName	Address	PhoneNo
Eleanor	Memphis	123-4567
Dave	Atlanta	321-4567
Mike	Boston	467-1122
Brian	Los Angeles	467-1234
Dan	Reston	587-4321
JoAnn	St. Louis	765-4321

Figure 15-5 The contents of CustomerTable

Recall that a primary key is a field that uniquely identifies each record in a relational table. The primary key of CustomerTable is PhoneNo, and the primary key of BoatTable is StateRegistrationNo. However, the PhoneNo field in CustomerTable and the CustomerPhoneNo field in BoatTable contain exactly the same information. See Figure 15-6.

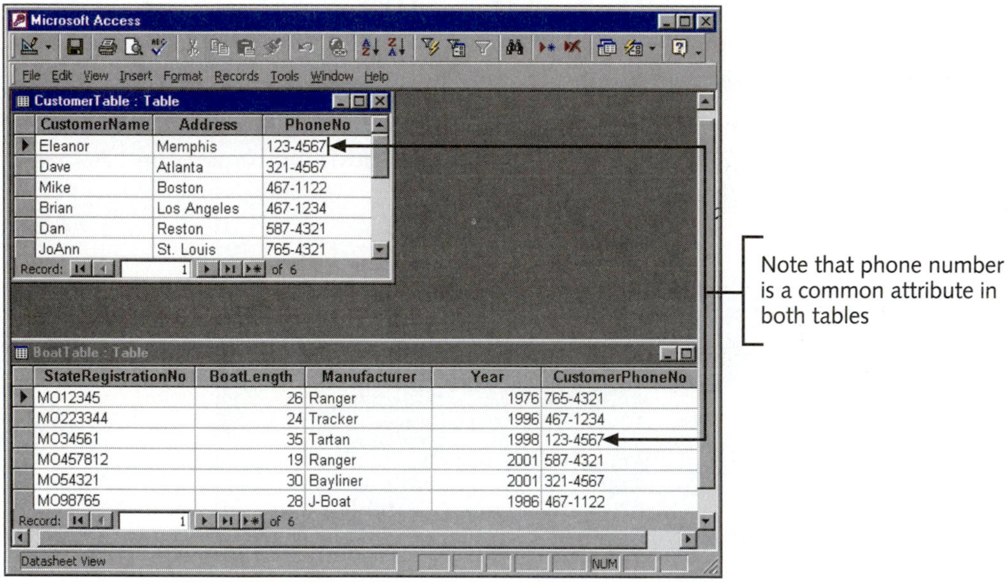

CustomerName	Address	PhoneNo
Eleanor	Memphis	123-4567
Dave	Atlanta	321-4567
Mike	Boston	467-1122
Brian	Los Angeles	467-1234
Dan	Reston	587-4321
JoAnn	St. Louis	765-4321

StateRegistrationNo	BoatLength	Manufacturer	Year	CustomerPhoneNo
MO12345	26	Ranger	1976	765-4321
MO223344	24	Tracker	1996	467-1234
MO34561	35	Tartan	1998	123-4567
MO457812	19	Ranger	2001	587-4321
MO54321	30	Bayliner	2001	321-4567
MO98765	28	J-Boat	1986	467-1122

Figure 15-6 The common field in CustomerTable and BoatTable

Tables in a relational database often share a common field. You use the common field to link information in one table to information in the other table. For example, if you know that the boat with state registration number MO12345 in BoatTable has the value 765-4321 for customer phone number, you can find the customer in CustomerTable whose primary key (PhoneNo) is 765-4321 and know the value of that customer's name and address. The CustomerPhoneNo field in BoatTable is called a foreign key. A **foreign key** is a field in one table (in this case, BoatTable) that serves as a primary key in a related table (CustomerTable). Foreign keys establish common attributes that allow you to link information in different tables. In Access, common attributes can be defined and depicted graphically in the Relationships window, as shown in Figure 15-7. (To open this window, click Tools on the menu bar, and then click Relationships.)

Using SQL to Join Tables in the Database

In Chapter 14 you learned how to specify SQL statements to retrieve, insert, update, and delete information in a single table. When two tables are involved, you use foreign and primary keys to link information in one table to information in another table. In relational database terms, this is called **joining** the tables. For example, the SQL statement to find and display the state registration number and manufacturer of all boats in BoatTable together with the name and phone number of each boat's owner is:

```
SELECT StateRegistrationNo, Manufacturer, CustomerName, PhoneNo
FROM BoatTable, CustomerTable
WHERE CustomerPhoneNo = PhoneNo;
```

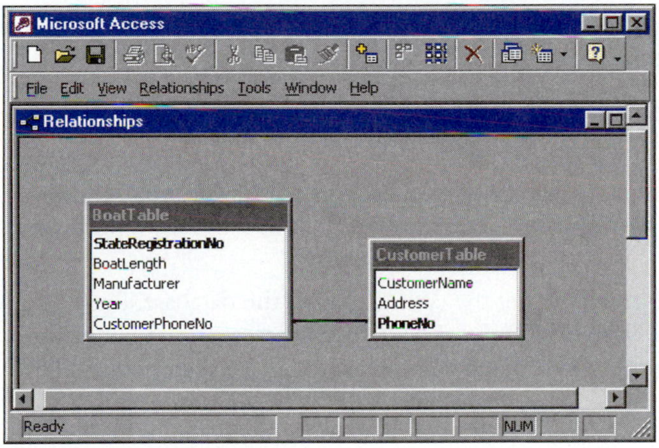

Figure 15-7   Relationships diagram for CustomerTable and BoatTable

Recall that the SELECT statement identifies the columns from the database that you want to see. Because these columns come from two different tables, the FROM clause includes the names of both tables involved in the query. The WHERE clause specifies the join condition—which in this case is a match between CustomerPhoneNo in BoatTable and PhoneNo in CustomerTable. Similarly, the SQL statement to display the state registration number, name, and address of the owner of the boat with state registration number MO98765 is:

```
SELECT StateRegistrationNo, CustomerName, Address
FROM BoatTable, CustomerTable
WHERE CustomerPhoneNo = PhoneNo
AND StateRegistrationNo = 'MO98765';
```

In this case, the WHERE clause specifies both the join condition *and* the primary key value for the item of interest. In general, WHERE clauses can specify any number of conditions that must be satisfied. You will use SQL statements of this type when you work with multiple tables in a relational database.

Establishing a Common Connection to CustomerAndBoatDatabase

In Chapter 14, you learned how to create and use a CustomerDA class to access a single table in a relational database. Recall that the CustomerDA class established a connection to CustomerDatabase, and that the CustomerDA class was the only class to utilize that connection. Now, two DA classes—one for Customer and one for Boat—should work together through a common connection to CustomerAndBoatDatabase. To establish a common connection, you need a new class, named CustomerAndBoatDatabaseConnect. The sole responsibility of this class is to manage the connection to the database. The class begins by importing the java.sql package. A string representing the ODBC data source name and a reference variable for the connection are then defined.

```
import java.sql.*;
public class CustomerAndBoatDatabaseConnect
{
    // The Data Source name is "CustomerAndBoatDatabase"
    static String url = "jdbc:odbc:CustomerAndBoatDatabase";
    static Connection aConnection;
```

Next, the initialize method establishes the connection to the database. This method is similar to the initialize method shown in Figure 14-19. Now, however, the connection instance is returned to the calling program so that the connection can be shared with all the classes that need it. See Figure 15-8.

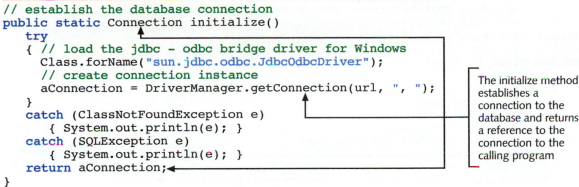

```
// establish the database connection
public static Connection initialize()
   try
   { // load the jdbc - odbc bridge driver for Windows
     Class.forName("sun.jdbc.odbc.JdbcOdbcDriver");
     // create connection instance
     aConnection = DriverManager.getConnection(url, ", ");
   }
   catch (ClassNotFoundException e)
      { System.out.println(e); }
   catch (SQLException e)
      { System.out.println(e); }
   return aConnection;
}
```

The initialize method establishes a connection to the database and returns a reference to the connection to the calling program

Figure 15-8   The initialize method of the CustomerAndBoatDatabaseConnect class

The only other method needed in this class is one to terminate the connection.

```
// close the database connection
public static void terminate()
{
    try
    {
        aConnection.close();
    }
    catch (SQLException e)
        { System.out.println(e); }
}
```

Modifying the Customer Problem Domain Class

To create a database application that deals with both CustomerTable and BoatTable, you modify the Customer class from Chapter 14 to reflect the linkage between the two tables. First, you include a boat reference attribute. This enables a customer instance to know about its associated boat instance. In the constructor, you initialize the boat reference to null. Then you include setter and getter methods to set and retrieve this value. For this application, you use the common database connection established by the CustomerAndBoatDatabaseConnect program. See Figure 15-9.

15

```java
// Customer with Boat reference attribute and DA methods
import java.util.Vector;
import java.sql.*;

public class Customer
{
    // attribute definitions
    private String name;
    private String address;
    private String phoneNo;
    // reference variable for Boat instance
    private Boat boat;

    // DA static methods ********************************
    public static void initialize(Connection c)
        {CustomerDA.initialize(c);}
    public static Customer find(String key) throws NotFoundException
        {return CustomerDA.find(key);}
    public static Vector getAll()
        {return CustomerDA.getAll();}
    public static void terminate()
        {CustomerDA.terminate();}

    // DA instance methods ********************************
    public void addNew() throws DuplicateException
        {CustomerDA.addNew(this);}
    public void delete() throws NotFoundException
        {CustomerDA.delete(this);}
    public void update() throws NotFoundException
        {CustomerDA.update(this);}

    // constructor with parameters
    public Customer(String aName, String anAddress, String aPhoneNo)
    {
        // invoke accessors to populate attributes
        setName(aName);
        setAddress(anAddress);
        setPhoneNo(aPhoneNo);
        setBoat(null);   // initially no boat
    }

    // get accessors
    public String getName()
        { return name;}
    public String getAddress()
        { return address;}
    public String getPhoneNo()
        { return phoneNo;}
    public Boat getBoat()
        { return boat;}
```

Include a boat reference variable

Use the shared database connection

Initialize the boat reference to null

Include a get accessor method to get the value of the boat reference

```
// set accessors
public void setName(String newName)
   { name = newName;}
public void setAddress(String newAddress)
   { address = newAddress;}
public void setPhoneNo(String newPhoneNo)
   { phoneNo = newPhoneNo;}
public void setBoat(Boat aBoat)
   { boat = aBoat;}

public String tellAboutSelf()
{
  String customerDetails = "Owner is " + name +
       "living in " + address +
       "with phone " + phoneNo;
       return customerDetails;

 {
}
```

Include a set accessor method to set the value of the boat reference

Figure 15-9   The Customer class

Introducing the BoatDA Class

The CustomerAndBoatDatabase application will find, add, delete, and update records in BoatTable. For this reason, you need a BoatDA class. The class imports the necessary packages and defines a boat reference variable and a Vector of boat reference variables. (The getAll method will use the Vector.) Variables are then defined for the database connection and the boat attribute values.

```
import java.util.Vector;
import java.sql.*;

public class BoatDA
{
   static Vector boats = new Vector();
   static Boat aBoat;

   // declare variables for the database connection
   static Connection aConnection;
   static Statement aStatement;

   // declare variables for Boat attribute values
   static String stateRegistrationNo;
   static double length;
   static String manufacturer;
   static int year;
   static String phoneNo;
```

15

Understanding the initialize and terminate Methods of the BoatDA Class

The initialize method of the BoatDA class uses the database connection established by the CustomerAndBoatDatabaseConnect class to create an instance of the Statement class. Recall that the Statement class contains methods that execute SQL statements. The other BoatDA methods will use the Statement class instance to retrieve, insert, update, and delete information in BoatTable. The terminate method closes the statement instance. See Figure 15-10.

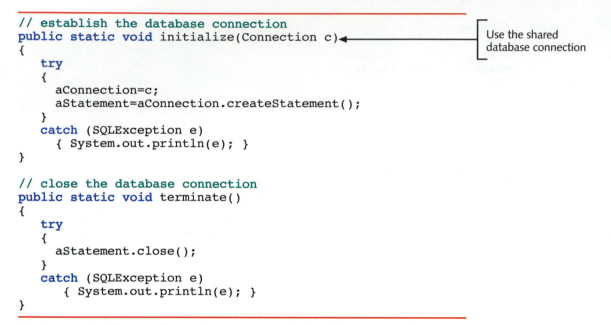

```
// establish the database connection
public static void initialize(Connection c)          Use the shared
{                                                     database connection
    try
    {
        aConnection=c;
        aStatement=aConnection.createStatement();
    }
    catch (SQLException e)
        { System.out.println(e); }
}

// close the database connection
public static void terminate()
{
    try
    {
        aStatement.close();
    }
    catch (SQLException e)
        { System.out.println(e); }
}
```

Figure 15-10   The initialize and terminate methods of the BoatDA class

Understanding the find and getAll Methods of the BoatDA Class

The find method of the BoatDA class defines a SELECT statement that retrieves a particular record from BoatTable. The argument list specifies the primary key of the record to be retrieved.

```
public static Boat find(String key) throws NotFoundException
{
    aBoat = null;

    // define the SQL query statement using the state reg key
    String sqlQuery = "SELECT StateRegistrationNo, BoatLength, " +
                      "Manufacturer, Year " +
                      "FROM BoatTable " +
                      "WHERE StateRegistrationNo = '" + key + "';";
```

Information in the result set is extracted and used to create a corresponding boat instance. This instance is then returned to the calling program. If the desired record cannot be found in the table, a NotFoundException is thrown.

```java
// execute the SQL query statement
try
{
    ResultSet rs = aStatement.executeQuery(sqlQuery);

    // next method sets cursor & returns true if there is data
    boolean gotIt = rs.next();
    if (gotIt)
    {
        // extract the data
        stateRegistrationNo = rs.getString(1);
        length = rs.getDouble(2);
        manufacturer = rs.getString(3);
        year = rs.getInt(4);

        // create Boat instance
        aBoat = new Boat(stateRegistrationNo, length,
                         manufacturer, year);
    }
    else
    {
        // nothing was retrieved
        throw (new NotFoundException("not found "));
    }
    rs.close();
}
catch (SQLException e)
    { System.out.println(e); }
return aBoat;
}
```

The getAll method of the BoatDA class is similar to the find method but returns a Vector of boat references rather than a single instance. See Figure 15-11.

15

```java
public static Vector getAll()
{
    Vector boats = new Vector();
    // define the SQL query statement for get all
    String sqlQuery = "SELECT StateRegistrationNo, BoatLength, " +
                      "Manufacturer, Year FROM BoatTable"
    try
    {
        // execute the SQL query statement
        ResultSet rs = aStatement.executeQuery(sqlQuery);
        boolean moreData = rs.next(); // next method sets cursor &
                                      // returns true if there is data
```

```java
        while (moreData)
        {
            // extract the boat data
            stateRegistrationNo = rs.getString(1);
            length = rs.getDouble(2);
            manufacturer = rs.getString(3);
            year = rs.getInt(4);

            // create Boat instance
            aBoat = new Boat(stateRegistrationNo, length,
                                manufacturer, year);
            boats.addElement(aBoat);
            moreData = rs.next();
        }
        rs.close();
    }
    catch (SQLException e)
        { System.out.println(e); }
    return boats;
}
```

Figure 15-11   The getAll method of the BoatDA class

Understanding the addNew Method of the BoatDA Class

The addNew method of the BoatDA class is similar to the addNew method of the CustomerDA class in Chapter 14, though boat attributes, rather than customer attributes, are of
interest. The addNew method begins by extracting boat attributes from the boat instance
received in the argument list.

```java
public static void addNew(Boat aBoat) throws DuplicateException
{
    // retrieve the boat attribute values
    stateRegistrationNo = aBoat.getStateRegistrationNo();
    length = aBoat.getLength();
    manufacturer = aBoat.getManufacturer();
    year = aBoat.getYear();
    phoneNo = aBoat.getCustomer().getPhoneNo();
```

Assume for a moment that the extracted values are MO33333, 25, Tartan, 1999, and 764-7414.
The SQL statement to insert this information into BoatTable is:

```
INSERT INTO BoatTable
    (StateRegistrationNo,BoatLength,Manufacturer,Year,CustomerPhoneNo)
VALUES
    ('MO33333', 25, 'Tartan', 1999, '764-7414')
```

Recall that the INSERT statement identifies the table and columns into which data will be
inserted. You specify column names in parentheses, separated by commas. The VALUES clause
identifies, in order, the values to be inserted into those columns. You also specify values in
parentheses, separated by commas. Remember that you must enclose string (or text) values in
single quotes. When you define an INSERT statement in a Java program, you must include

the parentheses, single quotes, and commas so that when values are substituted for variable names, the resulting SQL statement will be syntactically correct. In the following code, notice how the sqlInsert string concatenates string literals with variables to achieve the desired effect.

```
// create the SQL insert statement using attribute values
   String sqlInsert = "INSERT INTO BoatTable (StateRegistrationNo, "
                    + "BoatLength, Manufacturer, Year, "
                    + "CustomerPhoneNo)" +  "VALUES ('"
                    + stateRegistrationNo + "', "
                    + length + ", '" + manufacturer + "', "
                    + year + ", "" + phoneNo + "')";
```

```
//System.out.println(sqlInsert); display the SQL statement
```

 Defining SQL statements like the one above can be confusing. By including a System.out.println statement, you can see what the SQL statement actually looks like, and this can help you debug the code. Once you have the program working properly, you can delete (or comment out) the System.out.println statement.

Before executing the INSERT statement, you should confirm that the database does not already contain the boat. Recall that the definition of a relation forbids two records to have the same primary key. You invoke the find method to find a record with the primary key value of the boat to be added. If it finds the boat record, a DuplicateException is thrown. If it does not, the SQL statement is executed.

```
    // see if this boat already exists in the database
    try
    {
      Boat b = find(stateRegistrationNo);
      throw (new DuplicateException(:"Boat Exists "));
    }

    // if NotFoundException, add boat to database
    catch(NotFoundException e)
    {
      try
      {
        // execute the SQL update statement
        int result = aStatement.executeUpdate(sqlInsert);
      }
      catch (SQLException ee)
         { System.out.println(ee); }
    }
```

Understanding the update and delete Methods of the BoatDA Class

The update and delete methods extract attributes from the boat instance received in the argument list, then define appropriate SQL statements. Recall that the syntax for an UPDATE statement identifies the name of the table to be updated, followed by a SET clause where you specify the columns that will be updated and new values that will be assigned to them. You do not have to specify a value for each column in the table, but only for those columns containing a value that should be changed. For example:

```
UPDATE BoatTable SET BoatLength=30, Manufacturer='Tartan', Year=2002
WHERE StateRegistrationNo = 'MO123345';
```

The update method for the BoatDA class is shown in Figure 15-12.

```
public static void update(Boat aBoat) throws NotFoundException
{
    // retrieve the Boat attribute values
    stateRegistrationNo = aBoat.getStateRegistrationNo();
    length = aBoat.getLength();
    manufacturer = aBoat.getManufacturer();
    year = aBoat.getYear();

    // define the SQL query statement using the boat reg number key
    String sqlUpdate = "UPDATE BoatTable " +
                       "SET BoatLength = " + length +
                       ", Manufacturer = '" + manufacturer + "' " +
                       ", Year = "  + year +
                       "WHERE StateRegistrationNo = '" +
                       stateRegistrationNo + "'";
    // see if this boat already exists in the database
    // NotFoundException is thrown by find method
    try
    {
        Boat b = Boat.find(stateRegistrationNo);

        // if found, execute the SQL update statement
        int result = aStatement.executeUpdate(sqlUpdate);
    }
    catch (SQLException e)
        { System.out.println(e); }
}
```

Figure 15-12   The update method of the BoatDA class

Similarly, recall that the syntax for a DELETE statement specifies the table name and the primary key value of the record to be deleted. An example of a statement to delete a record from BoatTable follows:

```
DELETE FROM BoatTable WHERE StateRegistrationNo = 'MO12345';
```

The delete method for the BoatDA class is shown in Figure 15-13.

```
public static void delete(Boat aBoat) throws NotFoundException
{
    // retrieve the state registration no (key)
    stateRegistrationNo = aBoat.getStateRegistrationNo();
```

```
      // create the SQL delete statement
      String sqlDelete = "DELETE FROM BoatTable " +
                         "WHERE StateRegistrationNo = '" +
                           stateRegistrationNo + "'";

      // see if this boat already exists in the database
      // NotFoundException is thrown by find method
      try
      {
         Boat b = Boat.find(stateRegistrationNo);

         // if found, execute the SQL update statement
         int result = aStatement.executeUpdate(sqlDelete);
      }
      catch (SQLException e)
         { System.out.println(e); }
}
```

Figure 15-13   The delete method of the BoatDA class

Both the update and delete methods invoke the find method to determine whether the database has a boat with the state registration number specified in the SQL statement. If so, the SQL statement to update (or delete) that record is executed. Otherwise, the find method throws a NotFoundException.

Modifying the Boat Class to Work With BoatDA

You can now extend the functionality of the Boat problem domain class to take advantage of the capabilities in BoatDA. The Boat class needs four static methods to invoke the initialize, find, getAll, and terminate methods in the BoatDA class, and three instance methods to invoke the DA addNew, update, and delete methods. The only other change in the Boat class is a slight revision of the tellAboutSelf method. The code for the revised Boat class is shown in Figure 15-14.

15

```
// Boat with Customer reference and DA methods
import java.util.Vector;
import java.sql.*;

public class Boat
{
   // attributes
   private String stateRegistrationNo;
   private double length;
   private String manufacturer;
   private int year;

   // reference variable point to Customer for this boat
   private Customer customer;
```

```java
    // constructor
    public Boat(String aStateRegistrationNo, double aLength,
                    String aManufacturer, int aYear)
    {
        setStateRegistrationNo(aStateRegistrationNo);
        setLength(aLength);
        setManufacturer(aManufacturer);
        setYear(aYear);
        // initially no Customer for this boat
        setCustomer(null);
}

// custom method to assign a Boat to a Customer
public void assignBoatToCustomer(Customer aCustomer)
{
    setCustomer(aCustomer); // point this Boat to Customer instance
    customer.setBoat(this); // point the Customer to Boat instance
}
// DA static methods *******************************
public static void initialize(Connection c)
    {BoatDA.initialize( c );}
public static Boat find(String key) throws NotFoundException
    {return BoatDA.find(key);}
public static Vector getAll()
    {return BoatDA.getAll();}
public static void terminate()
    {BoatDA.terminate();}

// DA instance methods *******************************
public void addNew() throws DuplicateException
    {BoatDA.addNew(this);}
public void delete() throws NotFoundException
    {BoatDA.delete(this);}
public void update() throws NotFoundException
    {BoatDA.update(this);}

// set accessor methods
public void setStateRegistrationNo(String aStateRegistrationNo)
    { stateRegistrationNo = aStateRegistrationNo; }
public void setLength(double aLength)
    { length = aLength;}
public void setManufacturer(String aManufacturer)
    { manufacturer = aManufacturer; }
public void setYear(int aYear)
    { year = aYear;   }
public void setCustomer(Customer aCustomer)
    { customer = aCustomer;   }

// get accessor methods
public String getStateRegistrationNo()
    { return stateRegistrationNo; }
public double getLength()
    { return length; }
public String getManufacturer()
    { return manufacturer; }
```

```java
public int getYear()
    { return year; }
public Customer getCustomer()
    { return customer; }

// tellAboutSelf returns attributes in a String instance
public String tellAboutSelf()
{
    String boatDetails = "Boat is State reg number " +
                         getStateRegistrationNo() +
                         " length " + getLength() +
                         " Manufacturer " + getManufacturer() +
                         " Year " + getYear();

    return boatDetails;
  }
}
```

Figure 15-14   The Boat class

Modifying the CustomerDA Class

You can now change the CustomerDA class to support joining the information from Boat-Table and CustomerTable. The CustomerDA class begins much as it did before, but now includes a boat reference variable and variables to represent boat attributes.

```java
public class CustomerDA
{
    static Vector customers = new Vector(); // contains cust references
    static Customer aCustomer;
    static Boat aBoat;

    // declare variables for the database connection
    static Connection aConnection;
    static Statement aStatement;

    // declare variables for Customer attribute values
    static String name, address, phoneNumber;

    // declare variables for Boat attribute values
    static String stateRegistrationNo, manufacturer;
    static double length;
    static int year;
```

The initialize and terminate methods of the CustomerDA are identical to their counterparts in the BoatDA class and are not repeated here.

Understanding the find and getAll Methods of the CustomerDA Class

You can extend the capability of the find method of the CustomerDA class to retrieve data from both tables. To do so, you first change the SQL statement. In the WHERE clause, specify both the join condition *and* the primary key value for the customer of interest. You use

15

the values in the result set to create a boat instance and a customer instance. The boat instance invokes the assignBoatToCustomer method to establish the two-way relationship with its customer instance. The customer instance, which now includes a pointer to the boat instance, is then returned to the calling program. The find method of the CustomerDA class is shown in Figure 15-15.

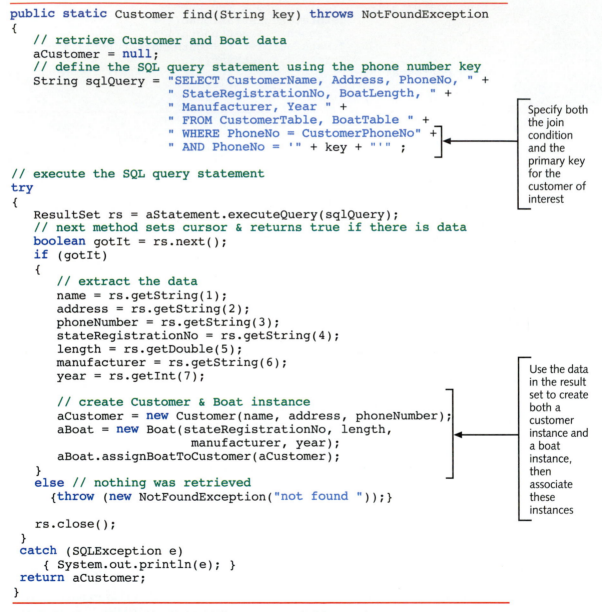

```java
public static Customer find(String key) throws NotFoundException
{
    // retrieve Customer and Boat data
    aCustomer = null;
    // define the SQL query statement using the phone number key
    String sqlQuery = "SELECT CustomerName, Address, PhoneNo, " +
                      " StateRegistrationNo, BoatLength, " +
                      " Manufacturer, Year " +
                      " FROM CustomerTable, BoatTable " +
                      " WHERE PhoneNo = CustomerPhoneNo" +
                      " AND PhoneNo = '" + key + "'" ;
```
Specify both the join condition and the primary key for the customer of interest

```java
// execute the SQL query statement
try
{
    ResultSet rs = aStatement.executeQuery(sqlQuery);
    // next method sets cursor & returns true if there is data
    boolean gotIt = rs.next();
    if (gotIt)
    {
        // extract the data
        name = rs.getString(1);
        address = rs.getString(2);
        phoneNumber = rs.getString(3);
        stateRegistrationNo = rs.getString(4);
        length = rs.getDouble(5);
        manufacturer = rs.getString(6);
        year = rs.getInt(7);
```
Use the data in the result set to create both a customer instance and a boat instance, then associate these instances
```java
        // create Customer & Boat instance
        aCustomer = new Customer(name, address, phoneNumber);
        aBoat = new Boat(stateRegistrationNo, length,
                         manufacturer, year);
        aBoat.assignBoatToCustomer(aCustomer);
    }
    else // nothing was retrieved
        {throw (new NotFoundException("not found "));}

    rs.close();
}
catch (SQLException e)
    { System.out.println(e); }
return aCustomer;
}
```

Figure 15-15   The find method of the CustomerDA class

Note that as before, the find method still returns a single customer instance, but with one important difference. As shown in Figure 15-16, this instance now contains a reference to the customer's boat instance.

This means that it is not necessary to execute a separate SQL statement to find the boat in BoatTable. The values of its attributes, by design, are already available. Including a boat attribute in the Customer class definition makes this possible. Including the boat attribute establishes the aggregation (or composition) relationship "customer has boat." The assign–BoatToCustomer method in the Boat class establishes which boat belongs to the customer. The ability to return a single customer instance, yet have related information available, is one of the strengths of the object–oriented approach.

The getAll method is similar to the find method but returns a Vector of customer references rather than a single customer reference. Note that both the find method and the getAll method now return information about both a customer and that customer's boat.

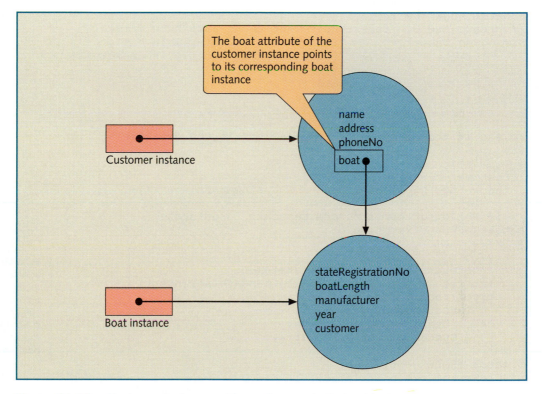

Figure 15-16   Customer instance with a reference to its boat instance

Understanding the addNew Method of the CustomerDA Class

Recall that there is a mandatory one-to-one relationship between Customer and Boat. This means that there must be a customer record for every boat record, and conversely, there must be a boat record for every customer record. The addNew method in the CustomerDA class must enforce this requirement.

It does so in the following way: After inserting a customer record into CustomerTable, the addNew method of the CustomerDA class invokes the addNew method of the BoatDA class to insert the associated boat record into BoatTable. This modification preserves the integrity of the database. See Figure 15-17.

```java
public static void addNew(Customer aCustomer) throws DuplicateException
{ // retrieve the customer attribute values
  name = aCustomer.getName();
  address = aCustomer.getAddress();
  phoneNumber = aCustomer.getPhoneNo();
  aBoat = aCustomer.getBoat();
  // create the SQL insert statement using attribute values
  String sqlInsert =      "INSERT INTO CustomerTable " +
                          "(CustomerName, Address, PhoneNo) " +
                          "VALUES ('" +
                          name + "', '" +
                          address + "', '" +
                          phoneNumber + "')";

  // see if this customer already exists in the database
  try
  {
    Customer c = find(phoneNumber);
    throw (new DuplicateException("Customer Exists "));
  }
  // if NotFoundException, add customer to database
  catch(NotFoundException e)
  {
    try
    { // execute the SQL update statement
      int result = aStatement.executeUpdate(sqlInsert);
      try // add the boat
        {aBoat.addNew();}
      catch(DuplicateException de)
        { System.out.println(de); }
    }
    catch (SQLException ee)
      { System.out.println(ee); }
  }
}
```

When the addNew method inserts a record into the customer table, it also inserts a record into the boat table

Figure 15-17 The addNew method of the CustomerDA class

Understanding the delete and update Methods of the CustomerDA Class

The delete method of the CustomerDA class also must preserve the integrity of the database by enforcing the mandatory one-to-one relationship between Customer and Boat. When a customer record is deleted from the database, the corresponding boat record also must be deleted. See Figure 15–18.

```java
public static void delete(Customer aCustomer) throws NotFoundException
{
  // retrieve the phone no (key)
  phoneNumber = aCustomer.getPhoneNo();
  // create the SQL delete statement
  String sqlDelete = "DELETE FROM CustomerTable " +
                  "WHERE PhoneNo = '" + phoneNumber + "'";

  // see if this customer already exists in the database
  try
  {
    Customer c = Customer.find(phoneNumber);
    // if found, execute the SQL update statement
    int result = aStatement.executeUpdate(sqlDelete);
    try // delete the customer's boat
      {aCustomer.getBoat().delete();}
    catch(NotFoundException nfe)
      { }// do nothing
  }
  catch (SQLException e)
     { System.out.println(e); }
}
```

When the delete method deletes a record from the customer table, it also deletes a record from the boat table

Figure 15-18   The delete method of the CustomerDA class

The update method of the CustomerDA class remains unchanged from Chapter 14, as the purpose of this method is to update information in CustomerTable only.

Testing the New CustomerAndBoatDatabase Application

TesterOne tests the classes in the CustomerAndBoatDatabase application. First, TesterOne declares necessary reference variables. Next, TesterOne invokes the initialize method of the CustomerAndBoatDatabaseConnect class to establish the connection to the database. TesterOne passes this connection to the Customer and Boat initialize methods.

```java
public class TesterOne
{
    static Customer aCustomer;

    public static void main(String args[])
```

15

```
        {
            Vector customers;
            Boat aBoat;

            // initialize the databases
            Connection c = CustomerAndBoatDatabaseConnect.
    initialize();
            Customer.initialize(c);
            Boat.initialize(c);
```

This is shown graphically in the sequence diagram in Figure 15-19.

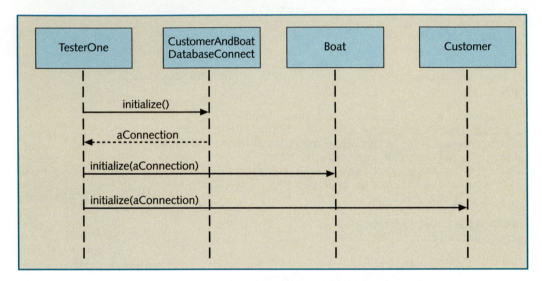

Figure 15-19   Sequence diagram to connect to the database

TesterOne then attempts to retrieve the customer and boat information from the database for the customer whose phone number is 123-4567. TesterOne invokes the find method of the Customer class, which invokes the find method of the CustomerDA class. Recall that the find method in the CustomerDA class executes a SELECT statement that joins the two tables and retrieves information about both the desired customer and the customer's boat. The Customer and Boat classes use this information to create corresponding customer and boat instances. TesterOne then calls its own printDetails method to display the customer and boat details.

```
        try // get a customer & their boat
        {
            aCustomer = Customer.find("123-4567");
            printDetails();
        }
        catch(NotFoundException e)
            { System.out.println(e); }
```

The sequence diagram in Figure 15–20 illustrates this process.

In the printDetails method, the customer instance invokes its tellAboutSelf method to report customer details, then navigates to the associated boat instance to invoke the Boat tellAbout-Self method.

```java
private static void printDetails()
{
    System.out.println("Found " + aCustomer.getName() +
                        " and associated boat:");
    System.out.println("   " + aCustomer.tellAboutSelf());
    System.out.println("   " + aCustomer.getBoat().tellAboutSelf() +
                        "\n");
}
```

To test the possibility that an attempt to find a record in the database might be unsuccessful, TesterOne tries to retrieve information from the database for the customer with phone number 000-0000. In this case, no such customer exists in the database. The SQL query produces a result set with no data, and the CustomerDA class throws a NotFoundException error. TesterOne catches the exception and displays the message "Did not find 000-0000."

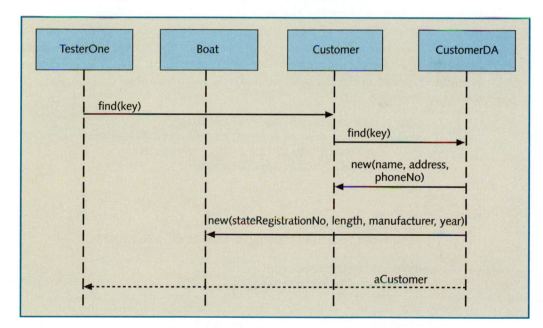

Figure 15-20   Sequence diagram to find a customer and that customer's boat

```java
try // try to get a non-existent customer & their boat
{
```

```
        aCustomer = Customer.find("000-0000");
        printDetails();
    }
catch(NotFoundException e)
    { System.out.println("Did not find 000-0000\n"); }
```

Next, TesterOne tests the CustomerDA getAll method, which executes a query that joins information in the two tables and returns information about all customers and boats in the database via a Vector of customer reference variables. A for loop is used to report the details of each element in the Vector.

```
// get all customers & their boats
customers = Customer.getAll();
for(int i = 0; i < customers.size(); i++)
{
    // get customer reference
    aCustomer = (Customer) customers.get(i);
    printDetails();
}
```

TesterOne then creates a new customer instance (with phone number 339-4990) and a new boat instance. The boat instance invokes its assignBoatToCustomer method to associate itself with its customer instance. The customer instance then invokes its addNew method. Recall that the addNew method of the CustomerDA class executes an INSERT statement to add customer information to CustomerTable, and then invokes the addNew method of the BoatDA class to insert information about the boat into BoatTable. If a duplicate customer or boat already exists in the database, the addNew method throws a DuplicateException, and the entire operation ends.

```
// add a new customer and their boat
aCustomer = new Customer("Ed", "KC", "339-4990");
aBoat = new Boat("MO112233", 25, "S-2",1984);
aBoat.assignBoatToCustomer(aCustomer);

try
{
    aCustomer.addNew();
    System.out.println("Ed and his boat added\n");
}
catch(DuplicateException e)
    { System.out.println(e); }
```

To verify that the new customer and boat have been added to the database, TesterOne invokes the find operation to find the newly added customer.

```
try // now, find the new customer & their boat
{
    aCustomer = Customer.find("339-4990");
    printDetails();
}
catch(NotFoundException e)
```

```
    { System.out.println("Did not find 339-4990\n"); }
```

To test the delete method, TesterOne calls the delete method of the CustomerDA class to delete the newly added customer from the database. The delete method executes a DELETE statement to delete the customer record from CustomerTable, then invokes the delete method of the BoatDA class to delete the associated record in BoatTable. TesterOne then calls the find method of the CustomerDA class to verify that the customer record has been deleted from the database.

```
    try // now, delete the new customer & their boat
    {
       aCustomer.delete();
       System.out.println("Ed deleted\n");
    }
    catch(NotFoundException e)
       { System.out.println(e); }

    try // now, try to find the deleted customer & their boat
    {
       aCustomer = Customer.find("339-4990");
       printDetails();
    }
    catch(NotFoundException e)
       { System.out.println("Did not find 339-4990\n"); }
```

Similarly, TesterOne tests the update method. TesterOne first issues a command to find the record in the database for the customer with phone number 123-4567. The find method returns the desired customer instance, which includes a pointer to the associated boat instance. TesterOne invokes a setter method to change the address of this customer instance, then invokes the update method to change this record in the database. Next, TesterOne invokes a setter method to change the length of the boat instance, then calls the update method for the boat instance to change the boat record in the database. If the customer or boat cannot be found in the database, a NotFoundException is thrown, and the entire operation is aborted. TesterOne confirms that the database has been updated by calling the find method to locate the revised customer record.

15

```
    // change Eleanor's address to Miami and her boat length to 40
    try
    {
       aCustomer = Customer.find("123-4567");
       printDetails();
       //change customer address
       aCustomer.setAddress("Miami");
       aCustomer.update();
       //change boat length
       aCustomer.getBoat().setLength(40);
       aCustomer.getBoat().update();
       System.out.println("Eleanor updated\n");
    }
    catch (NotFoundException e)
```

```
      {System.out.println(e);}

   try // now, try to find the Eleanor & her boat
   {
      aCustomer = Customer.find("123-4567");
      printDetails();
   }
   catch(NotFoundException e)
   {
      System.out.println("Eleanor not found");
   }
```

Finally, TesterOne calls the terminate methods of the Customer and Boat classes to close their respective statement instances, then calls the terminate method of the CustomerAnd-BoatDatabaseConnect class to close the connection to the database.

```
   // close the database
   Customer.terminate();
   Boat.terminate();
   CustomerAndBoatDatabaseConnect.terminate();
```

The output of the TesterOne program is shown in Figure 15-21.

Found Eleanor and associated boat:
   Owner is Eleanor living in Memphis with phone 123-4567
   Boat is State reg number MO34561 length 35.0 Manufacturer Tartan Year 1998

Did not find 000-0000

Found Brian and associated boat:
   Owner is Brian living in Los Angeles with phone 467-1234
   Boat is State reg number MO223344 length 24.0 Manufacturer Tracker Year 1996

Found Dan and associated boat:
   Owner is Dan living in Reston with phone 587-4321
   Boat is State reg number MO457812 length 19.0 Manufacturer Ranger Year 2001

Found Mike and associated boat:
   Owner is Mike living in Boston with phone 467-1122
   Boat is State reg number MO98765 length 28.0 Manufacturer J-Boat Year 1986

Figure 15-21   **Output of the TesterOne program**

Found JoAnn and associated boat:
   Owner is JoAnn living in St. Louis with phone 765-4321
   Boat is State reg number MO12345 length 26.0 Manufacturer Ranger Year 1976

Found Dave and associated boat:
   Owner is Dave living in Atlanta with phone 321-4567
   Boat is State reg number MO54321 length 30.0 Manufacturer Bayliner Year 2001
Found Eleanor and associated boat:
   Owner is Eleanor living in Memphis with phone 123-4567
   Boat is State reg number MO34561 length 35.0 Manufacturer Tartan Year 1998

Ed and his boat added

Found Ed and associated boat:
   Owner is Ed living in KC with phone 339-4990
   Boat is State reg number MO112233 length 25.0 Manufacturer S-2 Year 1984

Ed deleted

Did not find 339-4990

Found Eleanor and associated boat:
   Owner is Eleanor living in Memphis with phone 123-4567
   Boat is State reg number MO34561 length 35.0 Manufacturer Tartan Year 1998

Eleanor updated

Found Eleanor and associated boat:
   Owner is Eleanor living in Miami with phone 123-4567
   Boat is State reg number MO34561 length 40.0 Manufacturer Tartan Year 1998

15

Figure 15-21   **Output of the TesterOne program (continued)**

Hands-on Exercise 1

1. If you have not already done so:
   a. Create a Chapter15Example1 folder on your system.
   b. Locate **CustomerAndBoatDatabase.mdb** in the Example1 folder for this chapter on the book's CD, and copy it to the folder you created in Step 1a.

2. To register this database with the ODBC:
   a. Click **Start** on the taskbar, point to **Settings**, and then click **Control Panel**.
   b. Double-click **Administrative Tools**, if necessary, and then double-click the **ODBC Data Sources** icon. The ODBC Data Source Administrator dialog box appears.
   c. Click the **User DSN** tab, select **MS Access Database** from the list of data source names, and then click **Add**. The Create New Data Source dialog box appears.
   d. Make sure that Microsoft Access Driver (*.mdb) is selected, and then click **Finish**. The ODBC Microsoft Access Setup dialog box appears.
   e. In the Data Source Name text box, type **CustomerAndBoatDatabase**, and then click the **Select** button.
   f. In the right pane of the Select Database window, open the folder on your system that contains the CustomerAndBoatDatabase.mdb file.
   g. Click **CustomerAndBoatDatabase.mdb** in the left pane, and then click **OK**.
   h. Click **OK** to close the ODBC Microsoft Access Setup dialog box, click **OK** to close the ODBC Data Source Administrator dialog box, and then close the Control Panel window.

3. To ensure that the database copied from the CD is not write-protected, check the properties of this file.
   a. Start Windows Explorer, and locate the **CustomerAndBoatDatabase** file.
   b. Right-click **CustomerAndBoatDatabase**, and then click **Properties**. The CustomerAndBoatDatabase Properties dialog box appears.
   c. If the Read-only attribute box is checked, click the box to uncheck it, and then click **OK**. If the Read-only attribute box is not checked, click **Cancel**.

4. Copy all of the java source files in the Example1 folder for this chapter on the book's CD to the Chapter15Example1 folder on your system.

5. Compile TesterOne using the software recommended by your instructor.

6. Run TesterOne and verify that the program output is as shown earlier in Figure 15-21.

IMPLEMENTING A ONE-TO-MANY RELATIONSHIP IN A DATABASE APPLICATION

In the previous example, you learned how to implement the one-to-one relationship between Customer and Boat in a relational database application. Other one-to-one relationships on the Bradshaw Marina class diagram (such as the one between Boat and Slip) would be implemented similarly. Recall, however, that the relationship between Dock and Slip is a one-to-many relationship. That is, a dock contains many slips, and a slip belongs to exactly one dock. You will now learn how to implement the one-to-many relationship that exists between Dock and Slip. The application you are about to develop will allow the business owner to get a report that provides all available information about a dock, including details about each of its slips.

Understanding the Tables in DockAndSlipDatabase

Before beginning the Java programs that retrieve dock and slip information, look at the structure of the relational database tables that will be involved in this application.

To examine these tables:

1. Create a Chapter15Example2 folder on your system.

2. Locate **DockAndSlipDatabase.mdb** on the book's CD in the Example2 folder for this chapter, and copy it to the folder you created in Step 1.

3. Start Microsoft Access, and open **DockAndSlipDatabase.mdb**. Notice that the database contains two tables: DockTable and SlipTable.

4. Open **DockTable** and view its contents. Notice that it contains four columns—DockId (the primary key), Location, Electricity, and Water. DockId is an integer representing the dock number. Location is a string representing the dock location. The Electricity and Water columns indicate whether the dock has electricity and water. In the Java class definitions, these variables have been treated as true/false (boolean) values. However, Microsoft Access does not directly support the boolean data type. Therefore, within the database an integer value of 1 is used to indicate that the service is available, and 0 indicates that it is not. See Figure 15-22.

5. Open **SlipTable** and view its contents. Notice that it contains five columns—SlipNo, DockId, Width, SlipLength, and BoatID. Slips on each dock are numbered sequentially beginning with 1. This means that *both* SlipNo and DockId must be known to uniquely identify a slip. SlipNo and DockId, taken together, form what is known as a concatenated primary key. A **concatenated key** is comprised of more than one field (or column) in the database. See Figure 15-23.

An integer value of 1 indicates electricity (or water) is available; an integer value of 0 indicates it is not

15

Figure 15-22   The contents of DockTable

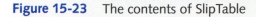

Both SlipNo and DockId are needed to uniquely identify a slip

Figure 15-23 The contents of SlipTable

6. Note that the DockId column in SlipTable is a foreign key to information in DockTable. Similarly, BoatID is a foreign key to information in BoatTable (although this information is not needed in this application). Figure 15-24 depicts the relationship between DockTable and SlipTable.

Establishing a Common Connection to DockAndSlipDatabase

As with the CustomerAndBoatDatabase application, you need a separate program to establish a single connection to DockAndSlipDatabase. The PD and DA classes that require access to the database then share this connection. Except for the specified data source name, the DockAndSlipDatabaseConnect program is identical to the CustomerAndBoatDatabaseConnect program, and therefore is not discussed here. The code for this program is included in the Example2 folder for this chapter on the book's CD.

Modifying the Dock and Slip Classes

You were first introduced to the Dock and Slip classes in Chapter 9 (see Figures 9-14 and 9-15). You will now modify these classes to support object persistence in a relational database application.

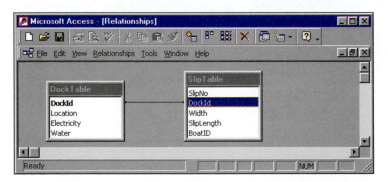

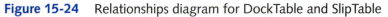

Figure 15-24 Relationships diagram for DockTable and SlipTable

Within the Dock class, you add a statement to import the Connection class of the java.sql package, then define the standard initialize, terminate, find, and getAll methods. The Dock class does not currently require methods to insert, update, or delete dock records. The fact that docks (and slips) will be added, removed, or updated rarely is something that would have been discovered during analysis. For simplicity, these methods are not included in the following examples. The last modification to the Dock class is to include a tellAboutSelf method. The revised source code for the Dock class is shown in Figure 15–25.

```java
// Chapter 15 - implement Dock has Slips

import java.util.*;
import java.sql.Connection;

public class Dock
{
   // attributes
   private int id;
   private String location;
   private boolean electricity;
   private boolean water;

   // implement slip association with Vector class
   private Vector slips;

   // constructor
   public Dock(int anId, String aLocation,
                  boolean anElectricity, boolean aWater)
   {
     setId(anId);
     setLocation(aLocation);
     setElectricity(anElectricity);
     setWater(aWater);
     slips = new Vector(10); // start with 10 slips
   }

   // DA static methods ********************************
   public static void initialize(Connection c)
      {DockDA.initialize(c);}
   public static Dock find(int key) throws NotFoundException
      {return DockDA.find(key);}
   public static Vector getAll()
      {return DockDA.getAll();}
   public static void terminate()
      {DockDA.terminate();}

   // set accessor methods
   public void setId(int anId)
      { id = anId;}
   public void setLocation(String aLocation)
      { location = aLocation;}
   public void setElectricity(boolean anElectricity)
      { electricity = anElectricity;}
```

15

```java
    public void setWater(boolean aWater)
       { water = aWater;}

    // get accessor methods
    public int getId()
       { return id;}
    public String getLocation()
       { return location;}
    public boolean getElectricity()
       { return electricity;}
    public boolean getWater()
       { return water;}
    public Vector getSlips()
       { return slips;}

    public String tellAboutSelf()
    {
       String hasElectricity = getElectricity()?"Has Electricity":
                               "Has No Electricity";
       String hasWater = getWater()?"Has Water":"Has No Water";
       return ("Dock " + getId() +
          " Location is " + getLocation() + ", " +
          hasElectricity + ", " + hasWater);
    }

    // custom method addSlipToDock
    public void addSlipToDock(Slip aSlip)
    {
       slips.addElement(aSlip); // connect dock to slip
       aSlip.setDock(this);     // connect slip to dock
    }
}
```

Figure 15-25   The Dock class

The Slip class from Chapter 9 already includes the code necessary to associate a slip with its dock. Slips (like docks) rarely will be added, removed, or updated; thus the Slip class does not need insert, delete, or update methods. Furthermore, in the DockAndSlipDatabase application, slip information is needed only when dock information is retrieved. The find and getAll methods of the DockDA class will retrieve information about a dock and all of its slips, which means that the Slip class does not need find and getAll methods of its own. Accordingly, you do not need to modify the Slip class and you do not need a SlipDA class.

Introducing the DockDA Class

The DockAndSlipDatabase application will need to access information in DockTable. For this reason, you need a DockDA class. The DockDA class is similar to the other DA classes with which you have worked, except that it does not require methods to insert, delete, or update dock information. The class begins by importing the necessary packages, then defining dock and slip reference variables and a Vector of dock references. Next, it defines variables for the database connection, followed by variables to hold slip and dock attribute values.

```java
// Chapter 15 - implement Dock has Slips

import java.util.Vector;
import java.sql.*;

public class DockDA
{
    static Vector docks = new Vector();
    static Slip aSlip;
    static Dock aDock;

    static Connection aConnection;
    static Statement aStatement;

    // declare variables for Slip attribute values
    static int slipNo;
    static int width;
    static double slipLength;
    static int dockId;

    // declare variables for Dock attribute values
    static int id;
    static String location;
    static boolean electricity;
    static boolean water;
    // Yes/No variables needed to convert boolean to text for dbms
    static int electricityYN;
    static int waterYN;
```

Methods to initialize and terminate the connection to the database are identical to those used previously in other DA classes and are not repeated here. The code for these methods is included on the book's CD.

Understanding the find Method of the DockDA Class

The find method of the DockDA class defines the SQL statement needed to extract dock and slip information from the database. The WHERE clause specifies both the join condition and the primary key for the dock of interest. The ORDER BY clause specifies that the information returned by the query is to be sorted in order by slip number.

```java
public static Dock find(int key) throws NotFoundException
{
    aDock = null;
    // define the SQL query statement
    String sqlQuery = "SELECT DockTable.DockId, Location, " +
                      "Electricity, Water, " +
                      "SlipNo, Width, SlipLength " +
                      "FROM DockTable, SlipTable " +
                      "WHERE DockTable.DockId = " + key +
                      "AND SlipTable.DockId = DockTable.DockId" +
                      "ORDER BY SlipNo";
```

The result set contains dock attributes and slip attributes for every slip on the designated dock. You can picture the result set as a temporary table of its own. If you direct the SQL query to find Dock 1, for example, the result set would include the information shown in Table 15-1.

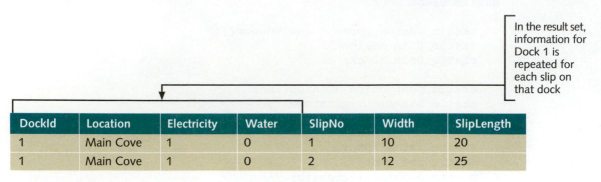

In the result set, information for Dock 1 is repeated for each slip on that dock

DockId	Location	Electricity	Water	SlipNo	Width	SlipLength
1	Main Cove	1	0	1	10	20
1	Main Cove	1	0	2	12	25

Table 15-1   Result Set of the find Method When DockId = 1

Notice that the information for Dock 1 is repeated for each slip. However, as the system retrieves items from the result set, it should obtain the dock attributes and create a dock instance only once. You can avoid unnecessary handling of the dock attributes by using a boolean variable named dockCreated. You initially set the value of dockCreated to false, then check its value within the while loop. The first time through the loop, the value of dockCreated is false, so dock attributes are extracted and used to create a dock instance. You then set the value of dockCreated to true so that subsequent passes through the result set will not process dock attributes. Note that you must convert the attributes for electricity and water, which are stored in the database as integers 0 or 1, to their boolean equivalents. A private integerToBoolean method handles this task.

```
// execute the SQL query statement
   try
   { // get the dock
     ResultSet rs = aStatement.executeQuery(sqlQuery);
     // next method sets cursor & returns true if there is data
     boolean dockCreated = false;
     boolean more = rs.next();
     while(more)  // loop for each row of result set
     {
         if (dockCreated == false) //create the dock if 1st time thru
         { // extract the Dock data
           dockId = rs.getInt(1);
           location = rs.getString(2);
           electricityYN = rs.getInt(3);
           waterYN = rs.getInt(4);
           // convert ints to booleans
```

```
            electricity = integerToBoolean(electricityYN);
            water = integerToBoolean(waterYN);
            // create Dock instance
            aDock = new Dock(dockId, location, electricity, water);
            dockCreated = true;
        }
```

Slip attributes are retrieved on each pass through the result set, and a corresponding slip instance is created each time. Recall that the constructor method in the Slip class establishes a two-way connection between a slip and its dock by invoking the addSlipToDock method.

```
        // extract the Slip data
        slipNo = rs.getInt(5);
        width = rs.getInt(6);
        slipLength = rs.getDouble(7);
        aSlip = new Slip(slipNo, width, slipLength, aDock);
        more = rs.next();   // set cursor to next row
    }
```

If the dock specified in the SQL statement cannot be found in the database, the system throws a NotFoundException. If all goes well, the dock instance, complete with a Vector of its slip instances, is returned to the calling program.

```
    if(dockCreated == false)
      throw (new NotFoundException("Dock not found "));
    }
    catch (SQLException e)
        { System.out.println(e);}
    return aDock;
}
```

Understanding the getAll Method of the DockDA Class

The getAll method of the DockDA class is similar to the find method. This time, however, the SQL query returns dock and slip information for all slips in the marina, sorted in order by dock and then by slip.

```
public static Vector getAll()
{
   Vector docks = new Vector();
   // define the SQL query statement for get all
   String sqlQuery = "SELECT DockTable.DockId, Location, " +
                     "Electricity, Water, " +
                     "SlipNo, Width, SlipLength " +
                     "FROM DockTable, SlipTable " +
                     "WHERE SlipTable.DockId = DockTable.DockId " +
                     "ORDER BY DockTable.DockId, SlipNo";
```

In this case, the result set includes the information shown in Table 15-2.

15

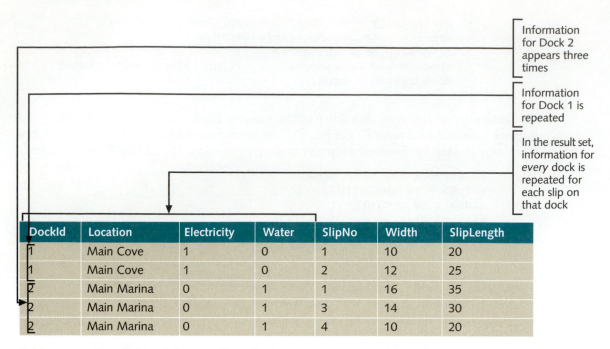

Information for Dock 2 appears three times

Information for Dock 1 is repeated

In the result set, information for *every* dock is repeated for each slip on that dock

DockId	Location	Electricity	Water	SlipNo	Width	SlipLength
1	Main Cove	1	0	1	10	20
1	Main Cove	1	0	2	12	25
2	Main Marina	0	1	1	16	35
2	Main Marina	0	1	3	14	30
2	Main Marina	0	1	4	10	20

Table 15-2 Result Set of the getAll Method

Note that dock information is again repeated for each slip. However, the system should retrieve dock information and create a dock instance only once for each dock. The code takes this into consideration by incorporating what is known as control-break logic. A **control break** occurs when there is a change in the value of a variable used to group a list of items. In this case, dock number is the grouping variable (or control field). When the dock number changes, information about a different dock needs to be extracted.

As shown in Figure 15-26, the variables thisDockId and prevDockId determine when a control break (change in the dock number) occurs. The program initially sets the value of this-DockId equal to the dock ID obtained from the first row of the result set. Each time through the outer while loop, the program stores this value of the control field in prevDockId, then extracts the remaining dock attributes from the result set and creates a dock instance. A reference to the dock instance is added to the vector that will be returned to the calling program. The inner while loop executes until there is either a change in the dock ID (a control break) or the end of the result set is reached.

On each pass through the inner while loop, the program extracts slip attributes from the current row of the result set and creates a slip instance. Recall that when a slip instance is created, the addSlipToDock method is invoked to associate the slip with its dock. The program then moves the cursor to the next row of the result set and sets the value of thisDockId equal to the dock ID obtained from this row of the result set. When the inner while loop detects a change in the dock number, control returns to the outer while loop and the entire process is repeated.

```
try
{
    // execute the SQL query statement
    ResultSet rs = aStatement.executeQuery(sqlQuery);
    // next method sets cursor & returns true if there is data
    boolean moreData = rs.next();   //initialize cursor
    // read initial value of control field
    int thisDockId = rs.getInt(1);

    while (moreData)
    {
        // store value of control field
        int prevDockId = thisDockId;
        // extract the Dock data
        location = rs.getString(2);
        electricityYN = rs.getInt(3);
        waterYN = rs.getInt(4);
        // convert int to boolean
        electricity = integerToBoolean(electricityYN);
        water = integerToBoolean(waterYN);
        // create Dock instance
        aDock = new Dock(thisDockId, location, electricity, water);
        docks.addElement(aDock);
        // get slips for this dock
        while ( prevDockId == thisDockId && moreData )
        {
            // extract the Slip data
            slipNo = rs.getInt(5);
            width = rs.getInt(6);
            slipLength = rs.getDouble(7);
            // create Slip instance
            aSlip = new Slip(slipNo, width, slipLength, aDock);
            // set cursor to next row
            moreData = rs.next();
            // get next value of control field
            if (moreData)
                thisDockId = rs.getInt(1);
        }
    }
    rs.close();
}
catch (SQLException e)
    { System.out.println(e);}
return docks;
}
```

Outer while loop executes until the end of the result set is reached

Dock attributes are extracted on each pass through the outer while loop

Inner while loop executes until a new dock is encountered (or the end of the result set is reached)

Slip attributes are extracted on each pass through the inner while loop

15

Figure 15-26 Control-break logic in the getAll method of the DockDA class

The control–break logic should now be clear. The outer while loop executes once for each new value of the dock ID. On each pass, the outer while loop extracts dock attributes and creates a dock instance. The inner loop executes once for each slip on that dock. On each pass, the inner while loop extracts slip attributes and creates a slip instance. When the end of the result set is reached, a Vector of dock instances is returned to the calling program. Each dock instance contains a Vector of references to its slips.

Testing the DockAndSlipDatabase Application

TesterTwo tests the classes in the DockAndSlipDatabase application. First, TesterTwo defines necessary variables and establishes the connection to the database. Next, it attempts to find Dock 1. If it finds the dock in the database, the find method returns a reference to that dock instance. The dock instance includes references to its slips. The printDetails method displays information about the dock and its slips. Next, TesterTwo attempts to find Dock 2 and, if successful, displays information about Dock 2 and its slips. Finally, TesterTwo invokes the getAll method, which produces a list of all docks and the slips that belong to each of them. The source code for TesterTwo is shown in Figure 15-27, and the output from this program is shown in Figure 15-28.

```java
// Chapter 15 TesterTwo - illustrate Dock has Slips association

import java.util.Vector;
import java.sql.*;

public class TesterTwo
{
    static Slip aSlip;
    static Dock aDock;
    static Vector docks, slips;

    public static void main(String args[])
    {
        // initialize the databases
        Connection c = DockAndSlipDatabaseConnect.initialize();
        Dock.initialize(c);

        // find dock 1 & its slips
        try
        {
            System.out.println("RESULTS of find dock 1:");
            aDock = Dock.find(1);
            printDetails();
        }
        catch(NotFoundException e)
            {System.out.println(e);}
```

```
        // find dock 2 & its slips
        try
        {
           System.out.println("\nRESULTS of find dock 2:");
           aDock = Dock.find(2);
           printDetails();
        }
        catch(NotFoundException e)
            {System.out.println(e);}

        // test getAll for docks & slips
        System.out.println("\nRESULTS of getAll:");
        docks = Dock.getAll();
        for(int i = 0; i < docks.size(); i++)
        {   // list slips for this dock
           aDock = (Dock) docks.elementAt(i);
           printDetails();
        }
        // close the database
        Dock.terminate();
        DockAndSlipDatabaseConnect.terminate();
    }

    private static void printDetails()
    {
       System.out.println("\n  " + aDock.tellAboutSelf());
       slips = aDock.getSlips();
       for(int j = 0; j < slips.size(); j++)
       { // list slips for this dock
          aSlip = (Slip) slips.elementAt(j);
          System.out.println("     " + aSlip.tellAboutSelf());
       }
    }
}
```

Figure 15-27 The TesterTwo program

15

RESULTS of find dock 1:

 Dock 1 Location is Main Cove, Has Electricity, Has No Water
   Slip 1 Width is 10, Length is 20.0
   Slip 2 Width is 12, Length is 25.0

RESULTS of find dock 2:

 Dock 2 Location is Main Marina, Has No Electricity, Has Water
   Slip 1 Width is 16, Length is 35.0
   Slip 3 Width is 14, Length is 30.0
   Slip 4 Width is 10, Length is 20.0

RESULTS of getAll:

 Dock 1 Location is Main Cove, Has Electricity, Has No Water
   Slip 1 Width is 10, Length is 20.0
   Slip 2 Width is 12, Length is 25.0

 Dock 2 Location is Main Marina, Has No Electricity, Has Water
   Slip 1 Width is 16, Length is 35.0
   Slip 3 Width is 14, Length is 30.0
   Slip 4 Width is 10, Length is 20.0

Figure 15-28   Output of the TesterTwo program

Hands-on Exercise 2

1. If you have not already done so:
   a. Create a Chapter15Example2 folder on your system.
   b. Locate **DockAndSlipDatabase.mdb** in the Example2 folder for this chapter on the book's CD, and copy it to the folder you created in Step 1a.

2. Register this database with the ODBC using the procedure described in Step 2 of Hands-on Exercise 1, and ensure that it is not write-protected.

3. Copy all of the java source files in the Example2 folder for this chapter on the book's CD to the Chapter15Example2 folder on your system.

4. Compile TesterTwo using the software recommended by your instructor.

5. Run TesterTwo and verify that the program output is as shown in Figure 15-28.

IMPLEMENTING AN ASSOCIATION CLASS IN A DATABASE APPLICATION

You have learned how to implement one-to-one and one-to-many associations in a relational database application. To develop a complete database application for Bradshaw Marina, however, you must also implement the Lease association class. The Lease class, along with its AnnualLease and DailyLease subclasses, was first introduced in Chapter 8. In Chapter 9, you learned how to create and use the Lease class when persistence was not an issue. You will now learn how to implement the Lease association class in a relational database application.

Understanding the Tables in CustomerLeaseSlipDatabase

This application involves three database tables: CustomerTable, LeaseTable, and SlipTable. Before developing the Java programs needed for this application, review these tables.

To open the database tables:

1. Create a Chapter15Example3 folder on your system.

2. Locate **CustomerLeaseSlipDatabase.mdb** in the Example3 folder for this chapter on the book's CD, and copy it to the folder you created in Step 1.

3. Start Microsoft Access, and open **CustomerLeaseSlipDatabase**. Notice that the database contains three tables: CustomerTable, LeaseTable, and SlipTable.

4. View the contents of CustomerTable, LeaseTable, and SlipTable. You will find that they contain the data shown in Figure 15-29.

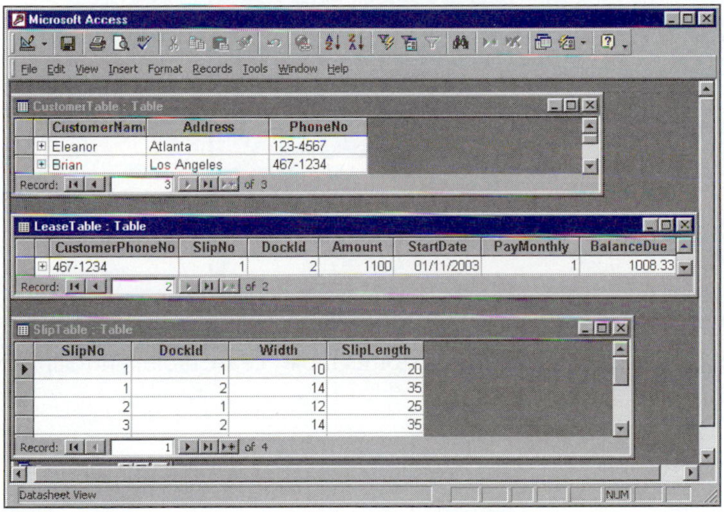

Figure 15-29 The contents of CustomerTable, LeaseTable, and SlipTable

5. Recall from Chapter 9 that there is exactly one lease between each customer and slip. For this reason, you can use customer phone number as the primary key for LeaseTable. Customer phone number is also the primary key for CustomerTable, which means that you can use the customer phone number in LeaseTable as a foreign key to information in CustomerTable.

6. Also observe that LeaseTable contains columns for slip number and dock ID. These columns serve as a concatenated foreign key to records in SlipTable. Figure 15-30 depicts these relationships.

The CustomerLeaseSlip application involves four problem domain classes—Customer, Slip, Lease, and AnnualLease. It also involves three data access classes—CustomerDA, SlipDA, and AnnualLeaseDA—as well as a tester class and a class to establish a connection to the database. For classes that have been discussed previously, only the modifications needed for the CustomerLeaseSlip application will be discussed here.

Establishing a Connection to CustomerLeaseSlipDatabase

As with DockAndSlipDatabase, you need a program that establishes a single connection to CustomerLeaseSlipDatabase. The PD and DA classes involved in this application will share this connection. The CustomerLeaseSlipConnect program is identical to the other connect programs in this chapter (except, of course, for the specified data source name) and is not discussed here. The code for this program is included on the book's CD.

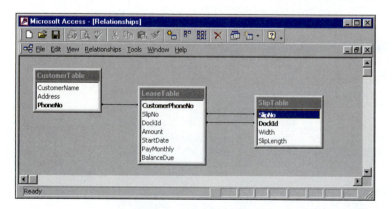

Figure 15-30 Relationships diagram for CustomerTable, LeaseTable, and SlipTable

Modifying the Customer Class

For this application, you need to associate a customer instance with its lease instance. To do this, add a lease reference to the list of attributes defined in the Customer PD class. Recall that the Lease class is an abstract class, which means that you cannot create lease instances. Instead, you must create instances of one of its subclasses (AnnualLease or DailyLease). In this example, the lease instance is of the AnnualLease type. The constructor initially sets the value of the annual lease reference variable to null. You include setter and getter methods to set and retrieve the annual lease reference. The revised source code is shown in Figure 15-31.

```java
// Customer with lease attribute added

import java.sql.Connection;

public class Customer
{
    // attribute definitions
    private String name;
    private String address;
    private String phoneNo;

    // reference variable for Lease instance
    private AnnualLease lease;

    // constructor with parameters
    public Customer(String aName, String anAddress, String aPhoneNo)
    {
        // invoke accessors to populate attributes
        setName(aName);
        setAddress(anAddress);
        setPhoneNo(aPhoneNo);
        setLease(null);// initially no lease
    }

    // DA static methods ******************************
    public static void initialize(Connection c)
        {CustomerDA.initialize(c);}
    public static Customer find(String key) throws NotFoundException
        {return CustomerDA.find(key);}
    public static void terminate()
        {CustomerDA.terminate();}

    // get accessors
    public String getName()
        { return name;}
    public String getAddress()
        { return address;}
    public String getPhoneNo()
        { return phoneNo;}
    public AnnualLease getLease()
        { return lease;}
```

15

```java
// set accessors
public void setName(String newName)
    { name = newName;}
public void setAddress(String newAddress)
    { address = newAddress;}
public void setPhoneNo(String newPhoneNo)
    { phoneNo = newPhoneNo;}
public void setLease(AnnualLease aLease)
    { lease = aLease;}

// tellAboutSelf
public String tellAboutSelf()
{
    String customerDetails = "Owner is " + name +
            "living in " + address +
            " with phone " + phoneNo;
    return customerDetails;
}
}
```

Figure 15-31   The Customer class with lease attribute

Modifying the Lease and AnnualLease Classes

The Lease problem domain class from Chapter 8 requires similar modification. The Lease class must associate a lease with its customer and its slip. Accordingly, you add a slip reference variable and a customer reference variable to the attribute list, and initially set them to null in the constructor. Include getter and setter methods to retrieve and set these reference variables. Recall that Lease is an abstract class, and you cannot create lease instances. In this application, LeaseTable contains information about instances of the AnnualLease subclass. Accordingly, the Lease class does not require DA methods. The modified Lease class definition is shown in Figure 15-32.

```java
// Lease with Slip and Customer references

import java.util.*; // for Date and Calendar classes
public abstract class Lease
{
    // attributes
    private double amount;
    private Date startDate;
    private Date endDate;
    // references to customer and to slip
    Customer customer;
    Slip slip;

    // constructor
    public Lease(Date aStartDate)
    {
        setStartDate(aStartDate);
        setEndDate(null);
```

```
      setAmount(0);
      // no customer or slip yet
      setCustomer(null);
      setSlip(null);
   }
   // abstract method subclasses must override
   public abstract double calculateFee(int aLength);

   // set accessor methods
   public void setAmount(double anAmount)
      { amount = anAmount; }
   public void setStartDate(Date aStartDate)
      { startDate = aStartDate; }
   public void setEndDate(Date anEndDate)
      { endDate = anEndDate; }
   public void setCustomer(Customer aCustomer)
      { customer = aCustomer; }
   public void setSlip(Slip aSlip)
      { slip = aSlip; }

   // get accessor methods
   public double getAmount()
      { return amount; }
   public Date getStartDate()
      { return startDate; }
   public Date getEndDate()
      { return endDate; }
   public Customer getCustomer()
      { return customer; }
   public Slip getSlip()
      { return slip; }
}
```

Figure 15-32   The Lease class with slip and customer attributes

The AnnualLease subclass from Chapter 8 includes the DA methods necessary to support this application. As shown in Figure 15-33, only four DA methods are needed: initialize, terminate, find, and addNew.

```
// AnnualLease with DA methods

import java.text.*;
import java.util.*;
import java.sql.Connection;

public class AnnualLease extends Lease
{
   // attribute in addition to those inherited from Lease
   private double balanceDue;
   private boolean payMonthly;

   // constructor
```

15

```java
public AnnualLease(Date aStartDate,
        int aSlipWidth, boolean isPayMonthly)
{
    // invoke superclass constructor
    super(aStartDate);
    // use calendar to add 1 year to start date
    Calendar aCalendar = Calendar.getInstance();
    aCalendar.setTime(aStartDate);
    aCalendar.add(Calendar.YEAR, 1);
    // invoke superclass method to set end date
    setEndDate(aCalendar.getTime());
    // invoke superclass method after getting fee amount
    setAmount(calculateFee(aSlipWidth));
    // invoke AnnualLease methods
    setPayMonthly(isPayMonthly);
    if (payMonthly)
        setBalanceDue(getAmount() - getAmount()/12);
    else
        setBalanceDue(0);
}
// DA static methods ********************************
public static void initialize(Connection c)
    {AnnualLeaseDA.initialize(c);}
public static AnnualLease find(String key) throws NotFoundException
    {return AnnualLeaseDA.find(key);}
public static void terminate()
    {AnnualLeaseDA.terminate();}
// DA non-static method
public void addNew() throws DuplicateException
    {AnnualLeaseDA.addNew(this);}

// custom method calculateFee
// overrides abstract method in Lease
public double calculateFee(int aWidth)
{
    double fee;
    switch(aWidth)
    {
        case 10: fee = 800;
        break;
        case 12: fee = 900;
        break;
        case 14: fee = 1100;
        break;
        case 16: fee = 1500;
        break;
        default: fee = 0;
    }
    return fee;
}

// set accessor methods
public void setPayMonthly(boolean isPayMonthly)
{  payMonthly = isPayMonthly; }
public void setBalanceDue(double anAmount)
```

```
    { balanceDue = anAmount; }

    // get accessor methods
    public boolean getPayMonthly()
    { return payMonthly; }
    public double getBalanceDue()
    { return balanceDue; }

    public String tellAboutSelf()
    {
        Date startDate = super.getStartDate();
        Date endDate = super.getEndDate();
        DateFormat x = DateFormat.getDateInstance(DateFormat.SHORT);
        String stringStartDate = x.format(startDate);
        String stringEndDate = x.format(endDate);

        String leaseInfo = "Lease amount: " + super.getAmount() +
                           "Start Date: " + stringStartDate +
                           "End Date: "   + stringEndDate;

        String annualLeaseInfo = "\n Balance Due: " +
                              Double.toString(getBalanceDue()) +
                              "Pay Monthly: " + getPayMonthly();

        return ( leaseInfo + annualLeaseInfo);
    }
}
```

Figure 15-33   The AnnualLease class with DA methods included

Modifying the Slip Class

The Slip class must associate a slip with its corresponding lease and customer. To accomplish this, you add an annual lease reference to the attribute list and set its value to null in the constructor.

```
public class Slip
{
    // attributes
    private int no;
    private int width;
    private double slipLength;
    private int dockId;   // added dockId
    private AnnualLease lease;

    // constructor with 3 parameters
    public Slip(int aNo, int aWidth, double aSlipLength, int aDockId)
    {
        // invoke accessors to populate attributes
        setNo(aNo);   // throws NumberFormatException
        setWidth(aWidth);
        setSlipLength(aSlipLength);
```

15

```
        setDockId(aDockId);
        setLease(null);  // initially no lease for this slip
    }
```

Include setter and getter methods to set and retrieve the lease reference.

```
    // set accessor methods
    public void setNo(int aNo)
        { no = aNo; }
    public void setWidth(int aWidth)
        { width = aWidth; }
    public void setSlipLength(double aSlipLength)
        { slipLength = aSlipLength;}
    public void setDockId(int aDockId)
        { dockId = aDockId; }
    public void setLease(AnnualLease aLease)
        { lease = aLease;}

    // get accessor methods
    public int getNo()
        { return no;}
    public int getWidth()
        { return width;}
    public double getSlipLength()
        { return slipLength;}
    public int getDockId()
        { return dockId;}
    public Lease getLease()
        { return lease; }
```

Three DA methods—initialize, terminate, and find—are needed as well. These methods are similar to those used in other problem domain classes. The only notable exception is that the find method includes two parameters in its parameter list—one for slip number and one for dock ID. Recall that slip number and dock ID, taken together, form the concatenated primary key for SlipTable, and for that reason you need both pieces of information to locate a particular slip in the database.

```
    // DA static methods *********************************
    public static void initialize(Connection c)
    {SlipDA.initialize(c);}
    public static Slip find(int aSlipNo,int aDockId)
        throws NotFoundException
            {return SlipDA.find(aSlipNo, aDockId);}
    public static void terminate()
        {SlipDA.terminate();}
```

You also need to define a custom method that associates the slip with its corresponding lease instance. This method, named leaseAnnualSlip, enables the Slip class to take responsibility for much of the processing involved in the "customer leases slip" application. The leaseAnnualSlip method requires three arguments—a customer reference variable (indicating the customer for whom the lease is being made), a date reference variable (indicating the start date for the lease), and a boolean variable (indicating whether the lease will be paid in monthly install-ments or in full at the time the lease is made). The start date and payment information, together with the width of the slip, are used to create a new instance of the AnnualLease class.

```
// custom method leaseSlip creates AnnualLease instance
public AnnualLease leaseAnnualSlip(Customer aCustomer,
                Date aStartDate, boolean isPayMonthly)
{
    // create AnnualLease instance and assign it to lease attribute
    // width is an attribute of this slip
    lease = new AnnualLease(aStartDate, width, isPayMonthly);
```

The annual lease instance invokes its setSlip and setCustomer methods to associate itself with the slip and customer instances. Then, the customer instance invokes its setLease method to associate itself with the newly created annual lease. A reference to the annual lease instance, which now contains references to its customer and slip, is then returned to the calling program.

```
    // tell lease to set its slip to this slip
    lease.setSlip(this);
    // tell lease to set its customer
    lease.setCustomer(aCustomer);
    // tell customer to set its lease
    aCustomer.setLease(lease);
    return (lease);
}
```

Introducing the SlipDA Class

As you will recall, the database application illustrating the one-to-many relationship between the Dock and Slip classes did not need a SlipDA class. In that application, the find and getAll methods of the Dock class performed the task of locating all of the slips for a dock. In the CustomerLeaseSlip application, however, you must find a particular slip so that it can be leased to a customer. Thus, you now need a SlipDA class.

The SlipDA class begins by declaring variables for slip attributes and those needed to estab-lish the database connection. This is followed by initialize and terminate methods, which are identical to those in the other DA classes.

```
public class SlipDA
{
    static Slip aSlip;

    // declare variables for the database connection
    static Connection aConnection;
    static Statement aStatement;

    // declare variables for Slip attribute values
    static int slipNo;
    static int slipWidth;
```

15

```
static double slipLength;
static int dockId;

// establish the database connection
public static void initialize(Connection c)
{
    try
    {
        aConnection = c;
        aStatement = aConnection.createStatement();
    }
    catch (SQLException e)
        { System.out.println(e); }
}

// close the database connection
public static void terminate()
{
    try
    {
        aStatement.close();
    }
    catch (SQLException e)
        { System.out.println(e); }
}
```

The only other method the SlipDA class needs is a find method. The find method defines a SELECT statement that returns information from SlipTable for a particular slip. Items extracted from the result set are used to create a new slip instance. This slip instance is returned to the calling program.

```
public static Slip find(int aSlipNo, int aDockId) throws
                        NotFoundException
{
    aSlip = null;
    // define the SQL query statement
    String sqlQuery = "SELECT SlipNo, DockId, Width, SlipLength " +
                      "FROM SlipTable " +
                      "WHERE SlipNo = " + aSlipNo +
                      "AND DockId = "  + aDockId ;
// execute the SQL query statement
try
{ // get the dock
  ResultSet rs = aStatement.executeQuery(sqlQuery);
  // next method sets cursor & returns true if there is data
  boolean gotIt = rs.next();
  if (gotIt)
  { // extract the data
    slipNo = rs.getInt(1);
    dockId = rs.getInt(2);
```

```
        slipWidth = rs.getInt(3);
        slipLength = rs.getDouble(4);
        // create Slip instance
        aSlip = new Slip(slipNo, slipWidth, slipLength, dockId);
      }
      else // nothing was retrieved
        {throw (new NotFoundException("not found "));}
      rs.close();
    }
    catch (SQLException e)
      { System.out.println(e);}
    return aSlip;
  }
```

Introducing the AnnualLeaseDA Class

In the CustomerLeaseSlip application, you must find and insert information about annual leases in the database. This means that you need an AnnualLeaseDA class. The Annual-LeaseDA class begins by declaring variables for annual lease attributes, then defines standard initialize and terminate methods.

```
public class AnnualLeaseDA
{
    static Customer aCustomer;
    static Slip aSlip;
    static AnnualLease aLease;
    static int payMonthlyYesNo;
    // declare variables for Customer attribute values
    static String name, address, phoneNumber;
    // declare variables for Slip attribute values
    static int slipNo, slipWidth, dockId;
    static double slipLength;
    // declare variables for Lease attribute values
    static double amount, balanceDue;
    static java.util.Date startDate;
    static boolean payMonthly;

    // references to customer and to slip
    Customer customer;
    Slip slip;

    // declare variables for database connection
    static Connection aConnection;
    static Statement aStatement;

    // establish the database connection
    public static void initialize(Connection c)
    {
        try
```

15

```
        {
            aConnection = c;
            aStatement = aConnection.createStatement();
        }
        catch (SQLException e)
            { System.out.println(e); }
    }

    // close the database connection
    public static void terminate()
    {
        try
        {
            aStatement.close();
        }
        catch (SQLException e)
            { System.out.println(e); }
    }
}
```

Understanding the find Method of the AnnualLeaseDA Class

The find method of the AnnualLeaseDA class structures a query that retrieves information from three tables: CustomerTable, LeaseTable, and SlipTable. Recall that the primary key of both LeaseTable and CustomerTable is customer phone number. Recall also that the SlipNo and DockId attributes in LeaseTable together comprise a concatenated foreign key that you can use to join LeaseTable with SlipTable. The WHERE clause uses these relationships to specify the matching conditions and the join conditions for the query.

```
public static AnnualLease find(String key) throws NotFoundException
    { // retrieve Lease, Customer and Slip data
        aCustomer = null;
        // define the SQL query statement
        String sqlQuery = " SELECT CustomerName, Address, PhoneNo, " +
                          " LeaseTable.SlipNo, Amount, StartDate, " +
                          " PayMonthly, BalanceDue, " +
                          " SlipTable.DockId, Width, SlipLength " +
                          " FROM CustomerTable, LeaseTable, SlipTable " +
                          " WHERE PhoneNo = '" + key +"'" +
                          " And CustomerPhoneNo  = '" + key +"'" +
                          " AND LeaseTable.SlipNo = SlipTable.SlipNo" +
                          " AND LeaseTable.DockId = SlipTable.DockId" ;
```

Items from the result set are processed in a straightforward manner. Because boolean variables are stored as zeros and ones in the database, you must convert the payMonthly attribute to its boolean equivalent.

```
    // execute the SQL query statement
    try
    {
```

```
ResultSet rs = aStatement.executeQuery(sqlQuery);
// next method sets cursor & returns true if there is data
boolean gotIt = rs.next();
if (gotIt)
{ // extract the customer data
  name = rs.getString(1);
  address = rs.getString(2);
  phoneNumber = rs.getString(3);
  // extract the Lease data
  slipNo = rs.getInt(4);
  amount = rs.getDouble(5);
  startDate = rs.getDate(6);
  int monthlyYesNo = rs.getInt(7);
  if(monthlyYesNo == 1) // convert 0/1 to boolean
     payMonthly = true;
  else
     payMonthly = false;
  balanceDue = rs.getDouble(8);
  // extract the Slip data
  dockId = rs.getInt(9);
  slipWidth = rs.getInt(10);
  slipLength = rs.getDouble(11);
```

The information obtained from the result set is used to create customer, annual lease, and slip instances. The annual lease instance invokes the setCustomer method to establish a link with the customer instance, the slip instance invokes the setLease method of the Slip class to establish a link with the annual lease instance, and the customer instance invokes the setLease method of the Customer class to establish a link with the annual lease instance. Provided there are no errors, the annual lease instance is then returned to the calling program.

```
// create Customer, Lease & Slip instances
aCustomer = new Customer(name, address, phoneNumber);
aLease = new AnnualLease(startDate, slipWidth,
                  payMonthly);
aSlip = new Slip(slipNo, slipWidth, slipLength, dockId);
aLease.setCustomer(aCustomer); // link lease to customer
aSlip.setLease(aLease); // link slip to lease
aCustomer.setLease(aLease); // link customer to lease
aLease.setSlip(aSlip); // link lease to slip
}
else // nothing was retrieved
  {throw (new NotFoundException("not found "));}
rs.close();
}
catch (SQLException e)
  { System.out.println(e);}
return aLease;
}
```

15

Understanding the addNew Method of the AnnualLeaseDA Class

The addNew method of the AnnualLeaseDA class adds a record to LeaseTable. The argument list receives a reference to the annual lease instance that will be added. The lease amount, balance due, payment type, and start date, along with references to the slip instance and customer instance that are associated with this lease, are extracted from the annual lease instance.

```
public static void addNew(AnnualLease aLease) throws DuplicateException
  { // retrieve the lease attribute values
    amount = aLease.getAmount();
    balanceDue = aLease.getBalanceDue();
    payMonthly = aLease.getPayMonthly();
    startDate = aLease.getStartDate();
    // convert date to String for database insert
    DateFormat x = DateFormat.getDateInstance(DateFormat.SHORT);
    String stringStartDate = x.format(startDate);
    aSlip = aLease.getSlip();
    aCustomer = aLease.getCustomer();
```

The program extracts the customer phone number from the customer instance, then extracts the slip number and dock ID from the slip instance. You must convert the monthly payment indicator (stored in the instance as a boolean value) to its integer equivalent (as that is the way it will be stored in the database).

```
    // retrieve the customer's phone no
    phoneNumber = aCustomer.getPhoneNo();
    // retrieve the slip no and dock id from the slip
    slipNo = aSlip.getNo();
    dockId = aSlip.getDockId();
    // convert boolean to integer
    if(payMonthly)
        payMonthlyYesNo = 1;
    else
        payMonthlyYesNo = 0;
```

Before executing the SQL statement that inserts this information into LeaseTable, the system checks to see if the lease with this primary key value already exists in the database. If so, the system throws a DuplicateException. Otherwise, it adds the lease record to the database.

```
    // create the SQL insert statement using attribute values
    String sqlInsert = "INSERT INTO LeaseTable " +
                       "(CustomerPhoneNo, SlipNo, DockId, Amount, " +
                       "StartDate, PayMonthly, BalanceDue ) " +
                       "VALUES ('"        +
                       phoneNumber + "', '" +  slipNo + "', '" +
                       dockId + "', '" + amount + "', '" +
                       stringStartDate  + "', '" + payMonthlyYesNo +
                       "', '" + balanceDue + "')";

    // see if this lease already exists in the database
    try
```

```
{
  AnnualLease a = AnnualLease.find(phoneNumber);
  throw (new DuplicateException("Lease Exists "));
}
// if NotFoundException, add lease to database
catch(NotFoundException e)
{
    try
    { // execute the SQL update statement
      int result = aStatement.executeUpdate(sqlInsert);
    }
    catch (SQLException ee)
    { System.out.println(ee); }
}
```

Testing the CustomerLeaseSlipDatabase Application

TesterThree begins by importing classes from the java.util, java.text, and java.sql packages. Classes within these packages contain methods to handle date and calendar information, and to establish the database connection. TesterThree then declares instances of the AnnualLease, Customer, and Slip classes. Next, it establishes a connection to the CustomerLeaseSlip database and passes this connection to the initialize methods of the Customer, Slip, and Annual-Lease classes.

```
import java.util.*; // for Date and Calendar classes
import java.text.*; // DateFormat class
import java.sql.Connection;

public class TesterThree
{
    public static void main(String args[])
    {

        AnnualLease aLease = null;
        Customer aCustomer = null;
        Slip aSlip = null;

        // initialize the database
        Connection c = CustomerLeaseSlipConnect.initialize();
        Customer.initialize(c);
        Slip.initialize(c);
        AnnualLease.initialize(c);
```

TesterThree attempts to add a new record to LeaseTable—in this case to show that a customer is leasing the first slip on Dock 1. The find method of the Customer class locates the record in CustomerTable for the customer with phone number 123-4567, then the find method of the Slip class locates the record in SlipTable for Slip 1 on Dock 1. Each find method returns an instance corresponding to the information in the database tables. The slip instance invokes its leaseAnnualSlip method, which creates a new annual lease instance.

15

```
// get a customer and slip
try
{
    aCustomer = Customer.find("123-4567");
    System.out.println("Customer Information:");
    System.out.println(" " + aCustomer.tellAboutSelf());
    aSlip = Slip.find(1, 1);
    System.out.println("\nSlip Information:");
    System.out.println(" " + aSlip.tellAboutSelf());

    // lease the slip to the customer
    Calendar aCalendar = Calendar.getInstance();
    aCalendar.set(2003, Calendar.AUGUST, 26);
    Date aStartDate = aCalendar.getTime();
    boolean payMonthly = false;
    aLease = aSlip.leaseAnnualSlip(aCustomer, aStartDate,
                payMonthly);
}
catch(NotFoundException e)
    {System.out.println(e);}
```

TesterThree then calls the addNew method of the Lease class to add the new lease to the database. If a lease for this customer already exists in the database, a DuplicateException is thrown.

```
// add the new lease to the database
try
{
    aLease.addNew();
    System.out.println("\nNew lease record added!");
}
catch (DuplicateException e)
    {System.out.println("\nLease already exists!");}
```

Next, TesterThree attempts to retrieve the newly added record from LeaseTable. The program passes the phone number 123-4567 to the find method of the AnnualLease class. The find method locates the lease record in LeaseTable and returns a reference to an annual lease instance containing that information. Recall that each annual lease instance contains references to its associated customer and slip instances. These references invoke appropriate tellAboutSelf methods, which display the customer, lease, and slip details. TesterThree then closes the connection to the database.

```
// find the lease on the database
    try
    {
        aLease = AnnualLease.find("123-4567");
        aLease.aLease.getCustomer();
        aLease.aLease.getSlip();
        System.out.println("\nLease Information:");
        System.out.println(" " + aLease.tellAboutSelf());
        System.out.println(" " + aCustomer.tellAboutSelf());
```

```
            System.out.println(" " + aSlip.tellAboutSelf());
         }
         catch(NotFoundException e)
            {System.out.println(e);}

         Customer.terminate();
         Slip.terminate();
         AnnualLease.terminate();
         CustomerLeaseSlipConnect.terminate();
      }
```

The output of TesterThree is shown in Figure 15-34.

Customer Information:
  Owner is Eleanor living in Atlanta with phone 123-4567

Slip Information:
  Slip 1 Width is 10, Length is 20.0
New lease record added!

Lease Information:
  Lease amount: 800.0 Start Date: 8/26/03 End Date: 8/26/04
  Balance Due: 0.0 Pay Monthly: false
  Owner is Eleanor living in Atlanta with phone 123-4567
  Slip 1 Width is 10, Length is 20.0

Figure 15-34   Output of the TesterThree program

Hands-on Exercise 3

15

1. If necessary, create a Chapter15Example3 folder on your system, and then locate **CustomerLeaseSlipDatabase.mdb** in the Example3 folder for this chapter on the book's CD, and copy it to the folder you created.

2. Register this database with the ODBC using the procedure described in Step 2 of Hands-on Exercise 1, and ensure that it is not write-protected.

3. Copy all of the java source files in the Example3 folder for this chapter on the book's CD to the Chapter15Example3 folder on your system.

4. Compile TesterThree using the software recommended by your instructor.

5. Run TesterThree and verify that the program output is as shown in Figure 15-34.

Summary

- Relational databases often include multiple tables. Information in different tables can be linked (or joined) when the tables share a common attribute.

- A primary key is an attribute (or combination of attributes) that uniquely identifies a single record in a relational database table.

- A foreign key is an attribute (or combination of attributes) in one table that serves as a primary key in a different (or foreign) table.

- Primary and foreign key columns often represent the common attributes used to link information in different tables.

- A concatenated key (primary or foreign) is one that consists of more than one attribute (or column) in the database table.

- Retrieve information in multiple tables by specifying a join condition in the WHERE clause of an SQL statement, provided the tables share a common column.

- Use an ORDER BY clause in an SQL statement to sort the information returned by a query.

- When multiple tables are required for a database application, create a separate class to manage the connection to the database. Modify PD and DA classes to use this connection. Include appropriate SQL statements and processing logic in the DA methods. Add attributes and accessor methods to PD classes to reflect table linkages.

- When multiple tables are involved, incorporate measures in the DA insert and delete methods to preserve the integrity of the database.

- When using multiple tables, DA find and getAll methods return a single instance of the specified type. This instance, however, will normally include one or more references to other instances of other types. Retrieve information from the database tables by navigating these instances.

- A control break occurs when there is a change in the value of a variable that is used to group records. Processing grouped data is very common in business applications.

Key Terms

concatenated key	foreign key	joining
control break		

Review Questions

1. Consider a relationship between Person and Pet. Assume that every pet has exactly one owner and that a person may own zero or many pets. Explain how you would implement these relationships in Java.

2. Assume that the information to be tracked in the Pet and Person application includes pet identification number, pet name, pet type (dog, cat, etc.), person social security number, person name, person address, and person phone number. How would you structure the tables in a relational database for the Pet and Person application? In other words, what columns would you include in the pet table and what columns would you include in the person table?

3. Identify the column (or columns) in each table that would serve as a primary key for the Pet and Person application.

4. Identify the column (or columns) in each table that would serve as foreign keys for the Pet and Person application.

5. Which DA methods would you suggest including in the Person class? Which would you include in the Pet class? Why?

6. Suppose that a list of all persons and their pets is needed. Give the SQL statement needed to extract this information from the database.

7. Suppose a person whose social security number is 111-11-1111 acquires a new cat named Molly, and that Molly's identification number is C123. Give the SQL statement needed to insert the new pet record into the pet table. Assume that information for this owner is already in the person table.

8. Explain the steps that you would take to protect the integrity of the database when a new pet is to be added to the database.

9. Explain the steps that you would take to protect the integrity of the database when an existing owner is to be removed from the database.

15

10. Can you think of a time when it would be necessary to add or remove a pet record from the pet table and NOT add or remove a person record from the person table? Explain how you would address this situation.

Discussion Questions

1. As you learned in Chapter 9, one-to-one associations have two directions. Consider the association between boats and slips: A boat occupies exactly one slip, and a slip is occupied by at most one boat. How would you structure the tables for a BoatAndSlip relational database application?

2. Recall that to implement the one-to-one association between Customer and Boat in the CustomerAndBoatDatabase application, you included a boat attribute in the Customer class and a customer attribute in the Boat class. You included an assign-BoatToCustomer method in the Boat class to establish the relationship in both directions—that is, this method associates a customer with the boat, and associates the boat with its customer. Why not include an assignCustomerToBoat method in the Customer class to set the customer for this boat? What, if any, is the advantage of assignBoatToCustomer? Why not have both?

3. In the CustomerAndBoatDatabase application, you included a boat attribute in the Customer class and a customer attribute in the Boat class. The find method of the CustomerDA class for this application finds both the customer and the customer's boat. Given that a reference to a customer is present, why not use BoatDA instead of CustomerDA to find the boat associated with the customer? What are the pros and cons of doing it each way?

4. Relational databases implement relationships using foreign keys. Java applications implement relationships using reference variables. Now that you have had some experience with both, discuss what you see as the major differences between using object references as attributes and using foreign keys in relational databases. What are the similarities?

Projects

Questions 1 and 2 refer to the programs and database you used in Hands-on Exercise 2.

1. In Access, open DockAndSlipDatabase and add several new slips to SlipTable. Leave the BoatID column in SlipTable empty to indicate that these slips are unoccupied. Modify the TesterTwo, Dock, and DockDA programs in Hands-on Exercise 2 to retrieve information about all of the unoccupied slips, including the location and availability of water and electricity on the associated dock. (Hint: To select rows in SlipTable that do not have a value in the BoatID column, include the condition *SlipTable.BoatID IS NULL* in the WHERE clause of an SQL statement.)

2. Extend the capabilities of the DockAndSlipDatabase application so that when the find method of the Dock class is invoked, information is available not only about a dock and its slips, but also about the boat that occupies the slip and the customer who owns the boat. To do this, you will need to add BoatTable, CustomerTable, and LeaseTable to DockAndSlipDatabase. (An easy way to do this for BoatTable, for example, is to open CustomerAndBoatDatabase, select BoatTable, and use "copy and paste" features to copy it to DockAndSlipDatabase.) Modify TesterTwo to invoke the find method for Dock 1 and report all dock, slip, boat, and customer details. Then invoke the find method for Dock 2 and report all corresponding details. You do not need to invoke the getAll method in this version of TesterTwo.

3. Refer to the programs and database you used in Hands-on Exercise 3. Suppose that Bradshaw Marina wants to track each lease that a customer makes over time. For example, a customer with phone number 123-4567 could have one lease with a start date of August 26, 2003, and another lease with a start date of August 26, 2004. With this in mind, modify the LeaseTable you used in Hands-on Exercise 3 to track multiple leases for each customer. Write a tester program that adds a second lease for the customer with phone number 123-4567.

4. For Project 3 at the end of Chapter 9, you developed an application to track boat service records. Recall that each boat might have zero or more services, and each service applies to one boat. The attributes of BoatServiceRecord are invoice number, service date, service type, and total charges. The project you created for Chapter 9 included the BoatServiceRecord class plus Boat and Customer, with the capability to associate the customer with the boat, and a method in the Boat class named recordBoatService to instantiate BoatServiceRecord. Convert this project to a relational database application. Write a tester program that inserts several service records into ServiceTable, making sure that at least one boat has more than one service record. The tester program should then retrieve records from the boat table (for the boats that have been serviced) and report information about the boat, its owner, and all service performed on that boat.

15

PART 5

Deploying the Three-Tier Application

CHAPTER 16

Combining the Three Tiers: GUI, Problem Domain, and Data Access Classes

In this chapter you will:

♦ Review three-tier design and the development process
♦ Combine a GUI, one problem domain class, and one data access class
♦ Use multiple GUIs and add an instance to a database
♦ Use a GUI with multiple problem domain classes

In this chapter, the first chapter of Part 5, you will learn how to combine the problem domain classes, GUI classes, and data access classes to form a complete information system module that provides a user interface, required system functionality, and object persistence needed in client-server applications.

You just completed Part 4, in which you learned how to use data access classes to provide object persistence. Chapter 14 showed you that object persistence can be achieved in various ways, although most business applications today require a relational database. A problem domain class is designed to interact with a corresponding data access class that implements object persistence. As you changed from sequential files to indexed files to a relational database, the problem domain class and the tester program did not have to change in Chapter 14. The only change required was to the data access class. In Chapter 15 you learned how to implement more complex data storage requirements using a relational database and multiple data access classes.

When you completed Part 3 earlier, you learned how to create GUI classes that implement a graphical user interface that can respond to user actions. The GUI classes are created using built-in Java classes that you combine to form a window with pull-down menus and panels containing buttons, lists, and labels. The GUI classes interacted with your problem domain classes, but object persistence was only simulated.

The next two chapters in Part 5 take the OO development concepts and techniques you have learned about problem domain classes, GUI classes, and data access classes and combine them to form a complete system module. This chapter demonstrates how to implement modules of the Bradshaw Marina application as a standalone system. Chapter 17 demonstrates how to implement three-tier application modules on the Web.

REVISITING THREE-TIER DESIGN

In Chapter 4 you learned about three-tier design as an architecture for structuring OO applications. The three tiers include GUI classes, problem domain classes, and data access classes. The user interacts with GUI class instances, and the GUI instances interact with problem domain classes and instances. Problem domain classes and instances interact with data access classes that handle storing and retrieving data from files or databases. Figure 16-1 shows how the three tiers interact to find a customer.

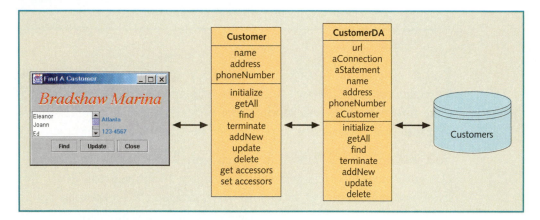

Figure 16-1   Three-tier design to find a customer

Having three tiers separates the functionality required for the user interface, the business application objects, and the database implementation. System maintenance is simplified as many changes made to the GUI do not affect the problem domain classes and data access classes. Similarly, many changes made to the data access classes do not affect the problem domain classes or the GUI. For example, the database management software can be upgraded or changed by modifying data access classes, but the problem domain and GUI classes are not affected. Similarly, the graphical user interface can be upgraded or changed without affecting the other tiers.

Three-tier design also provides benefits for distributing applications across the network. GUI classes can reside on the client machine, problem domain classes and instances can reside on a server, and the database can reside on another server. In this way, three-tier design lends itself to client–server architectures.

Three-Tier Design and the Development Process

Three-tier design provides a framework for organizing the system development process that is emphasized in this book. Recall that OO system development is done *iteratively*, with some analysis, some design, and some implementation occurring before continuing with more analysis, more design, and more implementation. OO systems analysis involves defining the requirement for the system—the use cases and problem domain classes required. Each use case is expanded into multiple scenarios that define what functions the system provides to users. The problem domain classes are initially defined in terms of their attributes and a few key methods. Additional details about the problem domain classes are added during each iteration.

OO system design involves adding details that specify how the system will be physically implemented. One detail involves the user interface: How will the user interact with the system to complete each use case? Therefore, GUI classes are designed to allow the user to interact with problem domain instances to complete a task. Another design detail involves object persistence: How will a database be used to store and retrieve data so objects are available over time? Therefore, data access classes are designed. User interface design and the physical design of the database are system design issues. Writing code to define problem domain classes, GUI classes, and data access classes is a system implementation issue (see Figure 16-2).

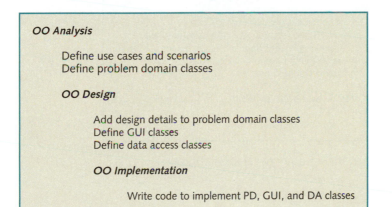

Figure 16-2   OO analysis, design, and implementation phases

The system development process as demonstrated for Bradshaw Marina starts with planning the project and defining the problem. The next step is defining use cases and problem

16

domain classes. Therefore, Chapter 4 described the business system requirements for Bradshaw Marina and introduced the use case diagram and class diagram. Figure 16-3 shows these steps at the beginning of the development process.

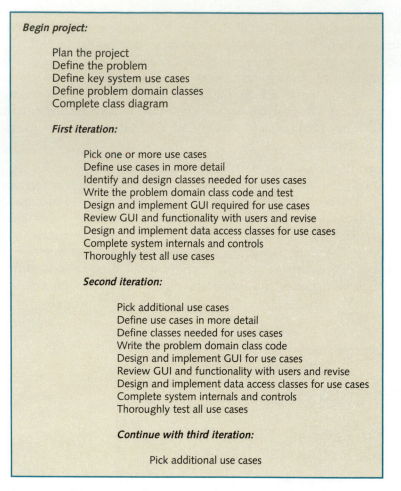

Begin project:

    Plan the project
    Define the problem
    Define key system use cases
    Define problem domain classes
    Complete class diagram

First iteration:

    Pick one or more use cases
    Define use cases in more detail
    Identify and design classes needed for uses cases
    Write the problem domain class code and test
    Design and implement GUI required for use cases
    Review GUI and functionality with users and revise
    Design and implement data access classes for use cases
    Complete system internals and controls
    Thoroughly test all use cases

Second iteration:

    Pick additional use cases
    Define use cases in more detail
    Define classes needed for uses cases
    Write the problem domain class code
    Design and implement GUI for use cases
    Review GUI and functionality with users and revise
    Design and implement data access classes for use cases
    Complete system internals and controls
    Thoroughly test all use cases

Continue with third iteration:

    Pick additional use cases

Figure 16-3   Steps in the iterative development process

Because you use an iterative approach to development, you can begin by focusing on some important use cases in the first iteration. In the Bradshaw case, you identified the problem domain classes involved in the use cases, and you implemented initial versions of them using Java. You added a constructor and accessor methods that all classes need, and you added some of the key custom methods. You tested the problem domain classes each time you added more functionality. You added validation and exception handling. You added subclasses, interfaces, custom exceptions, and association relationships. These techniques were covered in

Chapters 5 through 9. You did not worry about the user interface or about object persistence, but you did do some analysis, some design, and some implementation.

In a system development project, you would not try to implement all problem domain classes in detail all at once. Instead, you would identify the key classes needed for one or more of the use cases required in the system. Then you would implement those classes. You might move ahead by designing the user interface for those use cases, creating some GUI classes needed by users to interact with the system. As you saw in Part 3, the GUI classes could take the place of the tester programs you initially wrote to use to test the problem domain classes. In other words, you could simply plug in the GUI class in place of the tester program. Therefore, you did some design and some implementation for the user interface in the iteration.

In Chapter 11 you did not have to change the problem domain classes at all to add the GUI. In Chapter 12 you modified the problem domain classes so they would simulate using a data access class. Then you modified the GUI classes so they operated independently of any data access. At that point, most of your problem domain tier and your GUI tier were complete for those use cases.

Then your attention turned to object persistence and database management. You added data access classes that took the place of simulated object persistence. In the case of a relational database, you designed the database, created the database tables, and included foreign keys to join the tables. However, the data access classes can become complex, and in many cases database specialists are called in to work on them. You have done some design and some implementation for data access in the iteration.

When the three tiers are complete, final adjustments are made and they are now ready to be combined into a working system module. That is what you will learn how to do in this chapter.

Iterative development for the project continues, however. One approach is to begin the next iteration focusing on another use case. With Bradshaw Marina, the first iteration might focus on customers and their boats. The second iteration might focus on docks, slips, and leases. The third iteration might focus on reports and queries.

You might divide the project team based on specialties for each iteration. One team member might focus on problem domain classes and continue to refine the use cases and scenarios. Another team member might write the code and test the problem domain classes, while another might specialize on the GUI tier. Another team member might focus on the data access tier. As long as the team coordinates its work based on the use cases and problem domain classes, it is easy to divide the work when using iterative development and three-tier design.

16

COMBINING A GUI, ONE PD CLASS, AND ONE DA CLASS

The first example combining a GUI class, a problem domain class, and a data access class that you will implement involves the Customer class. The example uses a GUI named FindCustomer to retrieve information about a specific customer, similar to an example first shown in Chapter 11. Recall that the Customer class was introduced in Chapter 5 and was the first problem domain class implemented for the Bradshaw Marina system development project. Several key use cases involve customers, including Add new customer and Maintain customer information. The Customer class is also involved in other use cases, such as Lease slip, Transfer lease, and Renew slip lease.

Several versions of the Customer class have been used in this book, so you should review where and why the different versions were created (see Figure 16-4). In Chapter 5, the Customer class included a parameterized constructor and standard accessor methods. Although Customer was not modified in subsequent chapters, you learned that it could include a tellAboutSelf method, multiple constructors, validation and exception handling, and other features. In Chapter 9 you learned how to implement the association relationships between Customer and Boat and between Customer and Lease. Additional attributes and methods were added to implement the association relationships.

o   Customer implemented, enhanced with features
o   GUI implemented emphasizing usability (works with standard Customer)
o   Customer upgraded to simulate data access
o   GUI upgraded to work with final Customer (using simulation version)
o   Data access class developed and tested
o   Three tiers combined, tested, and evaluated

Figure 16-4   Steps for implementing the Customer class

The Customer Class in Chapters 11 and 12

In Chapter 11, GUI examples used the Customer class based on the simple Chapter 5 version. The Customer class did not have to be modified to be used by the GUI classes to add or find a customer because the GUI class created customers to be used for testing. The GUI class simply substituted for the tester program.

In Chapter 12, however, the Customer class was modified to demonstrate how the GUI tier could interact with a problem domain class independent of the approach used for data access. In other words, the GUI tier relied on the Customer class to get and return any needed Customer instances. Some data access methods were added to Customer, and Customer created some Customer instances from hard-coded data included in the Customer class definition. Now the GUI tier could be tested as though there was a data access tier, but the data access tier was simulated by the problem domain class.

The static methods added to Customer in Chapter 12 included initialize, which created six Customer instances and added their references to a Vector, and getAll, which returned the Vector of customers:

```
// Customer static methods added in Chapter 12
// create a Vector instance & populate with 6 new customers
   public static void initialize()
```

```
{
    customers = new Vector();
    Customer aCustomer;
    aCustomer = new Customer("Eleanor", "Atlanta", "123-4567");
    aCustomer = new Customer("Mike", "Boston", "467-1234");
    aCustomer = new Customer("Joann", "St. Louis", "765-4321");
    aCustomer = new Customer("Dave", "Atlanta", "321-4567");
    aCustomer = new Customer("Brian", "Los Angeles", "467-1234");
    aCustomer = new Customer("Dan", "Reston", "587-4321");
}
// return vector of customers
public static Vector getAll()
{ return customers; }
```

These methods are static methods, but they are also called *class methods* because they can be invoked by using the class name instead of by using an object reference. For example, to ask the class to initialize and then to return the Vector of customers, a tester program or GUI class would send the following messages:

```
Customer.initialize();
Vector customers = Customer.getAll();
```

After invoking those static methods, the tester program or GUI class would have access to a Vector containing references to all of the customers. The FindCustomer GUI class could put the customer names in a GUI list, for example.

An AddCustomer GUI also interacted with the Customer class in Chapter 12. Each time a new customer was added by the AddCustomer GUI, the constructor of Customer added a reference to the new instance to the Vector of customers that simulated the database:

```
// constructor with parameters
public Customer(String aName, String anAddress, String aPhoneNo)
{
    // invoke set accessors to populate attributes
    setName(aName);
    setAddress(anAddress);
    setPhoneNo(aPhoneNo);
    // simulate adding instance to the database
    customers.add(this);
}
```

The Customer Class in Chapter 14

In Chapter 14 the Customer class was used to demonstrate data access classes that implement sequential files, indexed files, and a relational database. The GUI tier was set aside, and tester programs were used to test the Customer problem domain class and its interaction with a data access class. Therefore, the Customer class was completed so it would work with a corresponding data access class named CustomerDA. This Customer class is shown in Figure 16-5.

16

```java
// Customer class for Chapter 16 example 1 ready for three-tiers
// Identical to Customer class in Chapter 14

import java.util.Vector;
public class Customer
{
   // attribute definitions
   private String name;
   private String address;
   private String phoneNo;

   // constructor with parameters
   public Customer(String aName, String anAddress, String aPhoneNo)
   {
      // invoke accessors to populate attributes
      setName(aName);
      setAddress(anAddress);
      setPhoneNo(aPhoneNo);
   }

   // DA static methods *******************************
   public static void initialize()
      {CustomerDA.initialize();}
   public static Customer find(String phoneNo)
         throws NotFoundException
      {return CustomerDA.find(phoneNo);}
   public static Vector getAll()
      {return CustomerDA.getAll();}
   public static void terminate()
      {CustomerDA.terminate();}

   // DA instance methods *****************************
   public void addNew() throws DuplicateException
      {CustomerDA.addNew(this);}
   public void delete() throws NotFoundException
      {CustomerDA.delete(this);}
   public void update() throws NotFoundException
      {CustomerDA.update(this);}

   // get accessors
   public String getName()
      { return name;}
   public String getAddress()
      { return address;}
   public String getPhoneNo()
      { return phoneNo;}

   // set accessors
   public void setName(String newName)
      { name = newName;}
   public void setAddress(String newAddress)
      { address = newAddress;}
   public void setPhoneNo(String newPhoneNo)
      { phoneNo = newPhoneNo;}
```

```
    public String tellAboutSelf()
      {
        return (getName() + ", " + getAddress() + ", "
          + getPhoneNo());
      }
}
```

Figure 16-5 Customer class definition from Chapter 14 that interacts with CustomerDA

Customer now includes four static methods and three instance methods that interact with the data access class named CustomerDA. The customers Vector, the hard-coded customer data, and the addition to the constructor have been removed. Customer no longer simulates data access; instead, it interacts with an actual data access class. This example was fully explained in Chapter 14. The four static methods are:

```
// DA static methods ********************************
public static void initialize()
   {CustomerDA.initialize();}
public static Customer find(String phoneNo)
      throws NotFoundException
   {return CustomerDA.find(phoneNo);}
public static Vector getAll()
   {return CustomerDA.getAll();}
public static void terminate()
   {CustomerDA.terminate();}
```

The initialize and getAll methods were included in the Chapter 12 version with different implementations. The find and terminate methods are new. Note that all four methods, when invoked, simply pass on the request to the CustomerDA class, which does the actual processing. In this way, the Customer class is always invoked by the tester program or by the GUI class, and the Customer class always passes on the request to CustomerDA.

Three instance methods are also included. These are invoked when the request is to add a new instance, update an instance, or delete an instance from the database. These methods also simply pass on the request to the data access class, supplying a reference to the Customer instance. They throw exceptions if a new customer already exists or if a deleted or updated customer is not found.

```
// DA instance methods ********************************
public void addNew() throws DuplicateException
   {CustomerDA.addNew(this);}
public void delete() throws NotFoundException
   {CustomerDA.delete(this);}
public void update() throws NotFoundException
   {CustomerDA.update(this);}
```

16

Reviewing the CustomerDA Class

Chapter 14 demonstrated several versions of CustomerDA. It introduced the version of CustomerDA using a relational database (in Example 4). Chapter 15 continued the discussion about relational database implementation with data access classes, and CustomerDA was modified to allow an association relationship between Customer and Boat and Customer and Lease. You will use the Chapter 14 version for the first example in this chapter, and that version of the CustomerDA class definition is shown in Figure 16-6.

```java
// CustomerDA for Chapter 16 Example 1 -
// Same as Chapter 14 Example 4

import java.util.Vector;    // for Vector of customers
import java.io.*;           // needed for file i/o
import java.sql.*;          // for SQL

public class CustomerDA
{
    static Customer aCustomer;

    // The Data Source name is "Chapter16CustomerDatabase"
    static String url = "jdbc:odbc:Chapter16CustomerDatabase";
    static Connection aConnection;
    static Statement aStatement;

    // declare variables for Customer attribute values
    static String name;
    static String address;
    static String phoneNumber;

    // Implement the four static methods in Customer *************
    // initialize, find, getAll, and terminate

    // establish the database connection
    public static void initialize()
    {
        try
        {
            // load the jdbc - odbc bridge driver for Windows
            Class.forName("sun.jdbc.odbc.JdbcOdbcDriver");
            // create connection instance
            aConnection = DriverManager.getConnection(url, "", "");
            // create statement object instance for this connection
            aStatement = aConnection.createStatement();
        }
        catch (ClassNotFoundException e)
            {System.out.println(e);}
        catch (SQLException e)
            { System.out.println(e);    }
    }
```

```java
// find an instance in the database
public static Customer find(String key) throws NotFoundException
{
    aCustomer = null;

    // define the SQL query statement using the phone number key
    String sqlQuery = "SELECT Name, Address, PhoneNo " +
                      "FROM CustomerTable " +
                      "WHERE PhoneNo = '" + key +"'";

    // execute the SQL query statement
    try
    {
        ResultSet rs = aStatement.executeQuery(sqlQuery);

        // next method sets cursor & returns true if there is data
        boolean gotIt = rs.next();
        if (gotIt)
            {
                // extract the data
                String name = rs.getString(1);
                String address = rs.getString(2);
                String phoneNumber = rs.getString(3);

                // create Customer instance
                aCustomer = new Customer(name, address, phoneNumber);
            }
        else
            {
                // nothing was retrieved
                throw (new NotFoundException("not found "));
            }
        rs.close();
    }

    catch (SQLException e)
        { System.out.println(e);}

    return aCustomer;
}

// get all instances from the database
public static Vector getAll()
{
    Vector customers = new Vector();
    // define the SQL query statement for get all
    String sqlQuery = "SELECT Name, Address, PhoneNo " +
                      "FROM CustomerTable ";
    try
```

16

```
        {
            // execute the SQL query statement
            ResultSet rs = aStatement.executeQuery(sqlQuery);
            boolean moreData = rs.next();
            // next method sets cursor & returns true if there is data
            while (moreData)
            {
                // extract the data
                name = rs.getString(1);
                address = rs.getString(2);
                phoneNumber = rs.getString(3);
                // create Customer instance
                aCustomer = new Customer(name, address, phoneNumber);
                customers.addElement(aCustomer);
                moreData = rs.next();
            }
            rs.close();
        }

        catch (SQLException e)
            { System.out.println(e);}

        return customers;
    }

    // close the database connection
    public static void terminate()
    {
        try
        {   // close everything
            aStatement.close();
            aConnection.close();
        }
        catch (SQLException e)
            { System.out.println(e);    }
    }

    // Implement the three instance methods in Customer ************
    // addNew, delete, update

    // add new instance to database
    public static void addNew(Customer aCustomer)
            throws DuplicateException
    {
        // retrieve the customer attribute values
        name = aCustomer.getName();
        address = aCustomer.getAddress();
        phoneNumber = aCustomer.getPhoneNo();

        // create the SQL insert statement using attribute values
        String sqlInsert = "INSERT INTO CustomerTable " +
                           "(Name, Address, PhoneNo)" +
                           "  VALUES ('" +
```

```
                              name          + "', '" +
                              address       + "', '" +
                              phoneNumber   + "')";

    // see if this customer already exists in the database
    try
    {
        Customer c = find(phoneNumber);
        throw (new DuplicateException("Customer Exists "));
    }

    // if NotFoundException, add customer to database
    catch(NotFoundException e)
    {
        try
        {
            // execute the SQL update statement, a 1 return good
            int result = aStatement.executeUpdate(sqlInsert);
        }

        catch (SQLException ee)
            { System.out.println(ee);    }
    }
}

// delete an instance from the database
public static void delete(Customer aCustomer)
        throws NotFoundException
{
    // retrieve the phone no (key)
    phoneNumber = aCustomer.getPhoneNo();

    // create the SQL delete statement
    String sqlDelete = "DELETE FROM CustomerTable " +
                       "WHERE PhoneNo = '" + phoneNumber +"'";

    // see if this customer already exists in the database
    // NotFoundException is thrown by find method
    try
    {
        Customer c = Customer.find(phoneNumber);

        // if found, execute the SQL update statement, a 1 return
        // is good delete
        int result = aStatement.executeUpdate(sqlDelete);
    }

    catch (SQLException e)
        { System.out.println(e);    }
}

// update instance in the database
public static void update(Customer aCustomer) throws
        NotFoundException
{
```

16

```
                    // retrieve the customer attribute values
                    phoneNumber = aCustomer.getPhoneNo();
                    name = aCustomer.getName();
                    address = aCustomer.getAddress();

                    // define the SQL query statement using the phone number key
                    String sqlUpdate = "UPDATE CustomerTable " +
                                       " SET Name      = '" + name +"', " +
                                       " Address   = '" + address +"' " +
                                       " WHERE PhoneNo = '" + phoneNumber +"'";

                    // see if this customer already exists in the database
                    // NotFoundException is thrown by find method
                    try
                    {
                        Customer c = Customer.find(phoneNumber);

                        // if found, execute the SQL update statement, a 1 return is
                        // good delete
                        int result = aStatement.executeUpdate(sqlUpdate);
                    }

                    catch (SQLException ee)
                        { System.out.println(ee);  }
        }
}
```

Figure 16-6   CustomerDA class definition for Example 1

The CustomerDA class is explained in detail in Chapter 14. Note that the data access class has the same four static methods as the Customer class with these method headers:

```
public static void initialize()
public static Customer find(String key) throws NotFoundException
public static Vector getAll()
public static void terminate()
```

The data access class also has the same three instance methods as the Customer class, but they are static methods in the data access class with these method headers:

```
public static void addNew(Customer aCustomer)
        throws DuplicateException
public static void delete(Customer aCustomer)
        throws NotFoundException
public static void update(Customer aCustomer)
        throws NotFoundException
```

The implementation of these methods is included in the data access class, so when asked, the Customer class or a customer instance passes on the request to CustomerDA. CustomerDA returns the result to Customer, and Customer returns the result to the tester program or GUI class. Now you can complete a GUI class to implement the first example.

Updating the FindCustomer GUI

The final tier for the example is the GUI named FindCustomer. A version of FindCustomer was introduced in Chapter 11, and it was designed to interact with the original Customer class. Therefore, FindCustomer in Chapter 11 included some code to create Customer instances. It is almost ready to work with the Customer class from Chapter 14, but a few modifications are required. The new FindCustomer GUI is shown in Figure 16-7.

Figure 16-7   The FindCustomer GUI

FindCustomer extends the JFrame class and implements the ActionListener interface. It declares reference variables for GUI components, a Vector of customers, and a found customer:

```
public class FindCustomer extends JFrame implements ActionListener
{
    // variables needing class scope
    Vector customers, customerNames;
    JList customerList;
    JLabel customerAddressText, customerPhoneText;
    JButton findButton, closeButton;
    Customer aCustomer;
```

The main method adds one additional statement that invokes the initialize method to create a database connection. FindCustomer invokes the static Customer method that, in turn, invokes the static CustomerDA method where the database connection is actually established. The other statement in the main method creates an instance of FindCustomer:

```
public static void main(String args[])
{
    Customer.initialize();  // create database connection
    FindCustomer frame = new FindCustomer();
}
```

As you learned in Chapters 11 and 12, the statements that instantiate and arrange panels, buttons, labels, and lists are placed in the constructor. An anonymous inner class is included to handle the window closing event, as before. FindCustomer invokes the getAll static method

16

of Customer to get a Vector containing references to all customers in the database. In the Chapter 11 version, the Vector was populated by invoking another method of FindCustomer that used hard-coded data (deleted from this version). The name of each customer is then obtained from each instance using the getName method as before. Finally, the names are added to the JList named customerList so the user can select a customer name:

```
// build JList
customers = Customer.getAll();// get vector of all customers
customerNames = new Vector(); // names used for JList
for(int i = 0; i < customers.size(); i++)
{
    //get customer reference, its name, and add to Vector
    aCustomer = (Customer) customers.get(i);
    String customerName = aCustomer.getName();
    customerNames.add(customerName);
}
// create the list
customerList = new JList(customerNames);
// add scroll bars to the list
JScrollPane scrollPaneCustomerList = new
                     JScrollPane(customerList);
```

Note that this code does not change from the Chapter 11 version except for substituting the Customer getAll method. Now that you have three tiers, FindCustomer asks for the Vector from Customer, and Customer passes the request on to CustomerDA. CustomerDA queries the database for each customer record and uses the record to instantiate a Customer instance. A reference to the instance is put in the Vector. When all customers are instantiated, CustomerDA returns the Vector to Customer, which returns it to the FindCustomer GUI. FindCustomer can now get information from any customer using standard accessor methods. Figure 16-8 shows a sequence diagram that illustrates the interaction of the three tiers. The complete FindCustomer GUI class definition is shown in Figure 16-9.

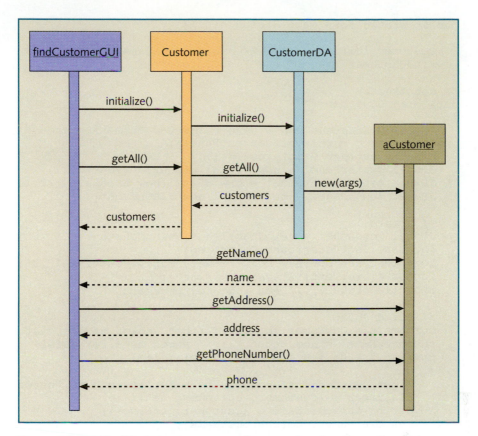

Figure 16-8   FindCustomer sequence diagram showing three-tier design

```
// Chapter 16 Example 1 - FindCustomer GUI
// Modified from Chapter 11 Example

import java.awt.*;
import javax.swing.*;
import java.awt.event.*;
import java.util.Vector;

public class FindCustomer extends JFrame implements ActionListener
{
    // variables needing class scope
    Vector customers, customerNames;
    JList customerList;
    JLabel customerAddressText, customerPhoneText;
    JButton findButton, closeButton;
    Customer aCustomer;
```

16

```java
public static void main(String args[])
{
    Customer.initialize();  // create database connection
    FindCustomer frame = new FindCustomer();
}
// constructor
public FindCustomer()
{
    // Use GridLayout and 3 panels for the Frame instance
    Container c = this.getContentPane();
    c.setLayout(new GridLayout(3,1));
    JPanel centerPanel = new JPanel(new GridLayout(1,2));
    JPanel centerRightPanel = new JPanel(new GridLayout(2,1));
    JPanel lowerPanel = new JPanel(new FlowLayout());

    // create logo
    JLabel logoLabel = new JLabel(" ",SwingConstants.CENTER);
    logoLabel.setForeground(Color.red);
    logoLabel.setFont(new Font("TimesRoman", Font.ITALIC,36));
    logoLabel.setText("Bradshaw Marina");
    c.add(logoLabel); // add logo to the Frame

    // build JList
    customers = Customer.getAll();// get vector of all customers
    customerNames = new Vector(); // names used for JList
    for(int i = 0; i < customers.size(); i++)
    {
        //get customer reference, its name, and add to Vector
        aCustomer = (Customer) customers.get(i);
        String customerName = aCustomer.getName();
        customerNames.add(customerName);
    }
    // create the list
    customerList = new JList(customerNames);
    // add scroll bars to the list
    JScrollPane scrollPaneCustomerList = new
                        JScrollPane(customerList);

    // create labels for address & phone
    customerAddressText = new JLabel("           ");
    customerPhoneText = new JLabel("          ");

    // add list and labels to the panels
    centerPanel.add(scrollPaneCustomerList);
    centerRightPanel.add(customerAddressText);
    centerRightPanel.add(customerPhoneText);
    centerPanel.add(centerRightPanel);
    c.add(centerPanel); // add center panel to the Frame

    // create & add Buttons for bottom panel
    findButton = new JButton("Find");
    closeButton = new JButton("Close");
    lowerPanel.add(findButton);
    lowerPanel.add(closeButton);
```

```
        c.add(lowerPanel);

        this.setSize(300,200);
        this.setTitle("Find A Customer");
        this.setVisible(true);

        // register frame as listener for button events
        findButton.addActionListener(this);
        closeButton.addActionListener(this);

        // create anonymous inner class for window closing event
        this.addWindowListener(new WindowAdapter()
            {
                public void windowClosing(WindowEvent event)
                    {shutDown();}
            }
        );
    }
    // actionPerformed is invoked when a Button is clicked
    public void actionPerformed(ActionEvent e)
    {   // see which button was clicked and findCustomer or shutDown
        if(e.getSource() == findButton)
            {findCustomer();}
        if(e.getSource() == closeButton)
            {shutDown();}
    }
    private void findCustomer()
    {
        // get index of list item selected
        int i = customerList.getSelectedIndex();
        // get corresponding customer reference
        aCustomer = (Customer) customers.get(i);
        // put customer info in labels
        customerAddressText.setText(aCustomer.getAddress());
        customerPhoneText.setText(aCustomer.getPhoneNo());
    }
    private void shutDown()
    {
        Customer.terminate(); // release database resource
        System.exit(0);
    }
}
```

Figure 16-9 FindCustomer class definition

The other FindCustomer methods are actionPerformed, which is unchanged, and shut-Down. The shutDown method invokes the terminate static method of Customer that passes on the request to CustomerDA, shutting down the database connection.

CustomerDA throws the NotFoundException and DuplicateException, so these must be included for the example to run. They are identical to the exceptions used for CustomerDA in Chapter 14.

Hands-on Exercise 1

1. Locate Customer.java, CustomerDA.java, FindCustomer.java, NotFoundException.java, and DuplicateException.java in the folder named Example1 in the Chapter16 folder and compile them using the software suggested by your instructor. Set up the database connection for the Microsoft Access database using Control Panel as instructed in Chapters 14 and 15. The database in the folder is named Customers.mdb, and the name used in CustomerDA is Chapter16CustomerDatabase. Run and test the example.

2. Create a second version of FindCustomer named FindCustomerByPhone that lists phone numbers in the JList and then finds a customer's name and address. Run and test the example.

3. Add the capability to update a customer's name or address to your FindCustomerByPhone GUI. Change the labels used for name and address to text fields and include buttons for find, update, and close. Recall that the phone number is the key value in the customer table, so it should not be changeable. Run and test the example.

4. The FindCustomer GUI gets the Vector of customers from Customer (which gets it from CustomerDA) and then gets the needed customer reference from the Vector. In other words, CustomerDA is only accessed initially. Create a GUI named FindOneCustomer that allows the user to type a phone number in a text field that is used to find the customer instance in the database. In other words, initialize the database but do not use the getAll method. Instead, use the Customer find method when the user clicks the find button. Run and test the example.

USING MULTIPLE GUIS AND ADDING AN INSTANCE TO THE DATABASE

The second three-tier example includes multiple GUIs and adding an instance to the database using a data access class. This example is based on Example 1 in Chapter 12. A main menu is included that allows the user to either find a customer or add a new customer. The FindCustomer GUI above is modified slightly to work with the main menu, as it was in Chapter 12. An AddCustomer GUI is added to the example based on the example in Chapter 12. The MainMenu GUI is identical to the example in Chapter 12. The same two custom exceptions are required: NotFoundException and DuplicateException. The MainMenu, FindCustomer, and AddCustomer GUIs are shown in Figure 16-10.

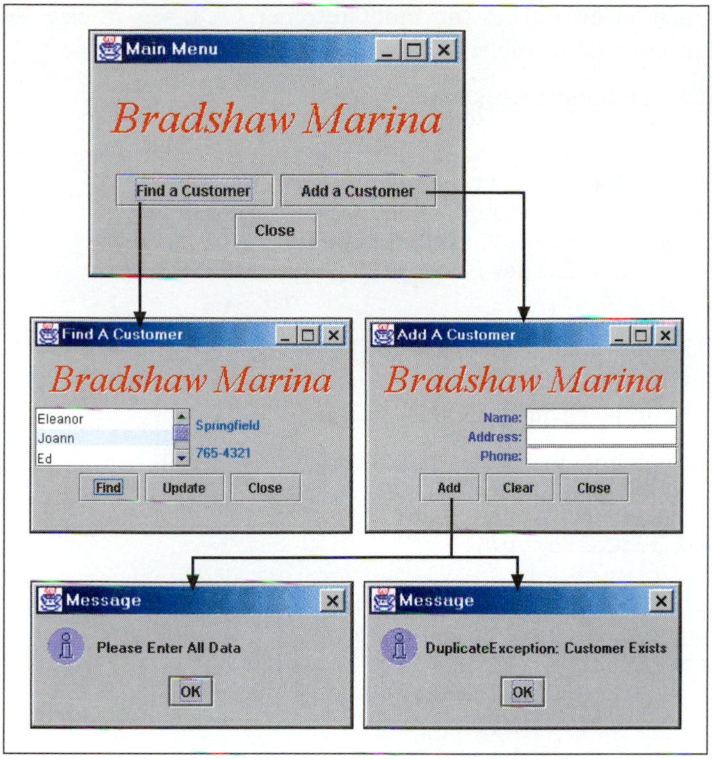

Figure 16-10   MainMenu, FindCustomer, and AddCustomer GUIs

Note that Customer and CustomerDA as defined in the example above *do not have to be modified* for this second example. Both Customer and CustomerDA already include the capability to add a new customer when asked. You are simply plugging in a new set of GUIs to handle user interaction.

Reviewing the MainMenu GUI

The MainMenu GUI class is identical to the version described in Chapter 12. MainMenu extends JFrame and implements the ActionListener interface. It has a main method that instantiates MainMenu. Therefore, when the example runs, it starts with MainMenu. There are three buttons that allow the users either to find a customer, add a customer, or close the application. The actionPerformed method invokes one of three methods when a button is clicked: findCustomer, addCustomer, or shutDown.

16

The findCustomer method instantiates the FindCustomer GUI, sets its size, sets its title, makes it visible, and makes itself invisible:

```java
private void findCustomer()
{
    FindCustomer findCustomerFrame = new FindCustomer(this);
    findCustomerFrame.setSize(300,200);
    findCustomerFrame.setTitle("Find A Customer");
    findCustomerFrame.setVisible(true);
    this.setVisible(false);
}
```

Note that the FindCustomer constructor accepts a reference to the MainMenu instance from the keyword **this** iso it can know about the main menu. This is one aspect of Find-Customer that will have to be changed for this example.

The addCustomer method instantiates the AddCustomer GUI, sets its size, sets its title, makes it visible, and makes itself invisible. AddCustomer also accepts a reference to the main menu:

```java
private void addCustomer()
{
    AddCustomer addCustomerFrame = new AddCustomer(this);
    addCustomerFrame.setSize(300,200);
    addCustomerFrame.setTitle("Add A Customer");
    addCustomerFrame.setVisible(true);
    this.setVisible(false);
}
```

Note that MainMenu *does not interact* with Customer or CustomerDA. There is no database interaction and no initialize, terminate, or getAll method invocation. FindCustomer and AddCustomer handle data access. The complete MainMenu class definition is shown in Figure 16-11. (This class definition is identical to the example in Chapter 12.)

```java
// MainMenu Chapter 16 Example 2 -- Multiple window navigation
// From Chapter 12

import java.awt.*;
import javax.swing.*;
import java.awt.event.*;

public class MainMenu extends JFrame implements ActionListener
{
    // variables needing class scope
    JButton findCustomerButton, addCustomerButton, closeButton;

    public static void main(String args[])
    {   MainMenu frame = new MainMenu(); }
```

```java
// constructor
public MainMenu()
{
    Container c = this.getContentPane();
    c.setLayout(new GridLayout(2,1));
    JPanel lowerPanel = new JPanel(); // default FlowLayout

    // create logo
    Font defaultFont = c.getFont(); // get font so can restore
    JLabel logoLabel = new JLabel(" ",SwingConstants.CENTER);
    logoLabel.setForeground(Color.red);
    logoLabel.setFont(new Font("TimesRoman", Font.ITALIC,36));
    logoLabel.setText("Bradshaw Marina");
    c.add(logoLabel); // add logo to the Frame

    // create Buttons for bottom panel
    findCustomerButton = new JButton("Find a Customer");
    addCustomerButton = new JButton("Add a Customer");
    closeButton = new JButton("Close");

    // add the buttons
    lowerPanel.add(findCustomerButton);
    lowerPanel.add(addCustomerButton);
    lowerPanel.add(closeButton);
    c.add(lowerPanel); // add lower panel to the Frame

    // register frame as listener for button events
    findCustomerButton.addActionListener(this);
    addCustomerButton.addActionListener(this);
    closeButton.addActionListener(this);

    this.setSize(300,200);
    this.setTitle("Main Menu");
    this.setVisible(true);

    // create anonymous inner class for window closing event
    this.addWindowListener(new WindowAdapter()
        {
            public void windowClosing(WindowEvent event)
                {shutDown();}
        }
    );
}
// actionPerformed is invoked when a Button is clicked
public void actionPerformed(ActionEvent e)
{
    // see which button was clicked
    if(e.getSource() == findCustomerButton)
        {findCustomer();}
    if(e.getSource() == addCustomerButton)
        {addCustomer();}
    if(e.getSource() == closeButton)
        {shutDown();}
}
```

16

```
   private void findCustomer()
   {
      FindCustomer findCustomerFrame = new FindCustomer(this);
      findCustomerFrame.setSize(300,200);
      findCustomerFrame.setTitle("Find A Customer");
      findCustomerFrame.setVisible(true);
      this.setVisible(false);
   }
   private void addCustomer()
   {
      AddCustomer addCustomerFrame = new AddCustomer(this);
      addCustomerFrame.setSize(300,200);
      addCustomerFrame.setTitle("Add A Customer");
      addCustomerFrame.setVisible(true);
      this.setVisible(false);
   }
   public void shutDown()
      {  System.exit(0);  }
}
```

Figure 16-11 MainMenu class definition

Reviewing the AddCustomer GUI

The AddCustomer GUI was first introduced in Chapter 11 along with FindCustomer. It was modified in Chapter 12 to be part of a multiple GUI example. AddCustomer is similar to FindCustomer except there is a method named addCustomer in place of findCustomer. The GUI components, the action listeners, the anonymous inner class, and the actionPerformed method are similar. There are some changes made to AddCustomer to allow it to work with the MainMenu GUI. These changes are emphasized here, and similar changes need to be made to FindCustomer. The AddCustomer class definition is shown in Figure 16-12.

```
// Chapter 16 Example 2 AddCustomer GUI
// Based on Chapter 12 Example

import java.awt.*;
import javax.swing.*;
import java.awt.event.*;

public class AddCustomer extends JFrame implements ActionListener
{
   // variables needing class scope
   JTextField customerNameText, customerAddressText,
         customerPhoneText;
   JButton addButton, clearButton, closeButton;
   Customer aCustomer;
   MainMenu parentMenu;

   // main not required - instantiated by MainMenu

   // constructor
```

```java
public AddCustomer(MainMenu menu)
{
    parentMenu = menu;        // set reference to main menu
    Customer.initialize();    // create database connection

    Container c = this.getContentPane();
    c.setLayout(new GridLayout(3,1));
    JPanel centerPanel = new JPanel(new GridLayout(3,2));
    JPanel lowerPanel = new JPanel(new FlowLayout());

    // create logo
    JLabel logoLabel = new JLabel(" ",SwingConstants.CENTER);
    logoLabel.setForeground(Color.red);
    logoLabel.setFont(new Font("TimesRoman", Font.ITALIC,36));
    logoLabel.setText("Bradshaw Marina");
    c.add(logoLabel);

    // create TextFields for name, address & phone
    customerNameText = new JTextField();
    customerAddressText = new JTextField();
    customerPhoneText = new JTextField();

    // add labels and TextFields to the panels
    centerPanel.add(new JLabel("Name: ",SwingConstants.RIGHT));
    centerPanel.add(customerNameText);
    centerPanel.add(new JLabel("Address: ",SwingConstants.RIGHT));
    centerPanel.add(customerAddressText);
    centerPanel.add(new JLabel("Phone: ",SwingConstants.RIGHT));
    centerPanel.add(customerPhoneText);
    c.add(centerPanel);

    // create & add Buttons to bottom panel
    addButton = new JButton("Add");
    clearButton = new JButton("Clear");
    closeButton = new JButton("Close");
    lowerPanel.add(addButton);
    lowerPanel.add(clearButton);
    lowerPanel.add(closeButton);
    c.add(lowerPanel);

    // register frame as listener for button events
    addButton.addActionListener(this);
    clearButton.addActionListener(this);
    closeButton.addActionListener(this);

    this.setSize(300,200);
    this.setTitle("Add A Customer");
    this.setVisible(true);

    // create anonymous inner class for window closing event
    this.addWindowListener(new WindowAdapter()
        {
            public void windowClosing(WindowEvent event)
                {shutDown();}
        }
```

16

```
        );
    }
    // actionPerformed is invoked when a Button is clicked
    public void actionPerformed(ActionEvent e)
    {
        // see which button was clicked
        if(e.getSource() == addButton)
            {addCustomer();}
        if(e.getSource() == clearButton)
            {clearForm();}
        if(e.getSource() == closeButton)
            {shutDown();}
    }
    private void addCustomer()
    {
        String customerName = customerNameText.getText();
        String customerAddress = customerAddressText.getText();
        String customerPhone = customerPhoneText.getText();

        if(customerName.length() == 0 ||
            customerAddress.length() == 0 ||
            customerPhone.length() == 0)

            JOptionPane.showMessageDialog(this,
                    "Please Enter All Data ");
        else
            {
            aCustomer = new Customer(customerName,
                            customerAddress, customerPhone);
            try    // addNew() adds customer to database
            {
                aCustomer.addNew();
                JOptionPane.showMessageDialog(this,
                    "Customer Added");
                clearForm();
            }
            catch(DuplicateException e)
            {
                // display exception information
                JOptionPane.showMessageDialog(this, e.toString());
                // do not clearForm so user can still see data
            }
        }
    }
    private void clearForm()
    {
        customerNameText.setText("");
        customerAddressText.setText("");
        customerPhoneText.setText("");
        customerNameText.requestFocus();
    }
```

```
// return to main menu
public void shutDown()
{
    Customer.terminate();          // release database resources
    parentMenu.setVisible(true);   // show main menu
    this.dispose();
}
}
```

Figure 16-12　The AddCustomer class definition

The first difference you will note is AddCustomer declares a reference variable to Main-Menu named parentMenu along with the other variables needing class scope. Another difference is AddCustomer does not have a main method. Instead, it is instantiated by MainMenu, and its constructor accepts a reference to the main menu as a parameter, which is assigned to the parentMenu reference variable. Additionally, the constructor also invokes the static Customer initialize method to create the database connection:

```
// constructor
public AddCustomer(MainMenu menu)
{
    parentMenu = menu;        // set reference to main menu
    Customer.initialize();    // create database connection
```

The addCustomer method is more involved than the findCustomer method in FindCustomer. The complete explanation is included in Chapter 12. It gets string data from the three text fields. Then it validates the three strings to be sure they have characters. If valid, Customer is instantiated using the three values from the text fields.

The Customer constructor does not add the new customer to the database, so in a try-catch block, addCustomer invokes the addNew method. Recall that the addNew method is an instance method of Customer, which passes on the addNew request to CustomerDA. CustomerDA uses an SQL INSERT statement to add the new customer record to the database. A try-catch block is required because the addNew method throws a DuplicateException if the key to the new customer (the phone number) already exists in the database. If the exception is caught by addCustomer, a message dialog is displayed:

```
private void addCustomer()
{
    String customerName = customerNameText.getText();
    String customerAddress = customerAddressText.getText();
    String customerPhone = customerPhoneText.getText();

    if(customerName.length() == 0 ||
       customerAddress.length() == 0 ||
       customerPhone.length() == 0)

        JOptionPane.showMessageDialog(this,
                "Please Enter All Data ");
```

16

```
        else
        {
        aCustomer = new Customer(customerName,
                           customerAddress, customerPhone);
        try   // addNew() adds customer to database
        {
           aCustomer.addNew();
           JOptionPane.showMessageDialog(this,
               "Customer Added");
           clearForm();
        }
        catch(DuplicateException e)
        {
           // display exception information
           JOptionPane.showMessageDialog(this, e.toString());
           // do not clearForm so user can still see data
        }
        }
   }
```

A final difference is the shutDown method. It closes the database connection by invoking the static Customer terminate method. Then the main menu is made visible:

```
public void shutDown()
{
   Customer.terminate();        // release database resources
   parentMenu.setVisible(true); // show main menu
   this.dispose();
}
```

Updating the FindCustomer GUI for Example 2

The FindCustomer GUI class used in Example 1 is modified slightly for Example 2. First, a MainMenu reference variable named parentMenu is declared, the main method is removed, and the constructor accepts a MainMenu reference variable as a parameter. Next, the constructor assigns the MainMenu reference to parentMenu and invokes the Customer initialize method. These changes are identical to those in the AddCustomer GUI above:

```
public class FindCustomer extends JFrame implements ActionListener
{
   // variables needing class scope
   Vector customers, customerNames;
   JList customerList;
   JLabel customerAddressText, customerPhoneText;
   JButton findButton, closeButton;
   Customer aCustomer;
   MainMenu parentMenu;

// main not required: instantiated by MainMenu
```

```
// constructor (with main menu parameter)
public FindCustomer(MainMenu menu)
{
    parentMenu = menu;              // set reference to main menu
    Customer.initialize();          // create database connection
```

The only other change is to the shutDown method. It is also the same as in AddCustomer above:

```
    private void shutDown()
    {
        Customer.terminate();           // release database resource
        parentMenu.setVisible(true);    // show main menu
        this.dispose();                 // dispose
    }
```

Hands-on Exercise 2

1. Locate Customer.java, CustomerDA.java, FindCustomer.java, AddCustomer.java, MainMenu.java, NotFoundException.java, and DuplicateException.java in the folder named Example2 in the Chapter16 folder and compile them using the software suggested by your instructor. You can use the same database that you used in Hands-on Exercise 1. An additional copy of the database is included in the Example2 folder. Run and test the example by adding several new customers. Try adding a customer with a duplicate phone number. Try adding a customer with a required value left blank. After you have added a few customers, make sure you can find them.

2. Modify your FindCustomerByPhone GUI from Hands-on Exercise 1 so it can be integrated into the example. The changes required are similar to the changes made to FindCustomer in this example. Modify MainMenu so that it allows the user to choose to find a customer based on a phone number and then to update the customer. Run and test the example.

3. Integrate the FindOneCustomer GUI from Hands-on Exercise 1 into this example by modifying it and by modifying MainMenu. Run and test the example.

4. Review how to add and use a menu bar and pull-down menus with a GUI as explained in Chapter 10. Modify MainMenu so it uses a menu bar as well as the buttons. Run and test the example.

16

USING GUI WITH MULTIPLE PROBLEM DOMAIN CLASSES

Example 3 uses two problem domain classes—Customer and Boat—in a query that requires joining two tables in the relational database, instantiating both boats and customers, and creating the association between instances. In this example, CustomerDA is modified to instantiate customers and boats based on an SQL query.

The GUI example is similar to an example in Chapter 12, but the original nonabstract Boat class is used without Sailboat and Powerboat subclasses. It also works without a MainMenu GUI. The GUI for the example is shown in Figure 16-13.

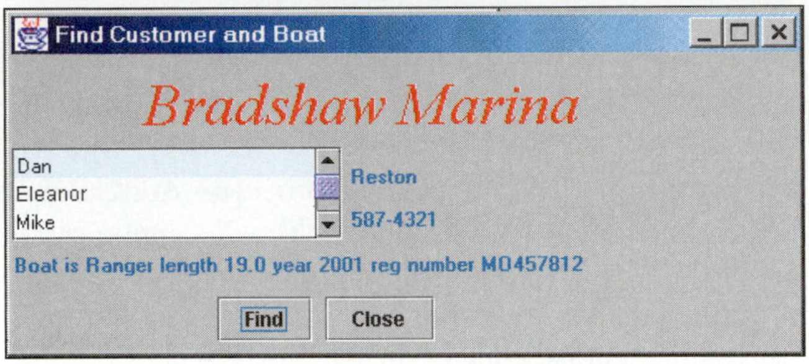

Figure 16-13   FindCustomerAndBoat GUI for Example 3

CustomerDA is based on the example in Chapter 15 and uses a relational database named CustomerAndBoatDatabase.mdb from Chapter 15. The database includes two tables, CustomerTable and BoatTable, including a foreign key in BoatTable named CustomerPhoneNo to allow the tables to be joined.

Reviewing the Boat and Customer Classes With an Association Relationship

Establishing an association relationship between Customer and Boat requires including a Boat reference variable in Customer and a Customer reference variable in Boat. The multiplicity is one-to-one in both directions, and this example was introduced in Chapter 9 and used for a data access class example in Chapter 15.

The Customer class in Examples 1 and 2 above needs to be modified to include a Boat reference variable, a getBoat method, and a setBoat method. In the constructor, the boat reference variable is set to null. No other changes are required.

The Boat class used in Chapter 15 included DA static methods and DA instance methods similar to the Customer class. This example does not require the use of BoatDA except that Boat methods refer to BoatDA. Therefore, you will need BoatDA for the example to compile. The complete class definition for Boat is shown in Figure 16-14.

```java
// Boat class for Chapter 16 Example 3
// from Chapter 15

import java.util.Vector;
public class Boat
{
   // attributes
   private String stateRegistrationNo;
   private double length;
   private String manufacturer;
   private int year;

   // reference variables point to Customer for this boat
   private Customer customer;

   // constructor
   public Boat(String aStateRegistrationNo, double aLength,
               String aManufacturer, int aYear)
   {
      setStateRegistrationNo(aStateRegistrationNo);
      setLength(aLength);
      setManufacturer(aManufacturer);
      setYear(aYear);
      // initially no Customer for this boat
      setCustomer(null);
   }
   // custom method to assign a Boat to a Customer
   public void assignBoatToCustomer(Customer aCustomer)
   {
      setCustomer(aCustomer); // point this Boat to the Customer
      customer.setBoat(this); // point the Customer to this Boat
   }
   // DA static methods ********************************
   public static void initialize()
      {BoatDA.initialize();}
   public static Boat find(String key) throws NotFoundException
      {return BoatDA.find(key);}
   public static Vector getAll()
      {return BoatDA.getAll();}
   public static void terminate()
      {BoatDA.terminate();}

   // DA instance methods ******************************
   public void addNew() throws DuplicateException
      {BoatDA.addNew(this);}
   public void delete() throws NotFoundException
      {BoatDA.delete(this);}
   public void update() throws NotFoundException
      {BoatDA.update(this);}

   // set accessor methods
   public void setStateRegistrationNo(String aStateRegistrationNo)
      { stateRegistrationNo = aStateRegistrationNo; }
```

16

```java
public void setLength(double aLength)
   { length = aLength;}
public void setManufacturer(String aManufacturer)
   { manufacturer = aManufacturer; }
public void setYear(int aYear)
   { year = aYear;   }
public void setCustomer(Customer aCustomer)
   {   customer = aCustomer;   }

// get accessor methods
public String getStateRegistrationNo()
   { return stateRegistrationNo; }
public double getLength()
   { return length; }
public String getManufacturer()
   { return manufacturer; }
public int getYear()
   { return year; }
public Customer getCustomer()
   { return customer; }

// tellAboutSelf returns attributes in a String instance
public String tellAboutSelf()
{
   return "Boat is " + getManufacturer() + " length "
          + getLength() + " year "
          + getYear() + " reg number "
          + getStateRegistrationNo();
}
}
```

Figure 16-14   Boat class definition ready to use with Example 3

Modifying the CustomerDA Class to Associate With Boats

This example is similar to the CustomerDA used with the FindCustomer GUI example. However, the CustomerDA class must be modified to accommodate a Boat reference for Customer. The complete example available on disk and explained in Chapter 15 includes changes to handle the boat reference in the following methods: find, getAll, addNew, delete, and update. This example only uses the getAll method, so changes to CustomerDA for Boat reference variables and changes to the getAll method will be described here.

The reference variables declared in CustomerDA include Customer variables and Boat variables because CustomerDA instantiates boats when the getAll method is invoked. The class definition begins declaring these variables:

```java
public class CustomerDA
{
   // Vector of customers, Customer reference and Boat reference
   static Vector customers = new Vector();
   static Customer aCustomer;
   static Boat aBoat;
```

```
            // declare variables for Customer attribute values
            static String name, address, phoneNumber;

            // declare variables for Boat attribute values
            static String stateRegistrationNo, manufacturer;
            static double length;
            static int year;
```

The database connection variables are then declared. Note that this example names the database source Chapter16CustomerAndBoatDatabase.

```
    // The Data Source name is "Chapter16CustomerAndBoatDatabase"
    static String url = "jdbc:odbc:Chapter16CustomerAndBoatDatabase";
    static Connection aConnection;
    static Statement aStatement;
```

The getAll method is invoked when the requester requires references to all customers. Customer instances include a Boat reference, so when CustomerDA instantiates customers it must also instantiate boats and assign the corresponding boats to the customers. Then the Vector of Customer references can be returned to Customer, which returns it to the Find-CustomerAndBoat GUI.

The getAll method uses an SQL query that joins CustomerTable and BoatTable using the common field for phone number. The ResultSet includes seven fields in each record, three for Customer and four for Boat. A try-catch block is used to execute the query and iterate through each record, instantiating a Customer and a Boat from each record. Each boat is assigned to its corresponding customer and the Customer reference is added to the customers Vector, which is finally returned. The complete getAll method is shown in Figure 16-15.

```
public static Vector getAll()
{   // retrieve Customers and their boats
    // define the SQL query statement that joins tables
    String sqlQuery = "SELECT CustomerName, Address, PhoneNo, " +
                      " StateRegistrationNo, BoatLength, " +
                      " Manufacturer, Year " +
                      " FROM CustomerTable, BoatTable " +
                      " WHERE PhoneNo = CustomerPhoneNo";
    try
    {   // execute the SQL query statement
        ResultSet rs = aStatement.executeQuery(sqlQuery);
        boolean moreData = rs.next()
        // next method sets cursor & returns true if more data
        while (moreData)
        {   // extract the data
            name = rs.getString(1);
            address = rs.getString(2);
            phoneNumber = rs.getString(3);
            stateRegistrationNo = rs.getString(4);
            length = rs.getDouble(5);
```

16

```
            manufacturer = rs.getString(6);
            year = rs.getInt(7);
            // create Customer instance
            aCustomer = new Customer(name, address, phoneNumber);
            // create Boat instance
            aBoat = new Boat(stateRegistrationNo, length,
                                manufacturer, year);
            // assign boat to customer
            aBoat.assignBoatToCustomer(aCustomer);
            // add customer reference to customers Vector
            customers.addElement(aCustomer);
            // set cursor to next record
            moreData = rs.next();
        }
        rs.close();
    }
    catch (SQLException e)
        { System.out.println(e);}
    return customers;
}
```

Figure 16-15   The revised CustomerDA getAll method

Introducing the FindCustomerAndBoat GUI

The FindCustomerAndBoat GUI is similar to FindCustomer used in Example 1. It includes a main method that establishes the database connection and instantiates the GUI. The constructor instantiates GUI components and completes the creation of the frame. A boatInfo-Label is included to hold information about the customer's boat.

The findCustomer method is similar to Example 1, except when the Customer instance is identified, its Boat reference variable is also obtained from the customer instance. The Boat reference is used to get boat information by invoking the boat's tellAboutSelf method. The sequence diagram illustrating FindCustomerAndBoat is shown in Figure 16-16. The Find-CustomerAndBoat class definition is shown in Figure 16-17.

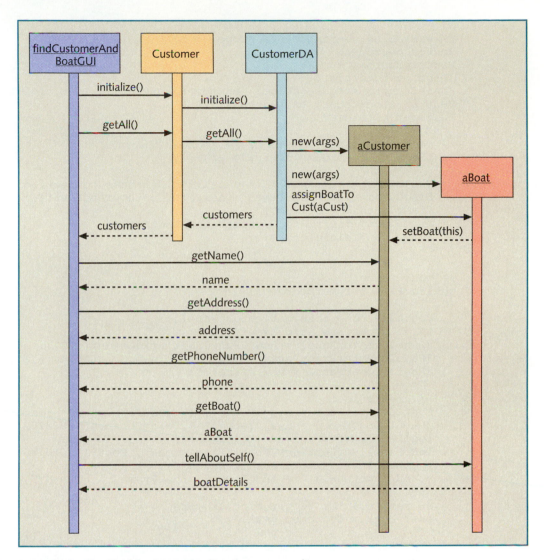

Figure 16-16 FindCustomerAndBoat sequence diagram

```
// FindCustomerAndBoat - Chapter 16 Example 3

import java.awt.*;
import javax.swing.*;
import java.awt.event.*;
import java.util.Vector;

public class FindCustomerAndBoat extends JFrame
                 implements ActionListener
```

16

```java
{
    // variables needing class scope
    Vector customers;
    Vector customerNames;
    JList customerList;
    JLabel customerAddressLabel, customerPhoneLabel, boatInfoLabel;
    JButton findButton, exitButton;
    Customer aCustomer;

    // main method because there is no main menu GUI
    public static void main(String args[])
    {
        Customer.initialize(); // establish database connection
        FindCustomerAndBoat frame = new FindCustomerAndBoat();
        frame.setSize(450,250);
        frame.setTitle("Find Customer and Boat");
        frame.setVisible(true);
    }

    // constructor
    public FindCustomerAndBoat()
    {
        Container c = this.getContentPane();
        c.setLayout(new GridLayout(4,1));
        JPanel centerPanel = new JPanel(new GridLayout(1,2));
        JPanel centerRightPanel = new JPanel(new GridLayout(2,1));
        JPanel lowerPanel = new JPanel();

        // create logo
        Font defaultFont = c.getFont(); // get font so can restore
        JLabel logoLabel = new JLabel(" ",SwingConstants.CENTER);
        logoLabel.setForeground(Color.red);
        logoLabel.setFont(new Font("TimesRoman", Font.ITALIC,36));
        logoLabel.setText("Bradshaw Marina");
        c.add(logoLabel); // add logo to the Frame

        // retrieve the Vector of customers
        customers = Customer.getAll();

        // store customer names in a vector
        customerNames = new Vector();
        for(int i = 0; i < customers.size(); i++)
            {
                aCustomer = (Customer) customers.get(i);
                String customerName = aCustomer.getName();
                customerNames.add(customerName);
            }
        // create a list containing customer names
        customerList = new JList(customerNames);
        // add scroll bars to the list
        JScrollPane scrollPaneCustomerList =
                        new JScrollPane(customerList);
        centerPanel.add(scrollPaneCustomerList);
        // create Labels for address, phone & boat info
```

```java
        customerAddressLabel = new JLabel();
        customerPhoneLabel = new JLabel();
        boatInfoLabel = new JLabel();
        // add labels to panels and panels to the frame
        centerRightPanel.add(customerAddressLabel);
        centerRightPanel.add(customerPhoneLabel);
        centerPanel.add(centerRightPanel);
        c.add(centerPanel); // add center panel to the Frame
        c.add(boatInfoLabel);

        // create Buttons for bottom panel
        findButton = new JButton("Find");
        exitButton = new JButton("Close");
        // add the buttons
        lowerPanel.add(findButton);
        lowerPanel.add(exitButton);
        c.add(lowerPanel); // add lower panel to the Frame

        // register frame as listener for button events
        findButton.addActionListener(this);
        exitButton.addActionListener(this);

        // create anonymous inner class for window closing event
        this.addWindowListener(new WindowAdapter()
            {
                public void windowClosing(WindowEvent event)
                    {shutDown();}
            }
        );
    }
    // actionPerformed is invoked when a Button is clicked
    public void actionPerformed(ActionEvent e)
    {
        // see which button was clicked
        if(e.getSource() == findButton)
            {findCustomer();}
        if(e.getSource() == exitButton)
            {shutDown();}
    }
    private void findCustomer()
    {
        // get list item index and customer reference
        int i = customerList.getSelectedIndex();
        aCustomer = (Customer) customers.get(i);
        // get customer details
        customerAddressLabel.setText(aCustomer.getAddress());
        customerPhoneLabel.setText(aCustomer.getPhoneNo());
        // get boat details
        Boat aBoat = aCustomer.getBoat();
        String boatInfo = aBoat.tellAboutSelf();
        boatInfoLabel.setText(boatInfo);
    }
```

16

```
public void shutDown()
{
    Customer.terminate();
    System.exit(0);
}
}
```

Figure 16-17   FindCustomerAndBoat class definition

Hands-on Exercise 3

1. Locate Customer.java, Boat.java, CustomerDA.java, FindCustomerAndBoat.java, NotFoundException.java, DuplicateException.java, and BoatDA.java (needed to compile the example but not to run it) in the folder named Example3 in the Chapter16 folder, and compile them using the software suggested by your instructor. This example uses a database named CustomerAndBoatDatabase.mdb in the Example3 folder, and the name used in CustomerDA is Chapter16CustomerAndBoatDatabase. Set up the database connection for the Microsoft Access database using Control Panel as instructed in Chapters 14 and 15. Run and test the example.

2. In Hands-on Exercise 1, you added a GUI that searched for a customer by phone number as an alternative to searching by name. Create a similar GUI named FindCustomerAndBoatByPhone. Run and test the example.

3. In Hands-on Exercise 1, you added a FindCustomer GUI that searched for a customer based on a specified phone number. Create a similar GUI for this example, but without the ability to update customer information.

4. Include a MainMenu GUI that works with the three FindCustomer GUIs you have implemented for this Hands-on Exercise. Include a menu bar and drop-down menus as well as buttons.

Summary

■ Three-tier design is a strategy for creating OO applications that are easy to maintain because the three tiers communicate using messages while hiding their implementations. One tier can be modified without affecting the other tiers. In previous chapters, you learned how to create and test each tier. In this chapter, you learned how to combine the three tiers into a working application module.

- Three-tier design provides a framework that lends itself to iterative development, where some analysis, some design, and some implementation are completed and then the process repeats with more analysis, more design, and more implementation. A good approach to use to complete an iteration is to define and create problem domain classes, then GUI classes, and then data access classes for one or two use cases at a time. That is the process followed in this book.

- The first example was FindCustomer, which demonstrated one GUI, one problem domain class, one data access class, and a database with one table. The example reads from the database but does not update it.

- The second example included multiple GUIs, including MainMenu, AddCustomer, and FindCustomer. One problem domain and one data access class are used, but the example involves adding records to the database.

- The third example was FindCustomerAndBoat; it uses a database with two tables and two corresponding problem domain classes with an association relationship. The CustomerDA class looks up customer records and boat records based on a relational join in the database, and then instantiates and associates customers and boats.

Review Questions

1. Explain how system maintenance is simplified with three-tier design.

2. Explain how three-tier design provides benefits for distributing an application across a network.

3. Explain how three-tier design can be used to define the tasks done in each iteration of the development process.

4. In Figure 16-1, which of the methods in Customer are static methods? Which are instance methods?

5. In Figure 16-1, which of the methods in CustomerDA are static methods? Are there any instance methods in CustomerDA?

6. Review Figure 16-2. In which life cycle phase would you define needed code for a problem domain class that included a constructor and standard accessor methods?

16

7. Again referencing Figure 16–2, in which life cycle phase would you define needed code for problem domain class static methods such as initialize, find, and getAll?

8. In which life cycle phase would you define the needed GUI classes? The needed data access classes? The needed database schema?

9. Explain how defining, coding, and testing the PD classes; defining, coding, and testing the GUI classes; and defining, coding, and testing the DA classes involve several analysis, design, and implementation iterations within an iteration that completes a use case.

10. Review the sequence diagram shown in Figure 16–8. Why does it include Customer (not underlined) as well as aCustomer (underlined) on the same diagram?

11. Again consider the sequence diagram shown in Figure 16–8. This interaction instantiates customers from the database so the user can find them. Therefore, update and addNew methods are not invoked. If the example did update or add a new customer instance, where would the messages from the GUI point: to Customer, to CustomerDA, or to aCustomer? Why?

12. What is the difference in function for problem domain setter methods and the update method?

13. What is the difference in function for the problem domain class constructor and the addNew method?

14. The MainMenu GUI from Chapter 12 is used without revision in this chapter even though data access classes and a relational database are included. Briefly list the changes that were made to FindCustomer and AddCustomer compared with the versions used in Chapter 12.

15. The FindCustomerAndBoat GUI did not use the Sailboat and Powerboat subclasses in this chapter, although the example did include the subclasses in Chapter 12. Briefly describe the changes you would have to make to the example to include the subclasses.

Discussion Questions

1. Discuss the strategy used in one iteration for Bradshaw Marina to create PD classes, GUI classes, and then DA classes. Why does it make sense to create the GUI classes before the data access classes? Or does it matter? What are a few reasons that different team members might focus on each activity?

2. Consider the design approach used for CustomerDA in Example 3. The getAll method returned a Vector of customers, but only after instantiating boats and associating boats and customers. The find method also instantiated boats. In the complete Bradshaw Marina system, what other responsibilities for instantiation might CustomerDA have? What are some additional methods that might be included to handle all of the requirements? (*Hint*: Is the find method different from findCustomerAndBoat or findCustomerAndLease?)

3. Given the discussion in Question 2, what are some additional methods that might be included in BoatDA? In SlipDA? In DockDA? In LeaseDA? To what extent would well-conceived use cases and scenarios help define the methods needed?

4. Consider the following design strategy: Have each PD class setter method invoke the update method so any change to attribute value is updated in the database immediately. What would be a specific problem with this strategy related to the constructor? What would be a specific problem with this strategy related to database management?

Projects

1. Consider an application that contains the Student class. A student has an ID, name, phone number, grade point average, and major. Draw a class diagram showing the Student class and the StudentDA class, including methods required for data access. Create a three-tier application with a relational database, a MainMenu GUI, a GUI for adding a student, and a GUI for finding and updating a student. You will need a database containing one table with test data, a Student class, and a StudentDA class. Create a tester program to test the classes and the database as shown in Chapter 15. Then add the MainMenu, AddStudent, and FindAndUpdateStudent GUI classes.

2. Recall the Person and Pet example from Project 1 in Chapter 9. It was also used as an example in the Chapter 15 Review Questions. Implement the database for the example with two tables—a person table and a pet table. The pet table should have a foreign key corresponding to the person ID field so that you can join the tables. Create a Person class, a Pet class, a PersonDA class, and a PetDA class. Note that you will need a PersonAndPetDatabaseConnect class similar to the examples with multiple data access classes in Chapter 15. As sample data, add at least four person records and four pet records to the database. Assume initially that a person has zero or one pets and a pet is owned by one and only one person. Write a tester program that tests the Person and Pet classes' getAll methods and find methods. Write another tester program that tests the Person and Pet addNew, update, and delete methods.

16

3. For the Person and Pet example in Project 2, design and implement GUI classes to replace the tester programs. Include a MainMenu GUI, an AddPerson GUI, an AddPet GUI, a FindPerson GUI, and a FindPetAndPerson GUI. Continue to assume that a person is not required to have a pet, but a pet must be associated with one person. Therefore, FindPerson will return only person information, even a person who does not have a pet. But because each pet must be associated with a person, the FindPetAndPerson GUI can include person information for each pet. The AddPerson GUI can be similar to AddCustomer, but AddPet should allow the user to select from a list the person who owns the pet. *Hint*: Because you need both PetDA and PersonDA to share the same database connection, have MainMenu invoke the initialize method of PersonAndPetDatabaseConnect to get the connection reference. Then design the constructor for each GUI instantiated by MainMenu so it accepts the connection reference as a parameter. For example: **public** FindPerson(MainMenu menu, Connection aConnection).

4. Consider what changes are required to modify the Person and Pet example so the association relationship is one-to-many—a person can own many pets. Create a FindPersonAndPet GUI that will display one or more pets for a person, and add it to the example created for Project 3. (*Hint*: The database does not need to be changed, but you will need to change the Person and PersonDA classes.)

17

Deploying Java Applications on the Web

In this chapter you will:

♦ Learn about the client-server model of computing

♦ Create input forms for Web applications using HTML

♦ Write Java servlets to process HTML forms and interact with databases over the Web

♦ Install a simple Web server to test your servlets

♦ Validate HTML input forms using JavaScript

♦ Use HTML, Java servlets, JavaScript, and Java Server Pages (JSPs) to develop a Web site for Bradshaw Marina

♦ Explore other technologies that support Web application development

Throughout this text, you have learned to write many kinds of Java programs, ranging from very simple to reasonably complex. Just as importantly, you have learned how to develop business applications using an object-oriented approach. From the beginning, you have followed a three-tiered design, keeping problem domain, data access, and GUI classes separate from one another. In the previous chapter, you learned how to connect these components to create a working system. As you will see, one of the many benefits of this approach is the relative ease with which you can deploy applications that use these components on the Web.

Establishing an effective presence on the Web is critical to the success of many businesses, and deciding which technologies to use for Web application development is just as important. Java is an excellent choice for Web development due to its security features, networking capabilities, and portability. **Portability** simply means that programs you write in Java will run on any implementation of the JVM, regardless of the hardware platform.

In this chapter, you will learn how to use Java and several related technologies to develop a Web application for Bradshaw Marina. You will use HTML to create input forms that gather information from visitors to the Bradshaw Marina Web site. You will then write special Java programs, called servlets, that use this information to interact with the Bradshaw Marina database and provide dynamic content to the user. You will also see how to use JavaScript and Java Server Pages to extend the capabilities of the Web site.

Web application development is both challenging and rewarding. Many different technologies are involved; some of them are complex and all of them change rapidly. This chapter introduces you to some basic Java-related technologies and illustrates how you can use them to develop a Web application for Bradshaw Marina. The concepts and techniques you will learn are powerful and fundamental to developing Java applications for the Web.

Understanding the Client-Server Model of Computing

Web applications are based on a form of distributed processing known as **client-server computing**. Simply stated, in a client-server model the client requests an action and the server performs it. Whether you realize it or not, you are familiar with this form of computing—you use it every time you surf the Internet. When you initiate a request for your browser to locate a particular Web site (such as *www.course.com*), your computer is the **client**. The computer that responds to your request and returns the desired Web page is the **server**. Sometimes, more than one server is needed to fulfill a client request. For example, when you shop online, the Web server that responds to your request for product information may interact with a database stored on a separate server. In client-server lingo, this is called a three-tiered, distributed architecture—the client represents the first tier, the Web server is the second tier, and the database server is the third tier. This is a common arrangement; before developing your own Web applications, you must understand what happens in a client-server exchange based on this model.

Examining a Typical Client-Server Exchange

Figure 17-1 illustrates a typical exchange in a three-tiered, distributed architecture. The client computer first issues a request to the Web server. The request specifies the address of the Web page to be loaded and could include information supplied by the user, such as the quantity of a product to be purchased. The Web server gathers necessary data from the database server (such as prices and credit limits), carries out the logic needed to fulfill the request (such as calculating shipping charges and total price), and returns a response to the client.

Figure 17-1 shows how processing is distributed among the three tiers. The client runs the Web browser software and is responsible for the user interface. The Web server is responsible for the business logic. The familiar problem domain and data access classes reside here, together with Java servlets. A **servlet** is a Java program that resides on the Web server and responds to client requests. The Web server passes database query requests to the database server, which contains the database and any specialized software needed to execute queries. The database server is responsible for executing the queries and returning the result to the Web server. The Web server performs any additional processing needed before sending the result back to the client. The client is responsible for displaying the result to the user.

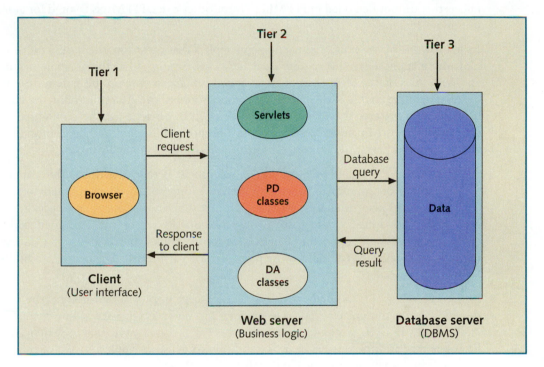

Figure 17-1 A typical exchange in a three-tiered client-server architecture

Notice that the distribution of responsibilities across the three tiers closely follows the approach you have seen throughout this text—the user interface, problem domain, and data access activities are separated. This is not an accident; by adopting this approach from the beginning, we greatly reduced the number of changes that are necessary to make things work in a Web environment. The most significant changes will occur in the user interface, which in a Web application is commonly handled by using either Java applets or HTML. **HTML (Hypertext Markup Language)** is used to format information that is displayed in a Web browser.

17

Creating the User Interface: Thin-client Applications

Deciding whether to use applets or HTML to create the user interface for a Web application requires careful consideration. As you discovered in Chapter 10, it is usually a simple matter to convert an existing GUI application into an applet. The decision between applets and HTML, however, should be driven by the functionality and performance you want for the Web application. Applets are required when a Web application uses animation or special effects that cannot be coded in HTML. In most other cases, HTML is favored for at least two important reasons.

First, browsers place security restrictions on applets that can make them difficult to use, particularly in applications that require database access. Among other things, applets cannot read and write files on the client. Although an applet can access data on the system from which it originates, doing so in a Web application can be troublesome. At a minimum, the client must be running a browser that supports the JDBC-ODBC bridge and be configured with the proper ODBC driver and data source name. This poses difficulties on the client side and creates a need for client-side support—a situation you should generally avoid.

Second, one of the design goals in Web development is to create **thin-client** applications. These applications minimize processing demands on the client, as opposed to **fat-client** applications that place higher levels of responsibility on it. For an applet to access a database on a server, the applet would have to originate on the server and be downloaded to the client, along with any supporting files needed for the applet to execute properly. Downloading takes time and adversely affects site performance, particularly for clients with limited processing power.

Using HTML avoids difficulties with database access, improves performance by decreasing download time, minimizes client-side support, and is consistent with a thin-client approach. Additionally, HTML works in situations where applets do not, such as when clients run browsers that are not Java-enabled. Try to limit your use of applets in Web applications to cases in which they are truly needed.

EXPLORING HTML: A SIMPLE EXAMPLE

Later in this chapter, you will discover how to create a Web site for Bradshaw Marina. First, however, you need to become familiar with basic HTML and simple servlets in a three-tiered client-server environment. Your first Web application will access data in the CustomerTable. Recall from Chapter 15 that this table has three columns—name, address, and phone number—with phone number serving as the primary key. In this Web application, an HTML form is used to obtain a phone number from the client. The Web browser then instructs the Web server to execute the servlet designed to process the form. The servlet requests the server to locate the record in CustomerTable whose primary key is this phone number, and then returns the corresponding name and address to the client.

Using HTML Tags

HTML code consists of **tags** that serve as keywords. Tags are contained within angle brackets, such as the <html> tag that marks the beginning of an HTML file. Many tags occur in pairs to designate the beginning and ending point of a particular kind of formatting. For example, the HTML code to center the words "Welcome to Bradshaw Marina" is:

```
<center>Welcome to Bradshaw Marina</center>
```

The <center> and </center> tags apply the centering format to any text that appears between them. Note that ending tags begin with a slash (/).

HTML has an abundance of formatting tags, and you will use many common ones in this chapter. Each tag will be explained as you encounter it in the examples; an alphabetical list of these tags is shown in Table 17-1. More information on HTML, including a complete list of tags, is available in a number of texts and online resources.

Table 17-1   HTML Tags Used in This Chapter

Tag	Meaning and Attributes
<! - - ... - - >	HTML comment
<body> </body>	Marks beginning and end of body
 	Line break
<center> </center>	Center
<em> </em>	Italics (emphasis)
<font> </font>	Font ■ color — font color ■ size — font size
<form> </form>	Form ■ action — specifies URL to invoke when form is submitted ■ method — indicates "post" or "get" request ■ name — name that uniquely identifies the form
<h1> </h1>	Level 1 heading
<h2> </h2>	Level 2 heading
<h3> </h3>	Level 3 heading
<head> </head>	Marks beginning and end of header
<hr>	Horizontal rule
<html> </html>	Indicates document is an HTML file
<img>	Image file ■ src — specifies location of image source file

17

Table 17-1 HTML Tags Used in This Chapter (continued)

Tag	Meaning and Attributes
<input>	Input element to include on a form ■ type — specifies type of input element to include (required), such as "text" for textfield, "Submit" for submit button, and "button" for command button ■ name — name that uniquely identifies input element ■ value — value assigned to input element
<p> </p>	Paragraph
<script> </script>	Specifies use of a Web scripting language ■ language — name of scripting language
<strong> </strong>	Bold
<table> </table>	Table ■ cellpadding — controls padding within cells ■ cellspacing — controls spacing between cells ■ align — aligns table (center, left, right) ■ bgcolor — sets table background color
<td> </td>	Table data cell ■ width — controls width of cell
<title> </title>	Title of the Web page (appears at the top of the browser window)
<tr> </tr>	Table row element ■ align — aligns table row

Using HTML to Create an Input Form

Your first HTML example explains how to create a document that generates the input form shown in Figure 17-2. The HTML code needed to render this form is shown in Figure 17-3.

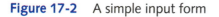

Figure 17-2 A simple input form

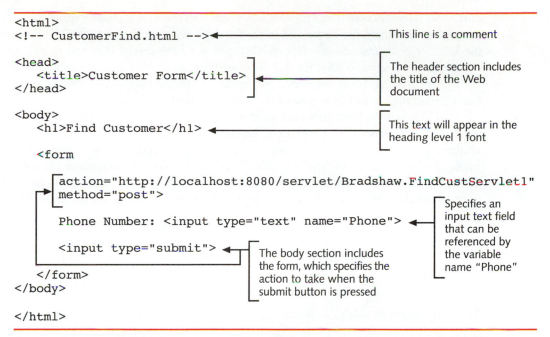

```html
<html>
<!-- CustomerFind.html -->            This line is a comment

<head>                                The header section includes
   <title>Customer Form</title>       the title of the Web
</head>                               document

<body>                                This text will appear in the
   <h1>Find Customer</h1>             heading level 1 font

   <form

      action="http://localhost:8080/servlet/Bradshaw.FindCustServlet1"
      method="post">                  Specifies an
                                      input text field
      Phone Number: <input type="text" name="Phone">   that can be
                                      referenced by
      <input type="submit">           the variable
                       The body section includes   name "Phone"
                       the form, which specifies the
   </form>             action to take when the
</body>               submit button is pressed

</html>
```

Figure 17-3   HTML code to generate the simple input form (CustomerFind.html)

The HTML file begins with <html> and ends with </html>. These tags indicate to the browser that everything between them is HTML. The second line of code is a comment statement. Comments in HTML are placed within a single tag that begins with <!- - and ends with - - >.

HTML files consist of two sections: a header and a body. The <head> … </head> tag pair indicates the beginning and ending of the header. Among other things, the title of the Web page is specified in the header. The title is placed between the <title> and </title> tag pair. The body of the HTML file is designated between the <body> … </body> tag pair. The <h1> … </h1> tag pair specifies a level one heading. HTML headings vary in size from h1 to h6, with h1 being the largest heading and h6 the smallest. Text rendered in an h1 heading appears in a larger font than an h2 heading, h2 headings are larger than h3 headings, and so forth.

The <form>… </form> tag pair specifies an input form. An input form enables you to collect information from people who visit your site. The action attribute of the <form> tag specifies the **Uniform Resource Locator (URL)** of the file on the Web server that processes the information gathered in the form. A URL takes the form of *protocol://hostname:port/file*. The URL in Figure 17-3, *http://localhost:8080/servlet/Bradshaw.FindCustServlet1*, specifies usage of the **Hypertext Transfer Protocol (HTTP)**. HTTP is the standard communication protocol used by most Web browsers and Web servers. The host name *localhost:8080* refers to

17

port 8080 on your computer. The Web server you will use in this chapter treats your computer as both the client and the server, and listens for client requests at port 8080. The file portion of the URL, */servlet/Bradshaw.FindCustServlet1*, points to the servlet that will process this form; *servlet* tells the system to look for the *Bradshaw.FindCustServlet1* class file in the folder on the Web server that has been designated for servlets. *Bradshaw.FindCustServlet1* indicates that the FindCustServlet1 class file is part of the Bradshaw package. (You will learn more about the servlet folder and the Bradshaw package shortly.) When the user clicks the Submit Query button, the FindCustServlet1 program is invoked to handle the client request. The method attribute of the <form> tag indicates the nature of the request. The value of the method attribute is either "post" or "get." Use "get" when you need only to retrieve information from the server, such as another HTML document. Use "post" to send information from the form to the server, as when you call a servlet to process information entered on an HTML form.

Between the <form> … </form> tags, use <input> tags to specify the GUI elements you want to include in a form. The type attribute specifies the kind of GUI element you want to use and must be included in an <input> tag. You can create many common GUI elements in HTML, including textfields, buttons, radio buttons, check boxes, and selection lists. Information on how to specify these elements is available in a wide array of HTML resources.

The name attribute of the <input> tag is optional, but when used, it assigns a variable name to the GUI element so it can be referenced by script code and servlets. The first <input> tag in Figure 17-3 specifies that a textfield should be placed to the right of the text "Phone Number:"—which serves as a label for the textfield. The name attribute ensures that the textfield can be referred to by the variable name "Phone." The second <input> tag specifies that a special button, called a submit button, is to be included on the form. When clicked, the browser submits the data on the form to the Web server, using the URL specified in the action attribute to locate the Web file designed to process the form.

Unlike Java, HTML is case insensitive. However, it is good practice to be consistent in your HTML code and use either all lowercase or all uppercase. In this text, we use lowercase for HTML tags. HTML is also forgiving if you fail to use quotation marks to enclose values you assign to attributes. In other words, <INPUT TYPE = TEXT> is equivalent to <input type = "text">. In this text, we include quotation marks to improve readability. As with Java, the use of indentation and white space is optional.

WRITING A SERVLET TO PROCESS THE FORM

In Figure 17-2, clicking the Submit Query button invokes a Java servlet named FindCustServlet1. Recall that a servlet is a Java program that runs on a Web server and responds to client requests. In this example, the servlet uses the phone number a user enters to find a record in a relational database, then formats a response to the client that includes other information within that record. The FindCustServlet1 program is shown in Figure 17-4.

```java
// Figure 17-4
// FindCustServlet1.java

package Bradshaw;
import java.io.*;
import javax.servlet.*;
import javax.servlet.http.*;
import java.sql.*;

public class FindCustServlet1 extends HttpServlet
{
    public void doPost(   HttpServletRequest request,
                          HttpServletResponse response )
              throws ServletException, IOException
    {
        String cName, cAddress, cPhone;

        // establish output stream for response to client
        PrintWriter output = response.getWriter();
        response.setContentType( "text/html" );

        // get phone number from HTML page
        cPhone = request.getParameter( "Phone" );
        if (cPhone.equals(""))
        {
            output.println("<h3> Please click the Back button and " +
                          "fill in the Phone Number field.</h3>" );
        }
        else
        {
            try
            {   // connect to the database
                Customer aCustomer = null;
                Connection c = CustomerConnect.initialize();
                Customer.initialize(c);
                // retrieve the desired record
                aCustomer = Customer.find(cPhone);
                // format a response to the client
                output.print("<h2>Record found!</h2><br>" +
                            "Name: " + aCustomer.getName() + "<br>" +
                            "Address: " + aCustomer.getAddress() +
                            "<br>" + "Phone: " + aCustomer.getPhoneNo());
            }
            catch (NotFoundException e)
            {
                output.println("<h3>Customer not found. " +
                              "Please click the Back button and " +
                              "try again!</h3>");
            }
        }
        output.close();
    }
}
```

17

Figure 17-4: Source code for FindCustServlet1

The servlet begins with a package statement, followed by the necessary import statements:

```
package Bradshaw;
import java.io.*;
import javax.servlet.*;
import javax.servlet.http.*;
import java.sql.*;
```

Up to this point, you have used import statements to take advantage of standard Java packages such as java.awt and java.swing. In this example, you are creating a package of your own. The package statement indicates that this servlet will be part of a group of related programs that belong to a package called Bradshaw. A servlet does not have to include a package statement. However, using a package to group the classes in a Web application helps to organize the files needed to deploy the site. When used, the package statement must be the first line of code in the program, other than comments.

The next four lines of code import the Java packages needed to make the servlet work. The javax.servlet and javax.servlet.http packages will be imported in every servlet you write, as they contain classes that all servlets need. The java.io package is imported in order to use the PrintWriter class in formatting a response to the client. The java.sql package is imported to support database access.

The servlet class definition begins by extending class HttpServlet. All of the servlets you write in this text will extend this class, which provides support for the HTTP. As previously noted, HTTP is the standard request-response protocol over which Web browsers and Web servers communicate.

```
public class FindCustServlet1 extends HttpServlet
```

The servlet in Figure 17-4 contains only one method, the doPost( ) method. Recall that the HTML form that invokes this servlet specifies a post request. When an HTML form issues a post request, the Web server looks for a doPost( ) method in the servlet specified in the action attribute, then executes the code in it. The method signature for the doPost( ) method is shown in Figure 17-4. This method receives references to two objects: one of type HttpServletRequest and the other of type HttpServletResponse. These objects encapsulate information about the request from the client, including information entered on the input form, and the response to the client. Because various problems can occur over the network, the doPost( ) method may throw either an IOException or a ServletException.

```
public void doPost(   HttpServletRequest request,
                      HttpServletResponse response )
             throws ServletException, IOException
```

If the HTML file had issued a get request rather than a post request, the Web server would look in the specified servlet for a doGet( ) method. Except for the method name, the signatures for a doGet( ) method and a doPost( ) method are identical.

Examining the doPost( ) Method

The doPost( ) method in this example declares three String reference variables—one to hold the customer phone number, one for the customer name, and one for the customer address. The following lines of code establish a character output stream through which a response to the client can be formatted. The getWriter( ) method establishes the output stream, and the setContentType("text/html") method ensures that the response to the client over the output stream is appropriately formatted for rendering by the Web browser.

```
String cName,cAddress, cPhone;

// establish output stream for response to client
PrintWriter output = response.getWriter();
response.setContentType( "text/html" );
```

The phone number that the user enters on the HTML input form is extracted from the HttpServletRequest object using the getParameter( ) method. This method has a single String argument that refers to the name of an element on the HTML form. Recall that the `<input type = "text" name = "Phone">` tag in the HTML file assigned the variable name "Phone" to the input textfield. The following Java statement assigns the text that was entered in the "Phone" element to the cPhone reference variable.

```
// get phone number from HTML page
cPhone = request.getParameter( "Phone" );
```

Before attempting to find the phone number in the database, the servlet confirms that a phone number was entered. If not, an error message is sent to the client through the output stream. Notice that information sent through the output stream includes embedded HTML formatting tags. These tags are rendered by the browser as they are in any HTML file.

```
if (cPhone.equals(""))
{
    output.println("<h3> Please click the Back button and " +
                   "fill in the Phone Number field.</h3>" );
}
```

If a phone number was entered, an attempt is made to connect to the database using the familiar methods of the Bradshaw Marina problem domain and data access classes. The find method of the Customer class is called to locate the record in CustomerTable whose primary key matches the phone number specified in the HTML input form. If the record is found, the name and address are retrieved from the database and included in the response to the client. If the record is not found, an error message is formatted and sent to the client. The output stream is then closed.

```
else
{
    try
    {   // connect to the database
        Customer aCustomer = null;
        Connection c = CustomerConnect.initialize();
```

17

```
        Customer.initialize(c);
        // retrieve the desired record
        aCustomer = Customer.find(cPhone);
        // format a response to the client
        output.print("<h2>Record found!</h2><br>" +
                     "Name: " + aCustomer.getName() + "<br>" +
                     "Address: " + aCustomer.getAddress() +
                     "<br>" + "Phone: " + aCustomer.getPhoneNo());
    }
    catch (NotFoundException e)
    {
        output.println("<h3>Customer not found. " +
                       "Please click the Back button and " +
                       "try again!</h3>");
    }
}
output.close();
```

INSTALLING THE JAVASERVER WEB DEVELOPMENT KIT (JSWDK)

Before you can successfully execute a servlet, it must be running on a Web server. The JSWDK, supplied by Sun Microsystems, includes the javax.servlet and javax.servlet.http packages that support servlet technology, as well as a simple Web server you can use to test your servlets. Although this Web server lacks features that would make it acceptable for commercial use, it provides all the functionality needed to test the servlets you will write in this chapter.

To download and install the JSWDK files on your machine:

1. Point your browser to the following URL:
   http://java.sun.com/products/servlet/archive.html
   Note: This URL is subject to change. If necessary, refer to the java.sun.com home page to find a link for downloading the JSWDK.

2. You see a dialog box for downloading the final release (version 1.0.1) of the JavaServer Web Development Kit. Select a platform (Windows 95/NT or UNIX), and click **continue**.

3. The terms and conditions of the license agreement appear. Click **ACCEPT**.

4. Click **FTP Download** to download the JSWDK zip file. The File Download dialog box appears.

5. Make sure that the **Save this file to disk** option button is selected, and then click **OK**. The Save As dialog box appears.

6. Accept jswdk1_0_1-win.zip as the default file name, and then click **Save**.

7. When the download is complete, use a program such as WinZip to unzip the zip file. Extract the files to the root directory of your hard disk, preserving the folder names embedded in the zip file. This creates an installation folder (and several subfolders) on your system.

Organizing Files for the Example Web Application

You can organize files for a Web site in many ways. It is good practice to group HTML files for a particular site in a single folder, and to place Java classes in a separate folder. As you saw in the previous example, you can use the Java package statement to group classes for a Web application. Recall that doing so requires the use of subfolders, which further improves file organization. Web servers have specific procedures for installing servlets; in this chapter, you will learn how to install servlets for the simple Web server that comes with this text. If you later decide to deploy your site on a different Web server, refer to that server's documentation for installation instructions.

The folder, or directory, structure of the example files in this chapter is shown in Figure 17-5. Some of these folders were created when you installed the JSWDK. Others will be created as you install the example programs.

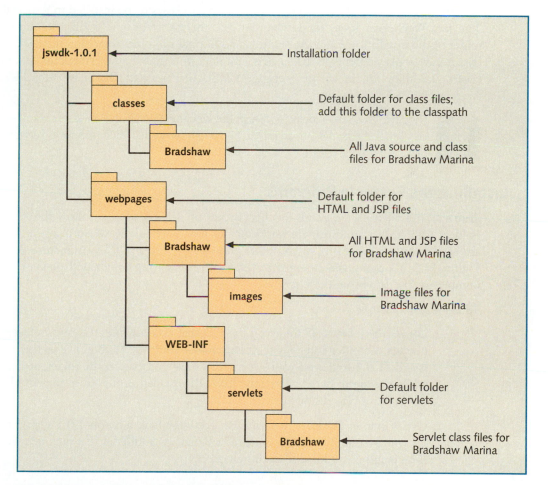

Figure 17-5   Folder stucture for example programs

When you installed the JSWDK, a folder named jswdk-1.0.1 was created on your system. This folder is known as the installation folder. The Web server you will use, called the Java WebServer, expects to find HTML files in the webpages subfolder of the installation folder. An additional subfolder, named Bradshaw, is used to separate the HTML files for the Bradshaw Marina application from those used in other Web applications. Thus, the webpages\Bradshaw subfolder will contain all the HTML and image files for the examples in this chapter. Although you have not yet worked with Java Server Pages (JSPs), JSP files also belong in this subfolder.

The Java WebServer expects to find class files in the classes subfolder of the installation directory. In this chapter, an additional subfolder named Bradshaw is used to separate the Bradshaw Marina classes from those in other Web applications. The Bradshaw subfolder is necessary because of the use of the package statement in the Java source files. Thus, the classes\Bradshaw subfolder will contain all the Java source and class files for the examples in this chapter.

When a site is deployed, Web servers require servlet classes to be installed in a special folder. The Java WebServer looks for servlet class files in the webpages\WEB-INF\servlets subfolder of the installation folder. As before, an additional subfolder matching the package name (Bradshaw) is placed beneath the servlets subfolder. You must copy servlet class files from the classes\Bradshaw folder to the webpages\WEB-INF\servlets\Bradshaw subfolder before running the Web application.

 The Java WebServer looks for files in the webpages\WEB-INF\servlets subfolder of the installation folder. Within an HTML file, you refer to this folder simply as *servlet*.

Installing the Example Programs

To install the example programs for this chapter on your hard disk, follow the steps below. Folders (directory structures) are important in Java, particularly when package statements are used to group programs, so you must preserve the file and folder structure depicted in Figure 17-5. Copying the example programs to the wrong folder will prevent you from compiling and executing these servlets.

To install the example programs:

1. Locate the Chapter17 folder on the CD that accompanies this text. Select the **classes** subfolder and copy the entire folder (not just its contents) to the **jswdk-1.0.1** folder on your system. You must copy the entire folder, because when the zip utility extracted the JSWDK installation files from the zip file, it did not create a classes subfolder.

2. Use Windows Explorer to verify that you now have a jswdk-1.0.1\classes folder on your system. This folder contains a Bradshaw subfolder that includes the Java source and class files used in this chapter.

3. Return to the CD and navigate back to the Chapter17 folder, and then navigate to the webpages subfolder. Select the **Bradshaw** subfolder and copy the entire folder (not just its contents) to the **jswdk–1.0.1\webpages** folder on your system.

4. Use Windows Explorer to verify that you have a jswdk-1.0.1\webpages\Bradshaw folder on your hard disk. This folder contains the HTML, JSP, and image files needed for the examples in this chapter.

5. Return to the CD and navigate back to the Chapter17 folder, and then navigate to the webpages\WEB-INF\servlets subfolder. Select the **Bradshaw** subfolder and copy the entire folder (not just its contents) to the **jswdk–1.0.1\webpages\WEB-INF\servlets** folder on your system.

6. Use Windows Explorer to verify that you have a jswdk-1.0.1\webpages\WEB-INF\servlets\Bradshaw folder on your hard disk. This folder contains the servlet class files for the examples in this chapter.

7. Locate the **BradshawDatabase.mdb** file on the CD and copy it to a folder of your choice on your hard disk. The servlets in this chapter use this database.

8. Register the BradshawDatabase.mdb file with the ODBC, using **BradshawDatabase** as the data source name. If you need help with this step refer to Hands-on Exercise 1 in Chapter 15. If you do not properly register the database, the Web server will not be able to locate the database.

Compiling the Example Programs

The example programs for this chapter have already been compiled for you. If you recompile these programs, the software you use may have difficulty locating all the necessary classes due to the use of package statements. If so, refer to the instructions in the Readme.txt file of the Examples folder for this chapter on the book's CD.

Remember that the Web server you are using requires servlet class files to be in the webpages\WEB-INF\servlets subfolder of the installation folder. You must copy servlet class files to this folder (or one of its subfolders) each time you compile a servlet. For modifications to a servlet to take effect, you must stop the Web server, compile the servlet, copy the servlet class file to the servlets folder, and then restart the Web server.

Running the Example Programs on the Java WebServer

A client can only access a servlet if the servlet is running on a Web server. Programs to start the server are included on the CD. To install these programs and start the Java WebServer:

1. Locate the **startserver.bat** file on the CD and copy it to the **jswdk–1.0.1** folder on your system. The Confirm File Replace dialog box appears. Click **Yes**.

2. Locate the **runserver.bat** file on the CD and copy it to your desktop.

17

3. Double-click the **runserver** icon on your desktop. An MS-DOS window opens. After a few seconds, the Web server responds with the message "endpoint created: localhost/127.0.0.1:8080," which indicates that the Web server is up and running.

> **NOTE** If you see an "Out of environment space" message, in Windows 98 right-click the **MS-DOS** icon in the upper-left corner of the MS-DOS window. Click **Properties**, and then click the **Memory** tab. Change the Initial environment setting from its default value to **2816**. Click **OK** to change the value, and then click **OK** again to close the Properties window. Close the MS-DOS window, and then repeat Step 3.

4. Once the server is running, minimize the MS-DOS window. (Do not close it.) Open your Web browser, enter the following URL, and then press **Enter**: **http://localhost:8080/Bradshaw/CustomerFind.html**.

5. The CustomerFind.html document appears in the browser, as shown in Figure 17-2. Enter the phone number **123–4567** in the input form, and click the **Submit Query** button. You see the output shown in Figure 17-6.

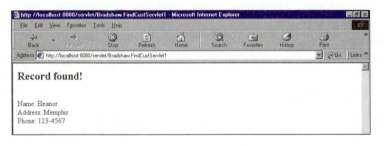

Figure 17-6   Output of the first example program

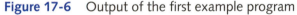

USING JAVASCRIPT TO VALIDATE AN HTML INPUT FORM

In the previous example, the servlet validates the input form by making sure that a phone number was entered. This means that an HTTP request-response sequence must be completed to inform the user of a data-entry mistake. You can improve the performance of the Web application by shifting the responsibility for form validation to the client. Although this step adds a little "fat" to the client, you enhance performance by eliminating an HTTP request-response communication when a phone number is not entered.

Web scripting languages such as JavaScript are often used for form validation. Although JavaScript looks very much like Java, it is an entirely different language. You can add JavaScript code to any HTML file to enhance functionality—in this case, code will be added to the CustomerFind.html file to verify that a phone number has been entered. Figure 17-7 shows the CustomerFind2.html file, which includes the JavaScript code necessary to validate the form.

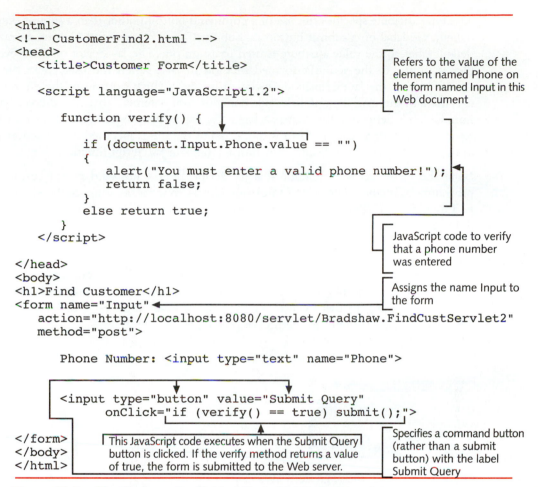

Figure 17-7   The CustomerFind2.html file (with JavaScript code)

The primary difference between CustomerFind and CustomerFind2 is the inclusion of <script> and </script> tags, and the JavaScript code between them. In this case, the <script> tag is placed within the header of the HTML file. The language attribute specifies JavaScript1.2 as the scripting language. The verify( ) function will be explained shortly. First, examine the <form> tag; it now includes a name attribute that assigns the name "Input" to the form. As with other name attributes you have seen, assigning a name to the form means that you can reference it by name in script code. Second, notice that the <input> tag has been changed to:

```
<input type="button" value="Submit Query"
       onClick="if (verify() == true) submit();">
```

The type attribute specifies the use of a command button (rather than a submit button). By default, the label on a submit button is "Submit Query." Command buttons do not have a default label, so the value attribute is used to assign one. The JavaScript onClick event handler is similar to the actionPerformed method in Java. When the user clicks the Submit Query button, the JavaScript code specified in the onClick portion of the <input> tag is executed. In this case, the onClick code contains an if statement that calls the verify( ) function, which is defined in the <script> tag at the top of the program. If the verify( ) function returns a result of `true`, the form is submitted to the URL specified in the action attribute of the <form> tag. The submit( ) function is a built-in JavaScript function.

Note also in the verify( ) function that JavaScript uses the keyword `function` to define a procedure or method. The verify( ) function checks to see if the value of the element identified by the name "Phone" on the input form is equal to the empty string. Note the use of dot notation:

```
document.Input.Phone.value
```

This expression refers to the value of the Phone element in the Input form of the current Web document. If no phone number was entered, the alert method is invoked to display a message reminding the user to enter one (see Figure 17-8), and a value of `false` is returned. The alert method is a built-in method of JavaScript.

Figure 17-8   Alert message from JavaScript

If the phone number the user entered is not equal to the empty string, a value of `true` is returned and the form is submitted to the server.

Although the JavaScript verify( ) function is defined within the header of the HTML file, it does not execute until it is invoked by the onClick event handler. Also, the modified version of the HTML file invokes a different servlet—FindCustServlet2. This servlet and FindCust-Servlet1 have only one difference: The `if` block that checks for an empty phone number in FindCustServlet1 is removed from FindCustServlet2. The source code for FindCustServlet2 is shown in Figure 17-9.

```java
// Figure 17-9
// FindCustServlet2.java

package Bradshaw;
import java.io.*;
import javax.servlet.*;
import javax.servlet.http.*;
import java.sql.*;

public class FindCustServlet2 extends HttpServlet
{
    public void doPost(   HttpServletRequest request,
                          HttpServletResponse response )
              throws ServletException, IOException
    {
        String cName,cAddress, cPhone;

        // establish output stream for response to client
        PrintWriter output = response.getWriter();
        response.setContentType( "text/html" );
        // get phone number from HTML page
        cPhone = request.getParameter( "Phone" );
        try
        {   // connect to the database
            Customer aCustomer = null;
            Connection c = CustomerConnect.initialize();
            Customer.initialize(c);
            // retrieve the desired record
            aCustomer = Customer.find(cPhone);
            //format response to the client
            output.print("<h2>Record found.</h2><br>" +
                        "Name:     " + aCustomer.getName() + "<br>" +
                        "Address: " + aCustomer.getAddress() + "<br>" +
                        "Phone:   " + aCustomer.getPhoneNo());
        }
        catch (NotFoundException e)
        {
            output.println("<h3>Customer not found. " +
                        "Please click the Back button and " +
                        "try again!</h3>");
        }
        output.close();
    }
}
```

Figure 17-9   Source code for FindCustServlet2

Hands-on Exercise 1

Run the example program that shifts the responsibility of form validation to the client.

To run the example program:

    1. If it is not already running, start the Java WebServer.

2. Open your browser and point to the following URL:
   http://localhost:8080/Bradshaw/CustomerFind2.html.

3. When the form appears, leave the phone number blank and click the **Submit Query** button. You see the alert message shown in Figure 17-8. Click OK.

4. Enter **123-4567** for the phone number and the click Submit Query to verify that the servlet is working properly. The output is similar to Figure 17-8.

DEVELOPING A WEB APPLICATION FOR BRADSHAW MARINA

Now that you have seen how to use some of the basic tools, you can develop a Web site for Bradshaw Marina. The Web site will enable customers to view information about their boat and lease on the Web.

First, a welcome page is needed to describe the features of the marina. This page will include a link that enables customers to log on and access information in the Bradshaw Marina database. The welcome page is shown in Figure 17-10.

Figure 17-10   Bradshaw Marina welcome page

To protect unauthorized access to customer information, visitors are required to enter a customer identification number (in this case, a phone number) as a password. See Figure 17-11.

Figure 17-11   Bradshaw Marina login page

The phone number is checked against the database. If the number is found, the customer's name and address is retrieved from the database and displayed in the browser. If the password cannot be found in the database, an error message is displayed, as in Figure 17-12.

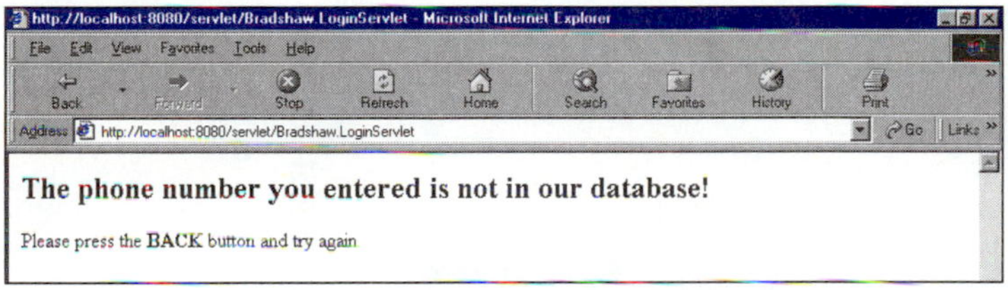

Figure 17-12   Bradshaw Marina invalid password page

17

Bradshaw Marina wants to keep its customer information current, so once a customer has logged on, he or she is asked to verify that the name and address retrieved from the database are correct. If not, the customer is allowed to make changes, as shown in Figure 17-13. These changes are used to update the Bradshaw Marina database.

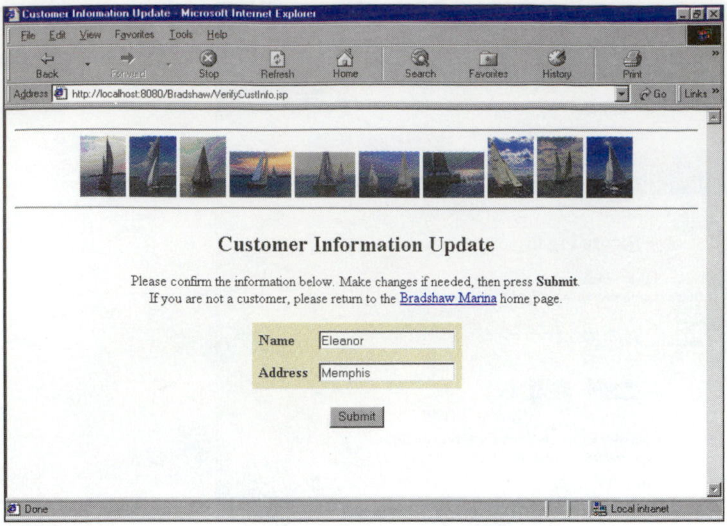

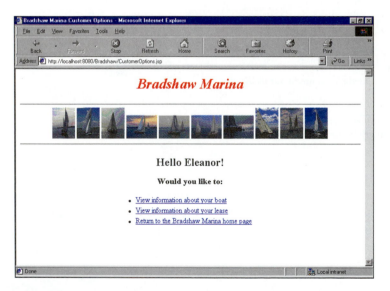

Figure 17-13   Bradshaw Marina verify customer information page

After verifying the name and address, a customer can view information about his or her boat, view information about his or her lease, or return to the Bradshaw Marina home page, as shown in Figure 17-14.

Figure 17-14   Bradshaw Marina customer options page

If a customer chooses to view information about his or her boat or lease, it is displayed from the Bradshaw Marina database, as illustrated in Figures 17-15 and 17-16.

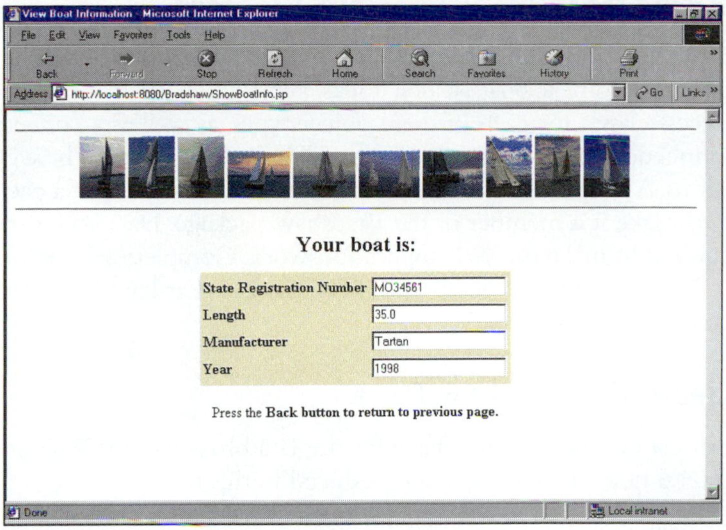

Figure 17-15 Bradshaw Marina view boat information page

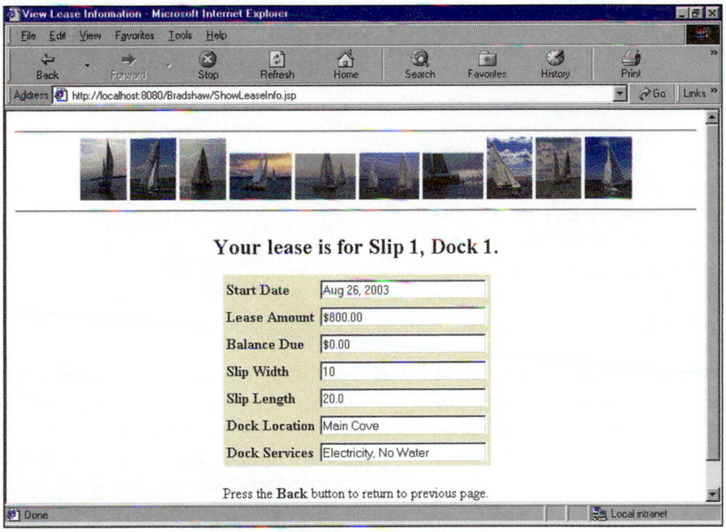

Figure 17-16 Bradshaw Marina view lease information page

This Web site uses a combination of HTML forms, Java servlets, JavaScript, and a new technology known as Java Server Pages (JSPs). The following sections explain how to create and deploy this Web site.

Modifying the Bradshaw Marina PD and DA Classes

The Bradshaw Marina Web application uses data from the Bradshaw Marina database to display information about customers, boats, leases, docks, and slips. As such, it requires problem domain and data access classes for each of these object types, as well as a connect program that establishes a connection to the database (which will be on the server). These classes need very few modifications. A simple but noteworthy change is the inclusion of a package statement in each class to make it a member of the Bradshaw package. Data access methods are limited to those required to make the Web application work. Complete source files for these classes are on the CD. Because these classes have been discussed at length elsewhere in this text, they are not discussed in this chapter.

Using HTML to Create the Welcome Page

The HTML file that creates the welcome page for the Bradshaw Marina Web site is shown in Figure 17-17. Several new HTML tags are introduced in this file.

```
<html>
<head>
   <title>Welcome to Bradshaw Marina</title>
</head>
<body><center>
<h1><em><font color="red">Welcome to Bradshaw Marina</font></em></h1>
<hr>
<img src="images/sabtart_07.gif">
<img src="images/stardrag_04.gif">
<img src="images/sabtart_22.gif">
<img src="images/sabtart_01.gif">
<img src="images/sabtart_04.gif">
<img src="images/sabtart_06.gif">
<img src="images/sabtart_19.gif">
<img src="images/stardrag_01.gif">
<img src="images/sabtart_32.gif">
<img src="images/stardrag_08.gif">
<hr></center>
<p>Bradshaw Marina is located on Clinton Lake in the rolling hills of
central Missouri. Because construction near its shores is restricted
by the U.S. Army Corps of Engineers, Clinton Lake provides an ideal
natural wildlife habitat as well as a beautiful, park-like setting for
boaters. Bradshaw Marina has slips to accommodate up to 450 sailboats
and 150 powerboats. </p>
<strong>Bradshaw Marina provides:</strong><br>
<table align="center" cellspacing=5 cellpadding=3>
```

```
<tr>
   <td><li>
      Docks with electrical service only
   </li></td>
   <td><li>
      Docks with both electrical service and water
   </li></td>
</tr>
<tr>
   <td><li>
      Covered slips (all of which have electricity)
   </li></td>
   <td><li>
      Annual leases, with monthly or yearly payment options
   </li></td>
</tr>
</table>
<center><br>If you are a Bradshaw Marina customer, please log in.
<table align="Center" bgcolor="lightgoldenrodyellow">
<tr>
   <td width=100 align="Center">
      <a href="Login.html">
      <strong><font size="+1">Log In</font></strong></a>
   </td>
</tr>
</table></body></html>
```

Figure 17-17 HTML file for the Bradshaw Marina welcome page

The <em> ... </em> tag pair formats text between the tags in italics. You can use the <font>...</font> tag pair to select a particular font style, size, and color. Here, the <font> tag is used to set the font color to red. The <hr> tag is a single tag that creates a horizontal line. The <p > ... </p> tag pair identifies a paragraph. The paragraph tag is used to set off text that spans multiple lines. The <strong> ... </strong> tag formats text in boldface, and the <br> tag creates a line break.

The <strong>...</strong> and <em>...</em> tag pairs have replaced the <b>...</b> and <i>...</i> tag pairs used in early versions of HTML for boldface and italics. Although <b>...</b> and <i>...</i> still work in most browsers, these tags have been **deprecated**, which means that eventually they will not be supported. Thus, their use is discouraged.

The <img> tag identifies an image file to be loaded. In the Bradshaw Marina Web site, there are ten image files. Each is loaded with a separate <img> tag. The src attribute of the <img> tag identifies the name of the image file. In all examples in this chapter, the image files for Bradshaw Marina are stored in the images subfolder of the webpages\Bradshaw folder.

The <table> ... </table> tag pair creates a table. Tables help organize information and improve the appearance of the page. The cellpadding and cellspacing attributes are used to format spacing within the table. Each row of the table is defined within a <tr> ... </tr> tag

17

pair. The table in this example has two rows, so there are two sets of <tr> …</tr> tag pairs; each set defines a cell within the table. There are four cells in this table, two in each row. Each cell uses an <li> … </li> tag pair to create a bulleted list item.

The <a> … </a> tag pair specifies an anchor, or link, to a different HTML document. The href attribute specifies the URL of the Web page that will be rendered when the user clicks the link. In this example, when the user clicks the Log In link, the browser loads the Login.html document.

A second table positions the link in the center of the page in a pale yellow background. Note the use of the align and bgcolor attributes in the <table> tag: The align attribute is self-explanatory, and the bgcolor attribute sets the background color of the table. For a list of available color names, consult other HTML resources. As before, the cellspacing and cell-padding attributes help you fine-tune the vertical and horizontal spacing of items in the table. The width attribute of the last <td> tag specifies the width of the cell in pixels. The `size = "+1"` attribute of the last <font> tag increases the font size by one point.

Using HTML to Create the Login Page

The HTML file that creates the login page is shown in Figure 17-18.

```
<html>
<head>
    <title>Log In to Bradshaw Marina</title>
    <script language="JavaScript1.2">
        function verify() {
            if (document.Input.Phone.value == "")
            {
                alert("You must enter a phone number!!");
                return false;
            }
            else return true;
        }
    </script>
</head>
<body>
<center>
<hr>
<img src = "images/sabtart_07.gif">
<img src = "images/stardrag_04.gif">
<img src = "images/sabtart_22.gif">
<img src = "images/sabtart_01.gif">
<img src = "images/sabtart_04.gif">
<img src = "images/sabtart_06.gif">
<img src = "images/sabtart_19.gif">
<img src = "images/stardrag_01.gif">
<img src = "images/sabtart_32.gif">
<img src = "images/stardrag_08.gif">
<hr>
```

```
<h2>Please log in</h2>
<p>Enter your phone number in 999-9999 format.<br>
   If you are not a customer, please return to the
   <a href="index.html">Bradshaw Marina</a> home page.</p>
<form name="Input" method="post"
   action="http://localhost:8080/servlet/Bradshaw.LoginServlet" >
   <table border=0 bgcolor="lightgoldenrodyellow" cellpadding=10 >
   <tr>
      <td><strong>Phone number</strong></td>
      <td><input type="text" name="Phone" value="" size=20></td>
   </tr>
   </table>
   <table border=0 cellspacing=15 >
   <tr>
      <td><input type="button" value = "Log In"
            onClick = "if (verify() == true) submit();"></td>
      <td><input type="reset" value = "Clear"></td>
   </tr>
   </table>
</form>
Please wait after pressing <strong>Log in</strong>
while we retrieve your records from our database.<br>
<em>(This may take a few moments)</em>
</center>
</body>
</html>
```

Figure 17-18 HTML file for the Bradshaw Marina login page

The file begins by defining a JavaScript verify( ) function. (This function is identical to the one defined earlier in the CustomerFind2.html program.) To maintain a consistent look and feel across the pages of the Web site, the same images, colors, and basic style elements are used. The page includes a link back to the Bradshaw Marina home page.

As in the previous example, the most important part of this file is the form used to obtain the user's phone number. The form is similar to the one used earlier, but uses a table to improve its appearance. When the user clicks the Log In button, the JavaScript onClick event handler calls the verify( ) function. As before, if the phone number is not left blank, the verify( ) function returns a value of **true**, and the built-in JavaScript submit( ) function is called. The submit( ) function invokes the servlet specified in the action attribute of the <form> tag—in this case, the LoginServlet.

Writing a Servlet to Complete the Login Request

The servlet invoked by the form on the login page is shown in Figure 17-19.

17

```java
// LoginServlet - Chapter 17
package Bradshaw;

import java.io.*;
import javax.servlet.*;
import javax.servlet.http.*;
import java.sql.*;

public class LoginServlet extends HttpServlet
{
    public void doPost(   HttpServletRequest request,
                          HttpServletResponse response)
                throws ServletException, IOException
    {
      try
      { // connect to database
          Connection c = CustomerConnect.initialize();
          Customer.initialize(c);
          AnnualLease.initialize(c);
          Dock.initialize(c);

          try
          {   // retrieve data from DB
              String phone = request.getParameter( "Phone" );
              Customer aCustomer = Customer.find(phone);
              Boat aBoat = aCustomer.getBoat();
              AnnualLease aLease = AnnualLease.find(phone);
              Slip aSlip = aLease.getSlip();
              int dockId = aSlip.getDockId();
              Dock aDock = Dock.find(dockId);

              // get the ServletContext and set attributes
              ServletContext sc = getServletContext();
              sc.setAttribute("customer", aCustomer);
              sc.setAttribute("boat", aBoat);
              sc.setAttribute("lease", aLease);
              sc.setAttribute("dock", aDock);
              sc.setAttribute("slip", aSlip);

              // redirect the response to a JSP
              response.sendRedirect
                 ("http://localhost:8080/Bradshaw/VerifyCustInfo.jsp");
          }
          catch( NotFoundException nfe)
          {
              String line1 = "<h2>The phone number you entered"+
                             " is not in our database!</h2>";
              String line2 = "<p>Please press the <strong>BACK" +
                             "</strong> button and try again.</p>";
              formatErrorPage(line1, line2, response);
          }
      }
```

```
    catch (Exception e) //not connected
    {
        String line1="<h2>A network error has occurred!</h2>";
        String line2="<p>Please notify your system " +
                        "administrator.</p>";
        formatErrorPage(line1, line2,response);
    }
}

public void formatErrorPage( String first, String second,
    HttpServletResponse response) throws IOException
{
    PrintWriter output = response.getWriter();
    response.setContentType( "text/html" );
    output.println(first);
    output.println(second);
    output.close();
}
}
```

Figure 17-19 Login servlet for the Bradshaw Marina Web site

The servlet begins with a package statement that identifies the class as a member of the Bradshaw package, followed by the necessary import statements. As with all servlets in this text, the class extends the HttpServlet class.

```
package Bradshaw;
import java.io.*;
import javax.servlet.*;
import javax.servlet.http.*;
import java.sql.*;

public class LoginServlet extends HttpServlet
```

The LoginServlet is invoked by Login.html using a post method, and therefore includes a doPost( ) method to handle the request. The doPost( ) method first attempts to establish a connection to the database and initialize the required classes. If the attempt is not successful, a network error page is formatted and sent to the client. Otherwise, the getParameter( ) method extracts the phone number from the HTML form. The find( ) method of the Customer data access class uses the phone number to locate the customer's record in the database. The version of the CustomerDA class used in this example comes from Chapter 15 and includes a find method that returns information about both the customer and the associated boat. The getBoat( ) method of the Customer class is used to extract the boat instance.

```
public void doPost(  HttpServletRequest request,
                     HttpServletResponse response)
            throws ServletException, IOException
{
    try
    { // connect to database
        Connection c = CustomerConnect.initialize();
```

17

```
Customer.initialize(c);
AnnualLease.initialize(c);
Dock.initialize(c);

try
{    // retrieve data from DB
     String phone = request.getParameter( "Phone" );
     Customer aCustomer = Customer.find(phone);
     Boat aBoat = aCustomer.getBoat();
```

Similarly, the phone number is used to locate the customer's lease in the database. The find( ) method of the Lease class returns information about both the customer's lease and slip. The getSlip( ) method of the Lease class is used to extract the slip instance, and the getDockId( ) method of the Slip class is used to get the dock number. The find( ) method of the Dock class uses the dock number to locate the dock record in the database.

```
AnnualLease aLease = AnnualLease.find(phone);
Slip aSlip = aLease.getSlip();
int dockId = aSlip.getDockId();
Dock aDock = Dock.find(dockId);
```

If any attempt to locate database records fails, recall that a NotFoundException is thrown. The corresponding catch block formats a response to the client, indicating that the record could not be found in the database.

```
catch( NotFoundException nfe)
{
    String line1 =    "<h2>The phone number you entered"+
                      " is not in our database!</h2>";
    String line2 =    "<p>Please press the <strong>BACK" +
                      "</strong> button and try again.</p>";
    formatErrorPage(line1, line2, response);
}
```

As for the next few lines of code, recognize that the information extracted from the database in this servlet will be shared among other programs in the Bradshaw Marina Web site that have not yet been discussed. Sharing this information enables users to move freely back and forth among the various Web pages without losing information or having to look it up again. This provides important continuity to the Web site.

```
// get the ServletContext and set attributes
ServletContext sc = getServletContext();
sc.setAttribute("customer", aCustomer);
sc.setAttribute("boat", aBoat);
sc.setAttribute("lease", aLease);
sc.setAttribute("dock", aDock);
sc.setAttribute("slip", aSlip);
```

This sharing is made possible through the ServletContext interface. The getServletContext( ) method returns a ServletContext object that enables direct interaction with the server. The setAttribute( ) method of the ServletContext interface allows the servlet to set an attribute that can be shared by other servlets. The setAttribute() method has two arguments. The first is a string that identifies the name of the attribute, and the second is the object to be shared. In this servlet, the setAttribute( ) method is used to share the customer, boat, lease, slip, and dock instances that have been retrieved from the database.

The following line of code invokes the sendRedirect( ) method of the HttpServletResponse class:

```
response.sendRedirect
        ("http://localhost:8080/Bradshaw/VerifyCustInfo.jsp");
```

This method simply redirects the browser to the URL specified in the argument list. In this case, the browser is redirected to a Java Server Page named VerifyCustInfo.jsp.

Introducing Java Server Pages

A **Java Server Page (JSP)** is an HTML file with embedded Java code. As you saw in previous examples, formatting responses to the client requires embedding HTML code in a servlet, which is easy if the responses to the client from the servlet are very short. However, generating output in HTML format with Java servlets becomes more cumbersome as the complexity and volume of the response grows. As you will see, JSPs can do anything a servlet can do, and vice versa. However, JSPs have the advantage of not requiring embedded HTML code in a Java program. Furthermore, because you can use HTML editors to create Java Server Pages, you can develop JSPs with little knowledge of HTML tags. All JSP files carry a .jsp file extension.

Using a Java Server Page to Return Dynamic Content

The code for the VerifyCustInfo.jsp file invoked by the LoginServlet is shown in Figure 17-20.

```html
<html><head>
    <title>Customer Information Update</title>
    <script language="JavaScript1.2">
        function verify() {
            if (document.Input.Name.value == "")
            {
                alert("You must enter a name!!");
                return false;
            }
            if (document.Input.Address.value == "")
            {
                alert("You must enter an address!!");
                return false;
            }
            return true;
        }
    </script>
</head>
```

17

```
<%@ page import = "Bradshaw.*" %>
<% Customer aCustomer =
       (Customer) getServletContext().getAttribute("customer"); %>
<body><center><hr>
<img src = "images/sabtart_07.gif">
<img src = "images/stardrag_04.gif">
<img src = "images/sabtart_22.gif">
<img src = "images/sabtart_01.gif">
<img src = "images/sabtart_04.gif">
<img src = "images/sabtart_06.gif">
<img src = "images/sabtart_19.gif">
<img src = "images/stardrag_01.gif">
<img src = "images/sabtart_32.gif">
<img src = "images/stardrag_08.gif">
<hr>
<h2>Customer Information Update</h2>
<p>Please confirm the information below. Make changes if needed, then
press <strong>Submit</strong>.<br>If you are not a customer, please
return to the <a href="index.html">Bradshaw Marina</a> home page.</p>
<form name="Input" method="post" action=
   "http://localhost:8080/servlet/Bradshaw.UpdateCustomerServlet">
   <table border=0 bgcolor="#FAFADD" cellpadding=5>
   <tr>
      <td><strong>Name</strong></td>
      <td><input type="text" name = "Name"
             value="<%= aCustomer.getName() %>"></td>
   </tr>
   <tr>
      <td><strong>Address</strong></td>
      <td><input type="text" name = "Address"
             value="<%= aCustomer.getAddress() %>"></td>
   </tr>
   </table>
<p><input type="button" value="Submit"
   onClick = "if (verify() == true) submit();"></p>
</center></form></body></html>
```

Figure 17-20 The VerifyCustInfo.jsp file for the Bradshaw Marina Web site

The JSP begins like any other HTML file, with the familiar <html> and <head> tags. As before, JavaScript is used to perform form validation, this time making sure that a customer has not supplied empty values for the name or address.

The tags that begin with <% and end with %> are JSP tags. JSP tags that begin with <%@ page define attributes of the page; tags that begin with <%= insert the value of a Java expression into the page; and tags that begin with <% enclose executable Java statements. The first JSP tag in this program imports the classes in the Bradshaw package and makes them available to the rest of the page.

```
<%@ page import = "Bradshaw.*" %>
```

The following line of code is also a JSP tag:

```
<% Customer aCustomer =
        (Customer) getServletContext().getAttribute("customer"); %>
```

Notice that the text inside the tag is an executable Java statement. This line of code uses the getAttribute( ) method of the ServletContext interface to retrieve the customer object that was placed on the ServletContext by the LoginServlet. Because objects placed on the ServletContext interface can be of any type, the object retrieved from ServletContext must be cast back to the Customer type. With this single line of code, all of the information stored in the Customer object, including its methods, is available to this JSP.

The remainder of the JSP contains a form and is similar to the other HTML files for the Bradshaw Marina Web site, with one exception. The <input> tags for the textfields use the value attribute to put information into the textfields. The value attribute uses JSP tags to put the values of customer name and address into the textfields after being extracted from the database. It does so by using the getName( ) and getAddress( ) methods of the Customer class to extract appropriate values from the object that was placed on the ServletContext. The <%= tag is used here to assign the value returned by the Java expression to the value of the textfield.

```
<input type="text" name = "Name" value="<%= aCustomer.getName() %>">
```

The form includes a submit button. When clicked, the button invokes the onClick event handler, which in turn calls the JavaScript verify( ) function to validate the form. If the customer has changed his or her name or address to an empty value, an alert message appears. Otherwise, the information on the form is submitted to UpdateCustomerServlet, which updates the database to reflect any other name and address changes the user has made.

Using a Servlet to Update the Bradshaw Marina Database

The UpdateCustomerServlet source file is shown in Figure 17-21.

```
// Figure 17-21
// UpdateCustomerServlet.java

package Bradshaw;
import java.io.*;
import javax.servlet.*;
import javax.servlet.http.*;
import java.sql.*;
```

17

```java
public class UpdateCustomerServlet extends HttpServlet
{
   public void doPost(   HttpServletRequest request,
                         HttpServletResponse response )
            throws ServletException, IOException
   {
     try
     {   /* retrieve the customer attribute from the ServletContext
            and cast it to an object of type Customer */

         Customer aCust =
            (Customer) getServletContext().getAttribute( "customer");

         // get the name and address values from the HTML page
         String name = request.getParameter("Name");
         String addr = request.getParameter("Address");

         /* if name or address from HTML page does not match
            info in DB, update DB */
         if (!name.equals(aCust.getName()) ||
                          !addr.equals(aCust.getAddress()))
         {
            aCust.setName(name);
            aCust.setAddress(addr);
            aCust.update();
         }
         // invoke the CustomerOptions.jsp program
         response.sendRedirect
            ("http://localhost:8080/Bradshaw/CustomerOptions.jsp");
      }
      catch (NotFoundException e)
      {   } //do nothing
   }
}
```

Figure 17-21 UpdateCustomerServlet source file for the Bradshaw Marina Web site

The servlet begins just as the other servlets did:

```java
package Bradshaw;
import java.io.*;
import javax.servlet.*;
import javax.servlet.http.*;
import java.sql.*;

public class UpdateCustomerServlet extends HttpServlet
{
   public void doPost(   HttpServletRequest request,
                         HttpServletResponse response )
            throws ServletException, IOException
```

The doPost( ) method of UpdateCustomerServlet first uses the getAttribute( ) method to retrieve the customer attribute from ServletContext. Recall that the customer information in this object originated from the Bradshaw Marina database. The servlet then uses the get-Parameter( ) method to retrieve the values for name and address that the user enters on the input form.

```java
public void doPost(   HttpServletRequest request,
                      HttpServletResponse response )
          throws ServletException, IOException
{
   try
   {   /* retrieve the customer attribute from the ServletContext
          and cast it to an object of type Customer */

       Customer aCust =
           (Customer) getServletContext().getAttribute( "customer" );
```

If the name or address from the input form differs from the information retrieved from ServletContext, the Bradshaw Marina database is updated with the new information. If no change has occurred, no update occurs.

```java
// get the name and address values from the HTML page
String name = request.getParameter("Name");
String addr = request.getParameter("Address");

/* if name or address from HTML page does not match
   info in DB, update DB */
if (!name.equals(aCust.getName()) ||
                    !addr.equals(aCust.getAddress()))
{
   aCust.setName(name);
   aCust.setAddress(addr);
   aCust.update();
}
```

The sendRedirect( ) method is then invoked to redirect the browser to a different JSP—the CustomerOptions.jsp file.

```java
// invoke the CustomerOptions.jsp program
response.sendRedirect
    ("http://localhost:8080/Bradshaw/CustomerOptions.jsp");
```

17

Using Java Server Pages to Complete the Application

The CustomerOptions.jsp file is shown in Figure 17-22.

```
<html>
<head>
<%@ page import="Bradshaw.*" %>
<% Customer aCustomer =
   (Customer) getServletContext().getAttribute("customer"); %>
<title>Bradshaw Marina Customer Options</title>
</head>
<body>
<center>
<h1><em><font color = "red">Bradshaw Marina</font></em></h1>
<hr>
<img src = "images/sabtart_07.gif">
<img src = "images/stardrag_04.gif">
<img src = "images/sabtart_22.gif">
<img src = "images/sabtart_01.gif">
<img src = "images/sabtart_04.gif">
<img src = "images/sabtart_06.gif">
<img src = "images/sabtart_19.gif">
<img src = "images/stardrag_01.gif">
<img src = "images/sabtart_32.gif">
<img src = "images/stardrag_08.gif">
<hr>
<h2>Hello
<%= aCustomer.getName() %>!
</h2>
<p>
<h3><strong>Would you like to:</strong></h3>
<table>
<tr><td><li>
<a href="ShowBoatInfo.jsp">View information about your boat</a>
</li></td></tr>
<tr><td><li>
<a href="ShowLeaseInfo.jsp">View information about your lease</a>
</li></td></tr>
<tr><td><li>
<a href="index.html"> Return to the Bradshaw Marina home page</a>
</li></td></tr>
</table>
</p>
</center>
</body>
</html>
```

Figure 17-22 The CustomerOptions.jsp file for the Bradshaw Marina Web site

This JSP is similar to the VerifyCustInfo JSP presented earlier, but simpler. As before, this JSP imports the Bradshaw package, then retrieves the customer attribute from ServletContext. The only other JSP tag in the file is shown below:

```
<%= aCustomer.getName() %>
```

This JSP tag is used to retrieve the customer's name and include it in the Web page. Three links are provided on the page: one that allows the customer to view information about his or her boat; one that allows the customer to view information about his or her lease; and one that allows the customer to return to the Bradshaw Marina home page. A table is used to organize the links as a bulleted list in the center of the page.

```
<table>
<tr><td><li>
<a href="ShowBoatInfo.jsp">View information about your boat</a>
</li></td></tr>
<tr><td><li>
<a href="ShowLeaseInfo.jsp">View information about your lease</a>
</li></td></tr>
<tr><td><li>
<a href="index.html"> Return to the Bradshaw Marina home page</a>
</li></td></tr>
</table>
```

If the user chooses to view information about his or her boat, the ShowBoatInfo JSP is called. If the user chooses to view information about his or her lease, the ShowLeaseInfo JSP is called.

The source code for the ShowBoatInfo.jsp file is shown in Figure 17-23.

```
<html><head>
   <title>View Boat Information</title>
</head>
<%@ page import="Bradshaw.*" %>
<%   ServletContext sc = getServletContext();
   Boat aBoat = (Boat) sc.getAttribute("boat"); %>
<body>
<center>
<hr>
<img src = "images/sabtart_07.gif">
<img src = "images/stardrag_04.gif">
<img src = "images/sabtart_22.gif">
<img src = "images/sabtart_01.gif">
<img src = "images/sabtart_04.gif">
<img src = "images/sabtart_06.gif">
<img src = "images/sabtart_19.gif">
<img src = "images/stardrag_01.gif">
<img src = "images/sabtart_32.gif">
<img src = "images/stardrag_08.gif">
<hr>
<h2>Your boat is:</h2>
<form>
<table border=0 bgcolor="#FAFADD" cellpadding=2>
<tr>
```

17

```
<td><strong>State Registration Number</strong></td>
<td><input type="text"
      value="<%= aBoat.getStateRegistrationNo() %>" >
</td>
</tr>
<tr>
<td><strong>Length</strong></td>
<td><input type="text"
      value="<%= aBoat.getLength() %>" ></td>
</tr>
<tr>
<td><strong>Manufacturer</strong></td>
<td><input type="text"
      value="<%= aBoat.getManufacturer() %>" ></td>
</tr>
<tr>
<td><strong>Year</strong></td>
<td><input type="text"
      value="<%= aBoat.getYear() %>" ></td>
</tr>
<tr>
</table>
<p>Press the <strong>Back</strong> button to return to previous page.
</p>
</center>
</form>
</p>
</body>
</html>
```

Figure 17-23 The ShowBoatInfo.jsp file for the Bradshaw Marina Web site

This JSP extracts the boat attribute from ServletContext, then uses methods of the Boat class to obtain the values for state registration number, length, manufacturer, and year. Once again, a table is used to format the page. No links to other Web pages are included (although they could have been), and the user is instructed to click the Back button to return to the previous page.

The code for the ShowLeaseInfo.jsp file is similar, and is shown in Figure 17-24.

```
<html>
<head>
    <title>View Lease Information</title>
</head>
<%@ page import="Bradshaw.*" %>
<%@ page import="java.text.*" %>
<%   ServletContext sc = getServletContext();
    AnnualLease aLease = (AnnualLease) sc.getAttribute( "lease" );
    Slip aSlip = (Slip) sc.getAttribute( "slip" );
    Dock aDock = (Dock) sc.getAttribute( "dock" );
```

```
    boolean electricity = aDock.getElectricity();
    boolean water = aDock.getWater();
    String services = electricity?"Electricity":"No Electricity";
    services += ", ";
    services += water?"Water":"No Water";
    DecimalFormat twoDigits = new DecimalFormat("$#,##0.00");
    DateFormat x = DateFormat.getDateInstance(DateFormat.MEDIUM);
%>
<body>
<center>
<hr>
<img src = "images/sabtart_07.gif">
<img src = "images/stardrag_04.gif">
<img src = "images/sabtart_22.gif">
<img src = "images/sabtart_01.gif">
<img src = "images/sabtart_04.gif">
<img src = "images/sabtart_06.gif">
<img src = "images/sabtart_19.gif">
<img src = "images/stardrag_01.gif">
<img src = "images/sabtart_32.gif">
<img src = "images/stardrag_08.gif">
<hr>
<h2>Your lease is for Slip <%= aSlip.getNo() %>, Dock <%= aDock.getId
() %>.</h2>
<form>
<table border=0 bgcolor="#FAFADD" cellpadding=2>

<tr>
<td><strong>Start Date</strong></td>
<td><input type="text"
    value="<%= x.format(aLease.getStartDate()) %>"  size=25>
</td>
</tr>
<tr>
<td><strong>Lease Amount</strong></td>
<td><input type="text"
    value="<%= twoDigits.format(aLease.getAmount()) %>" size = 25>
</td>
</tr>
<tr>
<td><strong>Balance Due</strong></td>
<td><input type="text"
  value="<%= twoDigits.format(aLease.getBalanceDue()) %>" size = 25>
</td>
</tr>
<tr>
<td><strong>Slip Width</strong></td>
<td><input type="text"
    value="<%= aSlip.getWidth() %>"  size = 25>
</td>
</tr>
<tr>
<td><strong>Slip Length</strong></td>
<td><input type="text"
    value="<%= aSlip.getSlipLength() %>" size = 25 >
```

17

```
</td>
</tr>
<tr>
<td><strong>Dock Location</strong></td>
<td><input type="text"
      value="<%= aDock.getLocation() %>" size = 25>
</td>
</tr>
<tr>
<td><strong>Dock Services</strong></td>
<td><input type="text"
      value="<%= services %>" size = 25>
</td>
</tr>
</table>
<p>Press the <strong>Back</strong> button to return to previous page.
</p>
</center>
</form>
</p>
</body>
</html>
```

Figure 17-24 The ShowLeaseInfo.jsp file for the Bradshaw Marina Web site

Hands-on Exercise 2

To run the Bradshaw Marina Web application:

1. If it is not already running, start the Java WebServer.

2. Open your browser and point to the following URL:
   http://localhost:8080/Bradshaw/index.html.

3. Experiment with the Web site and test its functionality.

EXPLORING OTHER TECHNOLOGIES FOR WEB APPLICATION DEVELOPMENT

In this chapter you have learned how to use HTML, Java servlets, JavaScript, and Java Server Pages to create simple Web applications. You have been introduced to basic features of these tools, but you have only scratched the surface of their full power and capabilities. Use the concepts and techniques you have learned to expand your knowledge and skills.

Many other technologies support Web development, and they are too numerous to list here. However, you should be aware of the following tools:

- **Active Server Pages (ASPs)** are a form of server-side scripting and are similar to JSPs.

- **Dynamic HTML (DHTML)** enables some data to be maintained on the client, which decreases the server and network loads and improves overall performance.

- **Extensible Markup Language (XML)** is similar to HTML. It allows programmers to develop their own tags and elements to fit the needs of specific applications and data structures.

- **XHTML (Extensible Hypertext Markup Language)** combines features of HTML and XML and thus provides a transition between the two languages.

- **Common Object Request Broker Architecture (CORBA)** technology allows an object on one system (such as the client) to invoke the methods of objects on other systems (such as the server).

- Multimedia tools, such as Flash

- Other server-side scripting languages, such as Perl

- Other client-side scripting languages, such as VBScript

We encourage you to explore these technologies on your own.

Summary

- One advantage of the Java programming language is portability. Programs you write in Java will run on any implementation of the JVM, regardless of the hardware platform, making Java an excellent choice for Web application development.

- Web applications are based on the client-server model of computing. In this model, a client requests an action and a server performs it.

- A common client-server arrangement is a three-tiered, distributed architecture. This includes the client, the Web server, and the database server. In this arrangement, the client runs the Web browser and is responsible for the user interface, the Web server handles the business logic, and the database server is responsible for the database and specialized database management software.

- In Web applications, thin clients are generally preferred. Thin-client applications minimize processing demands on the client.

- HTML and applets are commonly used to develop the user interface for a Web application. Applets may be required when animation or special effects are needed. In other cases, HTML is preferred because it overcomes security restrictions placed on applets, improves performance, minimizes the need for client-side support, and supports the goal of a thin-client application.

17

- HTML tags are used to format text that will appear in a Web browser.

- HTML forms are used to gather information from visitors to a Web site and can be used in conjunction with Java servlets to handle client requests.

- Servlets are Java programs that reside on a Web server and respond to various kinds of client requests. The most common requests are "post" and "get." A "post" request is used with servlets to process information entered on an HTML form.

- Servlets can only be executed on a Web server. Web servers have specific procedures for installing servlets.

- JavaScript is a programming language that adds functionality to an HTML document. Among other things, you can use JavaScript to validate information on an input form before it is submitted to a server.

- Java Server Pages (JSPs) are HTML files with embedded Java code. JSPs run on the server and can do anything that servlets can do. JSPs have the advantage of not requiring embedded HTML tags within a Java program.

- A GUI application can be rewritten as an applet but is subject to security restrictions and other limitations placed on applets.

- Java servlets, JSPs, JavaScript, and HTML are commonly used to develop Web applications. However, many other technologies are also available.

Key Terms

Active Server Page (ASP)

client

client-server computing

Common Object Request-Broker Architecture(CORBA)

deprecated

Dynamic HTML (DHTML)

Extensible Hypertext Markup Language (XHTML)

Extensible Markup Language (XML)

fat client

Hypertext Markup Language (HTML)

Hypertext Transfer Protocol (HTTP)

Java Server Page (JSP)

portability

server

servlet

tag

thin client

Uniform Resource Locator (URL)

Review Questions

1. Why is Java a good choice for Web application development?

2. Explain the general role of the client and the role of a server in a client–server application.

3. What are the tiers in a three-tiered, distributed architecture? What are the primary responsibilities of each tier?

4. What is a servlet? How does it differ from other Java programs?

5. Which Java packages are required in all servlets?

6. What is HTML? What is it used for?

7. Describe how HTML forms are used in Web applications that require access to databases stored on the server.

8. What are the two most common kinds of requests issued from an HTML form?

9. What is the difference between a post request and a get request?

10. Explain the following URL: http://localhost:8080/servlet/Bradshaw.UpdateBoatInformation.

11. What does the Java package statement do?

12. Why are package statements helpful in programs that will be used on the Web?

13. Why is HTML often favored over applets for handling the user interface in a Web application? Under what circumstances would applets be a better choice?

14. Java and HTML both contain deprecated methods. What does it mean for a method to be "deprecated?" Can you use deprecated methods in your programs? If so, what are the implications? If not, why not?

15. What is a Java Server Page?

16. What is JavaScript? What is it used for?

17. The doPost( ) method in a servlet has two parameters. One is an HttpServletRequest object and the other is an HttpServletResponse object. Explain the purpose of these two objects.

18. What is the purpose of the ServletContext interface?

17

Discussion Questions

1. Explain the client-server model of computing, including a description of a typical client-server exchange in a three-tiered, distributed architecture.

2. Compare and contrast Java servlets and Java Server Pages. How are they alike? How do they differ? When would you favor using one over the other?

3. What is meant by a "thin client" application? Why is it desirable in many Web applications?

4. Explain the difference between JavaScript and Java Server Pages. Under what circumstance would you use JavaScript rather than Java Server Pages? Is JavaScript the same thing as Java? Do Java Server Pages actually use Java?

5. Explain the relationship between `method = "post"` in an HTML file and the `doPost( )` method in a Java servlet.

6. Explain how information can be shared among different servlets and Java Server Pages in a Web application.

Projects

1. The Bradshaw Marina Web site allows customers to view information about their boats, but not to verify it. Modify the Web site so that customers can update all their boat information except the state registration number (primary key). Assume that changes in boat information will not affect the slip assignment.

2. Develop your own personal Web page. Include an option for visitors to register with your site by providing their name, address, phone number, and e-mail address. Use Microsoft Access to create a Visitors database to hold this information, using an e-mail address as the primary key. Then, use the techniques you have learned in this chapter to insert a record into the database when a visitor registers with your site. Use JavaScript to make sure that the e-mail address is not left blank. Include the ability to detect duplicates, and prompt the user to "try again" if one is detected.

3. Create a Web page that sells a product of your choosing. Include links that provide pictures of your product, descriptions, pricing information, and so on. Provide the capability for a user to make a purchase. When a purchase is made, capture the user's name, address, and credit card information, along with the product order quantity. Record all purchase information in a Microsoft Access database. Use JavaScript to validate the order form before it is submitted.

Glossary

abstract class — a class that cannot be instantiated and only serves to allow subclasses to inherit from it

abstract method — a method without any statements that must be overridden by a corresponding method in a subclass

accessibility — specifies which classes can access variables and methods: public (all classes have access), private (access only from within this class), and protected (subclasses and classes within the same package have access); default is that classes within the same package have access

accessor method — a method that provides access to attribute values

action event — an event resulting from clicking a menu item or a button

active object — an object that is executing or controlling part of an interaction

Active Server Page (ASP) — a form of server-side scripting; similar to a JSP

activity diagram — a UML diagram useful for showing the steps followed in a use case or scenario

actor — the person or entity using the system

adapter class — a class that extends a listener interface and implements the interface methods as null

anonymous inner class — a class defined within a class that is not given a name

argument — a value being passed to a method; the value is received into a parameter variable declared in the method header

arithmetic operators — symbols used for addition, subtraction, multiplication, and division (+, -, *, /, %)

assignment compatible — concept that the value of one variable may be assigned to another variable

assignment operator — (=); assigns the value on the right side of the equal sign to the variable named on the left side

assignment operators — the assignment operator (=) together with the arithmetic operators (+, -, *, /)

association class — a class that exists as a byproduct of an association relationship

association relationships — how objects of different classes are associated with each other

attribute — characteristic of an object that takes on a value

attribute storage — making an instance persistent by storing its attribute values in a file

block of code — statements between an open curly brace ({) and closed curly brace (})

breakpoint — a flag set by the programmer that instructs the debugger to pause program execution at a particular line of code

byte stream — a data stream consisting of Unicode characters

bytecode — the code produced when you compile a Java program

C++ — a programming language that adds OO features to become a superset of C

cardinality — entity relationship diagram term for multiplicity

casting — the process of changing the data type of a value

catch block — a block of code beginning with the keyword **catch** that executes if the specified exception is caught

character stream — a data stream in the default format of the system where the data is stored; it is automatically translated into Unicode when read by Java

class — objects are classified as a type of thing

class definition — Java code written to represent a class containing attribute definitions and accessor methods

class diagram — a UML diagram showing classes and their relationships

class header — a line of code that identifies the class and some of its characteristics

class method — a method not associated with a specific instance; a static method

class variable — a variable not associated with a specific instance; a static variable

client — the computer that issues a request in a client-server model of distributed processing

client object — the object invoking a method

client–server computing — a form of distributed processing in which a client requests an action and the server performs it

Common Object Request Broker Architecture (CORBA) — a technology that allows an object on one system (such as the client) to invoke the methods of objects on other systems (such as the server)

component–based development — refers to the fact that components interact in a system using a well-defined interface but might be built using a variety of technologies

compound expression — consists of two expressions joined using the logical operators and (&&) and or (||)

concatenated key — a key (primary or foreign) that is comprised of more than one field (or column) in the database

concatenation operator — (+); joins values together into a string

concrete class — a class that can be instantiated, as opposed to an abstract class

conditional operator — (?); a shortcut to writing an if-else statement

constant — a variable with a value that does not change; uses the keyword **final**

constructor — a special method that is automatically invoked whenever you create an instance of a class; it has no return type and has the same name as its class

control break — a change in the value of a variable used to group a list of items

custom exception — an exception that is written specifically for an application that extends the Exception or Throwable classes

custom method — methods written to do some processing; in contrast, accessor methods are written to store and retrieve attribute values

data source name — a name used by JDBC instead of the actual database name

data stream — a flow of bytes to or from an I/O device

data wrapper — a class that when instantiated contains primitive data *inside* an object instance; a wrapper class exists for each of the primitive data types (Boolean, Byte, Character, Double, Float, Integer, Long, and Short)

database — one or more files organized into tables to facilitate queries; each table column represents an attribute and a row represents a record (or an instance)

debugger — a set of tools that monitors the progress of a program at runtime and enables the programmer to isolate errors

decrement operator (--) — subtracts one from a variable

default constructor — a constructor method consisting of a header and an empty code block

deprecated — methods, tags, or other language elements that eventually will not be supported; the use of deprecated elements is discouraged

doc comment — a special comment statement used by the javadoc utility to generate program documentation in HTML format; the resulting HTML pages contain pertinent information about the classes, methods, and variables used in a program

dynamic binding — occurs when the JVM resolves which method to invoke when the system runs

Dynamic HTML (DHTML) — enables some data to be maintained on the client, which decreases the server and network loads and improves overall performance

dynamic model — a model such as the sequence diagram that shows objects interacting

encapsulation — occurs when an object has attributes and methods combined into one unit

escape sequence — the backslash character (\) followed by a second character such as "t" for tab or "n" for new line

event listener — an object that is listening for events from event source objects with which it has registered

event source — the object that triggers an event

exception — an object instance; more specifically, an instance of the Throwable class or one of its subclasses

Extensible Hypertext Markup Language (XHTML) — combines features of HTML and XML and thus provides a transition between the two languages

Extensible Markup Language (XML) — XML is similar to HTML and allows programmers to develop their own tags and elements to fit the needs of specific applications and data structures

external event — something that happens outside the system that results in system processing

fat client — a division of work in a client-server model that places heavy processing demands on the client

file — a collection of related records

file system — the hierarchical organization of directories (or folders) that exist above the package-level folder; they control the Java classpath

finally block — a block of code beginning with the keyword `finally` that will execute regardless of whether an exception is caught

foreign key — an attribute (or combination of attributes) in one database table that serves as a primary key in a different database table

format mask — an argument passed to the DecimalFormat constructor that determines how a number will be displayed

generalization/specialization hierarchy — a hierarchy of superclasses and subclasses; sometimes called an inheritance hierarchy

get accessor method — a method that returns attribute values

getter — get accessor method

GUI object — an object that is part of the user interface to the system

Hypertext Markup Language (HTML) — a language used to format information that is displayed in a Web browser

Hypertext Transfer Protocol (HTTP) — the standard communication protocol used by most Web browsers and Web servers

identifier — the name of a class, method, or variable

immutable — values that cannot be changed or mutated

incremental development — life cycle approach where some of the system is completed and put into operation before the entire system is finished

increment operator — (++); adds one to a variable

information hiding — occurs when encapsulation hides the internal structure of objects, protecting them from corruption

instance — a specific object that belongs to a class (synonym of object)

instance method — a method associated with a specific instance; a nonstatic method

instance variable — a nonstatic variable; each instance maintains its own copy of the variable

instantiate — to create a new instance of the class

Integrated Development Environment (IDE) — software that provides editing, debugging, and graphical tools used to develop systems

interface — a Java component that defines abstract methods and constants; classes that implement the interface must override the abstract methods

interpreter — a program that reads a file containing program code and executes it

Java — a pure OO language developed by Sun Microsystems

Java Database Connectivity (JDBC) — Sun Microsystems' protocol for database connectivity

Java Development Kit (JDK) — the Java software system consisting of a compiler, debugger, the JVM, and packages containing hundreds of prewritten classes

javadoc tag — a code used to identify certain kinds of information needed by the javadoc utility in creating HTML pages from the doc comments; begins with the @ character

javadoc utility — a utility program in the Java software development kit (SDK) that generates program documentation in HTML format based on the placement and content of doc comments

Java Server Page (JSP) — a technology that allows you to embed Java code within an HTML file

Java Virtual Machine (JVM) — the Java interpreter that executes bytecode

joining — the linking together of tables in a relational database that share a common attribute

keyword — a word that has special meaning in a programming language and is used in writing statements

layout manager — a class that determines the way GUI components are arranged on a container

lifeline — a dashed line representing a sequence of time that an object exists on a sequence diagram

literal — a value defined within a statement

logical model — model showing what is required in the system independent of the technology used to implement it

logical operators — OR (||) and AND (&&)

look and feel — the overall appearance of GUI components

loop counter — a variable used to count the number of times a loop is executed

message — a request sent asking an object to invoke, or carry out, one of its methods

method — what an object is capable of doing

method header — the first line of a method that identifies the method and describes some of its characteristics

method overriding — invoking the method of a subclass in place of the method in the superclass if both have the same signature (name, return type, and parameter list)

method signature — the method name and its parameter list

mnemonic key — a character you press together with the Alt key to generate a menu item action event

model — depicts some aspect of the real world

model–driven approach — a systems development approach where developers create graphical models of the system requirements and the system design

model–driven development — creating logical and physical models during analysis and design to describe system requirements and designs

modulus operator — *see* remainder operator

multiple inheritance — the ability to "inherit" from more than one class

multiplicity — the number of associations possible between objects (*see* cardinality)

naturalness — a benefit of OO because people more naturally think about their world in terms of objects

nested if — an if statement written inside another if statement

nested loop — a loop within a loop

nonstatic — another term used for instance variables and methods

nonstatic method — a method associated with a specific instance; an instance method

null — a Java keyword representing a constant containing binary zeroes

object — a thing that has attributes and behaviors

object identity — each object has a unique address, meaning you can find it, or refer to it, and send it a message

object-oriented analysis (OOA) — defining system requirements in terms of problem domain objects and their interactions

object-oriented approach — defines a system as a collection of objects that work together to accomplish tasks

object-oriented design (OOD) — designing the system in terms of classes of objects and their interactions, including the user interface and data access classes

object-oriented information system development — analysis, design, and implementation of information systems using object-oriented programming languages, technologies, and techniques

object-oriented programming (OOP) — writing program statements that define or instantiate classes of objects that implement object interactions

object persistence — making an object instance exist over time by storing the instance or its data in a file for future retrieval

object serialization — a Java technique to accomplish object storage

object storage — making an instance persistent by storing the instance in a file

one-dimensional array — an array consisting of elements arranged in a single row (or column)

Open Database Connectivity (ODBC) — a protocol that provides methods to Microsoft's Access database

overloaded method — a method within the same class having the same name as another, but with a different parameter list

overridden method — a method with the *same signature* as an *inherited* method

package — a group of related classes, similar to a class library; when working in an IDE, designate the package as the folder that contains your program

parameter — a variable declared in a method header that receives an argument value

parameterized constructor — a constructor method that receives arguments, usually used to populate attribute values

persistent objects — objects that are available for use over time

physical model — model showing how a system component will be implemented using a specific technology

polymorphic method — a method in one class with the same signature as a method *in a second class*

polymorphism — in OO, refers to the way different objects can respond in their own way to the same message

portability — the ability to write a program once and have it run on any implementation of the JVM, regardless of the hardware platform

post-test loop — a loop that tests the terminating condition at the end of the loop

pre-test loop — a loop that tests the terminating condition at the beginning of the loop

primary key — a field that is used to uniquely identify a record

primitive data type — one of the eight basic Java data types

primitive variable — a variable declared with one of the eight primitive data types

problem domain object — objects that are specific to the business application

project — a mechanism within an IDE for grouping related programs so that they are easier to find, manage, and work on; project structures are not recognized by the JVM and other systems software

protected access — attribute values can be directly accessed by subclasses (as well as by other classes in the package)

prototype — a model (or mock-up) of some portion of an information system; the prototyping strategy is to develop core features first, and get the look and feel of them before implementing other features

random access file — a file with its records organized so that you can access a record by specifying its record number

record — a collection of related variables

reference variable — a variable that uses a class name as a data type and refers to or points to an instance of that class

register — an event listener object invokes a method in an event source object in order to be notified when an event occurs

relational database — data organized into tables which may be related to each other

remainder operator — (%); one of the arithmetic operators used to produce a remainder resulting from the division of two integers

reuse — a benefit of OO that allows classes to be developed once and used many times

scenario — one of several variations to the steps followed in a use case

sequence diagram — a UML diagram showing object interaction

sequential file — a file with its records stored in sequential order, one after the other

server — the computer in a client-server model of distributed processing that receives client requests and performs the desired actions

server object — the object whose method is being invoked

servlet — a special kind of Java program that resides on the Web server and responds to client requests

set accessor method — a method that populates attributes

setter — set accessor method

Simula — the first programming language using OO concepts

SmallTalk — the first general-purpose OO programming language

spiral model — life cycle approach that emphasizes the iterative nature of development by showing the project as a spiral starting in the middle and working out

standard method — *see* accessor method

statechart — a UML diagram showing the transitions that objects make from state to state

state event — something that happens when the state of an object in the system changes that results in system processing

static — keyword used in a variable definition or a method header to associate it with a class instead of individual instances

static method — a method not associated with a specific instance

static model — a model such as the class diagram that shows system constructs but no interactions

Structured Query Language (SQL) — a standard set of keywords and statements used to access relational databases

subclass — a class that inherits from a superclass

superclass — a general class that a subclass can inherit from

system analysis — to study, understand, and define the requirements for a system

system design — process of creating physical models showing how the various system components will be implemented using specific technology

system requirements — define what the system needs to accomplish for users in business terms

tag — a keyword in HTML, JSP, ASP, XML, and other markup languages that identifies special kinds of formatting or commands to be carried out when a Web page is rendered by the browser

temporal event — an event that occurs at a specific point in time that results in system processing

thin client — a division of work in a client-server model that minimizes processing demands on the client; generally a thin client is preferable to a fat client for Web applications

three-dimensional array — an array that conceptually has rows, columns, and pages

three-tier design — a method of system design that requires that the collection of objects that interact in an OO system are separated into three categories of classes (problem domain classes, GUI classes, and data access classes)

try block — a block of code beginning with the keyword `try`; code that invokes a method that may throw an exception is placed in a try block

two-dimensional array — an array that conceptually has both rows and columns

Unicode — a standard character set used by Java that uses two bytes for each character; accommodates all of the characters in the major international languages

Unified Modeling Language (UML) — an accepted standard for OO analysis and design diagramming notation and constructs

Uniform Resource Locator (URL) — specifies the location of a document to be loaded by the Web browser; most often take the form of *protocol://hostname.port.file*

use case — a system function that allows the user to complete a task

use case diagram — a UML diagram showing use cases and actors

watch variable — a variable whose value is monitored and displayed by the debugger when program execution is suspended at a breakpoint

waterfall method — life cycle approach where all of analysis is completed before design can start, and all of design is completed before programming can start

wildcard — the asterisk character (*) indicates all classes when used with an import statement

workspace — a collection of windows that support certain types of activities within an IDE, such as editing or debugging

Index

7. Export Regulations. All Software and technical data delivered under this Agreement are subject to US export control laws and may be subject to export or import regulations in other countries. You agree to comply strictly with all such laws and regulations and acknowledge that you have the responsibility to obtain such licenses to export, re-export, or import as may be required after delivery to you.

8. U.S. Government Restricted Rights. If Software is being acquired by or on behalf of the U.S. Government or by a U.S. Government prime contractor or subcontractor (at any tier), then the Government's rights in Software and accompanying documentation will be only as set forth in this Agreement; this is in accordance with 48 CFR 227.7201 through 227.7202-4 (for Department of Defense (DOD) acquisitions) and with 48 CFR 2.101 and 12.212 (for non-DOD acquisitions).

9. Governing Law. Any action related to this Agreement will be governed by California law and controlling U.S. federal law. No choice of law rules of any jurisdiction will apply.

10. Severability. If any provision of this Agreement is held to be unenforceable, this Agreement will remain in effect with the provision omitted, unless omission would frustrate the intent of the parties, in which case this Agreement will immediately terminate.

11. Integration. This Agreement is the entire agreement between you and Sun relating to its subject matter. It supersedes all prior or contemporaneous oral or written communications, proposals, representations and warranties and prevails over any conflicting or additional terms of any quote, order, acknowledgment, or other communication between the parties relating to its subject matter during the term of this Agreement. No modification of this Agreement will be binding, unless in writing and signed by an authorized representative of each party.

FORTE(TM) FOR JAVA(TM), RELEASE 3.0, COMMUNITY EDITION SUPPLEMENTAL LICENSE TERMS

These supplemental license terms ("Supplemental Terms") add to or modify the terms of the Binary Code License Agreement (collectively, the "Agreement"). Capitalized terms not defined in these Supplemental Terms shall have the same meanings ascribed to them in the Agreement. These Supplemental Terms shall supersede any inconsistent or conflicting terms in the Agreement, or in any license contained within the Software.

1. Software Internal Use and Development License Grant. Subject to the terms and conditions of this Agreement, including, but not limited to Section 4 (Java(TM) Technology Restrictions) of these Supplemental Terms, Sun grants you a non-exclusive, non-transferable, limited license to reproduce internally and use internally the binary form of the Software complete and unmodified for the sole purpose of designing, developing and testing your Java applets and applications intended to run on the Java platform ("Programs").

2. License to Distribute Software. Subject to the terms and conditions of this Agreement, including, but not limited to Section 4 (Java (TM) Technology Restrictions) of these Supplemental Terms, Sun grants you a non-exclusive, non-transferable, limited license to reproduce and distribute the Software in binary code form only, provided that (i) you distribute the Software complete and unmodified and only bundled as part of, and for the sole purpose of running, your Programs, (ii) the Programs add significant and primary functionality to the Software, (iii) you do not distribute additional software intended to replace any component(s) of the Software, (iv) for a particular version of the Java platform, any executable output generated by a compiler that is contained in the Software must (a) only be compiled from source code that conforms to the corresponding version of the OEM Java Language Specification; (b) be in the class file format defined by the corresponding version of the OEM Java Virtual Machine Specification; and (c) execute properly on a reference runtime, as specified by Sun, associated with such version of the Java platform, (v) you do not remove or alter any proprietary legends or notices contained in the Software, (v) you only distribute the Software subject to a license agreement that protects Sun's interests consistent with the terms contained in this Agreement, and (vi) you agree to defend and indemnify Sun and its licensors from and against any damages, costs, liabilities, settlement amounts and/or expenses (including attorneys' fees) incurred in connection with any claim, lawsuit or action by any third party that arises or results from the use or distribution of any and all Programs and/or Software.

3. License to Distribute Redistributables. Subject to the terms and conditions of this Agreement, including but not limited to Section 4 (Java Technology Restrictions) of these Supplemental Terms, Sun grants you a non-exclusive, non-transferable, limited license to reproduce and distribute the binary form of those files specifically identified as redistributable in the Software "RELEASE NOTES" file ("Redistributables") provided that: (i) you distribute the Redistributables complete and unmodified (unless otherwise specified in the applicable RELEASE NOTES file), and only bundled as part of Programs, (ii) you do not distribute additional software intended to supersede any component(s) of the Redistributables, (iii) you do not remove or alter any proprietary legends or notices contained in or on the Redistributables, (iv) for a particular version of the Java platform, any executable output generated by a compiler that is contained in the Software must (a) only be compiled from source code that conforms to the corresponding version of the OEM Java Language Specification; (b) be in the class file format defined by the corresponding version of the OEM Java Virtual Machine Specification; and (c) execute properly on a reference runtime, as specified by Sun, associated with such version of the Java platform, (v) you only distribute the Redistributables pursuant to a license agreement that protects Sun's interests consistent with the terms contained in the Agreement, and (v) you agree to defend and indemnify Sun and its licensors from and against any damages, costs, liabilities, settlement amounts and/or expenses (including attorneys' fees) incurred in connection with any claim, lawsuit or action by any third party that arises or results from the use or distribution of any and all Programs and/or Software.

4. Java Technology Restrictions. You may not modify the Java Platform Interface ("JPI", identified as classes contained within the "java" package or any subpackages of the "java" package), by creating additional classes within the JPI or otherwise causing the addition to or modification of the classes in the JPI. In the event that you create an additional class and associated API(s) which (i) extends the functionality of the Java platform, and (ii) is exposed to third party software developers for the purpose of developing additional software which invokes such additional API, you must promptly publish broadly an accurate specification for such API for free use by all developers. You may not create, or authorize your licensees to create, additional classes, interfaces, or subpackages that are in any way identified as "java", "javax", "sun" or similar convention as specified by Sun in any naming convention designation.

5. Java Runtime Availability. Refer to the appropriate version of the Java Runtime Environment binary code license (currently located at http://www.java.sun.com/jdk/index.html) for the availability of runtime code which may be distributed with Java applets and applications.

6. Trademarks and Logos. You acknowledge and agree as between you and Sun that Sun owns the SUN, SOLARIS, JAVA, JINI, FORTE, and iPLANET trademarks and all SUN, SOLARIS, JAVA, JINI, FORTE, and iPLANET-related trademarks, service marks, logos and other brand designations ("Sun Marks"), and you agree to comply with the Sun Trademark and Logo Usage Requirements currently located at http://www.sun.com/policies/trademarks. Any use you make of the Sun Marks inures to Sun's benefit.

7. Source Code. Software may contain source code that is provided solely for reference purposes pursuant to the terms of this Agreement. Source code may not be redistributed unless expressly provided for in this Agreement.

8. Termination for Infringement. Either party may terminate this Agreement immediately should any Software become, or in either party's opinion be likely to become, the subject of a claim of infringement of any intellectual property right.

For inquiries please contact: Sun Microsystems, Inc. 901 San Antonio Road, Palo Alto, California 94303

(LFI#91205/Form ID#011801)

SUN MICROSYSTEMS, INC.
BINARY CODE LICENSE AGREEMENT

READ THE TERMS OF THIS AGREEMENT AND ANY PROVIDED SUPPLEMENTAL LICENSE TERMS (COLLECTIVELY "AGREEMENT") CAREFULLY BEFORE OPENING THE SOFTWARE MEDIA PACKAGE. BY OPENING THE SOFTWARE MEDIA PACKAGE, YOU AGREE TO THE TERMS OF THIS AGREEMENT. IF YOU ARE ACCESSING THE SOFTWARE ELECTRONICALLY, INDICATE YOUR ACCEPTANCE OF THESE TERMS BY SELECTING THE "ACCEPT" BUTTON AT THE END OF THIS AGREEMENT. IF YOU DO NOT AGREE TO ALL THESE TERMS, PROMPTLY RETURN THE UNUSED SOFTWARE TO YOUR PLACE OF PURCHASE FOR A REFUND OR, IF THE SOFTWARE IS ACCESSED ELECTRONICALLY, SELECT THE "DECLINE" BUTTON AT THE END OF THIS AGREEMENT.

1. LICENSE TO USE. Sun grants you a non-exclusive and non-transferable license for the internal use only of the accompanying software and documentation and any error corrections provided by Sun (collectively "Software"), by the number of users and the class of computer hardware for which the corresponding fee has been paid.

2. RESTRICTIONS. Software is confidential and copyrighted. Title to Software and all associated intellectual property rights is retained by Sun and/or its licensors. Except as specifically authorized in any Supplemental License Terms, you may not make copies of Software, other than a single copy of Software for archival purposes. Unless enforcement is prohibited by applicable law, you may not modify, decompile, or reverse engineer Software. You acknowledge that Software is not designed, licensed or intended for use in the design, construction, operation or maintenance of any nuclear facility. Sun disclaims any express or implied warranty of fitness for such uses. No right, title or interest in or to any trademark, service mark, logo or trade name of Sun or its licensors is granted under this Agreement.

3. LIMITED WARRANTY. Sun warrants to you that for a period of ninety (90) days from the date of purchase, as evidenced by a copy of the receipt, the media on which Software is furnished (if any) will be free of defects in materials and workmanship under normal use. Except for the foregoing, Software is provided "AS IS". Your exclusive remedy and Sun's entire liability under this limited warranty will be at Sun's option to replace Software media or refund the fee paid for Software.

4. DISCLAIMER OF WARRANTY. UNLESS SPECIFIED IN THIS AGREEMENT, ALL EXPRESS OR IMPLIED CONDITIONS, REPRESENTATIONS AND WARRANTIES, INCLUDING ANY IMPLIED WARRANTY OF MERCHANTABILITY, FITNESS FOR A PARTICULAR PURPOSE OR NON-INFRINGEMENT ARE DISCLAIMED, EXCEPT TO THE EXTENT THAT THESE DISCLAIMERS ARE HELD TO BE LEGALLY INVALID.

5. LIMITATION OF LIABILITY. TO THE EXTENT NOT PROHIBITED BY LAW, IN NO EVENT WILL SUN OR ITS LICENSORS BE LIABLE FOR ANY LOST REVENUE, PROFIT OR DATA, OR FOR SPECIAL, INDIRECT, CONSEQUENTIAL, INCIDENTAL OR PUNITIVE DAMAGES, HOW-EVER CAUSED REGARDLESS OF THE THEORY OF LIABILITY, ARISING OUT OF OR RELATED TO THE USE OF OR INABILITY TO USE SOFTWARE, EVEN IF SUN HAS BEEN ADVISED OF THE POSSIBILITY OF SUCH DAMAGES. In no event will Sun's liability to you, whether in contract, tort (including negligence), or otherwise, exceed the amount paid by you for Software under this Agreement. The foregoing limitations will apply even if the above stated warranty fails of its essential purpose.

6. Termination. This Agreement is effective until terminated. You may terminate this Agreement at any time by destroying all copies of Software. This Agreement will terminate immediately without notice from Sun if you fail to comply with any provision of this Agreement. Upon Termination, you must destroy all copies of Software.

7. Export Regulations. All Software and technical data delivered under this Agreement are subject to US export control laws and may be subject to export or import regulations in other countries. You agree to comply strictly with all such laws and regulations and acknowledge that you have the responsibility to obtain such licenses to export, re-export, or import as may be required after delivery to you.

8. U.S. Government Restricted Rights. If Software is being acquired by or on behalf of the U.S. Government or by a U.S. Government prime contractor or subcontractor (at any tier), then the Government's rights in Software and accompanying documentation will be only as set forth in this Agreement; this is in accordance with 48 CFR 227.7201 through 227.7202-4 (for Department of Defense (DOD) acquisitions) and with 48 CFR 2.101 and 12.212 (for non-DOD acquisitions).

9. Governing Law. Any action related to this Agreement will be governed by California law and controlling U.S. federal law. No choice of law rules of any jurisdiction will apply.

10. Severability. If any provision of this Agreement is held to be unenforceable, this Agreement will remain in effect with the provision omitted, unless omission would frustrate the intent of the parties, in which case this Agreement will immediately terminate.

11. Integration. This Agreement is the entire agreement between you and Sun relating to its subject matter. It supersedes all prior or contemporaneous oral or written communications, proposals, representations and warranties and prevails over any conflicting or additional terms of any quote, order, acknowledgment, or other communication between the parties relating to its subject matter during the term of this Agreement. No modification of this Agreement will be binding, unless in writing and signed by an authorized representative of each party.

Java(TM) 2 Software Development Kit (J2SDK), Standard Edition, Version 1.3.x

---

SUPPLEMENTAL LICENSE TERMS

These supplemental license terms ("Supplemental Terms") add to or modify the terms of the Binary Code License Agreement (collectively, the "Agreement"). Capitalized terms not defined in these Supplemental Terms shall have the same meanings ascribed to them in the Agreement. These Supplemental Terms shall supersede any inconsistent or conflicting terms in the Agreement, or in any license contained within the Software.

1. Software Internal Use and Development License Grant. Subject to the terms and conditions of this Agreement, including, but not limited to Section 4 (Java(TM) Technology Restrictions) of these Supplemental Terms, Sun grants you a non-exclusive, non-transferable, limited license to reproduce internally and use internally the binary form of the Software complete and unmodified for the sole purpose of designing, developing and testing your Java applets and applications intended to run on the Java platform("Programs").

2. License to Distribute Software. Subject to the terms and conditions of this Agreement, including, but not limited to Section 4 (Java (TM) Technology Restrictions) of these Supplemental Terms, Sun grants you a non-exclusive, non-transferable, limited license to reproduce and distribute the Software in binary code form only, provided that (i) you distribute the Software complete and unmodified and only bundled as part of, and for the sole purpose of running, your Programs, (ii) the Programs add significant and primary functionality to the Software, (iii) you do not distribute additional software intended to replace any component(s) of the Software, (iv) you do not remove or alter any proprietary legends or notices contained in the Software, (v) you only distribute the Software subject to a license agreement that protects Sun's interests consistent with the terms contained in this Agreement, and (vi) you agree to defend and indemnify Sun and its licensors from and against any damages, costs, liabilities, settlement amounts and/or expenses (including attorneys' fees) incurred in connection with any claim, lawsuit or action by any third party that arises or results from the use or distribution of any and all Programs and/or Software.

3. License to Distribute Redistributables. Subject to the terms and conditions of this Agreement, including but not limited to Section 4 (Java Technology Restrictions) of these Supplemental Terms, Sun grants you a non-exclusive, non-transferable, limited license to reproduce and distribute the binary form of those files specifically identified as redistributable in the Software "README" file ("Redistributables") provided that: (i) you distribute the Redistributables complete and unmodified (unless otherwise specified in the applicable README file), and only bundled as part of Programs, (ii) you do not distribute additional software intended to supersede any component(s) of the Redistributables, (iii) you do not remove or alter any proprietary legends or notices contained in or on the Redistributables, (iv) you only distribute the Redistributables pursuant to a license agreement that protects Sun's interests consistent with the terms contained in the Agreement, and (v) you agree

to defend and indemnify Sun and its licensors from and against any damages, costs, liabilities, settlement amounts and/or expenses (including attorneys' fees) incurred in connection with any claim, lawsuit or action by any third party that arises or results from the use or distribution of any and all Programs and/or Software.

4. Java Technology Restrictions. You may not modify the Java Platform Interface ("JPI", identified as classes contained within the "java" package or any subpackages of the "java" package), by creating additional classes within the JPI or otherwise causing the addition to or modification of the classes in the JPI. In the event that you create an additional class and associated API(s) which (i) extends the functionality of the Java platform, and (ii) is exposed to third party software developers for the purpose of developing additional software which invokes such additional API, you must promptly publish broadly an accurate specification for such API for free use by all developers. You may not create, or authorize your licensees to create, additional classes, interfaces, or subpackages that are in any way identified as "java", "javax", "sun" or similar convention as specified by Sun in any naming convention designation.

5. Trademarks and Logos. You acknowledge and agree as between you and Sun that Sun owns the SUN, SOLARIS, JAVA, JINI, FORTE, and iPLANET trademarks and all SUN, SOLARIS, JAVA, JINI, FORTE, and iPLANET-related trademarks, service marks, logos and other brand designations ("Sun Marks"), and you agree to comply with the Sun Trademark and Logo Usage Requirements currently located at http://www.sun.com/policies/trademarks. Any use you make of the Sun Marks inures to Sun's benefit.

6. Source Code. Software may contain source code that is provided solely for reference purposes pursuant to the terms of this Agreement. Source code may not be redistributed unless expressly provided for in this Agreement.

7. Termination for Infringement. Either party may terminate this Agreement immediately should any Software become, or in either party's opinion be likely to become, the subject of a claim of infringement of any intellectual property right.

For inquiries please contact: Sun Microsystems, Inc. 901 San Antonio Road, Palo Alto, California 94303

(LFI#90955/Form ID#011801)